Praise for A SENSE OF DUTY

A SENSE OF
DUTY

A SENSE OF
DUTY

Our Journey from Vietnam to America

QUANG PHAM

Dec '2011 —

For Stacie
Blair —

Thank you
for your service
and I look
forward to reading
your memoir
soon.

Best,
Quang

PRESIDIO PRESS TRADE PAPERBACKS

NEW YORK

For my mother, Nguyễn Thị Niệm,

and my father, Phạm Văn Hòa

2010 Presidio Press Trade Paperback Edition

Published in the United States by Presidio Press, an imprint of The Random House
Publishing Group, a division of Random House, Inc., New York.

PRESIDIO PRESS and colophon are trademarks of Random House, Inc.

LIBRARY OF CONGRESS CATALOGING-IN-PUBLICATION DATA
Quang Pham.
A sense of duty : our journey from Vietnam to America / by Quang Pham.
p.   cm.
ISBN 978-0-89141-876-4
1. Quang Pham.   2. Vietnamese conflict, 1961–1975—Personal narratives,
Vietnamese.   3. Pham, Van Hoa d. 2000.   4. Vietnamese Americans—Biography.
5. Refugees—United States—Biography.   I. Title.
E184.V53Q36 2005
959.704'3'092—dc22   2004063383

Printed in the United States of America

www.presidiopress.com

2 4 6 8 9 7 5 3 1

Text design by rlf design

CONTENTS

AUTHOR'S NOTE

Out of respect, the names of elderly Vietnamese appear in this book in the Vietnamese language format, with the family name listed first. My father's name appears as Pham Van Hoa while mine is written as Quang Pham. With several exceptions, I have also chosen not to include accent marks.

Most of the spelling of geographical locations (cities, provinces) is in the form of the American English language usage of the time. Da Nang, Sai Gon, and Viet Nam are written in the Vietnamese language format and not connected together.

I am grateful for the following works which I consulted during my research on the Vietnamese Air Force, the signing of the Paris Peace Accords, the fall of Saigon, and the reeducation camps: *No Peace, No Honor: Nixon, Kissinger and the Betrayal in Vietnam,* Larry Berman (The Free Press, 2001); *U.S. Marines in Vietnam: The Bitter End 1973–1975,* George R. Dunham and David A. Quinlan (Headquarters, U.S. Marine Corps, 1990); *Reeducation in Postwar Vietnam: Personal Postscripts to Peace,* Edward P. Meltzner (Texas A&M University Press, 2001); *A Gift of Barbed Wire: America's Allies Abandoned in South Vietnam,* Robert S. McKelvey (University of Washington Press, 2002); *Flying Dragons, The South Vietnamese Air Force,* Robert C. Mikesh (Schiffer, 2005); *The A-1 Skyraider in Vietnam: The Spad's Last War,* Wayne Mutza (Schiffer, 2004); *Their War: Perspectives of the South Vietnamese in American Literature and in Their Own Words,* Julie Pham (a paper, 2000); *A Better War: The Unexamined Victories and Final Tragedy of America's Last Years in Vietnam,* Lewis Sorley (Harcourt & Brace, 1999).

I have changed the names of several people in the book to protect their privacy. To my knowledge and memory, everything else is true.

ACKNOWLEDGMENTS

A special thank-you to my wife, Shannon, and our daughter, Willow. Thanks also to my mother, my sisters, my high school and UCLA friends, my Marine Corps buddies, Vietnam veterans and writers Bernie Edelman and Mike Tharp, and Rod and Laura McDermott, who were the first to support me in my run for Congress. Thanks to my in-laws, Jim and Eretta Ryan, who support me like their own son. My father's Vietnamese Air Force colleagues, students, and senior officers were extremely helpful. I am grateful to my literary agent Flip Brophy and my editors Ron Doering and Ryan Doherty. To Colonel John Braddon, USMC (Retired), thank you for rescuing my father on April 27, 1964, in Do Xa, Republic of Vietnam. Otherwise, life for the Pham family might have turned out quite differently.

A SENSE OF
DUTY

FOR FATHER, FOR COUNTRY

I WAS BORN A VIETNAMESE IN AN OLD FRENCH HOSPITAL SIX months before President Lyndon B. Johnson ordered thousands of U.S. Marines into my country. That tiny scimitar-shaped peninsula in Southeast Asia still considers me a citizen (for military conscription purposes only) even though I escaped three decades ago. Ask me where my hometown is on a map and I can still show you. But it now bears the name Ho Chi Minh City. Saigon is gone—but then again, it isn't. I can't tell people why that happened without choking up. John F. Kennedy said, "Victory has 100 fathers and defeat is an orphan." As a half-orphan of that war, I chose to find out on my own. Vietnam will remain a part of me for as long as I live, as will my love for *nuốc Mỹ*, Vietnamese for the United States, and now *my* country.

When I turned twenty I became an American by choice. Actually I was already a by-product, derived from a failed U.S.-backed regime fighting to keep the "dominoes" from falling in Asia. I could have kept my green card and maintained a legal-resident status. (Out of principle a few Vietnamese who remain bitter toward the United States still refuse to become naturalized.) But I knew I had to be a citizen in order to join the military as an officer. My childhood dream was to become a pilot like my father. Unknowingly, the pursuit of that dream would enable me to pay back the rewards of my precious new citizenship and to seek the truth about my father's service in a long-ago war. Or as he once wrote, "It was either simple coincidence or you may call it destiny. You're in the same Marine unit that I flew support for and was rescued by in the early days of the war."

It was no coincidence.

This book is not a personal condemnation of six U.S. presidents, the U.S. Congress, arrogant Pentagon leaders from the supposed "greatest generation," or hippie antiwar protestors for their roles in the multisided quagmire known as "Vietnam." Nor will it patronize a press corps that, in my opinion, ultimately took sides while covering Southeast Asia, later claiming credit for swaying the American public that helped prevent the early deaths of many more.

Neither will these pages vindicate former leaders of South Vietnam for losing their country in such a rapid, public, and humiliating way. Certainly this book will not honor the victorious Communists, long on military tactics but short on domestic reforms and human rights. Hell-bent on punishing the losers, they have wasted nearly three decades after victory over the mightiest nation on the earth. Their insistence on ideological purity over the well-being of their people has kept Vietnam years behind emerging Asian countries.

This is simply a story about a refugee boy who grew up without his father and became confused by an enduring nostalgia for Vietnam. Buoyed by a calling inscribed just before his birth, he bought into the American Dream, despite prejudice and other obstacles. Yet he would find an unexpected reconciliation through his father, the man he sought to honor but who expected no such payback.

In 1975, a week before North Vietnamese forces overran Saigon, my mother, my three sisters, and I fled Vietnam. Our country was falling apart; our hopes for freedom in our own nation were dashed. Unbeknownst to us, we would join the ranks of the thousands of families of the prisoners of war (POWs).

Images of desperate refugees scaling the U.S. Embassy fence, clinging to the skids of helicopters, and jamming leaky fishing boats have been seared into our consciousness. Some Americans celebrated our loss, while a handful gave their all to evacuate as many South Vietnamese as they could.

My mother raised the four of us in California by herself. When we landed in the United States, she was thirty-nine, spoke no English, and had never traveled abroad. We spoke French, but I thank God, and Buddha, that we didn't go to Paris to live with my aunt, because there I wouldn't have been able to realize my dreams.

As it turned out, our worst fear at the time we left had come to pass. My father was incarcerated after the war: he was sentenced to more than twelve years in prison camps—after he was told by his communist captors to report for thirty days. After listening (or pretending) to communist indoctrination (the euphemism was "reeducation") for a few months, he spent the remaining years in hard-labor prison camps facing beriberi, dysentery, malaria, starvation, beatings, and death. He and those of his generation thought the United States would stand by them forever. He had served in the military during his country's twenty-one years of post–World War II existence—his entire adulthood. But once he arrived on these shores he never received a welcome home, veteran's benefits, or a pension.

Despite all that, our family did survive the war, while many others didn't. (Approximately 3 million Vietnamese from both sides died in the war.) For the fortunate refugees who escaped, this country gave us a new life filled with opportunities as no other could have. For the prisoners and for those stranded South Vietnamese, the war was supposed to be over but the peace did not come for years.

When I was in the Marine Corps I shuddered at the thought of dying for my country; I wanted to make the enemy die for his. In a way, my native country died for me so that my generation could be spared more fighting, more killing. I am still not sure if it had to happen that way, but I can't rewrite history. Millions suffered in the aftermath, while I and others like me merely "struggled" here. There can be no comparison of our fates, and so our family, minus my father, had taken the less painful route.

When my father died in 2000, his old comrades showed up in force to honor him, as did some of my Marine friends. The afternoon I gave his eulogy was the hardest day of my life: I had lost my father a second time. Swaying behind the lectern at the funeral home, I stared at the standing-room-only crowd of mostly older South Vietnamese veterans long removed from the horrors of combat. The men who had served with my father in squadrons and in the prison camps were there: Bao, Hoi, Thanh, Tien, Tri, Xuong, among many more. They had draped a large yellow flag with the three bright-red horizontal stripes over his coffin. I had to eulogize him in English. I had neglected my native tongue far too long to be able to speak eloquently of his life and legacy in Vietnamese.

After the formal funeral service ended, one person after another came up and told me tales about my father. As I stood next to his casket opened for final viewing, a lifetime of memories were shared with me; some were clear, others hazy. My father's colleagues remembered him as a young, suave fighter pilot and a hothead, eager to show off by briefing his missions in English for the American advisers, and ready to fight anyone, anywhere, anytime. Then he changed. Toward the end of the war he became quiet and nervous in the cockpit, always twitching and touching the flight controls, exhibiting signs of war-weariness.

Yet my father's greatest trait, his sense of humor, his love for teasing and jokes, stayed with him until the end. Not even the Communists could break his spirit. In 1992, just months after he landed in the United States, he penned an open letter to his (South) Vietnamese Air Force (VNAF) buddies where he poked fun at General Rau Kem or "Stiff Mustache," their lavender scarf-donning former air force commander, Nguyen Cao Ky. If asked why he didn't leave before Saigon fell, he'd say . . . "I got stuck. If the lamp posts could walk, they would have gotten out of Vietnam too. Stop asking stupid questions." He also wrote, "I noticed many air force friends have changed their Vietnamese names to Anthony, Steven, William . . . they must be working for Americans, so changing their names for easier pronunciation made sense. If my name was 'Phuoc,' I wouldn't change it because it already has an English equivalent."

I don't think my family fully understood the military tradition of honoring its dead. Nor do they realize the sacrifice my father made during the war and the price he paid for losing our country. But if we don't know ourselves, how could we expect anyone else to understand?

My father was put to rest with full military honors from a country that no longer existed. The honor guard, in ersatz uniforms (long-sleeved blue shirts and trousers), neatly folded the flag of the former Republic of Vietnam into a triangle. The veterans began humming the familiar hymn of what was once the world's fourth-largest air force: *Ôi phi công danh tiếng, muôn đời. O pilot famous for life.* Tears streaked down my cheeks. I hadn't heard the tune since I was a little boy living on Tan Son Nhut Air Base in Saigon. The senior man in attendance presented that flag to me and quietly saluted with his wrinkled hand and bent elbow. He mumbled in Vietnamese: "On behalf of a grateful nation for your father's service, please accept this flag. . . ."

There was no longer such a nation, but by then I knew what he meant.

What did my father do to deserve such honor? Why did these veterans bother with the ceremony? After all, his country had lost the war as its leaders —its so-called best and brightest—scrambled out of Saigon in the first wave, some along with women and children. That was after the fifty-five-day rout in the spring of 1975 when its army of 1 million quickly disintegrated. Blame the United States? That was readily done, and many South Vietnamese still do. Wounds lingered for decades in this country as well. Abandonment of an ally? After more than two decades, $150 billion in aid, and 58,235 U.S. dead, how much more could it have given? Public support for Iraq plummeted after only one year and one thousand dead. How long could the war have been prosecuted? Why didn't my father leave like the rest of us when he could have flown out or boarded any other plane?

I almost didn't get to meet my father at all. I came into this world just after the U.S. Congress had passed the Tonkin Gulf Resolution in August 1964. That triggered massive air strikes against North Vietnam for putative gunboat attacks on the USS *Maddox* and *Turner Joy*. Shortly afterward a reluctant United States dragged itself into full-scale war in Vietnam. Congress, with only two dissenting votes in the Senate, overwhelmingly gave President Lyndon B. Johnson carte blanche.

On April 27, 1964, my father, then 2d Lt. Pham Van Hoa (pronounced "hwa") of the VNAF, was shot down flying in support of the largest heliborne assault up to that point flown by U.S. advisers in their secret war. Rescued and rededicated to his profession, he would fight the good fight in the skies over South Vietnam for another decade before his luck, like that of so many of his countrymen, would eventually run out. For more than twelve grueling years, and indeed for the rest of his life, my father would pay dearly for being on the losing side. His North Vietnamese captors called him unpatriotic, traitor, blood-debtor, American puppet, pirate pilot, and cheap mercenary. They forced him to write numerous confessions denouncing his affiliation with the Saigon government. (His former allies and their journalistic chroniclers, safely home in the United States, portrayed the South Vietnamese as corrupt, incompetent, shadowy figures who had not been worth backing.)

Somebody had to bear the blame for all the death and destruction. Besides the dead, somebody else needed to pay the price for losing. Someone had to accept responsibility.

South Vietnam did have its share of cowards, draft dodgers, and deserters. There were dishonest, incompetent, weak men in the Republic of Vietnam armed forces. From what I've been told at firsthand by a former CIA agent, as well as historians and veterans, they held the highest ranks of leadership. But it was the field-grade officers (my father's group) and those below who bore the brunt of the fighting. For the most part, the latter did their best, given the circumstances, and those who managed to survive kept fighting year after year.

There was no end until the end.

No military is ever perfect. The U.S. military itself faced desertion, drug, morale, and racial problems in Vietnam during its final years in the country and for a decade after its withdrawal. The few U.S. veterans, mostly military advisers who actually flew, fought, ate, and slept alongside the South Vietnamese, spoke respectfully of them. Some of the advisers (who still felt the same years later) became four-star generals like H. Norman Schwarzkopf and Anthony Zinni, both eventually heading the U.S. Central Command. Others included military author Lewis Sorley and Earl Woods (the father of Tiger Woods).

No one was more emphatic than retired U.S. Army Gen. Barry McCaffrey. "In no way denigrating the Americans, but the best assault troops I ever saw in my life [in three conflicts] were the Vietnamese Airborne soldiers. Hands down, the best air support I ever saw in combat, bar none, were Vietnamese [Air Force] A-1 Skyraiders. We cheered when we got them."

Hollywood made one-sided movies, often dismissing Army of the Republic of Vietnam (ARVN) soldiers and mocking them as troops who ran away from skirmishes. In *Apocalypse Now,* the arrogant Colonel Kilgore visits a dying Viet Cong guerrilla with a group of U.S. soldiers and an ARVN soldier. Kilgore knocks the ARVN soldier to the side and yells, "Get out of here before I kick your fucking ass." In *Full Metal Jacket,* several U.S. Marines fighting in Hue City exchange their thoughts on the South Vietnamese. "I'm not real keen on some of these fellers who are supposedly on our side. I keep meeting them coming the other way. We keep getting killed for all these people and they don't even appreciate it. If you ask me, we shooting the wrong gooks." Later in the movie, an ARVN officer is a pimp, offering young Vietnamese prostitutes to the Marines taking a break from combat.

What was I to think of my father's colleagues who had escaped and were preparing to retire by the time he got to this country. Several even considered him stupid for not leaving when he could.

As I grew up in the United States, I almost believed what I had heard and what I had read, but I never stopped loving my father. I didn't know what he had done to deserve more than twelve years in captivity. Did he commit atrocities? After all, the longest a U.S. POW was held in Vietnam (Jim Thompson) was nine years. I couldn't figure out how my father had survived such suffering. I didn't think he could adjust to a peacetime United States after I became aware of the post-traumatic stress disorder (PTSD) that U.S. veterans were undergoing. (In World War I it was "shell shock"; in World War II it was "battle fatigue." In Korea, "operation exhaustion" was the expression.)

By 1987, when my father was still in captivity, I had evolved from one of the "first to flee" to becoming one of the "first to fight." After I graduated from the University of California, Los Angeles (UCLA), and became a U.S. Marine 2d lieutenant in training, I sat through hours of eye-glazingly long lectures in Quantico, Virginia, about history and warfare. Unavoidably, the subject of Vietnam would come up in a "law of war" class sandwiched between strategy and tactics courses. The infamous picture of a South Vietnamese general executing a Viet Cong twenty years earlier triggered lively discussions about morality and rules of engagement. We were given no further explanations. No history. No context. A still photograph that arguably helped turn the tide against the war and South Vietnam had not lost its power.

I was handed a reading list approved by the commandant of the Marine Corps. The Corps wanted its rank and file to be intellectual warriors, while we lieutenants only cared about leading troops and earning medals (and getting laid). Depending on rank, each Marine was supposed to read a certain number of books per year from a list put out by Marine Corps Headquarters. I hardly knew anyone back then who read any of those books except for James Webb's *Fields of Fire* and Philip Caputo's *A Rumor of War*—one a memoir, and the other a novel. Both were bestsellers (and with very different perspectives) penned by combat Marine lieutenants in Vietnam. Also on the list were Sun Tzu's *The Art of War,* Stephen Ambrose's *Band of Brothers,* and *How We Won the War* by North Vietnam's Gen. Vo Nguyen Giap. I remember flipping through the first few pages of Giap's thin book before wanting to punch something or somebody. Instead, I took off on a long run alone, on paved roads surrounding the woods and buildings named for dead Marines, sick at heart while recalling that last night in Saigon. Even my beloved Corps had bought into communist propaganda.

Now I am forty, about my father's age when South Vietnam was defeated, and I think I understand. I am living a comfortable life, mostly because my father had gotten us out of Vietnam when he did and because of the Americans who helped us along the way. My journey through the Marines introduced me to U.S. veterans who had bravely fought for my cause, despite growing opposition back home. On my personal odyssey I've discovered many heroic acts, including ones that touched our family deeply. Of course I knew little of all of this until recent years. I needed time. I was too busy trying to prove my patriotism. For most Vietnamese and other immigrants, getting an education, paying taxes, obeying the law, and owning a home—the American Dream—were enough for us, the "model minority."

For me, however, there was an unfinished mission. Every U.S. conflict since Vietnam has been compared with it, rightly and wrongly. There's a Vietnam generation that is still fighting the war, exchanging barbs all the way to the voting booth in every national election.

As I entered that debate, something was still missing. What happened after the war? Who really won and who really lost? Have we learned anything? Even the Vietnamese elders in the United States had been silent. What should they tell the younger generation about the war and their roles in it? Reeducation camps remain a taboo topic, especially in modern Vietnam, its government making no mention of them. Tourists can't visit the former prison camps, and the Communists vehemently deny their existence.

Maybe my father's postwar predicament has distorted my understanding of Vietnam.

For the first few years after his capture, I thought my father was dead. Perhaps from grief, or anger, I couldn't conjure any positive attitudes toward the South Vietnamese. It was easier to blame them the same way we are now pointing fingers at the Iraqis for not holding their own against the insurgents. I could not summon enough strength to deal with my own emotions until my father came back into my life. All too soon, before my personal *shantih* could be achieved, he left again.

More than two years after his death, I finally got an opportunity to honor my father in public. The ceremony was in front of a new war memorial, with a full band and military helicopter flyover (courtesy of my Marine buddies on a "training" mission), the way this nation honors its own veterans. (The Westminster Vietnam War Memorial's dedication took place soon after U.S. troops had "liberated" Baghdad in April 2003. Ironically, it had also been three decades since Henry Kissinger signed the Paris Peace Accords that sent American boys home and thus catalyzed what would be a slow, sure death for South Vietnam.)

The memorial was not The Wall in Washington, D.C. It was a smaller memorial in California, where two 11-foot bronze statues of a GI and a slightly shorter resolute South Vietnamese soldier stand side by side with their M-16s, facing a flaming urn, and with two flagpoles behind the soldiers.

They stand together in Westminster, designated an all-American city but now popularly known as Little Saigon, much to the dismay of longtime white residents. Once a decaying suburb in the middle of conservative Orange County, it had evolved into the bustling, explosive de facto capital of Vietnam War refugees. Its *pho*-like flavor of pre-1975 Saigon politics is slipping away slowly as a new generation comes of age.

If truth was the first casualty of the Vietnam War, then this memorial should serve to announce one of its honest legacies. The statues' thousand-yard stares peer out to the west, where the Pacific Ocean connects North America and Vietnam, where the present meets the past with its anger, guilt, and shame. Westminster is also where 15,000 disgruntled refugees marched against a Vietnamese American video store owner who flew the communist flag and displayed a picture of Ho Chi Minh in public. This is where aging men spend their days sipping French coffee, smoking cigarettes, and talking about what might have been. Here the cultural and generational gaps sometimes seem to be widening rather than narrowing. Here, finally, is where my father felt most at ease in this country, playing tennis, shuffling mah-jongg tiles, or eating noodles with his former military comrades.

After the ceremonial fly-by and a series of speeches by veterans, a Vietnamese singer wearing camouflage-pattern pants took center stage. As she bellowed the anthem of the former Republic of Vietnam, the yellow flag with its three red stripes ascended slowly in the background:

Này công dân ơi! Quốc gia đến ngày giải phóng.
O People! The country nears its freedom day.

Ten thousand attendees rose to their feet, nearly all in tears, including me, even though I couldn't recite more than the first verse. Next "The Star Spangled Banner" was sung as Old Glory rose in a slight breeze. I knew every line.

I had come to Westminster to honor my father, the same way I had paid my tribute to the Americans at The Wall in Washington, D.C. The first time I visited the Vietnam Veterans Memorial was in 1986. It was difficult to stand before the names of those who gave their lives to fight for my freedom. They were not even from my country. Why didn't they go to Canada? Why didn't they question their orders? Where would I be now if they hadn't fought the Communists?

On the other hand, I knew that Americans were not the only ones who fought the Communists in Vietnam. Nearly 245,000 South Vietnamese died in defense of their country, about four for every U.S. forces death. Another 65,000* political victims were executed, while thousands more perished in the reeducation camps from disease, exhaustion, malnutrition, or suicide. I saw all the marked graves—those not bulldozed by the Communists after their victory—on the outskirts of Saigon when I returned there a decade ago.

I remember as a boy visiting my father's squadron and shaking hands with the other pilots all wearing green flight suits, pistols on their hips.

The first Americans I ever met were the advisers in his unit.

In the final years of the war my father would leave the house before dawn, sometimes arriving home in time for dinner. His job was to dump ordnance on Viet Cong (VC) positions, drop flares at night, and ferry troops and supplies. I used to think that was probably why the Communists kept him in captivity for so long after the war: a day for each VC he killed.

I wish my father were still alive. He died just eight brief years after leaving Vietnam. For all that—and despite the fact that he sometimes felt betrayed by the United States—he wouldn't have missed the memorial's dedication ceremony for anything. He fought alongside the Americans in Vietnam and was proud to have done so.

He didn't die in combat. I used to wish he had so I could have been rid of the burden of explaining what happened to him. In the United States, there is more recognition for dying than for surviving a war unless you are a POW celebrity like Jessica Lynch. No one questions the dead about commitment, duty, or sacrifice. My father accomplished a much more difficult challenge by surviving years of captivity, only to become a *nobody,* a cipher, in this country.

That's what happens when you lose a war and your country. The winners take away your family, your freedom, your people, and your flag. They tried to erase my father's mind, to destroy his dignity, to "enlighten" him about communism. But they could not take away his soul.

There is no memorial yet for my war, the Persian Gulf War that supposedly "kicked the Vietnam syndrome" in 1991 (or so President George H. W. Bush said to Congress). But Westminster's Vietnam War memorial is an es-

---

*In 1985, University of California at Berkeley researchers Jacqueline Desbarats and Karl D. Jackson published their research among Vietnamese refugees in the *Wall Street Journal.*

sential piece of our history. It honors my father and those fallen fighters who answered the call of duty during a time of turmoil for both countries.

He never looked back and no longer will I. It took thirty years, but my questions have been answered. The United States provided my family a second chance to live in freedom and peace and to get to know each other again; it did not forget about my father and his fellow detainees. And for that we are indebted. This is our story.

Top left: *Hoa at aircraft mechanic school, Rochefort, France, 1955. (Author's Collection)*
Top right: *VNAF Aviation Cadets Hoa and An at the Statue of Liberty, Christmas 1957. (Courtesy of Ly Ngoc An)*
Bottom: *Hoa as a student pilot in a B-25, Reese Air Force Base, Texas, 1958. (Author's Collection)*

FIRST FLIGHT

WHEN I WAS SIX I TOOK MY FIRST AIRPLANE RIDE. MY entire immediate family came along, as well as an older cousin. We were so excited we kept talking about the excursion for days in advance, and I could hardly sleep the night before. A white mosquito net covered my small body and blurred my half-asleep vision. Waking and turning, I tried to count the different cricket sounds through the night; their cadence rang in unison like a kinetic, unseen symphony. In the distance, faint explosions occasionally interrupted the cricket chirping but didn't silence them. Just like the people in my neighborhood, the insects were used to war. On most nights I would sleep right through the detonations. On this night I wished I knew what the crickets were saying.

I wasn't alone. My mother lay nearby, and my sisters slept in the same room; that's the way it was in our country. Families lived together and slept together. Our grandparents had lived with us until they passed away in 1969, within a year of each other. But little did we know that one day the Vietnamese diaspora would sprinkle us all over the world; we would all have our own houses.

Summer vacation had begun and we were heading for the low mountains of Da Lat, some 200 miles north of Saigon, to cool off for the day. When I was growing up, we hardly ever had any family vacations, so this would be a rare treat.

Because the countryside was dangerous, especially at night, for us air travel was safer—and we knew the pilot. That day the rain came and went, washing away the red clay on the pothole-filled dirt road leading to the airport. At the airport we moved among airplanes worth millions of dollars, yet we only had to step outside the gate to see a country mired in poverty. Our driver had dropped us off near an old, yellow half-cylindrical aluminum hangar from which we watched dozens of planes taxiing for takeoff and landing. We weren't at the civilian passenger terminal. We stood on the military side of Tan Son Nhut Airport, one of the busiest in the world in 1970.

We boarded a World War II–era C-47, the military version of the DC-3, a reliable, twin-engine transport. On its fuselage was the South Vietnamese national insignia, a white star on a blue disk surrounded by an outer red ring, with red and yellow sidebars. A national vertical yellow flag with three red horizontal stripes was painted on its rudder. The other passengers included families of military men, some in uniform. After a quick safety briefing by a crew member, we sat quietly on the red canvas seats usually reserved for airborne troops.

As the plane lumbered down the runway and took to the air, I looked out the window while gripping my mother's hand. She was also holding my older sister Thi, who sat on her other side. I could barely make out smoggy Saigon receding beneath the wings. Soon green rice fields and grass-roofed villages appeared. We were flying low enough to see tiny farmers and their water buffaloes dragging wooden plows. Growing up in the city, I had only seen buffaloes and fields in newspaper photographs.

After about fifteen minutes, the pilot in the left seat motioned to me to come into the cockpit. I unbuckled my belt and stumbled up the aisle, nearly tripping over the rollers on the floor. He picked me up and placed me on his lap. I could smell his signature Aqua Velva after-shave lotion and sweat. I hesitated to touch the controls even as he assured me that it was all right to steer the plane. He smiled to the copilot as I cautiously reached out and slightly pushed on the steering column.

There in front of me was our beautiful country. Tall, sharp mountains guarded deep green valleys, and the brown Mekong River wound sinuously through its delta to the sea. Large thunderclouds were scattered throughout the skies, ready to strike lightning and dump rain on those below. The plane was buffeted by the stormy air. The hazy countryside appeared so peaceful. But unbeknownst to me at that age was that our people, of the north and south, had been at war for almost two decades, the two sides supported by opposing superpowers. They had to choose sides or, unfortunately for many, face the wrath of all.

The pilot was my father. He had become one of the most experienced pilots in the VNAF. He pulled out a cigarette and turned his head to the left to blow the smoke out the small, sliding cockpit window. He hoisted me up by the waist so I could see over the nose of the aircraft. It was dizzying to be staring straight down at the ground as it moved underneath us.

We landed and spent the day in Da Lat. The return trip took nearly two hours, but I could hardly wait for us to land so I could go brag to my friends. I was hooked on flying that day. It would take another twenty years before I would become like my father, soaring over the plains of Texas, serving *my* country as a military aviator.

Top left: *My parents on their wedding day, Saigon, 1963. (Author's Collection)*
Top right: *With my mother and my older sister Thi, Saigon, 1966. (Author's Collection)*
Bottom left: *The only picture of all four kids with their father in Vietnam. Tan Son Nhut Air Base, Saigon, 1972. (Author's Collection)*
Bottom left: *Mama's boy at age one and his mother Nguyen Thi Niem, Saigon, 1965. (Author's Collection)*

CHAPTER 2

THE SHAMEFUL END

Today, America can regain the sense of pride that existed before Vietnam.
But it cannot be achieved by re-fighting a war that is finished as far as
America is concerned. These events, tragic as they are, portend neither the
end of the world nor of America's leadership in the world.

—President Gerald Ford, Tulane University, April 23, 1975

T HE SECOND TIME I BOARDED AN AIRPLANE, FIVE YEARS
later, was sheer terror for me.

As President Ford commented on the events unfolding in Vietnam, the rowdy crowd at Tulane University roared and gave him a standing
ovation. They were cheering the impending loss of my homeland, even
though most of them—like their predecessors of the 1960s—would never
feel the lasting impact of the Vietnam War. The military draft had ended and
U.S. troops and POWs had come home two years earlier. So why were they
celebrating our misery?

President Ford must have known the end was near. Two weeks earlier,
Congress had denied his request for $722 million in aid to South Vietnam.
American support finally came to an end as the North Vietnamese sped
toward Saigon with eighteen combat divisions backed by tanks for the "final
offensive." Their actions were in clear violation of the 1973 Paris Peace Accords, even though everyone knew at the time of signing that the accords
were a joke. Except for Henry Kissinger, who eventually took home the
Nobel Peace Prize, while his corecipient, North Vietnamese counterpart, Le
Duc Tho, rightfully declined. The United States withdrew its remaining

troops, and its 901 POWs were rightly released, but there would be no peace or honor to follow.

Images of the impending slaughter began airing in early March 1975. Long-ingrained photographs of barefoot rice farmers toting AK-47s had morphed into professional soldiers in green pith helmets armed to the teeth. They roared through the South Vietnamese central cities the way the U.S. Marines stormed Kuwait City sixteen years later, then Baghdad a dozen years after that.

Halfway around the world my family, along with the several thousand fortunate South Vietnamese who would live to tell about it, watched the unfolding of those tragic events. For us it was the worst of times. It seemed like the end of the world to me, even though I was only ten years old. That night remains as clear to me today as it was then. Every once in a while something triggers that haunting memory, and I am struck immobile.

On a recent Christmas vacation, my wife and I flew to Vermont to visit her family. Her father, Jim, and her sister Amy's husband, Bill, greeted us in the terminal. They were dressed in full snow garb, while we Californians strolled off the plane in skimpy jeans and thin turtlenecks. Snow had fallen, and it was freezing cold as we drove north through Connecticut and Massachusetts, with temperatures dipping into the teens. Steady flakes struck the windshield of Bill's SUV as visibility diminished to less than a quarter-mile.

I was riding in the back, barely able to make out road signs through the fog and snow. Jim put on a holiday CD, prepping us for the Christmas eve feast ahead: Nat King Cole sang, and then Bing Crosby did "White Christmas." My body went numb and my vision blurred. Flashes of Saigon came to life, and its night landscape filled my memory. I could hear the sound of helicopters approaching overhead.

"Daddy, can you skip that?" Shannon promptly asked Jim. She probably felt me squirming next to her, sliding across the leather seat like a car fishtailing across an icy road, uncontrollably and unpredictably. She understood. She had seen me react like this before when we were watching Vietnam documentaries on the History Channel.

To this day I cannot listen to "White Christmas." It is not because it's a terrible song. Indeed, it is still recognized as one of America's most favorite tunes. Written by Irving Berlin for a movie Crosby made with Fred Astaire called "Holiday Inn" in 1942, Crosby sang it often, especially during his visits with GIs during World War II, bringing many to tears, yearning for home.

But in Vietnam that week, his song signaled the end.

Some sicko must have thought of using such a sweet song as a warning. A simple, "Let's get the fuck out of here," over Armed Forces Radio, would have worked as well. Instead the announcer broadcast "It's 105 degrees and the temperature is rising," then played Crosby's hit to warn the remaining Americans in Saigon to head to the U.S. Embassy for the evacuation.

That was on April 29, 1975, the day before the end. The ARVN's ragtag 18th Division, the last unit standing before Saigon, was decimated at Xuan Loc despite putting up a valiant fight. A few VNAF pilots managed to get airborne and put up a heroic but futile final battle against the enemy.

I can't seem to get the night I left Saigon out of my mind. I still wonder what President Ford was thinking when he gave that speech acknowledging our impending loss. Could he have known how tragic this disaster really was to those of us who were there? Why were the Marines already waiting off the coast? Was there a secret negotiation for the evacuation, the way Kissinger had bypassed the South Vietnamese government at the 1973 Paris Peace Conference?

At the end of March 1975, the mood in Saigon became somber after Hue City fell so quickly to the NVA. This time, the Marines weren't there to fight door to door as they did during the 1968 Tet offensive. Danang was swollen by then with 2 million refugees, all scrambling south for safety along single-lane Route 7B while getting pounded by merciless North Vietnamese Army (NVA) artillery. Nearly 40,000 innocents died in the "convoy of tears," even though victory was within reach of the Communists. (This slaughter has gone almost unmentioned in the thousands of books about the war.) The NVA must have wanted to send a final signal to Saigon and Washington. Fleeing South Vietnamese were so afraid of the Communists that some hung desperately onto the landing gear of the last passenger jet plane leaving Danang and were crushed in its wheel wells. North Vietnam had committed its army to unrestricted killing to end the war, and the United States did nothing to stop this.

My Saigon elementary school classes had been canceled for two weeks, since the attack on the Presidential Palace on April 8. On that day, I nearly became a war casualty. It was my closest brush with death in Vietnam, having hunkered down in our family bunker many times.

I was attending my last class as a student in Saigon, where I had been learning to speak decent French after four long, tongue-twisting years. Final exams. Yes, even fifth-graders had to take them. I had cruised through the first test by 9 a.m. I took a short break and stared out the large window to the left of the classroom. Large trees hid the barbed-wire fence on top of the gates surrounding the Presidential Palace across the street. But I knew that the fence and the armed guards were there, having seen the palace many times on my way home from school. It was the equivalent of attending a public school on Pennsylvania Avenue, right across from the White House.

As I gazed out the schoolroom window, I savored dreams of a long summer, fishing in the bomb craters carved by VC artillery and B-52 Arc Light strikes. No more Mr. Bui and his disciplinary slaps; no more Mademoiselle Juneau and her Gallic bickering: *merci beaucoup* and *au revoir*. I was daydreaming when my teacher handed me the second exam.

Ka-Boom.

My ears rang as if someone had lit a firecracker inside my head. The concussion of the first bomb sucked the air from my tiny lungs while I struggled to hold on to my chair, gasping to catch a breath. A wall of air pushed me to the ground. The entire classroom, focused and silent a minute before, now looked like an insane asylum, with screaming kids scurrying every which way to get under desks. Even Mr. Bui crawled on his knees in front of the class, seeking shelter. I remained under my desk, having experienced numerous VC attacks on Saigon before, although none ever this close.

Ka-Boom.

The second explosion convinced me to stay put. Bracing myself against my chair, I heard the shriek of a diving jet fighter overhead. The shock wave shook the room viciously and sent books and notes flying everywhere. I thought it was all over. Peeking out from under my desk, I saw red antiaircraft fire fly skyward and heard a staccato of automatic weapons. These last rounds must have come from a guard post on the palace's grounds shortly after the second bomb struck. I wondered if anyone from my school had died. Two of my sisters were also in class that morning; my mother was here too, but she was teaching in a classroom on the other side of the school.

The deadly roars of the jet soon faded. There were no more explosions, just chaos inside my classroom. I was still in shock and scared, like the rest of my classmates. Many I would never see again. The ever-firm Mr. Bui remained under his desk. He looked awkward and funny to me, and probably to the other kids, too, and we all laughed, even under the morning's terrible spell of fear. Classes were canceled by noon, and we were all sent home. A curfew took effect shortly after.

My mother and sisters were all unhurt. We began to recover from the shock of being under attack. A few days later my father announced what had happened. The pilot who had bombed the Presidential Palace had been in the VNAF, one of our own. I was devastated; those pilots were my only heroes.

The true price of attending school next to the president's residence came to light that day. I suppose my experience was not an anomaly. In the modern world coup d'états and assassination attempts on presidents in their homes are not uncommon, and South Vietnam's turbulent history included a few.

For the Vietnamese the war was a part of our life whether we liked it, whether we had supported it, or whether the United States, China, or the Soviet Union had had enough. Civilians living in a war zone were subject to its horrors, much as the Israelis, Palestinians, Afghanis, Iraqis, and Kosovars were in subsequent years. Governments called the shots and soldiers carried out the orders. As an adult, I would puzzle over why some Americans had thought the war in Vietnam was a mistake when Ho Chi Minh and his supporters had tried to unite our countries at any cost. (If South Korea was worth defending for fifty years, why wasn't South Vietnam? Kuwait was worth liberating, so oil must be worth more than rice and rubber. Time will tell if the war in Iraq will be able to absorb more American blood.)

After the rogue jet attack panic began to spread like blood from a fatal wound. Fear was something we could touch and smell in our neighborhood, especially when soldiers and tanks crowded the streets in front of our house. The atmosphere at the base housing at Tan Son Nhut Air Base was thick with rumors and jet fuel fumes. Most children remained indoors, and families were glued to radios listening to the BBC for the latest update on the imminent invasion by North Vietnam. Our neighbors were gone; I didn't know when they had left and I never found out.

Tuesday, April 22, 1975, dissolved into a dark and sticky Saigon night. Under pressure from U.S. Ambassador Graham Martin, President Nguyen Van Thieu had resigned the day before. This had ignited widespread terror in Saigon and those with money and connections began to leave. Our family had the latter, but only by luck.

A cousin of my father, who had worked at the U.S. Embassy, told him to get us out of Saigon as soon as the evacuation began; thus we were among the very first to flee. My father came home from the airfield at about 11 p.m. My mother had been asleep for about two hours when my father, driving wildly, brought his Lambretta scooter to a screeching halt in our driveway.

My mother tried to get my sisters and me out of bed all at once. Lights were out, darkness surrounded us, but I knew exactly where my belongings were. Since we had gone through so many attacks on previous nights, the drill was set. Well prepared for war, we followed our instincts at the sound of an explosion, a shrieking air raid siren, or my mother's voice in the middle of the night. The sound of the Lambretta engine outside punctuated the silence; our dog, Milou, began to bark mournfully. Before I could even begin to fathom what was happening, he sensed our imminent departure. My mother hurried back and forth between the drawers and the suitcases on her bed, stuffing them at random. Her long silhouette was cast against the back wall, a precursor of her lasting impact on my life, replacing my father's role. She held a kerosene lamp in one hand and packed the luggage with the other. The room was barely lit as the tiny flame flickered and then slowly disappeared. I stumbled to the living room and reached for the light switch.

"Turn the damn lights off!" screamed my father. By now my mother had gone outside with my sisters. Standing alone in the dark bedroom, I wondered why we were packing our belongings and hurrying to go somewhere. I thought this was another attack and that we should be running toward our bomb shelter down the hallway from our bedroom. Not this time, though. I then realized that everyone was waiting for me. I grabbed my jacket and slipped on my sneakers. I took my favorite toy, a steel model A-37 Dragonfly, and ran to the porch. My sisters all had half-asleep, blank stares on their faces, but Thu, my two-year-old baby sister, was crying loudly.

"Where are we going, Mother?"

"I don't know yet, but we have to leave now. We'll be all right, sweetheart." My mother sounded nervous, yet she never would have guessed our fate that night, let alone envisioned bringing up her children in a strange land beginning only a week later.

My father wore his usual green flight suit and black boots. He was very quiet. He mustered a few words to get all of us on his scooter. Milou, our skinny, dirty-white poodle, stared at all of us. He looked sad. He was the only dog we'd had that had not been stolen at Tan Son Nhut. I sat in back, holding on to my mother for dear life, as we took up every inch on that worn leather seat.

My father kicked the overloaded scooter into gear with all six of us aboard, and we started weaving toward the dirt alley. I looked back at our house and wondered if I would ever see it again. The sandbags above our homemade bomb shelter seemed to be sliding off the roof; the shadows of the trees in the front yard shifted with the wind; the fragrance from our green

mango tree floated in the air. Our house. Our home. I got one last look before
the scooter sped away. Milou ran after us, but we couldn't take him along.
We lost him in a dust cloud kicked up by the scooter. We abandoned him, the
same way the United States left South Vietnam, like a dog that just didn't fit
into its plans.

We sped across the base through a slight breeze. Most of the lights were
out for security. In the distance flares and tracers lit the skies; artillery shells
exploded sporadically, reminding us of the danger closing in. It was an un-
usually frenzied morning. Until I saw *The Great Santini* years later, I never
thought of myself as a military brat. That morning in 1975 was like the fictional Colonel "Bull" Meachum hurrying his family out of bed to move to another base. Except we weren't singing "Battle Hymn of the Republic" or the
"Marine Corps Hymn." The military called it a "permanent change of station" (PCS) move. But our move could have been abbreviated PCC, for "permanent change of country." No movers came, and there were no packers, no
moving trucks, no farewell parties, and no goodbyes to our neighbors. It was
simply an escape in the middle of the night.

As we lurched through Tan Son Nhut, I looked for familiar signposts and
tried to catch last glimpses of my receding childhood. It had been filled with
joy amid the fear of death. We had moved onto the base in 1972 from a
Saigon suburb, and I had enjoyed that move more than my sisters did. The
fires of my childhood dreams that set me on the path of becoming a pilot
were stoked daily as I watched VNAF aircraft returning from missions. I
would go to the squadron with my father and fantasize about *Twelve O'Clock
High,* a popular World War II series shown on Armed Forces Television.
The hangar, the post exchange (PX), the movie theater, the ruined tanks on
the playground, the old warplanes—all had been my favorite hangouts.
From the back of the scooter, and trying not to slide off the seat, I saw the tall
grass waving in the wind, the place that had once made a perfect hideout
from enemies during a chase game with my friends next door.

We finally reached the darkened airport gym. A bus was parked in the
front lot, its oil-smelling diesel engine idling. My father stopped the scooter
and walked over to a group of men standing at the rear of the bus. I could not
hear the conversation, but I sensed the importance of the moment from the
look on my mother's face as she stood there, quietly holding my youngest sister. He walked back and whispered a few words into my mother's ear.

"OK. It's time to go, kids. I'll see you later." My father then reached into
his pocket and pulled out several strange green bills. He handed the money

to my mother and picked up two bags of clothes and his attaché case containing his military records and family photographs. I had my belongings in his green helmet bag, standard issue for military aviators everywhere. He winked at me and rubbed my head. We boarded the hot and crowded bus without him. I managed to get to a window and inhaled a breath of fresh air. I looked out into the darkness and found my father's face. He stood there waving and, as we pulled away, disappeared into the darkness.

The bus moved slowly. I was sure the driver couldn't see the road because his lights, and all the lights on base, were off that night. Then we stopped. Minutes went by. An hour passed. I began to suffer from extreme claustrophobia in the steamy, packed-sardine atmosphere of the bus. (Years later, I would have a panic attack in pilot survival training during a simulated imprisonment, a throwback to this moment.) I had lost sight of my mother and sisters. They were somewhere on the bus but no longer right next to me. But I saw my father again briefly, this time talking to some Americans also in flight suits. How could I have known it would take seventeen years before I would again see his face?

Finally, the bus doors swung open and everyone quickly piled out. It was still dark as I stumbled off the bus, searching for my mother and sisters. I found them, staggering along two families in front of me. I didn't know where I was on the tarmac until I felt the hot air from the propellers of a large camouflage-painted aircraft. From the profile, I knew it was a C-130 Hercules like the one my father flew. But it was not from the VNAF. Its fuselage had faint U.S. Air Force (USAF) insignia. Its ramp was down and two USAF crewmen tried to control the crowd rushing the aircraft. I smelled the familiar odor of aviation fuel as the Hercules' four turbine engines idled, ready for an immediate takeoff.

I held my mother's hand as we sat on the steel floor of the plane, layered with tracks and rollers used to load cargo. The canvas seats were rolled up on the sides of the cabin. No seats, no meals, no stewardesses. The only lighting came from several red and green lights in the cargo bay. There must have been over 200 people on an aircraft that ordinarily carries half that number. Improbably, the reasonable thought occurred to me as we waited that Vietnamese people are smaller than Americans, so more of us could fit on this airplane. In front of the crowd sitting on the floor was some sort of dark canvas tarp. I could not figure out what it was, though it took up room where several rows of people could have been.

The ramp screeched up and the engine noise of the plane quieted for a few minutes as the pilot began to taxi. The two crewmen struggled through the crowd to their takeoff seats near the two open windows, one on each side of the aircraft. I held on tightly to the floor railings to keep from bouncing every time the aircraft rolled over a bump on the tarmac.

The pilot made what seemed like a sharp turn followed by an immediate acceleration, signaling the takeoff roll. The Hercules roared down the runway. My butt felt every jolt until we were airborne. It seemed to take forever before the landing gear was raised. I would later learn that a long takeoff roll meant we were dangerously heavy. Looking out the dirty Plexiglas bubble window that night, I saw nothing but a faint orange glow bruising a dark sky. I could not catch a last glimpse of Saigon's bright lights, the lights of my hometown.

The crewman on the left stood up and took a large pistol from beneath his seat. A flare gun. He looked downward from the window, perhaps searching for a surface-to-air missile. "What a way to go," I sighed to myself; getting shot down on my way out of Vietnam wasn't exactly my childhood dream of flying. (Several VNAF aircraft would eventually be shot down on the penultimate day of the war by NVA troops firing shoulder-held SA-7s. But ours wouldn't be one of them.)

I wondered what it would feel like to get hit by a missile and tumble out of the sky from our altitude. (No parachutes.) But why would they shoot at us civilians, I wondered naively. Why was flying over Saigon considered dangerous territory? How come we had left at such an odd time? Why didn't my father come with us? The exhausting evening caught up with me and I slowly slid down the cold metal wall and slept.

I woke up to a bright blue sky shining through the window above me. I rubbed my eyes and glanced at my mother and sisters, who were all still asleep and looked drained. Most of the passengers were still sleeping on the floor of the plane. The two crewmen were sitting at their seats, facing the crowd, but without their flare pistols in hand.

In the light I didn't recognize any faces. Strangers. Who were these people? I thought we knew everyone who lived in my neighborhood. I looked toward the front of the crowd for that strange-looking tarp. But it was gone. Instead, there were more people than I remembered being there only a few hours earlier. To my shock and surprise, I recognized several men in the new group. They had served with my father in the VNAF, but they were not wearing their uniforms now. Dressed in civilian clothes and crouched on the floor, the men appeared to be in disguise. Major Binh and Colonel Trung were there. My stare caught the attention of Major Binh, father of my school-mate Tuan. I waved hello to him, but he didn't acknowledge it. Tuan also turned away quickly. I knew that both had seen me. Why were these men on the aircraft with us? How come my father hadn't joined us?

A horrifying thought flashed through my mind. *My father has been left behind!* I woke my mother and told her of my fears. She started crying; the plane's engines drowned out her sobs. I began to cry. Then my mother spotted another familiar face in the crowd and she whispered something to Thi. I didn't recognize the woman until my mother reminded me. Miss Mai was a well-known entertainer in Saigon; now dressed in dowdy clothes and hardly resembling a TV star, she sat huddled two rows behind us. Mai managed a fake smile, as though glad to be recognized by a fan.

The plane nosed over and banked sharply as gravity pulled me against my mother. We were descending, and the engine noise lessened for a moment. Where were we landing? The gears stuttered down noisily and the crewmen signaled the restless crowd to hang on to each other. Two hundred people shifted forward and then backward, as the Hercules touched down and reversed its propellers to slow down. I smelled tire rubber burning. It was a rough landing. I saw swaying palm trees passing the plane as we came to a temporary halt before making a turn off the runway.

The engines idled and the rear ramp was lowered to reveal two military police cars. The men were Asian and they wore khaki uniforms, but I still could not figure out where we were. We hadn't flown to Hanoi, I hoped. The crewman on the ramp motioned us to stand up as he pointed to the rear of the aircraft. My legs were numb after being cramped for hours on the steel rollers. My empty stomach growled for anything to eat. Where were we? Where was my father? Was he meeting us here? What was going to happen to us? Was the war over? My ten-year-old mind had questions that would multiply over the years and preoccupy my adult life.

My father could have easily gotten on that aircraft or flown one like it to the Philippines or Singapore. Others had done just that, but they were among the minority of servicemen who fled early, as I would learn decades later. Eventually over 125,000 South Vietnamese, or less than 1 percent of the entire population, would fearfully depart Saigon over the ensuing week. President Thieu allegedly took millions in gold with him to Taiwan, Britain, and then the United States. Yet he lived modestly until his death in 2001 (unlike many former leaders of the Vietnam era and their excuses, he died in silence).

Former premier Nguyen Cao Ky (by then a private citizen) vowed to fight to the death—but then flew his helicopter with a three-star general to a U.S. Navy ship off the coast. Who was left behind to fight the charging Communists? Where were our mighty American friends? Who remained to lead a desperate nation? I could only wonder.

The Marine Corps would later teach me much about duty and honor. But I already learned about both from my father the night I left Saigon.

Packed like sardines. Evacuation flight to freedom, C-141 to Guam, April 1975. (Courtesy of United States Marine Corps)

CHAPTER 3

GONE AGAIN

*I told myself I'd probably leave at the last minute. But I couldn't leave too
early. As an officer, you have your pride, your duty. You can't change the
past. [Looking at his son in uniform] Besides, if I had left, maybe he
wouldn't have turned out the way he did.*

—My father commenting in a *U.S. News & World Report* article written shortly
after his arrival in the United States in 1992

I PLACED MY FATHER'S WORN, DARK VINYL ATTACHÉ CASE ON
the top of my desk, and opened it. It contained his personal documents,
including those I took with me the night we left Saigon. I spun its two
rusting three-number locks to "ooo" with my thumbs, sliding them outward
then flipping the lid open. At first, I wondered if he had used a certain combination to lock the case, perhaps his old squadron designation, or his prisoner number, or the number of years he had lost in captivity. Then I realized
that honoring such dates would have presented too many possibilities, and at
his age would have been impossible to recall.

Now I know how wrong I had been about him all along.

A man who witnessed war most of his life, what would my father have remembered most? Was he ready to refight the Vietnam War and win back
our homeland? Was he haunted by all the death and destruction, the kind

that troubled many U.S. servicemen? Would he remember the faces of those Americans who trained him, fought with him, and evacuated his family to safety? What would he say to them now after all this time?

Maybe he simply wanted to forget all those bad times.

I kept hoping and wondering all those years, first waiting for him to appear among the crowds evacuated to the Guam and Arkansas refugee camps where we were flown after Saigon fell, then for the few letters that finally came. I finally gave up. I needed to get on with my own life, to walk out from his shadow once and for all. By becoming a *real* American through the U.S. Marine Corps, I would perhaps shed the last threads of bitterness and resentment whenever the word "Vietnam" was mentioned.

But that didn't happen, because the Marines have not forgotten about Vietnam either.

Just look at the 2004 presidential campaign. Only the Communists seem to be able to put the war behind them. Echoes of Vietnam resonate again as Americans are being tested as to their commitment to a war in another faraway land. The prism of Iraq forces us again to examine the same old questions: Who won? Who really lost in Vietnam? Or, as one prominent *Washington Post* columnist put it, "Who cares?"

I fucking care.

The full impact of war usually takes time to unfurl. It may take years, even decades. That, at least, was the case for me. I believe my father felt the same way.

Now that my father is gone again, I realize I had joined the Marines for him and for South Vietnam, as much as I did for any sense of patriotism to America. I wanted to relieve him of a loser's guilt, a husband's regret, a father's remorse. Most of all, I wanted him to know that he stood for respectability—for duty, honor, and country—and that he taught me those lessons early on. I don't know if I succeeded. My father used to stare at me when I was in uniform, perhaps reminding him of the U.S. Marine who had prevented him from leaving Saigon aboard one of the departing helicopters.

I had hoped that people would come to see my father in a different light—not to feel sorry for him but to appreciate him as the American public has come to acknowledge the sacrifice made by U.S. Vietnam veterans. Giving them their due. No longer blaming them for the quagmire.

Nobody ever welcomed my father home, in Vietnam or in the United States; nobody ever thanked him for serving or acknowledged his suffering.

Not even me, and I knew better. I thought I had more time. I had wanted one more promotion, had to make one more business trip, get one more bonus check before I made time to tell him how much I appreciated all he went through for us.

The attaché case holds most of his important documents, many needed as proof for senior citizen discounts in his new country. He needed all the help he could get at his age. Despite serving his country for two decades, not even counting the twelve-year imprisonment and hard labor, he had no pension. Nor could he rely on U.S. Veterans' Administration (VA) hospitals to treat him the way they finally accepted Filipino veterans.*

My father had lost a war *and* his country, and along with this all benefits (assuming the South Vietnamese government would have provided any). Yet he never once complained to me. Perhaps he thought his American Marine son would make snide remarks to him, the way the U.S. advisers did in the war.

When I was growing up in this country, I hated him for not coming along with us the night we left Vietnam. I loathed him for not being there when my mother bounced from job to job while learning English. My sisters and I hid in fear under the covers at night, locked inside a small, rundown apartment in a shoddy part of town, not knowing what to say or whom to call when someone knocked on our door at night.

I detested him whenever we stood in line at the grocery store, food stamps in hand, clutching several Twinkies while being scolded by the clerk as if we children on welfare were not allowed to enjoy such treats.

I could not stand the hundreds of times I was asked where he was. Almost everyone assumed he had abandoned us (most of the kids in my neighborhood came from single-parent families) or they thought he had died in the war. I often resorted to the latter, mumbling the easier answer.

We hardly interacted at all with the Vietnamese families who were still intact after the evacuation. None of his VNAF buddies wanted to deal with a single mom and four small kids. All of them had their own obstacles to overcome here. When we were scattered from Saigon, every man, woman, and child was for him or herself. The Vietnam tragedy began to resemble one of

---

*In 2003, President George W. Bush signed into law an act enabling World War II Filipino veterans living in the United States to receive VA medical care. Some Filipino veterans had been waiting for nearly sixty years since the U.S. victory over Japan.

those giant anthills in the Ia Drang Valley, their inhabitants running aimlessly in every direction without a leader. When we fled every family was on its own.

Yet I can remember the times I was questioned about whether the "so-called" reeducation camps really even existed. A U.S. Vietnam veteran mockingly asked if reeducation had been "just classroom lectures" or "retraining." I wonder why few of my father's peers, formerly detained, talked to their children or wives about what they endured in Vietnam. It must have been easier to gather at coffee shops in Little Saigon, to be with friends who survived the war, to reminisce about pre-1975 life, than to face their Americanized families. Once my father and I were united, I stopped wondering, waiting for him to open up, to let out that primal scream about losing his fellow soldiers, all respect, the war, his country, and another twelve years of his life. But he never did. He would never say anything bad about his new land, even in private.

Surely the years apart from his family must have been difficult for my father to forgive. He couldn't even pretend to make up for lost time with his children, especially as an old man in a strange land. And perhaps I didn't try hard enough, nor did my sisters or my mother. I guess I was hoping he would call me up one day and we would go fishing and he would tell me all about his life, from his birth and through the war, and he would reveal his true feelings about this country.

I watched *Coming Home, The Deer Hunter, Platoon, We Were Soldiers,* all of it, hoping to get a glimpse of what my father went through. I should have spent time with him. Rather than reading all those Vietnam War books and memoirs by American veterans and journalists, I should have asked him about his new life and its difficulties. The stories portrayed in the movies and books usually ended by the U.S. withdrawal in 1973. Only a few even attempted to capture the painful evacuation of Saigon.

In newsreels at the time, the U.S. Embassy resembled a wasp's nest with insect-like choppers repeatedly taking away desperate humans clinging to the helicopter skids. Many watched their freedom slip away from behind armed Marines and chain-link fences.

I caught a tiny glimpse of my past while watching *Miss Saigon,* only to be disappointed again with another love tale between a GI and a Vietnamese bar girl.

I still seethe when I think of the day I lost my country of birth. I also wanted to know why South Vietnam wasn't able to defend itself. After all, Vietnamization* had been announced in 1969, a full six years before the end.

But seeing those movies and reading those books did help me understand what Americans went through, for it was not *their* war or *their* country that they were fighting for. I wanted to know why some Americans served, while others avoided military service during that era. To many who opposed U.S. involvement South Vietnam was not worthy of America's sacrifice. To some, not even now, when history clearly shows that the Communists' atrocities had begun as early as the late 1940s. Even Jane Fonda has apologized. In his memoir *My Losing Season,* novelist Pat Conroy wished he had served as a Marine in Vietnam and protested the war "after he had done his duty." Why do presidential candidates still have to justify decisions made in their youth nearly four decades ago?

Perhaps Vietnam still haunts because Americans cannot stand losing, and America has never accepted losers in any of its wars, except those who came from my country. We refugees remind them of loss every time they see us.

The politicians were blamed first. Richard Nixon held the U.S. Congress responsible. The U.S. military was once blamed, but that perception has changed over time. To this day, Gen. William Westmoreland still faults the press for undoing his war efforts. Finally, it has become much easier just to point the finger at the South Vietnamese, for those once in charge are now either too old to refute the accusation or they are dead; their children are too busy with daily life, dealing with their own generational and adjustment issues. Who else is left to blame?

FOX News pundit Bill O'Reilly compared the Iraqis with the South Vietnamese during an interview with President George W. Bush on September 27, 2004.

O'REILLY: The South Vietnamese didn't fight for their freedom, which is why they don't have it today.

BUSH: Yes.

O'REILLY: Do you think the Iraqis are going to fight for their freedom?

BUSH: Absolutely.

---

*Vietnamization referred to the process of turning the war back to the South Vietnamese military as U.S. troops withdrew. In 1965 the United States had taken over conduct of the war.

To me, the most hurtful comment came from retired U.S. Army Col. David Hackworth, the nation's most decorated soldier in Korea and Vietnam, in a 2002 interview with *Proceedings*.

> We failed to understand that we couldn't rely on the Afghan supporting force, which was a basic lesson out of Vietnam. We never trusted the South Vietnamese on an operation. If it were an anvil-and-hammer operation, we'd never put the South Vietnamese as the hammer or the anvil, because they wouldn't be there for the job.

The United States will end up blaming the Iraqis, too. (General John Abizaid, chief of U.S. Central Command, has repeatedly stated that "Iraqis must depend less on the U.S. military, even if that means a bigger risk of violence in coming months. After all, it's their country, it's their future.")

At least in Vietnam, the United States was *asked* to come help. We will never know what would eventually have happened to Vietnam had this country stayed out of Southeast Asia. General Douglas MacArthur's principle, "Always avoid a land war in Asia," was violated and another intervention was embarked upon.

My father's briefcase had been sitting at the bottom of the closet collecting dust and waiting for time to heal my lingering sense of loss. I had put it away to forget, to stop tormenting myself for wasting the short time that I had him back, to help me to move on with my life. Yet there remained an occasional urge for me to riffle through it since he'd left us.

I actually believed my father would escape another brush with early death. For most of his life, he seemed invincible, in war and in captivity and in poverty. Maybe he ran out of lives.

The lock on the briefcase no longer worked; there were no more secrets to hide. The rusty clasps swung open like a coffin door unlocking, inviting me back to his past, to a stack of loose papers, layered on top of weathered brown, unclasped manila folders. Old letters with dry ink like scrimshaw across the onion paper dating back decades. Some were written to him, others were in his hand. I quickly perused several addressees; many letters came from one address in Ho Chi Minh City. I was tempted to try to find details of his life away from my mother, my sisters, and me. I wanted to know because, now that he was gone again, I was ready.

But I hesitated. I felt his stoic gaze on me. A blown-up wood-framed photo of my father as a handsome lieutenant dressed in VNAF service blues stands atop my bookshelf. He is in America but he is not smiling. He was here to learn how to fly while his family was back in a war zone. Next to his portrait lies the neatly folded Republic of Vietnam (RVN) flag given to me at his funeral. I recall being a schoolboy in Saigon, beaming with pride, standing tall with my classmates, singing "Quốc Ca," the national anthem, watching that flag run up the wooden pole before classes began. The words called for citizens to rise up, to prepare for the liberation; it had been written in 1945, when the French were still seeking to reclaim an empire in Indochina. It is still played, and sung tearfully, at Vietnamese expatriate gatherings worldwide. We have not forgotten. RVN flags still flutter at official state and local functions, much to the dismay of the present Consulate General of Vietnam in San Francisco.

An open box with incense sticks ready to be lit stands near the flag. A chevron-shaped pair of silver pilot's wings rests next to an empty bowl reserved for food and fruit offerings to Confucian gods.

I tried to read through the private letters, the ones written to him by the "other" woman and the mother of his second son and my half-brother An, but I could not do it. A dead man deserves his privacy. I put the letters back in the envelope where they remain.

I looked through the stack of loose papers. A résumé simply listed his job history as a teacher's aide and aircraft mechanic—no mention of his pilot career. Two blue passports, one granted by the Socialist Republic of Vietnam, the other from the United States, stuck to each other like two squares of rice paper. Near the bottom of the attaché case was a crumpled document with the words "Camp Nam Ha" at the top left. It stated his 1987 release date from captivity (for the alleged "crimes" of fighting against the people and for "befriending America, the Enemy").

Some of his paperwork winded me; the emotional power of paper and words was too raw for me to absorb. The first time I saw the internment documents I couldn't believe he had kept them. Why would someone want to hold on to those memories of suffering, those "reminders of failures," as he called them.

Several times I asked him what he did in the war. He kept his counsel, but in the notes I found years later, he had repeatedly scribbled: "Why do you want to know what I did in the war? Who wants to know?" He reached out to me from the grave, reasserting his right to silence.

I found several versions, both handwritten and typed, of a single letter like the one below.

Dear Son,

You must know how much it means to me when you decided to give me a chapter in your book. It will be written by a former South Vietnamese Air Force pilot in D- English. If it doesn't matter to you what I did was a failure, then I will tell you some stories of the past. All I've been doing is to get along with all of you. Things have changed. No one can estimate to what extent. I was a coward. For you guys see me become a loser, my old combat friends will see me with another eye.

All I can tell you now that it was fear and shame of what I thought. I was just lucky that I didn't have my picture posted on the wooden frame displayed along with the other officers in the Airborne Division, Marines at the roundup point in front of Ben Thanh Market after April 1975.

This is the only chance to tell about the old days of what I felt, thought, remembered of what I went through to you or anyone else who wishes to know of the past in the Vietnam War. Another reason, either simple coincidence or you may call it destiny, is you're in the same Marine unit that I used to fly support for and was rescued by in the early days of the U.S. involvement in Vietnam.

What the hell did I fight in the war for? Was it for a better living? Nah, it wasn't. My monthly wage was half of those who drove a Lambretta tricycle in downtown Saigon. An American will spend that amount in Vietnamese piasters in one night at the Continental Palace Hotel on drinks and girls. It was still better than the troops and families defending an outpost with steamed rice and fish sauce.

It was not a war between North and South Vietnam. It was part of the Cold War. It must not be forgotten that a war had been going on for 21 years in a very small country at that time with no name on the world map.

What I did in the war was a failure, don't you think? Who wants to know about us? No one wants to hear about the Vietnam War no more. Everything involved is degrading . . . the Communist leader slamming his shoes on the desk at the UN meeting, colonels repairing bicycles in the streets, lieutenant colonels selling sweet black bean soup.

I am sorry I had taken offense. There is no more sense of getting angry now. Twenty years have gone by.

*Dear Son, that is quite a big question you gave me. Who cares? Give the
old man a break!*
  —*Pham Van Hoa,* 1995

I sorted through the rest of the remaining loose papers, finally fingering a
thick vellum certificate, worn out along its folds with broken gold borders
lining the formal calligraphy. None of my U.S. Marine awards even come
close to resembling this one, I thought. I immediately noticed the signature of
President Nguyen Van Thieu at the bottom right. Even though I have not
had any formal education in my native language for years, I could still deci-
pher and appreciate the significance of the award.

"Bao Quoc Huan Chuong. National Order of Vietnam, Fifth Class,
awarded on January 28, 1968, to First Lieutenant Pham Van Hoa."*

Two audiocassettes mailed to me by my Vietnam veteran friend and journalist Bernie Edelman rest at the bottom of the briefcase. I played the first
one and leaned back on my chair. My father's voice came to life as if he were
in the room, sharing his life the way I had always hoped. Maybe this was his
way of opening up, able to communicate with a stranger, a veteran like
Bernie, even though their paths had never crossed in Vietnam.

I had to hit the stop button twice.

On the tape, my father paused and his voice cracked noticeably, answering
the questions posed by Bernie for a book on the Vietnam War. I had to clench
my teeth and kept swallowing.

"The U.S. Marines [later] had their own Cobra gunships," my father's
voice intoned. "They didn't trust us, the South Vietnamese fighters. But we
still went on an operation called Do Xa. D.O.X.A. We were on airborne alert.
The helicopters didn't have enough firepower, so they requested support
from us. I went in and got hit, and I crashed."

Through my years of studying Marine Corps and Vietnam War history, I
had never even heard of Do Xa.

I immediately powered up the computer and Googled "Do Xa." Several
search results popped up. I clicked on the one headlined, "Do Xa Troop Insert by the Purple Foxes," and scrolled through pictures of Marines and their
relic choppers. A narrative of the assault on Do Xa crowded the web pages,
recalling a battle scene from 1964. I continued reading until I came across

*The National Order was South Vietnam's highest military decoration.

two pictures of a downed A-1 Skyraider fighter-bomber. A chill went up my spine as I stared in disbelief. The memories of the stench of oily smoke and the thwop-thwop of my Sea Knight helicopter rotors over Kuwait forced themselves into the present, and I transported myself back forty years. I went back to a time when my father flew in another war, supporting the U.S. troopers and the ARVN.

CHAPTER 4

FIGHTER PILOT

A FLIGHT OF FOUR PROPELLER-DRIVEN T-28S CIRCLED OVER-head before landing on Danang's asphalt runway.

Four young VNAF pilots proudly stepped out of their aircraft, the core of the newly formed 2d Fighter Squadron (2d FS). They sported cowboy hats; their flight suits had the new squadron patch emblazoned with a growling tiger centered on a white five-pointed star. (The squadron's call sign was Phi Ho or Flying Tigers.) Each had a .38-caliber pistol on his hip. Flight leader Tuong had dark suntanned skin; his call sign was Tuong "Muc" or "Inky." Si was one of the tallest pilots in the VNAF, whose call sign was Si "Co" or "Stork." Round-faced Long was slightly heavy, Long "Heo" or "Piggy." Then there was my father, Hoa "Diên" or "Crazy." (While in flight school in the United States in the late 1950s, my father earned his call sign due to his penchant for brawling.)

For the next fifteen days, the flight would be providing quick-response close air support* for the northern region of South Vietnam, I Corps.

By order of Air Support Operation Center 1 (ASOC 1), arriving VNAF pilots had to report to a U.S. intelligence officer immediately after landing. A USAF first lieutenant, the "IO," was in his comfortable and cool air-conditioned office. My father had a difficult time understanding why his de-tachment had to dictate a postflight intelligence report, especially to a U.S. officer not in his chain of command.

"Five structures destroyed, five damaged, casualties unknown. Ordnance

---

*In late 1961, USAF advisers (known as "co van") arrived in South Vietnam. A detachment called Farm Gate helped stand up the 2d FS at Nha Trang. U.S. pilots also flew combat missions, in viola-tion of the 1954 Geneva Accords that had divided Vietnam into two countries.

expended—two cluster bombs, two 100-pound bombs." The IO was never pleased with that simple a report. He often asked with a doubtful and mocking attitude, "How do you know that's ten total?"

"That's what we estimated before we left the area," my father promptly replied, shifting under the weight of the parachute, life raft, clipboard with maps, gunbelt, helmet, and survival gear that all pilots had to wear. "We know how to count from 1 to 100 in Vietnamese, French, and English!"

"How can you be sure of your postflight reports?" the IO asked. It was clear he didn't believe the pilots. It was beyond his comprehension that they could really bomb their own country and people. It wasn't a problem so much of language but of trust. Neither the IO nor my father knew that the numbers were being sent back to the Pentagon for U.S. Secretary of Defense Robert McNamara. His "whiz kids" would crunch the data into pie charts and statistics that may have made sense at the Ford Motor Company but not in Vietnam.

Officially, the VNAF pilots were permitted to use the U.S. facilities while deployed at the air base, but their first time in the mess hall was not pleasant.

"Who let the Vietn'ese guys in here?"

My father immediately stopped and put down his food tray. He couldn't tell who yelled out the insult. The USAF airmen all stared at him and the other Vietnamese pilots. He tried to keep his cool, his voice under control. By now he was used to this condescending attitude; it reminded him of his days in the United States when he had trained there.

Since the T-28, an old trainer, had an empty seat in the back, my father offered the IO (not a pilot) a chance to see the real war up close. Taking unauthorized passengers on combat missions had been forbidden by the squadron commander, but my father wanted this officer to have something to talk about back home before the end of his tour. The IO came to the flight line the next morning, dressed in sharply starched fatigues and clutching his camera. He wore a gunbelt and survival equipment. After a complete briefing of safety and bailout procedures they took off. The officer was thrilled to see the beautiful countryside, something he may not have seen before. Then he got airsick and threw up all over the backseat. The flight quickly came to an end. It remains unclear whether what the IO observed on that flight was ever incorporated into a Pentagon briefing.

Most of the 2d FS missions revolved around close air support for the ARVN and prestrike sorties for U.S. Marine Corps helicopters ferrying ARVN troops. Circling overhead, the helicopters would quickly spiral down to insert the troops before the VC could flee. Along with the 1st FS, the VNAF fighters would strike suspected VC outposts in coordination with an airborne forward air controller (FAC).

American involvement, even at this early stage, meant that Vietnamese pilots had to adopt to the fighting style of their new allies. The lessons learned from the French in their 1945–1954 fight against the Viet Minh had no place in the new paradigm.

For the ARVN, that meant depending on fire support (especially air power), heliborne operations, and a bottomless supply chain. The "American" way of fighting had proved its successes on the battlefields of World War II, and in Korea. Yet the application of firepower would prove not to work in Southeast Asia. Regardless, for South Vietnam, accepting U.S. military and economic aid meant that was the "only" way.

It was also in the interest of Vietnamese officers to "please" their U.S. advisers. As former Premier Ky later observed in his memoir *Buddha's Child,* "When advisers went home, they usually received the highest decoration, a medal that only their Vietnamese counterpart was in a position to recommend. Such decorations were important to careers, so many American advisers promoted their own interests by reporting that an ARVN general was terrific and ran a crack unit."

At the battalion and squadron levels, relations between U.S. advisers and their South Vietnamese counterparts proved to be less self-serving. But at a high level, this two-way denial would keep the military status quo as well as work to increase South Vietnam's dependence on the United States (until the fall of Saigon).

In January 1963 there was a skirmish south of Saigon at the village of Ap Bac, resulting in the shooting down of several U.S. Army helicopters. U.S. advisers were highly critical of their ARVN counterparts for ignoring the recommendation to attack to relieve a besieged unit. That failure led to the death of a U.S. Army captain.

At about the same time, my parents, after years of an off-and-on relationship, finally married. My father (when not flying missions) was a frequent and debonair fixture of Saigon nightlife and could not have been more different from my mother. A quiet college graduate, she preferred teaching during the day and reading books at night. There would be no honeymoon, since my father immediately returned to his squadron and my mother promptly moved in with her new in-laws. (They didn't charge her rent.)

In an attempt to confuse the VC, the VNAF renamed the 1st FS as the

514th and the 2d FS became the 516th. The older T-28s, showing their age, began shedding their wings during bombing runs. They had been designed as trainers, not built for the stresses of routine bombing and strafing, so the decision was made to convert the 516th FS to Skyraiders as well as to move the squadron north to Danang. Fortunately for my father, he picked a number from a hat and was transferred to the 514th FS in Bien Hoa, where he would be closer to my mother and my sister living in Saigon.

In 1960, the U.S. Navy delivered the first of thirty single-seat, AD-6 Skyraiders (also known as A-1H, "ADs," "Able Dogs," and "Spads") to replace the aging F-8s of the 1st FS. Six VNAF students, all experienced F-8 pilots, were sent to the U.S. Naval Air Station at Corpus Christi, Texas, to undergo transition training. The Skyraider was the only tactical fixed-wing aircraft used by U.S. forces and those of South Vietnam simultaneously during the war. At that time, U.S. Navy pilots were still flying the Skyraiders off aircraft carriers. The U.S. Marines had traded in their Skyraiders for jets a few years after the Korean conflict.

The Skyraider carried 8,000 pounds of ordnance, more than the four-engine B-17 of World War II fame. It had four 20mm cannons on its wings. Powered by a 2,700-horsepower engine and a 14-foot, 4-bladed propeller, the aircraft cruised at 320 knots. Long viewed as the finest close air–support aircraft ever built, the lumbering Skyraider would become the airplane most closely identified with the VNAF: with over 350 delivered between 1960 and 1972, South Vietnam's young air force had finally upgraded its offensive capabilities to meet the increasingly deadly VC. The VNAF pilots nicknamed the Skyraider *Trau Dien* or "Crazy Water Buffalo," an appropriate airplane for my father, "Crazy" Hoa.

Soon after my father joined the 514th, a party was thrown at the Bien Hoa officers' club for USAF Maj. J. Stalling, who would soon be going back to the States after completing his one year advisory tour. American and Vietnamese pilots celebrated together with vast quantities of "7th Fleet" booze (89 proof American whiskey) and, brought in at the last minute, "shoum shoum," the local white-rice brandy. Everyone had a good time.

As the camaraderie between USAF and VNAF pilots steadily improved not all cultural gaps could be bridged. Two of the chief complaints against the VNAF pilots were that they flew too little at night and slacked off during the siesta between noon and 3 p.m. The fact that many VNAF pilots could go home at night to their families didn't help matters.

But some understood. A USAF colonel commented in a 1965 *Aviation*

Week & Space Technology article: "I don't blame them for taking their siestas and holidays. We come here for a year, and then we go home. For these guys, there is no end in sight; not even the prospect of an R&R (rest & relaxation) leave in Hong Kong."

Another adviser empathized, "They [the VNAF] take their siestas all right, but, fortunately for us, so do the VC."

Late one afternoon, on his third day in-country, USAF Capt. Clark James arrived at the 514th FS wearing a natty tan class B 505 uniform with short sleeves. He fit the popular image of a West Point graduate—short cropped hair, close shave, heavily starched shirt, and mirror-shiny shoes. No one in the squadron recognized James, since he hadn't attended the going-away party for his predecessor.

As the tropical sun sank below the *nipa* palms and the heat let up, my father and another 2d lieutenant, Tien, stepped outside the operations room. They constituted one of two standby ground-alert crews for the afternoon in case a mission was laid on. They watched as ground maintenance personnel loaded bombs onto the Skyraiders down the flight line. As James strolled up full of confidence, they both knew right away that he was Major Stalling's replacement. They also could tell James was a very young U.S. officer.

After a formal salute nobody relaxed. James, the new adviser, seemed to be bothered by what he saw.

"Do you think there are no more VC?" he asked.

My father and Tien looked at each other in disbelief. My father knew right away that the new adviser was ready for action, eager to get involved, and his arrogance would be tested soon enough (pilots usually waited a few days after arriving to adjust to jet lag). Just before dark a new flight schedule was published for the next day. My father walked down to the squadron operations officer's office to personally bring the good news.

"Sir, Captain James should get his familiarization flight first thing tomorrow."

In Saigon, meanwhile, President Ngo Dinh Diem's popularity had declined. The Binh Xuyen, Cao Dai, and Hoa Hoa religious sects opposed his favoritism toward Catholics, and so chaos erupted. In protest, a Buddhist monk doused himself with gasoline and immolated himself. Malcom Browne, an Associated Press (AP) reporter, captured the shocking image later seen worldwide. In November 1963, President Diem and his brother Nhu were murdered in a coup widely believed by the Vietnamese to have been backed by President Kennedy. A number of VNAF fighter planes attacked the presidential compound in Saigon in support of the coup. (In February 1962, two Skyraiders had bombed the Presidential Palace in another coup attempt.) Three weeks later, former Marine Corps marksman Lee Harvey Oswald fatally shot Kennedy in Dallas. Both shooters, Oswald and an ARVN major who killed Diem, were murdered soon after their crimes. Later, after Senator Robert F. Kennedy was fatally shot in 1968, talk spread among superstitious South Vietnamese for years about an evil curse on the Kennedys for the murders of Diem and Nhu: two brothers for two brothers, one president for another, the spooky incantation was uttered.

Increase in violence against the government and civilians and subsequent coups in South Vietnam led to President Lyndon B. Johnson's decision to send combat troops less than eighteen months later.

After the 1963 coup, the 514th FS received another adviser, Maj. Richard Howard. At fifty, he was older than the other advisers, who tended to be in their late twenties or early thirties. It was only when U.S. Secretary of Defense McNamara visited Vietnam in March 1964 that the pilots of the 514th realized that Howard was part of the specific precautions put in place to thwart the coup-happy VNAF.*

During a squadron meeting, the Vietnamese commanding officer proudly declared, "Today we get rid of McNamara!" What he meant was that McNamara's visit was coming to an end and that he was leaving Vietnam, but the literal translation sounded as if the VNAF pilots were planning to do "something." Right after the meeting, Howard ran to the phone to make a call and soon after, all aircraft were grounded at Bien Hoa for two hours. No one was allowed off base and, reportedly, there was a bad traffic jam at Tan Son Nhut Air Base in Saigon as well. Somebody must have been afraid of another unauthorized mission by the VNAF.

*My father never took part. He didn't belong to the military-political inner circle.

CHAPTER 5

SKYRAIDER
DOWN

F ROM THE LONE 7,800-FOOT RUNWAY AT THE OLD FRENCH
barracks in Danang, it took from just ten to forty-five minutes to fly
to the Demilitarized Zone, or DMZ, depending on whether it was in
a jet fighter or a helicopter. Located forty miles south of Hue City, Danang
would later become a major offloading point for the U.S. military machine,
especially for Marines. With Khe Sanh to the northwest and China Beach
just east, this was the I Corps, soon to become the second-bloodiest killing
field in the Marines' history. And in 1964 the bleeding had begun in earnest.

Major John Braddon, USMC, thirty-four years old, arrived in Vietnam in
January 1964, as part of Marine Medium Helicopter Squadron 364, or
HMM-364. He was among the 16,000 or so U.S. advisers of all ranks and

races who were sent to help in the war effort. He left his wife, Jean Anne, and four young children behind in Santa Ana, California.

HMM-364 flew twenty-four ugly but reliable single-engine CH-34 Sea Horse helicopters. The squadron had fifty pilots (nearly twice the size of present-day units) and over 200 Marines. The Marines came to train the VNAF on helicopter tactics that had been honed in Korea a decade earlier. The intention was to turn the helicopters over to the VNAF upon leaving Vietnam. Higher headquarters had made a premature announcement that all Marines would depart by June, the month that the United States was planning to end all direct participation in Vietnam.

Like most American advisers, Braddon knew his job and did it well, but he had mixed feelings about his Vietnamese charges. He told his Marines, "These are good Vietnamese guys. They don't speak the same language as we do. But they're members of our squadron, and we're going to treat them that way."

But ARVN soldiers had a shaky reputation. Braddon remembered some of them running back into his helo as soon as he had dropped them off in a landing zone (LZ). At times his crew chief had literally kicked them out of

Flight of two VNAF A-1 Skyraiders from the 514th FS, 1963. (Wayne Mutza Collection)

2d Lt. Pham Van Hoa, VNAF Skyraider pilot, 1964. (Courtesy of U.S. Air Force)

the chopper. "Occasionally they would shoot at us as we lifted off," he recalled.

On April 27, 1964, HMM-364 was ordered to lift a battalion of ARVN soldiers into a VC stronghold known as Do Xa, south of the Ashau Valley and fifteen miles northwest of Quang Ngai. Held by the VC for a decade after the fall of Dien Bien Phu, it served as a "gate" for communist forces to enter central Vietnam via the Ho Chi Minh trail which ran along the border with Laos. Brigadier General Nguyen Don, the Viet Cong commander for central Vietnam, based his headquarters there.

ARVN Col. Nguyen Van Hieu,* the chief of staff for the II Corps commanding general, led the planning of Operation Sure Wind 202. The assault on Do Xa would become the deadliest heliborne assault made before U.S. combat troops arrived in any appreciable numbers. The U.S. Army provided five UH-1B Huey gunships to provide escort for the large Marine flight, which included two additional VNAF H-34s. The entire flight would ren-

---

*Hieu became a two-star general and a division commander in 1968. One of the better ARVN generals, he was mysteriously assassinated a few weeks before the fall of Saigon.

dezvous to refuel and load at the Quang Ngai airfield, 100 miles south of Danang, before proceeding to Do Xa.

U.S. Army Capt. Jack "Woody" Woodmansee, a 1956 West Point graduate and classmate of "Stormin' Norman" Schwarzkopf, was in his final month of a one-year tour in Vietnam. As leader of the Huey gunship detachment Dragon Flight, Woodmansee had clocked his share of combat time escorting Marine helicopter units based in Danang. Formed in December 1963, his unit had also supported the U.S. advisory teams in I Corps and two ARVN divisions. At that time the U.S. Marine Corps didn't have armed helicopters; its doctrine called for fixed-wing aircraft for escort, but there were none in Vietnam.

At Danang, my father landed his Skyraider fighter-bomber on the western end of the runway. He had flown up with his wingman from Bien Hoa for the joint heliborne mission with the U.S. Marines. He had done this many times before, flying with the 2d FS (T-28s) and his current unit, the 514th FS.*

The weather had been perfect on that spring day as Braddon and his Marine flight flew to Do Xa. Braddon was the leader of a two-aircraft flight to act as search-and-rescue birds, ready to pick up downed aircrew members if necessary. He had a clear view of the entire flight from his position high above the large formation.

Approaching the LZ, Woodmansee's gunship flight raced 2 miles ahead and performed "recon by fire," stirring up antiaircraft fire from the hidden VC below. Red tracers from VC machine guns crisscrossed beneath the Hueys as their door gunners fired back—immediately silencing several gun positions. The lead helicopter crew chief threw out smoke grenades to mark hostile fire positions for the other four gunships as they emptied their Emerson kits, four 7.62mm machine guns controlled by the copilots, and two pods of seven rockets each. The crew chiefs and door gunners fired M14 rifles and tossed hand grenades from treetop height. This large H-34 flight was on its final approach when Woodmansee got on the radio and warned them off. "Give us some time to clean up this mess!" he shouted. The LZ was still too hot.

After another pass Dragon Flight was running out of ammunition, while the Marine flight leader was pushing to land the attacking infantry force. Woodmansee hoped to convince the marine pilots to fly back to Quang Ngai

---

*At the time, he also helped stand up the 518th FS, the VNAF's third Skyraider unit.

so that Dragon Flight could rearm itself. He really wanted to talk the Marines out of going into the original LZ altogether: almost out of ammunition, all he could do was call the FAC to have the VNAF Skyraiders pound the LZ while the helos flew back to Quang Ngai.

As soon as Woodmansee could see the LZ he knew it was suicide. Enemy guns were alongside mountain ridges surrounding the LZ on three sides, with only the westerly approach open. Numerous caves could be seen in the mountainside cliffs. The machine guns were emplaced a few hundred feet up the sides of these cliffs.

Woodmansee flew close to the VC gunners, no more than about 30 feet above them. He could see dun-colored pith helmets and green uniforms, unlike the black pajama-clad VC guerrillas he had expected. They had readied their shoulder-sling-mounted .50-caliber machine guns with concentric gun sights like the ones Woodmansee had seen on World War II ships. He expended what ammunition he had left to mark the LZ for the FAC. "OK, right where the smoke is, there's a .50-cal and a bunch of guys in a tunnel," Woodmansee said, and then pulled off to watch the aerial bombardment. He had the best view in the house as the first Skyraider began its steep dive.

"I got it," exclaimed the FAC, orbiting overhead in a small L-19 Bird Dog observation plane.

My father had been flying a narrowing gyre above the choppers when his flight of Skyraiders got the radio call to attack. He turned his plane toward the LZ and threw the switches to arm his bombs and guns. Rolling into a deep 40-degree attack dive, he let loose several 20mm cannon bursts and unleashed two 250-pound bombs. They struck the bottom of the hill to the north of the LZ but missed their intended targets. The VC gunners greeted him with a barrage: tracers flew like red fireflies over his white aircraft. Veering off the target, my father wrenched to his left and looked back. He saw the tracers chasing his flight of two planes, the rounds getting closer and closer to their marks.

Hovering safely away from the bomb bursts, Woodmansee told the FAC to move the Skyraiders up the mountainside. It was a tough mission; the VNAF pilots were trying to hit a pinpoint target with "dumb" gravity bombs on the side of a mountain, almost impossible to do under the best circumstances.

My father climbed back to a safer altitude to swallow his fear and make a second pass. The VC machine guns kept firing, taunting him to come back.

He put the stick down, leading the Skyraider into a steeper dive than before, cannons blasting away as communist tracers zinged up again from the ground. This time, another gun across the valley, on the south side, opened up, punching holes in the plane from the engine cowling across the fuselage. The gun could track the Skyraider all the way down its bombing run. Rounds also punctured the wings, and just missed the cockpit area. His bird was on fire. Now he had to make a decision—stay with the aircraft or bail out over "bad guy" territory 15 miles from friendly forces. He didn't have much time or altitude to decide.

Braddon was with the Marine flight when he saw the Skyraiders hit the target. He didn't know where they had come from but he knew the aircrafts' capabilities. (He had himself flown Skyraiders earlier in his career.) As he watched the attack, he saw a Skyraider pull out of its dive, smoke billowing from its engine. The VC guns kept pumping, hoping to finish off the crippled aircraft as it fluttered away from the LZ. Thick black smoke silhouetted the stricken plane against the cobalt sky as its pilot struggled to maintain a level flight path. Braddon immediately pushed his stick to the right and followed the smoke trail and radioed the flight leader that he was breaking off.

Woodmansee figured that Braddon needed an armed escort because they were all flying over enemy territory. He followed Braddon's H-34 and soon there were two U.S. helos chasing their smoking VNAF ally. None of this had been planned or practiced.

The other Skyraider rolled in on top of the VC, who began to scatter from the hills to track my father's plane. They were probably anticipating his parachute descent or his crash-landing nearby. The other Skyraider's pilot made several passes, shooting his 20mm cannons and providing cover while my father's damaged plane quickly descended from 1,000 feet where he had leveled out after his bombing dive.

Inside the cockpit seconds ticked away as it began to fill with smoke. The powerful Skyraider was losing power and altitude fast. As he struggled to see the instruments while controlling the aircraft, my father began to panic—but then his training kicked in. Emergency procedures ran through his mind in the English he had been taught, then quickly translated into action. He reached up and slid back the canopy to allow the smoke to clear. He could see fire emerging from the engine cowling. Behind the flames and surrounding him were hills and rocky terrain crenelated by 8,500-foot peaks. Flames then broke through the firewall and seared his face, scorch-

Hoa's downed Skyraider. Note .50-caliber bullet holes on fuselage. Do Xa, Vietnam, 1964.
(Courtesy of Warren R. Smith)

ing his eyebrows. The world through his windshield was growing quickly in size: the engine quit.

Not knowing his exact altitude above the ground, my father decided to stay with the aircraft and dead-stick it to the flattest surface he could find. Thoughts of my pregnant mother and my sister ran through his mind as he quickly went through emergency procedures for engine failure and fire in flight. For the first time since he'd joined the VNAF a decade earlier, he thought he was going to die. He was twenty-eight years old.

He had no clue that U.S. helicopters were following him. He could hear his Vietnamese wingman making Mayday calls when suddenly a dirt airstrip flanked by tall hills appeared to his left. He quickly lowered his flaps to slow his heavy plane, gliding in at over 150 knots. Careful not to stall the aircraft or nose it over, he "slipped" the aircraft, stepping hard on one rudder and pushing the opposite stick to quickly descend so that he wouldn't overshoot his intended landing spot. With the landing gear still up, the Skyraider hit the ground hard, and its large propeller blades wrapped around the cowling before its oversized engine broke away, as designed. The right wing wrapped around a large tree and stopped the aircraft from nosing into an irrigation ditch. My father must have forgotten to lock his seat belts, for he lunged forward on impact: his head struck the dashboard, splitting both his lips, bruising his forehead, and cracking his sunglasses. His left knee hit the lower dashboard, hard.

The Skyraider skidded to a stop, kicking up dirt and smoke. My father quickly climbed out of the cockpit. He was dizzy, and his left leg was throbbing with pain. He could not believe he had survived the crash-landing. Minutes before he was piloting a 22,500-pound metal projectile at 300 knots, the engine's roar and the boom of gunfire deafening him. Now he sat in total silence on a loamy field. The VC who had seen him go down would reach him soon, he thought.

Braddon's H-34, empty except for a copilot, crew chief, and door gunner, had barely been able to keep up with the Skyraider even as it had lost altitude and airspeed. Woodmansee's Huey was even farther behind, hustling along at just ninety knots per hour. Glancing through his dirty windshield for enemy fire from below, Braddon had focused on the smoking Skyraider as it suddenly dropped below his window, disappearing from his view just before it struck the ground, kicking up red dust mixed with the black cloud of its own burning fuel. Braddon had just witnessed his first aerial casualty of the Vietnam War.

Landing his H-34 near the crashed Skyraider, Braddon could see blood on my father's face as he approached the helo under his own power. "The lucky guy made it out," he thought as his crew chief reached out, grabbed the Vietnamese pilot's arm, and pulled him in. No one said anything; the helicopter rotors were too deafening to even try to speak. The Skyraider pilot collapsed on an empty row of canvas seats, and without delay the crew chief radioed Braddon to take off. Not knowing exactly where he was, Braddon immediately lifted up and flew east at maximum airspeed to Quang Ngai. He called the base to inform the medics of an incoming casualty. Woodmansee trailed the H-34. Both U.S. pilots knew there was still much work ahead: to them, the VNAF pilot was done as far as this mission was concerned. The Americans would have no idea of his fate as they dropped him off at Quang Ngai and repositioned their helos for the second attempt on Do Xa.

Back in Saigon my mother held my sister while battling morning sickness.

Her brother came knocking on the door with news that her husband's plane had been shot down over Do Xa a few hours earlier—he did not know whether her husband was dead or alive. She felt dizzy, falling into her brother's arms as he helped her lean back onto a couch. She moaned as pain gripped her stomach.

USAF Air Commando Course, C-123 Class, 1966, Hurlburt Airfield. My father is kneeling in center with bandage on his pinkie. Ho Dang Tri is to his right. (Courtesy of U.S. Air Force)

CHAPTER 6

HERE COMES JOHNNY

M Y FATHER HAD BEEN FORTUNATE, BUT SO HAD MANY Skyraider pilots who also walked away from crash-landings over the years. It was one tough aircraft, designed to handle heavy enemy fire and hard landings. After Major Braddon dropped him off in Quang Ngai, a VNAF C-47 from my father's old transport group flew him to Danang. He recovered in a military hospital when VNAF commander Nguyen Cao Ky, his former CO in the transport group, was in the area visiting wounded soldiers. (By the spring of 1964, after a few more coups, Ky was on his way to becoming South Vietnam's prime minister.) He saw my father in the hospital and promptly authorized him to be flown back to Saigon to Grall, the top hospital in the country once reserved only for rich Frenchmen. My grandparents and my mother were able to visit him while he recovered nearby instead of in far-off Danang. No medical bill ever came.

But first, upon receiving the news of my father's arrival in Saigon, my mother went to the Tan Son Nhut morgue, looking for his body to identify. In those days, the Vietnamese military had a difficult time notifying families of injured or deceased soldiers: news coming from the front lines was sketchy, often incomplete and sporadic. But the duty officer redirected her to the city, and then her brother drove her to Grall, where they both ran to my father's hospital ward. They found him sitting upright on his bed smoking a cigarette and smiling. He managed to crack a quick joke. His head was wrapped with white bandages, both his legs were covered with dressings. My uncle recalled seeing "Hoa's two white buggy eyes and no brows amid a burned face."

There must have been a reason that I was not born fatherless. After her husband came home from the hospital, my mother kept his bloodstained flight suit for several years in our closet in Saigon. That was it for history. No one ever told us that a U.S. helicopter, a U.S. Marine helicopter no less, had rescued him. I had to put the pieces together forty years later.*

After the crash my father came home from the hospital a different man. Now he snapped at my mother over little things. It seemed to her that the crash had changed him, removing a certain lightness from his character. They argued often, even late into my mother's pregnancy with me.

My father was grounded for several months after his crash, as stipulated by VNAF regulations. No blame was assigned—his downed Skyraider was categorized as a combat loss. Now, for the first time in his career, he had a desk job, and he didn't know how to shuffle military paperwork.

My father earned two Vietnamese Gallantry Crosses and two Air Gallantry Crosses while flying close air–support missions, and his unit won the U.S. Presidential Unit Citation (PUC), the first awarded to a South Vietnamese military organization. The citation is the highest U.S. military unit award, given to units with outstanding performance in action.†

But when my father returned to the Skyraider cockpit, he wasn't the same aggressive pilot he had been. He was uncomfortable, his hands trembled on engine startups, yet he managed to keep his jitters to himself, at least for a while. Somehow, he was selected to join the 83d Special Operations Group (SOG), along with his 2d FS buddies Ly Ngoc An and Tran Ba Hoi. The unit was under the direct control of General Ky. Ultimately, the 83d SOG was to carry out air strikes against North Vietnam. Trained by the U.S. Navy in naval commando tactics, SOG pilots were to fly northward at night over the South China Sea at an altitude of 200 feet then turn at certain checkpoints and head toward land, above the 17th parallel. Practice missions were flown at night and often completed just before dawn. The war was expanding, and the growing number of VNAF fighter pilots would do their share by striking Ho Chi Minh's forces in their homeland.

*For his bravery at Do Xa, Braddon won a Silver Star and his copilot received a Distinguished Flying Cross, the first time that Marine Corps aviators had received such decorations in Vietnam. Woodmansee was recommended by HMM-364 for a Navy Cross, but Marine brass quickly disapproved. They apparently did not want to award the first Navy Cross in Vietnam to an "army" aviator. Both officers returned for second combat tours in Vietnam. Braddon became commanding officer of VMFA-334, an F-4 fighter squadron. Woodmansee spent a year as a White House fellow before going back to Vietnam to command another helicopter unit. He retired as a three-star general.

†In the Marine Corps, no unit would earn a PUC after the Vietnam War until the I Marine Expeditionary Force took Baghdad in April 2003 as part of Operation Iraqi Freedom.

On August 5, 1964, the USS *Maddox* incident* in the Tonkin Gulf led President Lyndon B. Johnson to authorize direct air strikes against North Vietnam.

Every combat flier in Vietnam, Vietnamese or U.S., wanted to take part in the retaliatory strike against North Vietnam. While the VNAF fliers were told that their propeller-driven aircraft wouldn't stand a chance against North Vietnamese antiaircraft defense system, the U.S. Navy continued sending its Skyraiders into North Vietnam from 7th Fleet carriers operating on Yankee Station. VNAF Skyraider pilots would only get their chance the following spring, after USAF, U.S. Navy, and U.S. Marine pilots had their opportunity. The fighting in the air was starting to shift to the Americans even before ground combat troops would arrive.

On September 27, 1964, the Year of the Dragon, I came into this world in a small room in Saint Paul's Hospital in downtown Saigon. A few weeks later, on a dark night over the Gulf of Tonkin, my father flew a training mission alongside An's wings. They were part of a large flight of Skyraiders practicing commando raids against makeshift North Vietnamese targets. With 200 feet on the radar altimeter, they had plenty of nose-up trim, the small aerodynamic adjustments that took pressure off the control stick. Airspeed exceeded 300 knots. There was no terrain to use for checkpoints. Over the black, horizon-less ocean, navigation was by time and distance, clock and map.

The pilots' eyes feverishly flashed between the maps on their kneeboards strapped to their thighs, and their instruments—especially the altimeter. No help came from the dimmed cockpit lighting. Little chatter took place between airplanes. Pilots had to focus for hours and tensions ran high during the flight. Some pilots kept a death grip on the controls, the kind that held the stick so tight that knuckles would lock. The death grip could lead to over-controlling the aircraft, and at low altitudes, pushing a stick forward just a quarter-inch for a few seconds would mean instant death.

My father was already tense before he got into his plane. Maybe he had gone back to flying too soon after his crash; maybe he was worn down by the war; maybe his mind was on my mother, my sister, and me. At the time little was known of the 83d SOG. Their pilots stood out, dashing young men wear-

---

*Controversy has raged for decades over whether the USS *Maddox* was actually attacked by North Vietnamese gunboats, as Johnson claimed, or whether the "attack" was simply promoted by his administration to justify his war aims.

ing black flight suits with fancy unit patches and polka dot purple scarves. All were volunteers, somewhat cocky, and believed they were invincible.

Their camouflage Skyraiders had no national insignia but bore the words *than phong,* or "kamikaze" (Japanese "divine wind") inscribed on both sides. Their leader, Ky, wore his signature lavender scarf.

According to An, on that fateful night my father heard an abnormal engine noise, louder than usual. Nothing seemed right. The plane was shaking. He couldn't tell if his engine was about to quit. (No one was talking on the radios—not even the U.S. advisers.) That engine noise increased. He was shaking by then, and sweat formed on his forehead, dripping down his neck. The flight was 50 miles off the coast of South Vietnam; the mission still had another forty-five minutes to go.

Finis. Xong roi. Done.

He pulled up from 200 feet and climbed to 3,000, took a deep breath, and tried to collect himself. He still had to fly back to Bien Hoa. He radioed his flight leader and dialed in the Bien Hoa military navigational beacon. An pulled up as well and quietly led the lonely flight of two back to land. After nearly three years of continuous combat, my father's days as a fighter pilot had come to an end.

Later in the Vietnam War, what befell my father would come to be called post-traumatic stress disorder (PTSD), a clinical condition that still afflicts tens of thousands of U.S. veterans. All he knew was that, for the time being, he couldn't fly anymore. For my father, flying was like riding a tiger: if he got off its back, he would be eaten alive. So he just stayed on and kept riding.

By mid-1964, ARVN losses had exceeded 13,000, on track to pass the 21,000 deaths the previous year. Civilian casualties hovered near 250,000.* With such losses, it was uncertain whether the South Vietnamese would be able to hold their own against a growing insurgency. I can't even imagine how life would have turned out had those young Americans not come to our aid. On the other hand, was it worth all the death and destruction seen in the following decade when the outcome may already have been inevitable?

---

*South Vietnam's casualty statistics are from *Street Without Joy* by Bernard Fall.

CHAPTER 7

NO ONE-YEAR TOURS

NOT MANY KNEW THE REASON WHY MY FATHER LEFT the fighter community. The 83d SOG's executive officer reassigned him to the Tactical Air Control Center in Saigon, but my father knew his career goal to command a squadron was in jeopardy. His superior was Col. Nguyen Ngoc Loan, one of the rare senior pilots who flew combat missions with the 514th as well. Loan, a French Air Force Academy graduate, was one of the few truly admired VNAF officers. He was small in stature but a tough individual who took a liking to my father.

On February 8, 1965, the VNAF made national history: General Ky handpicked twenty-four pilots from various squadrons and led the first air strike into North Vietnam. In this raid every Skyraider took hits and one was shot down. The mission boosted VNAF morale, and more important, improved the reputation of the VNAF among U.S. leaders. The Vietnamese would be rewarded with more aircraft and training.

By then my father had started to miss flying, and regretted his decision to quit a few months earlier even though it was made during a busy time in his newly married life. He wished he had flown north with his buddies. He asked for a transfer back to the Skyraider community, but it was denied. Colonel Loan, who also flew the C-47 to keep up his flight hours, made the decision that would restart my father's career, restoring my father's flying status but with one condition: my father had to go back to the C-47. My father was more than happy to oblige, getting up to speed quickly and regaining his aircraft commander status.

The war was evolving rapidly. Operation Rolling Thunder, the bombing of North Vietnam, had begun* and increased VC attacks on U.S. airfields in Danang and Pleiku required added security. Although there were still plenty of ARVN troops on hand to defend the bases, American ground troops were called in.

On March 8, 1965, two battalions of U.S. Marines from the 9th Amphibious Brigade waded ashore unopposed in Danang. Vietnamese girls donning white *ao dai* (traditional silk dress with pants) presented leis to the Marines in front of worldwide press coverage. Bui Diem, chief of staff for South Vietnam's prime minister, was required to write the communiqué "inviting" U.S. troops into South Vietnam—as the Marines were landing. At the time, a Gallup poll reported only one in four Americans thought "sending troops to Vietnam had been a mistake."

Lyndon Johnson wanted to show the North Vietnamese that he was serious, and he thought that the sight of U.S. Marines coming ashore would send a strong signal. That amphibious walk in the park marked the official beginning of the "Americanization" of the war and relegated the South Vietnamese military to the sidelines.

Now the U.S. military's footprints would be everywhere in Vietnam, from the buildup at Tan Son Nhut to Bien Hoa, Cam Ranh Bay to Nha Trang, Danang to Chu Lai. (It took about ten men at these massive facilities to support the one combat "grunt" out in the boonies who did the actual trigger pulling.) Command and control, logistics, supply personnel (known during the war as REMFs—"rear-echelon motherfuckers") made up most of the 3 million Americans who served in Vietnam between 1960 and 1975. Along with the men and materiel came the post exchange (PX), military stores (with surpluses that would end up on the black market), barbershops, bowling alleys, movie theaters, mess halls, and brothels. Certain parts of Vietnam, including Saigon, were transformed into the likes of Olongapo and Subic Bay in the Philippines; tawdry but welcome escapes for the U.S. military personnel (and civilians) and other foreigners.†

U.S. airmen, Marines, sailors, and soldiers and the journalists who covered them arrived en masse. Everyone wanted a piece of the action, to get that

---

*The U.S. dropped three times the tons of bombs and expended twice the artillery fire power used in all of World War II. Unexploded ordnance and land mines still pose a danger in Vietnam, probably the most bombed country in history.

†Some 80,000 Amerasians were born in Vietnam during the war, many left behind after the fall of Saigon.

combat tour, to send war dispatches from the front lines. Career advancements were on the line, and getting the Vietnam ticket punched was a must. It was the biggest game in town. Civilian contractors erected bases overnight, laid down runways, opened up harbors, paved dirt roads, and made billions in the process. Oversized military vehicles crowded dirty streets and forced civilians off the roads. Many thought it would take six months, maybe a year to "kick some ass, take names, and go home."

In faraway and dangerous outposts, Marine and army infantry (grunts) lived spartanly, often supplied only by helicopter. They occasionally gained a brief rest and recreation (R&R) trip to the rear. With General William Westmoreland's strategy of "search and destroy" while running up "body counts" of dead Viet Cong, the United States was seen as "winning the hearts and minds" if not the war itself. The U.S. Marines practiced their Combined Action Program, where a squad of Marines would live and serve within a village.

Even Australia, Canada, New Zealand, and South Korea eventually sent over 300,000 troops to fight. But more and more U.S. troops joined the war, peaking at 560,000 in 1969.* The personnel policy meant one-year combat tours; individuals rotated into units already in-country. Even though some volunteered for extended or additional tours, the mind-set of these troops and ARVN soldiers unfortunately differed greatly: there was no such thing as a one-year combat tour for the South Vietnamese military.

Western journalists landed well before the U.S. buildup. British author Graham Greene had written *The Quiet American* in 1955, keenly observing the unintended consequences of the arrival of Americans in Indochina. Bernard Fall, a French scholar and writer who had become a U.S. citizen, wrote *Hell in a Small Place* and *Street Without Joy,* notable books about the siege at Dien Bien Phu and the beginning of U.S. involvement in Vietnam. Fall later died while accompanying U.S. Marines on a mission outside Hue. (My father was mentioned in his second book, though not by name. He was in a footnote to history, recorded as, "4 helicopters and one AD-6 [Skyraider] are shot down, 18 other helicopters hit [over Do Xa].")

The American press put its flag up in Saigon, attending the popular routine known as the "five o'clock follies," the bitter name news writers gave to the daily command briefings during the war. The war gave meteoric boosts

---

*It took four years for U.S. forces to reach 560,000. During the 1990 pre–Gulf War buildup, it took just over four months to reach the same number.

to the careers of David Halberstam and Neil Sheehan, two of the most well-known journalists of the era and both Pulitzer Prize winners. Others were CBS newscasters Dan Rather and Morley Safer, who brought home the images of Marines burning the grass-roof village at Cam Ne with their Zippo lighters. Many of today's network news anchors made their brief "I was there" appearances. Some journalists spent as much as five years in Vietnam, like Richard Pyle of AP who became the Saigon bureau chief. His colleague, George Esper, held the record of ten years, finally getting kicked out after the fall of Saigon. The AP had the largest number of journalists covering the war, including Pulitzer winners Peter Arnett and Horst Faas, the photographer.

While I have been grateful for the many articles, books, and news clips generated by this august collection of chroniclers, I wasn't always sure which war they were covering. They certainly received much acclaim, especially considering that many other newsworthy and watershed events were taking place in the United States and the rest of the world during the Vietnam War. What they didn't write about was the war my father and his South Vietnamese colleagues fought or the reign of terror the Viet Cong brought to families like mine.

It took many years after reading many books, but I finally came to this conclusion: American journalists wrote about Americans and America's War in Vietnam for Americans back home. The history of what happened to the South Vietnamese remains in the hands of expatriates, but I don't expect any revisionists to come to our camp thirty years after the war. Careers were made on a certain style of reporting; positions were clearly staked out. Hindsight and regrets would undo everything, so nothing new will change those attitudes, but I am hopeful that future generations of reporters will be more open to different perspectives.

After the Americans arrived the fighting didn't stop for the South Vietnamese. My father continued ferrying troops to the front and hauling supplies to outposts. On many return trips his plane would be full of "silent passengers."

"You know they're there, you know their names. But they don't talk to you. And you can't talk to them," my father recalled.

Tin coffins with dead ARVN soldiers, usually from I Corps (many were picked up at Phu Bai), needed to be flown to Saigon where family members could properly bury them. Some of the corpses had already begun to rot on the tarmac in the broiling sun. Out in the fields the rains would cover the bodies in mud, then later wash away the sludge, exposing the dead to be found. There were so many stacked up; so first come, first out was the policy. The yellow flags with the red stripes were draped over each one.

As the transport planes rose above 8,000 feet or so the pressure changed—in unpressurized aircraft. The gases in the coffins would undo the lids, opening them slowly in gruesome waves. (The crew in back would watch in silence, as if the dead had acknowledged their deed.) Pressure changes speeded the decomposition of the bodies and thus made it difficult for families to identify the remains.

The smell of death got into the ears, hair, nostrils, and flight suits. My father tried stuffing his nostrils with cooking oil, and that helped a bit. But the stench finally was so strong that two or three showers didn't do the trick, and occasionally flight suits had to be thrown away. Yet he never refused a coffin mission.

"When I die, drape my country's flag over my coffin and bury me fast enough before I smell," he once said. My father got his final wish.

In January 1966 my father and several other VNAF pilots and crew members were selected to train in the United States. It would be his second trip to the States. The airmen were to be qualified on the C-123 (although this plane was not to be delivered to the VNAF until 1970) at the Hurlburt Air Commando School in Florida. The fast and new C-123, a twin-engine, short-field transport aircraft that looked like a whale, had replaced the C-47.

The United States was quite different from the one he remembered from his first visit. Now civil rights marches, drugs, and rock and roll music made the headlines; the antiwar movement was under way, and the press reported it daily. My father saw the news every day in his bachelor officers' quarters, and it never failed to predict bad things for South Vietnam's war efforts.

The VNAF crew had come to Hurlburt to learn the newest commando tactics. They were to return to Vietnam to fly covert missions into the north, such as dropping off agents and saboteurs the way the earlier, failed CIA-backed missions had done. Low-level navigation, night missions, parachute drops, and no-communication flights were to be the standard.

My father was definitely "back in the saddle."

By the 1960s there were thousands of nonmilitary South Vietnamese in this country, not counting the war brides. Most had come to study at universities, managing to avoid the draft back home. While American conscientious objectors fled to Canada and Oxford, some South Vietnamese men went to the United States or France. Some opted to remain in the United

States after their studies and several joined the antiwar movement with their new American friends.

It was a difficult nine months for my mother. She had turned thirty, alone with two small children, and was teaching full-time. Luckily, both sides of our families were nearby and both grandmothers and her sisters pitched in. Even though mail took weeks to get from the United States to Vietnam, she received many letters from my father, including numerous Polaroid shots from a new camera that he had bought at the PX. She sent back traditional black-and-white photos of herself and my sister and me at the Saigon zoo and in front of the Continental Palace, another familiar Saigon landmark.

Meanwhile, my father's old friends in the VNAF fighter community were suffering heavy casualties. The 514th FS lost a third of its pilots (nine out of thirty were killed in combat) in 1967 to enemy fire. That was the same rate as a U.S. Navy squadron operating from carriers on Yankee Station. The only time my mother saw my father cry was the night his friend "Stork," the squadron mate from the 2d FS, was shot down and killed. He often attended funeral services, in his uniform, and sometimes gave the bad news to the family and the eulogy at the funeral. (Two of his Lubbock, Texas, classmates also died. The VNAF motto became "Fly until you die.")

His good friend An had a near-fatal mishap while taking off with a full load of bombs for a mission in North Vietnam. Right after taking off from Tan Son Nhut as part of a large strike, An nearly died when his engine blew up. Fighting fire and smoke, he managed to set his Skyraider up for landing when the smoke overwhelmed him. Luckily his wings had been leveled and the impact brought him back to consciousness, and the 500-pound bombs had not yet been armed. (His plane skidded off the runway atop 3,000 pounds of explosives.) An lost a hand, however, and was badly burned. But once again General Ky took care of one of his pilots: he authorized An to be flown to the United States where he received world-class medical care. An entered this country without any immigration paperwork. His flying days were done; he would serve as a military attaché in Washington, D.C., and as a psychological warfare officer until the end of the war. During his recovery his VNAF friends nicknamed him An "Cut" or "One-Hand" An.

In May 1966, a young VNAF pilot from the 516th Fighter Squadron named Nguyen Quoc Dat was shot down on his twenty-sixth mission over North Vietnam. Hit by heavy antiaircraft fire, he too made a crash landing in the sturdy Skyraider and survived. Unfortunately, though, the North Vietnamese nabbed him immediately. They thought he was a U.S. flier, maybe an orphan adopted by a GI, since he was carrying a Texas driver's license from his training days.* And he had on "Jockey" underwear. He was taken to the Hoa Lo prison, or "Hanoi Hilton," where other U.S. POWs were being held. Nicknamed "Max" by fellow POWs, he would earn the distinction of becoming the only VNAF pilot held at Hoa Lo. Later that year, two Americans, Navy Lt. Paul Galanti and Marine Capt. Orson Swindle, would join Max in captivity. Orson was on his 205th, and last, mission, and Galanti his ninety-seventh. Assigned to kitchen and other menial duties, Max would sneak food and medicine to his fellow POWs. The Americans would never forget him. All three reconnected in this country after their release in 1973, thanks partly to the efforts of a Texas billionaire named H. Ross Perot.

Returning to Saigon in September 1966, my father rejoined the 83d SOG as part of its transport group. By then, the 83d had its full complement of Skyraider, transport, helicopter, and observation pilots, all handpicked. Yet before he got to fly into North Vietnam, the unit was disbanded and its pilots ordered back to regular units. Due to infighting and mistrust, President Thieu supposedly didn't want anyone, including Vice President Ky, to have the luxury of a special-operations air unit available for use to possibly unseat him. After all, VNAF pilots had taken part in coups before.

Around this time VNAF Skyraiders stopped flying bombing missions into the north altogether. For one year, they had been ordered to remain south of the 19th parallel, just north of the DMZ (at the 17th parallel), leaving those missions to U.S. pilots. It appeared that U.S. military leaders had grown leery of an overzealous Nguyen Cao Ky taking the war to the north beyond their control.

The Tet offensive of 1968 gave me my first taste of war. I have an early memory of a loud explosion and AK-47 gunfire that disrupted our holiday celebrations. My mother took my sister and me to my aunt's house in a safer part of Saigon. It was reported then that the VC had taken over the city. My father grabbed his personal weapons which he kept at the house, a U.S. M14 rifle, and several pistols, and remained on base for three weeks. We didn't hear from him during that time. Until Tet, and outside of occasional grenade attacks, Saigon had been fairly insulated from the war. Near the DMZ, U.S.

---

*VNAF and other foreign military pilots took their English language training at Lackland Air Force Base in San Antonio.

Marines courageously held their outpost at Khe Sanh, where ten NVA divisions surrounded the hills as the Viet Minh had the French at Dien Bien Phu. In Hue City, U.S. Marines and ARVN troops fought house to house in fierce combat and retook this old imperial capital. (It was then learned that the VC had murdered about 3,000 civilians, even though little of the atrocity was mentioned in Western press.)

On February 1, 1968, at the height of the Tet offensive, Brig. Gen. Loan, by then appointed by Vice President Ky as national police chief and head of the RVN equivalent to the CIA, executed a Viet Cong officer in front of an NBC television crew and an AP photographer named Eddie Adams.* In a fraction of a second, a South Vietnamese military hero would be forever transformed into a barbarous symbol of the war. Even though the Viet Cong had been decimated by ARVN and U.S. forces, Walter Cronkite still declared the war as "unwinnable."

---

*Already a well-revered photojournalist, Adams would win the 1969 Pulitzer Prize in photography. The picture made front-page headlines in leading U.S. newspapers the following day.

CHAPTER 8

ON OUR OWN

ICHARD MILHOUS NIXON'S 1969 INAUGURAL SPEECH CON-
spicuously was devoid of the word "Vietnam."

Reducing the U.S. presence had been a Nixon campaign promise,
but its corollary, Vietnamization, giving the Vietnamese greater responsibility in prosecuting the war, would take time to achieve. The need for U.S. advisers and B-52 bombardment never really went away. The invasions of
Cambodia and Laos (an ARVN-led operation called Lam Son 719) in 1970
and 1971 to cut off North Vietnam's supply chain only created more uproar
in the United States and the world over the war in Vietnam.

The VNAF finally received its first jets, in the form of a squadron of supersonic F-5s, and a year later, three squadrons of A-37 attack jets were formed.
Maintenance on these high-tech aircraft proved more difficult than that for
the propeller-driven planes and the necessary civilian-contractor support
("tech reps"), also used by the U.S. military, ensured dependence on the
United States. Other South Vietnamese military services also expanded in ca-
pability with the goal of replicating the military philosophy, tactics, and structure of their great ally. Unfortunately, this meant inheriting the associated
costs and complexity. By 1970 the South Vietnamese government remained
totally supported by, and completely dependent on, the United States.

My father was on flight status for his twelfth consecutive year. While some
of his peers had returned to the United States for the U.S. Air Force Command and Staff College, followed by a staff or instructor tour at the national
military academy, he stayed and helped start another new unit, the 817th
Combat Squadron or *Hoa Long*. The 817th flew the AC-47 "Spooky," or
"Fire Dragon," gunship armed with three 7.62mm quick-firing miniguns
designed to rain deadly fire onto an enemy on the ground. The USAF had

left the gunships behind as it upgraded to the newer C-130 "Spectre" (still in service today in Iraq).

The "Fire Dragons" boosted morale for besieged ARVN troops, flew combat support missions for air base defense, and compiled a combat record comparable with that of U.S. squadrons.

While my father flew missions for the VNAF, my mother took care of my sisters and me at home with the help of a nanny who cooked, cleaned, and did general chores. My family had a television set (a rarity in Vietnam then), and we watched Neil Armstrong walk on the moon in July 1969. The United States seemed so far away, so advanced, and so incredible. And we saw the daily television reporting of the war. I remember reports of South Vietnamese and U.S. soldiers still bravely fighting the Communists and dying in numbers.

My mother would take my older sister and me with her on a Honda moped to school, masterfully dodging the Saigon traffic. We were attending Le Qui Don public school, across the street from the Presidential Palace.

We students were very competitive, and lots of homework was given out. I studied hard after school with the help of my mother at night. I loved to read. I borrowed anything I could, Vietnamese folklore, short stories, anything. One of my favorites was the biography of Saburo Sakai, the World War II Japanese ace who shot down sixty-four Allied planes. He was a descendant of the samurai, the ancient Japanese warrior class. He had risen from the enlisted ranks to become a pilot like my father. After the war, he lived a hard life, as did many Japanese veterans, before becoming a Buddhist acolyte and owner of a small print shop. Sakai also befriended various Americans he once battled in the air. He died in 2000, at age eighty-four, a month before my father passed away.

Looking back, it was strange to cheer for this famous pilot, a former enemy of the United States. I guess his story was familiar; he reminded me of VNAF pilots, Asian men flying prop-driven fighters. My friends enjoyed the book as well, which had been translated into Vietnamese and passed around among military brats. The VNAF pilots in the mid-1960s who had painted their Skyraiders with a "kamikaze" logo must have also read Sakai's book.

I remember watching the American Forces Vietnam Network, the English-language channel for servicemen. Between news broadcasts were episodes of *Twelve O'Clock High* (the television show in the 1960s, not the movie) and *Combat,* another show about World War II. (*Star Trek* was then on the air, too.) The GIs won most of the battles; the airmen braved walls of flak and held tight formations while dropping their bombs, but I didn't take to Captain Kirk or the weird-looking Dr. Spock with his funny ears; outer space adventure was beyond our realm. At the movies, my father and I saw *The Longest Day,* the 1962 epic of the 1944 Normandy landing, with Vietnamese subtitles. My friends and I would make drawings of the amphibious landing in Normandy, with parachutists descending onto the beach and ships congregating offshore. My mother took my sisters and me to two other American-made movies, *The Wizard of Oz,* which frightened me for days, and *Willy Wonka & the Chocolate Factory,* one of my favorites. For children, the universal appeal of candy and chocolate transcended nations and war.

Like every Asian movie buff of those years, I became an avid fan of Bruce Lee movies, spoken in Chinese with Vietnamese subtitles. He looked larger than life, and as a well-muscled Asian movie star with good looks, he became one of the very few "positive" Asians on the big screen. Of course, I didn't know of his previous American television role as Kato, sidekick to the Green Hornet. Later, during my Marine career, I first didn't understand why it seemed that every other Asian-American naval aviator I knew had a call sign of "Kato."

In early 1972 my family moved onto Tan Son Nhut Air Base, mostly for security reasons. Our new military home was much bigger than the house we had shared with my father's parents. It was about 2,500 square feet, a one-story dwelling on a 10,000-square-foot lot. It reminded me of U.S. military housing for officers (except for the Marine Corps, long notorious for outdated and substandard quarters). We lived in the field-grade officer housing section (my father being a major), which was across the street from former Prime Minister Ky's house.

I remember crossing the street to play soccer with my friends, children of junior officers, who lived down the street from Ky's house. But no kid would dare go near there. I was tempted once when urged by my friends but I did not accept the "mission"; a battle-ready tank sat outside his front door, though I never saw anyone in it. (After the 1971 election, when he failed to defeat Thieu for the presidency, Ky essentially sat out the remainder of the war as a private citizen.)

In February 1972 President Nixon visited China after his national security adviser, Henry Kissinger, had met secretly with the Beijing government. Both Nixon and Kissinger wrote in their memoirs of China's probable motives in seeking détente with the United States. By the end of 1969, North

Vietnam had expelled tens of thousands of Chinese advisers, "volunteer" workers, and soldiers, and had clearly begun to align itself with Moscow. Given the confrontations with the Soviet Union on the Manchurian border, therefore, Beijing most likely wanted the United States to remain engaged in Southeast Asia despite China's official support for the Hanoi regime. A shift in policy was needed, and the United States saw the potential in a new Chinese market after supporting China's entry into the United Nations.

In a declassified taped conversation from the U.S. National Archives in 2003, Nixon and Kissinger mulled over the situation in Vietnam in preparation for the presidential election of 1972.* It worried Nixon that "losing" South Vietnam (thus making him the first U.S. President to lose a war) would cost him his reelection. "If we settle it, say, this October [1972], by January '74 no one will give a damn," Kissinger coldly said to Nixon.

There were other reelection concerns for the Nixon administration besides *realpolitik*. Nuclear arms limitation negotiations were under way with the Soviets. The situation in the Middle East involving Israel and Egypt (the Yom Kippur War in 1973), along with the subsequent oil crisis, were looming.

South Vietnam, the "domino theory," "our ally," "stemming the tide of communism," no longer mattered as much. Détente with the Soviets and a direct channel to China meant that Vietnam remained the burr under the saddle of U.S. foreign policy. It was time for "a peace with honor" and the beginning of a treachery in Paris a year later. More bloody fighting would follow as the Saigon government "had to hold on," at least until the U.S. election in November 1972 was over (and ideally after the next in 1976). To Kissinger, U.S. support for South Vietnam only had to buy enough time for a "decent interval."

Several weeks after my family moved into its base housing, my father had me help him do a "home improvement" project. Next to our dining room was a cement stairway entry that led to an underground bunker, about 15 feet deep and big enough to hold twenty people. I hesitantly went down into the bunker while holding my father's hand. It was claustrophobic and creepy down there and it felt like being inside a tomb. The ceiling was made from

*Transcribed by Ken Hughes of the University of Virginia Center of Public Affairs.

pieces of pierced-steel planks, probably left over from military runway construction. I could see sunlight through the circular holes, so the bunker wasn't totally dark.

We went back up to the dining room and stood above the bunker, which was like a basement with an outside entrance. My father pointed to a pile of empty sandbags on the driveway. "See those bags? I want you to fill them up with dirt from our front yard. I'll stack them on top of the [steel] planks." He didn't need to explain to me why. Already at age seven, I had seen many sandbagged bunkers in South Vietnam. I assumed the probability for survival increased with the bags' protecting us unless we took a direct hit. It took me all day of shoveling hard dirt and rocky sand into those green bags. By evening, my father had neatly stacked three layers of sloppily filled sandbags atop our home bunker. We were going to be hunkering down like the rest of our fellow South Vietnamese.

By spring of 1972, my father had become executive officer or XO (i.e., second in command) of the 425th Transport Squadron. Earlier, as part of Nixon's Vietnamization initiative, the VNAF had received hundreds of airplanes, helicopters, and thousands of spare parts: the VNAF's inventory quadrupled to more than 2,000 aircraft and 60,000 personnel. C-123s replaced C-47s as the lead transport aircraft. My father, who had already qualified in the C-123 in 1966, took part in training new students. Along with USAF advisers, he helped bring two other squadrons on line, the 421st and 423d, before assuming his duties with the 425th, which was made up entirely of VNAF-trained pilots. Even though the VNAF had grown to be the fourth largest air force in the world, just behind the U.S., the Soviet, and Chinese forces, that would contribute to the overblown assessment of South Vietnam's true military capabilities. As an example, many of the older Skyraiders, and other aircraft, were put into storage due to a lack of spare parts but were still counted in the general inventory.

In April of 1972 North Vietnam launched a 130,000-man, all-out assault (also known as the Easter offensive) throughout South Vietnam. Retreating southern troops converged on the city of An Loc, 60 miles northwest of Saigon, with a handful of U.S. advisers among thousands of ARVN soldiers. Along with Soviet T-54 tanks and advanced antiaircraft cannon, portable, SA-7 surface-to-air missiles (SAMs) had made their appearance for the first time, which immediately knocked down vulnerable VNAF airplanes and helicopters. A combination of B-52 strikes and ARVN tenacity kept the attackers at bay during a siege that would last 70 days. The situation began to look alarmingly like Dien Bien Phu in 1954 and Khe Sanh in 1968. Without aerial resupply, the troops could not hold out.

The heavy NVA antiaircraft fire was the thickest ever seen over the skies of South Vietnam.

On April 15, the aircraft flown by the commanding officer of the 425th was shot down, killing all ten crew members. The plane had been filled with antitank munitions and it instantly exploded when hit by antiaircraft fire. (At the funeral, as my mother recalled, the commander's wife and his mistress argued in public and created an unforgettable scene.) My father then took command of the 425th; at age thirty-six, and with over 7,000 hours of flight time, he had finally achieved his goal of becoming a commanding officer. He promptly canceled all leave and ordered every pilot in the unit onto the flight schedule, and he led the next mission. As he announced to the squadron, "You have to do your job or quit flying and turn in your wings. I'll go first, then the new XO, then the next officer in rank. Then we'll repeat the order. No sick call, no sick mother excuses. If your name is on the flight schedule, you will fly. If it's your turn to die, that's it."

Sorties were flown around the clock. Then four days later the 425th lost another plane and another ten crew members. Morale plunged. My mother said that my father came home then white as a ghost. It was a good thing our family had moved onto the base so that we could at least see him some of the time.

Once again USAF pilots came to help. Several U.S. C-130s attempted to resupply An Loc, and three were shot down within ten days—which led to the U.S. squadron commander's prompt relief and being ordered back to the States.

The siege ended badly for the North Vietnamese, who suffered around 100,000 casualties, or two times South Vietnam's losses. General Creighton Abrams (who had relieved General Westmoreland as U.S. commander) reported: "Overall, the South Vietnamese have fought well under extremely difficult circumstances. They have made great progress in this area [the integration of air, armor, artillery, and infantry into a coherent whole] during the past year in particular." A distinguished Vietnam historian, the late Douglas Pike, cited the defense of An Loc as "the single most important battle of the war." The South Vietnamese military had risen to the occasion and answered lingering questions about its resolve to fight. The ARVN repelled the assault albeit with the hold of U.S. air power. The revered General Giap was "moved" out of his job as overall NVA commander. Saigon gained another three years.

Despite withstanding the Easter offensive, South Vietnam suffered a public-relations blow when American actress Jane Fonda visited North Vietnam in August 1972. A photograph of "Hanoi Jane" in a pith helmet and peering through the sight of an antiaircraft gun was seen around the world. She ended her visit by broadcasting a radio message from Hanoi.

(Her apology in 1988 would not prove good enough for thousands of American Vietnam veterans. In 1999, when she was profiled in a television show named "A Celebration: 100 Years of Great Women," there was an outcry across the United States. Senator John Kerry would experience the same outrage, especially from the Swift Boat veterans during his 2004 presidential campaign, though he never expressed regret. Some Vietnam veterans don't easily forget and forgive. Both incidents demonstrate that the Vietnam War is still being fought in the United States, among Americans in an unrelenting generational and political divide. Now as then, the Vietnamese people themselves hardly matter.)

Nixon overwhelmingly won reelection in November 1972 over George McGovern, a World War II bomber pilot and ardent antiwar senator. All that was left now to save in Vietnam were 600 or so American POWs. That would be the top agenda item in Paris before the North Vietnamese withdrew from negotiations in mid-December.

At the end of 1972, the VNAF received C-130s from the USAF, replacing all the C-123s. Once more, in order to quickly attain greater capabilities, the VNAF sacrificed gaining familiarity with the new equipment. My father, along with five other sets of aircrew, rapidly underwent the instructor pilot and tactics courses at Tan Son Nhut and other airfields in Southeast Asia. Two C-130 squadrons were manned, and he took the assignment as XO of the 437th Transport Squadron.

Five days after North Vietnamese negotiators abruptly left Paris, Nixon gave them and their fellow citizens an "early Christmas present." Over 120 B-52 bombers raided Hanoi and surrounding cities assisted by hundreds of U.S. Marine and Navy tactical aircraft in Linebacker II, the deadliest non-nuclear aerial strikes ever known to mankind. Twelve days later, the North Vietnamese bowed. Nixon had spoken and carried a gigantic stick, and the Communists listened.

In January 1973, the Paris Peace Accords were signed and both North and South Vietnam took a much-needed respite from full-scale fighting. The NVA used the cease-fire to rebuild, but my family saw more of my father.

Three key provisions (or concessions) in the accords would contribute to the fall of Saigon in 1975. First, the North Vietnamese were allowed to keep 150,000 soldiers south of the DMZ. Second, the United States would retaliate if North Vietnam violated the accords. Finally, and most important, the United States would continue to aid South Vietnam unconditionally. The latter two provisions would never happen.

CHAPTER 9

THIS IS THE END

S ADLY, NORMAL LIFE ONLY CAME DURING OUR LAST TWO years in Vietnam. My father was around more than he had been in previous years; it would be when I felt closest to my father. His flight time and overall VNAF training had been curtailed. A shortage of detonators, fuel, bombs, and spare parts kept much of the VNAF fleet grounded. My father's C-130 squadron rarely had more than two or three airplanes in "up status" out of sixteen. Overall, the VNAF operated at less than 50 percent of capacity and morale bottomed out. The other military services also faced cutbacks in ammunition and supplies and were ordered to ration what they had remaining.

Some of my father's duties required him to drive his squadron's jeep onto the flight line, stopping to inspect cargo, coveys of military personnel, and, sometimes civilians. He took me on some of these drives. He'd pull right behind combat aircraft being armed for missions and get out and talk to the pilots. He drove underneath the wings of huge cargo planes so that I could stare up at their engines, rivets, and fuel tanks, marveling at the size of these machines.

My father came home from work one night and told my mother during dinner that there was a Viet Cong being held at the base jail. I was eating at the table so I overheard. In my young mind, the Viet Cong remained this elusive mysterious enemy talked about on radio and television. To my surprise the next morning, my father looked over at me sitting in the right seat of his jeep and asked, "Do you want to see what a Viet Cong looks like?" I immediately nodded. We drove to the Tan Son Nhut prison as military policemen saluted my father, who was by then a lieutenant colonel. We strolled through the jail until we reached a desk in front of a locked door with a small window. My father said something to the guard as he opened the door. The Viet Cong captive stood up, looking at us expressionlessly. He was in his late twenties, had a hollow face and a rail-thin torso, and he wore a white T-shirt and black shorts. In my mind, it was completely opposite to my expectation. *The VC looked like us.*

During this short lull in the fighting, my father caught the fishing bug and he took me along half a dozen times on weekends. I would sit on the back of his Lambretta, hanging onto his waist with one hand and holding the fishing poles with the other. My arm would get tired from holding the poles, which bounced up and down at my side as we motored along unpaved roads. I was so worried about dropping them and disappointing my father that I bit my bottom lip and hung on, my arm numb with pain. On one trip, about ten of his friends and their sons rode on their scooters to the countryside where bomb craters carved out by B-52 raids had filled up with rainwater and become ponds. We were fishing for bluegills, catfish, or anything that bit. After a slow morning one of the men produced a hand grenade and dropped it into a fish pond. A loud explosion interrupted the tranquility as waves rippled across the water, and thirty seconds later dozens of fish floated to the top, some bleeding from their gills. A grenade proved to be the best bait any of us used that day, but I never tried it.

On another occasion my father took me fishing at a naval base on the Saigon River. He had graduated from simple bamboo fishing poles to more modern, Japanese-made open spinning reels mounted on fiberglass rods. He went after channel catfish, a Vietnamese delicacy but one not easy to hook. The bait was several 2-inch-long brown cockroaches that I had trapped the night before in our kitchen. I was given several small poles to fish around the pier pilings. As I gazed across the river waiting for action, I noticed a strange clump of brush moving toward the pier where we were fishing. It was floating against the outgoing tide. Suddenly, the Vietnamese sailors in the watchtower opened up their machine gun. Rounds flew over my head, striking the water around the vegetation, and finally blowing it to pieces. Empty cartridges were ejected onto the pier, clinking on the concrete. I dropped my poles, got on my knees, and covered my ears. Meanwhile, my father went about his business nonchalantly, casting with his pole as if nothing was happening around him. I didn't particularly enjoy my first "combat" fishing outing.

One of my biggest fears when growing up was swimming. Before I could go fishing with my father in deep water, I had to take swimming lessons at

Le Cercle Sportif, a popular former French retreat in Saigon. One of my uncles was a prominent lawyer in Saigon, so my parents would occasionally be
invited as my aunt's guests. My mother remembered U.S. ambassador Henry
Cabot Lodge in the late 1960s quietly reading a book on a lounge chair or eating in the dining room. The members were Americans, French, and well-off
Saigonese. My father occasionally played tennis there while my mother su-
pervised our swimming lessons after school.

The Communists had never planned to abide by the peace accords. Rocket
attacks were soon resumed, and I was glad my father had reinforced our
bomb shelter with sandbags. One night when my father was away flying, the
air raid siren shrieked through the Tan Son Nhut night. Seconds later, the
first incoming rockets landed close to our house, which was less than a third
of a mile from the flight line. The concussion shook us right out of our beds.
Our bedroom's broken wooden shutters flew open and shut with every blast.
My sister Thi's job was to shut off the gas line. My mother grabbed a prepo-
sitioned flashlight. My job was simple—to run down the hallway into the
bomb shelter in our dining room and grab a light with a long extension cord
on the way.

The shelling went on for what seemed like hours, but in actuality was
probably more like fifteen minutes. Before this attack I had been a macho
nine-year-old, seasoned in war games with my friends and comfortable
around military men and their hardware. And I had seen the war movies.
Yet, in front of my sisters and my mother, I started bawling nonstop, asking
where my father was. My sisters just looked at me without saying anything,
while my mother tried to calm me down. I couldn't stop shaking until the attack ceased. (If only my father could have seen his boy cry like a little sissy.) I
don't think my mother ever told him of this shameful episode.

In the middle of the so-called countrywide cease-fire, my parents entered
on their first entrepreneurial venture: they decided to raise chickens and sell
them to the vendors on the open market to make extra money. Later, as an
American, it was unfathomable for me that my parents had to even pursue
such an endeavor. My father was a lieutenant colonel, after all, and my
mother worked full-time as a teacher. Yet we needed the extra money. America tried to make the South Vietnamese military into a replica of her armed
services, but without any matching pay scales, or the elimination of endemic
corruption and desertion. Inflation rocketed and unemployment increased
after the U.S. military had departed.

My sisters and I chipped in to help, cleaning the chicken cages and picking up eggs each morning. It was fun for us children to have the feeling of living on a "farm" while our parents tended their chickens in flight suits and *ao dai* after returning from work. A few months later, my parents sold the remaining hens and got rid of the cages. It was simply too much work.

In August 1974 President Nixon resigned from office. The news sent a shock wave throughout South Vietnam, for he was seen as its last savior. To make matters worse, in the same year Congress reduced the amount of aid to South Vietnam by $300 million, signaling its impending abandonment. North Vietnam took notice and tested U.S. resolve under President Ford's new leadership. Ignoring the Paris Peace Accords, they quickly overran Phuoc Long Province in December without drawing a response from the United States. The new president mentioned "Vietnam" once in his state of the union address in early 1975.

My father finally took a staff assignment, leaving his C-130 unit to become the wing safety and standardization officer, flying missions only on occasion. For the final months of his career, he was not even attached to an operational unit. I am not sure he ever really knew the reasons why South Vietnam fell so quickly. He and other VNAF veterans told stories of aircraft flying half-loaded with fuel and bombs, and jet planes landing with blown tires that were never replaced. Clearly the VNAF was feeling the effects of U.S. disengagement, but the ARVN had grown to depend heavily on air support during the war. And without the high-tech and expensive support of the VNAF, the army could not hold out for long.

In March 1975, confident of U.S. indifference to the plight of South Vietnam, Hanoi unleashed an all-out assault to end the war. The province of Ban Me Thuot quickly fell and President Thieu (himself a former ARVN general) made the fatal decision to withdraw ARVN troops from the Central Highlands. Already paranoid about a coup, he desperately wanted elite units to defend Saigon, and so the northern regions were practically deserted.

Having family members nearby in a war zone was a luxury for the South Vietnamese that the average U.S. soldier did not have. That's what happens when you fight a war in your own backyard. But as the "family syndrome" came into play, the withdrawal to the south turned into chaos. Soldiers abandoned their units to return home to help evacuate loved ones amid confusing orders from Saigon. Troops and refugees crowded Route 7B, a single-lane highway known as the "convoy of tears," as NVA artillery shells rained down from above. This time there would be no An Loc. No heroic stand. No reprieve.

James Willbanks, a retired U.S. Army officer on the staff of the U.S. Army Command and General Staff College, wrote of the collapse of South Vietnamese forces in his book *Abandoning Vietnam:*

> The loss of materiel and equipment was staggering. Hundreds of artillery pieces and armored vehicles had been destroyed on the road or abandoned in Pleiku. Only a handful of armored vehicles, including just thirty armored personnel carriers, made it to Tuy Hoa. Nearly 18,000 tons of ammunition, a month's supply for a corps, was left in depots in Ban Me Thuot, Pleiku, and Kontum. Scores of good aircraft were left for the enemy at Pleiku.

At the end of March 1975, President Ford dispatched Gen. Fred Weyand, army chief of staff, to South Vietnam to assess the imminent collapse. A week later, he reported to Ford and sent a copy to the National Security Council. An excerpt of Weyand's report, highlighting his assessment and recommendations, said as follows:

> The present level of U.S. support guarantees the GVN [Government of Vietnam] defeat. Of the $700 million provided for fiscal year 1975, the remaining $150 million can be used for a short time for a major supply operation; however, if there is to be any real chance of success, an additional $722 million is urgently needed to bring the South Vietnamese to a minimal defense posture to meet the Soviet and PRC (People's Republic of China) supported invasion. Additional U.S. aid is within both the spirit and intent of the Paris Agreement, which remains the practical framework for a peaceful settlement in Vietnam.
>
> One of the most serious psychological and attitudinal problem at all levels, military and civilian, is the belief that the South Vietnamese have been abandoned, and even betrayed, by the United States. The Communists are using every possible device of propaganda and psychological warfare to foster this view. Much of this emotion is keyed on the 1973 Paris Agreement and subsequent U.S. withdrawal. It is widely believed that the GVN was forced to sign this agreement as a result of a private U.S.-North Vietnamese deal under which the U.S.

was allowed to withdraw its forces and get its prisoners back in return
for abandoning South Vietnam. This sense of abandonment has been
intensified by what is widely perceived as a lack of public U.S. acknowledgement of South Vietnam's current plight or willingness to
provide needed support.

There is not and cannot be any guarantee that the actions proposed
will be sufficient to prevent total North Vietnamese conquest. The effort, however, should be made. What is at stake in Vietnam now is
America's credibility as an ally. We must not abandon our goal of a
free and independent South Vietnam.

While sitting on the sidelines militarily, the United States began devising
an evacuation plan for its personnel and several hundred specially selected
Vietnamese at the recommendation of Gen. Fred Weyand. CIA agents and
State Department personnel frantically worked around the clock inside the
U.S. Embassy in Saigon as the sand ran out of the hourglass. Sensing the collapse, North Vietnam's generals pushed even harder, sending southward
units previously held in reserve.

On April 10, Ford appeared before a joint session of Congress to appeal
for $722 million in military aid and for $250 million in economic aid and
refugee relief for South Vietnam. He received no applause as two Democratic freshmen congressmen (part of the 1974 post-Watergate class) walked out
before he finished. Congress denied his request.

Like thousands of South Vietnamese military men, my father spent the
last week in Saigon trying to get more family members out of danger. After
my mother, my sisters, and I flew out of Vietnam, he hustled back and forth
on his Lambretta from Tan Son Nhut to Saigon, trying to convince my maternal grandmother and one of my aunts to leave. Our exact whereabouts
was unknown to him; he only knew we had been in good hands when he saw
us depart on a U.S. C-130 on April 23.

The following day, President Ford gave a speech at Tulane University, declaring that "the war in Vietnam is over as far as America is concerned." Ambassador Martin notified Washington that the evacuation from Saigon of
U.S. personnel and critical Vietnamese should soon commence. U.S. Marines
had been flown off amphibious ships into the Defense Attaché Office (DAO)
compound next to Tan Son Nhut in preparation for the evacuation.

Years later my father said he was no hero by remaining until the end, but he never told me why directly. In an interview with Bernie Edelman, he said "Officers cannot leave early or they're cowards. I could have left. But everyone will know what day I left. I would have that on my mind all the time. No one normal could do that." One of his colleagues told me at a VNAF reunion in 2004, "I saw your father the day before the last day. He was still wearing his khaki uniform, ribbons and all. Damn, he wouldn't leave."

My grandmother, an aunt, and a cousin were driven by an air force friend to Tan Son Nhut on April 27. (Many of my father's friends had congregated at our house to hide in our bomb shelter.) While waiting to board an aircraft, my grandmother wanted to see my uncle one last time, so she, my aunt, and my cousin left the base to return home. They, too, never made it out.

Meanwhile, in the political world Gen. Duong Van "Big" Minh had assumed power from a weakened Tran Van Huong, who had replaced Thieu a week earlier. (After the 1963 coup that toppled the Diem government, Minh had temporarily risen to power.) False rumors also surfaced about Nguyen Cao Ky's attempting to take power.

Under orders from the United States, the VNAF sent its fleet of F-5 fighters to Thailand to avoid their capture by the advancing North Vietnamese. Transport aircraft manned by VNAF pilots also took part in the evacuation, often flown by many of my father's colleagues and former students. On the evening of April 28, three captured A-37 jets flown by North Vietnamese pilots (led by the defector who bombed the Presidential Palace on April 8) struck Tan Son Nhut Air Base, damaging a number of aircraft on the ground.

By April 29, NVA troops on the outskirts of Saigon were lobbing long-range artillery rounds and rockets into the air base. My father and a dozen of his comrades clambered into our home shelter to wait out the heavy shelling. At daylight next morning, several of those in the bomb shelter left and caught the last VNAF C-130 flights out of the country (at this point the aircraft were skirting debris on the runways as they took off for U Tapao Air Base in Thailand). My father was last seen in the shelter talking on the phone to my grandmother. Two others of his colleagues fled to Vung Tau, the coastal resort, where they boarded departing Vietnamese Navy ships.

U.S. Marine Sgt. Ted Murray checked on his Marines shortly after the NVA barrage ceased. Two of them had died during a rocket attack: Cpl. Charles McMahon, Jr., and LCpl. Darwin Judge were the last two Americans to die in combat in Vietnam.

Murray recalled that fateful morning:

I saw first-hand the delays and the needless paperwork that people
were put through before leaving. There was a Vietnamese woman
who waited at the guard gate to the compound. Von was her name
and her daughter was Van. I promised both of them on the 28th that
I would make sure that they left before we did. But that night, the airport was bombed by the Dragonfly [A-37] aircraft that had been captured by the NVA. [Von] had gone home already. I don't know if she
ever got a chance to get back in or not. . . . I was just a sergeant doing
my job to the best of my ability and doing things that could have gotten
many of us in trouble, putting people on planes without prior "authori-
zation" from the State Department or anyone else. Why? Because I
could. And that is one thing that I am extremely proud about.

Murray witnessed what were probably the final sorties flown by the
VNAF. On the morning of April 29, an AC-119 gunship made a last effort,
circling over Tan Son Nhut and firing its miniguns (which sounded like
cloth ripping) into the advancing NVA troops. The aircraft had been in
nearly constant combat source earlier that night, landing to refuel and reload
several times before an SA-7 antiaircraft missile struck the gunship shortly
after 7 a.m. The gunship exploded violently, and several open parachutes
were seen descending to the ground. Two Skyraiders from the 514th and
518th FS (my father's former units) also took to the air and made several
strafing runs. One would be shot down by antiaircraft artillery fire and the
other by an SA-7. These last combat missions brought the illustrious history
of a mighty air force, born and grown in war, to a sad ending.

Hundreds of VNAF fixed-wing aircraft fled to Thailand, while appearing like locusts on the horizon, VNAF helicopters rushed to land on the
overcrowded U.S. fleet in the South China Sea, only to be pushed overboard
to make room for others. General Ky flew Lt. Gen. Ngo Quang Truong* and
a dozen others in his personal helicopter, landing on the USS *Midway* shortly
after noon. Ky's aide-de-camp, Maj. Ho Dang Tri, one of my father's closest
friends, refused to leave; Tri's entire family stayed in Saigon.

The price of freedom was no longer a factor. Rear Admiral Lawrence
Chambers ordered the dumping of some $10 million worth of Huey helicop-

---

*Truong was I Corps commander and regarded by most Americans (including General Abrams) as
Vietnam's best field commander and the "second coming of General George S. Patton," according
to Ky.

ters to save one family. VNAF Maj. Bung Ly (with his wife and five children on board) successfully landed his O-1 observation plane—without a tailhook—on the aircraft carrier USS *Midway*.

It would take fifteen years before another Vietnamese would land aboard a U.S. Navy ship then as a Marine helicopter pilot.

My father decided to go back to Saigon one last time to attempt to bring out my grandmother. When she refused he headed back to Tan Son Nhut and tried to reenter the base. As he drove through Saigon, he passed the remnants of an army scattered throughout the downtown area. Members of the 18th ARVN Division, the last unit fighting at Xuan Loc, had retreated to the city. Soldiers ran about in their boxer shorts, their boots and uniforms left on the ground. M16s were thrown into the Saigon River.

My father, too, had changed out of uniform and into civilian clothes. Weaving in and out of traffic, he pushed his Lambretta as fast as it could go. Trying to avoid capture by infiltrators and advancing NVA troops, he managed to get to Tan Son Nhut in hopes of catching a departing plane.

Unbeknownst to him, the airport had been shut down after the rocket attacks had rendered the runways unsafe and unusable. The U.S.-led evacuation had shifted to Option IV, an all-helicopter extraction at the U.S. Embassy and the DAO compound. Bing Crosby's "White Christmas," the signal for the remaining Americans to evacuate, had been played a few hours earlier. My father managed to get to the front gates of Tan Son Nhut where he saw once-familiar faces, now wearing Viet Cong uniforms. He changed direction and headed to the DAO compound where giant U.S. Marine CH-53 Sea Stallion helicopters began landing shortly after 3 p.m. He stopped his Lambretta and ran toward the fence to join the terrified crowd.

Amid chaos and confusion, a shirtless Marine wearing a flak jacket pressed the muzzle of his M16 against my father's chest, quickly discouraging him from any thoughts of entering the compound. My father stood back and watched the fortunate Vietnamese who had been allowed to enter. A U.S. Marine had rescued my father eleven years earlier, and now another would keep him from catching a flight to freedom. Stranded and dejected, he watched with shame as more South Vietnamese soldiers ripped off their uniforms and threw their rifles into the river to evade capture by the approaching communist troops. On the night of April 29 my father drove back to my grandmother's house to await his fate.

Through the rest of the afternoon and into the morning of April 30 Marine and Air America (CIA) helicopters lifted nearly 7,000 Americans, South

Vietnamese, and third-country nationals to navy ships offshore. Operation Frequent Wind became the largest helicopter-based evacuation operation ever conducted. At 4:59 a.m., a CH-46 with call sign "Lady Ace 09" piloted by Capt. Gerry Berry radioed the amphibious command ship USS *Blue Ridge,* "Tiger, tiger, tiger." That signaled the departure of Ambassador Martin from Saigon. Martin had remained only until a direct order from President Ford was given for him to leave the embassy. At 7 a.m., Berry flew the second to the last group of Marines out of Saigon. "You could see fires. The (South Vietnamese troops) were retreating into the city and some of them were still putting up a good fight, especially in the north end of the city," Berry told me years later. "I could see NVA tanks entering the city. After twenty years of fighting, it was a tough thing to watch."

At 7:30 a.m., CH-46 call sign "Swiff 2-2" ferried the last eleven Marines off the embassy rooftop. By 11 a.m., two NVA T-54 tanks had crashed through the front gates of the Presidential Palace. A crewman ran into the palace and unfurled the red communist flag from the front balcony. President "Big" Minh and his three-day-old cabinet officially surrendered to a military journalist, Col. Bui Tin.*

When the announcement to surrender came over the radio, an ARVN colonel in uniform stood at the base of the Vietnamese Marine Memorial, saluted, and killed himself with a single pistol shot to the head. Several ARVN generals also committed suicide at various posts in South Vietnam. Family members had to take away my father's pistol because they feared he would kill himself.

My father peeked out at the streets of Saigon as the NVA rode into town. His mind was foggy, his actions unpredictable. Twenty-one years of his military service had come to an end. Thousands of his peers had given up their lives for South Vietnam, including the dozens of personal friends who had been shot down during the long years of fighting. A strange quiet fell on Saigon that evening. My father remained at my grandmother's for a month and a half before he would report for "reeducation" along with other South Vietnamese officers. For most Vietnamese the fighting had finally ended. For

---

*Fed up with censorship and lack of democratic development in Vietnam after the war, Bui Tin moved to France in 1990. In his memoir *Following Ho Chi Minh,* Tin recalled the day of surrender. "On April 30, 1975, he [Nguyen Van Hao, head of the National Bank of South Vietnam] told me that South Vietnam's gold reserves [16 tons], which President Nguyen Van Thieu was rumored to have transported out of country, in fact remained intact and under guard in the national treasury in Saigon."

several millions, however, the dying and the suffering would continue in the years after Saigon's "liberation."

Bui Diem, South Vietnam's ambassador to the United States, remembered this about South Vietnam's final days:*

"Is it possible for a great nation to behave this way?" That was the question an old friend of mine asked me in Saigon when the news came in August 1974 that [the U.S.] Congress had reduced the volume of aid. He was a store owner whom I had gone to school with in North Vietnam, a totally nonpolitical person. "You are an ambassador," he said. "Perhaps you understand these things better than I do. But can you explain this attitude of the Americans? When they wanted to come, they came. And they want to leave, they leave. It's as if a neighbor came over and made a shambles of your house, then all of a sudden he decides the whole thing is wrong, so he calls it quits. How can they just do that?" It was a naïve question from an unsophisticated man. But I had no answer for it.

The South Vietnamese people, and especially the South Vietnamese leaders, myself among them, bear the ultimate responsibility for the fate of their nation, and to be honest, they have much to regret and much to be ashamed of.

Two weeks after Saigon fell Henry Kissinger, in his 1975 memo addressed to President Ford (declassified in 2000), wrote, "When the United States entered the war during the 1960s, it did so with excesses that not only ended the career and the life of an allied leader but that may have done serious damage to the American economy. When we made it 'our war' we would not let the South Vietnamese fight it; when it became 'their war,' we would not help them fight it."

The memo was never sent to the President.

*From his memoir *In the Jaws of History.*

CHAPTER 10

OPERATION NEW LIFE

OUR C-130 LANDED BEFORE SUNRISE. ASIAN SOLDIERS wearing khaki uniforms entered the aircraft and led us down the rear ramp. They spoke in their own language to one another, but used English with the USAF crew. My mother huddled the four of us together as we found our own way off the airplane. It had been a rough, cramped flight. Like most other passengers, all of us were still groggy from the long flight. Once outside, we lined up in front of a series of tables with stacks of paper on them. As the sun came up, we were provided with milk and fruit, and U.S. uniformed military personnel helped us fill out paperwork and answer questions. We were then told to get on a bus and proceed to a huge terminal to wait.

My mother fell asleep before we kids did. I watched some families leave the terminal, going back onto buses. The military personnel had brought us dinners on paper plates. I wolfed down my first U.S. military cafeteria meal in no time. It didn't matter if the mashed potato, green beans, canned corn, and breaded chicken tasted bland compared to a bowl of *pho*, white noodles sprinkled with *nuoc mam*, fermented fish sauce. The milk definitely needed sugar. I was used to drinking hot water mixed with French condensed milk, which was sweet as can be. After dinner my sisters and I finally fell asleep and woke up an hour later, to find that everyone had left the terminal. The other refugees hadn't bothered to wake us up. We were on our own. A young

U.S. airman finally tapped my mother on the shoulder and told us to grab our belongings. A bus was waiting outside. We were the last family to walk out of the terminal. My mother never forgot his simple good deed: it was her first "live" impression of an American, and it had been extremely positive.

We stayed in the Philippines for just under twenty-four hours. Apparently there were many more inbound planes from Saigon, and we had to leave to make room. President Ferdinand Marcos refused to accept the influx of Vietnamese: he demanded that the United States get the refugees out of his country as soon as possible. Later in the week, Vietnamese Navy ships overflowing with refugees would be banned from docking in Subic Bay and were forced back to sea. They had to sail directly to Guam, adding another week of misery for those onboard. So much for the fellow Asian brotherly love!

Travel conditions improved, though. This time, we filed into a C-141, a four-engine jet transport with enough seats for everyone. There was no rush to run aboard. Everything was calmer than our departure from Tan Son Nhut the night before. The jet noise inside the cabin was deafening (there was no padding), so the crew passed out yellow foam-rubber earplugs. We began to feel safe, since enemy ground fire no longer threatened us.

We flew to Guam, while other refugees went to Wake Island.

The flight took less than two hours and we landed at sunrise again. Our plane touched down at Andersen Air Force Base, ironically home to the B-52s that had once pounded the NVA. There was hardly anyone at the terminal when we first got there; it was as if no one was expecting us. It turned out our plane had been one of the first to arrive, so the actual refugee camp (another bus ride away) was still getting ready. We were then driven to Camp Asan, an abandoned area that had once been a Marine Barracks.

In less than twenty-four hours, 400 or so Marines and Navy Seabees made the abandoned, faded-yellow Quonset huts habitable again.

Since we were in the first group to enter the camp, my mother had her pick of fifteen or so empty barracks. Typical of junior enlisted personnel housing, each Quonset hut held two rows of racks (twin-size beds) for about fifty people. We slept separated by a 5-foot-wide path down the middle. The first night on Guam I developed what turned into a recurring episode of bed-wetting. I used the green issue blanket and white sheets to wipe up the mess as quickly as I could. Then I ran out the back door to throw the blanket away before anyone could see me. The evacuation had taken an emotional toll on me, but I didn't know it then. However, I was old enough to know that boys my age no longer peed in bed.

Our week on Guam seemed like a month. Everyone was waiting for the "big battle" that never took place in Saigon. Denial was still the norm; there was talk of returning to Saigon when things "calmed down." More and more people arrived daily; buses ran round the clock. Those already in the camps kept waiting for new arrivals, hoping to see loved ones among the crowds. I ran into several schoolmates—some with their entire family and some, like me, without their fathers. We children congregated each night to watch American movies under the starry equatorial skies. The Marines had set up the camp to make our lives more comfortable, adding amenities each day, such as portable toilets and additional chow lines. A Vietnamese man, Tony Lam,* was designated the "camp manager" and served as the liaison between the refugees and the Marines. He spoke some English and was one of the very few among us who understood what the Americans were saying. The rest of us just followed gestures or Vietnamese slang that some GIs spoke.

The kids usually were first to line up for meals, and I ran to the head of the line three times a day. The military men were nice to the kids, always smiling. I couldn't understand them when they said something to me so I smiled back and gave them that reaffirming American "thumbs-up." Between meals our parents gathered near makeshift bulletin boards, where announcements and messages were left for incoming refugees.

Guam's beaches were rocky and shallow; the water was up to the knee or the waist from the shore to at least a mile out. I saw several teenagers wade out until they became dots on the horizon. Adults paced the beaches, staring out to the same horizon. The warm water soon attracted more bathers, including me. The beaches brought back memories of the coastal town of Nha Trang where my family took our second and last vacation. On our third day on Guam, I was scratched by something in the water. A few hours later, the infection had turned my right foot red and blue, and soon after a bluish coloring ran up to my thigh. My mother, as if she hadn't had enough on her mind, ran me over to the clinic, where a navy doctor squeezed some pus out of my ankle and gave me some medicine. I spent the next two days, mostly by

---

*Tony Lam also later served as "camp manager" at the Camp Pendleton refugee camp in California. In 1992, he became the first Vietnamese American to be elected to public office in the United States.

myself, resting in our empty building during the day, fighting a slight fever and feeling exhausted. Sometimes hours went by before someone came to check on me, and it was lonely.

More and more refugees arrived, and soon Camp Asan became full; tents were erected to handle the overflow. Chow lines took longer, so we began lining up sooner, usually holding places for the adults. Those with large families usually caused a ruckus, since they would take up more spots in front of families already in line. There were conflicts between adults and among the children, but the Marines and Seabees quickly broke them up. Each day my mother would run to the bus arrival area, hoping to catch a glimpse of familiar faces. The new arrivals piled off buses, exhausted and traumatized, just as we had looked a few days earlier. My mother would return to our hut each night looking disappointed. Not only did she not find my father, she hadn't run into any of our other relatives. She did, however, see several of my father's VNAF colleagues reunite with their families, and that made her even more sad. A USAF adviser who knew my father stopped by the camp many times to check with the VNAF pilots to see if anyone "had run into Hoa." No one had.

Shortly after noon on April 30, 1975, a crowd of mostly women and elderly refugees burst into tears. They had been huddling near the camp's operations center listening to the BBC. My mother was among the crowd. "The Communists have entered Saigon. It's all over." The radio announcement quickly spread throughout the camp. Our worst fears had been realized.

The next day my family left for its new life in the United States, fortunate to be among the 1 percent of the population that had escaped. The tropical scenery of Guam had given us a temporary illusion of Vietnam, but we had to move on. As in the Philippines, more refugees were arriving and we had to vacate our quarters to make room. My mother wanted to stay longer, in hopes that my father would catch up; we were told that families would be able to connect in the United States. As our plane rolled down the Andersen runway, I noticed two rows of dark-green jets, neatly parked, with no crewmen in sight, and no bombs to be loaded. They were the B-52s the South Vietnamese had thought were coming one more time.

We stopped in Hawaii at Hickam Air Force Base to refuel. As the plane descended, I remember staring out the window and seeing the tall buildings on Waikiki's beaches with the Diamond Head volcano at one end. Pearl Harbor was full of gray ships. When we touched down, I also saw many military planes including more parked B-52s. Hickam resembled a quiet Tan Son

Nhut with the mighty U.S. forces sitting idle. We made one more stop at San Francisco International Airport and finally arrived at Little Rock, Arkansas, nearly a full day after leaving Guam. Another bus took us to Fort Chaffee as its gates swung open to take in some 24,000 refugees over the next three months.

In the mid-1970s, Arkansas was well known for hogs and Tyson Foods. Vietnamese loved eating pork, including the ceremonial head, and we were desperate to quickly find things in common with our new hosts.

Life at Fort Chaffee began as at Camp Asan, minus the beaches and the uncertainty of the war's outcome. The base had row after row of wooden barracks, more sturdy than the Quonset huts on Guam. A soldier must have seen my mother and four young kids milling about the camp, for he assigned her an end room with a door lock so that our family could have some privacy. That was especially good for me, since I still could not stop my bed-wetting habit.

Citizens from nearby towns donated clothes and volunteered at the camp, teaching English to the refugees. One family in particular came to our aid. Retired Army Lt. Col. Dick Clohecy, a Vietnam veteran, and his wife Gloria met my mother one day when she was at the donation center looking for clothes for my sisters and me. The weather was cool in Arkansas compared to the tropics of Guam and Vietnam, so we needed more layers. Dick and Gloria lived in Gravette, a small town nearby on the Arkansas-Oklahoma border. (The nearest "big city" was Tulsa, 100 miles away.) I don't know how many people lived in Gravette in 1975 but the 2000 census showed 1,800 with 91 percent whites and less than $30,000 in income per household. The Clohecys had two teenage girls, so it wasn't that they were retired and had nothing better to do. They brought clothes, especially boys' pants and jackets for me, and came back weekly during our seven-week stay.

Outside the camps, public sentiment against Vietnamese refugees ran high even though at the time we did not directly feel it. The book on Vietnam had been closed for most Americans until the refugees arrived in unprecedented numbers; only the Cuban refugee resettlements had even come close in size, and the news reported the country split on what to do with the refugees.

In a May 1975 *New York Times* article, West Virginia Senator Robert Byrd commented that "barmaids, prostitutes and criminals" should be screened out as "excludable categories." Delaware Senator Joe Biden "charged that the [Ford] administration had not informed Congress adequately about the number of refugees." As if anyone actually knew during the chaotic evacuation. "They are better off in Vietnam," sniffed George McGovern in *Newsweek*. At the time unemployment in the United States hovered near double digits, so perhaps this had something to do with feelings against refugees.

In Larry Engelmann's 1997 *Tears Before the Rain: An Oral History of the Fall of South Vietnam,* Julia Vadala Taft, formerly in charge of the refugee re-settlement effort, recalled such opposition:

> "The new governor of California, Jerry Brown, was very concerned
> about refugees settling in his state. Brown even attempted to prevent
> planes carrying refugees from landing at Travis Air Force Base near
> Sacramento. . . . The secretary of health and welfare, Mario Obledo,
> felt that this addition of a large minority group would be unwelcome
> in the state. And he said that they already had a large population of
> Hispanics, Filipinos, blacks, and other minorities."

After a few weeks my mother began attending English and general classes about the American society. That left me free from sunrise to sunset, wan-dering all over the camp. There was an open grass field, and we kids congre-gated there to play soccer after meals. I got into games with kids around my age, playing goalie. Once, when I dove for an incoming ball, a charging player continued kicking after I had gathered the ball, until I was lying on the ground bleeding from my mouth. Luckily I lost no teeth. I stayed away from our barrack as long as I could, until the bleeding stopped, and ran back after dark. My thin mother, who had lost 15 pounds in the weeks since we left Vietnam, was livid when she saw the swelling on my lips. She took me inside, and unlike anytime before, screamed and slapped me until I cried. "Your fa-ther is not here so you better listen to me. Do what I say and don't talk back. I don't have time for this." She cried too.

By now U.S. military food was tasting great to me. I had never eaten so much before: even creamed chipped beef on toast or (known forever to GIs as "SOS"—"Shit on a shingle"), peanut-butter-and-jelly sandwiches, bur-gers, hot dogs, and cookies and cakes. I didn't particularly like tasteless corn flakes, not until somebody told me to put two teaspoons of sugar into the milk. Once in a while the mess hall would serve fish, but it didn't taste like the salty and flavorful catfish dishes in Saigon. Ice cream was the fa-vorite for the kids in the camp, and the GIs brought it out at night when we huddled to watch B-grade movies under the stars; the films didn't have Vietnamese subtitles, so the crowd would chuckle when the Americans laughed.

At Camp Talega, in the northeastern training area of Camp Pendleton, a former concert promoter, but now a refugee, Nam Loc, strummed his guitar and composed a tear-jerking song titled, "*Saigon Vinh Biet,*" or "Farewell Saigon."

Saigon oi, I have lost you in my life,
Saigon oi, my best time is far away.
What is left is some sad memory,
the dead smile on my lips, bitter tears in my eyes.
On the street, is the sun still shining?
On our path, is the rain still falling?
In the park, is my lover still there?
Going under the trees? Smiling or crying lonely?
Here, I am the bird losing her way.
Day by day my time just passes by
the life of an exile is painful.
O Saigon I call you
Saigon oi, I will be back, I promise!
My lover, I will keep my word always
Although here, passion begins at night,
the city lights are bright,
but you still are in my mind.

We refugees were extremely fortunate. Our biggest supporter, outside of Julia Vadala Taft, was the U.S. president. In May 1975, President Ford visited the camp and soon after refugees began leaving to start new lives across the country. I don't recall any other politicians, antiwar protestors, esteemed journalists, or celebrities visiting Fort Chaffee.

During our stay at the camp, more families were reconnected and those who arrived later found notes from loved ones who had been settled. But there was still no news of my father's whereabouts. More and more familiar faces showed up at the camps, mostly VNAF families we knew, but no one had seen my father.

The first English terms I picked up in the camp were "GI," "Salem,"

"Coke," and "sponsor." A sponsor (I pronounced it "spun-ser") was our ticket out of camp, for he or she signed the paperwork that allowed families to leave. The refugee task force's goal was to resettle as many refugees as it could within a few months of arrival.

One of my mother's brothers had escaped on one of the last planes out of Saigon: Uncle An, his wife Aunt Ly, and their daughter Dien were the only relatives we had in this country. They had studied in the United States in the 1960s and had been able to connect with one of Aunt Ly's classmates, who served as their sponsor. They left the refugee camp in early June and moved to the Los Angeles suburb of San Fernando Valley.

While my father had had the foresight to get us out of Vietnam early, my mother made an even more critical decision while we were in Fort Chaffee. Three of her sisters were living in Paris, and my mother was fluent in French. My older sister Thi and I had studied French since the second grade. My two younger sisters . . . well, they didn't speak any of it at all, but in some ways it would have been much easier to choose France as our destination. After talking with one of her sisters, my mother decided not to go to Paris and took a risk in choosing this country. Later she admitted, "I felt you kids would have much more opportunities in the United States, especially with your education. The French never saw Vietnamese as equals."

My uncle began posting ads for sponsors in newspapers in California but received no response for several weeks. His own sponsors, Ron and Bonnie Counseller, had two small children and couldn't have possibly taken on my family as well. My mother started to get nervous; other families, with both parents, began to leave in droves. She worried that a mother with four young children could be perceived as an extra burden on an American family. Finally, after three weeks, we found a sponsor. A man named Edward Minton called my uncle and we were on our way to the Golden State, despite the concerns of the governor and secretary of state. Our destination was Oxnard, "just north of Malibu." That was a local joke, we learned later: there was a world of difference between the two. Life had been a roller coaster for nearly two months, but the future looked as promising as it could get.

The last time the U.S. government had put so many Asians (this time 125,000) in camps was shortly after Pearl Harbor, and that was for a completely different reason. Japanese Americans had unconstitutionally been rounded up for internment at various camps even though they were U.S. citizens. In 1975, we Vietnamese refugees were just—refugees. Yet we received better treatment than our Asian-American predecessors and we got out of the camps after months, not years. How could a refugee ever pay back such kindness?

Top left: *New Americans. My refugee family in Oxnard, California, 1976. (Author's Collection)*
Right: *A Little League All-Star with my mother and youngest sister Thu, 1977. (Author's Collection)*
Bottom left: *(from left to right) Mark Adams, Mike Hiji, James Stewart, John Gadd, and I at our high school graduation. Oxnard, California 1982. (Author's Collection)*

CHAPTER 11

BASEBALL, MEMORIES, AND MOM

NAVY PETTY OFFICER EDWARD MINTON, HIS WIFE, THREE young daughters, and a son awaited us at his home, outside the Port Hueneme Naval Construction Battalion Center (CBC or Seabee) in Oxnard, California. His was a small, one-story house, with four bedrooms and a white picket fence. Slightly overweight and wearing thick, standard-issue GI black-frame glasses, Minton had a huge, warm smile. His wife hugged us, but her daughters were standoffish. We sat down and ate some sandwiches and attempted to communicate. The Mintons gave us one of the bedrooms, and we immediately fell asleep on top of the bedding. The next morning the Minton girls woke us up and began chatting, apparently more receptive to our presence than the day before.

In the mid-1970s, Oxnard was an agricultural working-class town of 150,000, nestled on the coast between Los Angeles and Santa Barbara. The early inhabitants were Chumash Indians who made a living near the beaches. Apparently a sugar beet factory owner in the 1800s, Henry T. Oxnard, frustrated by his dealings with bureaucrats, named the town after his family. His factory soon attracted many migrant workers to the area, including Chinese, Japanese, and Mexican immigrants. By World War II, a military base, Point Mugu Naval Air Station, was established just north of Malibu and 7 miles from our first apartment. After we moved there, once in a while, I would recognize a C-130 coming in for a landing. But the days of roaming the flight line with my father were long gone.

A few days after arriving, Minton took me with him to work at Port Hueneme. I had expected to see a military base like Tan Son Nhut, with planes and tanks; instead, we went to a kitchen, where he took me into a large refrigerator full of slabs of beef hanging from iron rods. Minton worked in the food service side of the U.S. Navy and his job was as a meat cutter. There I stood, lost inside a freezing room full of cow parts, wondering when I could go home. But he kept smiling and hacking away at the meat; neither one of us could say much to each other.

After a few days with the Mintons my mother decided we would be better off in town; there were simply too many of us living too close together for comfort. After we had spent a day at the county welfare office, Edward Minton drove us to a small rickety apartment on Aleric Street (rent at $175 a month), which was on the second floor, part of a rundown building with six units. There we kept to ourselves the first week, too scared to go outside. Our neighbors kept staring at us, and one family, in particular, had a single mother and five kids. They all had black hair, dark skin, and round eyes. They didn't look like the "other Americans" I had met in the refugee camps or the Mintons. They didn't speak English either, but they kept waving to us every time they saw us peeking out through the blinds.

Aleric Street hosted many hookers and pimps, drug pushers and sellers, all going about their business in broad daylight and at night. Years later, the city eventually changed its name to Cuesta del Mar Drive but that didn't erase its reputation from my memory or from that of anyone else who lived in Oxnard back then.

On our third night on Aleric loud explosions were heard after sunset. Rockets whistled and small firecrackers popped in our neighborhood like sporadic gunfire. I could hear people yelling and laughing outside. The noise continued for half an hour before subsiding, just as the incoming rounds had in Saigon (minus the concussions). I ran to the window and caught a glimpse of bright and colorful flashes in the distance; then a glow appeared low on the horizon, behind rows of apartments. I ran back into my bedroom (my mother and my youngest sister shared one of the other bedrooms) and I pulled the covers over our heads. My mother turned off the lights and we kept quiet. After a while the explosions faded and the yelling stopped. The next day we learned about the commotion: Fourth of July fireworks.

As for our friendly neighbors? They were Mexicans.

Welcome to América.

There was a convenience store down the block. My mother would occasionally walk there, and I would tag along. When she pulled out food stamps to pay for the groceries, the clerk would spitefully stare at her whenever she purchased any candy or goodies. One early evening, I noticed pretty women all dressed in short skirts, faces glistening with makeup, hanging out in front of the store, which stood on the corner of Hueneme Road, a main road a few blocks from the ocean. Strutting in their miniskirts and high heels, they smiled and puffed their cigarettes on the sidewalk. Men pulled up next to them in beat-up cars and drove away with the women. "Mom, what are those pretty ladies with red lipstick doing out there?" I asked. My mother grabbed me and said nothing. After that my sisters and I weren't allowed to go outside anymore after dark.

A month after arriving in Oxnard, my mother signed us up for summer school at a nearby elementary school. My sister Thi was eleven, I was ten, and my sister Uyen was six. My youngest sister, Thu, who was two, remained at home. My mother had already spent several weeks trying to teach us English by forcing Thi and me to copy words from a children's book she'd found. But it was all to no avail. We wrote page after page, trying at least to gain familiarity through writing out our new language. Although reading and speaking English weren't yet possible, I soon discovered I could do arithmetic faster than my American peers. I completed multiplication exercises on the blackboard faster than they did. For the first time in my life, I enjoyed competition, especially when winning out over peers (and gaining approval) in front of a strange audience. When the school decided to help us with language training, a U.S. Vietnam veteran who allegedly spoke Vietnamese was hired to help us with our studies. He couldn't understand us, and we could barely make out his broken Vietnamese slang, so the situation worsened. After a week he was let go. Our English as a second language, or ESL, lessons never materialized, and we had to swim or sink, learn English or make no friends. (Actually, French was our second language and English third.)

There were many boys my age in our neighborhood. Soon after arriving, they grabbed me to go play hide-and-seek in an alley behind our house. We communicated with one another by pointing, giving thumbs-up signs, drawing things in the dirt, tugging shirts, and using simple statements like "aaeeyy," "cool," "hey man," and "run." (The television show *Happy Days* and its lead character Fonzie were big hits. However, it took me a year to understand the meaning of "sit on it!") Two of the boys took my right hand and shaped my palm into a closed fist. Slowly, they pried open my middle finger, which also loosened the other knuckles. After several tries, they succeeded in raising my right arm with only my middle finger extended. All three of them jumped up and cheered and joined in the ceremonial graduation. There I was, bonding with my new American friends (a Mexican, a Japanese American, and a white kid) telling the world how I felt, even if I didn't yet know what the gesture meant. That first cultural lesson remained with me for a few days as I proceeded to flip everyone off in my neighborhood. An adult finally told me to stop, happily before I got a beating.

Once regular classes began in September 1975, I entered the sixth grade in Mrs. Dorothy King's class at Art Haycox Elementary School. Mrs. King was in her late fifties, and close to retirement. She spent extra time with my English lessons, often speaking more precisely and slower than she did with the other students. I remember her being protective of me, seating me toward the front of the class and scowling at students who mocked me. It didn't take long for the other students to call me a teacher's pet.

During recess one day I watched my peers play a variety of games. I decided to try my hand at one that I knew—marbles. In Vietnam boys shot marbles with two hands, one hand holding the marble on the tip of the other hand's middle finger, bent back like a slingshot. American kids flicked their marbles with their thumbs. I managed to win a few marbles while the other kids tried, without luck, to duplicate my style.

I learned that Bruce Lee was as popular an actor here as he was in South Vietnam. Boys often asked me if I knew kung fu or karate, then proceeded to motion with their hands to mimic the martial arts legend and yell something they thought resembled Chinese: "Waahh! Yaaa! Oueeiue!" I usually ad-libbed a few hand chops accentuated with a kick or two, then stopped, doing just enough to make the others wonder. It worked; no one challenged me to a fight until the end of the school year. However, one day after school, a popular kid named Javier, just slightly bigger, decided to find out. He followed me and a group of fifteen or twenty students tailed along. I knew my first "true" test in this new land was about to be given. Javier had started by pushing me in the back as I crossed the schoolyard on my way off campus. He mocked me and laughed. "You don't know any kung fu, man. Let me see you try some on me." The other students, several of whom I'd befriended, didn't cheer Javier. They just stood back and watched as Javier and I pushed each other around in a shouting match. I managed a broken reply, "I no chicken. You want fight. I fight." The shouting match went on for about five minutes as the spectators grew impatient. Most likely, they just wanted to see how the new kid from Vietnam would hold up.

His first punch landed on my shoulder, but I didn't even feel it because I was so pumped. Javier just stood as if he was waiting for me to cry. I leaned forward and struck him as hard as I could, on one of his shoulders as he had done to me. (In those days, a punch to the face was a serious move and this fight hadn't gone that far.) Javier then kicked me in the stomach. I fell backward, but quickly sprang to my feet and gave him the old one-two kick-and-punch combination that would have made Bruce Lee proud. The crowd grew in size and cheered for both Javier and me. The other kids weren't against me; they just wanted to see a good old-fashioned schoolyard brawl. Javier and I traded blows for a few more minutes, then we both simultaneously stopped to catch our breath. He looked at me probably to gauge if I had had enough. I realized he didn't want to lose face, either, so I held up my hands, palms open, signaling a truce. Javier and his group walked to the other side of the field as I gathered my books and went down the alley toward our apartment.

I had withstood my first challenge here, and a tie was all I needed.

In the spring of 1976, several kids in my neighborhood grabbed me to go try out for the Little League baseball at the Seabee base. I hardly knew what baseball was, but I decided to join them, without telling my mother. I hitched rides with my friends, since my mother hadn't yet received her California driver's license (she had learned how to drive in Vietnam when our family owned a Volkswagen Beetle for a year). Most of the kids already belonged to a team in the base's six-team league. They either were children or relatives of the coaches or they had participated the previous year.

I joined the "majors" with eleven- and twelve-year-olds. New kids had to attend a tryout where coaches would select several players to fill their rosters. At the tryout I borrowed another kid's glove and waited for my turn at bat. One of the coaches in the league threw batting practice as a small crowd, mostly parents and players already on teams, sat and watched prospective benchwarmers. My turn to bat finally came. I stood at the plate and held the bat with a reverse grip. I was right-handed so I held the bat the most natural way to me. As a result, I could hardly bring the bat around and badly missed the first few pitches. I could hear the hisses in the bleachers. They were probably wondering, "Where the hell did this boy come from?"

The kid playing catcher was nice. He told me to reverse my grip but that didn't help either. I could not time my swing and didn't even make contact despite ten or so pitches. The coach sent me to right field, which I later found out was the position for the worst players. Even there I failed to catch any fly balls, and, to make matters worse, managed to trip over myself chasing a fly ball, resulting in much laughter in the stands.

I didn't think I made any team, but when I got home one of the kids told me to call Chuck Morse, head coach of the Indians. Apparently he had "drafted" me. I knew I hadn't dazzled anyone during tryouts, but I just wanted to hang around my friends at the baseball field and to wear that Little League baseball uniform. I began to develop a desire to belong to something, to be identified as somebody, and to be accepted. In Vietnam athletics weren't nearly as high a priority as academics. There was no Little League, or soccer league, or Pee Wee Football. For me, though, team sports were my entrance into America. But I didn't like being laughed at by my peers or, worse, by their parents. Proving doubters wrong would be the thrust of my life for many years, starting at ballparks and on playgrounds.

Coach Morse was a swell guy. He must have been in his late thirties or early forties. He was overweight and never took off his dusty black windbreaker and filthy baseball hat, which had the initial "I" for Indians, his team. He had a son, Chuck Junior, who was a year older than me. Coach Morse drove a beat-up, dirty white van with no seats in the back. Several long bags full of bats and balls rested in the back, along with bases and cleats. He showed up at my door one day and briefly met my mother before taking me to practice. Obviously he won her trust in supervising me after school.

Even though Morse looked like what people today would call "white trash," I thought he was great. For two seasons he picked me up and drove me home on most game days. I rode my bike to the field for practices, which was about 3 miles from where we lived. He probably even paid my league fees, because I knew my mother didn't have the money. He treated me better than he treated Chuck Junior, whom he often scolded on the field and forced to run laps dragging a weighted bag belted around his waist. I can still hear his deep voice, yelling, "Jiminy Cricket, Pham! Bend your knees! Get down closer to the ball! Jesus H. Christ!" He didn't yell that much at me and when he did, it didn't matter. *What the hell was a Jiminy Cricket anyway?*

I managed a .000 batting average that season, but my worst experience took place during the last game, when Coach Morse stuck me in right field.

It was a bright Saturday afternoon, and the Indians had finished the season second to last. We had several good players who had made the all-stars, but by the end many of our best players had already left to hit the beaches for the summer.

I was playing right field when a rare pop fly headed my way. Judging its flight path, I ran underneath it, certain I was going to make this catch in front of a large crowd that was waiting for the championship game scheduled to play after ours.

Suddenly I felt my feet scrabbling under me as I looked up at the bright sky, attempting to locate a small, quickly falling, dark baseball. I raised my oversized mitt (which was too large for my hand) and it nearly blocked out the sky. I was about to make the catch when suddenly the ball disappeared. I then felt a heavy pain in my chest as I fell on my back. There was a hush in the crowd as Coach Morse ran toward me.

The sun was so bright that I had a difficult time seeing the faces of the adults now surrounding me. I could hardly breathe, but gathered enough strength to sit up after a few minutes. I sat there for a moment, not so much because of the pain, but because I was too embarrassed to get up and walk off the field.

Although that playing field back in 1976 wasn't exactly level, I was glad just to get onto one. The opposing pitchers weren't going to slow down their pitches for me, and the other teams' batters wouldn't hit the ball any slower or softer. I had to catch up.

(To hurt my fragile ego further, the public announcer never did say my name correctly. It was always "Kwang Fong or Kwung Fang.")

To improve, though, I also spent that summer playing baseball in the alley behind our apartment. The neighborhood kids and I decided to use a tennis ball in case we accidentally hit somebody's window. Since it traveled faster than a baseball, especially on hitting the pavement, my timing improved as well. I had the other kids pitch tennis balls to me, and we traded places in pitching and hitting. I was going to be prepared for the next season. I was tired of being laughed at.

I also watched the Los Angeles Dodgers on local Channel 11 whenever I could. Even though I didn't play first base, my favorite player was Steve Garvey, the sturdy first baseman with the good looks and a hot blonde wife: they seemed the Ken and Barbie of baseball. He became my first sports hero, and I wore his number 6. I was quickly buying into Mom, apple pie, and the all-American look even though in reality, I was a short, Asian benchwarmer living in a single-parent household eating rice for dinner.

Between sixth and seventh grade I got my first job, delivering a daily newspaper after school. The *Press-Courier* had been Oxnard's daily for many years, and my route took less than an hour each day because there weren't many subscribers in my Aleric neighborhood. My pay was $20 to $30 a month, depending on my ability to sign up new customers. I learned a little about selling as I knocked on doors and pitched the paper. It was also a chance for me to practice my English, speaking to adults by myself.

(President Jimmy Carter took office in January 1977. His first official act was to pardon all Vietnam-era draft dodgers, including those who fled the country (not including deserters or those who had gone absent without leave from their military units). For Americans, this act either marked the beginning of the healing or the continuation of division of that generation. With a signature, Carter "forgave" thousands of Americans. Years later several articles included the future President Bill Clinton in this group, although he was never charged with draft evasion.)

Baseball was on my mind again as my second baseball season rolled around in spring 1977. So was the laughter of those parents the previous spring. This time I was ready. Coach Morse put us through two weeks of practice as he tried me at nearly every position. By our first practice game against the Reds, the previous season's league champions, I had cracked the starting lineup, batting third and playing second base. A boy named Nathan, one of my closest friends on the team and a left-hander, batted clean-up and played first. And he had been one of my biggest supporters the previous season.

That game marked the beginning of the "new" Quang, Quang the athlete. In the first inning a runner stood on first with one out when I came to the plate. Only a handful of parents had come out to the practice game, but I recognized their faces. I didn't waste any time. The pitcher went into his windup. As he released the ball from some 40 feet, I saw its seam stitches more clearly than I ever had before. I belted the first pitch over the left fielder's head into some weeds. The sparse crowd clapped as I rounded first base, still in shock over my first-ever hit. The coaches (also acting as umpires) decided to hold me at second base, ruling my hit as a ground-rule double. The runner scored. I had earned my first run batted in as well. It didn't matter that it was a practice game. I had ended the dry spell, thrown the monkey off my back—pick a cliché! On my next at-bat I laid down a perfect bunt along the third-base foul line after receiving a signal from Coach Morse. (Like Buddha, his bunt signal usually included a rubbing of his ear and belly.) I also fielded several ground balls to second base without making an error.

Tied for first place, the Indians made the one-game championship playoff that year. I had started the entire season at second base. Late in the championship game, with the bases loaded, I hit a single up the middle and two runners came home. We held on to win the game and received individual championship trophies. I was elated, and to top things off Coach Morse, having coached the league champions, became the head coach for the CBC All-Stars. He selected me to play in the All-Star Series.

After the season I thanked Coach Morse for all he had done for me. He laughed and jokingly said, "Pham, just have your mother cook me a good Vietnamese dinner sometime." My mother never invited him over. I think she was a little scared of him, and he was married. I never saw him again after that. I wonder if he ever knew how much of a difference he made in a young boy's life.

CHAPTER 12

MY COMING-OUT PARTY

I T WAS THREE YEARS AFTER COMING TO THE UNITED STATES
before I finally felt comfortable speaking and writing English. Reading
comprehension would take a little longer. I had achieved a 3.8 grade-
point average by the end of my freshman year in high school, receiving As in
college preparatory classes, including Spanish. I guess my Vietnamese didn't
meet the college entrance requirement for a foreign language.

My mother worked several jobs during the day while completing her associate degree in accounting at night. I remember hardly seeing her during
those years except on the weekends. After she got her degree, she accepted a
new position working in the back room of a small bank. My older sister also
found a part-time job at the local shopping mall. I worked various part-time
jobs, from a clerk at a local state government office typing forms to a janitor
cleaning toilets and picking up trash at a local accounting company. With the
income we were now all bringing in, my family was able to move to a nicer
part of town on the north end of Oxnard.

Finally, gone were the days of having to use food stamps and receiving
welfare checks. Although grateful for these services, I was embarrassed every
time I went to the grocery store clutching food stamps. Even the federally
subsidized school-lunch program didn't feel comfortable. I would use the al-
lowance my mother gave me to pay for "discounted" lunches (20 cents),
which I hoped would make me appear to other children (paying the full 50
cents) as if I weren't poor. *For Christ's sake, I was the son of Lt. Col. Pham Van
Hoa.** I can't describe that feeling of low self-esteem and shame but I was

*I would learn that I wasn't the only Vietnamese refugee who was hung up on my pre-April 1975
status.

glad public assistance was there: without it our family would not have been able to make it here. My mother worked overtime so our family could jettison that stigma of poverty even though, in reality, we hovered right above the line.

My family made friends with only one other Vietnamese family (although there were several Vietnamese at my schools) during our first several years here. I played with one of the boys, who was a few years younger. We visited each other's house only once a month, and after a while we went our separate ways. Since the nearby navy bases brought Filipino sailors and veterans to the area, we went to school with many of their children, but only to toil in their shadow. The Filipino kids were called "Flips," while we garnered an acronym that pretty much marked us in the minds of the other kids.

"FOB" was short for "fresh off the boat." FOBs often didn't speak proper English (choppy, incomplete sentences lacking action verbs, and with no "s" in plurals); looked as if they were still traumatized (as if many Asians displayed much emotion anyway); and wore mismatched clothes from Goodwill stores or the Salvation Army. Most of all, FOB boys had the same haircut, the supposedly universal Asian "bowl cut." For my sisters, they dreaded the "à la garçon" bob. For me, becoming a Marine would not be the first time I had had a bad haircut.

There were other Asian-American students at my school: several Chinese and *sansei* kids, third-generation children of Japanese-American farmers and ranch owners (the Mexicans picking strawberries and other crops from the formers' fields). I made friends with some although I overheard some of the *sansei* boys refer to us Vietnamese as "those fucking FOBs" on many occasions. (It was bad enough having whites, blacks, and Mexicans make fun of us.)

During those days in Oxnard popular jeer aimed at Mexican students was "la migra," meaning "Immigration Service" or "Border Patrol." Heads would quickly turn when the taunts were screamed, then laughed about by ruthless pranksters of all colors. (At least I had a green card.) No doubt the Vietnamese refugees received special treatment and help from the government to immigrate and resettle, in contrast to some other immigrants. Maybe America felt badly about the events of April 1975 and was making things right for us few fortunate escapees.

By 1977 the plight of the Vietnamese "boat people" had caught the world's attention. Conditions in postwar Vietnam were horrendous: discrimination, human right violations, famine, and poverty had driven many to flee across the high seas in the years after the fall of Saigon. The refugees risked their lives in leaking, overcrowded fishing boats, and so U.S. Navy warships operating in the region were ordered to pick up refugees at sea.

Then, in late 1978, Vietnam invaded Cambodia and overthrew Pol Pot's regime (by then, about 2 million Cambodians had died in the "killing fields"). In early 1979 China and Vietnam fought a two-month border war. China had supported Pol Pot. So, facing discrimination and retaliation from the government, many ethnic-Chinese Vietnamese (the bulk of the entrepreneurs in the Cho Lon district in Saigon) fled by fishing boat. Thus over 60,000 of them ended up in refugee camps throughout Southeast Asia. Hostility grew as the boats continued to come to the shores of Asian neighbors, some boats being forced back to sea.

I wondered if the *Mayflower* pilgrims and the immigrants who came through Ellis Island were also called "FOBs."

Another jeer I often heard was, "Go back to Vietnam!" I wanted to yell my comeback, "I can't!" but I never did. Nobody would understand anyway. That's the difference between a refugee and an immigrant. *Hell, even the 15,000 or so who emigrated before the fall of Saigon could no longer go back.*

The United Nations estimated that more than a million people left Vietnam between 1976 and 1985, and as many as 300,000 died from drowning, hunger, sickness, thirst, and attacks.

In my spare time I continued my fascination with the military and aviation. With money from washing neighbors' cars and selling raffle tickets, I bought model airplane kits even though I wasn't very adept at putting the plastic parts together. *My* planes always ended up with extra glue, visible on their fuselages; their insignia were slightly crooked, and the propellers often didn't spin because parts were broken or somehow lost during assembly. Still, I could rattle off the types of airplanes that were flown in World War II by U.S., British, German, and Japanese pilots.

The only planes I knew my father had flown were the C-130 and C-123 transports. My mother kept a photo of my father's Air Commando training class, taken in the United States in 1966, along with pictures of him in Texas. I also had one headshot of him smiling and wearing a flight helmet with U.S. Air Force inscription. I knew transport pilots didn't wear helmets; I also knew bomber pilots didn't wear helmets because I had seen *Twelve O'Clock High*.

I rode my bike to the annual Point Mugu airshow featuring the Blue Angels, the U.S. Navy's flight demonstration team. I watched in awe their display of aviation precision, those beautiful blue jets soaring so close to each other. Other planes participated in the show, including vintage aircraft and modern fighters reenacting dogfights and strafing runs. Then, one time, a blue-gray aircraft appeared, a sleek, dual rudder, twin-engine fighter, with a short probe on its nose and "MARINES" painted on its fuselage. The plane looked like a space-age aircraft in contrast to the other jets at the show, even the A-4 Skyhawks flown by the Blue Angels. The crowd of mostly aviation enthusiasts was mesmerized, and so was I. The announcer finally said, "To your right coming in for landing is the McDonnell-Douglas YF-17, our latest fighter."*

I attended the same Point Mugu airshows regularly, even while I was in college. I remember walking up to pilots and asking them about their airplanes, the maximum speeds, and the weapons they carried. I remember my first meeting with a U.S. fighter pilot, the commanding officer of the navy's Top Gun squadron. He was speaking to a crowd of attendees, talking with his hands to demonstrate maneuvers and how he had shot down enemy aircraft. He then proceeded to pull out some books to sell, which were his memoirs! I later found out that he was the first ace in Vietnam and a future congressman.

I did, however, buy *Marine Air: First to Fight* from a former pilot named John Trotti. In the book were color photographs of Marine planes and helicopters and their pilots. I particularly liked the green camouflage color of the pilots' helmets. Marine pilots struck me as being different from air force or navy pilots. On the television series "Baa Baa Black Sheep," the pilots got into fistfights (like *Crazy* Hoa), won their dogfights with Japanese pilots, got drunk often, and always ended up with the navy nurses.

I would occasionally pull out my father's B-25 flight school yearbook from Class 1959-E at Reese Air Force Base in Texas. Along with his photos and records, the book was in one of the bags he gave us the night we left Saigon. My mother stored most of his documents in her bedroom closet but I kept the yearbook. It was the only item I could understand because it was like my high school yearbook. But I couldn't comprehend why my father had been training in the United States or why he was wearing the flight helmet. There were several pages of crumpled VNAF documents with short Vietnamese phrases and abbreviations typed on onion paper. I had no clue what they meant, nor was I interested in asking my mother.

*The YF-17 was the prototype of the F/A-18 Hornet, widely used in U.S. Navy and Marine Corps aviation since the 1980s.

My favorite part of his yearbook was the "A Student Pilot's Day" section, a chronology of black-and-white photographs with captions.

0500	Another day . . . [alarm clock]
0530	Breakfast, Hurry! [coffee, juice and toast]
0620	Flight Briefing [poring over flight plan]
0700	You Fly First!? [walking to airplane]
1200	On Final [cockpit view of runways]
1230	A Moment's Rest [lunch]
1300	Mail [opening mailbox]
1305	To Class [carrying brief case]
1400	Notes, Notes, Notes! [writing copiously]
1530	Ten Minute Break [smoking]
1625	P.T. [physical training]
1730	Dress for Supper [coming out of shower]
1815	Supper [food and smoking]
1900	Relax [pinball]
2000	Study [flight charts, maps]
2200	Dear Nancy [writing home]
2300	Lights out [alarm clock]

Back then, never once did I think I could do what my father did, achieving pilot's wings in a foreign country. Nor did I ever envision myself as a U.S. pilot even after I had attended the military airshows and seen the war movies and TV shows. FOBs couldn't possibly become fighter pilots, although I was really a FOP or "fresh off the plane." It also didn't occur to me until much later that all of the U.S. military pilots I saw were white—at the airshows, in the aviation books, and in films.

For Christmas in 1980, my Uncle An gave me Frank Snepp's *Decent Interval: An Insider's Account of Saigon's Indecent End Told by the CIA's Last Chief Strategy Analyst in Vietnam*. It was the first of many books on the Vietnam War that I would read. It took me years to finish the book; each time I would cringe at reading about the deceptions that took place before the fall of Saigon. Defying all censors, Snepp wrote the book just two years after the South Vietnamese capital fell. The CIA took him to court (all the way to the U.S. Supreme Court, where he lost) and he had to forfeit some $200,000 in royalties. Most of his marvelous writing was over my head at that time, but even then I began to sense there were more reasons why my family and thousands of Vietnamese had had to flee our native country. Our motherland hadn't just been "lost overnight."

After getting cut from the JV baseball team, basketball became my new athletic obsession. I bought a rim and bolted it onto a 3-by-3-foot piece of wood. I then hung it about 10 feet high in the alley behind our apartment complex. The apartment manager wasn't thrilled about that but she didn't say anything, since I allowed other kids to use it. The men in our neighborhood who worked night shifts also weren't too pleased with the sound of bouncing balls early on weekend mornings.

I shot hoops nearly every day. I practiced the fundamentals by watching varsity players do their warmups. I made sure I could do layups, pushing off on the correct foot as well as not traveling with the basketball. I shot free throws after school and played one-on-one with my new friend, Mark Adams. He was assured a starting position as the small forward. He often imitated Larry Bird of the Boston Celtics with his fade-away jump shot and pinpoint passing. I preferred the flashy guy with the big Afro—"Dr. J."

Oxnard High School was the ultimate melting pot. We had blacks, whites, surfers, "loadies" (or partiers), rich, poor, Mexicans, Japanese, Koreans, Chinese, and several Vietnamese. Our team exactly reflected the school's composition. Amazingly, all the players got along and we even hung out together outside of basketball. We didn't take shit from anyone, especially from the rich kids at nearby Thousand Oaks and Westlake high schools. We even had a small bunch of groupies who rooted for us at every game, at home and away (that is, when they weren't drunk or high on dope).

I was on the verge of getting cut from another sports team. My inability to bring the ball up court against a full-court press in practice proved to be my Achilles' heel. But my man-to-man defense and offensive skills otherwise held up. My make-or-break chance came during the fourth and final practice game against Santa Barbara High School. It would be an insignificant moment in the history of Oxnard High School athletics but unforgettable for me.

Late in the third quarter I was sitting near the end of the bench, second farthest from our coach, Rick. The varsity team and their head coach (Coach Smith) sat behind the scorer's table, just 20 feet away. Rick had already announced that he would post the final roster the next day. I had on my sweatshirt, and was ready to end my short-lived hoop dreams when he called me over. "Pham, you're going in for Dan as the two."

Boy was I glad I didn't have to run the point. I could hear my teammates trying to pump me up. A few minutes after I entered the game, a loose ball rolled past me and toward the scorer's table. Without hesitation, I headed for the floor, diving headfirst, but did not come close to even touching the ball which had ended up under the bleachers next to the scorer's table. My head banged into one of the table's legs; my vision temporarily went blank. My skin peeled off my knees. Everything seemed to slow including Coach Smith's voice. "Are you OK, Pham?" he asked while looking down at me. He extended his hand and I grabbed it, pulling myself off the floor, expecting laughter to cascade down from the stands. Instead, I heard Coach Smith and the varsity players enthusiastically say, "Way to hustle, man! Go get 'em!" Coach Rick ran over and gave me a pat on the back, smiling proudly.

On the next inbound, our team got a steal. I ran down the court and the point guard fed me the ball on the left wing. I came to a jump stop, put the ball in the air from about fifteen feet and—nothing but net. Our bench jumped up and down and I ran back on defense, fully charged. A few plays later, I got a steal and scored on a layup. Another jump shot followed. We lost by about twenty but on the bus back to Oxnard after the game, I felt I had turned the corner.

The next day I paced the hallways, anticipating the final roster which was to be posted after school. I could hardly wait, pestering Mark about my chances. He just laughed, reassuring me that the small bump on my head, a souvenir of the previous game, had earned me a spot on the team. Still, my heart pounded as I approached the locker room.

Twelve kids made the junior varsity team; my name was second to last.

By the fourth game of the season, with a 0–3 record, Coach Rick shuffled his lineup and announced a new starting point guard. Me. I never lost my starting job (despite many turnovers) and was often appointed as one of two team captains Rick selected before each game throughout the season. We finished 0–16, losing by ten to the league's champion, Westlake High, in the season's finale.

At the team banquet Rick made some remarks about our winless season. He said that the team had improved throughout the year and that was important. He decided not to give a most valuable player award (which would have gone to Mark). Instead, he held up a plaque and said something like, "Throughout the season, there was one player who rose up and took charge even though he hadn't become a starter. He was vocal at practice, in games, and during time-outs. He hustled and he played hard. He made me proud. I am pleased to present the 1981 team captain award to . . . Quang Pham."

In less than three years of high school, I had gone from a studious geek, speaking broken English, with a bowl haircut to a sort-of jock (OK, junior varsity still counted) and basketball team captain. I still had the bad Asian hairdo but there was something special in the air that day for this sixteen-year-old high school kid. I felt as if I belonged, that I had been accepted. For the first time since I arrived in this country, I could compete in the classroom and on the basketball court. As if my ego needed another boost, I found the girl that I had a crush on, a varsity cheerleader and a knockout, and asked her to an upcoming school dance. Used to rejections, I was not expecting it when she smiled and nodded, "I'd love to go with you." I hadn't even thought of the consequences since she had just broken up with her boyfriend, a good friend of mine and a varsity football lineman. I was lucky he didn't beat the pulp out of me.

"Bird Dog" became my new nickname for a short time. I didn't know what that meant until Mark whispered something to the effect that I "had moved in" on the lineman's ex so soon after his breakup. To me, she and I were just friends, but it was obvious I still needed much cultural training.

A couple of new Vietnamese students enrolled at Oxnard High School, but I never spent much time with them except for a quick hello once in a while. I had become a "somebody," but in reality I was really no different from the latest arrivals from Vietnam. Except that most had their fathers with them. At school I hardly ever ran into my older sister, Thi, who by then had become a senior with many boys vying for her attention. Some of them tried to befriend me, and I took advantage of their bribes to get close to her. I borrowed their Pontiac Firebirds, or asked them to buy me new rock-and-roll records in exchange for passing notes to Thi.

In the fall of 1981, just before my senior year, my mother bought our first home with help from my Uncle An and Aunt Ly. It was a small four-bedroom house on Doris Avenue two miles from the high school. The mortgage took most of her salary, so we basically lived on Thi's part-time wages and my monthly newspaper delivery check of some $400. My mother had incredibly achieved the American Dream of home ownership after just six years, and starting with nothing.

I still remember waking up with her every day at 4 a.m. to deliver the *Los Angeles Times*. Afterward, she would go to work at her bank and I would go to school, often nodding off by the early afternoon. My mother taught me how to drive with a stick shift, the way my father had taught her in a Volkswagen a decade earlier. The newspaper route had come from a friend who was two years older and already had his driver's license. He first had hired me as his "assistant." After two months, he decided it wasn't worth losing his beauty sleep over and was about to quit when I offered to take over the route.

We delivered newspapers to about 200 customers—she'd crisscross the streets in the wee hours, while I sat in the passenger seat throwing the rolled-up papers with my right hand. (The other "paperboys" were grown men in their forties and fifties, holding another job to make ends meet.) For those few months, I spent more time with my mother than I had since we left Vietnam, but I don't remember much of our conversations though since we were hardly awake those mornings.

My three years of delivering the *Los Angeles Times* brought our family extra money for the mortgage, and got me up early enough to attend morning basketball practices, leaving my afternoons free to play in games after classes. It was particularly difficult, however, to wake up on Saturday mornings after Friday night games and postgame parties. But my boss, Mr. Hendrickson, called my house every morning for three years, often two or three times, to get his young employee out of bed. He was my backup in case I was sick—which rarely happened. The route was for seven days a week, 365 days a year, and in three years I only missed a few days.

As an added benefit, my job enabled me to read the front and sports pages every day before school.

One day after school I came home and smashed all my model airplanes, and I threw them all away. I ripped posters of warplanes from my bedroom walls. I had come to feel that the model-building hobby was for geeks and nerds. I had become "somebody" now, a team captain and a varsity basketball player. I had only three things on my mind as I prepared for my final year of high school: babes, basketball, and my Volkswagen Bug.

As the only boy I had my own bedroom, while two of my sisters shared one and my youngest slept with my mother. That special treatment would not go unnoticed by my sisters, especially Thi. My mother had also imposed different standards on us—Thi had to come home by 10 p.m. while I could stay out until 11, which she greatly resented. We occasionally crossed paths at high school parties but she was the one who had to leave first. (She also got grounded when she came home with cigarette smoke on her breath.) Thi added another nickname to my long list, "Mama's Boy."

During our later high school years, my mother paid a lot more attention to Thi and me. Thi could not have boys visit her or call the house, with the exception of her attending the senior prom, while I violated my curfew twice before I was grounded, thus missing a huge party after our football team upset our cross-town rival.

On one occasion, I came home with alcohol on my breath after driving back from a party. I could taste it so I figured my mother would be able to easily smell it. That was *the* rule I could not break. I was hoping my mother had gone to sleep so I could sneak in through the garage as I had done before.

My mother stood like a madwoman in the living room when I staggered through the front door. She had been wide awake, her hair all mussed, her eyes already red from crying. Without saying a word she slapped me so hard that I saw stars. I could barely see my sisters in the background and their blurry faces. Nobody had ever struck me that hard, even after all those street fights with the other boys. She hit me again. Tears welled up in my eyes as I became angry. My chest tightened in angry response and my fists were clenched.

My mother must have seen the look on my face and my tensed body. She backed off. I could see my sisters looking down from the stairwell, their faces smiling at "Mama's Boy" crying again. My mother began to weep, covering her face, "If your father was here, you would not get away with this. God, in Vietnam, I would not have to put up with you undisciplined children. You uneducated and disrespectful imbeciles. Please send me back to Vietnam, God." That's when my sisters began to cry as well.

We children had heard her cries many times, but a reference to my father would bring a stop to every argument, his presence felt from some jungle camp 12,000 miles away. We all quietly retreated to our bedrooms.

My mother never struck me again after that, and I never drove home drunk again (at least while I lived with her).

I don't know how my mother ever did it, coming to the United States by herself and raising four kids. But it also never occurred to me that we were a single-parent household. Unlike the other kids with single parents in my neighborhood and in school, my father hadn't left us, we'd left him. As the years went by, though, my hopes of seeing my father again began to vanish, leaving room for me to go on with my life. My Vietnamese cultural knowledge and language were slowly slipping away.

CHAPTER 13

ABANDONED ALLY

Vietnam 1975–1982

JUST AFTER THE FALL OF SAIGON MY FATHER REMAINED IN hiding. Uncertain of the new government's intent, he kept mostly inside my grandmother's house in the Ban Co area of Saigon.

Saigon was then littered with U.S.-made military equipment and uniforms of ARVN soldiers who had escaped Vietnam or disappeared into hiding. Shredded papers were strewn across the streets, remnants of documents from the U.S. Embassy and other government buildings. Whole blocks of the city resembled ghost towns. In congested areas downtown, "liberators" from the north continued to pour in via every entry point into the city. The reek of diesel exhaust from tanks and trucks fouled the humid air.

My father stripped himself of everything linking him to the VNAF, the Saigon government, or the United States. He destroyed his ID card and ripped his names off his uniforms. He had given my mother most of his official documents the night we left Saigon, but he didn't know that my Aunt Nhang also kept some photos of my family in a secret box in my grandmother's house. Looting was in full swing as crowds gathered to cheer arriving NVA soldiers, hoping for possible amnesty down the road.

Old Glory and the South Vietnamese yellow flag with its three red stripes disappeared on May 1, 1975. Red flags with single gold stars now flew in front of the former Presidential Palace (renamed Reunification Palace) and on the antennas of tanks and armored vehicles clanking through the streets. The Communists promptly renamed Saigon Ho Chi Minh City (although to this day many residents and expatriates still refer to the old "pearl of the Orient" by its maiden name). The next day, communist cadres, broadcasting over loudspeakers and local radio stations, announced roundup points for former South Vietnamese government and military officials. Posters of the faces of South Vietnam's senior officers were posted at the Ben Thanh Market. The same procedures were carried out throughout the country, in every province. The *Who's Who* in South Vietnam would become "Hanoi's Most-Wanted."

Joining my father in the reeducation camps were thousands of VNAF veterans, about 90 percent of whom had stayed in Vietnam. They included Lt. Col. Nguyen Cau (call sign "Dupont"), a former C-47 navigator and commander of the "Monkey Mountain" radar center east of Danang. Cau spent the most camp time with my father, nearly a decade, and in six different facilities in northern and southern Vietnam. Other fellow inmates were "Piggy," who had been one of my father's wingmen in the 2d FS back in 1962, and Maj. Ho Dang Tri, "Tri Toc," a navigator and former aide-de-camp to Gen. Nguyen Cao Ky. Three decades later they all provided me with firsthand recollections of their years in captivity. My three uncles gave me their perspectives on the reeducation camps in the south.

In all, about a million South Vietnamese were sent to hundreds of reeducation camps throughout Vietnam. The detainees included thousands of journalists, judges, politicians, propagandists, teachers, and religious leaders. Although most of the civilians underwent three-day lectures, about 100,000 were sent to long-term reeducation.

Many ARVN soldiers (airborne troops, rangers, and Vietnamese Marines), especially those stationed in Military Regions I and II closer to the DMZ, never had a chance to escape. The three uncles had been captains in the artillery, infantry, and signal corps, respectively, and they, too, were sent to the reeducation camps. Somehow they would never cross paths even though prisoners were kept in groups according to rank.

Infiltrators, those who worked clandestinely for North Vietnam during the war, revealed their true identities and began shouting that "the new Vietnam would be good for everyone." For the first time since anyone could remember, the open market was empty—anticipation of a bloodbath kept everyone in their homes. Communist troops looted Tan Son Nhut, carrying out air conditioners, bicycles, refrigerators, and typewriters. Rumors of revenge on the "puppet" regime and "infidels" floated from door to door. Communist officials continued broadcasting over old Saigon radio stations and loudspeakers: "It's time to forgive and forget. The war is over. Turn yourselves in for reeducation. There's only one Vietnam."

Soon after victory, communist cadres called for ex-VNAF pilots to return to Tan Son Nhut and another location in the city. My father reported along with about 500 other men; they were uncertain how the new government was going to treat them. North Vietnam certainly did not abide by Geneva conventions, as evinced by their treatment of U.S. POWs, and if the victors were seeking revenge, the only enemies the Communists could get their hands on now were South Vietnamese.

The South Vietnamese were told that their pending incarceration would last between three and thirty days, depending on rank. Enlisted members attended a three-day reeducation course, the shortest, and were then released with official certificates of approbation. Lieutenants and captains were to report for ten days; majors and above prepared for thirty days.

After reporting to Tan Son Nhut, the prospective internees turned in all identification and arms that they still possessed. In longhand writing they answered a detailed questionnaire about their lives since 1945. There was no way they could lie on the questionnaires: a former captain in the VNAF administrative headquarters had been a Communist agent, and he knew everything about everybody. Cau estimated about 1 percent of the VNAF was VC. After completing the forms most were sent home to wait for further instructions.

My father was ordered to assist the cadres for two weeks. As one of the first flight instructors in the C-130, he and other crewmen translated its flight manual from English to Vietnamese. The cadres forced him to teach communist pilots how to operate this newest and biggest transport plane in the VNAF inventory.

According to USAF sources only ten C-130s could be flown out to Thailand and Singapore, so fourteen of them were left behind, and it was later revealed that the Communists operated about three of them, until spare parts ran out.

An armed cadre sat in the cockpit between my father and his new communist copilot. There was only enough fuel in the aircraft to fly brief training missions and not enough to flee to Singapore or the Philippines. My family and I did not know why my father didn't try to attempt to escape or to overwhelm the cadre member. Years later I was told that he'd had one chance. On one of the flights a junior cadre agreed to defect to Thailand with the crew; however, one of my father's crew members aboard didn't want to flee, since his family would have been left behind in Vietnam. My father turned the plane around and landed at Tan Son Nhut.

Yet successful escapes such as these did occur on at least two occasions. One C-47 pilot was able to convince his Communist copilot to flee to Ubon, Thailand. They flew at extremely low altitude and barely made it before their fuel tanks went dry. A helicopter crew also successfully defected.

It didn't take long before the cadres got fed up with flying lessons, so my father was transferred to other duties. Along with other detainees, gripping small brooms, he swept the parking lots and runways at Tan Son Nhut, where he had made thousands of takeoffs and landings. The summer heat was unrelenting on the asphalt runway and PSP ramps, a portent of harsher labor in the years ahead. Still, his famous humor did not go unnoticed.

He reported one day for sweeping duty wearing an extra dose of Aqua Velva aftershave lotion from his last bottle. He didn't want to "waste" the remaining drops. The cadres apparently weren't fond of his scent, so they gave him some extra hours of sweeping as punishment for being a wiseguy. An "enlightened" fellow VNAF officer told my father, "You're not used to manual labor, are you? To them [the Communists], that means glory." My father retorted, "If we did hard labor, we wouldn't have energy left to fly airplanes!" This was not a response designed to win Communist hearts and minds. And it didn't.

The cadres then ordered all the prisoners to stop speaking foreign languages, especially English. *Be proud of our mother language!* To that my father angrily countered, "American airplanes, American fuel, American training. If we spoke Vietnamese, we may make a mistake in communication that would make flying very unsafe. Even the Russians speak English when they're flying. It's the international aviation language."

There was no resistance to the massive incarceration. Like the others, perhaps still in shock over the rapid fall of Saigon, my father's mind was full of defeatist thoughts. Since he was a southerner, he hadn't been exposed to the nefarious communist ways, but his colleagues born in the north were leery because they had been made to witness executions, rapacious land reform, and other instruments of communist rule.

After they locked their heels in front of the victors on June 15, 1975, the South Vietnamese were required to fill out dozens of long forms listing all of their previous military assignments. They also had to write denunciations of their earlier allegiances. Cadres with nothing else to do compared the forms with previous versions (and with the knowledge of turncoats). Those who lied would be punished by beatings.

A few days after officially reporting to what amounted to a military police station, my father's prisoner group was trucked to Camp Suoi Mau (Spring of Blood) near Bien Hoa, his former duty station fifteen miles northwest of Saigon. His "thirty-day" sentence was quickly absorbed into his first year, consisting of hours of classroom propaganda on the "new way of thinking" and endless denouncement of the "puppet regime" and the "American imperialist dogs." Communist ideology and labor were praised throughout daily eight-hour study sessions. "How many kids did you kill, Mr. Hoa?" cadres would dully intone. "How many villages did you torch with napalm? How many bombs did you drop?"

While at Camp Suoi Mau my father wrote a letter to my grandmother dated March 27, 1976:

HT 1248/K-5-A8
Dear Mother,

I received permission to write you, sister Nhang [my mother's sister] and family. I am continuing my studies and it is going well. I will overcome all difficulties to be "reeducated" in order to become a citizen in our new society. The camp manager has allowed us to write and ask our families to send necessary items. I don't really know what to request except medicine and dry food. The clothes you sent were adequate, as it is getting hot again. I hope my brothers and their families continue to live near you for support. I will try my best to graduate from reeducation soon so I can return to society a better man. Please say hello to everyone.

Your Son, Hoa.

In his letters, my father was necessarily vague. He never mentioned his immediate family living in the United States. If his captors had learned that his wife, son, and daughters had escaped to this country, they may have held him longer. Once his responsibility, our freedom became his liability.

In the summer of 1976 a few senior prisoners were flown to the north on C-130s, while thousands more were sent crammed onto teeming cargo ships. My father boarded the *Song Huong,* packed in with about 1,000 other prisoners. The ship, named after the Perfume River at Hue City, in central Vietnam, and once used to transport pigs, would make numerous trips ferrying prisoners along the coastline of Vietnam. It took four days to steam from the port of Saigon to a small port in Nghe Tinh Province just north of the DMZ.

Conditions on the ships were horrendous. Men slept in the cargo hold and often got sick. With detainees living literally atop one another, many fell ill from having to lay in feces and vomit. To compound the prisoners' utter humiliation, the cadres forced them to wear the old Vietnamese Ranger "tiger-striped" camouflage uniforms.

After disembarking and stumbling ashore shortly after midnight, they were kept in an old warehouse built of corrugated tin and wood. Guards with dogs patrolled throughout the night to prevent escape. In the early morning the hungry, exhausted men were walked through a gauntlet of angry locals. Six- and seven-year-old children, schoolteachers, old men, and women spat on the prisoners, pelted them with rocks and cursed, "You bloodthirsty imperialist dogs! Do you know how many of our people you have killed? You are nothing but puppets of the Americans!" Cau and many prisoners believed the angry protests had been staged, so they just laughed and marched to their destination. How would these children know who they were?

The prisoners were then placed on a train headed toward the provinces of Son La (in the northwest corner of Vietnam near Dien Bien Phu and the Laotian border), Hoang Lien Son (near the top of Vietnam and the China border), and Lang Son (in the northeastern corner). They were locked inside cattle cars for two days. Years later Cau had a difficult time speaking about this: "It was like the Holocaust. First, we thought they were taking us to our graves. But soon we realized we would not be killed right away. They needed to profit from our labor." The cadres repeatedly announced through megaphones: "We're lenient. We're going to give you a chance to be reeducated first."

When they arrived at the provincial train depots, the prisoners were divided into subgroups and squeezed into the backs of trucks. The guards secured the canvas tarps to prevent attempted escapes. The trucks got them closer to their destination, but the last 15 miles was done in a forced march to their respective camps deep in the mountainous jungles. Hundreds of camps and subcamps ran along the base of the Hoang Lien Son Mountains where Mount Fansipan, the tallest peak in Southeast Asia, rose to over 10,000 feet. The French had called Fansipan and surrounding mountains the Tonkinese Alps. This mountain range also marked the border with China. Escape by foot was impossible, according to Cau. Unlike the south, which had only a "wet and a dry season," the north had all four distinct seasons: during summer, the humidity neared 100 percent; in winter, snow fell.

My father and Cau were herded to Son La, a sizable, ethnically mixed village 200 miles northwest of Hanoi and, incidentally, the site of a concrete French jail built in 1908. Opponents of the French colonial regime and, later, counterrevolutionaries were incarcerated under harsh conditions, including Le Duan, a founder and head of the Vietnamese Communist Party after Ho Chi Minh died in 1969. Numerous camps were established 2 to 3 miles apart, with each housing some 300 to 400 prisoners. Colonels and high-ranking civilians were held there; my father went to Camp 3, Cau to Camp 1, two of the most remote camps.

The lies of the Communists became apparent as my father's sentence went from thirty days to three years. The three-year sentences were the standard to "reeducate" former high-level officials, combining indoctrination and hard labor. Policy being to establish a self-sufficient army throughout Vietnam, the People's Army of Vietnam (PAVN) formed Group 776 to run the northern camps. The PAVN was determined to "grow" its own food at the expense of its prison camp detainees; death by hard labor and starvation didn't matter.[*]

Dropped in the middle of forests, the prisoners had to build their own camps, some from the latrines up. At night, guards barricaded the prisoners with fences built from bamboo trees and wood. No movement at night was allowed, so prisoners had to relieve themselves where they slept. Hard labor, malnutrition, and sickness inevitably led to many early deaths. Those who tried to escape and got caught were beaten to death with rifle butts and clubs; others were shot at night. No reasons were ever given.

The prisoners grew their own food, which was also provided to their guards. Daily rations included an occasional bowl of rice, salt, and six inches of starchy manioc root, which Cau said tasted like cardboard. Surplus rice was sold in the nearest markets by the guards to line their own pockets. The prisoners also caught whatever they could to eat, from rats to snakes, from scorpions to snails. Many died from amoebic dysentery from eating raw food.

In 1997, *Golf Digest*'s Tom Callahan reported that Lt. Col. Vuong "Tiger" Phong, a former ARVN province chief, died in September 1976 (from starvation and/or stroke) only a few months after arriving in the Lang Son labor camp. Ten months earlier, back in the United States, retired Special Forces Lt. Col. Earl Woods had nicknamed his newborn son Eldrick after "Tiger"

---

[*]Based on an interview with Robert DeStatte, formerly a senior analyst in the Defense Intelligence Agency's Special office for POW/MIA.

Phong (Woods had given Vuong this nickname because of his bravery in battle). Lieutenant Colonel Phong, possibly the most famous of all reeducation camp detainees, died never knowing that his nickname would be given to a world's top golfer.

In a 2003 interview with Michael Arkush for the VVA Veteran (Vietnam Veterans of America), Earl Woods remembered his former ally: "He was a courageous fighter and leader who was really nondescript," Woods said. "All he wanted to be was a schoolteacher. Neither one of us were these robotic, rigid professional soldiers. We had a job to do and we were doing it." When Saigon fell in 1975, Woods "vowed that if I had a child, I was going to nickname him Tiger in the hope that he would be on television and 'the other Tiger' would make the connection that he was my kid and would get in touch with me. I don't know how I knew but I just knew that my kid would be somebody great. I just knew that all the time."

After eighteen months of chopping wood and hauling burlap bags of rice back to his camp, my father began to wonder how long he could go on. He and other prisoners had dwindled to skin and bones, but their declining condition was of no concern to the cadres. "You've lived off the people. Now it's your turn to live off the land and do something with your hands. You are the lowest form of life in our country."

My father experienced his worst days in the camps sometime in 1977. His body was bloated, his face and hands were swollen. He struggled to take just three steps. He had been stricken with beriberi, a disease of eighteenth-century sailors caused by a lack of Vitamin B1. Left untreated, beriberi could be fatal. For reasons he could never figure out, the cadres then fed him a bowl of rice with sugar and let him rest. Recovery was slow at first but his natural vitality kicked in. Two days later, he was ordered back to work in the jungle.

(While my father was literally fighting for his life in a prison camp, I was a twelve-year-old refugee just beginning to stand up to the teasing and bullying I got in large doses. Vietnamese mystics might interpret my newfound boldness to the courage and energy transmitted from my abused, faraway father. Once this spiritual transfer was completed—and I had decided to stop taking shit from American kids—my father's mission had been accomplished. So his energy and his health returned.)

As a grown man and a U.S. Marine I know this could never have happened, but whatever it was, as a yellow boy in a strange land of blacks, browns, and whites, I appreciated whatever caused me to stop running away and backing down.

Prisoners were allowed to receive up to two packages a year weighing a maximum of 1 kilogram (2.2 pounds) each. Families sent vitamins, sugar, and medicine for flu, diarrhea, and infections, although there was always a question of whether the packages would reach the prisoners, who were moved to different camps every few months. My Aunt Nhang recalled those years:

> Whenever we got an address for him, it would change within months. He kept moving and there was no way we knew. The cadres allowed us to ship him one kilogram. I packed hand towels, cold and stomach medicines, soap and toothpaste. We had to go to a certain location and wait all day to ship the boxes. We sat on the ground. I didn't know when he would get the boxes so I never sent food. I don't know if he got every package. He was in many camps.

This shuffling of prisoners was done to keep them from becoming familiar with possible escape routes and to prevent them from getting to know one another well. False rumors, constant movement, and starvation were the control measures employed by the cadres who were afraid of prisoner revolts or escape attempts.

Ho Dang Tri recalled an episode when he ran into my father as prisoners were shuffled from camp to camp:

> On a cold day, we were gathering near a fire pit. The cadres were watching closely; they didn't want the prisoners from different camps to communicate with each other. I looked away and said to your father, "Hoa, why are you so skinny?" Your father replied, "I wouldn't talk. You think you're fat or something?" We laughed at our misery. Cadres then ran over and asked us about the exchange. We denied it, of course.

When China invaded Vietnam in early 1979, my father and his fellow inmates were nearly "liberated" by the invading troops. As the Chinese attacked along the China-Vietnam border, very near the labor camps, the internees were moved farther south to Hanoi to Camp Nam Ha, known to former U.S. POWs as Ba Sao. Nam Ha had three subcamps. Nam Ha A was the most humane, and Nam Ha C was for detainees soon to be released. My father and Cau were sent to Nam Ha B, the worst subcamp.

Even so, conditions in the camps closer to Hanoi were better. Death rates were lower, although sickness was still rampant. For the first time, visitors were allowed and on the occasion of Tet, Liberation Day, and Ho Chi Minh's birthday, the prisoners received a small portion of water buffalo meat. Buffalo skin was distributed the rest of the year, which needed to be boiled for ten hours before it could be eaten.

Many of the prisoners died between 1977 and 1979, mostly from executions, starvation, and untreated sickness. "They [the guards] kept the discipline of the camp by playing on our stomach," Cau sighed.

In 1980 one of my uncles (a former captain) was released early from the camps. His wife had died, so he had to come home to take care of his children. Then Amnesty International inspectors visited two camps outside of Hanoi-Ta Son and Nam Ha, and conditions improved after their departure. The outside world was finally able to see that Vietnam's victors had memorialized their win with fundamental human rights abuses. During the five years after the fall of Saigon, Vietnamese expatriates had little information on the plight of their loved ones. Information came from rescued "boat people," who would tell human rights advocates and journalists about those still in captivity. This in turn piqued the interest of specialists from the Defense Intelligence Agency (DIA), who flew to Southeast Asian refugee camps to further investigate possible U.S. POW "live sightings" reported by refugees.

Also in 1980, courtesy of my Great Uncle Minh's driver and his truck, my Aunt Nhang and one of my cousins visited my father for the first time since his captivity at a camp in Vinh Phuc Province. (Great Uncle Minh had served in the Communist Party during the war and had risen to become a minister in the Ministry of Propaganda.)

Despite his connection with a high-ranking communist official, my father remained in Nam Ha until 1982, on his third three-year term. With few exceptions, he and his fellow prisoners remained in custody without formally being charged, without trial, and without protection from criminal abuses by the guards. In 1982, my two other uncles were released from their camps in the south.

CHAPTER 14

QUANTICO-BOUND

Some people spend a lifetime wondering if they made a difference.
The Marines don't have that problem.

—President Ronald Reagan

IN THE FALL OF 1983 I PACKED MY BUG AND DROVE AN HOUR south of Oxnard to Westwood, home of the University of California, Los Angeles (UCLA) Bruins. I had spent the previous year at Ventura College (a community college) even though I had the grades as I simply forgot to apply to UCLA in time. No one had informed me that four-year college applications were due in November. I never once met with my high school counselor one-on-one; he was only pitching me vocational schools anyway.

On my last day of work delivering newspapers, I arrived early to thank the men who had folded my newspapers for three years. They couldn't believe I was actually headed for UCLA; college was beyond them. My boss, Mr. Hendrickson, thanked me and wished me luck. The next day my mother stood in the driveway and cried as I drove off to start my new life, leaving her with my two younger sisters in Oxnard (Thi had left home the year before for college).

There were many Asian Americans and foreign students from Asia at UCLA, nicknamed the "University of Caucasians Lost among Asians." Others called it "JewCLA." The funniest nickname, though, that I heard for UCLA originated with a decorated Vietnam veteran years after I had graduated. He referred to it as the "University of Corrupted Liberal Assholes."

Hollywood had powerful influence on me in those years, and I found that a major benefit of attending UCLA was its proximity to Hollywood studios. World-class movie producers like Francis Ford Coppola and George Lucas had graduated from UCLA and nearby USC (University of Southern California) film schools. World premieres took place in Westwood theaters, just a few blocks from campus. Screening tickets were plentiful and so was on-campus filming.

Vietnam War movies began to emerge in the late 1970s and early 1980s, mostly angry and bitter portrayals of veterans and the controversial war: for instance, *The Deer Hunter, Coming Home,* and *Apocalypse Now.* I can't say I enjoyed them. (Where were the real South Vietnamese?)

No other movie from that period touched me more than *The Killing Fields,* based on the true story of journalist Sydney Schanberg and his Cambodian guide, Dith Pran, during Cambodia's takeover by the Khmer Rouge. I squirmed in my seat, as I envisioned my father working in the fields like the suffering Cambodians in the movie.

A few weeks after the 1984 election, I drove to the Los Angeles Convention Center to attend a ceremony to become a U.S. citizen. After nine years of repeatedly checking the "no" box in numerous questionnaires asking whether I was a U.S. citizen, I finally could check "yes" and skip writing my "alien number." I hadn't done anything special to warrant citizenship, but in the United States, I only needed to stay out of trouble with the law and wait. (Of course I had to pass an oral test about U.S. history and government selected from 100 questions, and had to demonstrate some fluency in speaking and writing English.) Without preparation, many native-born inhabitants would fail the oral part of the exam. For my father and thousands of elderly immigrants, the oral test was later a gigantic obstacle, with many taking a crash course before the exam.

There must have been 10,000 people of all colors and creeds standing on the convention floor. A judge came out and within minutes, all of us had become citizens of the United States after taking our oath of allegiance.

I hereby declare, on oath, that I absolutely and entirely renounce and abjure all allegiance and fidelity to any foreign prince, potentate, state, or sovereignty of whom or which I have heretofore been a subject or citizen; that I will support and defend the Constitution and laws of the United States of America against all enemies, foreign and domestic; that I will bear true faith and allegiance to the same; that I will bear arms on behalf of the United States when required by the law; that I will perform noncombatant service in the Armed Forces of the United States when required by the law; that I will perform work of national importance under civilian direction when required by the law; and that I take this obligation freely without any mental reservation or purpose of evasion; so help me God.

I wondered whether native-born Americans had to take a similar oath, or that their allegiance was naturally assumed. I didn't dare to raise the question; I was just happy about no longer having to check the "no" box.

I drove back to campus feeling indifferent about my new citizenship. There was no celebration. I didn't change my name, like some immigrants who adopted American-sounding first names. I still looked the same, and didn't get a patriotic tattoo on my arm or put a flag decal on my rear car window.

A few weeks later my mother called and asked me to come home. When I got there she pulled out a watercolor portrait of my father with the inscription, "To my friend Hoa, Camp Nam Ha, 1984." The portrait had been given to my aunt in Vietnam and she immediately mailed it to my mother. In the portrait I could see my aging, stoic father in a white T-shirt, then into his third term of reeducation. He no longer looked like a fighting man, at least superficially. The delicate sketch was the surest proof that he was still alive.

Sometime in 1985 I came across an ad in the campus newspaper that read "many Asian extras needed for upcoming major motion picture. No experience required. Three days with good pay and meals. Call for more information." How could I pass up this chance for fame and fortune? How could any student who attended UCLA? This could be my "breakthrough."

I rang the Los Angeles number. After several minutes a woman came on the line. I eagerly spouted my name and my availability and asked her if she could tell me a little about the movie. "I can't tell you the name of the project or the director. But I can tell you that it's going to be a major 'Vietnam' movie. We need extras to play the enemy. You know, the Viet Cong." I quickly slammed down the phone, my Hollywood dreams instantly vanished.

By the first quarter of my second year I had surged above a 2.0 GPA. Besides economics classes, most of my electives were political science courses, as well as two art classes and nuclear arms control seminars. In the mid-1980s, UCLA hosted its share of social issues demonstrations, ranging from protestors railing against the apartheid in Africa to prophets declaring themselves as Jews for Jesus. You could not get through the main campus thoroughfare, Bruin Walk, without hearing about somebody's misery or society's injustice. I blocked out most of the propaganda, taking the offered fliers just to be nice, but only to toss them as soon as I got to my next class. No one raised hell about the human rights abuses in Vietnam then. None of the issues struck a chord with me until one day in April 1985, on the eve of the tenth anniversary of the loss of my former country.

I was scurrying across campus, late for class, when a harried student pressed a leaflet into my hand. It read, "Come Help Us Celebrate the 10th Anniversary of the Reunification of Vietnam." The crumpled flier had a picture of the tank crashing through the Presidential Palace gates in Saigon and the unforgettable helicopter on top of a Saigon building awaiting a chain of humans climbing a dangling ladder. I had become very familiar with both images.

I tore up the document, wadded it into a tight ball, and threw it in the surprised student's face. He was a white kid with unkempt long hair and had on clean but wrinkled clothes. He looked like a sanitized Vietnam War protestor from the 1960s.

"What the hell is wrong with you, man? Go to hell!" I thought about knocking a few of his teeth loose but I just walked away. How could he have possibly known anything about Vietnam?

Later that night, I stayed up and watched Ted Koppel's "Nightline" broadcast from Saigon (now Ho Chi Minh City). Henry Kissinger and Le Duc Tho exchanged their thoughts via a satellite connection. Neither had seen each other since signing that sham agreement. Kissinger seemed bewildered while Tho would not stop talking long enough to give his interpreter a chance to speak. I still understood enough Vietnamese to begin to realize how this Communist had "operated" in Paris. Then the satellite feed broke off and Koppel disappeared, leaving Charlie Gibson to continue the interview.

Later Koppel characterized the episode as having been the "worst 'Nightline' ever." I disagreed. It was fun to watch Kissinger squirm. I couldn't help but wonder if Tho was as dominant a figure back in 1973. There was no peace and no honor, and no Nobel Prize should have been awarded.

Watching the aging diplomats trade barbs that night, I thought about my father and wondered what he was doing in the reeducation camps. I had no idea where he was, and I missed him dearly. I must admit, though, that in the midst of my kaleidoscopic collegiate life, I had forgotten about him. But thanks to the never-ending American nostalgia for Vietnam, I had kindly been reminded. And I have not forgotten since.

A few months before the Bruin Walk flier incident, I was eyeing a summer internship at a Fortune 500 company during a campus job fair when I saw a Marine Corps officer recruiter. With the haircut, neatly pressed short-sleeved tan shirt, and blue trousers with red stripes, he stood out among the blue suits.

The job market was tight for everyone then except engineers. Under Reagan, defense spending had jumped dramatically and aerospace companies were interviewing every engineering graduate they could get their hands on. I didn't have the grades for the engineering program so I made economics my major. I knew nothing about John Maynard Keynes and Milton Friedman except that my debts kept growing every month. "Econ" became the major of choice for many nontechnical UCLA students like me.

The recruiter was poster-perfect. Tall, tanned, handsome, standing erect at his booth in the same aisle as IBM, Procter & Gamble, and Boeing, he was doing better business attracting sorority girls to his table than prospective officer candidates like me. I noticed that. The recruiter was talking to several other students, so I timidly sneaked behind one of them and grabbed a pamphlet. He saw me but continued with his conversation. As I walked away while skimming through the literature, a crisp and loud voice sounded off, "Hey young man, come here. What are you going to do when you graduate? What are your plans for the future?"

I turned around as he put out his hand. "What's your name? I'm Doug Hamlin, captain of Marines." "I . . . I . . . I just wanted to have the airplane pictures."

(I was stupefied. This was what I had aspired to do all my life. And I just didn't have the nerve to say it. Quang Pham from Oxnard/Saigon a Marine pilot? No way.)

"That could be you in that F-18 cockpit in three years," said Captain Hamlin in his sales pitch. He sensed my curiosity and he was good at this. "If you qualify for the PLC Program and make it through OCS," he finished.

I stood there for fifteen minutes telling him my background, and he shared his with me. Doug Hamlin had been his fraternity's president at the University of Michigan. He had joined the Corps in 1980 and was assigned to the local recruiting office in 1983. He had served with the 1st Marine Division (2d Battalion, 9th Marine Regiment) at Camp Pendleton as an infantry officer and was a quarterback on the battalion football team.

He went over the Corps requirements, and I felt intimidated. "To pass the Marine Corps Physical Fitness Test, you have to run three miles in under eighteen minutes, do at least twenty pull-ups and eighty sit-ups in under two minutes. You need to graduate with a 2.0 GPA and have at least a 1,000 on your SAT. Any major is fine. (Well, three miles in under twenty-four minutes, ten pull-ups, and sixty sit-ups before OCS. Plus you need to pass the Aviation Qualifications Test and a flight physical. You have 20/20 vision, correct?)

"Remember, Quang, you can go into business anytime. This is your one chance to do something for your country as a Marine officer." I had bought his sales pitch, but it would be another year before I would attend the longest summer camp of my life.

I spent the summer of 1985 working as an intern in San Diego for the General Dynamics Corporation. John Gadd's stepfather, Mel Barlow, was general manager of the electronics division, so John and I preferentially got our jobs. (John was my best friend in high school.)

I could not stop thinking about the Marine Corps and Captain Hamlin's words. The General Dynamics complex was in Kearney Mesa, a few miles from the Miramar Naval Air Station, and during two weeks in July, F-14 Tomcats would be launched in the morning, followed by a smaller plane in close pursuit. Bored with my summer assignment after only a month, I was mesmerized by the planes, so I asked questions around the office. Nobody knew what they were doing. A year later, I would find out the planes had been part of the filming for the movie *Top Gun*.

My junior year sped by in a blur. By December 1985, after meeting all the academic requirements, I made up my mind to attend OCS, with no obligation (as reemphasized by Captain Hamlin). I had been thinking about my citizenship and how joyless I had felt after the swearing-in ceremony. I remembered the quiet, studious Asian Americans in the physics laboratories, and although I respected their goals I wanted more than a secure job. I wanted to contribute, to belong, and not disappear into the working world as another faceless minority member—a perpetual foreigner with mediocre grades. I wanted to do something to make my parents proud, beyond making money, to know that their sacrifice had been worth something. I wanted to be a *real* American because I could no longer be a true Vietnamese, since my country of birth no longer existed.

At the time, the reasons for taking what for me was a highly unlikely step seemed clear enough. Even though I was then closer to completing a college degree, I had basically been drifting. Nothing seemed permanent for me. I could chase girls, drink beer, and play pickup hoops with the rest of my buddies, but I'd begun to see those things as temporary, rootless. I wanted to do something meaningful, make my new citizenship momentous.

Perhaps not having a father in my life made me look for stability in institutions—and the Marine Corps was *the* most institutional of institutions, with "210 years of tradition unimpeded by progress."

Mark Adams, my high school buddy and roommate, thought I had gone crazy. So did most of my friends, especially the Asian Americans on my intramural sports teams. "Why the fuck are you going into the Marine Corps? There are plenty of jobs in L.A. Aren't they a bunch of rednecks?" But I ignored them all.

On New Year's Eve of 1985 some friends and I went to the Rose Parade, and then the Rose Bowl game. We stayed up all night and the next day watching and celebrating UCLA's victory. That would be the last night I would party so hard in college; the next week I began my self-paced training program in preparation for OCS, still five months away. Three miles equaled twelve laps around the Drake Stadium track where Olympic-caliber athletes trained. The 1984 Olympics, held in Los Angeles, had given the athletic facilities at UCLA a major upgrade.

After the first two laps around the track I had to stop. I couldn't breathe. I hadn't run laps in nearly four years. After a five-minute halt to regain my breath, I resumed my run and managed to eke out eight laps. I then went over to the pull-up bars and then did sit-ups, which were the easiest. It was clear to me that my faint hope of succeeding at OCS required much more discipline than suggested by the relaxed officer candidates in the color photographs of the recruiting brochures. I had to be ready by June.

The Marine OCS program that I would join had been around since the 1930s; it was the number one route for Marine officer candidates. This Platoon Leaders' Class, or PLC, became known as the "Please Leave the Corps" program later in my career as PLC members received reserve commissions (and rushed out of the service). Thus, many would leave after three years except for aviators who owed four and a half years of service for the flight training that cost more than $1 million. Those who wanted to remain on active duty longer had to compete in a process called "augmentation." Naval Academy and most Reserve Officer Training Corps, or ROTC, graduates automatically got regular commissions, regardless of their academic grades. (It was known that only a few top OCS graduates would receive a coveted regular commission, and I had no such hopes.)

In early June I saw the movies *Top Gun* and *Platoon,* and both psychologically prepped me for induction into the armed forces. I could not help remember the references to the Vietnamese in *Platoon* and in other Vietnam movies: "Charlie," "dink," "gook," "slope," "zipperhead." I believed then that the GIs were referring to their Viet Cong enemy and not their allies in the south. But I would find out otherwise. (Dehumanizing the enemy was the norm; "Jap" was used in World War II. In Iraq, the locals are known as "hajis.")

After I took my final exams at UCLA, Mark Adams drove me to L.A. International Airport. I had carried exactly one backpack and one bag, per the instructions sent to me by Marine Corps Headquarters. About twenty-five of us showed up at the USO Terminal, coming from all walks of life in Southern California. Pictures of famous veterans and Bob Hope hung on the wall. Flags, photographs of airplanes and tanks, and recruiting posters adorned the walls. I felt patriotic and couldn't stop looking around me. The room reminded me of my bedroom in Oxnard, minus the flags.

Most candidates were college students, and several had already graduated. Three were prior-service enlisted Marines in the reserves. The recruiters, including Captain Hamlin himself, showed up to give us a final pep talk. I knew they had already filled their recruiting quotas, so it was up to us candidates to make it on our own.

Hamlin asked us all to say a few words about ourselves. Several candidates mentioned that their fathers had been Marines. A few, like me, were hoping for flight school. The confidence displayed by these young men was remarkable. I particularly recall a pock-faced bodybuilder from San Diego. He stood over 6 feet tall and had already cut his hair fairly short. He was built like a linebacker, packing about 220 pounds, or eighty pounds more than me at that time. This candidate stood up, veins standing out on his neck and muscles bulging from his polo shirt, and barked, "My goal is to finish as the number one graduate from OCS."

Even though I wanted to scream to these guys, "I am here because my father was one of the best pilots in the Vietnamese Air Force. Because he stayed behind until the end and he's still in prison. Because he had fought for twenty-one years. Because I feel I owe it to him to make him proud of me—wherever he is, whether he's still alive or dead."

Instead, I mumbled, "My name is Quang Pham and I come from Oxnard and my goal is to become a Marine pilot." No one said a word to me after my self-introduction. We boarded the plane and flew to Washington National Airport. A black Marine sergeant in green trousers and short-sleeved khaki shirt greeted us as we departed the plane. He was courteous, but spoke in a commanding voice. We grabbed our bags and followed him outside to an old white school bus with "United States Marine Corps" inscribed on its side. The humidity in the air slapped me in the face, hinting at the impending physical challenges awaiting us at Quantico.

As soon as the bus driver closed the door and pulled away from the civilian-filled terminal, our world changed. The courteous sergeant spoke again, but now in a thick Southern drawl: "What the fuck took you girlies so long to lollygag through my airport? You better move quicker than that or you'll be going home tomorrow! Now sit the fuck down and don't say a fucking word. Look straight ahead. There is nothing for you to stare at out the windows."

I had a hard time understanding him at first. Having grown up in California most of my life, I hadn't come across any black people from the South, so I had to strain to pay attention. The bus finally exited I-95 toward a wooded area, where it was still light as we came to a stop outside the Quantico base gate. A sentry exchanged some words with our bus driver. Our bus slowly rolled through the gate, above which I could barely make out the inscription, "Crossroads of the United States Marine Corps." I didn't understand what that meant but I could guess it was basically "make or break." My soft civilian reality quickly changed when the bus came to a halt on what seemed like a large hardtop basketball court.

"Get out of this fucking bus! Get on line! I say get on line, candidates!" screamed two drill instructors who had just climbed aboard. I grabbed my backpack and ran down the aisle, nearly tripping over the seat legs. Once outside, I saw dozens of other young men also being yelled at and I felt more comfortable with the harassment. *Hey, I can handle this. I saw* An Officer and A Gentleman. *Oh yeah, that was the Navy.*

The staff had us running back and forth, aligning our suitcases neatly then repeating the sequence endlessly. We would not get any sleep during the first thirty-six hours in Quantico. Looking back, the barking and yelling would eventually teach us to follow orders from our superiors, under stress and without hesitation. Discipline was the primary goal for the individual and for the team. OCS employed techniques to expose the physically and mentally weak, and to wash them out over a ten-week period. In Vietnam, such blind discipline, even in response to illegal orders, had led to atrocities in such places as Cam Ne and My Lai, the latter an Army atrocity. "Burn all dem hootches! Waste 'em motherfuckin' gooks! Get some!"

Of course I knew none of this back then. Now candidates can simply visit an official Marine Corps OCS website and download the "gouge," as the inside scoop is referred to in the military. (I also wish Captain Hamlin had given me the "gouge" about our treatment before I got to OCS but he hadn't—probably on purpose.) When I checked into Charlie Company, I wasn't the only one without the gouge. The military brats probably had gotten the gouge from their fathers or uncles. The prior-service types had already been through boot camp, while OCS was a serious boot camp for college "pukes" like me. During the Vietnam War, and long before, regular troops called OCS graduates "ten-week wonders."

As I stood there dumbfounded and in shock, another big, black sergeant got in my face. "Fang, Fong, Fam! Whatever your fucking name is! What the fuck are you doing in my Marine Corps? Are you a Viet Cong spy?"

I was stunned. I didn't know what to say. "No, sir!"

"Don't be calling me fucking sir. I work for a living. It's Sergeant Instructor to you, candidate P-Ham. That's it. Go ahead and cry. We don't want babies around here!" He towered over me, leaning into my face.

Tears came to my eyes; I couldn't even speak. I was ready to quit right then and go home. It was immediately obvious to me that I needed the Marine Corps a hell of a lot more than it wanted me.

With TBS classmates after 25-mile hump. From left to right. John Pettit, Chuck Protzmann, Bob Plantz, me, and John Pryce. (Courtesy of Frank Quattrocchi))

Second Lieutenant of Marines and Captain Doug Hamlin at commissioning ceremony. UCLA, 1987 (Courtesy of Thi Pham)

Solo flight in the T-34 "Turbo Weenie," Corpus Christi, 1989. (Author's Collection)

CHAPTER 15

THE FEW, THE PROUD

O N THE BUS RIDE TO QUANTICO, I COULD NOT GET THE recruiting slogan out of my head, "Yeah, I've got what it takes." A J. Walter Thompson recruiting commercial had been run in the 1980s, featuring an ironsmith hammering raw molten iron, forging it into a Marine sword. A bass voiceover crooned off a macho patriotic pitch: "We begin with raw steel . . . mold it with muscle, shape it with fire and sweat. Polish it to razor-sharp perfection. Maybe you have what it takes to be one of us—the few, the proud, the Marines."

All I could think of while standing at attention in front of the OCS barracks was how to get the hell out of the fire. Plus I had to go to the bathroom ("head") since the staff had ordered us to drain two canteens of water within minutes to keep us from becoming a "heat casualty."

Before OCS, I hadn't yet learned about the Marines' illustrious combat history aside from episodes of "Baa Baa Black Sheep" and John Wayne's Sergeant Stryker in *The Sands of Iwo Jima*. Most of the Vietnam War movies had revolved around the Army's experiences. Soon I would study the scripture of the Corps combat record in Vietnam.

In the face of overwhelming challenges and unclear objectives, Marines had fought valiantly in their longest war ever. They were as courageous as their "greatest generation" predecessors who had assaulted Pacific islands, hopping from one bloody battle to another. My mother had told me that "the VC were scared of the Marines. They were vicious." She was wary of my military venture but never tried to talk me out of it. Before I departed for OCS she added, "During the war, we never saw Marines in Saigon. They did all their fighting up north."

Yet the debacle in Southeast Asia would burden the Corps as it did the United States. And I felt the brunt of it, real or imagined, during my first four weeks at OCS.

Historian and retired Marine Col. Allan R. Millett determined that the Corps had 101,574 killed and wounded in Vietnam, almost 4,000 more casualties than in World War II. It was only in the number of dead (19,733 to 12,983) that World War II held the greater number.* Vietnam was not a simple "civil" war as depicted in history books and pundit columns. There was nothing civil about it.

When your name is Quang Pham and you check into Charlie Company (or C Company) at U.S. Marine OCS eleven years after the fall of Saigon, you don't expect any breaks. When the elite outfit you're trying to join has lost thousands of young men in the Quang Nam, Quang Ngai, Quang Tin, and Quang Tri provinces, you don't expect anyone to pronounce your name correctly, even if it was known how. I hoped these guys who were going to make my present a hell and determine my future realized that the war was over.

I was called a "VC" at Quantico, even though I had nothing to do with the U.S. debacle in Vietnam. I was only a kid, on the U.S. side, on the losing side, but to my Marine instructors I symbolized that loss and shame. My father was still paying for that loss at a prison camp. All I could do was remember that his predicament was infinitely worse than mine.

We candidates handwrote our biographies with emphasis on our accomplishments, which also inadvertently revealed our "potential" weak points as well: for example, if you didn't mention that you had leadership experience, then it could be assumed that you had poor leadership skills. My file contained my enlistment contract and OCS application with "MINORITY CANDIDATE" stamped across the top. (That hadn't been there when I signed the original paperwork.) On the second line, my birthday and my place of birth, "Saigon, Vietnam," were typed.† That's how the staff knew about my background. I didn't think the "minority" stamp was necessary if anyone had bothered to look at my face, my name, and my birthplace.

---

*Medical evacuation by helicopter (medevacs) played a major role in reducing the number of those killed in action (KIAs).

†In 2004, I received my military records from Marine Corps Headquarters and I interviewed my recruiter, Doug Hamlin, who had become one of my closest friends. When I pushed him for answers, Doug admitted that he and other recruiters worked to a quota system for minority and female officer candidates. Doug thought he would get more Asian-American candidates, especially at UCLA. He didn't.

The fourth platoon, my training platoon, was commanded by Capt. Barry Amos, an infantry officer who had washed out of flight school. His dislike of aviation types became evident the first week. "Let me see who my air candidates are. Raise your hand. Ah . . . Pham, I knew you'd be an Airedale." In the Marine Corps, everyone is first and foremost a rifleman. The infantry or the "grunts" made up the Corps and always would. The aviation candidates called Amos a "fallen angel" and "Captain Sunshine" for his cynical attitude. Gunnery Sergeant Robert Ramirez was the fourth platoon sergeant, and Sgt. Martin Anderson, the sergeant instructor, rounded out the staff. Both were physically shorter than average but were as lean and mean as Marines come.

Captain Amos also wanted to know if there were any "legacies" in the platoon. "Raise your hand if your father is a colonel or above." There was a line in the OCS application to list all "relatives who served or are serving in the armed forces" by rank, name, and service. I didn't write anything on my application. Somehow, I instinctively put up my hand thinking that my father would have been at least a colonel by 1986. Amos looked at me and sneered, "Colonel or above *in the U.S. military!*" (Sergeant Anderson did later threaten, "For many of you, that family military tradition will end this summer!")

After the first thirty-six hours of no-sleep shock treatment, I settled into the platoon's squad bay. It was a long linoleum-floored room, with bunk beds ("racks") neatly aligned. The training staff had private rooms. There was one communal bathroom (the head) with four toilets next to each other, a dozen sinks, and showers. In the middle of the squad bay was the rifle rack of securely locked M16s.

Fourth platoon began with sixty candidates, including twelve prior enlisted Marines, seven or eight aviation candidates, five minority members, and four lawyers. The candidates came from all parts of the country, although more came from the Midwest and the South. We had one Harvard graduate and a tough young candidate from Lebanon.

Candidates ran the gauntlet of uniform issue, reams of paperwork, and, yes, that first Marine haircut for three dollars that took less than three minutes. Soon we all had fuzzy "grapes" on our shoulders, some more lopsided than others. We wore camouflage-patterned utilities (cammies) with no rank and no Marine Corps emblem (eagle, globe, and anchor). We hadn't earned the title of "Marine" just yet. Our names were stenciled in black on white strips sewn onto our left shirt pockets.

Within the first week six candidates had dropped out for various reasons.

One was physically unfit and several had developed cellulitis from blisters on their feet (even the simple act of marching around the OCS parade deck had disqualified a handful).

The OCS staff graded its candidates in the following categories and their associated importance: academic 25 percent, physical fitness 25 percent, and leadership 50 percent. Peer evaluations, better known as "spear evals," came from candidates ranking one another in the top third or the last third in each squad (fifteen to twenty candidates) and in the platoon. Long before reality shows became big television hits, OCS candidates voted the "unsats" (unsatisfactory performers) off Quantico. The instructors acted as hosts; candidates played the "survivors." Those who made it through would receive lieutenant bars.

On the third night, we were ordered to drink two quarts of water but prohibited from making a head call. My bladder was about to burst, so I got up and ran back to my wall locker to relieve myself in my boots. The next morning I took the boots to the head and washed them before anyone could notice. Someone who slept near my rack had ratted me out on a spear eval. I had to squirm on the carpet in front of Amos to explain my predicament. He called me "unsat" and informed me that I had been ranked among the bottom three men in the squad that week. "What was I supposed to do? Hold it in or pee in my rack?" I thought the nark was a chickenshit. From that point forward, I learned to watch my back.

Integrity was the most important leadership trait. "Integrity violators" got the boot from OCS, with no second chance. That meant cheaters, liars, and thieves were automatically sent home. OCS was the first place that taught me about ethics. (I had not been a regular church attendee or Bible reader, and my mother never spoke about ethics at home. Her Confucian, later Catholic, discipline was enough.)

The OCS staff was the crème-de-la-crème, best from the Fleet Marine Force. Our company commander, Major Van Fleet, was a "mustang," once an enlisted Marine with combat experience in Vietnam who had earned an officer's commission. The Corps loved officers like Van Fleet, usually good with troops, gruff but approachable, firm but fair. The OCS commanding officer, in a colonel's billet, usually became a general officer. Ours was Col. Robert B. Johnston, a tough-as-nails two-dollar-steak colonel, also a highly decorated Vietnam veteran and originally an immigrant from Edinburgh, Scotland. He regularly finished the Physical Fitness Test in eighteen minutes, completing all three events: three-mile run, twenty pull-ups, and eighty sit-ups. He outperformed candidates twenty-five years younger than he was. It was motivating to see him run past us. In the Corps setting the example was paramount.

Every morning, reveille began before 5 a.m. A quick run through the chow line preceded physical training (PT). By sunrise the entire company of six platoons, including the female platoon, would assemble in front of a "colour sergeant," a senior enlisted member on exchange from the Royal Marines.

"Good morning, Charlie Company. Are you ready for some Marine Corps PT? Oohhrraahh! We will do three sets of UBDs (upper body development course) followed by the Fartlek Course (a 3- to 4-mile trail, consisting of nearly one dozen exercise stations, designed to build endurance). I will count the cadence, you will count the repetition. We will do twenty side-straddle hops. Reaaddy. Exercise! One, two, three!"

"One!" the number one echoed in the Quantico woods, screamed by 300 motivated (and mostly) bald candidates.

"One, two, three!"

"Two!" There was an enormous rush in my body listening to the bellows, synergized by the camaraderie.

After warming up platoons took turns running the trails, some days individually, some days in formation. Anyone who fell out of a formation run received a bad eval. Too many bad evals meant packing your bag and going home early, still with a peculiar haircut.

Major Van Fleet led us on a run once and he sang my favorite "Jody":*

Ho Chi Minh is a son of a bitch.
Got the blue balls, crabs, and the seven-year itch!
Gimme some, PT
Good for me, good for you!

Mama and Papa were lying in bed
Mama rolled over and this is what she said
Gimmme some, PT
Good for me, good for you!

Leaders in the platoon quickly emerged. Predictably, they were the prior-service members. They had the best polished boots, the most squared-away

*"Jody" was the mythic name of the SOB who would be "sneaking" your girlfriend or wife while you were off learning to be a Marine, soldier, sailor, or airman. I first thought "Jody" was a girl.

uniforms, the cleanest rifles. They also had an impressive military presence that I lacked, especially in public speaking. Until OCS, I had felt fairly comfortable with my English-language fluency. Yet I remained timid. I never had to bark orders to strangers or sing cadence or reply under stress. I had to think on my feet, react to obscene screaming, and make decisions in a satisfactory manner amid chaos. Outside of my childhood, my only exposure to the military had been airshows, movies, and television. The staff called the California contingent "Hollywood candidates." I could identify with that; there weren't any bases near Bel Air, Brentwood, or Beverly Hills.

Sometimes, under stress the left side of my brain reverted to my native tongue and my reaction was to say something in Vietnamese. It was a strange phenomenon and it only happened under the constant strain at OCS. The candidate who slept on the rack above mine, a lawyer from Texas, heard me mumble "something in Vietnamese" while I was tossing and turning. I was probably cursing at Amos.

The fourth week was the one I really had to survive. A fifth-week board would convene to determine the fate of the unsats. It seemed as if the staff took turns each week picking on certain candidates to push them to their outer limit. But it was in the fourth that the company went on its first forced march (or "hump"). Every candidate carried an M16, plus forty pounds of assorted military gear and a helmet. For me "humping" was a brand-new torture. A mile into the hump, I experienced pain in body parts I didn't even know I had. My neck ached from the weight of the steel helmet (Kevlar helmets came in the next year). My shins and my ankles felt as if they were going to snap with each step. The accordion effect, as the formation continually stretched out and then became compacted during the march, forced the rearmost platoon to run part of the hump to catch up. I couldn't fathom how Marines had charged up beaches in World War II or patrolled endlessly in the jungles of Vietnam. I was beyond exhaustion after only 3 miles, and nobody was shooting at me.

The motivating jodies helped relieve the pain and focused my mind on something else:

Gimme that ole' Marine Corps spirit
Gimme that ole' Marine Corps spirit
Gimme that ole' Marine Corps spirit
Cause it's good enough for me!

It was good at Belleau Wood
It was good at Tarawa
It was good at Inchon
And it's good enough for me!

Several candidates fell out of the hump and trailed the platoon. Afterward they all reported to Captain Amos. They were headed to the fifth-week board to face disqualification. I thought I'd be joining them, too, the way Amos spoke to me every time I had to face him.

(One time Amos closed the door to his office and had me stand at attention staring straight ahead. "Pham, I read your bio. I thought maybe you could talk about your father during the 'impromptu speech.' But you're too . . . too emotional. My brother was a B-52 tail-gunner in Vietnam and he got shot down. What do you think about that, huh?")

He was probably right, but I couldn't possibly have told my father's story then. I didn't fully understand it myself, and nobody understood or cared anyway. Despite my resolve, my vision blurred with tears: I was so upset that I could not control my emotions. I wanted to yell back, "Fuck you, I didn't kill your brother!" I tried to keep my cool, maintain my composure. But somehow, in the heat of the moment, my voice cracked and tears ran down my cheeks again. "Get the hell out of here, Pham."

As soon as I left his office, I wanted to punch myself for letting him get to me again. I didn't know if he was lying about his brother or if he was just "working" me over.

After four weeks candidates were given a twenty-four-hour liberty pass. I had made friends with Mark Henderson, an unassuming aviation candidate from Boulder, Colorado. His father had flown combat missions in Vietnam and reached the rank of colonel in the air force flying F-16s. We hitched a ride to nearby Quantico, a typical service town with restaurants and stores that catered to Marines and not much else. Q-Town looked like one of those old towns in Western movies. Candidates circled the downtown, got haircuts, and ate pizza. Then Mark and I decided to take the train up to Washington, D.C. After walking around Georgetown, we checked into the Key Bridge Marriott in nearby Arlington. We turned on the television, blasted the air-conditioning, and ordered room service. Even hotel food tasted so good after four weeks of Marine Corps chow. It was heaven. After frantically setting our alarm clocks and calling the front desk for a wake-up call, we quickly passed out. Returning to OCS late would result in major problems.

The fifth week did not begin well for many candidates in fourth platoon. One of the prior-service Marines, and first-ranked candidate in the platoon, had tripped on the obstacle course and had to be taken away by an ambulance. I had passed all my multiple-choice academic examinations and tackled all PT challenges—but I had developed a major case of hemorrhoids after our second hump. So it was back to sick call to see the doc, and the news was not good. "Candidate Pham, you need to get those removed. That means NPQ (not physically qualified). You can come back next summer," the navy physician on duty advised.

I froze. There was no way in hell I was going to go through this again.

I begged the doctor, "Sir, can you give me anything to relieve the itching? I've got another hump next week."

I had made up my mind. They're going to have to drag me out of OCS. Dead. I'm halfway home.

"OK, Candidate Pham, go to the dispensary and apply this ointment and use the suppositories every few hours. Got it?" (My platoon buddies reminded me to take my medicine: "Hey Pham, don't forget to take your butt drugs!" Nothing in any basketball locker room I'd ever heard approached the personal nature of OCS "pimping." But at least they cared.)

The hemorrhoids kept me up at night. I would lie awake thinking about my father and about the South Vietnamese soldiers who had died in Vietnam. I would be ashamed if I ever let them down. The negative perception about the ARVN would be cemented. The U.S. media and military would continue their bashing: *The ARVN was corrupt, inept and unwilling to fight. Now their kids aren't good enough to join our ranks.* Gunnery Sergeant Ramirez's voice echoed in my mind: *There is no room for marginal candidates, let alone marginal officers. I ain't gonna let none of you weaklings lead me!*

I was angry yet grateful that I was there in Quantico, proving that I had the mettle to join the ranks of the best. In hindsight, that's all anyone can ask in this country—an opportunity and not a guarantee.

We saw quite a few Hollywood movie clips and training films. It became a wash of images of Marines bayoneting and flame-throwing Japanese on South Pacific islands, Communists in Korea and more Communists in Vietnam. Under the dimmed classroom lights, I would recoil while my fellow candidates screamed *Oohhrraahh!* and *Get some!* I did it too to go along with the crowd. This fixation on the Asiatic as the enemy was not the Corps' fault.

It was not racism, it was reality. Our simulated field training exercises were from lessons learned in the last war, the Corps' experience in Vietnam. *Five NVA soldiers with a machine gun at grid coordinate AB234784. Your mission is to destroy the enemy by fire and maneuver and close combat. Fix bayonet! E-tool! Oohhrraahh!*

The military training was hurtful but truthful. That's one thing the Marine Corps never hid from us or the public. The Corps built men and killers and was extremely good at it. That was what parents of young enlisted Marines expected—competent lieutenants who would not get their sons killed in combat. Our motto, *semper fidelis,* or "always faithful," was constantly drilled into our heads.

Several candidates were dropped by the fifth-week board, though. My bunkmate, the lawyer candidate who was doing fairly well, developed bad shin splints and was sent home. I asked him if he was returning the following summer after graduating from the University of Texas law school. "Hell, no!" was his reply.

Every time we lost candidates the platoon had to reconfigure the squad bay. Empty racks were disassembled, stored away, and the remaining racks reset at proper intervals. The staff wanted not a trace of failure within our sight. The departing OCS candidates transferred to the R&S Platoon and no longer wore cammies; R&S did not stand for Reconnaissance and Surveillance as in the Fleet Marine Force. Here R&S meant failure, that is, Rest and Separation, where the unsats and "shitbirds" waited for their out-processing. Although R&S candidates still had fresh "high and tight" haircuts, their slumping shoulders, their broken bearing, spoke volumes about their fate. Every time we ran past the R&S platoon, Sergeant Anderson would shout: "I look to my right and who do I see? A bunch of sick, lame, and lazy."

Captain Hamlin and the other recruiters visited their far-flung OCS candidates at the halfway mark. I couldn't wait to meet with him in private to "choke" him for sending me to my summer hell. He remained confident of my success, however, far more than I was. I was curious about what he knew about what lay ahead for me. He just repeated, "Focus on the present, tackle one obstacle at a time. You'll get through it."

Something miraculously ignited inside me during the sixth week. The fuck-fuck games appeared funny to me now (and racial epithets had ceased after the initial welcome). My forty-pound pack, M16, and assorted combat gear felt lighter during longer humps. The obstacle course was easier, the endurance run less painful. I had cut six minutes off my initial time. I was still struggling in every aspect of OCS except in taking written examinations (and Motrins and suppositories).

After the reshuffling of the squad, Candidate Tim Pierson became my new bunkmate. He was a prior-service Marine. He pushed me every time I struggled, sometimes yelling in my face, "Come on, Pham! You can do it! Just think about finishing!" Based on his facial expressions during PT, I could tell he was having a hard time as well. Yet he had been ranked one of the top three in my squad. "Come on, Pham. You've got to understand. They're just fucking with you. You're gonna make it. Hang in there."

The first instance of favoritism I saw in the Marine Corps happened at OCS. A twelve-year gunnery sergeant, a salty and cocky fellow, suffered a stress fracture in his leg. He was given crutches and placed on light duty (no PT). He was permitted to continue the course and observed the rest of us while we went through the remaining small-unit field exercises and PT. Standing in the back of a corpsman's truck trailing the company runs (in case candidates needed medical assistance), he still had the balls to "motivate" us. "Come on, Pham, don't fall out!"

I wanted to tell him to shut the fuck up.

The staff allowed him to finish and graduate with the rest of us even though he technically had only completed 70 percent of the PT. I guess those stripes and rockers of his rank insignia meant something after all. But I had thought *all* candidates were being "screened and evaluated" fairly. I hadn't known that Marine officers who had graduated from the Naval Academy were also exempt from OCS.

Female candidates, naturally, had separate PT standards.

The company took all its major remaining tests in the ninth week: a second small-unit leadership exercise and a final obstacle and endurance course culminating in a 15-mile hump. As the company came to a halt after finishing our "Bataan death march," I knew I had survived. Those who fell out were doomed. Our sole black candidate, from South Carolina, nice fellow, had flunked several written exams. He kept to himself throughout the course. I was rooting for him, but to no avail. He and six others were dismissed at the ninth-week board. (The bodybuilder candidate was dropped at the seventh-week board.)

Henderson and I took a cab to the Key Bridge Marriott again the moment liberty was sounded on the Saturday before graduation. I was elated but I was still paranoid about being summoned to a "last-minute" secret board by

Amos. After dropping off our backpacks at the hotel, Henderson suggested that we visit The Wall across the Potomac, in Washington, D.C.

It was eerie to stand before the inscribed names of the 58,000 Americans who had died in Vietnam. What would their lives be like now, had they lived? I did not know a single one.

Out of the sixty candidates who began training with fourth platoon, thirty-five graduated. Two of the five minority members had made it: the Lebanese candidate and I. All four lawyers were dropped. Bill McGuire (a friend from Oxnard) and his mother Jane drove down from Alexandria, Virginia, to attend my graduation. I was glad to see familiar faces in the bleachers. Mark Henderson's father showed up in his air force blues with shiny silver pilot's wings.

I hadn't invited my mother and sisters. Maybe I didn't think I would make it. But as I marched with my platoon past the bleachers and reviewing stand to the Marines' Hymn, a monumental sense of accomplishment coursed through my body. I had overcome the toughest challenge I had faced in my new country up to that point. I had represented my father and former country well (albeit in the bottom third).

My feelings unavoidably turned to the man who wasn't there. My father would have loved this moment, I thought. The discipline and focus on close-order drill helped me hold back tears of regret. *Crazy* Hoa—now you got company, sir!

As the "eyes, right!" command was given, I could think of no greater joy, knowing that I had passed possibly the hardest screening and evaluation of any military organization in the world. Just as the lowest ranked graduate of medical school is still called "doctor," my place in the bottom third of my class meant I would be called "sir" if I decided to join the Corps. (Even Chesty Puller didn't kick ass at OCS, and look where John McCain ended up in life after finishing fifth from bottom at Annapolis.)

Graduating from OCS was one thing, contributing to my new country was another matter. I had undergone training the summer between my junior and senior years at UCLA. I had to return to finish my degree and decide on my future. With my OCS diploma in hand, I landed at LAX with a "high and tight," packing eight additional pounds of lean and mean muscles (almost surpassing the buck fifty mark). I now saw the world as a Marine sees it. I went on a run on Sunset Boulevard around the campus perimeter. The hills of Bel

Air next to UCLA looked like a "military crest" at twilight. I saw "avenues of approaches" and "cover." Every other civilian I ran into appeared unsat and overweight. Bruin Walk was a world away from Quantico's Brown Field.

My senior year in college was a blur, submerged beneath waves of memories of OCS, The Wall, and the bronze statue of Frederick Hart's three soldiers, arms around one another, searing my memory. I thought of their deaths. (To me, it was not for nothing. Even if they hadn't believed in the cause, at least they went honorably. I wondered how they would have viewed their portrayals by history and Hollywood.) By the end of 1986, I had made up my mind that I had to do something to make up for my survivor's guilt. I wanted to contribute to a cause, so I called my recruiting office and advised it of my decision to accept my commission the following summer.

Before I was to become a lieutenant, two headlines piqued my curiosity in the organization I was about to join. The Iran-Contra affair began making news in late 1986, and Marine Lt. Col. Oliver North, Annapolis 1968, was involved. I was intrigued. I didn't know Marines worked in the White House involved in foreign policy. I had taken college political science classes and so I followed the scandal closely. North was well-spoken, and his testimony was credible. But the more I read, the more troubled I became. No one had told me at OCS about Marines conducting "arms trading" and secret funding for the contra rebels fighting in Nicaragua. Could it be the disclosure of another secret war like Kennedy's early involvement in Vietnam?

In April 1987, a drawing of a Marine with a black eye (wounding the Corps reputation) made the cover of *Time*. Sergeant Clayton Lonetree, stationed at the U.S. Embassy in Moscow, was suspected of passing secrets to a beautiful Soviet agent. It was shocking news that served some of my college friends well who had been skeptical of my career decision in the first place. U.S. Marines are not supposed to do these sorts of things. Integrity, integrity, integrity. I had learned, along with many around the world, that the Marine Corps was the best fighting organization in the world. At least that's what they kept telling me. But there was no war going on. Marines weren't used to being political players; no former Marine had ever occupied the Oval Office.

As my college graduation and commissioning day neared, I didn't know who to ask to administer my oath of office. Military fathers usually participated in the ritual, or an instructor or a family friend. I had made friends with the UCLA Navy ROTC staff and midshipmen, so the Marine instructor had invited me to participate in their ceremony. I gladly accepted just to be a part of a special day with twenty-five other new navy ensigns and one other Marine lieutenant. I called Doug Hamlin, who had resigned his commission the week I returned from OCS, and was now selling advertising for *Guns & Ammo* magazine. (He was still in reserve.) Doug gladly obliged. On a sunny, warm June afternoon, in front of my mother, my sisters, and two dozen friends, I repeated the "I do solemnly swear to support and defend the Constitution of the United States" oath like millions of Americans before me. I wondered if my father would ever learn that his only son had followed in his footsteps, not in Vietnam but here.

*A Communist cadre "reeducating"
former South Vietnamese officers, 1975.
(Courtesy of Marc Ribaud/
Magnum Photos)*

*A rare picture from Communist
prison camp taken by my Great Aunt
Phu. My father after a day's hard work in
the prison camp, Vietnam, 1985.
(Author's Collection)*

CHAPTER 16

NO BAD DAY

ONE OF MY FATHER'S FELLOW PRISON CAMP DETAINEES had a son who had fled to Germany. The man always spoke about his own pending release and the day he would rejoin his family in Europe. Months went by, then years, but the man kept hoping. One day he had a stroke and died in his sleep while lying next to my father. After witnessing his friend's death, my father lived by his newly adopted motto, "No bad day."

Late in 1982 the prisoners held in the north were transported to southern Vietnam on trains. My father and his peers (Cau, "Piggy," and Tri) had originally believed that their release was imminent. But they had been lied to again. When the trains stopped in Quang Tri, just south of the DMZ where U.S. Marines had fought fierce battles fifteen years earlier, crowds surged around the train station. The prisoners raised their hands to show they were handcuffed to each other. But this time the residents cheered, cried, and threw fruit and snacks to the prisoners. Most of the prisoners broke into tears. They saw that not all South Vietnamese had forgotten their plight. They were still part of the history of their former country, though it could no longer be called Viet Nam Cong Hoa (South Vietnam) in public.

Cau was taken to Camp Z30-C and my father to Camp Z30-D. Both were in the Rung La jungle, about 100 miles north of Saigon. Reserved mostly for senior officials and "difficult" prisoners, the inmates of Z30-D were forced to carry on the dangerous work of clearing the mine fields around their camp.

In 1984, my father was sent back to the north to Camp Nam Ha while his friends remained in the south. All three of them were released in 1985 and eventually resettled with their families in the United States by the early 1990s. My father's mundane labor routine would continue for another three years.

With its economy still in shambles ten years after the war Vietnam's government finally decided to place the economy over ideology. Adopted in 1986, the *Doi moi* reforms meant Vietnam would reach out to its former enemy, the United States, for a jump start. It marked the beginning of the "new" Vietnam. Analogous to the POW "bargaining chips" at the 1973 Paris Peace Conference, Vietnam had something the United States still wanted— a full accounting of those Americans missing in action (MIA).

In the United States, POW/MIA advocates continued lobbying the White House, Congress, and the Pentagon to account for their loved ones. They met with Vietnamese Foreign Minister Nguyen Co Thach in New York. Newspapers reported that the Hanoi government had asked for $4 billion in exchange for dozens of "live" U.S. POWs. In early 1987, President Reagan phoned retired Army Gen. John Vessey Jr., a former chairman of the Joint Chiefs of Staff, to ask him to assume the role of special emissary to Vietnam for POW/MIA affairs. Vessey landed in Hanoi in August 1987 with orders not only to find out if there were any living U.S. POWs left in Vietnam, and get them out, but also to obtain the release of former South Vietnamese military and political leaders from the reeducation/prison camps.

When General Vessey raised the question of releasing former South Vietnamese military officers and political officials, Deputy Foreign Minister Nguyen Dy Nien told him that it would be too difficult. "It just couldn't be done at this time."

On the way to the airport after a three-day meeting, which had led to some agreement on the U.S. MIAs, Vessey was asked by the escorting officer from the Vietnamese Foreign Ministry whether he thought his trip was successful. Vessey quickly replied, "No, I don't."

"Why?"

"I was told that we wouldn't be able to get any movement on getting the former ARVN officers out of the prison camps."

The officer stopped at the airport before Vessey was to board his aircraft. He made a call and connected Vessey with Nien, to whom he again expressed his disappointment. Nien then conceded, "We will do it then. We will make it happen."

Nien added, "We couldn't release the ARVN prisoners from the prison camps because they would disrupt the country and possibly form a rebellion." (If Nien had visited the camps and seen the men of "skin and bones," the word could not possibly have occurred to him.) Vessey quickly interrupted, "We'll take every one of them into the United States." Nien reaffirmed, "OK, under that condition, we'll let them out."

Two months later, on September 30, 1987, my father was released after nearly 4,500 days in captivity. His fellow prisoners did not rejoice, believing this was yet another lie. My father scrounged some money and went to a bar near the train station. He told no one of his release. He treated himself to a small glass of rice wine and some peanuts before boarding. He soon got sick from the wine and threw up. After more than twelve years without a drink, his system couldn't handle the alcohol.

My great-aunt sent a telegram to my grandmother in Saigon (now Ho Chi Minh City) about my father's release. A few days later when my grandmother, aunts, uncles, and cousins greeted him at the train station, they hardly recognized the tall, brash, handsome air force pilot he had once been. His hair was now gray, his skin sunburned and wrinkled from working in the fields. But his signature smile remained the same.

They cried together like so many other families at the station. After an abbreviated reunion several cadres took away the newly released prisoners: they had to go register with the local police—and stay behind bars for two more days. After his release, my father was told to report on a weekly basis all his activities including his movements (restricted as they were), his contacts, and conversations, especially if with foreigners. Being released did not yet mean he was free.

Here is how Ho Dang Tri spoke about his years after his release.

The cadres prohibited us from working jobs that required interacting with outsiders, especially tourists. Senior officers were not allowed to work as barbers, *cyclo* drivers, or street vendors. They knew we spoke French and English and were afraid of us telling our story. They repeatedly interrogated us about our contacts with outsiders. Everywhere we went we had to report the people we met and their location. Weekly check-ins: "Who did you meet, what did you talk about, etc." After a few years, they did away with this rule.

While the U.S. involvement in Vietnam engaged six U.S. presidents, it would take another five administrations to untangle its aftermath. The last prison camp detainees (some held since 1975) were released in 1993, but taking their place were the artists, political dissidents, religious leaders, writers, and anyone else who spoke against the Vietnamese government. In December of 1992, President George H. W. Bush awarded General Vessey the Presidential Medal of Freedom for his accomplishments as special envoy. In 1993, Vessey made his final visit to Vietnam, and reported to President Clinton that all living American POWs and political prisoners of the former Republic of Vietnam were released.

CHAPTER 17

TRAINED TO KILL

GOVERNMENT RED TAPE DELAYED MY ORDERS TO THE Basic School (TBS) in Quantico, Virginia. Captain Hamlin's recruiter replacement informed me that the Gramm-Ruddman budget reduction legislation meant I would not be reporting to TBS until "further notice." The emotional high of my commissioning was followed by months of lull. I had quit my accounts receivable job; my $12,000 in student loans would become due six months after graduation. I had moved back to my mother's apartment in L.A. She had moved from Oxnard when she took a new job.

Meanwhile, I had no job and no life in Los Angeles.

The recruiter left a message suggesting that I resign my commission and forgo my five-month-old oath because there was no funding for training. I didn't call him back but, instead, applied for a position as an associate financial analyst with a national firm. I was hired and immediately joined a training class in Glendale. Naturally, my military orders arrived. I had to report to TBS by January 2, 1988, to join Bravo Company, Basic School Class 2-88. I went to my new civilian boss and promptly quit. I was not ready to trade my dream—my coveted flight school slot—for an entry-level corporate pencil-pushing job.

Snowflakes covered the road leading from I-95 to Camp Barrett. TBS sat across the highway from OCS, still within the confines of the base at Quantico. (The FBI Academy, and not much else, was nearby.) Thick woods, nothing like those in Southern California, ran unimpeded to the edges of the long, dark, winding road. I managed to hit an icy spot and spin 360 degrees twice in my new VW Jetta. Luckily, I struck nothing and no one saw me, or

I could have lost my flight slot right then and there. The Asian bad-driver stereotype nearly came true.

TBS was nothing like OCS. It had no entry gate, so there was no alcohol checkpoint for young lieutenants returning from liberty in Georgetown or Old Town in Alexandria. (If there were, the Corps would be short of young officers.) An alcohol-related driving offense was considered a career ender, but even here there were exceptions made for a few lucky "water-walkers."

TBS marked the biggest difference between the Marine officer corps and those of other services. Every new officer (except some pilots during the Vietnam era) graduated from TBS, including aviators, lawyers, supply officers, and administrative types. Since every Marine is a rifleman, officers had to be prepared to lead a rifle platoon if necessary. Real infantry officers would continue their studies with an additional nine weeks of the Infantry Officer Course following TBS. About a third of the class, including me, was headed for Pensacola, Florida, for flight training as an aviator or a naval flight officer ("backseater").

Bravo Company lived in Graves Hall, with two lieutenants per room in dormitory-like bachelor officers quarters (BOQ). Married lieutenants rented off-base housing but kept a room in the BOQ as well. Graves Hall was named after 2d Lt. Terrence C. Graves, a Medal of Honor winner killed in action in Vietnam in 1968. Graves was twenty-two when he died. A color portrait of him hung on the first floor.

Our days were packed with a meticulous training syllabus refined by a staff, as at OCS, that included the best officers in the Corps. Unlike OCS, we were accorded the appropriate military courtesy. No verbal abuse, no yelling. The school's commanding officer, Col. Terry J. Ebbert, had one lung; the other had been removed after a VC round had pierced his chest during the battle for Hue City in 1968. The executive officer was the ever-colorful Lt. Col. Gerry "Bear" Berry, the CH-46 helicopter pilot who had flown the most hours during the evacuation of Saigon. He could be depended on to motivate the aviation-bound officers with his exciting war stories. Flashing us his Rolex watch, he patently exclaimed, "You can never be too rich, too thin, or have too many medals!"

The new officers sat through hours of lectures on military history and tradition, and infantry tactics at the squad and platoon level. We fired practically every weapon in the Corps inventory: squad automatic weapon, M203 grenade launcher, M19 40mm (multiple) grenade launcher. I had never shot anything before except a friend's pellet handgun and a dozen rounds with the M16A1 at OCS. After two weeks at the pistol and rifle ranges, I had qualified with the Beretta 9mm pistol and M16A2 rifle. Marine marksmanship training was simply amazing. I was not a "gun freak" like many of my fellow officers, but from 500 yards, in the prone position and using a sling to tighten my grip on the M16, I fired nine out of ten rounds into a human silhouette.

Later in the training program, I threw hand grenades and called in artillery and air support. The company also went on long humps, culminating with a 25-miler. We took buses down to Norfolk, Virginia, and participated in a mock amphibious landing. I wasn't particularly fond of being on a ship or sitting in a steel amphibious assault vehicle that sank the moment it hit the water. But I told no one of my fears then and just sucked it up.

Midway through TBS, the aviation-bound officers were notified of their reporting date to flight school, which excited all of us. Our flying dreams were now only months away.

I met a Vietnamese tailor named Dinh at the uniform shop. He was a friendly man and always gave me extra time in fitting my uniforms. A month after starting TBS, the sister of a friend of mine invited a group of us lieutenants to a dance at nearby Mount Vernon College, then an all-women's school. We single lieutenants wanted to impress the coeds, so we decided to wear our dress blues. The only problem was that the uniforms would not be ready for two weeks. I walked over and spoke to Dinh. The next day, he fitted all nine of us and we were off to the Capitol Hilton.

To our surprise, the socialite women were not impressed with our form-fitting uniforms or our near-bald heads. And a couple of us got kicked out of the dance for rowdy behavior. We retreated to the bar and listened to the hotel pianist keying the "Marine Corps Hymn." (Before I left TBS, I stopped by to say goodbye to Dinh. It had been nice to know a fellow Vietnamese amid strangers. I would run into several more during my stints in Florida and Texas. Not all were clustered in ethnic enclaves.)

The first fake Vietnam veteran I met was one of my TBS classmates. He arrived as a member of the Navy Judge Advocate General (JAG) section and wore three rows of ribbons, including the Vietnam Service Ribbon. He was in his thirties and claimed to have taken part in the evacuation of Saigon. I was immediately impressed when I met him at the Hawkins Room (the TBS Bar), but then I did some quick arithmetic in my head and found that something did not jibe. A few years later, I read a piece in a military newspaper that the so-called JAG officer had been court-martialed for lying about his career. A former sailor, he had duped the Marine Corps and submitted phony records, and all legal cases involving this officer had to be overturned.

After six terrific months at TBS I was sad to leave Quantico. (I had graduated in the middle of my TBS class.) As much as I had hated the place two years earlier, I felt as though I finally "understood" what it meant to be a Marine officer. Even if I hadn't been guaranteed flight training in Pensacola, I would have remained in the Corps for at least a three-year stint. I flew back to California to see my mother and to participate as a "swordsman" in a wedding; this would be the first of dozens of sword arches I would form with my fellow Marines.

If I could sum up TBS in a one-sentence lesson, it would be: "Right or wrong lieutenant, make a fucking decision!"

I finally checked into Pensacola, the home of naval aviation, in August 1988, nearly thirty years after my father was one of the first fifteen VNAF pilots to receive pilot's wings in this country. Six weeks of aviation indoctrination awaited me, and I was eager to start.

Navy and Marine pilots often operated off aircraft carriers and flew over open ocean. If we crashed or ditched our aircraft, our lives depended on our ability to swim and survive at sea. For me swimming qualification posed the greatest obstacle to getting my wings. I shuddered at the thought of swimming a mile in a flight suit, treading water for ten minutes encumbered with helmet and flight gear, or exiting a helicopter underwater in what was called the "helo dunker" finale.

The government wanted one final assurance before it gave us its $1 million flight training. My second potential obstacle came as a surprise. Student pilots were randomly selected for an in-depth quality assurance flight physical by the Naval Aerospace Medical Institute (NAMI). Students could be disqualified by NAMI for weak eyesight (less than uncorrected 20/20), sinusitis, or other discovered disabilities. Luckily I wasn't picked; I needed my "anthro" measurements done.

An ancient machine measured the distances between my feet and knees, my knees to my hips, my fingers to my elbows, and my shoulders to fingertips. The Navy wanted to make sure that I could fit into tight jet cockpits and safely eject, without tearing off a leg.

No problem there, but then the Navy wanted to make sure I could reach all the switches while my safety harnesses were locked. That was the closest

I came to washing out of flight school, and it happened before I even climbed into a cockpit.

My arms are short. When the examining medical corpsman locked my harness and asked me to touch a certain switch, I could not reach it. I was at least 2 inches away. I was squirming in my seat, sliding back and forth to loosen myself from the harnesses. The corpsman and a flight surgeon observed silently. They could see I was struggling and sweating.

Miraculously, just before the corpsman gave up, I pulled a "Houdini." Somehow, between squirming and struggling in my seat, I came up with an extra 2 inches in reach and touched the wooden switch. The doctor signed my "up chit" and I ran out of the NAMI building as fast as I could.

I had a few weeks off after training so I frequented the area's pristine white beaches and nightlife. The legendary Trader Jon's was an old, run-down warehouse in downtown Pensacola. Martin Weismann, its owner, had turned it into an aviators' bar. On its walls were memorabilia and pictures of a who's who in naval aviation going back decades. Photographs of aces, astronauts, senators, and various naval aviators (now admirals and generals) hung from its ceilings and walls. The bar was a fire hazard, but nobody cared: the beer was cheap and the music raunchy. Hardly any women frequented the bar in the late 1980s when I was there, although the Blue Angels, based in Pensacola, had made the place their off-duty hangout. (Weismann once asked me to mail him a picture of me and the airplane that I would fly. I never did, knowing that some drunken patrons would laugh and tear it down.)

An F-14 guarded the front entrance of the nearby Naval Aviation Museum. A U.S. Navy A-1 Skyraider sat on the floor with its wings folded. I wandered through, admiring the planes I had only seen in books and on film. But among the grounded war birds a tiny plane suspended from the ceiling caught my eyes. Freshly painted, it had the familiar red and yellow VNAF insignia on its fuselage and the flag of the Republic of Vietnam on its rudder. The plane was VNAF Maj. Bung Ly's observation plane that had landed on the USS *Midway* during the fall of Saigon. A relic from my father's military service had found its way into my branch's museum.

I left and went for a drive along the beach. The sense of karma was overpowering. The VNAF will fly again!

About a fourth of the students opted for primary flight training in Corpus Christi, and I was one of them. I wanted to visit as many states in the nation as I could. (I also acted on the rumor that the Corpus-based flight instructors there were more relaxed; some were called "Santas" for doling out plenty of good evaluations, which meant it was easier to get jet-flight grades.) On the other hand, "Corpus" had its share of high winds that made crosswind landings for new pilots more challenging.

After a short T-34 ground school I was ready for my first flight in February 1989. There was a backlog of students, meaning a month's wait, so two other students and I set out for Mardi Gras in New Orleans. We drove straight from Texas and stayed with some female friends who were attending Tulane University.

After a few days of intoxication, I called the squadron duty officer to check on the duty schedule. "Lieutenant Pham, you are scheduled for 8 a.m. tomorrow for FAM-0 with Captain Close, flight three." I almost shit in my pants. "Ensign Smith, are you sure. Pham. P.H.A.M. Is this a joke? I'm not supposed to start for another month. I'm in New Orleans."

He didn't even pause.

"Then I'd get your ass in that car and start driving now."

The three of us frantically packed our bags. We took turns driving through an ice storm in eastern Texas. I spun out a couple of times so Rob, an ensign from Pennsylvania, took control of his Ford. "You California idiot. Don't you know how to drive in bad weather?" I just laid in the backseat and went to sleep trying to eliminate a monumental hangover from the Big Easy's finest "Hurricanes."

We three arrived back in Corpus Christi after midnight, and my first meeting with Captain Close (my primary flight instructor) was at 7 a.m. I woke up at 4 a.m. and went over the syllabus. FAM-0 involved a forty-five-minute briefing on the ground and a walk around the T-34. Close was to quiz me on systems knowledge and basic procedures. Flight school preparation meant memorization of statistics and flight procedures learned by rote. Students used three-by-five index cards to study—just like in college. I hadn't even prepared mine.

(I found Captain Close's picture hanging on the hangar wall. "Instructor Pilot of the Year, 1988. Captain Guy M. Close, USMC." Captain Close looked like a badass. Marines don't smile in their official photographs until they make general. He had two rows of ribbons consisting of an Air Medal, a Navy Achievement Medal, and decorations from a deployment to Beirut. One thought went through my fevered brain: "You are fucked, Lieutenant Pham. A 'down' in FAM-0, unheard of for a Marine flight student.")

If a student flunked an oral or written test, executed an unsafe procedure, or flew poorly, he would get a "down." Three downs and you were sent packing to find another military occupation specialty. Most flight students got at least one down during flight school, but I certainly could not afford one on my first event.

I walked into the ready room right before 7 a.m. There were two other instructors and Captain Close. No other student was there. "Hey, look who is here. Lieutenant Pham is showing up for . . . FAM-0. Pham for FAM," Captain Close joked as he extended his hand.

"Hey, you look tired. Where have you been?" he asked.

"Sir, we were in New Orleans and we just got back. I wasn't supposed to . . ."

"You guys drove back from Mardi Gras in this weather?" The other instructors broke into laughter. The ice storm had stopped, but light rain was falling that morning and the temperature dipped below forty degrees. "OK, let's get started, Pham. Tell me how to do a 'level speed change.' " I hadn't had the slightest clue about that maneuver. "What's the maximum airspeed of the T-34?" he continued. Silence. I was preparing to get a "ready-room down."

Close also decided he had enough. He started laughing and said, "Let's go get some breakfast. The scheduler made a mistake." I took a deep breath and followed him to the snack bar. I noticed that no one else was in the squadron area, the bad weather canceling the entire flight schedule. The joke was on me.

Three weeks later, I officially began my primary flight training. My goal was to fly F/A-18 Hornet or AV-8 Harrier jets, so I had to qualify for that kind of plane. Helicopters were second, and the C-130, my father's last assigned plane in 1975, was dead last for me. Each flight maneuver was graded as below average, average, and above average. Unsafe performance or poor "headwork" (in-flight decision making) led to a "down." To fly jets, a student needed at least thirty or so net "aboves" or a minimum grade of 3.045. The jokes were that forty "aboves" meant a good chance of getting jets; fifty resulted in a very good chance, and those with seventy or more would automatically become astronauts.

My first flight in the T-34 with Captain Close was close to perfect. He had allowed me to fly in the backseat while he flew a maintenance hop (a freebie exposure). He was thorough with his briefing and asked many questions. He then bought me lunch before we took off (I actually thought he wanted me to get sick and throw up). He turned out to be an extremely patient flight instructor and a great pilot. I was very comfortable in the cockpit and handled the radio calls without much difficulty. The flying itself was not demanding.

I came to believe that all students would graduate from flight school if they were provided extra training the way private students were who paid for lessons. In naval flight training, students had to achieve a certain proficiency within a limited number of flights. The challenges came in handling emergencies, such as simulated engine fire, engine failure, or "chip light" (ferrous material in the oil pan possibly indicating imminent engine or transmission failure). The students were judged on their "monkey" skills, keeping altitude, airspeed, and directional heading, and how they performed emergency procedures under stress. After two flights I had earned four "aboves," well on my way to achieving my goal of earning a ten for the familiarization (basic flying and landing) portion of the syllabus.

On May 2, 1989, I took off on my first solo flight in a T-34 over Corpus Christi Bay. Scattered clouds covered the southern Texas skies. I couldn't actually believe I was piloting a military aircraft by myself. I zoomed back and forth along the coastline before making five touch-and-go landings at an auxiliary field.

The local nightlife had a variety of venues, from country music–only bars to open-air gatherings near downtown, a fifteen-minute drive from the base. The first time I went to a country music bar with my buddies from Texas A&M University was actually fun.

I managed to strike out two weeks in a row in getting a girl to dance the two-step with me. I didn't own any cowboy boots or hats, nor did I wear a huge silver belt buckle, the outfits worn by many locals. But I didn't care. Finally a young lady said "Yes." A minute later I managed to step on her feet and knock her to the floor. *Marine Lt. "Q" wasn't quite as smooth as his VNAF father Lt. Crazy Hoa.* Hank Williams's voice will always remind me of my days in Texas:

> There's a tear in my beer
> 'cause I'm cryin' for you, dear

Another time a group of us were drinking outdoors and listening to a live rock band at Elizabeth's in downtown Corpus Christi. Commander Phil Sims, a reserve Navy pilot and laid-off Eastern Airlines first officer, was in town to do his drills as a flight instructor. As a reservist, Smith was definitely more laid-back than his active-duty counterparts. He bought students drinks and prophesied about his uncertain flying career. I'll never forget his smile and his sunburned red head as he raised a toast to me, "Long live the South. May the South rise again . . . South Vietnam!"

Growing up in California, the ultimate melting pot, I had heard many generalizations about the South. A relative repeatedly warned me before I departed for Quantico, "Don't go anywhere by yourself at night. The East Coast and the South are not like here. They don't like foreigners." Another colleague cryptically wondered, "Don't they still lynch people down there?" During my two years of living and training in Virginia, Florida, and Texas (and on my visits to Alabama, Georgia, and Louisiana), luckily, I never encountered anything to support those stereotypes, on base or off. Despite the good intentions of my California clan, I learned to judge people and regions myself, at firsthand if possible.

After some basic instrument training in the simulator and two additional flights, I was qualified to do acrobatic maneuvers. I could not help but be impressed with the training syllabus that in less than three months took a student with one hour in a Cessna to one qualified to fly basic dog fight maneuvers.

I flew with several female Navy pilots (Marines didn't have any until 1995) who were as good, if not better, than their male counterparts. A good-looking female flight instructor teased me in front of several male colleagues with, "So Q., I heard that you've got a good stick." I didn't know what to say so I kept quiet.

She was not in my flight, but I knew of her reputation as a Jekyll and Hyde: she could flip and turn into a nasty screamer once airborne. And I didn't need to show her my "stick." I could see her trying to fit in with the boys, flying and talking tough. I empathized with that.

I completed primary flight training in July 1989, with a jet grade slightly above the minimum and, miraculously, zero "downs." Captain Close had prepared me well. He used to tell me in the cockpit, "Quang, when you're flying a Hornet in California, don't forget us CH-46 bubbas in New River [in North Carolina]." That motivated me, and like Doug Hamlin, Close would serve as a mentor to me throughout my Marine career.

I did not get my first choice of jets. Due to the "needs of the service," our entire class in Corpus, consisting of Navy, Marines, and Coast Guard personnel, received helicopter assignments that week. Confident of my abilities, I wrote a letter to the commanding officer requesting a "pipeline" change to jets. He promptly denied my overture.

(I returned to Pensacola and completed another six months of training in the H-57 Jet Ranger helicopter.)

On March 30, 1990, I received my gold naval aviator wings and orders to California, along with my buddies Joe Heneghan and Keith Scholfield, formerly from Orange County. My assignment was to fly the CH-46 Sea Knight, also known as the "Mighty Battle Phrogs." I would not be "killing" or "shooting" anyone except in self-defense: the CH-46's mission was to ferry cargo and troops. The jet guys called us "trash haulers"—at least until they had to be medevaced or rescued.

A week later, I reported to Marine Helicopter Training Squadron 301 in Tustin, California, for basic training with the CH-46 helicopter before reporting to my regular squadron. The giant wooden hangar, once used to house World War II blimps, looked empty. A few CH-46s Sea Knight helicopters circled overhead, their pilots attempting a few more practice landings before the airfield closed. My heart was pounding. I had waited for more than two years to get to the mystical Fleet Marine Force (FMF). I got out of my car and tugged on my trousers, making sure I looked sharp. I wanted to make a good first impression and was ready to stand duty in case the squadron scheduled me that first weekend. I had heard of an unofficial rule in the military. *Give it to the FNG (Fucking New Guy).*

A tall, young-looking captain wearing a hydraulic fluid-stained flight suit walked out of the ready room. Gripping my orders with my left hand, I came to attention and saluted him as he walked by. He looked at me as if I had just come from Mars. He had a sympathetic grin on his face, then put out his hand. "I'm Drew. Call me Junior. Check in on Monday. Let's go to the club!"

Welcome to the Fleet Marine Force Lieutenant Q. Pham. Relax!

I could not have been more fortunate. I figured I could tolerate helicopters, as long as I was stationed in California. As a single guy, having Huntington Beach, Laguna Beach, and Newport Beach nearby almost guaranteed a social life.

My focus on flying helicopters wasn't as sharp as flying the T-34, and my performance showed it. My grades were average; I was just getting by. At that time, I saw no thrill in flying the CH-46, and knowing that some 5,000 U.S. helicopters had been shot down in Vietnam didn't help matters. (Nothing could be worse than a lackadaisical attitude confronted by an asshole.)

On my sixth flight in the CH-46, I encountered trouble for the first time in my short military career. My instructor was Capt. Kevin Cash, who had a thick moustache and was married to the daughter of a retired general. He had good flight credentials, and hung out with his favorite students. But I was not among them. Captain Cash would not call me by my name or rank. "Phlegm, Flam, that's your new call sign." One of my peers, a son of a retired colonel, was one of his favorites, and he added fuel to the fire by suggesting I be called "Donger" (the Asian exchange student character in the movie *Sixteen Candles*) or better yet, the "Khe Sanh bomber." I just ignored Cash, hoping the call sign would not stick. In two months, I would be on my way to my deploying unit anyway.

After a laborious premission briefing, Cash and I took off and flew down the beach toward Camp Pendleton. He threw emergency after emergency at me, cursing and screaming. "What the fuck are you doing, Phlegm? Watch the airspeed! Jesus Christ, I've got the controls." The abuse went on for ninety minutes, from takeoff to landing. There was a crew chief in the back, a senior corporal, who said nothing.

I had never been treated so badly. In flight school, I had flown with instructors with the worst reputation as "screamers," but Cash easily outdid them. I didn't think I had flown poorly; I was definitely prepared. I was soaked in sweat but kept my cool. We flew back to Tustin and he quickly left the helicopter.

"Sir, that was the worst treatment I have ever seen in my career," the crew chief told me as I angrily grabbed my helmet bag and jumped off the helicopter. I sensed a reprieve; someone had witnessed the atrocious verbal abuse. I also felt a bond with the corporal, a connection that existed in multicrew aircraft. There would be no more tears like those I'd shed in OCS. I had become a Marine officer and a qualified naval aviator, so court-martial or not, I was going to confront Cash about his behavior and settle it. Maybe mano a mano.

I could not find him on the flight line so I returned to the ready room to look for him there. I found my training evaluation that he must have quickly written before he bolted from the squadron. (We were supposed to debrief after each flight, but he was nowhere to be found.) I looked over my evaluation. Surprisingly, he gave me no below-average remarks; all averages. But why did he act like an idiot?

When Saddam Hussein's Iraqi forces invaded Kuwait on August 2, 1990, I had no clue where those places were. Half of Tustin base was leaving for the

Persian Gulf, including my buddy Joe Heneghan with his CH-53 squadron. Marine Medium Helicopter Squadron 161, or HMM-161, a CH-46 unit, shipped out within two weeks. Before HMM-161 left Tustin, its CO and the group commander handpicked pilots to fill its roster from other units, including two instructors from HMT-301: John D. ("J.D.") Harrigan and David ("Guido") Giannetta.

Three months had passed since U.S. forces began assembling in the Persian Gulf. No one was certain that war would take place. On base, rumors ranged from "everyone will be going" to "they'll be back after six months." By November, my chances to join Operation Desert Shield units would rise exponentially. I had successfully completed my CH-46 training despite Cash's continual harassment.

A request came down from our parent unit, Marine Aircraft Group 16 (Rear). HMM-161 needed a pilot to replace a captain who had to return home to be with his sick wife. I volunteered for the slot. And it's not that I was thirsty for war, but as a Marine, I felt that if there was going to be a war, then I needed to be there. I wanted to see if I could actually perform in combat, because there was no real test during peacetime. I figured that a combat record would shield me from potential detractors like Captain Cash. My run-in with him had caused me to temporarily doubt myself again, second-guessing my flying abilities. The only way to try myself was in a combat zone.

I didn't think I would be sent. I was so junior that HMM-161 would have had to spend many flight hours to train me once I got into the operational zone. There were so many other more qualified pilots on base. I thought, too, that Cash might pick up the phone or write a letter to keep me out. But I also discovered that in aviation at least, your flying reputation preceded you, not your other officer skills, your appearance, or how you are perceived by others. You may not make colonel but you could get away with being a fat Marine if you were a great pilot. A squadron CO could easily prevent a poor pilot from joining his squadron. He could also jettison a weak performer already in the squadron—or as Marines called it, "shit canning" someone.

I finally got my wish and my orders for Operation Desert Shield. To my surprise, no one else had "put up his hand" to go. I had also violated another military truism: never volunteer for anything.

I spent the next several days getting my immunization shots and writing a will. I gathered my flight gear, packed my belongings, and visited my mother in Los Angeles. She cried as I showed up for the last Vietnamese meal I would have for a while. I never told her that I had volunteered to go overseas.

My father waiting in Saigon to immigrate, 1990. (Author's Collection)

(I would have missed the war had I remained with my peers in my first unit, HMM-166. Incidentally, Cash transferred to HMM-166 and stayed home.) I did my best to assure my mother that I was going to a combat zone with the best military force there was. I was going with the U.S. Marine Corps. She just shook her head, not able to understand my absolute blind faith in the Corps. She confessed that the night we left Saigon, she never would have guessed that her only son would go off to war for this country. Neither had I.

Top: *"Highway of Death," Kuwait City, 1992. (Author's Collection)*
Second from top: Jay Leno visits Marines in Saudi Arabia, Thanksgiving, 1990. *(Author's Collection)*
Bottom: *Kuwait International Airport with my CH-46 crew on final day of the war, 2/27/91. From left to right, pilot Captain John D. Harrigan, Lance Corporal Kennedy (aerial gunner, kneeling), crew chief Lance Corporal Jesse Wills, me, and Sergeant Smith (aerial gunner, kneeling). (Author's Collection)*

CHAPTER 18

PAYBACK

MILITARY BUSES DROVE OUR CONTINGENT OF MARINES from El Toro to Norton Air Force Base, an hour away in Riverside County. I didn't know anyone. At Norton we straggled onto a C-5 Galaxy that would take us to our theater of war. About sixty Marines sat facing backward inside the giant cargo plane, which had only a handful of tiny windows. Flanking me were two sergeants major, both Vietnam veterans heading to a war zone once again. During the long flight, we shared Vietnam stories over the reverberating engine noise and foam-rubber earplugs. After twenty-four hours and stops in Westover, Massachusetts, and Rhein-Main in Frankfurt, Germany, the C-5 landed at Al Jubayl Airfield in Saudi Arabia, 120 miles south of the Kuwaiti border. Adrenaline rushed through my body. I felt as I had when I entered my first varsity basketball game, but the feeling was ten times as strong. Since I had left Tan Son Nhut, I'd never seen this many military aircraft in one place. Row after row of helicopters were parked tightly next to one another: AH-1W Cobra gunships, UH-1N Hueys, CH-53Ds, and CH-53E "Shitters" (they left trails of smoke), and my helo, the CH-46E "Phrogs." Several TWA and Tower Air 747s sat at one end of the runway; fuel trucks were filling C-141 and C-130 cargo planes. Al Jubayl was rocking.

One-fourth of the Corps entire rotary-wing force was in-country and another quarter was aboard ships in the Persian Gulf. Still more were coming from the Second Marine Aircraft Wing in North Carolina. As I left the giant cargo plane, a dry heat blew dust and sand into my face. One of the sergeants major bade me farewell: "Lieutenant, we're not going to lose this one!"

It was mid-November, but the Arabian sun was unforgiving, heating the tarmac to 105 degrees. Two of the HMM-161 junior pilots greeted me at the taxiway as I dragged my bulky flight and sea bags. I had met these guys at the Tustin officers' club, and I was glad they had come out to meet me. Captain Don Buczynski, or "Buzz," eighteen months senior to me, grabbed the heavier bag and smiled. "Welcome to the sandbox, Q.X." Later that night, the other pilot, Capt. Roy Santa Maria, asked me, "Dude, why the fuck did you volunteer to come here?"

"This country has been good to me. I need to pay back my citizenship." It may have sounded corny to some. Not to me. Not to Roy.

The U.S. Army had arrived in Saudi Arabia first, with the 82d Airborne Division jumping into Saudi Arabia just days after Iraq's invasion of Kuwait in early August. HMM-161 was part of the first Marine contingent that followed, and was the first transport helicopter unit to arrive in-theater. Its helicopters had been disassembled and stuffed into C-5s, three per plane. Activated in 1951 during the Korean War, the HMM-161 "Greyhawks" (or "The First") composed the oldest tactical helicopter unit in the Marine Corps. The squadron patch had a winged horse over a three-bladed rotor and the Latin words *Equitatus Caeli* ("Cavalry of the Sky") across its top. Black letters "YR" were painted on the rear pylon of every helicopter. ("Yankee Romeo" was used to identify the squadron.)

When the orders came down for deployment to Saudi Arabia, some squadron pilots were surprised that HMM-161 was the first to go. Two other units at Tustin, HMM-163 and HMM-268, had better in-house reputations and HMM-161 had been the destination for pilots soon to be rotated, or were, for various reasons, undeployable. According to pilots interviewed for this book, it took a lot of effort and last-minute addition of three Marine Aviation Weapons and Tactics instructors and five senior pilots to complete the HMM-161 team.

All twelve HMM-161 helos sported a fresh Earl Scheib desert camouflage paint scheme over their traditional green coats. Like every new guy who ever walked before me, my first squadron became "the best squadron in the Marine Corps." No aviator ever forgets his first squadron, especially if it's a combat outfit.

"Tent City" was only a few hundred feet from the flight line. Marine Corps tent cities looked the same in every war. It didn't matter if it was Vietnam, refugee camps set up by the Corps, or the Persian Gulf. Except I did notice that jungle green did not blend well with the brown desert. I lugged my belongings next to Buzz's cot on the sand floor; every flat surface in the tent was covered with a fine layer of dust. Flight suits, green T-shirts, and clean underwear hung from parachute cords strung together along the insides of our hootch. Some of the pilots had posted photographs of their wives and kids above their cots.

A mosque stood on the southeast corner of our city. Prayers droned from its speakers every few hours, according to Islamic doctrine. In the Vietnam War movies, I remember seeing U.S. troops blaring Jimmy Hendrix or The Doors. In Saudi Arabia, Marines listened to their favorite music on headsets connected to their portable cassette players. Several crew chiefs rigged their portables to the helicopter's communication system and blasted away during flight.

I grabbed several designer-water bottles from the squadron supply (S-4) tent and strolled through my new home away from home. Handwritten cardboard signs pointed to each squadron's living area in the compound, and I passed several rows of tents before I saw the sign for HMM-462, "Dude" Heneghan's CH-53 unit. As I poked my head into one of the tents, a familiar voice hollered. "Q! What the fuck are you doing here?" Joe Heneghan looked as if he had dropped ten pounds. Dirt covered his steel-toed black flight boots. He was wearing a filthy, sweat-salty flight suit with a pistol holster slung across his chest, and a light-brown gas mask cover on his left hip. Like everybody else at Jubayl, he no longer resembled a garrison Marine, with a spit shine and a "high and tight." He was ready for war, sir!

"This place blows, man." Before he'd received his orders, he was living a bachelor's dream in Laguna Beach, his hometown, surfing every weekend: he planned on only playing Marine for a living. As we sweated in the Saudi heat, he gave me a quick lowdown on food: one meal ready to eat (MRE) each day and hot chow for breakfast and dinner; water (drink lots of it); and which of our TBS classmates had made it to Jubayl. Joe was also nice enough to cover the frequently asked stupid new-guy questions.

I met most of the other squadron pilots at chow that night. The XO, call sign "Dawg," was a college football nut and a cool guy. A graduate of Florida State University, "Dawg" would post betting lines every Saturday and accepted wagers against his team. He tried to give me another call sign that night. "Pham, you're now Mongo." Mongo for Mongolian? Or Mongo for Mongoloid? Or for the Alex Karras character in Mel Brooks's *Blazing Saddles*?

The enlisted members of the squadron hung out at night in an area away from "officer country." I also noticed that they worked harder and had longer hours than the pilots. We pilots were the prima donnas who needed crew rest and a good night's sleep so we could fly safely. *Standard operating procedures (SOP)*.

The black enlisted Marines had decided to share one tent, which pissed off one of the more senior white officers. "Those 'dark greens,' they're making it a 'black' thing. We ought to make them move in with others." *Dark* green Marines? I'd been taught there was only one shade of Marine. And that was green.

The next day I checked out my "dry" flight vest with a survival kit and emergency radio, but no life preserver unit. Nearly all of our flying was over desert, so there was no need to add more baggage. We had to leave room on our body for the "chicken plates" or "bullet bouncers," body armor left over from the Vietnam era. The S-4 issued me my personal 9mm Beretta and a box of twenty-five rounds. I stuck it in the standard-issue black holster, strapped it on my hip, and, Shazaam! I was a gunslinger from the east.

I then strolled to the flight line to see the squadron's helos up close. Captain John D. Harrigan, the flight line officer, gave me a quick tour and introduced me to his right-hand man, flight line chief SSgt. Joe Robinson. Several crew chiefs were on duty, working on their respective helos: Sergeant Kelley, Corporal Oakley, and Lance Corporal Wills. They all looked so young but they had a comforting "edge" about them. They had been in-country for three months and they were salty.

I had noticed that the birds had extra electronic countermeasure equipment, "disco lights," on their rear pylons, designed to deflect incoming missiles. Two empty pods, normally loaded with chaff and flares, sat atop fuel stubs on both sides of the helo. The CH-46s had been somewhat improved since the Vietnam War. Beefier engines, tougher rotor heads, higher torque transmissions, off-the-shelf LORAN navigational devices, and makeshift Trimble GPS units essentially separated the Persian Gulf CH-46s from their early years in Vietnam.

Patches on bullet holes from Vietnam were still visible on most every fuselage. It was hard to believe these ancient helos were still flying. Still, the crew chiefs and mechanics worked around the clock to keep 161's fleet in "up" status. When the squadron had first arrived in August, the crew chiefs immediately noticed the fine sand's corrosive effect: the sand ate away the helo's turbine engine compressor blades and leading edges of the rotors. With the help of civilian contractors and technical representatives, the Marines devised a clear tape to cover the blades and filters for the intake manifolds.

It was amazing to watch the young Marines quickly adapt to the harsh fly-ing, living, and working environments (on some days, the temperature rose to over 130 degrees on the flight line). The young ones still went at it, on top of their helos, checking hydraulic fluid gauges on the rotors. Words of wis-dom: "If they're leaking, they've still got fluid in them."

It was obvious by 1990 that the Marine Corps needed to find creative ways of keeping the CH-46s in the air. The assembly line had been closed since the early 1970s, and no replacement model appeared on the horizon as the ven-erable helos surpassed their twenty-fifth anniversary (the first ones had rolled off the line in 1964). After more than $2 billion of research and development, Secretary of Defense Dick Cheney in 1989 tried to cancel the CH-46's re-placement, the V-22 Osprey, a hybrid aircraft that flies at airplane speed but can stop on a dime and land vertically like a helicopter. Today, Marines are still waiting for the Osprey, and still flying the "Phrogs" in the meantime.

The "Phrogs" had been the backbone of the Corps vertical-envelopment tactic, developed by U.S. forces in Korea and then honed by the French in Al-geria. The ability to lift combat Marines over a wide area and bypass the enemy gave commanders the flexibility to employ subordinate units to meet any mission.

Helicopter tactics mastered in Vietnam were not completely transferable to the Persian Gulf. Small-arms fire was the biggest threat to helicopters in Southeast Asia, but in the desert, the defensive tactic of spiraling down from 3,000 feet over an LZ didn't make sense. There was no terrain to hide behind. In the desert, the enemy could hear and see the helos from miles away. That meant pilots had to fly faster and lower, using terrain flight and nap-of-the-earth maneuvers. And we needed to be proficient at flying at night. Marine aircrews had been training for years in the California desert base of Twenty-nine Palms and at Arizona's Yuma ranges, but there were no mountains in the Arabian Peninsula or in Kuwait.

When you're flying in a cockpit with others, the other pilot can either save you or kill you (the crew chief in the back will usually save both asses up front). It didn't matter if I flew with Captain "Brick" or if I flew with a weapons and tactics instructor (WTI), I paid attention to their flying. At first, I did not take anyone's word or reputation for granted. I said something if the other pilot made me nervous or tried to show off by pushing the ancient CH-46 to its performance limit. Aviation is an unforgiving business; one mis-take can result in many deaths, and it doesn't matter if there is a war or if it is peacetime training. Our mission was to safely get from A to B on time, then back to A.

HMM-161 needed all the training it could handle. The squadron had no pilots with combat experience. Only a staff sergeant wore combat aircrew wings, and I could not remember if he had earned them in Lebanon or Vietnam.

Our CO had been with the Marine units off the coast of South Vietnam during the 1975 evacuation, but he didn't fly in that big mission. So it would be on-the-job combat training for just about everyone. On the first day of the war combat time mattered little; our squadron had none.

My first flight in Saudi Arabia was a troop-lift mission inserting Marines into a facility fifty miles north of Jubayl. There were no bodies of water like lakes and streams to be seen anywhere. *Sabkhas* were the most visible features used for navigation. Red markers dominated the maps—tall electrical wires and their stanchions. A huge cement plant that could be seen from miles away was there. Pilots referred to the giant plant as "Oz." A dirty gray haze covered the horizon, and fire and smoke billowed from black pipes marring the scenery. The reason our forces were deployed was made abundantly clear to me in that flight. I could feel it, see it, and smell it: oil, oil, and oil.

For most of December 1990, I flew training missions to increase my combat readiness percentage. Most flights involved one other aircraft. We would do low-level navigation and landings in the desert. I managed to fly one NVG hop bumping my total NVG time to 4.7 hours, hardly close to the twenty-five minimum hours to carry troops while wearing NVGs. At night, flying at 100 feet or below, the stanchions, poor landings, and vertigo became our biggest threats on training runs. Maybe I was destined to be a day-only combat helo pilot. An occasional chow and mail run to the forward areas where the grunts were dug in gave me a hint of the battle that lay ahead.

A host of celebrities visited the Marines during the Thanksgiving and Christmas holidays. The cast from "Major Dad" and Jay Leno were clearly HMM-161's favorites. The "Greyhawks" flew Leno from base to base to visit Marines scattered across the Arabian Peninsula. Arnold Schwarzenegger (President Bush's Physical Fitness Council chairman) sent the Marines weight-lifting sets—and we put them to good use. (Well, OK, I lifted weights twice while in Saudi.)

The celebrities came to see us, but there was no R&R or liberty. We were restricted to the airfield. No babes, no boob books, no booze, and no bullshit. We were focused on the mission at hand. Aircraft spare parts and flight hours were plentiful. There was no doubt in our mission. The United Nations was behind us, and so were the American people.

I had absolute trust in our president and our senior military leaders, especially, all of whom had experienced the debacle of Vietnam: Walter Boomer (a Marine three-star general who led all Marine aviation, infantry, and supporting units and one army brigade), H. Norman Schwarzkopf, and Colin Powell. They had remained in the military despite the difficult years following Vietnam. And the men and women under their command needed their leadership. Desert Storm would be the first time the United States had ever sent an all-volunteer military force into harm's way since before World War II.

However, each night, I noticed that the air force ground crews boarded a truck to leave the airfield. While Marines walked back to Tent City, the airmen headed somewhere else. "Sir, we're staying off-base at barracks with mattresses and air-conditioning," was the response. That blew my mind. (Go Air Force. Aim high. Sleep nice and cool.)

The January 17 deadline for Saddam Hussein to withdraw his troops from Kuwait quickly approached. My inbound mail volume increased twofold. Everyone was writing me—my mother, my sisters, the boys in Oxnard, my college buddies, and women to whom my college buddies had passed on my military mailing address. After a month in-country, I began generating form letters because I couldn't keep up with responses. Postage was free, so I mailed dozens of one-page synopses once a week. One thing was certain. Although I had wanted someone to write me love letters, I was damn glad I was single. War is a young man's game, and love during wartime is a liability. There was already enough stress on my mother and my sisters; I didn't need a girlfriend or a spouse to worry about me. I could tell married pilots from aircrew members in my squadron. The former were writing letters late at night to their wives and children.

> If I die in a combat zone
> Box me up and send me home
> Pin my medals on my chest
> Tell my mama that I did my best

When you're twenty-six years old, have no wife and kids, and you're doing what you've been dreaming all your life, death was for the other guy.

On the night of January 16, 1991, Joe stopped by my hootch around 10 p.m. "Q. It's starting tonight. I just overheard our CO." Several of us had thought there would be no shooting: Saddam Hussein would withdraw at the last minute and we'd all go home. I didn't want to take any chances, so I told Buzz and the pilots in my tent what Joe had told me. I had my flak jacket, my helmet, my gas mask, and chemical suit by my side. Ready for anything, I hit the rack.

The air raid siren shrieking through the cold Arabian night sounded like the ones I had heard in Saigon. (Must be the same manufacturer.) I sat up on my rack and looked at my watch. It was 3:00 in the morning. (Fucking A! The war is starting!) I slipped on my flight suit, grabbed my mask and the rest of my gear, and did a 40-yard dash to the bunker in back of our tent. Everyone else was awake and doing the same thing. I took a deep breath and donned my gas mask just outside the bunker. Within two minutes everyone was inside the sandbagged bunker. I heard no explosions.

My mind drifted back to 1973 when I had freaked out in the bunker with my mother and my sisters. I felt helpless back then; I was just a little boy. I just wanted the rocket attack to end. Now the sirens in Saudi Arabia continued whining. Ten minutes went by, then thirty. My bladder was full, but I wasn't about to go outside the bunker. We sat there in the dark peering at one another through gas mask lenses, looking like space aliens holed up in a cave. My breathing got heavy and my lens fogged. The "all clear" order finally sounded over the compound's loudspeakers. We had just survived our first Scud missile attack of the war.

Morning came fast that day. I grabbed a quick shave and headed to the operations area with all my military gear. The message board with all-important announcements was sitting on top of the operations officer's desk. I picked it up and flipped open the binder to the first message:

Z 170001Z JAN 91 ZFF-1
FM USCINCENT
TO ALL DESERT SHIELD FORCES
SUBJ: DESERT STORM MESSAGE TO OUR TROOPS
PLEASE GIVE THIS MESSAGE FROM USCCINCENT WIDEST DISSEM-
INATION POSSIBLE

SOLDIERS, SAILORS, AIRMEN, AND MARINES OF THE UNITED STATES
CENTRAL COMMAND. THIS MORNING AT 0300C WE LAUNCHED OP-
ERATION DESERT STORM, AN OFFENSIVE OPERATION THAT WILL
ENFORCE UNITED NATIONS RESOLUTIONS THAT IRAQ MUST CEASE
ITS RAPE AND PILLAGE OF ITS WEAKER NEIGHBOR AND WITH-
DRAW ITS FORCES FROM KUWAIT. THE PRESIDENT, THE CONGRESS,
THE AMERICAN PEOPLE AND INDEED THE WORLD STAND UNITED
IN THEIR SUPPORT FOR YOUR ACTIONS. YOU ARE A MEMBER OF THE
MOST POWERFUL FORCE OUR COUNTRY, IN COALITION WITH OUR
ALLIES, HAS EVER ASSEMBLED IN A SINGLE THEATER TO FACE
SUCH AN AGGRESSOR. YOU HAVE TRAINED HARD FOR THIS BATTLE
AND YOU ARE READY. DURING MY VISITS WITH YOU, I HAVE SEEN
IN YOUR EYES A FIRE OF DETERMINATION TO GET THIS JOB DONE
AND DONE QUICKLY SO THAT WE ALL MAY RETURN TO THE
SHORES OF OUR GREAT NATION. MY CONFIDENCE IN YOU IS TOTAL.
OUR CAUSE IS JUST! NOW YOU MUST BE THE THUNDER AND LIGHT-
NING OF DESERT STORM. MAY GOD BE WITH YOU, YOUR LOVED
ONES AT HOME, AND OUR COUNTRY—

H. NORMAN SCHWARZKOPF, COMMANDER IN CHIEF,
U.S. CENTRAL COMMAND.

I made a copy of the message to keep for myself. I still couldn't believe the shooting had started. Our six months in the sand had failed to dislodge Saddam Hussein. Now it would be our turn. The I Marine Expeditionary Force would take the lead into Kuwait.

Almost immediately proof of the violence of war visited itself upon us.

A French Jaguar bomber made an emergency landing at Al Jubayl shortly after sunrise. Marines rushed out to the flight line to see the damaged jet. The pilot had limped back to Saudi Arabia after a night bombing mission in Iraq. One of the bomber's tailpipes was damaged. The aviator stood on the tarmac, resplendent in a flowing white scarf and wowed Marine aircrew members as he re-created his harrowing run-in with a guided missile with his hands. The French were with us.

A flight schedule was hastily written, and I made the first cut. Sweat curled down my neck during the preflight briefing. My wet hands, under-neath flight gloves, shook from the cold air, further amplifying the vibrations on the stick. My voice cracked on the radio while I fumbled to turn on the electronic countermeasure equipment in our cockpit. After about fifteen minutes, my initial adrenaline rush leveled off as we reached 130 knots at 100 feet. Our section of two CH-46s had taken off in case we were needed to pick up downed jet pilots near the Saudi Arabia-Kuwait border. We flew for ninety minutes and returned to base without incident. That was my first log-book entry denoting flight time in a combat zone, and it was nothing to write home about.

In Los Angeles, my mother was a nervous wreck, constantly watching CNN for reports of choppers going down. (A dozen or so had already crashed during training missions leading up to the war.) She could not focus on her accounting job. In Saigon, my father was waiting for the paperwork that would allow him to go to the United States. No one had told him that I was in a war.

My mother was afraid the Communists would not permit my father to leave if they knew of my Marine Corps affiliation.

I could not believe it. Sixteen years after the war ended, the Commies still affected our lives. The Vietnam War certainly hadn't ended for my family.

On January 29, 1991, three Iraqi armored divisions attacked the small coastal town of Khafji and held it for thirty-six hours. To untested U.S. troops, and thanks to overblown Pentagon and media assessments, the Iraqi military loomed larger than life.

News quickly filtered down to Jubayl, 100 miles south. Buzz and I convinced ourselves that Iraqi tanks were rolling toward our position. Deterrence would have been minimal all the way to Bahrain.

Fortunately, understrength Marine reconnaissance units fought back. Along with Marine F/A-18s and air force A-10s, Jubayl-based Cobra gunships destroyed many enemy tanks.* One A-10 pilot, however, had mistaken a Marine light armored vehicle for an enemy rig and fired a Maverick missile, instantly killing eleven Marines—and that would not be the last incident from "friendly fire" in the "new technology" war. USAF 11 USMC 0.

In mid-February, Marine helicopter units leapfrogged some 80 miles north closer to the action to Tanajib. HMM-161 parked its helos at the small airport that had also served oil camps of the Arabian-American Oil Company in Saudi Arabia. We were 35 miles from the Kuwaiti border.

---

*Marine Capt. Randy "Spanky" Hammond destroyed twenty Iraqi vehicles of the war, including the first tank.

When the ground war finally arrived on February 24, 1991, I was on the schedule for a test flight. This was also the day of the biggest Marine helicopter lift since the Vietnam War. Over fifty helos from nine squadrons from three different wings including reservists took part in the operation, all without a rehearsal. The goal was to insert a company-sized antitank blocking force to the east of the 1st Marine Division. As the flight lifted off and the dust cloud settled, a CH-46 from HMM-161 remained on the ground, rolled on its side. Luckily no one was hurt. All Marines had safely gotten out and run from the crash site, taking no chances in case the machine gun rounds or the TOW missiles would explode. The helo was being piloted by two of our best pilots, one of them a WTI. News of the downed craft filtered through the squadron.

On the fourth day of the ground war I was posted on the flight schedule. My HAC, J.D., and I grabbed our NVGs, filled up our canteens, and flew with our section leader to Lonesome Dove, an expeditionary base near the "elbow" of Kuwait. We shut down and topped off our gas tanks and waited for our mission. Then the skies above us turned dark, ash sprinkled down on us from above, and oil residue and fine black dust crept into our eyes, our noses, and our ears. The fleeing Iraqis had set the oil fields ablaze.

An hour later we got the call. The 1st Marine Division had reached its final objective, Kuwait International Airport, and a medevac was needed. We immediately took off and radioed our Direct Air Support Center. No Cobra gunships were available to escort us; those guys were still busy killing Iraqi tanks. We were on our own.

In the flight to Kuwait International Airport, the smoke was so thick that the ceiling had dropped to 150 feet with less than a quarter-mile visibility. We dropped to 50 feet, slowing to fifty knots. Giant electrical-power stanchions loomed above us. We bumped up our altitude. Our door gunners were jittery. In the haze and smoke, flashes could be seen on both sides. We couldn't tell if they were vehicle headlights or muzzle flashes in the distance.

After about twenty-five minutes the haze began to clear a bit and there before me was the most magnificent sight I had ever seen. At 100 feet, our CH-46s roared over a column of hundreds of tanks, armored personnel carriers, and supply trucks converging on the airport, still 10 miles ahead. It was like a scene out of *Patton*. Victory was within reach. My helmet visor was down, so J.D. could not see my wet eyes. I was overwhelmed for a moment.

(Why couldn't we have done this in Vietnam?) I was about to enter Kuwait City airspace and experience the "other side" of liberation.

We approached the airport from the south keeping an eye out for any remnants of the Iraqi Army. A forward air controller (FAC) had cleared the LZ. On our second pass over the airport, J.D. shot a steep approach into a taxiway near the base of the tower. I looked over my right shoulder to make sure there was no communications antenna that we might hit. The enemy was nowhere to be found. Barrels of unmanned antiaircraft artillery stared silently at the skies a few hundred feet from our landing spot; their gunners had probably fled north the night before. Loose papers blew along the empty runways, which were pockmarked by coalition force air strikes. The terminal buildings looked as though they had been through an earthquake— collapsed walls, cracked windows, and open roofs.

As J.D. and I began to shut down our CH-46, two filthy men in green camouflage began running from one of the buildings toward our helo. They were too big to be the enemy, plus I recognized the jarhead hairdos.

I looked at J.D. as he took off his helmet. "Who the hell are those guys?" Gas masks and 9mm pistols dangling from their sides, I could see their white teeth and eyeballs peeking out through blackened faces. There lay the difference between aviators and grunts. J.D. and I were wearing our white crew- neck undershirts designed for use with our "charcoal" protective suits. We looked like two skiers about to go on our first run, still clean and fresh.

But these Marines *were* aviators.

J.D. finally chuckled, "Fuckin' Hofley and a 'Shitter' guy!" The Marines were Drew Hofley and Jack McElroy, two captains serving as FACs with the 1st Marine Division. The night before Drew and Jack had earned their com- bat pay. They were directing air strikes to repel an attack on the 1st Division combat operations center with the division commander in it. Cobra gunships directed by Lt. Col. Mike "Spot" Kurth destroyed the Iraqi column. Kurth would win the Navy Cross, the highest personal award given to Marines dur- ing Desert Storm. Captain Ed Ray won the other; McElroy was given the Bronze Star for these actions.

Two more CH-46s from HMM-161 landed a few minutes after we had shut down. "Guido" Giannetta strolled up with a huge grin on his face. Two Hueys soon followed. Everyone was joining the party even though the war wasn't officially over yet. In the distance smoke billowed on the outskirts of Kuwait City, floating toward Basra, in Iraq. The smoky skies had cleared somewhat, yet the haze, the brown Persian Gulf miasma, still covered the late-morning Arabian sun. My section leader took the wounded Marine we'd come for, and I took three Iraqi enemy prisoners of war. I saw their gaunt faces; I looked into their hopeless eyes. They had given up.

We took off for a field hospital in Saudi Arabia, and landed with just drops of fuel remaining in our tanks.

That night the cease-fire took effect. Two days later I flew over the "highway of death," the road leading from Kuwait City to Iraq. A traffic jam of fleeing Iraqi soldiers had been discovered by Marine attack pilots and promptly destroyed. The mile-long column of charred vehicles looked like a junkyard; no human remains could be seen. War was brutal. Kill, overkill, or be killed.

Two weeks later HMM-161 left Saudi Arabia. Our brief war had ended, and it was time to fly home. Our Delta airliner touched down at El Toro after dark; a large crowd awaited us as we left the plane. I saw the face of the one I had missed. Half of her hair had gone gray, she was noticeably thinner, and she looked as if she had aged ten years in just four months. Tears rolled from her eyes. Her husband had been released, and now her only son was coming home from war, alive and well.

God was with our family.

CHAPTER 19

COMING AND GOING

FTER THE LIBERATION OF KUWAIT, THE HOMECOMING parades and the victory celebrations in the United States did not stop for six months. No one had expected the war to end so abruptly or the overrated Iraqi Army to be destroyed by the coalition forces in such a convincing manner. The country had its first major clear-cut victory since 1945. Besides the local revelries, there was a ticker-tape parade in Manhattan and a victory march in Washington, D.C. Yellow ribbons were festooned on trees, outside houses, and on streetlights for months after the war ended.

While returning veterans were relishing the homecoming, many Marines were still abroad, participating in the relief of displaced Kurdish refugees in northern Iraq (Saddam Hussein was already reasserting his rule over his people). And on the way home to bases in Hawaii and California, Marines participated in a humanitarian operation in the Indian Ocean, helping Bangladesh recover from a major tropical cyclone. A Bangladeshi had spotted the amphibious task force off the coast and nicknamed it "angels from the sea," so the effort became known as Operation Sea Angel. Navy and Marine warriors were suddenly transformed into saviors.

For the Corps participants in Desert Storm, the rotation policy had been "first in, first home." What the brass didn't tell us was the second part: "first home, first back out."

The timing of HMM-161's next deployment became a lively topic in the ready room and among spouses of the Marines in our squadron. The destination of our deployment was no secret—a return trip to the Persian Gulf. Marines like to refer to deploying as going on a "cruise," going to "the boat" or "pumping" overseas. That meant a minimum of six months on the high seas, starting in San Diego, then steaming to the Persian Gulf and back, hopefully with a few exotic ports of call along the way.

It's not just another job, it's an adventure. See the world, meet interesting people . . . and kill them.

The U.S. force in readiness or "911 force" was the U.S. Marine Corps, and we had proven this once again. But in the annals of Corps history, Desert Storm had been the exception, an anomaly of force on force, open desert warfare, with unlimited air and armor unleashed on an unconcealed enemy. As convincing as the outcome in Kuwait was, no one could have guessed then the long-term effects of not going all the way to Baghdad.

But the victory was enough for this nation to finally purge itself of the guilt over the despicable homecoming it had given Vietnam War veterans two decades earlier. In its reception of Desert Storm veterans perhaps our country overcompensated, but as the beneficiary of this gesture, I loved every minute of it. So did Hollywood and the celebrities who had visited the troops in "the sandbox."

And so my Hollywood dreams abandoned long ago were about to finally happen.

Mark Adams had been working as a personal trainer (long before it was chic to have one) in Los Angeles, and one of his clients was a writer on *The Tonight Show*. At that time Jay Leno was subbing for Johnny Carson on Friday nights. During his visit to Saudi Arabia, Leno had literally "jumped" into a picture with me. Soon after, I mailed Mark a copy of that photograph as proof of my only cameo shot with a celebrity. Mark then gave it to his client (along with my home number) who mentioned it to Leno.

A week after I got home, Leno called my apartment. My roommate, Joe Heneghan, answered the phone. (Joe had returned to California at the same time I did, and the two of us immediately rented a pad in Newport Beach, ready to resume our normal lives again.)

"Hello, is this Quang?"

"No, this is Joe, his roommate. Let me get him on the phone."

"Hello Joe, this is Jay Leno from *The Tonight Show*."

"Yeah, right. And I'm John Wayne. Hey, Q, some dude calling himself Jay Leno wants to talk to you."

Leno could not have been any nicer on the phone or in person.

"Hi, Quang. I saw that photo of us together overseas. Welcome home. I'm hosting the show this Friday and would like to have you come down to the [show's] taping. Bring your girlfriend, and I'll have you onstage after my monologue."

I had only been in my squadron for four months but I knew better than to blindly accept that invitation as it was presented. Going on the show by myself, as if I had single-handedly won the war, would have meant never-ending ridicule for the rest of my career. I spoke with Leno and his staff and arranged for eight Marines from HMM-161 to attend the taping in uniform: four officers and four enlisted Marines. No one bothered to check with the brass. *Woops.*

I had a blast. Leno jokingly introduced us to his audience and they cheered. He then showed some pictures taken during his visit, thanked us for our service, and expressed his happiness at our safe return. He treated us with first-class hospitality, and I felt his sincerity behind the jokes and laughs. Sure, it was a superb publicity stunt for Leno, but he had been well on his way to taking over for Carson. He didn't need to do what he did.

(Hollywood is not so bad after all. It's showtime . . . and it's not about Vietnam!)

My fifteen minutes of fame quickly ended and my Marine Corps reality returned like a boomerang. We were given a week off upon returning to the States and then we were back at work, flying our helos over Southern California. We had little time to reflect on our fast and furious war.

I read through our squadron's record. HMM-161 lost no lives during the war, even a crashed helicopter was being shipped to North Carolina to be fixed and would return to flying status as part of another squadron. The Marine Corps could not afford to lose any more CH-46s—there were no replacements on the horizon.

In contrast to the war in Vietnam, where the Corps suffered the highest number of casualties in its history, twenty-three Marines died in combat (out of 121 Americans) in our 100-hour war, Desert Storm. Eighty-one Americans perished in accidents, and twenty-three more were listed as MIA.

In quiet moments, I would recall a briefing from our CO a few weeks before about the impending assault by Marines into Kuwait. Casualties were expected to be high; the ground campaign was expected to last sixty days or more. The Pentagon had ordered thousands of body bags—just in case. My squadron was prepared for mass casualty evacuations from the battlefield. When not ferrying troops or resupplying the grunts, our helicopters were configured to carry twelve canvas stretchers, plus a navy medical corpsman in the back. He would have provided first aid en route to a nuclear, biological, and chemical decontamination area or to the USS *Comfort* and USS *Mercy,* hospital ships stationed in the Persian Gulf.

None of the nightmare scenarios ever materialized.

Still, the public wanted to hear about the fighting from the troops themselves, so many speaking invitations came to the base and to my squadron. I gladly accepted a handful. I gave oral presentations combined with a color slideshow about my experiences in the war to local Rotary Clubs and at company meetings. I told the HMM-161 story as best as I could from the perspective of the secondmost junior pilot in the squadron, one not even privy to the big picture. A month after I got home, the Marine public affairs officer called me about a "unique" community relations event.

The Vietnamese American Community in nearby Little Saigon was requesting a Desert Storm veteran to appear at their annual ceremony to mourn the fall of Saigon. He chuckled. "I told the representative that the Marine Corps would do better than that. I said I will send him one of his own."

"Of course," I said. "Yes."

I pulled my service "A" uniforms out of storage: green polyester jacket and trousers, silver lieutenant bars, rifle and pistol shooting badges, gold aviator wings, and one token red and yellow ribbon awarded to everyone in the military during the Gulf War. That was the National Defense Service Ribbon, or more popularly referred to as the "fire watch ribbon." Personal and unit decorations were still awaiting approval from the brass.

In 1991, Little Saigon was the new official name for a 1-square-mile block of small restaurants and immigrant-owned businesses located in the city of Westminster (such Vietnamese concentrations would later take root in neighboring Garden Grove and Santa Ana). This area catered to the largest Vietnamese population outside Vietnam. Many of its residents had migrated from the refugee camps at Camp Pendleton 70 miles to the south, and others moved there from other parts of California and the rest of the country to be closer to their own, to be connected to their native community. I had no idea I had been living so close to so many old friends of my parents in their immigrant community only twenty minutes from my military base.

Every year since the mid-1980s, residents of Little Saigon gathered for a commemorative ceremony near the April 30 anniversary to remember loved ones and mourn the day they lost South Vietnam in 1975. Flags of the former Republic of Vietnam adorned the stage, hastily constructed in the middle of a shopping center parking lot. Red and yellow balloons swayed with the wind. The crowd swelled to over a thousand; radio and television reporters from local Vietnamese-language stations covered the event. Politicians gave patriotic speeches laced with fervent anticommunist rhetoric, even though only one of the dozen elected officials present that night had actually served in the military. None had been in Vietnam. In my mind, much of it was chickenhawk bullshit, obviously seeking to capitalize on the raw emotions of former refugees for future votes.

Forty-five minutes later, after long-winded speeches, the master of ceremonies, a former VNAF pilot, invited me onto the stage. Two young Vietnamese-American women wearing the traditional *ao dai* silk dresses greeted me with smiles and leis of flowers. I felt as if I were a U.S. Marine landing in Vietnam. *Déjà vu.*

The emcee said a few words in English and Vietnamese and told everyone about my academic and military background. I had not informed him of my father's predicament or about my family. He then asked, "Now that the lieutenant has returned from victory in Desert Storm, is he ready to fight and win back South Vietnam?"

I couldn't believe he asked that question.

With the microphone in my face, I could feel the hush in the audience, made up of mostly Vietnamese Americans. I imagined they wanted to hear a feverish *Da Dao Cong San!* Down with communism!

I temporarily froze, my reaction muted by the unrehearsed rhetorical challenge. I finally replied, "No comment," and stepped off the stage. At that moment, I realized that, just as for me, the war had not ended for many of my fellow refugees.

After my public appearance in Little Saigon, I began to wonder about my father's immigration status. I had not spoken to him directly, as my aunt's house in Saigon did not have a phone. My family was getting mail sent via France from Vietnam. A year earlier, the first group of former prison camp detainees had arrived in the United States under a special program called the Humanitarian Operation, better known as H.O. It had been over three years since my father was released from the prison camps, yet he was "still on the waiting list."

But I didn't realize that my parents had had a falling out and that my angry father never bothered to continue with the necessary paperwork. He could have left Vietnam at least a year earlier than he did. My mother had allegedly written a "dear John" letter to my father that was supposed to be hand-delivered by an aunt in Paris. Somewhere in the family loop communications broke down, accidentally or on purpose, with regard to my mother's feelings about my father. My aunt had torn up the letter and tried to explain to my father, but to no avail.

Just two months after returning from Saudi Arabia, we Marines of HMM-161 were notified that we would be returning to the Persian Gulf in May 1992 as part of the 11th Marine Expeditionary Unit (MEU), capable of conducting special operations. In the Marine Corps, the MEU was considered its crown jewel, the "tip of the spear."

My squadron would spend the next twelve months preparing for its overseas deployment. Our unit had to quickly transition from operating in a desert environment to flying from amphibious ships. We needed hundreds of hours of flight training, especially experience with NVGs, but our CH-46s were tired, their spare parts limited. The CH-46's rotors required intensive inspection for invisible cracks after every ten hours of flight time. The other deploying units had priority, so my squadron did not fly much in the months after the war.

For me, life as a Marine pilot stationed in Southern California in the early 1990s could not have been more perfect.

The Tustin base sat in the middle of Orange County, a bustling suburb with a population of 2.5 million. Booming high technology, tourism (Disneyland), and real estate industries bordered our base, the built-up area inching its way to our front gate and perimeter fences. The locals welcomed the Marines, except for a few residents who lived beneath our noisy flight paths and would call the base duty officer daily to complain.

Orange County was also "Republican country," home to John Wayne, the John Birch Society, and Congressman "B-1" Bob Dornan. It made a perfect fit for the anticommunist residents of Little Saigon.

As the training officer for the squadron, I decided to send myself to POW survival training before I sent the other pilots. I drove down to San Diego for my two-week training at Survival, Evade, Resistance & Escape (SERE) School. SERE staffers trained pilots and aircrew in techniques to avoid capture and to survive imprisonment as a POW. Most of the training took place in a classroom environment on beautiful Coronado Island, but the graduation finale was a three-day survival romp in a mock POW camp located in a mountainous area north of San Diego.

We arrived at the "prison" greeted by singsong Arabic music blasting through loudspeakers. The staff placed sandbags over our heads and forced us to crawl on our knees to our prison cells, a cement area that looked like a dog kennel. A navy chief knelt next to me and whispered a few words in my ears. "You're not an American pilot. What are you doing here?" I was stunned at his command of Vietnamese. I figured he was a Vietnam veteran and had recognized my name. I answered in English, in accordance with the classroom training I had just received. "I am an American."

"No, you are not. You're an impostor!" the chief shrieked, again in my ancient tongue. He pulled me by my elbows, stood me on my feet and pinned me against a corrugated-steel wall. I was slammed against the wall, which swayed as I leaned back on it. It was not rigid, intentionally designed to be flexible and absorb the full effect of a body slam.

My first instinct was to strike back, to pummel the chief, and ... flunk. But students had been warned that flunking out of SERE School meant losing flight status. "Students must resist and not react to training techniques." Simply stated, the staff could beat the crap out of me as much as they wanted, but I could not fight back, or else I would be grounded.

I had figured the chief was merely "training" me how to survive my first interrogation. Then something happened for the first time in my military career.

He slapped me with his open hand at least six times, until stars appeared in my vision. I bit my gums and my mouth was quickly filling with blood. The chief proceeded with his simulated interrogation. "You're a fucking liar. You're not an American pilot. You're an impostor and we're going to kill you."

I still figured he was just doing his job, and after a few more slaps, the chief sent me back to my cubbyhole, my dark prison cell, and I sat there for hours, hunched over a bowl of drinking water and feeling miserable as the temperature began to fall.

I had wanted to get the full training experience so I decided to escape, consistent with the fourth letter in the SERE acronym. Around midnight of our first night in captivity, I poked my head out of my cell to look for a place to run and hide. The gated prison was illuminated with bright spotlights. A watchtower, surrounded by barbed wire, stood in the middle of the camp. Before I could turn my head, two staffers pulled me out of my cell and took me to another part of the camp for additional "training." They laid me on my back and tied me up on a wooden board, securing my ankles and wrists with shackles so that I couldn't wriggle loose. A group of interrogators stood over me, but I could not see their faces as one of them was shining a bright flashlight into my eyes.

One of the men placed a small wet towel over my face. I could still breathe so I guessed the "torture" was just beginning. The men then tilted the end of the board where my head rested until my head was below the level of my feet. The men then asked me questions about my unit and my operating base. I gave them some bogus answers and repeated the textbook robotic reply: "Pham, Quang, first lieutenant, U.S. Marine Corps, 123-45-6789."

Then someone began pouring water into my mouth and nose. I felt like I was drowning. The men allowed me to quickly catch my breath then continued the procedure for what seemed like two or three minutes. More questions were screamed but I could hardly make out the words. My chest tightened as I struggled to free myself. My heart was pounding so hard I felt as if I was going to have a heart attack. I then blurted out "HMM-161, Tustin, California."

The prison guards had "broken" me. My physical limitations had been exceeded by the infamous "waterboard" torture, allegedly invented by the North Vietnamese. The staffers stopped the drill, allowed me to sit upright, unbuckled my ankle and wrist restraints, and escorted me back to my cell. I was soaking wet and cold; and to add insult to insult, I had accidentally kicked over my urine bowl and had to spend the rest of the evening drenched in my own piss.

At the graduation ceremony, the navy chief who spoke Vietnamese came up and shook my hand. "No hard feelings, Lieutenant. I married a Vietnamese woman during the war." He smiled then moved on to congratulate the next student. I left SERE school a few pounds lighter, with a swollen mouth and an incredible fear of being captured by the enemy.

The SERE training was the most physically abusive experience I have ever faced, and that includes OCS, but I thought it had prepared me well to do my job. As I thought of the POWs in the Hanoi Hilton and about my father's twelve years in the prison camps, another thought shook me: "I would not have survived in captivity for as long as they did."

Right after SERE training ended, I drove from San Diego to Twentynine Palms, a vast desert training base near Palm Springs. Our squadron had deployed there to gain NVG experience. There was no better place to do it than in Twentynine Palms or the "Stumps." Marine units from all over the country rotated through the Stumps to conduct combined-armed exercises where they would get live-fire training around the clock.

Under the starry skies and sometime moonless nights, our squadron flew in formations of two, four, and six helicopters, practicing our land navigation techniques, shooting our machine guns, and landing on the dry and dusty desert floor. Green-tinted views became a way of life at night. We never flew anywhere at night without the NVGs on top of our helmets. Flying at night unaided (without NVGs) was frightening, like driving at 100 miles per hour without the ability to see anything on the road. I don't know how the Vietnam-era chopper pilots flew at night in the jungles amid tall mountains and in bad weather. But they did it.

Our CO, Lt. Col. Tom Rollins, or "Tank," simply repeated our mission, "To be in the right [landing] zone, on time." I thought he had brilliantly and succinctly summed up our training objectives.

During a flight to Northern California to resupply a detachment on a training mission, one of our CH-46s crashed into the Pacific off Oxnard. Lance Corporal Johns, a twenty-year-old avionics technician, was killed in the mishap. (Naval aircraft accidents are referred to as mishaps.)

I had run into Johns two weeks earlier in the squadron spaces. He was always helpful in answering my questions about radios and was full of energy. News of the crash was sketchy. The crew had experienced a single engine failure (the CH-46s had two engines and could fly on one if proper emergency procedures were implemented), but continued the flight for a few minutes before the helicopter crashed into the ocean with three crewmen, six passengers, and 2,000 pounds of gear. Everyone who managed to exit from the sinking helicopter was rescued by a navy search-and-rescue helicopter, except Johns who went down to the bottom of the ocean inside the craft.

That would be the second crash in HMM-161 within a year, and both accidents would be blamed on pilot error. The mishaps reminded me of the ever-dangerous nature of my profession. Unlike fighter pilots who had ejection seats to save their butts or who usually killed only themselves when they made fatal mistakes, helicopter pilots who screwed up usually killed many people.

After the crash off Oxnard, the pilot who was the HAC departed the squadron, pending a mishap investigation and a Judge Advocate General (JAG) Manual investigation. The pilot had also been the squadron's legal officer, acting as a military paralegal. As a result of his departure, the XO summoned me to his office and asked me if I would like to move from my training officer job to become the legal officer. I had begun to think about my post–Marine Corps career and one of the options that caught my interest had been law school.

I gladly accepted my new assignment and spent several weeks at the Naval Justice School in San Diego to learn the nuances of my new job. I had no idea how busy I would be (when not flying) the next nine months in coordinating the administrative requirements of various nonjudicial punishment proceedings and more aircraft mishap JAG Manual investigations.

Our squadron kept pressing on with the training syllabus because we needed to be ready. Our training, no matter how dangerous, would continue. I could sense an increase in safety awareness after yet another CH-46 from a sister squadron crashed into the ocean off the coast of Africa. I certainly was extremely aware of my limitations and began nurturing a humble respect for my ancient helicopter. Or as one of my grunt lieutenant friends darkly reminded me, "The '46 is God's machine. That helo has sent more Marines to God than anything else I know."

In April 1992, HMM-161 flew aboard the USS *Tarawa* for the 11th MEU's final evaluation called fleet exercise (FleetEx). The squadron's full complement of aviation assets included six AV-8B Harrier "jump jets," four AH-1W Cobras, four UH-1N Hueys acting as gunships and as command-and-control helos, four CH-53E Super Stallions, and twelve CH-46E Sea Knights. Some of our fellow infantry mates from the 1st Battalion, 4th Marine Regiment (one-four or BLT 1/4) joined, as did our service support component. The MEU was a small army in its own right, with 2,200 Marines equipped to fight a seven-day war without resupply.

I was copiloting the second helicopter in a flight of four CH-46s as we approached the *Tarawa* for landing. The amphibious assault ship/helicopter carrier USS *Tarawa* was nicknamed "Eagle of the Sea" and it spanned the length of three football fields, rose over 20 stories with a flight deck 70 feet above the waterline. It served as a floating airport, barracks to house the combat Marine force, and could also launch surface amphibious assault vehicles (AAVs) from its well deck.

"Proud Eagle, Greyhawk 11 and flight 1 mile initial for the break," our CO radioed the ship's tower. The gray-painted CH-46's were close together in parade formation, within one rotor's arc from each other (25 feet). The four-ship armada was a beautiful sight to see as I prepared the landing checklist.

"Roger, Greyhawk flight. Winds 15 degree starboard at 15 knots. Clear to land spots two, four, five, and six."

The 11th MEU was evaluated on its ability to conduct a set of twenty-seven missions, with six hours from notification to execution—three hours to plan, three hours to rehearse. The staff was critiqued on its mission planning and briefing as well as its execution. The missions ranged from a full-scale war to an *in extremis* hostage rescue to noncombatant evacuations and humanitarian operations.

With the staff from our sister squadrons and higher headquarters acting as evaluators, HMM-161 managed to pass its required milestones, but the feat was not accomplished without another close call. After taking off from the *Tarawa,* a flight of six CH-46s had to rendezvous on a windy night before proceeding to their LZ. The aircrews were wearing NVGs but, somehow, two of the helos nearly collided in the air, further shaking the confidence of some of our pilots, especially the new ones. And me.

Ten days after operating off the Southern California coast, the 11th MEU was declared "mission ready" to deploy. I felt that the squadron had "barely" passed its required readiness tests, although no one would publicly admit to it and neither did I. Unit loyalty was among the most important traits of Marines (sometimes to their detriment).

HMM-161 flew home to Tustin as squadron members finalized their personal plans with their families, updating their wills and enjoying their waning days on land.

A week after our squadron flew off the *Tarawa,* a major sociological event happened in Los Angeles. The Rodney King trial resulted in the acquittal of four Los Angeles Police Department officers. Within hours of the court's decision, the "City of Angels" erupted into riots unseen since the 1960s. Stores were looted, buildings were set afire, and some 10,000 people were arrested. Korean-American liquor store owners (some had fought in Vietnam with the South Korean Marines) brandished sawed-off shotguns and semi-automatic rifles. They stood together on rooftops, vowing to defend their livelihood as looters approached their stores. Fires could be seen for miles as the rioting spread.

National Guardsmen, U.S. Army regulars, and U.S. Marines were mobilized to assist in quelling the riots. For a few days I thought that HMM-161, the most mission-ready transport helicopter squadron on the West Coast, might be summoned to fly resupply or run reconnaissance missions over the city. The thought of flying combat missions over my former college town had never crossed my mind since the day I signed up for the Corps.

Thankfully, our squadron never did receive a call to help, and the riots quieted after several days. Millions of dollars in damage had been done and race relations in Los Angeles had taken a step backward. The rest of the country watched in despair, quietly hoping the melee would not spread to their communities.

Captains Don "Buzz" Buczynski and Roy Santa Maria, the two pilots who welcomed me to Saudi Arabia, had taken on increased responsibilities in HMM-161. Buzz became the CH-46 check pilot and Roy the assistant logistics officer. One of Buzz's assignments was to give recommendations to the CO on the progress of copilots in their training syllabus to become HACs.

After three check flights with other senior pilots in the squadron, I flew a three-hour evaluation flight with Buzz. Upon landing, he debriefed me on my performance.

"Q. Pham. You're not the ace of the base but you're a safe pilot, well qualified to be a HAC in this squadron. Congratulations!"

"Welcome Home Dad." Our family reunion at LAX seventeen years after we left Vietnam, 1992. (Author's Collection)

I was extremely proud to earn my HAC papers. Now, I would be in charge of a multimillion-dollar helicopter. Along with the helo, I would be charged with the safety of a copilot, one or more enlisted crewmen in the back and, at times, a squad of Marine grunts. My turn to lead had arrived.

Two weeks before our scheduled departure date, my family finally received the news we had been awaiting for two decades to receive. My father's immigration paperwork was approved by the Vietnamese government and he would soon be joining my mother in Los Angeles. I could see the fear in my mother's eyes at that prospect. I could sense her nervousness, her body shaking at times when she spoke about my father. She was panicking, unsure about the long-awaited reunion with her husband. He was going to "live" with her, the two of them alone, since my sisters had moved to other cities and I was on my way to a six-month "pleasure" cruise. After all these years she wasn't sure that's what she wanted.

"Weaseling" my way out of the deployment would not be an option for me even though my unique family situation might have allowed me to stay home. Certainly, there were plenty more capable pilots at Tustin to take my spot if I were to decide to spend time with my father. I would have been allowed to join the next deploying squadron six months later. But, I didn't want special treatment; I didn't want to whine. I had to fulfill my destiny. The reunion with my father was going to have to wait at least another six months.

A week later, I drove to Monterey, California, to take part in my roommate Joe Heneghan's wedding to his fiancée Cindy. At the reception, I met the father of one of the bridesmaids who was a retired Navy SEAL captain and a Vietnam veteran. When he learned of my postponed reunion with my father, he became visibly angry. "Those goddamn Marines, don't they have any heart? They should give you some time off to see your father, for Christ's sake."

I didn't need *another* special favor, especially from a stranger, and a sailor. "I'm going to make some calls to San Diego tomorrow."

He kept his word. When I showed up at my squadron for work the next week, the XO summoned me into his office again. "Q, how come you didn't tell us about your father?"

"Sir, I didn't want any distraction. We're leaving in five days, plus I am not sure he will actually be here by then."

"OK, I talked to the CO. Just get your trash aboard the boat and meet us in Pearl Harbor. Go see the S-1 [administration] for orders and airline tickets."

I was elated. The Corps (and the navy) had taken care of me and my $300 American Airlines ticket to Honolulu where the *Tarawa* would be berthed at Pearl Harbor. And they gave me the rest of the week off to boot.

Two days before the USS *Tarawa* was scheduled to sail out of San Diego, my father finally arrived from Vietnam. As hundreds of passengers departed the Air Thai 747, my mother, my sisters, and I huddled near the international terminal at LAX. Mostly Asians, the passengers all looked weary from the eleven-hour trans-Pacific flight. Then, I noticed a thin, gray-haired, and slightly hunched man. He looked much older than the dominating and cocky pilot I had remembered. He appeared lost—an aging man in a strange land. Yet this would be his third time in this country.

The older man looked around, paused, and stared right at my mother, my sisters, and me. A huge smile creased his face and his wrinkled eyes sparkled with joy. The Communists had not broken his spirit. *My father was finally a free man.* We frantically rushed toward him. For the first time in seventeen years, the Pham family was united. We had absolutely no clue of the difficulties that still lay ahead for my father. It took nearly two decades, but apparently, the United States had not forgotten its duty and moral obligation toward its former allies.

CHAPTER 20

FROM THE SEA

DOMINATING THE ROW OF GRAY-HULLED WARSHIPS WAS my new home. I hurried up the gangplank, one bag in each hand, admiring the gigantic vessel towering above me. A "1" was painted on the departure end of its flight deck and on its superstructure (island tower). I dropped the bags at my sides, faced the ship's stern, came to attention, and saluted the national ensign (flag). The boarding procedure was the first in a long list of naval customs and traditions and lingo that jarheads would have to learn.

(Bow is front, stern refers to the rear end of the ship; port is left, starboard means right. Showers must be short. Water is precious and don't drop the soap. A captain in the navy outranks a captain in the Marines. Sailors are squids and so on.)

"Lieutenant Pham requesting permission to come aboard." I sounded off to the duty officer, a navy lieutenant junior grade, the equivalent of a Marine first lieutenant. He smiled and shook my hand. "Glad you made it. We pull out at eight a.m. tomorrow. Liberty is secured at midnight."

I fought my way up several flights of narrow stairs, passing sailors and Marines rushing off the ship for a few hours of precious downtime in Waikiki Beach. Walking through tight corridors crammed with cables and tubes overhead, I entered a section with "Officer Country" inscribed on a wooden board and secured above an oval hatch. My stateroom was located down the hall, one deck beneath the flight deck on the port side of the ship, (under landing spot 4 to be exact).

The *Tarawa* was a mammoth vessel, and for the first few weeks, rookie seagoing Marines like me would get lost finding our way around the ship. Compartments, decks, and frames were categorically numbered but still didn't make sense to me at first. I needed a personal guide but at my pay grade I didn't rate one.

Along with most of the pilots in HMM-161, my three roommates, a Harrier pilot and two Phrog drivers had left for liberty. I stuffed my bags atop a yellow metal locker and lay down on the left top rack, my twin-sized bed with a worn-out mattress to serve me for the next six months. Dozens of officers had slept on this rack since 1976, when the *Tarawa* was commissioned, so I made sure I had clean sheets.

My mind wandered back to the previous week's reunion with my father. He had finally come, then I was gone. He had reached freedom in America; I was off defending freedom (and oil) for America. After all the crying and hugging at the terminal, my father turned to me and asked the question only an aviator father would ask first. "So, Quang, what do you fly?"

"Helicopters, Dad. U.S. Marine CH-46s."

"Helicopters?" He looked in dismay. I later learned that in the VNAF, the best pilots flew A-1 Skyraiders and transports. Pilots with less ability got assigned to OV-1 Bird Dogs and helicopters.

By the look on my father's face as I was driving him from LAX to my mother's apartment forty-five minutes away, I could tell he was overwhelmed. He asked me to slow down, and I was only doing sixty. He had gotten dizzy looking outside as cars, billboards, and the Los Angeles skyline rushed by. At the age of fifty-six, he looked older than he was as he slouched in the back of my Jetta, falling asleep.

My mother did not talk either. She sat in the front passenger seat. Awkwardness filled the car, two separated lovers reunited and a son who could not decide whether to speak English or Vietnamese to his father.

We arrived at my mother's place just before dinnertime. Retreating to her kitchen, my mother cooked a Vietnamese meal later that night. Stewed pork in *nuoc mam, rau muong xao* (fried spinach), vegetable soup, and steamed rice filled our table. I couldn't even recall the last meal we had together as a family. While the meal would be my father's first supper with his family here, I was merely looking forward to stuffing my face. The dinner would be my last Vietnamese home-cooked food for a long time.

My mother stared at my father. He sat on the floor and watched television with his hands and his legs crossed. There was not much talking in the room by anyone. (What the hell were we supposed to do after all this time apart? My family needed a guidebook on family reunions.) My mother motioned me into her bedroom and whispered: "Look at him. He's sitting on the floor the way Communists taught him. He won't sit in a chair like normal people. I am scared, Quang."

(For Christ's sake, Mom. Give him a break. He just got here today!)

I felt like scolding my mother but I figured her babbling was her way of dealing with the uncomfortable situation. In a few weeks, when my sisters would leave, I'd be floating somewhere in the Pacific, and she would be all alone with my father in her apartment. And she was extremely anxious about that prospect.

My youngest sister Thu, not quite twenty, could not speak Vietnamese fluently, so she and my father conversed in English, to my mother's dismay. My two other sisters occasionally chimed in, both looking happy as ever.

My sisters and I slept in the living room for a few days, and my father slept in the second bedroom. In preparation for his arrival, my mother had neatly arranged the room, including a small desk, a chair, and a television. It was clear to everyone that my parents would have separate rooms, for the foreseeable future. I don't know what my father had in his mind but I knew that universal soldierly dream of Mary Jane Rottencrotch (fictional girlfriend) and the Great Homecoming Fantasy were not going to happen!

For the next few days, I drove my father around Los Angeles, helping him buy necessary items for men like aftershave, deodorant, razors, and cognac. We also stopped by a sporting goods store where my father selected an over-sized Wilson tennis racquet and several cans of balls. He tried on some shorts and tennis shoes as I followed him clutching shopping bags full of athletic clothing and sweatpants. He was ready to pick up life where he had left off in 1975.

(Game, set, match. Hoa!)

"Captain Phillips, arriving." Four loud bell gongs over the 1-MC loud-speaker brought me back to the present. Thoughts of my father vanished as I rose from my rack, nearly hitting my head on the overhead (ceiling). The U.S. Navy spoke a strange language, crafted 217 years earlier like the Marine Corps.

Navy Capt. Braden Phillips was the commander of the amphibious task force. He was a member of the 1968 Naval Academy class, which included Oliver North, former secretary of the navy and decorated U.S. Marine James Webb, and Marine Col. Mike Hagee, his counterpart on the *Tarawa*. Colonel

Hagee commanded the 11th MEU and had the title of commander of the landing force. He led all Marines in the task force.*

Phillips and Hagee hadn't crossed paths since their days at Annapolis taking German-language classes together.

The morning after I boarded the *Tarawa,* we were on our way. Marines and sailors stood at attention on the flight deck to pay tribute to our fallen comrades as our ship passed by the USS *Arizona* Memorial. I could not help but feel a deep sense of pride, a sense of camaraderie, standing next to my naval brethren.

During the first few days, getting my "sea legs" was top priority as the *Tarawa* headed for Okinawa in the Western Pacific, where the high seas could get rough in a hurry. During the week we sailed for FleetEx off the California coast, I had felt slightly queasy and had to sneak topside several times for fresh air. Miraculously, I struggled through it and also fought back my longtime fear of drowning. I forced myself to walk to the edge of the flight deck while the *Tarawa* was anchored and looked down at the sea 70 feet below. For me, confronting fear was always better than avoiding another phobia. Once the ship got under way there was no getting off the "boat." Sea-sickness was no excuse.

Before the Persian Gulf War, Marines and sailors stationed on the West Coast deployed to WestPac (Western Pacific) and conducted exercises with our allies in Australia, the Philippines, Japan, South Korea, and Thailand. Their counterparts on the East Coast sailed on Mediterranean (Med) Cruises. After the war with Saddam Hussein's military, deployments became "Gulf-Pac" cruises, combining the Persian Gulf and the Western Pacific. That meant less time spent in Eastern Asia—and, less fun.

As the *Tarawa* and her three sister ships sailed westward, Marine Corps history lessons from OCS and TBS came to light. We passed within miles of the once volcanic island of Iwo Jima. I stood on an upper deck of the *Tarawa* and stared at Mount Suribachi, site of the iconic flag-raising where "uncommon valor was a common virtue."

Within 100 miles of Okinawa, the site of another famous World War II Marine battle, HMM-161 prepared to launch aircraft for Exercise Valiant Usher 92, a simulated assault on the island.

As I sat in the left seat of the third CH-46 in a flight of six preparing to en-

---

*In 2003 General Hagee would become the thirty-third Commandant of the Marine Corps.

gage rotors, the sun rose brilliantly to the stern of the ship. The *Tarawa* was turning into the wind while keeping her point of intended movement (PIM) as far westward as possible. I was still flying as a copilot while awaiting my "cherry" or initial flight as a HAC.

"Tower, say winds." Somebody in the flight queried to make sure the winds were within limit to turn our rotors. Out of limit winds (above thirty knots and more than 30 degrees port or starboard of base recovery course) could cause rotors to droop and strike the helicopters.

"BRC two-nine-zero. Winds at 10 degrees port, twenty-five knots." BRC stood for base recovery course. Since the ship was always moving, a BRC was necessary so pilots could properly align their approaches, and along with the PIM, calculate the approximate location of the ship after a long flight without the ship in sight.

Upon hearing the flight leader's countdown for a simultaneous rotor engagement, I released the rotor brake, along with all the others in my flight. Every little item in our mission checklist had to be in sync. Two rotors resembling giant eggbeaters slowly whirled above me like Hula hoops, slightly flapping in the wind then spooling up to full speed. Loud rotor thump and steady vibrations shook the helicopter on its three wheels, bouncing it up and down on its hydraulic shocks.

Lines of grunts briskly walked toward the helicopters, the tips of their M16s covered with red blank-firing attachments. This was not a live-fire exercise, just a heliborne raid. Flight deck crews in colored vests crisscrossed the busy flight deck: brown (plane captain), green (landing signal enlisted, or LSE), purple (fuel), red (crash and ordnance), yellow (aircraft handlers), and white (medical personnel and visitors).

"Proud Eagle, Greyhawk 14 and flight for takeoff. Dash 1, 2+00 [of fuel], 16 souls aboard. Dash 2, 2+00, 17 souls. Dash 3 . . . ." The calls rippled through the radio waves.

"Winds at fifteen degrees port, twenty knots. Greyhawk flight cleared for takeoff."

I finished the takeoff checklist and placed my right hand on the power management system (PMS) switch, ready to turn it off in case our helicopter lost an engine. That was second nature for CH-46 pilots. Turning off the PMS enabled the good engine to obtain maximum power to resume level flight. The possibility of losing an engine on takeoff, with a full load of grunts, and fuel, made this a very dangerous part of the flight.

With a heavy load in the back, sometimes the CH-46 would temporarily "sink" below the flight deck as it flew out over the ocean and lost its lift over the flight deck.

After seeing the takeoff hand signals from the LSE, my HAC slid left, picked up airspeed, and followed Dash 2, the second helo in the flight, which had taken off fifteen seconds earlier from the spot in front of us. Soon, the entire flight rendezvoused at 300 feet and eighty knots on the starboard side of the *Tarawa*.

Two Cobras and two Hueys flew in the overhead delta (holding pattern). Their pilots were among a select group of fliers from Light Attack Squadron 367 based at Camp Pendleton, nicknamed "Scarface."

Two CH-53s had been circling a few miles away. The Shitters always took off first since they carried the most fuel, flew the fastest, and, most important, carried the most weight, including the 105mm howitzers. The helos came from Heavy Helicopter Squadron 466, or "Wolfpack," based at Tustin like HMM-161.

As the last CH-46 was taking off, the flight deck crew towed two AV-8 Harriers (from Attack Squadron 211 known as the "Wake Island Avengers," based in Yuma, Arizona) into their takeoff spots at the 300-foot line on the flight deck, their pilots ready to launch to join the helo flight for the insert into Okinawa.* At full throttle and without external fuel tanks or aerial refueling, Harriers often had an endurance of less than one hour. Thus they took off last and landed first.

The two Harriers roared off the *Tarawa* and screamed toward Okinawa to simulate an attack on the LZ ahead of the assault force's arrival. Two Cobras sped ahead of the six CH-46s and one Huey flew the mission commander while the other acted as a gunship. The CH-53s carried whatever the CH-46s couldn't.

Upon reaching a predetermined checkpoint, the flight leader called out a code word over the radio. My adrenaline was pumping through my veins. Flying in a big formation was a thrill unmatched in any other helicopter training, something I hadn't done much Stateside or during the war.

I turned to my right, flipped up my tinted sun visors, and looked back into the cabin. Our crew chief stood over the machine gun on the right side, while

---

*The Harrier is a fixed-wing attack jet that can take off and land vertically. It was originally designed and first used by British forces.

another crewman manned a similar gun on the left. Two rows of six green-and-black-camouflaged young Marines sat on red canvas seats, the white of their eyes staring at each other across the aisle. I guessed none of them was more than twenty, except for the sergeant.

One of the grunts smiled at me and gave me the thumbs-up sign. I returned his gesture and flashed him five fingers, signaling five minutes from the LZ. He looked motivated; grunts enjoyed flying in the back of helicopters, even though many of them have heard horror "sea stories" of heavily weighed-down Marines drowning, trapped in the back of fast-sinking helos. For CH-46 pilots, we had escape hatches located right next to our seats. Our crew chiefs could egress through their side openings. *The grunts were screwed.*

The flight slowed down to 100 knots at the initial point (IP). I reset the stopwatch on the dashboard. From the IP it would be less than three minutes to the LZ, a large clearing in the Northern Training Area on Okinawa.

The Cobra flight leader cleared the zone for landing. Six gray CH-46s landed 60 feet from each other, their rear ramps lowered to the ground. Grunts sprinted out the back of the helos, most likely screaming "Oohraahh" and "Get some!" They lay on the ground in the prone position with their M16s at the ready and formed a half-circle perimeter facing toward the area of anticipated enemy contact. They had been instructed to make sure they had been well cleared of the helos in case one had to land again. No one wanted the wheels of a twelve-ton helicopter on his back.

"You've got the controls, Q." My HAC relinquished the flight controls and allowed me to fly back to the ship. Helicopter pilots traded off flying; the HAC always made the decision to fly certain parts of the mission. My HAC raised the rear ramp, signaling to the flight leader's crew chief that we were ready for takeoff. Two clicks chimed over the radio, a signal that the last aircraft was ready to depart the LZ, its ramp's status not easily seen. The flight lifted off and safely flew back to the *Tarawa*. In a few hours we would return to the same LZ to pick up the grunts, ready for a ride back to the boat for a hot shower and greasy chow.

After leaving Okinawa, the *Tarawa* ARG sailed to Hong Kong for three days of liberty. A year earlier, the navy would have pulled into Subic Bay in the Philippines ("the P.I.") and emptied its ships of wound-up, horny Marines and sailors into the raunchy neighborhoods of Olangapo City. I had seen bawdy homemade movies shot by pilots during their R&R in the P.I. As in

Vietnam, there were thousands of unclaimed Amerasians there waiting for their fathers to return.

It didn't matter anyway. Earlier in 1992 the Filipino government decided to kick the U.S. military out of its country. Many had missed visiting the P.I., where $10 would get a young American a full night of pleasure, his laundry cleaned, plus a neck massage in the morning, but I would have taken a pass. I was not the "virtuous officer." I just decided to have fun by other means. I rebuked no one for their behavior. (What happens overseas stays overseas . . . until the divorce proceeding.)

The leg from Hong Kong to Singapore created some excitement for our Harrier pilots, especially through the Straits of Formosa. Tensions between China and Taiwan were high; Chinese-made Silkworm missiles posed a credible threat to the four-ship ARG. Two fully loaded Harriers were placed on five-minute alert with pilots in their seats. They took off once to intercept a simulated "Bear attack" flown by a U.S. Navy P-3 antisubmarine aircraft training nearby. (Bear was the code name for a Soviet-made long-range bomber that often shadowed U.S. Navy ships.)

En route to Singapore, someone announced that the *Tarawa* was 100 miles off the coast at Hue City in central Vietnam. It was nighttime, just after evening chow. I left my stateroom and climbed the stairs to three decks above the flight deck. There was no flying, so the flight deck was quiet. Only the watch officer and several Marines were there, checking the chains and tie-downs on the Harriers and helos. (A plane or helicopter blown into the ocean was a big no-no, second only to a man overboard.)

Ocean breezes cooled the sticky air. I stood next to thick chain railings, bracing myself as the giant 40,000-ton ship pitched and rolled in the dark seas sprinkled with white foam. A mile-long wake trailed the *Tarawa,* the ocean churned by its twin screws moving the ship along at twenty-two knots. A quarter-moon rose halfway up the horizon, casting a bright streak across the ocean. I glanced at the dark vastness, to the starboard side, but saw nothing. In the distance was my birthplace, so close yet so far away.

I didn't realize until much later that I wasn't the first Vietnamese to board the mighty *Tarawa.* In 1979, during the *Tarawa's* first WestPac deployment, its crew had rescued 400 Vietnamese drifting at sea in fishing boats and brought them to safety.

A Vietnam veteran once told me of a South China Sea superstition. Travelers would hear faint cries for help, voices of drowning boat people. Offerings and incense were thrown into the sea to honor the dead. I heard no such cries that night and I had nothing to throw into the sea. I had seen the hallowed grounds of the U.S. Marine Corps, the islands of valor in the South Pacific. Now I had traversed sacred waters, where some 300,000 of my fellow South Vietnamese had lost their lives trying to reach freedom in the years following the fall of Saigon.

I could feel a lump in my throat and tightness in my chest, but I could no longer shed a tear. I was a U.S. Marine, deployed at sea, merely sailing by my past and steaming toward my future. But I still wanted to pray for the dead. I finally went below.

While traveling between ports of call life on a navy ship was memorable. While sailors worked around the clock and aircraft mechanics turned wrenches through the night, some Marines got to work out, train on fast ropes, dry-fire weapons, and sleep. One officer even joked that "if you sleep twelve hours a day, the cruise would only be three months." Pilots laughed about their respite (MORP, for Marine officer rest period). Then there was chow, four times a day, as much as you could eat.

Junior Marines and sailors took turns working the officers' mess and doing our laundry. At first, I was not comfortable with the service so I decided to do my own late at night. Letting someone else wash my dirty clothes and flight suits was not the way I was taught but I had to live by the navy's way. *It's their ship!*

Fortunately for its "guests," the *Tarawa* did not have a stale odor like the other ships I've been on. It was by far the cleanest ship I've ever seen, its quarterdeck always shiny, its brass polished. Sailors chipped paint, mopped floors, swabbed decks, and stood watch. Besides the harmless and tireless jokes about the navy, I quickly grew to admire the "black shoes," a fond reference to those sailors who worked on ships for a living. But I saw theirs as a life of endless, confined toil. I could never be a sailor.

While in port in Singapore, I was promoted to captain along with six other peers. In a squadron full of lieutenants, the promotion meant I would not be too busy assigned duty as integrity watch officer while the ship was in port. I had ten new guys in tow, and half had families back home, so I wouldn't expect too much trouble from them. In addition to keeping an eye on my flock, another damper on my liberty plans was the ongoing investigation of the 1991 annual Tailhook Convention in Las Vegas, where drunken navy and Marine pilots had groped young female attendees.

(I had to coordinate with the MEU's JAG to schedule sexual harassment and "sensitivity" training. All pilots on the ship were asked whether they had attended Tailhook. I hadn't gone but I had been invited to attend as a guest of fighter pilot friends.)

After a month under way, I wrote my father to update him on our deployment and I got a letter back from him three weeks later.

Van Nuys, Calif., 7/22/92
Hi Quang,

Your mother and Thu are getting ready to send you letters and gifts. I want to drop you a few quick lines to say hello. Last week I went to San Jose and ran into many VNAF friends. There was a big reunion.

My friend Bao took care of me and helped me get my driver's license. Thu moved home from college for the summer, so I will not be alone while your mother is at work. I am waiting to hear back from a potential employer. I am hopeful that I will get the job.

I ran into former VNAF commander, Brigadier General Minh. He knows about your Kuwait Liberation Medal. If I don't brag nobody will know. Hope you enjoy your tour and see you soon.

Your Dad Hoa.

It sounded to me as if my father was adapting to his new life rather well, until I got letters from my mother indicating otherwise. She wrote to complain about my father's weekend bachelor-like escapades with his friends in Little Saigon. I felt helpless, floating on the open sea 12,000 miles away. I was glad my sister Thu was home for the summer to help bridge the gap between my parents as well as to spend some time with my father.

My mental distractions evaporated the moment the *Tarawa* entered a severe tempest in the Indian Ocean. Flight operations were canceled for three days. The giant ship was tossed in the ocean like a small leaf tumbling down a whitewater river. Marines walking in the corridors leaned forward and backward, struggling to brace themselves as the ship rolled and pitched. Inside the officers' mess, paper cups and plates flew off the dining table, spilling their contents all over the deck. In the ready room, a large television broke loose from its straps and nearly landed on one of the pilots sitting in the front row of leather chairs.

Between squalls flight deck personnel performed maintenance, since HMM-161 was expected to fly as soon as we reached the Persian Gulf. One morning, the ship ran into a powerful storm cell that could have easily blown people and aircraft (and our helos) overboard. My friend Roy was standing watch and he immediately sounded the storm alarm and cleared the flight deck. Fortunately everyone ran to safety in time thanks to Roy.

When the ship cleared the squall damage was glaringly visible. One of the CH-46s had not been properly secured, its rotors not being tied down. As a result, the rotor blades had rotated and flapped in the wind, striking the aft fuselage, causing significant damage to the helo, its blades, and transmission. Metal-shop mechanics fixed the fuselage damage; all other parts had to be replaced. Roy would later be blamed for the accident; somebody had to take the hit.

When the *Tarawa* finally reached the top of the Persian Gulf off Kuwait, the helicopter contingent flew into the army post, Camp Doha, erected after the Gulf War to host U.S. military personnel operating in the region. There was a huge parking lot at Doha that had been converted into a helicopter LZ with plenty of room for at least fifty helos. The Harrier detachment flew to Kuwait International Airport where it would fly training missions over the Kuwaiti desert and drop bombs on the Udari Range in northwestern Kuwait.

We were to participate in the joint exercises Operation Eager Mace and Operation Nautical Mantis with Kuwaiti and Saudi Arabian forces. The maneuvers should have been named Hotter than Hell.

It was August and the temperature, coupled with the high humidity from the Persian Gulf, was nearly unbearable. Sand flies and the occasional scorpion would scatter from underneath metal trash cans every time the bins were moved. It became obvious to me why Desert Storm (and the 2003 invasion of Iraq) took place in spring. Heat casualties would have decimated the ranks.

The next day a flight of four CH-46s flew from Doha to Al Jaber Airfield in southern Kuwait. We were to brief and fly a mission with the revamped Kuwaiti Air Force flying French Gazelle and Puma helicopters. Two senior pilots from our squadron were supposed to act as "liaisons" to the Kuwaiti pilots, teaching them briefing techniques, flight maneuvers, and tactics. A joint briefing was conducted between U.S. Marine and Kuwaiti pilots, interweaving English and hand signals over a large map spread across the sandy floor. After thirty minutes, it was clear to every U.S. participant in the briefing that the joint training was not going to be "Marine-perfect."

On the night of August 9, 1992, tragedy again struck HMM-161. A Cobra crashed into the Kuwaiti desert, killing Capt. John "Beav" Beving and 1st Lt. David "Davey" Jones. Both had taken off on an NVG navigational route; their wingmen had mechanical problems and had to cancel.

I flew a recovery crew to the crash site, which had already been visited by a medevac helicopter a few hours after the accident. The hop happened to be my first flight as a HAC. As I circled to land, I could see a black smoke trail about 100 yards long scorched against the dun desert floor and leading to small burned pieces of what once had been a helicopter gunship.

Beav had been a Desert Storm veteran, and Davey was on his first overseas tour. I hardly knew the two fallen aviators but I felt a great sense of loss, just as I had felt for Lance Corporal Johns in the CH-46 crash. Peacetime training missions were killing Marines—just as they have done throughout our history. *Train as you fight.*

After dropping off the recovery crew at Doha, my flight was a routine navigation training mission over the desert floor, interspersed with practice landings in various LZs. The terrain was familiar to me, since I had seen Kuwait from the air fifteen months earlier. The smoke had disappeared, the Iraqi Army defeated. But remnants of the war could still be seen, with the "highway of death" still littered with charred vehicles.

After two weeks ashore, the helicopter party departed Camp Doha and flew back to the *Tarawa* on August 16. The Harriers were scheduled to arrive the next morning before the ARG sailed southward.

Then tragedy struck again; our run of bad luck seemed unbreakable. A Harrier had gone down while on a night training run in Kuwait. Captain Mike "Rip" Vansickle died without attempting to eject. Like Davey, Rip left behind a wife and a young son. The news traveled to the *Tarawa* shortly after I hit the rack. Two CH-46s immediately launched and attempted to find the wreckage on the dark desert floor.

The Harrier crash was the fourth noncombat aviation class "A" mishap in HMM-161 within fifteen months. Eighteen months before Desert Shield, HMM-161 had lost another CH-46 in South Korea during its last WestPac deployment, killing all four Marines aboard. That made a total of five major crashes in four years, making HMM-161 the most accident-prone squadron in the Marine Corps—maybe in the entire U.S. military during that period.

I couldn't come up with a rationale; no one could explain the reasons for the tragedies. Inquiries were begun, hours of interviews and aircraft component engineering investigations were conducted. Except in one of the crashes, all the pilots had been excellent aviators, well experienced and well regarded.

Even so, naval aviation was and has always been an inherently dangerous and unforgiving business.

I sat down and wrote to the families of the deceased Marines and received wrenching letters from Beav's girlfriend and his parents.

Two days later, Marines and sailors stood on the *Tarawa*'s flight deck in a memorial service for the three fallen Marines. Then the ARG pulled into Bahrain, where another major announcement was made in the ready room.

HMM-161's top three officers, the CO, the XO, and the operations officer (OPSO), were relieved of their duties, effective immediately. No reasons were given, but we could figure this out on our own. The high accident rate had been unacceptable; aircraft losses and fatalities too many. The departing officers' replacements would arrive from stateside within ten days; until then the squadron would undergo a mandatory safety stand-down.

Morale bottomed. In the ready room the mood grew somber. We weren't flying. We were stuck in the Persian Gulf and there was nowhere to go, no war to fight, no one to kill except ourselves.

I saw my CO as he was packing his bags to go home. I never saw the XO and OPSO leave the ship. Tank looked devastated, his career finished. I had heard from many Marines that he would someday make general and I didn't doubt it. I saw him lead Marines and flew with him on several occasions; he was even better than his reputation. I felt the squadron had let him down, especially the senior officers on his staff, who should have worked harder to prevent the mishaps. But what did I know? I could only speculate until the information from eventual JAG Manual investigations was released.

In the Corps the leader, the CO, the commander, was always responsible, and Tank took his lumps like a professional, even at the nadir of his career.

As I handed him some last-minute legal paperwork requiring his signature, I managed to mumble, "Sir, I am really sorry about what's happening to you."

Tank looked at me and I thought he was going to break down. But there was no way in hell the salty, likable lieutenant colonel was going to melt. "Don't worry about me, Q. I'm through. You guys still have half a cruise to go, so you better get back at it. I'll be fine."

Listening to Tank at that moment, I had never felt prouder to be a Marine Corps officer. We didn't hug each other or shake hands; he must have felt my respect by the way I looked at him. He grabbed his belongings and left his stateroom; I saw him walk down the gangplank with his head held high.

Two lieutenant colonels and a major joined HMM-161, and the *Tarawa* finally set sail again. The new commanding officer, Lt. Col. John "BOFA" Lemoine, and new operations officer, Maj. Bruce "B.D." Coleman came from HMM-268; the new XO was a Huey pilot from Camp Pendleton. As the ship neared the mouth of the Strait of Hormuz, every pilot in the ready room cheered to the announcement over the 1-MC. We were ready to get out of the "Gulf of Gloom" and the "Desert of Despair" that took the lives of three of our buddies. The *Tarawa* was headed to Perth, Australia, and the 11th MEU was to conduct a joint exercise with the Australian military.

An hour later, I sensed a sharp right turn and had to grab a bulkhead to keep myself from falling over. When an 820-foot ship kicks in right full rudder, you feel it! The ship's captain came back onto the 1-MC and shared the latest news. "Attention, this is the captain. You are probably wondering why we took a right turn. Australia is not that way. [Laughter.] We have received a new mission from CentCom [Central Command]. We are headed for Mogadishu, Somalia."

I had no clue why we were heading to Somalia, although I had read that the U.S. Embassy there had been evacuated just before the Gulf War.

While crawling along the African coast, I received a second letter from my father.

Van Nuys, Calif., 8/30/92
Hi Quang,

Glad to hear from you. Congratulations on your new bars and on becoming aircraft commander. I flew A-1s low-level with no [night vision] goggles over water with only moonlight; the only difference was a lot of nose-up trim.

Last Friday night, Thu, her boyfriend, and I went to dinner at Bob's Big Boy — all you can eat. I felt like I was back in a USAF mess hall. Then we went bowling. Haven't played since 1966. I got 100, Thu 125, and her boyfriend 135. My VNAF buddies say "it's too late for me to start" 'cause I'm seventeen years behind. I try anyway.

It's sure sad when you lose a friend in the same squadron. I lost many of them. I either had to make a speech at the funeral or bring the bad news to their families in class A uniform with black ties. Stood honor guard too.

Haven't played much tennis lately. The U.S. Open's early matches have already started. Both [political] parties' national conventions are over. No one knows until November.

A quarter million people are homeless because of Hurricane Andrew in

Florida. Troops are sent down there for rescue, C-130s are flying all of sort of
supplies, food, and tents. If you're here, you'd probably be down there too.
   Well done Quang . . . I meant "Captain Quang."
   Your Dad, Hoa.

For the first time in my military career, I felt as if my father, the first member in my family, had fully understood what I was going through. He had been there, done that.

The 11th MEU had been assigned to assist with transporting 3,000 UN troops from Pakistan to Somalia to provide security and to protect the famine-relief food supply. HMM-161's CH-53s flew Captain Phillips, Colonel Hagee, and their staffs to Nairobi, Kenya, to meet with U.S. diplomats and military officers in the region.

As flight operations resumed, the mood in the squadron improved. HMM-161 was a deployed Marine squadron with combat experience; with a contingency on the horizon, pilots weren't about to quit in the middle of a deployment. There would be no union-led airline strike or a boycott.

Still, I couldn't get the crashes completely out of my mind.

The newly arrived CO and OPSO had been to Desert Storm with HMM-268, one of the best CH-46 squadrons in the Marine Corps. They rallied the squadron; we pilots rallied ourselves to continue our mission.

The new CO, whose call sign of BOFA stood for "breath of fresh air," allowed me to continue flying as a HAC, which made me feel more confident about my contributions to the squadron. As I expected, given our recent high accident rate, he brought a conservative approach to our routine. In order for two helicopter pilots to fly together, there had to be a minimum of 1,000 total flight hours in the cockpit between the HAC and the copilot. At that time, I had just passed the 700-flight-hour mark, and most of the ten copilots had less than 400. (On some of the missions my helo crew barely met the minimum.)

A Marine wisecrack ran through my mind: "If the minimum wasn't good enough, it wouldn't be the minimum."

With two CH-46s and two Cobras aboard, the USS *Ogden* and the USS *Schenectady* steamed toward Mombasa, Kenya, to support the MEU staff, while the USS *Tarawa* and USS *Fort Fisher* trailed behind. The former U.S. ambassador to Somalia, Robert Oakley, was named special envoy for Somalia and he flew in and out of African countries to coordinate with U.S. personnel in charge of Operation Provide Relief, a food-relief effort flown by C-130s.

The S-2 department (intelligence) briefed the pilots on anticipated threats in Mogadishu, which were minimal in September 1992, a full year before Task Force Ranger would lose sixteen soldiers in a fierce firefight depicted in *Black Hawk Down*. A civil war was taking place in Somalia amid a famine. Warlords ruled Mogadishu; Mohammad Aideed was one clan leader, his son, ironically, being a Marine reservist studying in California. Early daylight flights were preferred because it was believed that the Somalis slept late into the morning, still high from chewing *khat* (or *qat*), leafy amphetamine-laced leaves from a local plant.

A few days after the hard right, the *Tarawa* arrived 25 miles off the Somali coast, remaining beyond the horizon, unseen by Mogadishu inhabitants.

Our first mission was to fly Colonel Hagee, Captain Phillips, their staffs, and UN personnel into Mogadishu. Hagee was scheduled to meet with warlord Aideed, but I didn't know when he would actually do so.

The rules of engagement (ROE) were shaky; we could not mount our machine guns on our side doors because some bureaucrat didn't want Marine helicopters to show a "threatening" profile. Our crew took machine gun rounds on the flight, but it would have been impossible to mount the guns while in flight and fire back at the enemy effectively in time. Each Marine packed a Beretta 9mm pistol and twenty-five rounds. *If the threat was minimal, why are we taking personal weapons and preparing to defend ourselves?*

Two Harriers were being towed into their takeoff positions. Unlike conventional jets that are hurled off aircraft carriers, the Harriers only need a couple hundred feet and no catapult to get airborne. Ordnance personnel had loaded the Harriers with 20mm cannon rounds, cluster bombs, and a pair of MK-82 (500-pound) bombs. The Harriers' job was to escort the CH-46s from high above, yet not cross the Somali coastline. If the CH-46s took hostile fire, the Harriers would roll in as part of a tactical recovery of aircraft and personnel package. And an international incident would have made CNN.

No Cobra helicopters were allowed to escort our flight into Mogadishu; they circled off the coast. *Something didn't smell right.*

As the rotors began to turn, a salty mist splashed the front windows of my CH-46. The scent of the sea and the leaky hydraulic fluid hoses and the oily stench combined to heighten the senses of a combat-ready Marine helicopter crew. There was no other smell like it anywhere except on amphibious ships, in the "gator" navy. The sun rose behind a hazy sky, the horizon obscured by dirty brown clouds with sporadic black smoke rising from the ground.

Colonel Hagee and his staff boarded my helo and I radioed Brick, my section leader, "Dash 2 is set for liftoff."

I maneuvered the CH-46 into a hover and slid to the left, pointing the cyclic slightly down to pick up airspeed. Brick was a quarter-mile ahead, but I didn't need to fly too close to him. The flight would take less than twenty minutes; our directions were crystal clear: Fly a straight line to the southern end of the Mogadishu Airport; do not fly over the built-up area to the south.

Two miles from the coastline, Brick suddenly veered to the left and swung wide of our flight path. He did not make a radio call to me so I proceeded on course and did not follow him. I remained on course as confirmed by my copilot. He double-checked his map coordinates against our GPS heading indicator. The distance between the two helos widened. I had chosen to follow the S-2 briefer and not my section leader, an act that usually led to a nasty postflight debriefing. Plus I didn't want to fly over the small buildings just south of the airport.

Nothing unusual took place. The Harriers remained on our radio channel, circling high overhead. I could not see them but I knew they were just a quick call away from unleashing bombs on any Somalis who threatened us. As I touched down at the Mogadishu airport, I could see what appeared like "technicals" moving slowly on the ground, their guns pointed skyward. "Technicals" were makeshift combat vehicles such as Toyota Land Cruisers, Mercedes trucks, and flatbed pickups with sizable weapons manned by several Somalis. I also saw trucks with "UN" painted on their sides. I instructed my crew chief to keep an eye on one technical, sitting about 200 yards from our helos, its occupants observing our every move. If the technical had started firing, we would have taken hits. The best I could have done was to immediately take off from my position, exposing my helo to more fire.

I was very edgy during the forty-five-minute wait while the colonel was at his meeting. We kept both our CH-46s' engines on line, rotors turning. *Never shut down a helo in the field unless you absolutely have to. There is always a chance you will not be able to restart it.*

Our flight made several round-trips into Mogadishu that day, for over seven hours of flight time, all without incident. When we landed back on the ship both aircrews were summoned to see our CO.

"Who fucking broke off the flight path?" the CO demanded. Brick readily admitted that they had done so and tried to blame his copilot for getting him "lost." Later, he got a private ass-chewing from the CO. The HAC (and section leader) was in charge, not his copilot.

I informed the CO about the technicals and asked him about our sketchy ROE. "Sir, what is it going to take for us to mount the .50-cals? Does one of us have to be shot down?" The CO gave me his best reply. "I don't know, Q. But I will find out and let you know." He didn't try to bullshit me.

Our Mogadishu Miscellaneous Operational Details, Local Operations, ended after three weeks and the *Tarawa* ARG sailed toward Perth, Australia. En route, the ships dipped below the equator and their crews took part in a "Wog Day" initiation, a long-standing half-sadomasochistic naval tradition consisting of a bizarre combination of *Rocky Horror Picture Show* antics and a college fraternity pledge initiation. Participation was voluntary, but like most traditions in the military peer pressure ruled the day. Even though I felt ridiculous crawling on my knees for hours while getting spanked with canvas fire hoses by "trusty shellbacks" (those who have already gone through initiation), then, finally having to suck a cherry out of a fat navy chief's hairy belly button full of lard, I too succumbed.

A few years later, the navy would ban Wog Day. Carrier deployments would then include female sailors and Marines and ships would have access to the Internet, e-mail, and telephones. *Welcome to the new navy! And for the better.*

After forty-five days at sea, the *Tarawa* ARG finally pulled into Perth for seven days of R&R. Pepe, Torch, and I and the rest of the squadron roamed Perth and its surrounding areas. Everyone agreed that Perth had been our best port visit by far for three reasons: the natives spoke English, the women were beautiful (OK, a few) and overly friendly, and Foster's beer was cheap and abundant. When the *Tarawa* left Australia, several sailors and Marines were left behind. "Missing movement" was a major offense, punishable under Article 87 of the Uniform Code of Military Justice. But I was sure the guilty men had had a great time—and didn't plan on making the military a career anyway.

(On November 3, 1992, I overheard the news of Bill Clinton's surprising presidential election victory over George H. W. Bush. There was a silence in the ready room—the majority of Marines I knew were Republicans. I was an independent, like several officers in my squadron, and had voted for Bush again by absentee ballot. I only had a slight impression of Clinton, and mostly about his hanky-panky and avoidance of military service during the Vietnam War.)

The ARG stopped at Guam for thirty-six hours, enough to refuel and to get mail. I walked off the ship and flagged down a taxi. I told the driver to drive me by Camp Asan, site of a former refugee camp. I had torn a picture of the camp out of a Marine history book. The taxi driver recognized the location and drove me to it. The large yellow Quonset huts were no longer there; the camp was now a giant empty field next to beaches with ankle-deep surf. I stood outside the taxi for a few minutes, staring at what once had been a temporary home for me and my family seventeen years earlier.

I could remember the old camp filled with tormented refugees and friendly Marines. A little boy stood in line for chow with his friends, oblivious to why he had been taken there with his mother and sisters. I saw my youthful but frightened mother scanning the bulletin board, looking for a message about my father. I again felt the pain in my right leg, when something in the water had bitten me.

I shook myself out of my daze. My father was in California with my mother. *Life had turned out all right for the Pham family.*

As we sailed from Guam to Hawaii, I realized that some Marines were as superstitious as the Vietnamese. On Friday, November the 13, the *Tarawa* crossed the International Date Line. *Bingo, it was Friday the 13th again,* and no flight operations for two days due to a convenient "maintenance stand-down."

Mike "Vegas" Jones, a Harrier pilot, and his five detachment mates celebrated this bizarre circumstance by donning Jason Voorhees hockey masks (the character from the *Friday The 13th* movies) and watched the taped series on the television in our ready room.

Now, a dozen years after GulfPac 2-92, I remember how proud I was to be a part of HMM-161. We'd had a tough deployment, but according to retired Capt. Braden Phillips, "You guys made one helluva comeback!"

I also remember sleepless nights, tossing over nightmares of losing an engine on takeoff and having to ditch at sea, fighting my way out of a dark sinking helicopter filled with freezing ocean water. I'd imagined pushing on my emergency hatch to no avail, the water pressure on the outside preventing me from exiting. I would sink 2,000 feet to the bottom of the Pacific, maybe deeper into the Marianas Trench. I remember the night I flew an actual instrument approach through a storm to 200 feet above water but still could not see the ship. I had to fly another approach as we finally landed with low-fuel lights lit during the last fifteen minutes of the flight.

I don't know if anyone else in my squadron was as scared as I was after the series of accidents. If they were, they didn't show it or talk about it. I too could not lose my cool, display any weaknesses, in front of other Marines. I had made some off-the-cuff remarks but I kept most of it to myself. In reality I barely survived that deployment. If the *Tarawa* had turned around and returned to Somalia, as scuttlebutt had it, I don't know how I would have managed to keep flying. As it was, the only thing that kept me going was that I didn't want to let my fellow Marines down. I was part of them, part of HMM-161, and part of the 11th MEU—a United States Marine.

But I didn't want to die for them. I wanted to see my father again.

Two days before Thanksgiving 1992, the *Tarawa* arrived off the coast by Camp Pendleton. The Harriers flew on to Yuma, the Cobras and Hueys returned to Pendleton. The gung-ho grunts went ashore on AAVs and landing crafts; they would've swum if they had to.

HMM-161's twelve CH-46s and four CH-53s rumbled through the skies of southern Orange County, approaching Tustin with its two landmark wooden blimp hangars almost 200 feet tall. Sixteen helicopters broke overhead, landed on the runway, and taxied toward our squadron's flight line.

I could see my father wearing a suit standing in a crowd of family and friends gathering near the base of the tower. His smile was wider than I had ever seen. He must have seen our flight arrive.

Pilots and crew chiefs promptly shut down their helicopters. We exited our helos and stood in formation with the rest of the Marines of HMM-161. Our CO made some brief remarks and dismissed the squadron.

As the formation broke, I ran toward my father, elated to see him again. He was there to welcome me home just as my mother had when I returned from Desert Storm. (To my father, the "YR" identifier on my helicopter may have appeared similar to the "YK" on his rescuer's chopper in Do Xa.) My new friend journalist Mike Tharp stood nearby and watched the moment, having no idea how long I had waited to come home—the longest six months of my life.

CHAPTER 21

TRANSITION

A LOW MARINE LAYER (FOGGY OVERCAST) HUNG OVER THE
Southern California coast, keeping the late afternoon spring temperature cool. A flock of seagulls trailed the 65-foot fishing charter
boat, diving for dead bait slung overboard, as it slowly plowed its way into
the Newport Beach harbor. Two giant brown pelicans, their wings fully
spread, took off from the nearby rock-lined jetty covered white with guano
to join the feast, scattering the frenzied smaller birds. On board, dozens of
men and some women were packing their rods and reels after a fun day at
sea, with lots of bites but not many fish worth keeping.

It had been nearly twenty years since I last cast a rod with my father, when
we used to fish from the banks of the Saigon River. After his release from the
prison camps, I never learned if he had ever fished again in Vietnam. Growing up without him in Oxnard, I had learned to tie my own hooks with the
knots he taught me.

After returning from my USS *Tarawa* deployment, I tried to relive the
past, to reconnect with him through the threads that once bound us as father
and son. I looked at my father standing at the rear of the boat, puffing a
Salem. He didn't say much during the trip but he appeared content just to be
hanging out with me. The way he was slouching made me wonder whether
he actually had enjoyed a breezy Sunday bobbing at sea. Perhaps I saw an ap-
preciative smile on his face, thankful of my gesture.

Once we were both living in Southern California, I only saw my father
sparingly, every other weekend at most. He lived with two other Vietnamese
latecomers, an hour away in the San Fernando Valley north of Los Angeles,
hopping from one hourly wage job to another, trying to make ends meet with
some help from his children. Only three months after landing in this country,

he had found part-time work at a senior center. I was extremely proud of my father: his once oversized ego was still there but he was not angry at the world.

At age fifty-eight, he applied for a five-dollar-an-hour job as a gas attendant at nearby Van Nuys Airport. In his résumé, he did not list his VNAF pilot career with its over 7,000 flight hours, probably more than any aviator then operating at Van Nuys.

He didn't get the job pumping gas into corporate jets and private planes. I truly don't know how he got by, but he managed.

As I had envisioned during my deployment, my parents' marriage lasted only one year after my father arrived in the United States, with their divorce finalized in early 1994. My hopes for a *Brady Bunch*–like family union had been dashed; my expectations were unrealistic for a couple who had grown apart after seventeen years. My father was hungry for life, to regain the prime years that had been taken away. My mother had become fiercely independent; my sisters grew to be equally autonomous, each achieving her own personal and professional successes, totally contradicting Hollywood's depictions of Vietnamese women. A line from a rap song and a scene from Stanley Kubrick's *Full Metal Jacket,* one of the most popular movies among Marines then, came to mind. *Well, baby . . . me so horny . . . me so horny . . . me love you long time.*

I took my father, my uncle, and some of their friends to the annual Marine Corps El Toro Airshow, one of the largest of its kind in the world. I believed my father would enjoy that day more than our fishing expedition. For the first time since he had swept the runways at Tan Son Nhut (the initial days of reeducation), my father was walking on the tarmac of a military airfield, on Tustin's sister base. Rows of planes lined the taxiways; biplanes flew overhead, warming up the crowd for the Marine Corps Air Ground Task Force demonstration, and then came the Blue Angels.

We stopped by my helicopter and entered the cockpit of a static CH-46. I pointed to the ancient pressure gauges similar to those in aircraft he once flew. I wanted to show him the GPS system, but the crew had removed the expensive green box to keep stray military buffs from "borrowing" it.

We walked past row after row of helicopters and planes, from a Huey to a B-52, each filled with curious spectators, mostly fathers and young boys. Then he saw a four-engine, gray, propeller-driven airplane with a black flag ornamented with a skull and crossbones sticking out of the top opening. His eyes opened wide, his finger pointed toward the familiar bird. The aircraft was a KC-130 from Marine Aerial Refueler Transport Squadron 352, nicknamed the "Raiders."

A Marine captain from 352 took my father into the cockpit of the aircraft he last flew for the VNAF, the same type of plane that had unloaded 15,000-pound "daisy-cutter" bombs on advancing NVA troops in 1975. A CBU-55B fuel/air explosive asphyxiation bomb had also been pushed out the back of a VNAF C-130 on top of an advancing NVA Regiment. I don't know if my father actually flew these missions, but he later told me about these flights. He had been the XO of one of two VNAF C-130 squadrons and one of the first instructor pilots trained in the transporting of that deadly cargo.

As I watched from the middle console, my father quickly slipped into the left seat where aircraft commanders and instructors usually sat. He touched several knobs, reached above to feel the engine control levers, looking as comfortable as I had ever seen him since he'd come to this country. I only wished that the friendly Marine captain could have jumped into the right seat, fired up the engines, and flown around the El Toro landing pattern once for my old man's sake.

We left the C-130 elated and then lined up behind a large crowd to watch the Marine air-ground team conduct a simulated assault. AV-8 Harriers and F/A-18 Hornets rolled in on a mock objective a few hundred yards in front of the crowd. Marines set off loud faux explosions and set fuel drums ablaze to add verisimilitude to action. Then CH-46 helicopters inserted troops followed by CH-53s with howitzers dangling beneath them. Cobra gunships circled overhead; grunts rushed out of the back of CH-46s and fired blank rounds as they rushed toward the objective.

My father watched stoically. At that moment, amid the explosions, fires, and helicopter rotor noises, I looked at him and wondered if he was having a flashback to the war, a PTSD moment. Five minutes later, a civilian pilot took off in a Korean War–era F-86 jet to demonstrate the aerial maneuverability of the famed warbird. The Blue Angels were getting ready to follow the F-86. On the third pass in front of the crowd and over the El Toro runways, the F-86 pilot attempted a tight loop. As he rolled inverted, I thought to myself, "This doesn't look right. He's too low." A few seconds later, the F-86 leveled on the downside of his loop but pancaked into the ground, exploding in a fireball and killing the pilot.

As firetrucks and rescue crews rushed toward the crash site, my father stared at the runway and shook his head. I grabbed my backpack and with my father quickly headed for the parking lot trying to beat 500,000 other departing attendees.

(The airshow had been a bad idea. Go fishing, less trauma!)

Like most squadrons after an overseas deployment, some Marines leave the unit and others join. I had fulfilled my unspoken obligation—two deployments in my first two years in the Fleet Marine Force. I was due for further orders but I didn't want to leave Southern California because life was comfortable and I wanted to live near my father. I opted to fulfill a staff position at Marine Aircraft Group 16 as the "frag" officer, responsible for the coordination of helicopter support requests from the 1st Marine Division and other military and civilian organizations on the West Coast.

I was still an unmarried officer, "deployable" in the eyes of the Corps. After SERE School and Desert Shield and Desert Storm, I had learned never to volunteer again. Sure enough, a call came my way five months after I returned home. Major Roger Baty, the operations officer from HMM-268, the "Sea Dragons" and the next squadron to deploy, telephoned me one day at my office.

"Hey, Q. Roger here. How would you like to pump with us as our S-2?"

I was flattered, my pride swelled. HMM-268 was one of the best CH-46 squadrons on base; its former CO and operations officer had brought HMM-161 safely home from the *Tarawa* deployment. I quickly imagined myself briefing "Sea Dragon" pilots and leading a flight into Mogadishu, where Marines and army soldiers were taking part in Operation Restore Hope. And then within seconds, I shuddered at the thought, as I remembered my father and my new girlfriend, whom I had met through Buzz.

Let someone else go. I've done my time.

"Sir, I appreciate the call but I've got some family matters to take care of . . . you're not going to send me orders, are you?"

"Don't worry about it, Q. We'll find someone else." Major Baty was sympathetic and didn't try to lay a guilt trip or spout off a loyalty speech on me.

The next month, a request for nominees to interview for the aide-de-camp position for the new commanding general of the 3d Marine Aircraft Wing was posted on a message board. I jumped at the opportunity, not to further my career in the Corps, but to ensure that I would be able to remain in Orange County, to spend more time with my father. I would not have to deploy unless there was a big war like Desert Storm, when the entire wing and its general and his aide would have to go. I would remain in Southern California for at least a year, the standard tour for aides, before the next set of orders arrived.

After a quick lesson on etiquette and duties as an aide by my group commander, a colonel who had been an aide to the Commandant of the Marine Corps, I was ready to proceed to my interview. The colonel looked over my uniform and gave me one last assurance. "General Frat is tough. He can be mean and nasty. Do your best and don't make us helo bubbas look bad. He's not going to pick a helo driver as his aide; he's a fighter jock."

I drove to the general's headquarters, a new two-story building with a Marine Corps flag and a major general's red flag with two stars flying in front. The secretary asked me to wait in the lobby; I was the third candidate to interview for the position, jokingly referred to by squadron pilots as the general's "butt boy" or "coffee boy."

Major General Paul A. Fratarangelo finally called me into his office, shook my hand, and sat me down. He then put on his gold-rimmed glasses and scanned my short "military" résumé.

General Frat had just finished a tour as the second in command of the I Marine Expeditionary Force, the same parent unit of all Marines in Desert Storm (and Iraq in 2003). He also led Operation Provide Relief in Somalia. Before that he had served as a one-star inspector general on General Schwarzkopf's CentCom staff during the Gulf War and in Somalia. A former F-4 fighter pilot by trade, he had reached the pinnacle of a Marine pilot's career after twenty-nine years of service. He was about to take command of one of the three air wings in the Corps.

When I first saw General Frat, I was caught off guard. He didn't look or act like my notion of a general officer. He was my height, about five feet, eight inches, stocky, and losing his hair. And he smiled and called me by my first name and pronounced it correctly, much to my surprise. I had been told that in order to make general, officers had to be tall, act mean, and look tough and sharp in uniform. I remember briefly meeting Gen. Al Gray in 1988, a former commandant of the Marine Corps (CMC), during his visit to Corpus Christi while I was a flight student. Gray was short and had the same gregarious, approachable demeanor as General Frat. He was also responsible, along with former secretary of the Navy James Webb, for taking the Corps back to its warrior roots in the 1980s.

After six years as a Marine, my interview was the first time I had spoken to a general officer privately. In the Marine Corps, generals numbered only seventy or so in a body of 180,000, and they were worshipped. All general officers indirectly reported to the CMC, a four-star posted in Washington, D.C. All Marines knew the name of their current CMC and those of the first three, that being instilled in us since the first week of boot camp or OCS. Only the sergeant major of the Marine Corps, the highest enlisted rank, had equal name recognition.

Following my self-introduction, I told General Frat about the helicopter community and that some of the helo pilots had felt neglected, flying thirty-year-old whirlybirds while the jet jocks flew new Harriers and Hornets. I also joked about how some of the officers had been talking about the general's arrival at El Toro. He suddenly interrupted me in mid-sentence and became serious. "So, Quang, what do the [helo] guys around there think about me?"

This may sound like a self-defeating answer but I automatically responded without one second of hesitation.

"Sir, they think you're an asshole."

General Frat looked at me and I thought he was going to give me the old OCS boot and orders to Kuwait. My interview was over, my prospect for the aide's job and another year in California flew out of the general's office like an F/A-18 catapulted off a carrier.

I drove back to Tustin, parked my car, and walked up the steps of Marine Aircraft Group 16 Headquarters. A fellow captain came rushing toward me. "Go see the group commander, Q. General Frat picked you and you're to report to the wing headquarters on Monday."

Voilà. Easy as that.

But then after a few days as aide-de-camp, I thought I was going to be fired.

The general's staff was setting up his new office, including his personal computer and files. One afternoon, after the general had left the building, two Marines and a civilian government worker entered my office and asked for my help. They had wanted access to the general's PC to set up his password. The general had told me his call sign, BOZO, and for me to use it as his password. (That's a funny call sign, Bozo the Clown. I wondered how General Frat got that call sign.) I relayed the item to the information technology Marines.

The next morning General Frat attempted to use his PC for the first time. As he sat in his leather chair and entered his call sign, he was unable to gain access. "Quang, my computer is not working. What password did you use?"

"General, enter your call sign," I replied from my new desk, in a cubicle just outside his corner suite.

"It's not working. Come in here."

I walked into his office and sat down on his leather chair.

"DOZZO doesn't work. Try it and see." General Frat insisted.

I almost crapped in my cammies. I wasn't about to type "BOZO" in front of General Frat, so I agreed with him.

"Sir, let me call the G-6 (IT Department) and get someone up here. It'll be ready after you come back from chow," I assured him.

The IT Marines returned, fixed the temporary problem, and saved my ass that afternoon.

After the PC incident, I caused another politically incorrect snafu. General Frat had not moved into his general officer's quarters on base because the departing general and his family hadn't completely vacated it. He asked me to go check on the status of his house, which was a quarter-mile from the office, and I gladly obliged.

Arriving at his new quarters, I ran into two women, one Asian American, the other a middle-aged Caucasian. They were both in casual wear, their hair untidy. They were moving pots and pans, boxing kitchenware, and packing utensils.

"Are you ladies here to clean the house?" I opened my big mouth, confident of my new "butt boy" powers.

A silence filled the air.

"No, we are not! I am Mary Fields, wife of Colonel Fields, the chief of staff."

"And I am Jane Wilson, and my husband is Major General Wilson, the base commander," the second woman chimed in.

All was quiet in the general's quarters, both women looking at me to respond, showing no pity.

"I'm sorry . . . ma'am . . . ladies. Have a good day." I quickly disappeared, thinking General Frat's wife would get a call.

The women never ratted on me, and both were friendly toward me at subsequent social gatherings.

My aide job kept me busy but I was able to spend some more time with my father on the weekends. We would play tennis at the Mile Square Park public courts near Little Saigon then drive to Pho Bolsa Restaurant to eat lunch with his VNAF buddies. I had not seen so many of his old friends since I left

Vietnam. Their children were now thirty-year-old adults like me living in this country.

My father and I would play doubles against other partners, either two men or a couple about his age. I had to restrain myself from smashing overheads at the seniors while at the net; I was always a serve-and-volley player, too impatient to exchange baseline forehands or backhands. My father, on the other hand, was smooth and consistent, covering shots behind me, running back and forth from sideline to sideline, though not quite as fast as he was at Le Cercle Sportif in Saigon.

On one occasion after playing, we met up with a group of thirty VNAF veterans at a small Vietnamese restaurant. We had been sitting around sipping tea waiting for the arrival of a former general, someone important. I was getting hungry and a little pissed off. I was an aide-de-camp, and, by God, everybody should be on a time line, preferably one that I had drawn up. I was wasting my precious Saturday, not with my father, but at a goddamn restaurant waiting for an ex-general.

As the general entered the restaurant with his former aide, Ho Dang Tri (a close friend of my father's as I was later informed), both in their sixties and in civilian clothes, everyone in the restaurant hurriedly stood up. Except for my father. Someone belched out in Vietnamese, "Attention! Air Marshal Ky has arrived."

I immediately recognized the Clark Gable mustache, the flair in his walk, the cockiness in his face. General Nguyen Cao Ky, the former head of the VNAF and vice-president of South Vietnam. Even though I had lived across the street from his house at Tan Son Nhut, I had seen him only in photographs, in American textbooks. I was excited; I once thought of Ky as a hero, along with all the other VNAF fliers during the war.

My father slowly got to his feet and so did I.

Another veteran handed General Ky a beer. Ky then made a brief speech, commenting that he had just returned from a business trip to Hong Kong. He walked toward my father and they awkwardly shook hands. Then the former general turned to me and asked me what I flew.

"General, I fly 46s in the Marine Corps."

"Marine Corps huh . . . hmm . . . hmm." Ky shook his head. I wasn't sure what his body language meant but I was excited about meeting a former head of state and the top officer in the VNAF. He chatted with the other veterans, then strutted out of the restaurant, disappearing after a token appearance.

For the next hour across the luncheon tables, I listened to VNAF veterans exchange their thoughts on President Clinton and his impending normalization of trade and investment with Vietnam. I heard them talk about abandonment by the United States during the rout of 1975; I overheard others discuss their lives here; not all former fliers had stories to brag about.

The end of the Vietnam War had brought these veterans to the States, and, like my father, they all had to start life over. Their social status and their military rank no longer mattered; salutes were left in Saigon. Everyone began at the same starting point when they got here, the same as millions of immigrants before them. The earlier they had arrived after the war, the better off they had become.

As I eavesdropped on the animated conversations, my mind wandered back to an earlier social event for General Frat, in the privacy of the El Toro officers' club, swarming with servers and waiters and aides-de-camp. The crowd that night was also mostly Vietnam veterans, American Vietnam veterans, and they were reminiscing about their days of flying in the war. Most had retired as lieutenant colonels or colonels; some were now flying for major airlines or were filling corporate executive positions. They had served their country honorably and were about to enjoy the fruits of retirement after long successful careers. They had earned everything they were getting.

Back to what was going on around me in the Vietnamese restaurant, my father was having a ball, drifting from table to table, joking with everyone. The men in this small linoleum-floored eating place had also served their country, South Vietnam, with honor, but they were a long way from a comfortable retirement. Even so, the VNAF veterans eating three-dollar bowls of spicy noodles were as honorable as the Marine brass sipping merlot at the O' club.

I felt blessed that I could be a part of both worlds. I was built from both— my roots and my new country.

Another time, I went with my father to a crowded VNAF reunion in Anaheim, near Disneyland. The festivities were held at a giant hotel, a favorite of convention attendees. Red and yellow balloons, yellow flags with red stripes, and VNAF logos covered tables and walls inside the ballroom.

I came alone; my father brought his new girlfriend, some fifteen years his junior. The music was Vietnamese, the conversations were in Vietnamese, and I wasn't dating a Vietnamese woman at the time. It would have been too cumbersome to bring a non-Vietnamese to roam the ballroom, meeting my father's old friends.

Half of the veterans, men in their fifties, sixties, and seventies, wore makeshift VNAF uniforms or flight suits with their old VNAF squadron patches. My father wore a sports coat and tie, and so did I. Although I was repeatedly encouraged by my father's friends or the organizers of this and similar functions, I never once strutted in with my Marine Corps dress blues and medals at a VNAF event. It didn't feel right. I didn't want to appear as if I was trying to one-up the VNAF veterans, and, most important, my father. My war experience was *ti ti* (tiny) compared to his.

Most of my father's friends were cordial to me at the reunions, several expressing their envy of my access to military aircraft and the bases. A few made pointed remarks like, "So, Quang, you're flying for the Americans huh? How do they treat you? Better than they treated us?"

The old officers frequently encouraged me as my Marine career progressed. "Stay in for at least twenty. You'll get all those retirement benefits and get to go to the PX. I am proud of you. Make at least colonel. Your daddy was a lieutenant colonel. Show them [Americans] that we can do it too!"

At one reunion, my father was dancing the night away and, at age fifty-nine, still looked like a Vietnamese Fred Astaire doing the tango. He was having a blast, and I enjoyed watching his moves, knowing full well that I could not match his grace. He then returned to my table and grabbed me by the hand. "Come on, Quang, I want to introduce you to somebody." I instinctively followed him.

We pushed our way through the crowd, finally reaching the opposite side of the dance floor, away from all the hoopla. A circle of VNAF veterans crowded around a table, looking up watchfully as my father and I approached. The ballroom was dark, and it was late. I had to strain to look but I recognized him right away from the famous photograph.

There he was, sitting with a few older men, all slightly hunched over their drinks. He appeared shrunken, his shirt collar floating around his scrawny neck. He seemed diminished, not the same vigorous man who had stood erect wearing a flak jacket, helmetless, on the streets of Saigon's Cho Lon District in 1968. The man who had ignored American cameras and pulled the trigger of the pistol inches away from a Viet Cong officer's head—an image that forever changed the war.

Major General Nguyen Ngoc Loan, South Vietnamese National Police chief and ex-VNAF pilot. When he saw my father, he flashed a huge smile, then looked at me.

"General Loan. This is my son Quang. Pham Xuan Quang. He's also a pilot like us. He flies for the U.S. Marines." My father proudly introduced me in Vietnamese, acting with a respectful military protocol I had never seen before.

I bowed my head and extended my arm. *Chau xin chao bac.* I was trying to express my introduction in Vietnamese but wasn't sure I had greeted the general with the appropriate courtesy. *It's an honor to meet you, General.* He kept his seat and shook my hand, mumbling something too soft for me to hear. My father and I then returned to our table.

The strange meeting stuck in my mind but I never asked my father why he had introduced me to one of the most despicable South Vietnamese, according to many Americans of the Vietnam generation. My father never bothered to tell me either.*

Back at El Toro, I received some good news and bad news in early August 1993, a month after I began my aide tour. When I got to my office on a summer morning at 6:30 a.m., the phone on my desk rang. Usually early phone calls, coming from Washington, D.C., went directly to General Frat's unlisted number, available only to other generals and their aides.

I noticed the "I MEF" telephone number on the caller identification.

"Good morning, 3d Marine Aircraft Wing Headquarters, this is Captain Pham."

"Q! This is Rifle."

I hesitated for a moment.

Who the fuck is "Rifle" and why is he calling me at 6:30?

Then I realized it was Brig. Gen. Mike "Rifle" Delong, the deputy commander of the I Marine Expeditionary Force, and a hotshot Vietnam veteran and CH-46 pilot. General Delong had also commanded the prestigious MAWTS-1 "Top Gun" Squadron.

---

*In 2004, I visited Eddie Adams in his New York City studio a few months before he died from Lou Gehrig's disease. The Pulitzer-prize winning photojournalist, who had snapped the Viet Cong execution picture, was debilitated from the disease. He had to use a voice communication box to express his admiration for General Loan and his regrets for taking the photograph. His assistant then showed me a pictorial called "The Boat with No Smiles," a collage of pictures Adams had taken in 1977 as he boarded a Vietnamese boat that had been pushed back to sea by the Thai government. Adams relayed to me that the photos had been his proudest work, and which later were presented to Congress and helped persuade President Carter to pursue legislation to help the refugees. After an hour, as I got up to leave, Adams motioned me to look at his left shoulder. He then rolled up the sleeve of his polo shirt, revealing a large faded blue tattoo depicting an eagle, globe, and anchor, the Marine Corps emblem. I gave him the best compliment I could give a fellow Marine. "Semper fi, Eddie." He could still hear and a huge smile lit up his face.

Shit. Why is General Delong calling me? Who did I piss off now?

I had only met General Delong once, and he seemed to be happy to see a young CH-46 captain as General Frat's aide.

"Congratulations. Have you seen the message board this morning?" General Delong continued. "You were selected for augmentation."* He then jumped off the phone. I thought it had been nice of the general to personally call me.

I put the receiver down and ran down the hallway, where the administrative gunnery sergeant had hung the message board, basically daily announcements from different Marine commands around the world but predominantly from headquarters. I flipped through the first several pages, finally coming across a message with "RESULTS OF THE ORB 2-93 BOARD." I quickly scanned for familiar names, saw mine, but didn't recognize any others on the list except one: "GRATHWOL, PHILIP. 7562. MAG-36."

I had known about Phil's achievements in the Corps so I was not surprised that he was also selected. He was my roommate in flight school and one of my closest friends. The number 7562 was the military occupational specialty designation for CH-46 pilots. Only two had been selected from California- and Hawaii-based units. The selection rate was 6 percent for my specialty's year group.

I was surprised and honored. I knew that my old CO, Tank, had written outstanding officer fitness reports for me, ranking me third out of eighteen lieutenants in HMM-161 competing for augmentation. Tank had relied on his department heads to rank us, as well as a peer evaluation system where the lieutenants were asked to rank the top three among themselves. Back then, only ROTC, Annapolis graduates, and a few honors graduates of TBS received regular commissions. I had also received "A MUST FOR AUGMENTATION" on three other fitness reports. A board of four colonels had ranked me as the top candidate out of fifty-one officers in Marine Aircraft Group 16 during the interview portion of the process. Another major had commented on my performance as "clearly in the top 5 percent and functions at an advanced level."

Congratulatory phone calls and e-mails arrived sporadically throughout the day; the augmentation board's results had been highly anticipated be-

---

*Augmentation is the process used to manage the regular-officer population through time in service and occupational categories. Officer retention boards (ORBs) meet to select reserve commissioned officers for retention.

cause most of my peers had less than two years remaining on their tour. The economy was sagging; airlines were slow to hire helo pilots. The next day I began to sense a shift in the tone of best wishes.

One peer exaggerated the gossip. "Everyone in the squadron [my old unit] thinks you got 'augmented' because you're a minority and you're the general's 'coffee boy!' "

(How would they know? Did they sit on the board? Have they seen my fitness reports?)

I knew that the board had reached its conclusions before I even took the aide job but I wanted to make sure. I walked right into General Frat's office and asked him point-blank. "Sir, did you make a call to the augmentation board for me?"

"Quang, I did not do that and would not do that for anyone," General Frat tonelessly answered.

I tried to see the skeptics' point of view. There weren't many minority officers in the Marine Corps at that time, and even fewer were pilots. I wondered if the Corps had picked me because of my race.

I pushed the second-guessing aside and proceeded to assist General Frat with the demands of his official schedule. I accompanied him to many meetings, including the secretary of the navy's war games in Quantico, live-fire exercises, high-level aviation leadership boards, and community relations events in Orange County where I met dozens of elected officials and private citizens. I researched and wrote his speeches because he trusted me with helping him.

By far the best perk of being General Frat's aide was the opportunity to fly in the back of an F/A-18D Hornet, fresh off the McDonnell-Douglas assembly line in St. Louis. (OK, my dream as a fighter pilot didn't materialize but a supersonic backseat flight would beat any "E" ticket ride at Disneyland.) I pushed hard to fly as often as I could with General Frat, who was qualified to fly the Hornet and had to meet his annual flight-time requirement. I made sure the general *needed* me to accompany him everywhere, especially to meetings across the country when he would occasionally commandeer a Hornet.

I rushed through a week's worth of abbreviated training. I spent two hours in the F/A-18 simulator, went through the ejection seat qualification, and got my G-suit fitted perfectly to my body. I wanted to make sure that if something bad happened, I'd be able to land the jet or eject myself.

The big day finally came. The Marines of All-Weather Fighter/Attack Squadron 242 gave me their best support, well aware that I was only an opportunistic helo bubba looking for a fast joy ride. I never hid my motives. I could still remember, as a fourteen-year-old, seeing the sleek Hornet prototype coming in for a landing at the Point Mugu airshow. Fifteen years later, I was about to climb aboard a Hornet with only five flight hours in its life.

The leather on the rear ejection seat headrest smelled like a brand-new car, the avionics were state-of-the art technology. The plane captain handed me a pair of clear plastic booties so I would not "scuff" up his new jet. I had to laugh at myself; in my CH-46 squadron, the helos were filthy. (We would have had to wear the booties to keep our boots clean!)

General Frat took Runway 7 at El Toro.

"Bat 03, switch Departure, cleared for takeoff." The tower gave us our instructions.

He then slowly pushed the throttles forward with his left hand, then informed me over the cockpit communication system. The jet began its takeoff roll.

"OK, Q, I'm lighting the ABs [afterburners]."

I braced myself against the ejection seat, my straps pinning me to the cushion. I could hear a loud screaming noise at my back, where two General Electric engines, each with 18,000 pounds of thrust, rocketed down the runway, pulling me to the back of my seat. *Oohhrahhh.* The acceleration was unbelievable, the hangars blurred by me as the Hornet became airborne en route to Yuma, Arizona. *I could not keep up with the radio calls.* A minute later, we were at 18,000 feet. In a CH-46, I'd be lucky to get to 3,000 feet.

Fifteen minutes later, we were over Yuma's firing ranges. General Frat switched to "range control" for entry into the Restricted Area 2507 (bombing range requiring permission to enter). He looked around his left and right and I followed his head movement, thinking he was keeping an eye out for traffic. Suddenly, my head snapped, my vision blackened at the edges, the forces of gravity slamming me against my seat. I glanced at the dashboard and saw *only* 6.5 on the G-meter. I then recognized the maneuver from my days of flying the T-34 in flight school. We were in a tight loop. (Geez, my fifty-one-year-old general is trying to get me sick on my first jet hop. No chance in hell, sir!)

On October 31, 1993, Marine Corps Commandant Gen. Carl E. Mundy Jr., appeared on "60 Minutes" with Leslie Stahl and commented on minority officers:

"In the military skills, we find that the minority officers do not shoot as well as the nonminorities. Now how do you rationalize? I don't know. I can't explain that to you but we're going to find out. . . . They don't swim as well. And when you give them a compass and send them across the terrain at night in a land navigation exercise, they don't do as well at that sort of thing."

I had known about the show, having been informed by one of the show's participants, a black captain and former CH-46 pilot who had been accepted at Harvard Law School the previous spring. He alleged that he was called a "boy" by white officers in his squadron before he was "boarded," his flight status revoked.

I notified General Frat since several black officers appearing on the "60 Minutes" were serving in his command, the 3d Marine Aircraft Wing. He and I were attending a live-fire exercise in Twentynine Palms. The general appeared disgusted at the news, stating, "I can't believe we still have that shit in the Marine Corps! Those goddam rednecks!"

In 1993, a discomforting undercurrent began to flow within the Marine Corps about diversity and equal-opportunity programs. Marine minority-officer issues boiled to the top amid military downsizing, the Tailhook scandal, "Don't ask, don't tell," and the "women in combat" controversies.

As an aide-de-camp I had access to the "Early Bird," a daily headline news summary faxed to our offices daily, and other documents. I saw official data for minority personnel in the Corps, by rank. As of October 1992, out of 19,000 active duty officers, 90 percent were whites, 5 percent blacks, 3 percent Hispanic, and 2 percent "Other." The U.S. Army had 10,000 black officers in its ranks. I guess I was counted in the "Other." (Maybe that's why the Corps had stamped "MINORITY CANDIDATE" across my OCS application back in 1986.)

I watched the entire "60 Minutes" segment and recognized another black officer on it, a classmate from TBS. I tried to dispel the commandant's perception of minority officers' orienteering and marksmanship skills, even though I realized that he was referring to blacks versus whites in the interview. I compared my performance to the comments made by the commandant. I did so because I had believed in the Marine Corps as well as in our commandant.

"Minority officers do not shoot as well as the nonminorities." I had qualified as a sharpshooter (the middle ratings) with the 9mm pistol and the

M16A2, missing a rifle expert badge by one point. I had also requalified several times since TBS.

"They don't swim as well." Despite my fear of water, I had been designated as water survival qualified, or WSQ, the highest rating a Marine could get. I had successfully graduated from water survival during flight training (and three subsequent times), a feat much more difficult than becoming WSQ.

"When you give them a compass and send them across the terrain at night in a land navigation exercise, they don't do as well at that sort of thing." I had graduated in the top half of my basic school class and in the top 10 percent for military training, which encompassed all training regimens.

So why did the commandant say what he said? What data was he looking at?

I felt disappointed and let down, an outsider constantly having to struggle to fit in, never fully accepted. I took his remarks personally. The rumor mill criticism about my selection for augmentation was still bothering me. (My buddies called me "thin-skinned." I had rejected all racial call signs— they would only have reinforced stereotypes. "Q" was my call sign and I was comfortable with it.)

I still wanted to believe the Commandant had been misquoted, his sixty-second interview extracted for sound bites from a two-hour interview. As many "lifers" jumped to his defense, I desperately hoped that he had been quoted out of context. Marines I knew wanted this racially-tinged episode to disappear, buried under the carpet.

What about Asian Americans in the Corps, grouped under "Other"?

There weren't many in the Corps. I found out that as of 1991, there were six Vietnamese-American Marine officers, according to the *Navy Times.* I had met Van K. Tran,* a Vietnamese American CH-53 pilot from Texas who had received his wings a few months after I got mine. His father had been a VNAF veteran like mine. I also knew of several Asian-American Marine aviators, Roy Santa Maria, a Filipino American, and Roy "Kato" Akana, a Japanese American flying Harriers.

Asians didn't matter in the Marine Corps until the *New York Times, Washington Post, Los Angeles Times, Navy Times,* and *Good Morning America* showcased former officer candidate Bruce Yamashita, a Georgetown-trained

---

*As of this writing, Lt. Col. Van K. Tran is still on active duty in Virginia.

lawyer who charged that he had been racially discriminated against. He got booted from OCS two days before graduation, classified as a "leadership failure." OCS staffers called him racial names and told him to "go back to your own country!" and "during World War II, we whipped your Japanese ass!"

Hey, they called me a Viet Cong!

Yamashita waged a five-year legal battle against the Corps, with the help of civil rights groups, powerful Japanese-American veteran associations, and elected officials. In early 1994, under pressure from the office of the secretary of the navy, the Corps issued an apology and commissioned Yamashita as a captain.

I was livid. I was confused, I was torn. (I am damned if I excel and I am damned if I don't—the double-edged sword of equal-opportunity and minority programs.) I was getting tired of the constant pressure, the "Marine team player" image I had to uphold; my contributions and presence in the officer corps dismissed as token. The Kool-Aid was wearing off. The straw that broke my back took place at the 1993 Marine Corps Birthday Ball, which I had attended with my girlfriend at the time.

As I was heading to the restroom near the end of the evening, I heard something behind me that sent chills down my spine. "Chong. Yang. Fong. Fu." When I turned around, I saw two white Marine officers laughing, drinks in hand, one a first lieutenant, the other a captain and a peer of mine. They were wearing dress blues and so was I. Except I had an obnoxious gold braid called an "aiguillette" around my left shoulder. I guess I had to wear that so my general could spot his "butt boy" in a crowd. To be blunt, I stood out.

I was in no mood to joke around. "What the fuck did you guys just say?" I confronted my fellow officers.

They immediately stopped laughing, their eyes focused on my date who had heard the taunting. "Nothing, man, we didn't say anything."

"I didn't fucking think so." I walked away fuming. My hecklers had backed down, after exhibiting the worst kind of racism, the subtle, deniable type. I was ready to resign my commission and turn in my wings to General Frat that night.

I'm glad I waited. I began thinking about Doug Hamlin, Guy Close, Mark Henderson, Phil Grathwol, Joe Heneghan, Pepe, Torch, General Frat, and all my buddies in the Corps. The assholes were few and far between, no more than a few percent of the Marines I've met. Contrary to another word of warning by a civilian: "You've got to watch out for the enlisted guys, they don't have a lot of education." I had no run-ins with enlisted Marines; all of my hazers were officers. I couldn't possibly indict the whole Corps as Bruce Yamashita had done, taking his legal case to the public and making the Marine Corps look parochial. I still believed in *semper fidelis,* Always Faithful. I decided that I'd had enough.

I could have gone as far as I wanted in the Corps, but it was no longer worth the stress.

An officer recruiter I knew often repeated: "We've been around for over 200 years. Why the hell would we need you?" I agreed with him. No individual could "break" the Marine Corps.

In June 1994, after nearly seven years of service, I officially turned down my regular commission, resigning from my beloved Corps, quitting my profession of arms. I also declined a seat at the upcoming Amphibious Warfare School, a career-level school for 200 captains selected annually. I had made the alternate attendee list, only to be immediately offered orders by my monitor (assignment officer) once I had resigned. He too tried to persuade me, offering me practically every assignment. General Frat did not try to talk me out of my decision. Instead, he ordered me to visit four colonels who attempted to find out my reasons. One even spoke about the prospect of sending me through jet training. I was reminded of my helo affiliation and a popular phrase by rotor heads: Jets are for kids. Thanks but no thanks.

Right after my resignation, a bubbling nuclear crisis in the Korean Peninsula nearly resulted in me packing my bags to accompany General Frat and the 3d Marine Aircraft Wing to South Korea. We waited for our orders—to be prepared for combat operations should the North Koreans maintain their nuclear weapon development posture. The wing headquarters was going to be located at an airfield south of Seoul, its location and parts of OPLAN 5027, the war plans against North Korea, revealed to me by the G-2 in a top secret briefing. I had only a secret clearance. I had tried to apply for a top secret clearance but was told that since I still had relatives in Vietnam, a communist country, there was no way the U.S. government would grant me one.

After ten days, things cooled off and we stood down.

One of the best things I learned from the Marine Corps had remained with me since my days in Quantico: Make a decision. And stick with it.

In early 1995, I went on terminal leave (using my sixty days of paid vacation) from the Marine Corps. I had become a better U.S. citizen, more informed than the twenty-year-old who indifferently took his oath of citizenship a decade earlier. I also had three job offers in hand, one from one of the world's most esteemed pharmaceutical companies. I left the Corps with unquestionably more confidence but also harbored an enormous unresolved anger. For the first time in my life, I had retreated from confrontation. Yet I wanted to show myself and those few bigoted and jealous Marines that I no longer needed the Corps.

Expressing my thanks at the Vietnam Wall with its founder, Jan C. Scruggs, 1998. (Courtesy of Chau Tran)

CHAPTER 22

CAN'T GO BACK

AFTER SEVEN YEARS IN THE MARINE CORPS, I YEARNED TO be rebellious, unstructured, and borderline "unsat" again. I didn't want to have to worry about my trouser center line, my uniform, and my flight hours. I grew my hair long—my head started to look like a "bowl" again. I stopped shaving and tried to grow a goatee, able to showcase only a few whiskers after a week. I peeled off the red Marine Corps sticker on my car bumper. I stopped running, until a fellow drug sales representative challenged me to a jog, mockingly asking if the "Corps had really been that tough?"

(I ran his ass into the ground, leaving him choking in the diesel fumes of a city bus in midtown Los Angeles.) The competitive fires were still burning inside me.

In the midst of all the psychological conflicts, my new marriage was falling apart.

I hadn't spent much time with my father for most of the second half of 1994, too busy looking for a job, too embarrassed to tell him the true reason why I had left the Marines. I didn't want to have to answer his friend who had once asked, "So, Quang, you're flying for the Americans, huh? How do they treat you? Better than they treated us?"

Despite the residual bitterness, deep down inside, I knew the answer was a resounding, "Yes."

During my first several months as a civilian, I was adrift, starting all over again. Money wasn't a problem, but my new job schlepping prescription drugs quickly bored me. My civilian counterparts weren't exactly impressed with my Marine credentials; only a fraction had worn a uniform. I wasn't about to tell them the true reasons why I left the Corps. My new boss assigned me a sales territory in rough neighborhoods because I was an "ex-Marine." It didn't matter anyway; the doctors only wanted free drug samples and pizzas. My sales pitches lasted thirty seconds, eight sales calls a day equaled a day's work, which could be completed within hours.

A recurring headline drew deep interest from me—Vietnam, my birthplace. Talks of normalizing trade relations were rampant, with expatriate entrepreneurs rushing back to their homeland, looking to make the big bucks. I had other compelling reasons to visit, so I convinced my Marine buddy Scott "Goober" Dodson, himself an entrepreneur and ex-pilot, to come along. I really needed Scott to accompany me, since I had heard about human rights abuses in Vietnam and jailed dissidents. I wanted to go with a *real* American—the Vietnamese wouldn't dare touch Scott and maybe stay away from his *Viet kieu* (Vietnamese expatriate) sidekick, Quang the civilian.

Two nights before I left for Vietnam, my father dropped a 50,000-pound bombshell on me. He rang me at home, just before I crawled into my queen-size bed, no longer a twin rack.

"Quang, it's Dad." He hesitated for a minute.

"Yes, Dad?"

"When you get to Saigon, I want you to go see your brother. You have a brother there."

What the fuck, over? I couldn't seem to kick my Marine habits.

"Go see him, Quang. He's your brother."

I was expecting my father to tell me that my "new" brother was my age, someone from his past who had grown up like me.

"His name is An. He's almost three and he looks like you."

I thought to myself. "He's three now? So he must have been born in 1992, the year Dad got to the United States. Huh? What's going on?"

I decided not to interrogate my father, who sounded as depressed as I was. Yet I sensed that he was relieved about no longer having to withhold a family secret. I would meet An soon enough. I jotted down his mother's address and phone number.

"Go back to Vietnam!" The words of the Aleric Street bully rang in my ears. *OK, OK. . . .*

The day after I was officially discharged from the Corps I landed in Saigon. Nobody was waving flags and welcoming me home the way they did for us after Desert Storm. But I was sure glad to see my Aunt Nhang and all my long-lost relatives again.

"Homecoming." At the same Saigon intersection thirty years later with my sister Thi, 1995. (Author's Collection)

It was April 1995. The twentieth anniversary. Reunification. Liberation. Unfinished business . . . and new business.

I was simply visiting my birthplace and, at the last minute, a newly discovered brother made my travel itinerary. I went "home" to see distant relatives before they all died, to stroll the streets of my hometown, to use my native tongue, and possibly to blend in again. I went back to Saigon as a U.S. veteran, a Vietnam vet of a different kind. Was it me, the Vietnamese, clinging to old memories? Or was it me, the American, who grew up with portrayals of my homeland from Hollywood directors, politicians, journalists, and old soldiers—all of them foreigners? Or was it both?

In Vietnam two decades earlier I was not an immigrant, a refugee, or fresh off the boat. Back then I looked like everyone else. Back then no one ever mispronounced my name or made fun of it. Growing up back then, nothing made me stand apart from the other kids—until I came to the United States speaking the only English I knew: "OK, Salem, Coke, GI." Back then, had I remained in Vietnam, I might have had to fight a war as a child soldier in Cambodia or against China.

When my family left Vietnam, I didn't know then that we were leaving forever. Luckily for me, forever lasted only twenty years. I sat next to Goober on the Airbus jet from Hong Kong, and my stomach knotted as we circled through the bumpy skies over Tan Son Nhut Airport. Even while flying helicopters off the USS *Tarawa,* I wasn't this nervous. We began our descent, and images from my childhood flashed through my mind.

My family had lived on the airfield that I was now seeing below me. The plane landed, just as I had taken off in 1975, in darkness. My hopes of blending in didn't last long. The immigration officer stared at me and asked in English, "Is this you first time back from America?" I stammered a "yes" in Vietnamese, but he continued in broken English, as if the language we shared was too hard for me to comprehend. He didn't even bother to look up, pocketing the twenty dollar bill that I had slipped in between my passport pages and moving on to the next expatriate. Glancing at the skinny, hollow-eyed policemen in oversized polyester uniforms, I was glad my Marine Corps ID card and dog tags had been left in California. (The Corps wasn't with me to watch my back.)

When I ventured downtown after leaving the airport, long-forgotten smells washed over me: charcoal smoke, motorcycle exhausts, kerosene fumes, the pungent odor of *nuoc mam.* I was greeted by what seemed like every *cyclo* driver in Saigon. They all spoke to me in piecemeal English, then were surprised that I could pronounce Vietnamese words and that I wasn't a Taiwanese, Japanese, or Hong Kong businessman. My Western clothing and extra twenty-five pounds of weight over them helped differentiate me from the locals. Some drivers in their forties and fifties had served in the ARVN, and pedaling a *cyclo* was the best work they could now find. They spoke fondly of the years before 1975, bitterly about their time in reeducation camps, and enviously about their comrades living the good life in the States. The youngest were college students by day, *cyclo* drivers by night. It was eerie to think that, had I not gotten out of Saigon, I could now be pedaling for a living like one of them.

I went by my elementary school that stood next to the Presidential Palace, now the Reunification Palace. Standing there, I could still feel the phantom concussion from two 500-pound bombs sucking the air from my tiny lungs, dropped by a defecting pilot a few hundred yards from the school. (The VNAF Benedict Arnold later became the chief pilot for Vietnam Airlines.) The only familiar face still in the neighborhood was a nurse who told me most of my teachers had retired or had gone to the United States.

I visited my favorite park, where the old Marine statue with two Viet-namese carrying a machine gun (probably modeled after the famous Iwo Jima Memorial) stood near the Rex Hotel. But it was gone. Around the corner I stared at a statue of Ho Chi Minh holding a child, a reminder of my hometown's current name.

Disappointed, I retreated to the rooftop of the Rex Hotel, once the old U.S. officers' club. Several American veterans hustled in the lounge, back from a day trip shooting AK-47s at the Cu Chi tunnels, playing tourist and exorcising their demons. In the late afternoon sun, we sipped cold drinks together and imagined the view from this high terrace two decades earlier, as Marine choppers clustered like dragonflies over the old U.S. Embassy, extracting as many friends as they could. Strangely enough, of all the esteemed American journalists who had covered Vietnam over the war years, few were still *embedded* in country on that dark day. But they all converged on Saigon that week in 1995, for "Namstalgia" sake.

I finally found my way to my brother's home; his mother's shack was in a crowded section of Saigon, hundreds of Vietnamese squeezed into a square block. Five adults lived at her house, but I didn't know who they were. I looked at the woman's face and I became angry. (Was this the person who derailed my mother's marriage? Does my mother know about this?)

An's mother then left us alone for a few minutes. I didn't know what to say to a three-year-old boy who couldn't understand English. ("Hello? Sorry? How are you? Dad says hello.")

Compared with American children, An appeared sick, his arms and legs as thin as those of a one-year-old. I didn't know if he was undernourished. I wasn't a parent myself. I had to admit he looked like me and my father, resembling my father more than I did.

I had to leave after thirty minutes. My heart was not in the visit; I came only because my father had asked me. I gave An's mother $100 cash (U.S.) and rubbed his head as I quickly left her shack.

The strangest episode occurred later in my visit when I had dinner at my aunt's home with a second cousin in his late thirties. He was only a teenager when the war had ended, but later became a major in the People's Army of Vietnam. My innate U.S. Marines reaction to meeting a communist officer was confrontational at first, but I held back. Wrong reason, wrong place, and wrong time. Later in the evening, it really didn't make any difference in our relationship, since he had never shot at me nor I at him. Even so I couldn't shake his hand when I left.

I also met an aunt from Qui Nhon, my father's sister, who had lost everything after the war, and an uncle who spent nearly $10,000 (the per capita income then was about $400) to get his three sons to the States. He failed, and my cousins went to prison after trying to escape. They're still there.

Everywhere I went, there were signs and billboards announcing the celebration of April 30, marking it the day of "liberation" rather than "evacuation." In Little Saigon in Orange County, former refugees mourn this date every year as "Black April."

On every corner was a *pho* stand, selling hot white noodle soup in beef broth, now chic in the States. There was not much meat in the bowls. Every resident, it seemed, had something to sell. I was looking to buy back my childhood, but I found only a giant void in the black market.

The best salesman in Saigon I met was a tattered little boy offering bootleg, poorly bound copies of Graham Greene's *The Quiet American* near the Hotel Continental. He unloaded three of the novels on our group at $5 each, probably enough money to feed his family for a month. As he ran down the sidewalk, yelling with joy and clutching our greenbacks, I suddenly saw myself. Except for luck and fate twenty years earlier, I would have been hustling on the streets like him, a boy left behind to fend for himself and his family.

I would learn that discrimination against the children of former South Vietnamese officials, and against *Viet kieus* like me, would make my American "prejudice" experiences seem like a picnic.

Later in the week, I felt strong enough to visit the graves of relatives, especially my grandmother on my mother's side. On the road, I passed many marked cemeteries, unaware of many more that had been unearthed by Communists shortly after their "liberation."

I thought of the American Vietnam vets I knew. Some remained bitter; many went on with their lives and became very successful in military or civilian careers or comfortably retired. And quite contrary to the Saigon *cyclo* driver's perception, my father and many of his South Vietnamese colleagues who emigrated late (the H.O. group) worked menial jobs in the United States, facing their "golden years" without a pension or veteran's benefits. Most tragic was to watch their pride slip away. Once their VNAF parties had ended, some in the H.O. group were again *nobodies*.

To lose a war was one thing. To lose your country was another.

My week in Vietnam ended at the same place I had taken off in April 1975. Getting out was much easier the second time. As the Vietnam Airlines jet lifted off and banked left over the Saigon River, I sat by myself in the last row, half-dazed, staring down at the hazy countryside I had now left twice. I was looking at a place where sorrow had struck millions of lives, where policies and policymakers failed miserably, and where brave young Americans and South Vietnamese paid with their lives in a sincere effort to secure freedom for the Republic of Vietnam.

A month earlier, I had visited the Vietnam Wall in Washington, paying my respects again to those who had given everything they had in a futile effort that brought me as a boy to their land. They weren't wrong. Their leaders were wrong. As the tile-roofed houses and the brown rice paddies receded below, and twenty years of memories and feelings came rushing back, I could no longer hold back the tears.

Life goes on. Once again, I was on a plane heading for a place where I had found a chance to live. This time I was really going home, back to America, as an American.

CHAPTER 23

FINAL FLIGHTS

FIVE MONTHS AFTER I RETURNED FROM VIETNAM, AFTER the emotions had cooled, and nearly a year after submitting my resignation, I ran back to the Marine Corps. I no longer *needed* the Corps, but I *wanted* to be a part of it again. And I missed my Marine friends. In the midst of my divorce, it was my buddy "Stinky" Brennan who moved in as my new roommate, providing companionship and support for this grateful former jarhead.

And I wanted to get back into the cockpit again.

By mid-1995, the Pham family had been spread out all over the United States and the world, all of us living our own private lives and in our own homes. It was not what a typical Vietnamese family would do. Two sisters married and moved to Northern California, another to Washington, D.C. My father remained in Los Angeles County, me in Orange County. My mother, my sixty-year-old mother who had become a grandma, had left the States to pursue her own dreams. She too would join the "Corps." I had initially thought she was running away from all of us. I was wrong.

After their divorce, my parents would still see each other, remaining cordial at holiday and family gatherings. They actually seemed as if they got along better than when my father had first emigrated three years earlier. My mother had finally earned her B.A. degree in accounting, not for career advancement, but to qualify for the Peace Corps Program. She landed in the former Soviet Union, in the capital city of Almaty in the Republic of Kazakhstan following the footsteps of my uncle's 1975 American sponsors, Ron and Bonnie Counseller. She had admired them greatly. For two years and two subzero winters, she helped small businesses with her accounting skills.

She sounded happy (and freezing) every time I spoke to her across the globe. Her phone was always scratchy as if her lines had been tapped. My sisters and I jokingly called her a "spy" for the CIA; she would have been their oldest rookie ever and the only "free" Vietnamese in Russia who spoke three languages and knew something about military aviation.

With my family scattered everywhere, and my independent sales job a routine and my divorce a disappointment, I had become depressed and lonely. I found myself sitting in a family therapist's chair, embarrassed at first to enter his office and afraid someone might recognize me.

Marines don't need shrinks.

Fortunately for me, I had another friend besides my roommate Stinky. He was Dean Sawyer, a former undersized linebacker for the University of the Pacific, and my roommate during sales training at my new employer. He took me under his wings, explaining the pharmaceutical trade, and shared his "best practices," especially with the coeds.

By the fall of 1995, I was beginning to pull myself out of a twelve-month funk, and I decided to pursue two endeavors that had been close to my heart—a renewed relationship with my father and with the U.S. Marine Corps. At that juncture I was on good terms with neither.

For weeks after I returned from Vietnam I did not want to see my father. I was angry at him for telling me last, after he had revealed the existence of his second son to my sisters. Perhaps he didn't want me to think less of him; maybe he felt our relationship had only an artificial connection of fishing and flying and nothing more. Even though we enjoyed each other's company at functions and outings, my father and I did little talking one-on-one. I tried several times to ask what had happened in the years that he had been incarcerated. But he only gave a slight hint. After finding out about my half-brother, I wondered what other secrets he might have. I will never forget one sticky afternoon in Los Angeles, where he and I sat in an empty Vietnamese restaurant, calming each other over our marital failures. He did more consoling than me. (Father knew best.)

A year earlier, concurrent with my psychological wrestling match with the Corps, General Frat's second in command, the assistant wing commander, Col. Don "Buff" Beaufait, was also going through his own struggle, albeit with much more at stake than I. "Buff" had been second in command of Marine Hornets during the Gulf War. As a squadron CO, he had also led the 1986 airstrikes against Libya's Muammar Khadafi. He owned the distinction

Finally there with my son. My mother and my father at my promotion to major in the reserve, 1997. (Courtesy of C. Tran)

of being the first Marine to land a Hornet aboard an aircraft carrier and, like General Frat, had flown many F-4 combat missions in Vietnam.

Buff was a bona fide war hero, a nice guy, and an avid mako shark fisherman. He would also take the biggest pummeling by a Marine pilot as a result of the Tailhook scandal fallout.

I must profess to not knowing all the details of Tailhook, and, I don't condone the actions of some of the attendees, but I knew that Buff had been selected for brigadier general and that his promotion had been held up. Only five or six colonels got selected each year for general; their opportunities came after twenty-five years of outstanding service.

I don't know if General Frat would have picked up his third star (he retired as a two-star in 1997), but I knew that he had supported Buff. He wrote two letters requesting the brass to promote Buff to brigadier general, going against the politically correct pendulum.

His efforts were in vain but they were *semper fidelis* at its highest level.

Don Beaufait retired as a colonel and moved on to a successful private-sector career. At the peak of his career he had endured more turmoil than I could ever have imagined. Like my old CO, Tank, who was relieved of command during the 1992 deployment, Buff remained a professional, a true Marine until he took off the uniform. Both took their lumps in stride, never blaming anyone for their misfortunes, dealt with their adversities, and finished their careers.

Both of them gave me hope as I returned to the Corps as a reserve pilot, trying to undo my sour-note departure.

I finally found my niche; I was able to continue my private-sector career in pharmaceutical/biotech sales while taking to the air several times a month, 50 percent at night, sometimes more, sometimes less. I joined the Reserves, the weekend Marine Corps. I became a part of El Toro–based Marine Medium Helicopter Squadron 764, HMM-764, aptly called the "Moonlighters."

One thing I didn't know about HMM-764 was that the squadron could afford to be selective. It was the only reserve CH-46 squadron on the West Coast, and its longtime core members could unofficially blackball crappy aviators and, more important, jerks. By the time I interviewed with HMM-764's CO, Lt. Col. Ray "Weasel" Wersel, his OPSO, Maj. Robert "Hermbo" Hermes, and five other "players" in the squadron, they already knew about my reputation as an officer and as a pilot. After an hour-long semiformal interview, I left the squadron wondering if the Corps would take me back. I hadn't exactly been a pleasant Marine to be around during my last year on active duty, and some pilots in HMM-764 still remembered. (First impression wasn't important as a lasting impression. Don't burn your bridges.) I would finally grow up.

Later that afternoon, "Weasel" called me at home.

"Q, you're in. Congratulations!"

For the next four years, I served in HMM-764, deployed to the Caribbean, and flew NVG missions over Death Valley to insert Drug Enforcement Agency agents. The counter-narcotic efforts were coordinated through Joint Task Force 6 Headquarters, based in El Paso, Texas. The squadron also went to the "boat" and participated in summer live-fire exercises in Twentynine Palms.

Compared with the "1,000-hour" cockpit of my active-duty squadron, HMM-764's paired aircrew usually combined to exceed 3,000 flight hours, not counting the thousands of flight hours that nearly a fourth of the pilots had through their airline careers. I had no close calls; the "Moonlighters" crashed no helicopters and killed no Marines during my stint with the unit. My buddies from HMM-161, Pepe, Roy, Torch, and longtime friends Crash,

Guido, Hondo, and Stinky also joined the unit, and all of us had a blast, flying with each other, training in case we ever got activated for war.*

In October 1997, my father joined my mother and me at a HMM-764 Saturday drill. My CO, "Hermbo," presided over a promotion ceremony and administered the oath of office to four of us captains who were about to become majors. When Hermbo called me front and center, my parents followed. A decade after I became a Marine 2d lieutenant on a bright June day at UCLA, my father had finally witnessed one of my promotions. He pinned the oak leaf clusters onto my collars as I had once wished he could. Just as I had attended my father's VNAF reunions, he would also come to one of our HMM-764's Marine Corps Birthday Balls. We had come to terms with each other, me more so than he, because I had been the one with the issue.

There was no prouder moment for us collectively than in 1999, when I accompanied my father to the Los Angeles Convention Center for his U.S. citizenship ceremony. It was much more special than my lonely and indifferent trek in 1984. My father was thrilled; he had rehearsed his immigration oral interview question bank with me. I knew he wouldn't have any problem. As the two of us stood on the convention floor, a federal judge strolled onto the stage and gave a feverishly short, but patriotic, introduction. I recognized Judge David O. Carter, a Marine veteran who had been seriously wounded in Khe Sanh. I had met Judge Carter at a UCLA football rally; he was also a die-hard Bruin season-ticket holder and active in Marine Corps circles in Orange County. He was gracious to my father and me. He invited us back to his chamber and brought us coffee. We milled around with him for forty-five minutes, interrupting his usual busy day of presiding over serious legal cases.

In 1999 HMM-764 relocated to Edwards Air Force Base in the Mojave Desert. Its former home, and my base El Toro, was closing, victim of military downsizing; Tustin had closed two years earlier. I had begun an entrepreneurial endeavor and decided it was time to hang up my wings and leave the Corps. This time it was my choice again. This time it would be on good terms.

I flew my final flight in May that year. As the one-hour hop came to an end, I could feel the emotional rush of a decade-long association with Tustin,

---

*In 2004, HMM-764 was activated and sent to war for the first time in its history. During a six-month rotation in Iraq, the squadron flew hundreds of combat missions and returned home intact. Pepe, Torch, and Hondo remained in the unit, which is scheduled to return to Iraq in the spring of 2005.

El Toro, and the Marine Corps. The Corps had taken me on a whirlwind tour, a journey I could have never imagined. The people I had met—only the good ones came to mind—became my supporters, my mentors, my lifelong buddies. Their powerful sense of teamwork, duty, and mission accomplishment had permeated me, enabling me to rise above my problems, to reach down and grab hold when things got difficult, to realize my weaknesses, and to compensate for my shortcomings.

As the CH-46 reached the bottom of its final approach, I added power and pulled back gently on the stick, bringing the ancient chopper to a nose-high hover, then a smooth final touchdown. Mission complete. On that note, my military aviation career came to an end with a goal I had set long ago—to have the same number of landings as takeoffs.

In August of 2000 my father also flew his final hop. He had returned to Vietnam to attempt to bring my brother to the States. Shortly after arriving, he became ill and had to rush back here. He was immediately taken into surgery so physicians could remove a large tumor in his brain. He was also diagnosed with late-stage lung cancer, most likely as a result of a thirty-five-year smoking habit that he had kicked for four years. The damage was done; his remaining quality of life would be determined by the treatment he chose: chemotherapy, radiation, or watch and wait. The prognosis was less than one year.

My old man gave it his all. At age sixty-five, he left the hospital a week after major brain surgery. I picked him up in Los Angeles; he would be moving in with me in Orange County, sleeping in a spare bedroom next to my mother. I had been living with my mother; actually, she moved in with me after she completed her Peace Corps tour. For six weeks, I lived under the same roof as my parents, something I hadn't done in twenty-five years. I was still a single man, although I had fallen head over heels for Shannon Ryan, a Floridian whom I met at a medical industry trade show in Vegas. During my father's sickness, Shannon (now my wife) was able to meet him on two occasions; both times remain dear to me.

As I worked my way through the city traffic, my sick and dying father gave the best praise I could have ever wished for. During the commute, I had to conduct a teleconference with the management team of my fledging Internet pharmaceutical marketing startup called MyDrugRep.com (now Lathian Systems). I was its chairman and CEO. I had neglected some of my corporate duties while tending to my father during his hospitalization. He must have listened attentively to my comments, specifically directed to my chief financial officer and my vice-president of marketing. Like most of the dot-bombs, I had managed to allow our company to burn through most of a $5 million investment from our investors, Hummer Winblad Venture Partners. My company was going bankrupt, my father was dying.

But I couldn't afford to fall apart, my father still needed me.

As I finished the call, my father shook his head in amazement. Tears welled in his eyes. "Oh, I'm so proud . . . so proud of you, Quang."

On Friday, November 10, 2000, at 7:10 p.m., my father took his last breath. He had lapsed into a ten-day-long coma, resulting from a massive stroke amid radiation therapy treatment. Around the world, in every clime and place, Marines celebrated the Corps' 225th birthday. Except me. I was crying. In Vietnam an eight-year-old boy would also grow up—like my sisters and me—without knowing his father.

Full circle. With my father's rescuer, retired Marine Col. John Braddon, 2004. (Author's Collection)

CHAPTER 24

FULL CIRCLE

P EOPLE HAVE TOLD ME THAT WITH DEATH COMES CLOSURE. It was the opposite for me. My father's passing away raised more questions and created a greater void inside me, a burning desire to ask him the $64,000 question. Fortunately, my friend Bernie Edelman had the foresight and the opportunity to get the answer when he interviewed my father in 1999.

More than three years after my father's death I pulled the audiocassettes out, the ones that Bernie had mailed me, slowly rewinding them to the beginning, and listening several times.

"When you think back, were all the fighting and the bloodshed worth the price?" Bernie inquired as only a professional journalist and veteran like him could phrase it. He drew reactions from my father that I never dared to pursue.

My father paused, then answered, "The way I see the war—it needed to end some way or another. When I was fighting the war in Vietnam, I still had many relatives in the north. My wife also had relatives in the north. And my friends had relatives in the north. Both sides had families on the other side. I don't know how the Communists felt.

"But we [in South Vietnam], we knew that we're not going to win the war. We just kept it that way forever until we [would] die. That was it. In 1954 some South Vietnamese went to the north. From the north a million fled south. I could not figure out the war, so let's just end it that way. Yeah, we're the losers. But the war must end somehow. The killing has been going on for quite a long time. And now you don't know who the winner is."

I didn't expect my father to say those words. I thought he would still be gung-ho about how we (the South Vietnamese) could have won, how the

United States had abandoned us and how we need to keep fighting communism today.

I had been wrong all along about my father, and now I know the reasons why. I may still be wrong but I can surmise that my father saw the humanity in his supposed enemy, the Communists. He experienced firsthand kindness from my Great Aunt Phu and Great Uncle Minh, the high-ranking communist official, who brought him food and medicine while he was incarcerated in the north and from the prison camp cadre who fed him rice and sugar that saved him from beriberi.

My father's refusal after imprisonment to blame anyone for the betrayal, his lack of bitterness, his avoidance of hatred were his greatest legacies, affecting me more than his sense of humor and his military service. He somehow managed to move on, until his final days, even calmly telling my sister Thi during one of her visits to the hospital before he went into surgery: "I'm not afraid to die. I've lived a full life, I have no regrets."

There was another person I needed to meet to fulfill my filial duties.

After reading the Do Xa (the battle where my father was shot down in 1964) narrative posted at HMM-364's website, I sent its webmaster an e-mail. The next day, retired Marine Maj. Frank Gulledge, fondly known as Uncle Frank, forwarded former Marine helicopter pilot John Braddon and crew chief Warren Smith's e-mail addresses. I promptly contacted them, and they responded with utter but pleasant surprise.

Smith had missed the April 27, 1964, Do Xa Operation because he had been on liberty. A few days later, he flew into an open field to salvage parts from several helicopters shot down during the operation. My father's VNAF A-1 Skyraider was also there. He walked around wreckage, marveling at the line of bullet holes carved by VC machine guns. He took several photographs of the A-1 and kept them in his Vietnam memorabilia box for over three decades. After several long conversations, he mailed two 8 × 10-inch original photographs of the wrecked plane to me.

After I interviewed retired Marine Col. John Braddon over the phone, I jumped on a commercial flight to Washington, D.C., to meet my father's rescuer. I hailed a cab from the city to Dulles International Airport.

At age seventy-four, John Braddon still sounded like a tough Marine fighter pilot (he only flew helicopters for one tour), proudly volunteering at the new Smithsonian Air and Space Museum (the Steven F. Udvar-Hazy

Center) near Dulles Airport. As I approached the docent desk, I hesitated for a moment to make sure it was him. I glanced at the pages that I had printed from the Internet. Braddon's headshot was taken in 1964, when he was a young major flying H-34 helicopters with HMM-364 in Danang. A shock of gray hair now fell across his forehead, just above steely blue eyes that could still clearly see across the gigantic museum hangar without glasses.

I did not think Braddon would believe me, so I brought along the tape of my father's interview by Bernie as well as his military records and his flight school yearbook. He too brought his Marine cruise book, with photos of his helicopter squadron and their year in Vietnam, in and out of combat. We traded war stories, his much longer than mine.

We had only chatted for a few minutes, when Braddon began introducing himself to fifteen or so visitors for a walking tour. I decided to tag along at the back, already familiar with most of the history of the aircraft on display. Unlike the other senior docents, Braddon didn't need a microphone. His voice radiated across the hangar deck, bouncing off immaculately restored war birds as if he was briefing his aircrew before a mission. His eyes sparkled; his voice reflected a pride in aviation history, and he was living proof from having flown several of the aircraft on display. He didn't need a script; he was history.

Between his tours Braddon and I sat down for a quick lunch. I played the portion of the tape where my father spoke about his crash-landing near Do Xa. While eating, I couldn't tell if Braddon had heard my father's cracked voice: "The U.S. Marines [later] had their own Cobra gunships. They didn't trust us, the South Vietnamese fighters. But we still went on an operation called Do Xa. D.O.X.A. We were on airborne alert. The helicopters didn't have enough firepower, so they requested support from us. I went in and got hit, and I crashed."

The museum was abuzz with announcements and more visitors. So I replayed my father's "Do Xa" comment.

I had come in person to ask Braddon only one question.

"Sir, why did you do it? You had to provide search and rescue for eighteen U.S. Marine helicopters. Why leave your flight and go after a Vietnamese pilot?"

Without a pause, Braddon interrupted me. "When I saw your father go down, I went after him . . . no hesitation . . . because he had supported us."

I shook Braddon's hands and thanked him—for his service, and for rescuing my father. I stopped thinking about what if he hadn't.

It was still early in the afternoon. As the museum shuttle driver weaved through traffic back to Washington, I could see the Marine War Memorial in Arlington, forever emblazoned in our nation's conscience and in my life. In the United States fallen soldiers will always be remembered. From the Tomb of the Unknown Soldier to the Korean War Memorial, I've visited them all.

The U.S. Capitol stood in the distance, far removed from military memorials, at the opposite end of the National Mall. The men and women inside that building retain the power to declare and end wars, past and present. I wish more of them could have experienced the effects of war and its lingering wounds. I wish I could someday meet those who voted for President Johnson's Tonkin Gulf Resolution in 1964 and those who torpedoed President Ford's plea in 1975 to help a collapsing South Vietnam.

The White House stood in the middle, its occupiers needing to be held accountable for their foreign forays.

I shake myself free of the bitterness. "The war had to end. We had been killing each other for so long." My father's voice echoes in my mind. *It's over! Let it go!*

Instead, I need to thank Congress for passing the Refugee Act and subsequent legislation that has enabled over a million Vietnamese to live here in freedom. Refugees are still coming, nearly thirty years after the war, from the last camps in the Philippines. A thirty-four-year-old Australian lawyer named Hoi Trinh is helping resettle the remaining 1,800 Vietnamese refugees. Some have been toiling in the camps for fifteen years.

I remember the images on the Internet of northwestern Vietnam where my father once wasted the prime of his life laboring in prison camps, trying to survive his incarceration. The fruits of his labor and those held in the camps of Son La and Hoang Lien Son (now called Lao Cai and Yen Bai) provinces were evident. Manioc plants had given way to rice fields and tea plantations. Ethnic minorities—Red Dzao, Nung, Zay, Black Thai, and various H'mong tribes—indigenous Vietnamese wearing colorful outfits—are able to live a meager and simple life.

The area where my father was imprisoned has become a hot destination for Western tourists, especially adventurers and photographers. Tall mountains guard endless fields split by the famed Red River, where, according to legend, the first Vietnamese (the "Lac") lived. The Hoang Lien Son Moun-

Accepting the Republic of Vietnam flag on behalf of my family at my father's funeral in California, 2000. (Author's Collection)

tains, the "Tonkinese Alps," look as beautiful as any destinations I've seen in person or on video. The entire area symbolizes peace and serenity. I doubt if any of the tour guides knew the grounds they were traversing had once been the soil upon which thousands perished. I wonder if visitors wonder why so many Vietnamese had to endure such revenge at the hands of their own people, the victors who had declared peace in April 1975.

A verse of the VNAF Hymn echoed in my head. *Ôi phi công danh tiếng, muôn đời. O pilot famous for life.*

I look up at the blue skies. Not a plane is in the air. I do not hear the afternoon traffic passing by. Life around me seems to have slowed down.

I imagine a VNAF A-1 Skyraider swooping low over the Mall then popping into a victory roll, but I force it out of my mind.

My head is clear, my breaths come free. I feel a sense of relief as I have never felt before.

EPILOGUE

I had no idea what to expect when *A Sense of Duty* was first published in 2005 on the thirtieth anniversary of the fall of Saigon. No first-time writer ever does, I suppose. Part memoir, part military history, part family history, part war story, part immigrant-life story, and, ultimately, part of the American journey that many have experienced in our country, my book gave the South Vietnamese a voice, a voice that I dearly wanted to be heard. And that was what I had wanted to accomplish the most.

By spring 2004, it had taken me a decade to wrestle with Vietnam in my head—and only a slim proposal containing two short sample chapters to show to editors. By then the literature about Vietnam in the English language already had more than 3,500 books from nearly every angle—every American angle.

Something was still missing. In a feverish rush after my agent sold the proposal, I finished the book in a four-month sprint. All the emotions were set free and I felt a great sense of relief.

My biggest postpublication worry was that a Vietnam veteran would challenge my writing at a book-signing event. But that never happened. The reception was overwhelming: Americans wanted to hear about the South Vietnamese. I received by far the most e-mails from readers who had served in Vietnam as part of the U.S. military.

Below is one of those e-mails, which I have slightly edited for clarity.

Dear Quang,

I just finished reading your book. . . . I found it to be extremely interesting and well written. When I was in Vietnam (27 May 1967 to 14 June 1968 in I Corps—Chu Lai to the DMZ), I had a less than stellar opinion of the Army of the Republic of Vietnam (ARVN) and the civilians. I considered all *civilians, and half the ARVN, to be VC. I made no attempt to learn anything about the people and the culture. This was a mistake for me, for during the years after my return I met and became friends with many Vietnamese. And have developed a strong respect for their character, work ethic, and family devotion.*

I was unmoved by the abject poverty and misery I witnessed there. I was only concerned about the safety of my fellow Marines and myself. Kill the enemy, not be killed by him. It was forty years after my initial arrival in Vietnam that my wife and I visited there last May. I was so pleased to see the marked improvements in the country and the greatly higher standard of living and education.

What your book did for me was give a view of the Vietnamese experience of the war, which I never even considered during the war and only thought I understood in the ensuing years. Your search for answers and understanding has helped me understand myself a bit more, and for that I am grateful.

Like many Vietnam vets, I am still conflicted about the experience. I hope these brief words, perhaps poorly expressed, show my appreciation for what I am sure must have been an extremely difficult project. Thank you for sharing your story.

Semper fi—Fred Williams, Florida

The second biggest group of readers who contacted me were the South Vietnamese veterans and their children, some of them my age. Surely the book would have had greater reach if it had been published in Vietnamese. Nevertheless, letters such as the one below kept coming.

Quang,

I have uncles that were in the VNAF and ARVN that either died during the war or were sent to re-education camp for years afterward, so I know what those vets had gone through. My girlfriend's dad is still in Vietnam and he spent 1975 to 1988 in various camps around Vietnam because he was a general in the ARVN. We visited him last year and luckily he is still in good health and good spirited even for what he had to endure.

For years I felt that the ARVN was not treated fairly and was made a scapegoat for the American failure there. I thought I was the only one that figured this out but have no way of expressing it. I'm glad that you put out the time to write your book and gave your lectures to people that have no idea what our soldiers had to go through.

Thanks again and let me know if you are ever in San Diego for any of your lectures or book signing or if you are close to town. I would like to attend it or have a chance to meet with you in the future. Take care.

Minh Nguyen

So much news from overseas still triggers my memories of Vietnam. And I am not the only one who is still obsessed with that conflict.

The first Americans I met were military advisers, much like the ones who are training military forces in Iraq and Afghanistan. That year, 1970, the United States was in the process of Vietnamization—turning the war over to the South Vietnamese as U.S. troops simultaneously departed.

I remember as a boy visiting my father's South Vietnamese Air Force squadron and shaking hands with U.S. pilots who wore reassuring smiles, green flight suits, and pistols. Today, six years into the war in Iraq, memories of Vietnam come back when I hear our president talk about his eventual plans to withdraw U.S. troops from Iraq or send 30,000 more to Afghanistan after a fraudulent election.

If U.S. troops cannot extinguish the insurgencies and end the carnage from improvised explosive devices (IEDs), should we expect the Iraqis and Afghans to fare much better with less training? They too are doomed as independent military forces if the United States makes the same critical mistakes it made with the South Vietnamese.

Lewis Sorley, author of *A Better War,* wrote about one Vietnamese officer who had forty-seven different U.S. advisers. The United States essentially micromanaged South Vietnamese military and political affairs while Vietnamization's key assumption—that the South Vietnamese could successfully fight entirely on their own without U.S. advisers and air power—was never tested until the very end of the war.

In the current wars, we should hand over responsibilities to the Iraqis and Afghans at a faster pace and put them to the test while U.S. troops are still in country. Taxpayers have to wonder what our trillion-dollar wars will bring to the American, Afghani, and Iraqi people. These wars require more than partisan politicking in favor of either withdrawing our troops now or staying the course.

If our success in World War II had given America false hopes for Vietnam, then Desert Storm, my war, imparted to a new generation of bystanders unrealistic expectations of war in Iraq and Afghanistan: quick and overwhelming victories with low casualties by using smart weapons and an all-volunteer military.

When we liberated the Kuwaitis, the United States had its first clear-cut military victory since 1945, despite Congress shirking its duty to declare war ever since the "day which will live in infamy," December 7, 1941. Led by veterans who remembered too well the lessons of Vietnam, the Pentagon overestimated enemy strength in the Persian Gulf, then "pooled" and fooled the media. The [Colin] Powell Doctrine required an overpowering force, strong public support, and a clear exit strategy.

Together, it all worked.

Iraq's military in 1991 had loomed larger than life, combat-proven in a long war against Iran and deeply entrenched in Kuwait behind twelve-foot-high sand walls, hoping to bog down the American-led attack in oil-filled fiery traps. After thirty-seven days of unrelenting aerial assault, it took us four days to reach Kuwait City.

The result was a desensitized conflict and a ticker-tape victory parade in Manhattan, à la World War II. I had wanted to march in that parade, to sweep a girl off her feet and kiss her, but all I got was a set of orders back to the Persian Gulf and a cheap Kuwait Liberation Medal.

At first, I, too, fell victim to hindsight and history. As a boy who fled Saigon sixteen years earlier, I had been on the losing end of the longest and most divisive war America has fought. Images of refugees scrambling to board the last outbound choppers played in my mind. Yet beneath our helicopters that day over Kuwait, thousands of allied tanks, armored personnel carriers, and troops were converging on the capital like a scene out of the movie *Patton*. Liberation was much sweeter than evacuation.

While waiting for the injured to be loaded at the bombed-out Kuwait International Airport on that penultimate day, I stared at the smoke billowing through the brown miasma toward Basra, in Iraq. I never expected to see that awful place again. I was wrong.

In the annals of military history, Desert Storm had been the exception, an anomaly of force on force, open desert warfare, with unlimited air and armor unleashed on an unconcealed enemy. Call it a perfect war planner's dream, an Xbox 360 bestseller. As convincing as the outcome was in Kuwait, no one then could have guessed the long-term effect of not going all the way to Baghdad.

The biggest impact may be the increasing gap between those in uniform and those wearing civvies. With two open-ended wars sans a draft, apathy is on the rise in America, especially in areas without a high military or veterans presence. War seems distant from daily life, war protesting a vanishing act. No risk, no rebellion. Just get a job with health insurance.

My desert-tan flight suit no longer fits; my black-green-red-white Kuwait Liberation Medal is lost in my closet. When I last checked, eBay listed many similar medals, with a starting bid as low as ninety-nine cents. Will the Iraqis award U.S. troops the Liberation Medal or the Iraq Occupation Medal? How about the Afghans?

Finally, we have not heard the last about Vietnam. It appears that we are on our way out of Iraq by 2011. But Afghanistan is an entirely different story.

America's longest allies in any of its wars can offer us lessons for Afghanistan a generation after their own war. Ordering more U.S. troops to their country was not necessarily an effective strategy. Yet no one paid much attention since they had been a part of the most corrupt, inept, and maligned military in history, according to American experts.

Who were these allies and what can President Barack Obama learn from their experience before making his decision on escalating the war in Afghanistan?

They are the South Vietnamese, the "other" Vietnam veterans, many of whom have immigrated to the United States since the end of the Vietnam War. They fought in our longest and most divisive conflict. They were trained by the American military and accompanied by American advisers in the field. More than 250,000 died during their 10,000-day war; thousands more were maimed. In the end they lost their country in the most rapid, public, and humiliating way.

At a time when journos, generals, and politicos are comparing and contrasting Afghanistan and Vietnam, the voice of the South Vietnamese is missing in action. Often ridiculed as "Marvin the Arvin" for ARVN (Army of the Republic of Vietnam), they are the only allies we've ever abandoned on the battlefield—so far. Their legacy may be destiny for the Afghanistan Security Forces.

After the war, there was no national reconciliation in Vietnam. Losers left town if they could; those stuck behind faced retaliation and were marched into the reeducation camps (including my father, for twelve years). Some were imprisoned for nearly two decades. Others died in silence.

But some of the losers in Vietnam did speak, and some of what they said may be useful today.

The late Army historian Colonel Harry Summers wrote in his 1995 book, *The New World Strategy:* "The United States cannot do for an ally what it is unwilling to do for itself. The real danger is that the U.S. response will be so overwhelming, and its attitude so impatient and condescending, that it smothers what will and self-reliance does exist."

After the war, a South Vietnamese officer was asked, "What mistakes do you think the Americans made in preparing [the] South Vietnamese to fight the war?"

"Two things," the officer replied. "First, when American troops came to Vietnam, they try to do everything. And they make the South Vietnamese lose the initiative. . . . So the South Vietnamese don't rely on themselves. They rely on the Americans."

Americans would find revealing the conclusions of a little-known 1978 report by the Rand Corporation. In a study prepared for the Defense Department's Office of the Historian, three researchers, including internationally acclaimed terrorism expert Brian Jenkins, debriefed twenty-seven South Vietnamese generals, diplomats, and politicians a year after they lost their country. The report's stand-alone conclusion: South Vietnamese officials agreed that the overarching cause for the debacle was the American role in the drama.

Two years ago, Jenkins said the report was disregarded because after Watergate, Americans both in and out of government were tired of hearing about Vietnam. Moreover, "the Army abandoned any counterinsurgency tactics and strategy from the Vietnam War because it did not want any more Vietnams," recalled Jenkins, himself a former Special Forces captain in Vietnam.

Since the Vietnam War, the U.S. military has so insulated itself from criticism that its leaders shunned two decades of experience in Indochina and failed to include any meaningful optempo guidelines in its latest counterinsurgency manual. The manual hadn't been updated until General David Petraeus and a few others re-wrote it in 2006—for the first time in twenty years for the Army and twenty-five years for the Marine Corps.

The counterinsurgency manual mentions Mao Zedong and North Vietnam's *dau tranh* ("the struggle"), but nothing about the South Vietnamese. One vignette covers a pacification lesson, but from American civilian and military perspectives only.

In the Rand study, another South Vietnamese officer recalled: "When South Vietnam scored a success, Americans took the credit. When the North scored a success, it was always Ho Chi Minh or General Giap."

The *Los Angeles Times* reported that American military advisers conceded in 1972 "that U.S. Air Force eagerness to keep itself heavily involved in the

Indochina War has often squeezed out the Vietnamese Air Force, even when it had planes available and pilots eager to fly."

After eight years of war, the Afghans are becoming war-weary and perhaps skeptical. Sending 30,000 more combat troops may produce the same negative effect as in Vietnam, where the U.S. military stayed involved for too long, no matter what the tactical results, thus eroding the national identity of its Vietnamese allies.

America is better off maintaining a smaller footprint and committing only with advisers and aid. The only guaranteed outcome of another escalation in Afghanistan is more American casualties. And more Afghan deaths.

So then you may ask, "What's next for you, Quang?" Well, I have had enough of professional politicians making their decisions on my behalf. In 1965, Congress passed the Gulf of Tonkin Act, which escalated the war in Vietnam, and Congress denied aid to South Vietnam in its final hours of existence. Congress gave President George W. Bush the authority to go to war without much oversight.

Many in Congress have no idea about the impact of war for many decades to come. I can do a better job and I will be entering the political realm.

As a healthcare entrepreneur, Marine Corps veteran, and active member of the community, I am running for Congress because these are challenging times for our country. We face uncertainties overseas and at home. Career politicians have failed us. We need a fresh voice and a new choice.

I joined the Republican Party for its principled stance on less government, lower taxes, and sensible and strong national defense. I believe in individual choice, liberty, and the right to pursue happiness. I believe in personal responsibility and respect for others.

We need more independent, fiscally conservative leaders in Washington with strong values and real-world business experience. We need leaders who will help create jobs, advance entrepreneurship, reward innovation, improve education, and reduce our staggering national debt. We need leaders who have a deep understanding of the national security issues plaguing our country and who have served our nation firsthand in harm's way.

When I arrived in America as a boy from Vietnam, I had lost my country, my freedom, and my father. Yet the American Dream was still attainable. It took dedication, encouragement, hard work, and perseverance. And it can still be done. We need leaders who will emphasize self-sufficiency and who will inspire others to seek opportunities—not just government handouts.

Will my American Dream take me to the hallowed halls of Congress? Stay tuned and check ASenseOfDuty.com to get the latest campaign news. Win or lose, there is no other place that I would rather live with my family than in the United States of America, where anything is *still* possible.

Quang Pham

ORANGE COUNTY, CALIFORNIA
NOVEMBER 2009

GLOSSARY

AK-47: Assault rifle firing 7.62mm rounds. Standard issue for the North Vietnamese Army (NVA), the Viet Cong (VC), and Soviet-bloc countries

ARG: Amphibious ready group

ARVN: Army of the Republic of Vietnam

BOAT: Navy ship or "the boat"

BOQ: Bachelor officer quarters

CLASS "A" (MISHAP): A serious aircraft mishap typically involving loss of life or a major financial loss, defined as $1 million (U.S.) or greater

CO: Commanding officer

DMZ: Demilitarized Zone

FAC: Forward air controller (one who coordinates air strikes)

FNG: Fucking new guy

HAC: Helicopter aircraft commander

KIA: Killed in action

LZ: Landing zone (usually in reference to helicopters)

MEU: Marine expeditionary unit (comprising an infantry battalion, reinforced squadron with helicopters and Harriers, and a service support component embarked aboard amphibious ships)

MIA: Missing in action

NVA: North Vietnamese Army

NVGs: Night-vision goggles

OCS: Officer Candidate School

POW: Prisoner of war

PSP: Pierced-steel planking (for runways and taxiways)

RVN: Republic of Vietnam (South Vietnam)

SAM: Surface-to-air missile

SRV: Socialist Republic of Vietnam (since 1976)

TBS: The Basic School (six-month training course for new second lieutenants)

UN: United Nations

USAF: U.S. Air Force

VC: Viet Cong

VNAF: (South) Vietnamese Air Force

XO: Executive officer (or second in charge)

APPENDIX

Citation

The White House

By Virtue of the Authority Vested In Me as President of the United States and as Commander-In-Chief of the Armed Forces of the United States, I Have Today Awarded the Presidential Unit Citation to the 514th Tactical Fighter Squadron Republic of Vietnam Air Force for Extraordinary Heroism and Outstanding Performance of Duty

The 514th Tactical Fighter Squadron, a unit of the Republic of Vietnam Air Force, is cited for extraordinary heroism and outstanding performance of duty in combat against an armed enemy of the Republic of Vietnam throughout the period 1 January 1964 to 28 February 1965. Participating in daily actions in support of Republic of Vietnam ground operations, the courageous men of the 514th Tactical Fighter Squadron carried out their attacks on military targets with indomitable spirit and determination. The fierce determination to destroy the enemy displayed by the men of this unit was exemplified in the 6,000 sorties, and 13,000 flying hours compiled in support of ground operations during this period. Frequently, aircraft were landed just long enough to secure additional armament before continuing their attacks against Communist aggressors threatening their homeland. The determined and daring attacks launched by the valiant men of the 514th Tactical Fighter Squadron against the heavily armed and fanatical Communist insurgents, in the face of fierce ground fire, had a demoralizing effect upon the enemy, raised the morale and fighting spirit of the supported ground troops, resulted in inestimable damage to the Communist aggressors in the loss of men and materiel, and were instrumental in stemming the tide of Communist aggression against the Republic of Vietnam during this period. While a ground count of the many enemy killed and wounded was impossible, the heavy losses inflicted upon the enemy by this unit are known to have been significant, severely restricting his ability or desire to conduct sustained ground operations.

Despite being called upon to provide key personnel to cadre the organization of three additional fighter squadrons during this period, the 514th Tactical Fighter Squadron continued to carry out every assigned mission. The actions of the 514th Tactical Fighter Squadron reflect conspicuous gallantry and extraordinary heroism in keeping with the finest traditions of the military service and reflect great credit on the Republic of Vietnam.

—Lyndon B. Johnson

PHOTO: © YUEN LUI STUDIO.

Quang Pham, a businessman and Marine Corps veteran, is running for the U.S. Congress in California's 47th District. He is a popular public speaker and has appeared on national radio and television programs. Visit his website at www.ASenseOfDuty.com.

FAIR FORMS

Essays in English Literature from Spenser to Jane Austen

Transported with celestiall desyre
Of those faire formes . . .

EDMUND SPENSER, 'An Hymne of Heavenly Beautie'

FAIR FORMS

*Essays in English Literature
from Spenser to Jane Austen*

EDITED BY MAREN-SOFIE RØSTVIG

ROWMAN AND LITTLEFIELD
TOTOWA, NEW JERSEY

First published in the United States 1975
by Rowman and Littlefield, Totowa, New Jersey

Library of Congress Cataloging in Publication Data

Røstvig, Maren Sofie.
    Fair forms; essays in English literature from
Spenser to Jane Austen.

    Includes bibliographical references.
        1.   English literature—Addresses, essays, lectures.
    1.   Title.
PR403.R6   820'.9'2   74-17472
ISBN 0-87471-598-9

Printed in Great Britain

Contents

List of Illustrations

Preface

Structural analysis is a key that unlocks many doors, and so no wonder the study of literary theory has been structurally oriented from its very beginning and at no time more so perhaps than today. To deplore the lack of proper attention to structure therefore may seem utterly perverse, if not frivolous. I would nevertheless argue that the theoretical interest in structure has failed to influence practical criticism to the extent that one would have expected in view of its professed importance. If one considers the sustained energy with which critics have pursued poetic imagery, for example, or the uses of irony, it is at once apparent that the concept of structure, vital though it is, has elicited no comparable massed attempt to unravel its many complexities. Efforts along these lines have been sporadic rather than sustained; they have seldom been taken far enough, nor have they been worked into some kind of survey or connected argument about the role of structure in pre-Romantic literature.

It may be futile to call for any such survey; the very nature of the task may make it impossible to perform. Even Swift's seven sages shut up close in seven chambers for seven years (with or without computers) would most likely have had to admit defeat. But what one may legitimately expect is a keener awareness of the role of structure in individual textual analyses, and a more systematic attention than one usually finds.

It is possible, however, that this awareness is in the process of becoming more widely shared. The studies collected here, for example, are sharply focused on structure, not because the editor insisted on some kind of unifying principle, but quite simply because this was the direction taken by each contributor. As a consequence this volume displays a wide range of structural approaches extending from a classical investigation of narrative structure in a novel by Jane Austen, to the structural complexities (often of a numerological kind) of Spenser's *Fowre Hymnes* and Milton's 'On the Morning of Christ's Nativity'.

Einar Bjorvand's investigation of the complex patterns of cross references within Spenser's *Fowre Hymnes* enables the reader to perceive and interpret the overall thematic movement with far greater precision than has been so far achieved. The analysis was partly carried out by means of Mr Bjorvand's recently published concordance to Spenser's poetic *progressio quaternaria*.

Each essay is, of course, self-contained, but the two studies of Milton's *Nativity Ode* are complementary. These trace various sequential arrangements, sometimes of a balanced or symmetrical character, and sometimes of the kind usually referred to as numerological. As these essays indicate, the two types of arrangement may be so closely connected that it is singularly illogical to admit the one and reject the other in the manner of some American Milton scholars. But in the case of Dryden's *Essay of Dramatick Poesie* and Fielding's *Tom Jones* the structural analyses submitted here contain no references to the now largely forgotten subject of symbolic numbers. They depend, instead, on an analysis of the author's use of structural allusions. While we are thoroughly familiar with the technique of tracing verbal echoes or related image-clusters, we have failed to perceive the point that it was possible for a *structure* to be imitated and consciously echoed not merely as a matter of convenience, but in order to invoke the associations invested in it. As H. Neville Davies shows, this is what Dryden did when he decided on the form for his *Essay of Dramatick Poesie*, and once we grasp the import of the selected form we realise that Dryden's essay is an ambitious defence of London as a cultural centre in the mid-1660s.

Although my own study of *Tom Jones* touches on the topic of structural allusion in its discussion of Samuel Johnson's *Rasselas*, structural analysis is largely a point of departure for the discovery of Fielding's use of various aspects of the myth of Hercules. The action of the central section (Books VII–XII) is seen to constitute an exact narrative version of the theme so popular among Renaissance and neoclassical painters of the Choice of Hercules.

The essay which concludes the volume—Grete Ek's analysis of Jane Austen's *Pride and Prejudice*—argues that the opposition between Darcy and Elizabeth is apparent rather than real. Beneath the antithetical framework we recognise a substructure based on a gradual revelation of facts that contradict the dramatic illusion of the first half of the novel. The resolution, therefore, terminates a process of clarification rather than one of substantial change.

If this volume as a whole carries a message, it must be that the mechanics of literary design, if examined with due care, may afford important new insights into basic thematic concerns. It is implicit in this message that the gap between numerological and more traditional approaches to structure should be bridged, since strictly speaking it does not exist.

Oslo   M.-S. R.
22 April 1974

I

Spenser's defence of poetry

SOME STRUCTURAL ASPECTS OF THE
FOWRE HYMNES

EINAR BJORVAND

IN his teaching that 'every one that exalteth himself shall be humbled; but he that humbleth himself shall be exalted', Christ has epitomised the crucial predicament of the devout Christian. The truly righteous man is to be known—not only to God, but also to his fellow Christians —through protestations of sinfulness, and by his confession and repudiation of former errors. 'God, be merciful to me a sinner', prayed the publican, smiting his breast. Yet, plainly this behaviour may become a kind of self-praise: the Pharisee too may adopt the attitude of the repentant publican, but he will remain a Pharisee. 'For faith consists not in a body bending but in a mind believing.'[1]

What then of the penitent sinner who speaks to us through the dedicatory epistle to his *Fowre Hymnes*? Is he a publican or a Pharisee? Has he humbled his mind as well as his body? The question is of interest because the answer may shed light on the structure of the *Hymnes* and help us to decide whether they are arranged in a sequence of steady and gradual ascent, or whether the second pair should be seen as contrasted to the first pair. Spenser certainly takes great care to place his 'lewd layes' well into the past. He has created a myth which associates, very appropriately, passionate love with youth and allows it to be superseded, with growing maturity, by love of God. He promises 'to amend, and by way of retractation to reforme' the product of erring youth.[2] But Spenser's statement that the first pair of the *Hymnes* was written early in his career should not be taken at its face value; for the mass of both external and internal evidence leaves little doubt that the hymns of earthly love and beauty were in fact written, or rewritten, after the publication of the *Amoretti* in 1595.[3] Furthermore, the dedication might seem to invite the conclusion that Spenser, now in his forties and at the end of his poetical career, had come to embrace a religious outlook on life that involved a rejection of sexual love. But such a view would make nonsense of Spenser's praise of the two Countesses as representatives of love and beauty 'both in the one and the other kinde'.[4]

The theories outlined above seem to corroborate the supposition that despite Spenser's tone of high moral seriousness, the 'retractation' should be regarded as a conventional cliché.[5] But the fact that such retractions were in fashion does not deprive the dedication of its claims on our attention. Several considerations may have guided Spenser in his phrasing of the dedicatory epistle. It may be designed to safeguard his hymns from moral censure. But we should also be aware that the preamble functions as a prologue to the hymns and may be intended to play its part in shaping the attitude of the reader. Perhaps its most obvious effect is to put the reader on the alert, watching keenly for implicit as well as explicit contrasts and cross-references within the subtly organised structure of the *Fowre Hymnes*.

It seems a reasonable deduction, at all events, that Spenser's major concern was not merely to render his first pair of hymns harmless by neutralising their moral blemishes, but that he was much more concerned with the artistic unity of his work as a whole. Critics have tried to account for this essential unity, which is perceptible in the *Fowre Hymnes*, either by interpreting the last two hymns as a complement to the first two,[6] or by regarding the account of love and beauty in the first pair as a description of lower steps on the Neoplatonic ladder of love.[7] But both of these tidy assumptions require further inspection. After all, the poet-speaker of the last two hymns can hardly be said to be recommending the experiences recorded in the first two hymns as necessary or even desirable 'steps' on the ladder to heavenly love and beauty. In fact, the transition from the first to the last pair of hymns suggests a Christian conversion rather than a gradual ascent. The first two hymns record a stage in the poet's life, a stage which he eventually outgrew when he 'put away childish things'. It may be argued that we are nearer to the true relationship between the two pairs by saying, with Robert Ellrodt, that 'if a structural unity is discovered in the *Fowre Hymnes*, it will be the unity of a diptych with parallel but contrasted themes on each leaf, not the continuous ascent of a Platonic *scala*'.[8] There are others besides Ellrodt who have glimpsed a system of contrasts and verbal echoes in the *Hymnes*, but the rich complexity of Spenser's scheme seems never to have been investigated.

Spenser was not content simply to state his present attitude to his 'early' hymns and then offer them as a warning to others 'of like age and disposition'. He also had to ensure that the reader would be willing to accompany the poet on his ascent to the vision of heavenly love and beauty. The first pair of hymns was needed both to point a contrast between earthly and heavenly love and also to give the true story of man's journey to harmony with God and his fellow men. Surely, until man realises that he *is* a sinner, until he can pray with the publican, 'God, be merciful to me a sinner', he is denied the divine grace needed for his ascent.

The discussion of the relationship between the two pairs of hymns touches on Spenser's conception of the function of his poetry. Does his poetry have the power not only to 'show the way' but also to 'intice any man to enter into it'?[9] How can Spenser make sure that the reader will not prefer love's 'Paradize' of pleasure in the first hymn to the 'sweete pleasures' of the 'soueraine light' in the last hymn? Spenser must have realised the rhetorical inadequacy of a mere appeal to the reader not to renew his 'passed follies'; a far wiser poetic strategy would be to permit the first pair to be, not simply a record of youthful errors, but part of a design to 'intice' the reader into choosing the right path. Such a design would enable Spenser to defend his poetry in the eyes of both God and man. The first two hymns prepare the way for the second pair and 'the two later hymns are designed to gain strength and meaning from the two former. The method is a complex system of parallels and contrasts'.[10]

Some contrasts and parallels strike the reader immediately: 'two Hymnes of earthly or naturall loue and beautie' are followed by 'two others of heauenly and celestiall'. Furthermore, each hymn praises one guardian deity, Cupid and Venus in the first two hymns, and Christ and Sapience in the 'heauenly' hymns. Thus the masculine love-god, Cupid, who has descended to earth from '*Venus* lap aboue', is paralleled by the loving Christ descending 'out of the bosome of eternall blisse'. Similarly, the maternal queen of beauty, Venus, characteristically remaining 'aboue', is paralleled in the last hymn by the heavenly, feminine figure of Sapience. But the pattern of parallelism and contrast can be seen to be more complex than this. It has been shown that in retrospect the *Fowre Hymnes* may be seen as displaying similar and clearly related patterns of falling and rising, and that there is an intricate interplay of parallel and contrasted verbal elements between the hymns.[11] But so far no attempt has been made to show

how the complex pattern of thematic and verbal contrasts and parallels is underscored by the stanzaic design of the hymns. The two later hymns represent a fresh start rather than a continuous progression from the former two. They may thus be seen to run parallel with the first pair, and the parallelism is brought out, not only in the thematic movement of the hymns, but also by their structure. Such a parallel structure throws new light on related and antithetical aspects of theme, imagery and form, and thus, ultimately, on the relationship between the two pairs.

The detection of a parallel structure in the *Fowre Hymnes* should come as no great surprise since a similar structural arrangement has been demonstrated in the *Epithalamion*.[12] The structure of *Epithalamion* is probably concentric, the first stanza matching the last stanza, the second stanza the penultimate one and so on. In the *Fowre Hymnes*, however, an exactly symmetrical arrangement of stanzas would distort the general thematic movement which clearly indicates that each of the 'earthly' hymns should be paired with its 'heavenly' counterpart.

For Spenser the publican's behaviour was only a part solution. As I hope to show, Spenser was concerned to vindicate his poetry, and he wrote and revised his *Fowre Hymnes* according to a structural pattern that allows even the first two hymns to form by parallelism and contrast, foreshadowing and antithesis, a glorification of God in his Trinity of supreme love, beauty, and wisdom.

II

Many readers, turning from the dedication to the introductory stanzas of *An Hymne in Honour of Love*, seem to have been surprised by the Petrarchan description of love. The Petrarchan elements in the first two hymns have been taken as evidence of the inclusion of older material.[13] But the modern reader sees a contrast between Petrarchism and Neoplatonism which may not have been there for Spenser.[14] And if we assume that Spenser had outgrown Petrarchism by the time he was preparing his hymns for publication, the question arises why he did not leave out the Petrarchan stanzas. However conventional the courtly tradition was, there were other ways open to a poet of his experience and achievement. Spenser must have had some good reason to stress the tyrannical aspects of love. If he wanted his first pair of hymns to fall into a pattern of contrast and parallelism with the second pair, and if he wanted at the same time to make his poems seem to describe his psychological development, the firmly established courtly tradition was well suited to his purpose.

The description of the tormented lover who forgets all other claims on his attention and sees no dangers in the pursuit of love, who invariably overestimates the beauty of his mistress and exaggerates his happiness when well-favoured or his misery when rejected, must have been felt to correspond to at least a traditional psychology of love. The descriptions of the tyrannical Cupid playing with human destinies and of the loving Christ suffering to restore man to his former happiness may be consciously designed to point the contrast between earthly and heavenly love. Spenser may also have brought out this general pattern of contrast between earthly and heavenly love as clearly as he did in order to encourage the reader to pair stanzas or groups of stanzas in his two hymns of love.

One of the problems facing the critic who attempts to uncover the parallel structure of the hymns is what to make of the introductory stanzas. There are six introductory stanzas in *An Hymne in Honour of Love,* but there are only three in *An Hymne of Heavenly Love.* A quick glance through the introductory stanzas of the *Hymne of Love* will, however, reveal that this part of the hymn falls into two parts of three stanzas each; three for the lover's complaint and promise 'to sing the praises' of Cupid's name, and three invoking Cupid, the Muses and Nymphs, and the ladies. In the *Hymne of Heavenly Love* the invocation and repudiation of his 'lewd layes' in the three introductory stanzas, are followed by three stanzas in praise of the three persons of the Trinity. Thus the first three stanzas after the introduction of the *Hymne of Heavenly Love* describing the Father (stanza 4), the Son (stanza 5), and the Holy Spirit (stanza 6), parallel the invocation of Cupid (stanza 4), the Muses and Nymphs (stanza 5), and the young ladies (stanza 6) in the *Hymne of Love.*[15] But stanzas 4 to 6 of the *Hymne of Heavenly Love* also have further significance. Renaissance artists frequently designed their works so as to place particular emphasis on the sovereignty of the centre. 'Almost as a regular practice, they would devote the central place to some principal figure or event, or make it coincide with a structural division of the poem.'[16] If the sixteen introductory stanzas are disregarded, the three stanzas in praise of the Trinity become the three central stanzas of the *Fowre Hymnes,* with the Son in the triumphant mid position. The positioning of the Trinity at the centre of the *Fowre Hymnes* may be seen to be even more telling if the stanzas of the *Hymnes* can be seen to group themselves around this centre in a way which would enhance the formal perfection of the work and also form a key to our understanding of the thematic development of the whole sequence.

Stanza 7 (lines 43–49) in each hymn of love forms an introduction: to the *rule of tyranny* in the *Hymne of Love* and to the *rule of grace* in the *Hymne of Heavenly Love*.[17] Cupid, the great 'god of might', the 'subduer of mankynd', may be seen as the antithesis to the Holy Spirit who is praised as the eternal 'spring of grace and wisedome trew'. The contrast becomes apparent when the poet-speaker of the *Hymne of Love,* impressed and over-awed by the power of Cupid, humbly asks, who 'can expresse the glorie of thy *might?*', while the poet-speaker of the *Hymne of Heavenly Love* hopes to be inspired by the Holy Spirit to 'tell the marueiles by thy *mercie* wrought' (my italics).

Stanzas 8 to 10 (lines 50–70) of the two hymns offer parallel accounts of the birth and early activities of Cupid and the creation and 'eternall blis' of the prelapsarian angels. The ambivalence which surrounds Cupid, born of plenty and want, is contrasted with the 'infinite increase of Angels bright' created by the 'fruitfull loue' of God in his own likeness. While Cupid is stirred to rise from Chaos in 'which his goodly face long hidden was / From heauens view, and in deepe darknesse kept' (*HL* 9), the angels inherit 'the heauens illimitable hight', 'adornd with thousand lamps of burning light' (*HHL* 9). While the angels enjoy 'eternall blis', Cupid wakes up in a sublunary world of time indicated by the presence of Clotho. The 'hardie flight' of winged Cupid (*HL* 10) through the dark waste forms a clumsy imitation of the easy flight and 'nimble wings' of the angels (*HHL* 10) who wait on God and 'behold the glorie of his light'. The contrast is underscored by the selection of rhymewords. 'Bright-light-hight-spright' abound in the *Hymne of Heavenly Love*, while 'light' in stanza 10 of the *Hymne of Love* occurs only to stress the absence of light in Cupid's world ('yet wanting light'). The most frequent rhymewords in the *Hymne of Love* are 'fyre-desyre-flame', but when the poet 'turns to heavenly love, fire and flame [and desire] are conspicuously absent (except for the hellfire in *HHL*, line 89) until the very end of the poem when their meaning is presumably divinised by the identification of Love with Christ'.[18] By the end of stanza 10 the contrast between Cupid and the angels has been established in terms of the contrast between time and eternity, earth and heaven, darkness and light.

The story of the birth of Cupid may also have another significance. The glory and mystery of the 'wondrous cradle' of Cupid's infancy reminds us of Christ's nativity:

> where he encradled was
> In simple cratch, wrapt in a wad of hay,
> Betweene the toylefull Oxe and humble Asse.
> (*HHL* lines 225–27)

To grasp this contrast between the exaltation of Cupid and the humility of Christ helps our understanding of their separate roles.

Cupid is said to be older than his own nativity (*HL* line 54), like Christ, who before his birth was coeternal with God the Father. The parallelism is underlined in the structure of the two hymns since the stories of the nativities of Cupid and Christ are both to be found in the second stanza after the introduction. To readers accustomed to interpreting the second Psalm as the allegory *par excellence* of the Son as eternal godhead, direct and oblique reference to the *second* person of the Trinity in the *second* stanza of the hymn proper may have been felt to be appropriate. Furthermore, both Cupid and Christ are born in time, Cupid through Venus and Christ through the Virgin, and 'while Cupid is "begot of Plentie and of Penurie" (*HL, l.* 53), Christ also expresses the paradox of the richness and poverty of Love ("And in what rags, and in how base aray, / The glory of our heavenly riches lay," *HHL, ll.* 228–229)'.[19] Simply to see the similarities, however, is not enough. It is true that the description of Cupid as 'elder then [his] owne natiuitie' and 'the eldest of the heauenly Peares' (*HL* lines 54 and 56) may seem to link him with Christ, but on the other hand the denomination 'eldest' has no meaning in relation to the *eternal* Son. This becomes clear in the *Hymne of Heavenly Beautie* where Sapience is described as 'peerelesse maiesty' (*HHB* line 186). The seeming splendor of Cupid is reduced to earthly vainglory, and he becomes an earthly parody rather than a type of Christ. Spenser frequently uses the technique which Milton brought to perfection in *Paradise Lost*, where, for instance, Satan 'High on a throne of royal state' (II, 1), is implicitly contrasted with God 'High throned above all highth' (III, 58).[20] Dryden takes the same process one stage further by alluding to Milton's description of Satan when, in *MacFlecknoe*, the 'Prince of dulness' appears 'High

on a Throne of his own Labours rear'd' (lines 106–7). 'Satan not
God is the original imitated' and 'the proper wit of the poem is that
Flecknoe can only parody a parody of God'.[21] When used by an
intelligent poet the technique of presenting praise that finally appears
as dispraise is a powerful one.

The Son in the third hymn becomes man to serve man while Cupid
descends only to rule over man. And surely, while dualism is an essential characteristic of earthly love, the poverty of Christ is self-imposed.
Christ is 'derived not from a desire for something lacking nor from a
mixture of contraries but from single Plenty alone'.[22] Spenser stresses
the ambiguous and controversial nature of Cupid. He makes the
reader associate him both with the angels and with Christ, but the
final effect of the cross-references is not to give an exalted impression
of Cupid but to increase awareness of the utter inadequacy of this god
of love.

Stanzas 11 to 14 (lines 71–98) strengthen the impression of Cupid's
role as both type and parody. Stanza 11 starts in much the same vein
as that in which stanza 10 ended. Cupid was surrounded by darkness
until

> *His owne faire mother, for all creatures sake,*
> *Did lend him light from her owne goodly ray:*
>
> *(HL lines 72–3)*

and his situation is echoed in the description of the angels (*HHL* 11)
who spend their time in the eternal light of God who 'his beames
doth still to them extend'. Stanzas 12 to 14 of the *Hymne of Heavenly
Love* describe the civil war in heaven and relate how order was
restored as God 'blew away / From heauens hight . . . / To deepest
hell' the rebel angels. The parallel stanzas in the *Hymne of Love*
describe the civil war among the elements and relate how Cupid
managed to

> *place them all in order, and compell*
> *To keepe them selues within their sundrie raines,*
> *Together linkt with Adamantine chaines.*
>
> *(HL lines 87–9)*

It is interesting to note that Cupid in his creative activity uses the
same kind of force that God resorted to in expelling the angels. Milton
seems to have been aware of the connection since he uses the same

phrase in *Paradise Lost* but applies it to Satan who was thrown down from heaven 'to dwell / in adamantine chains' (I, 47–8). The harmoniously ordered elements reappear in the description of order and harmony in the created universe in *An Hymne of Heavenly Beautie* (lines 36–49). There the stress is not on the contrary forces of the elements but on their upward movement. The thematic parallel at this point between the two hymns of love is reinforced by the mutual rhymes: 'fyre-conspyre-fyre-yre' in stanza 12 of the *Hymne of Love* are echoed by 'yre-aspyre-fyre' in stanza 13 of the *Hymne of Heavenly Love*. It is significant that the creative activities of Cupid parallel the activities of God, not as a creator, but as a destroyer.

Stanzas 15 to 17 of the *Hymne of Love* (lines 99–119) declare that man 'breathes a more immortall mynd' than other creatures. And since beauty, 'borne of heauenly race', is the nearest resemblance man can find on earth to 'th' immortall flame / Of heauenly light', beauty will be the object of all his earthly desires. Adding depth to this idea of man's 'immortall mynd' stanzas 15 to 17 of the *Hymne of Heavenly Love* relate how God made man in his likeness according 'to an heauenly patterne' and 'endewd [him] with wisedomes riches, heauenly, rare'. The basic pattern of contrast is emphasised by the rhymes. 'Spright' is a rhymeword in stanza 16 of both hymns, but while God 'breathd a liuing spright' into man, the lover in the first hymn possesses only a 'deducted spright'. 'Aspyre' is another telling rhymeword since its only occurrence in the third hymn is in a reference to the aspiring pride of the rebel angels (*HHL* 13).[23] The seventeenth stanzas of both hymns are linked because both employ the rhymewords 'see-bee' in the couplet. The 'fragile men' of the *Hymne of Love* are, of course, so 'enrauisht' at the sight of the earthly reflection of heavenly beauty that they completely forget its source (*HL* 17). One may be reminded of St Paul's warning about those who 'worshipped and served the creature more than the Creator'.

Man did not know how to make proper use of his 'wisedomes riches', and so he fell

> *Into the mouth of death to sinners dew,*
> *And all his off-spring into thraldome threw.*
> $$(HHL\ 18,\ 123\text{–}4)$$

The 'thraldome' of fallen man strongly recalls the sad predicament of Cupid's subjects who 'lye languishing like thrals forlorne' (*HL* 20, 136). And the 'neuer dead, yet euer dying paine' of the sinners (*HHL*

18, 126) may remind the reader of the torment of lovers whose inner flame

> *suckes the blood, and drinketh vp the lyfe*
> *Of carefull wretches with consuming griefe.*
>
> (*HL* 18, 125–6)

Cupid is the 'tyrant Loue' who makes the lovers' pains his play and who seeks 'their dying to delay' (*HL* 20). The tyranny of Cupid as well as the sufferings of fallen man may be said to last until Christ has identified himself with the sinner-lover in the incarnation when

> *He downe descended, like a most demisse*
> *And abiect thrall, in fleshes fraile attyre.*
>
> (*HHL* 20)

Again the image of thraldom is evoked, but this time the lover, already identified as fallen man, is released from his thraldom when his role as thrall is taken over by Christ. 'The parallel to the lover's anguish is that of Jesus.'[24] This is clearly brought out by stanzas 21 to 24 (lines 141–68) of the two hymns of love. The lover is Cupid's poor

> *vassall, whose yet bleeding hart,*
> *With thousand wounds thou mangled hast so sore.*
>
> (*HL* 21)

Yet, if he could raise his head and look at the suffering Christ, his own wounds and 'bleeding hart' would be soon forgotten at that

> *huge and most vnspeakeable impression*
> *Of loues deepe wound, that pierst the piteous hart*
> *Of that deare Lord . . .*
>
> (*HHL* 23)

Christ wanted to put an end to man's hellish misery, 'for mans deare sake he did a man become'; Cupid, however, has increased the lover's pains, 'enfrosen' the 'disdainefull brest' of the beloved (stanza 21 in both hymns). The lover in the *Hymne of Love* complains of the injustice of Cupid who, in spite of the poet's high praise, does not 'moue ruth in that rebellious Dame' but is content to 'let her liue thus free', and the poet 'to dy'. The poet-speaker in the *Hymne of Heavenly Love* is shocked at the gross crime of those who 'slew the iust, by most vniust decree' (stanza 22 in both hymns). The injustice of Christ's executioners 'doing him die, that neuer it deserued', is paralleled by the injustice of Cupid who does not scruple to 'afflict as well the not deseruer' (stanza 23 in both hymns). And we could hardly wish for a sharper contrast than that between the god who on his 'subiects most doest tyrannize' and Christ who willingly suffered on the cross to 'free his foes, that from his heast had *swerued*' (stanza 23). Cupid, however, wants first of all to make sure 'if they will euer *swerue*' before he restores 'them vnto grace' (my italics). While Christ granted grace freely because man had 'swerued' and could never be in a position to deserve it, Cupid, the feudal lord, wants to make sure that his subjects are deserving and true servants before he restores them to his favour (stanza 24).

While Christ suffers in order to lift man up, Cupid makes man suffer in order to assert his own power. The poet's final explanation of Cupid's harsh treatment of his subjects is that it makes them 'better to deserue' his grace

> *And hauing got it, may it more esteeme,*
> *For things hard gotten, men more dearly deeme.*
> *(HL* 24)

If this is true, Cupid shows greater psychological cunning than Christ, who generously 'our life hath left vnto vs free' (*HHL* 27).

The parallel between the pains of the lover and those of Christ is emphasised even by the choice of rhymewords. We have already seen how words like 'deseruer', and 'swerue—deserue' in the *Hymne of Love* (stanzas 23 and 24), are echoed by 'deserued-swerued' in the *Hymne of Heavenly Love* (stanza 23). Similarly, the set 'hart-part-smart' in stanza 21 of the first hymn is paralleled by 'hart-part-dart' in stanza 23 of the third hymn. (Rhymewords from the set 'hart-part-smart-dart' and their plural equivalents are frequent in descriptions of the relationship between Cupid and the lover, see stanzas 1, 5, 18, and 21 of the *Hymne of Love*). Once we have become aware of this pattern we may also respond to the rhymes 'blame-shame-became' and 'tree-decree' in stanza 22 of the *Hymne of Heavenly Love* as echoes of the similar sets 'name-Dame-flame' and 'thee-me' in stanza 22 of the *Hymne of Love*.

This sequence of stanzas shows how Spenser was able to use the traditional lover's complaint in an exciting new way to epitomise the essential predicament of fallen man. By this point it should have become clear to the reader that the pagan world of the first hymn is identical with the fallen world, and that this intimate relationship between the hymns is signalled by 'the strategic recurrence of words and images'.[25]

The central stanzas of the *Hymne of Love,* stanzas 22 to 23 (central if we include the introductory stanzas), express the lover's complaint about Cupid's tyranny over mankind, and establish a crucial contrast between the two hymns since the central stanza of the *Hymne of Heavenly Love,* stanza 21, relates the story of how for 'mans deare sake' Christ 'did a man become'. In this way the central stanza of the *Fowre Hymnes* (*HHL* 5) describes Christ as the second person of the Trinity, Christ in his heavenly aspect, while the central stanza of the third hymn itself describes Christ as man, Christ in his earthly aspect.

In stanzas 25 to 28 of the *Hymne of Love* (lines 169–196) true love is contrasted to 'loathly sinful lust', and in stanza 28 the true lover in his 'refyned mynd' admires 'the mirrour of . . . heauenly light'. In the corresponding stanzas in the third hymn we are admonished to admire Christ who is the 'glorious Morning starre', the 'lampe of light' and the most 'liuely image' of the face of God. We are exhorted to love Christ who

> *our life hath left vnto vs free,*
> *Free that was thrall, and blessed that was band.*
>
> (*HHL* 27)

He has saved us from the second death and given us something far more real than a reflection in a mirror:

> *the food of life, which now we haue,*
> *Euen himselfe in his deare sacrament.*
>
> (*HHL* 28)

While the readers of the *Hymne of Heavenly Love* are urged to prove their love of Christ through love of their fellow human beings and to contemplate the love and mercy of Christ (29–32, 197–224), the lover in the *Hymne of Love* concentrates on the reflection of beauty which he has seen, to the exclusion of its source. On this image printed 'in his deepest wit' he 'feeds his hungrie fantasy' (*HL* lines 197–8). In so doing he seems to lose all power of judgement and to be constantly deceiving himself:

> *Thrise happie man, might he the same possesse;*
> *He faines himselfe, and doth his fortune blesse.*
>
> (*HL* 30, 209–10)

It has been argued that here 'as in line 240 "faines", i.e. "feigns" probably means imagines rather than pretends. We may compare lines 216–17 where the lover's "fayning eye" is conjuring up a *mental* and perhaps an idealised, but not a wholly false image of his lady's beauty'.[26] But surely, the choice of an ambiguous word like 'faines' may be interpreted as a discreet author's comment anticipating the radical criticism of the earthly lover in the last pair. The word occurs twice in the *Hymne of Heavenly Beautie* (lines 216 and 273), and on both occasions it refers to a false imagination. In fact, the epithet 'thrise happie' is probably an example of prolepsis, the reader of the *Hymne of Heavenly Beautie* knowing better who should be considered 'thrise happie' when he finds the echo:

> *thrise happie man him hold,*
> *Of all on earth, whom God so much doth grace,*
> *And lets his owne Beloued to behold:*
> *For in the view of her celestiall face,*
> *All ioy, all blisse, all happinesse haue place.*
> (*HHB* lines 239–43)

And if this does not suffice to bring out the full measure of the lover's folly, the utter inadequacy of his self-centred, earthbound love and its ill effects on his judgements, here is how he regards his faint, earthly reflection of beauty:

> *His harts enshrined saint, his heauens queene,*
> *Fairer then fairest, in his fayning eye.*
> (*HL* lines 215–16)

It is the discovery of this 'complicated web of recurrent elements' in the hymns which enables the reader to see the happiness and beauty in the transient world of the earthly lover in its true perspective.[27]

The Christian lover is inspired with an unselfish love that reaches out to his fellow men and up to Christ. He knows that his faith and fortune depend on the love and grace of Christ; thus he urges the reader to

> *Lift vp to him thy heauie clouded eyne,*
> *That thou his soueraine bountie mayst behold,*
> *And read through loue his mercies manifold.*
> (*HHL* 32)

But the earthly lover is shut in by his selfish, earthbound love. His 'galley' is 'charged with forgetfulness'. He is concerned only with his

own temporary happiness and can trust only himself and his own
powers.

> *Then forth he casts in his vnquiet thought,*
> *What he may do, her fauour to obtaine;*
> *What braue exploit, what perill hardly wrought,*
> *What puissant conquest, what aduenturous paine,*
> *May please her best, and grace vnto him gaine.*

(*HL* 32)

Readers familiar with the third hymn will once more observe the
contrast between earthly and heavenly love. 'For the "brave exploits"
of the one there is the "humble carriage" of the other' (*HHL* 34).[28]

The traditional, and implicitly critical, review of the lover's psychic
development and religious adoration of his beloved in the *Hymne of
Love*, is interrupted by the apparently serious praise of Cupid in
stanza 33. This is the only stanza in the *Fowre Hymnes* which is one
line short. It is difficult to spot this startling irregularity as the fourth
line, although metrically regular, exceeds the normal line length by
more than one third and is carried over into an indented fifth line,
while the fifth line proper is missing. In the Quarto edition (1596)
the layout normally adopted is to print four stanzas on each page so
that the stanzas on two facing pages will match each other in exact
symmetry.[29] The normal procedure with long lines is to print the
remaining words or letters at the end of the line immediately above
or below it. The obvious effect of carrying the fourth line of stanza 33
over into the next line is to keep an illusion of symmetry in spite of
the 'missing' line, thus making the discrepancy less easily detectable
at first glance. The effect may, of course, merely be the result of a
compositorial error; failing to find enough room to continue the
excessively long line at the end of the lines preceding and succeeding
it, the compositor has carried the line over, and because of the symmetry thus achieved, may have failed to notice his mistake. Such a
theory, however, presumes that the proof-reader would have failed
to notice the irregular indentation. (Note that B3r on which *HL* 33 is
found, and B2v, the page facing it, were also facing each other in the
outer forme of sheet B.) In view of the fact that the *Fowre Hymnes* is
more carefully printed than any other of Spenser's works printed in
his lifetime, this seems improbable. Some commentators even suppose
that Spenser assisted at the printing. That the omission should be
accidental is unlikely also because it is repeated in the Folio edition

of 1611. There is nothing in the syntax to indicate that a line should be missing: it makes perfectly good sense as it stands. The 'error' therefore would seem to be intentional. Corroborative evidence may be deduced from the division of the long line: 'Through seas, through flames, through thousand / swords and speares'. This division may be seen to produce an additional 'internal' or visual rhyme: 'thousand-withstand-hand'. It may thus be argued that instead of an incomplete rhyme-scheme, ababcc, we are left with a new variation: aba(c)bcc. My belief that this division and its possible effect are the results of conscious design is strengthened by the fact that the long line is divided in exactly the same way in the Folio edition of 1611. This effect is lost in the text of the *Variorum Edition* where the line is divided: 'through thousand swords / and speares'.

These considerations make me conclude that the 'error' is Spenser's own and that he made it deliberately. In so doing he relied on a tradition according to which it was perfectly acceptable for a poet to depart from the established stanzaic form to emphasise his themes. Among the early poems of Sir Thomas More, for example, there is a sequence of nine stanzas designed to accompany nine illustrations on a tapestry. The first seven of these stanzas have seven lines, but the eighth, entitled 'Eternity', has eight lines, no doubt to make the form of the stanza as well as the stanza number accord with its subject matter, the number eight symbolising eternity.[30]

Although I do not wish to attach symbolic significance to the number of lines left in Spenser's stanza, one may observe that the overestimation of the powers of Cupid in the long fourth line results in a stanza which is as inadequate as the god which it praises. We should also note that what may initially seem a failure on Spenser's part to calculate the number of lines in his stanza correctly, agrees with the main fiction of the dedication—that the first two hymns were composed at the beginning of his career when he was young and inexperienced. This technical or poetical failure, however, may also serve as a sign of spiritual failure. The spiritual failure of the poet may be formally expressed through his lack of elementary, technical skill and such a failure is suggested by the excessive praise of Cupid. One may object that Cupid is praised even more excessively elsewhere and particularly in the last stanza of the hymn, and without similar formal indications of error. One possible solution is that it may perhaps be significant that the formal error occurs in this particular stanza. We know from earlier studies of Spenser that his structures were often highly complex and carefully worked out. As I have already noted, this is stanza 33 and thirty-three was, more than any other number, associated with Christ, since Christ was popularly believed to have been thirty-three years old when he died. Since we have seen that the two hymns of love contain several contrasted descriptions of Christ and Cupid, Spenser may have wished to provide this formal indication of the inadequacy of Cupid and the error of his followers by making his 'mistake' in this particular stanza. This interpretation is enforced when we turn to stanza 33 of the *Hymne of Heavenly Love* and find there a description of the birth of Christ. The description of the life and sufferings of Christ in stanzas 33 to 35 is a little puzzling since it seems in many ways to be a mere repetition of what has already been said in stanzas 20 to 23. The popular import of the number thirty-three and the need to establish a contrast to the first hymn are two considerations that may have prompted the repetition. The reader should also note the contrast between the extravagant praise of the power and glory of Cupid and the plain description of the simple and low birth, and the painful and miserable life of Christ. This is a clear example of the contrast between pride and humility.

In stanza 33 Cupid is praised not only as the lover's god, but also as his guide. But, as Spenser takes care to point out, this guide is blind. There were at least two ways of depicting Cupid: either as blind with a bandage over his eyes, or as seeing. Erwin Panofsky informs us that 'the bandage of blindfold Cupid . . . [was introduced] wherever a lower, purely sensual and profane form of love was deliberately contrasted with a higher, more spiritual and sacred one, whether marital, or "Platonic," or Christian'.[31] He also asserts that 'the Renaissance spokesmen of Neoplatonic theories refuted the belief that Love was blind . . . and used the figure of Blind Cupid, if at all, as a contrast to set off their own exalted conception'.[32] This may seem to fit in very nicely with the idea that Cupid is deliberately contrasted with his heavenly and Christian counterparts. To make matters a little more complicated, however, Edgar Wind has pointed out that the 'tradition that saw in the blind Cupid a symbol of unenlightened animal passion, inferior to the intellect' was reversed by people like Marsilio Ficino, Pico della Mirandola, Lorenzo de' Medici and Giordano Bruno.[33] They saw in blind Cupid a symbol of a superior form of love, either for the reason mockingly given in *A Midsummer Night's Dream*:

> *Love looks not with the eyes, but with the mind;*
> *And therefore is wing'd Cupid painted blind.*[34]
> *(I, i)*

or for the reason given by Pico: 'Love is said by Orpheus to be without eyes because he is above the intellect.'[35] It is this last interpretation of Cupid's blindness which is implied in Benivieni's *Canzone d'Amore* in the two last lines of stanza II:

> *O Love, on my weak wings, bestow*
> *The promised pinions, and the blind way show!*[36]

Thus there are two ways of interpreting Cupid even when he is described as blind, either as blind passion without reason, or as a higher intellectual vision blinding the eyes of the body only to activate the eyes of the mind.

Certainly, the Cupid of *An Hymne of Love* may be interpreted as blind in a bad sense. He is the blind god who guides the lover so that he does not 'see his feares', and his blindness reminds us of Christ's saying that 'if the blind lead the blind, both shall fall into the ditch'. The significance of the reference to Cupid as the lover's *guide* both in stanza 33 and in the last stanza of the *Hymne of Love* is underlined by the reference to man's departure from the ways of God as 'mans misguyde' in the *Hymne of Heavenly Love* (line 144).

It seems likely that Spenser was aware of the Neoplatonic interpretation of the blindness of Love, but he did not choose to invest his Cupid with the kind of mystical blindness with which Benivieni furnished his god of love. But if Spenser knew the tradition Benivieni refers to, and if the two pairs of hymns were composed according to a conscious pattern of parallels and contrasts, we would expect a reference to Benivieni's and Pico's 'blind way' in the last pair. And our expectation is not disappointed. In the *Hymne of Heavenly Love* the poet declares that if the reader gives himself to Christ he will be so inflamed with love that all earthly things will

> *Seeme durt and drosse in thy pure sighted eye,*
> *Compar'd to that celestiall beauties blaze,*
> *Whose glorious beames all fleshly sense doth daze*
> *With admiration of their passing light,*
> Blinding the eyes and lumining the spright.
> *(HHL* 40, 276–80; my roman)

The reader is actually told to renounce earthly love

> *with which the world doth blind*
> *Weake fancies, and stirre vp affections base.*
> (*HHL* 38, 262–3)

In the *Hymne of Beautie* we are told that love has such power over man that 'it can rob both sense and reason blynd' (*HB* line 77), and in the *Hymne of Heavenly Beautie* the reader is encouraged to

> *Mount vp aloft through heauenly contemplation,*
> *From this darke world, whose damps the soule do blynd.*
> (*HHB* 20, 136–3)

Thus the description of Cupid as blind reinforces the antitheses between earthly and heavenly love, and the contrast is given added emphasis by the formal incompleteness and the significant placing of the stanza in which this description of Cupid is found. At the same time, however, the very ambiguity of Cupid's blindness in the Renaissance suggests that he is presented not only as the negation of the true vision but also as a foreshadowing of that higher, inner vision which is granted to those who seek heavenly love and beauty.

Among those who pursued their love even into Hell itself, Orpheus is the supreme example:

> *And* Orpheus *daring to prouoke the yre*
> *Of damned fiends, to get his loue retyre.*
> (*HL* 34)

The corresponding stanza in the *Hymne of Heavenly Love* focuses on the sufferings of Christ to redeem man from Hell:

> *His cancred foes, his fights, his toyle, his strife,*
> *His paines, his pouertie, his sharpe assayes.*
> (*HHL* 34)

This contrast and parallelism between Cupid and Orpheus, and Christ may have a further significance. Since they are both mentioned at this crucial point in the *Hymne of Love*, they may serve not only as a contrast but even as a foreshadowing of Christ. Orpheus descending to Hell to free his Eurydice from death, and Cupid making way 'both through heauen and hell' for those who obey him, are both reminiscent of Christ, who descended even to the realm of the dead to redeem fallen man. The fact that there are no classical allusions in the third hymn[37] supports an interpretation of Orpheus and Cupid as types of Christ, since the type must disappear on the arrival of the anti-type. It is supported also by the early Fathers of the Church who argued 'that the pagan legend of Orpheus in some way prefigures the story of Christ's ministry, and that just as the coming of Christ outdates the Old Law, so Christ the new Orpheus replaces the old Orpheus of Helicon and Cithaeron'.[38] We know that 'well into the Middle Ages writers compared the actions of Orpheus and Christ in the underworld, showing that what Orpheus had begun, Christ had finished',[39] and medieval commentaries on Ovid identified Orpheus with Christ, notably the *Ovide Moralisé* where 'the whole legend [of Orpheus] is taken as a figure for Christ's harrowing of hell'.[40]

Whether we choose to interpret Orpheus as a type of Christ or not, it seems safe to say that both in the way he is described and through the significant position he occupies, he seems to remind the reader of Christ and to lead him on to the third hymn. But by the time he gets there he will realise that Orpheus is outdated and outshone by the true God, who alone possesses the power to bring his beloved out of Hell. If Spenser has succeeded in achieving this response in the reader, he has succeeded in vindicating his poetry against the accusations of allegedly bad effects on readers.

In stanza 35 of the *Hymne of Love* (lines 238–44) the lover is approved of by his mistress and experiences feigned 'heauens of ioy' which make him forget his previous pains to such an extent that

> *Had it bene death, yet would he die againe,*
> *To liue thus happie as her grace to gaine.*

When paired with stanza 35 of the *Hymne of Heavenly Love* this looks like a clear travesty of the pains of Christ, who died on the cross 'with bitter wounds through hands, through feet and syde', and who alone can grant man grace and secure him joy in heaven.

The transitory and imaginary nature of the lover's paradise is brought out clearly in stanzas 36 to 39 of the first hymn (lines 245–73), where his illusory paradise is turned into a 'wretches hell' through the fears of rivals that 'torment / His troubled mynd with more then hellish paine!' In stanzas 36 to 39 of the third hymn the self-centred love of the earthly lover is replaced by the self-effacing love of the Christian, who is urged to forget himself and 'melt into teares' at the sight of the suffering Christ. The Christian is told to shun

All other loues, with which the world doth blind
Weake fancies, and stirre vp affections base.

(38, 262–3)

This is a striking comment on the earthly lover's 'fayning fansie'
which gives rise to all kinds of 'affections base': envy, fear, and mistrust (stanza 38).

The contrast between amorous love and Christian love is brought
out even in the description of the lover's relationship to his fellow
beings, particularly when we recall the description of Christian
charity in stanzas 29 to 31 of the *Hymne of Heavenly Love*. To the
lover whose only pain is his own possible dissatisfaction and whose
only aim is his own happiness, his fellow beings are important only
as potential rivals and competitors. Cupid's relationship to the lovers
is mirrored in their relationship to their neighbours. The lord-vassal
relationship between Cupid and his subjects does not encourage a
relationship of mutual love and charity among his subjects. Conversely,
Christ's suffering love for man is mirrored in the mutual love among
his followers.

The description of the lovers who have to go through a painful
Purgatory before they reach Love's paradise and take part in a banquet of sense where 'they doe feede on Nectar heauenly wize' and lay
their heads in the 'snowy bosome' of Pleasure, may be compared to
the last stanzas of the *Hymne of Heavenly Love*. There is no mention
of any Catholic Purgatorium for Christ has gone through all their
pains, and 'all the worlds desire' is purged away, not through pains
but through love of Christ. The last decisive difference between
earthly love aroused by earthly beauty and 'celestiall loue /
Kindled through sight of those faire things aboue' (*HHL* 41), is that the one
trusts in the senses while the other has had recourse to the 'bright
radiant eyes' of the spirit. The 'bright and glorious' sun of Cupid's
paradise (*HL* 40) is nothing

> *Compar'd to that celestiall beauties blaẓe,*
> *Whose glorious beames all fleshly sense doth daẓe*
> *With admiration of their passing light,*
> *Blinding the eyes and lumining the spright.*
>
> (*HHL* 40)

In stanza 42 of the first hymn the lover has come full circle. He has
joined with Pleasure in a paradise which seems to be identical with
the 'siluer bowres' of Venus.[41] But the sensuous pleasures enjoyed

by the lovers are clearly contrasted to the pleasures of the Angels (*HHL* 11) and to the 'sweete pleasures' enjoyed by those who seek heavenly beauty (*HHB* 43).

The last stanza of the *Hymne of Love* reveals to what extent the first hymn is 'lewd' not because there is anything wrong with amorous love *per se*, but because its advocate in this hymn has lost his sense of proportion. He does not seem to be conscious of a wider perspective. He is not aware of the existence of a sun which is even more glorious than the one he can perceive with his eyes, and he allows his spiritual eyes to be blinded by the transitory glory of what can be experienced with the senses. There is no room for Christian love because earthly love has so taken possession of the lover that it has taken the place even of religion. Certainly, any Christian would be expected to react to a poet offering to sing of Cupid's 'immortall praise / An heauenly Hymne, such as the Angels sing' (*HL* 44, 301–302). There must be something seriously wrong when Cupid takes the place properly belonging to God himself. The poet offers to raise Cupid's name

> *Boue all the gods, thee onely honoring,*
> *My guide, my God, my victor, and my king;*[42]

And if this is not enough to alert the reader and make him aware of his folly, the last stanza is paralleled and implicitly negated in the first stanza of the *Hymne of Heavenly Love*.[43] In this stanza the poet asks to be lifted up to 'heauens hight' to see the admirable works of God

> *That I thereof an heauenly Hymne may sing*
> *Vnto the god of Loue, high heauens king.*
> (*HHL* 1, 6–7)

The rhymes 'sing-honoring-king' in the last stanza of the *Hymne of Love* echo not only the rhymes 'sing-king' in the last introductory stanza of that hymn, but are also echoed in the first couplet of the *Hymne of Heavenly Love*. And the lovers who play with Pleasure 'without rebuke or *blame*' and are 'deuoyd of guilty *shame*' (my italics) in the third stanza from the end of the *Hymne of Love* are proved false by the reappearance of the rhymes 'flame-blame-shame' in the retraction of the third stanza of the *Hymne of Heavenly Love*, just as they are contrasted to the suffering Christ (*HHL* 22), who alone was without 'all blemish or reprochfull *blame*' and was treated 'with despightfull *shame*' by man (my italics).

If we accept this parallel reading of the two hymns of love, even the poet's last prayer to Cupid to accept his 'simple song, thus fram'd in praise of thee' may be significant. It is beautifully 'fram'd' for instance in the sense that the rhymes of the last couplet, 'mee-thee', echo the rhymes of the first couplet, 'bee-thee'. It is also interesting to note that stanza 33 of the first hymn, which seems to establish the contrast between Cupid and Christ in such a significant way, is followed by eleven stanzas which bring us to the obvious blasphemy of stanza 44. This seems appropriate since eleven was the number of transgression and hence of sin. Above all, however, we should note the predominance of the number four in the sum total of the forty-four stanzas, since the number four is 'the number *par excellence* of the created universe'.[44]

We have seen how Spenser has turned the pagan world of the first hymn into the world of fallen man. The strange mixture of Neo-platonism and traditional courtly love poetry which has puzzled his critics has enabled Spenser to align his first hymn with the third and thus to show the way from heathen gods to Christ, from fallen man to redeemed man, from the rule of tyranny to the rule of grace. The rule of Cupid is allowed to foreshadow the rule of Christ in a way that enabled contemporary readers to read the hymns in much the same way that they were used to reading the Bible, for 'in the Old Testament the New is concealed, and in the New the Old is revealed'.[45] Before man can smite his breast and cry 'God, be merciful to me a sinner' and receive grace, he must be conscious of sin. We might say that the first hymn seeks to convince the reader of the necessity of grace by showing him the misery of life without grace.

III

According to Plato 'all communion between mortals and gods was established...through the mediation of Love'.[46] Thus the hymn to Cupid has prepared the way for the hymn to Venus, and the hymn to Christ serves as a necessary precursor to the *Hymne of Heavenly Beautie*. For, 'however much anyone is illuminated only by the light of nature and of acquired science, he cannot', Bonaventura teaches us, 'enter into himself that he may delight in the Lord in himself, unless Christ be his mediator'.[47]

The *Hymne of Heavenly Beautie* begins where the *Hymne of*

Heavenly Love ends.[48] 'Rapt with the rage of [his] own rauisht thought' the poet-speaker ascends the ladder of increasing beauty until he reaches God's 'mercie seate' and a vision of heavenly Sapience. The poet-speaker of the *Hymne of Beautie* is sufficiently well-informed to know about the heavenly origin of true beauty. He passes from love considered as stemming from beauty to beauty as the cause of love but concentrates on the effects of beauty as immediate cause to the exclusion of beauty as ultimate cause. Thus he remains firmly on earth and is largely content to admire how the heaven-born souls form their 'fleshly bowres'.

The speaker of the *Hymne of Beautie* is also in a sense beside himself not 'with the rage' of his 'rauisht thought' but with 'wontlesse fury' and Cupid's 'raging fyre' (*HB* and *HHB* 1). The lover in the *Hymne of Beautie* entreats Venus to 'vouchsafe' to illuminate his 'dim and dulled eyne' with her 'loue-kindling light' enabling him to inspire 'admiration of that heauenly light' in his readers (*HB* 2–3). The transported speaker in the *Hymne of Heavenly Beautie* petitions the Holy Spirit to 'vouchsafe' to inspire him with 'some sparkling light' of the 'eternall Truth' so that he may teach the 'hearts of men'

> *to loue with ʒealous humble dewty*
> *Th' eternall fountaine of that heauenly beauty.*
> (*HHB* 3)

The *third* stanza of the *Hymne of Heavenly Beautie* provides commentary on the *third* stanza of the hymn to Venus. This is emphasised by the choice of identical rhymes: 'Beauty-dewty' and 'delight-sight-light' in the third stanza of the second hymn are echoed by the rhymes 'sight-delight' and 'dewty-beauty' in the third stanza of the last hymn.

The lover wants his hymn to beauty to serve an additional purpose. His hopes are that it will please his lady so 'that she at length will streame / Some deaw of grace, into [his] withered hart' which 'wasted is with woes extreame' (*HB* 4). The speaker of the *Hymne of Beautie* is not really interested in the heavenly origin of beauty, but concentrates on its manifestations in the beauty of the beloved. Thus while 'the movement of the earthly hymn is down,. . .the movement of the heavenly hymn is up'[49] The poet in the *Hymne of Heavenly Beautie* takes as his point of departure the discovery of beauty in the well-ordered universe. Comparing himself to the young falcon he hopes to ascend even to 'contemplation of th' immortall sky' (*HHB* 4).

In stanzas 5 to 9 of the *Hymne of Beautie* (lines 29–63), the poet describes how the great 'workmaister' made everything according to the 'goodly Paterne' of perfect beauty. Flowing from the 'bright starre' of Venus this beauty streams into the *res creatae*. With it Venus points Cupid's 'poysned arrow, / That wounds the life, and wastes the inmost marrow' (*HB* lines 62–3). In the corresponding stanzas of the last hymn the reader is invited to observe the purposeful and beautiful organisation of the 'endlesse kinds of creatures' which people the universe, and in an ascending movement he is urged to admire the well-ordered elements and 'last that mightie shining christall wall, / Wherewith he hath encompassed this All' (lines 41–2). The frail mind of mortal man can reach only a partial understanding of the infinite beauty and wisdom of God, but by reading in the *liber creaturarum* (lines 127–33), man may form some idea of the beauty of those heavens 'much higher in degree'.

The structure of parallelism and contrast does not seem to work on a stanza by stanza pattern in these sections. But the procedures of the narrators are clearly related in a less complex way. The speaker of the heavenly hymn ascends to discover perfect, heavenly beauty in God, and the speaker of the earthly hymn imitates this procedure by peeling off layers of inessential qualities of beauty to disclose the true nature of earthly beauty. The speaker of the second hymn is preoccupied with that beauty which is 'in earth layd vp in secret store' and its effects on man. He is primarily concerned to establish (in stanzas 10 to 15) that the beauty which can

> *Moue such affection in the inward mynd,*
> *That it can rob both sense and reason blynd,*
> (*HB* 11, 76–7)

is not an 'outward shew of things, that onely seeme' (line 91). But even that beauty which arouses the desire of earthly lovers 'is heauenly borne and can not die' (line 104). This does not mean that he takes an interest in its origin, but it helps him to explain the psychological effects of beauty. The poet-speaker of the *Hymne of Heavenly Beautie*, however, has to pursue his search through the hierarchy of the heavens which

> *by degrees redound,*
> *And rise more faire, till they at last ariue*
> *To the most faire, whereto they all do striue.*
> (*HHB* 11, 75–7)

In stanzas 16 to 21 of the *Hymne of Beautie* we are told how the soul descended from 'that great immortall Spright' to be 'embodied' in 'fleshy seede' and then framed 'her house' to make it a 'pallace fit for such a virgin Queene' (line 126).

> *For of the soule the bodie form doth take:*
> *For soule is forme, and doth the bodie make.*
> (*HB* 19, 132–3)

Consequently, a fair body is the certain outward sign of a fair soul. But, the poet hurries to inform us,

> *oft it falles, that many a gentle mynd*
> *Dwels in deformed tabernacle drownd.*
> (*HB* 21, 141–2)

While the poet in the second hymn stresses the body as the mirror of the beautiful and immortal soul, the poet of the *Hymne of Heavenly Beautie* sees the acts of God as the true

> *looking glasse, through which he may*
> *Be seene, of all his creatures vile and base,*
> *That are vnable else to see his face.*
> (*HHB* 17, 115–17)

If we can look at the bright beams of the sun only through a mirror,

> *how can we see with feeble eyne,*
> *The glory of that Maiestie diuine.*
> (*HHB* 18, 123–4)

The second hymn recommends that we observe beautiful bodies because 'all that faire is, is by nature good' (*HB* 20). The speaker of the heavenly hymn urges the reader to observe God's works as a means of experiencing His goodness, and he ends on very much the same note as the speaker of the earthly hymn: 'for all thats good, is beautiful and faire.' (*HHB* 19).

The Christian's journey does not end here. By means of 'perfect speculation' and 'through heauenly contemplation' he mounts aloft, and imitating the eagle he fixes his eyes on 'that bright Sunne of glorie' (*HHB*, 20). The comparison between the eyes of the eagle and the speculative mind of the Christian contemplator is found in *The Faerie Queene*.[50] When Mercy accompanies the Red Cross

Knight to the hermitage of Contemplation they find him to be an 'aged Sire' with 'snowy lockes':

> *All were his earthly eyen both blunt and bad,*
> *And through great age had lost their kindly sight,*
> *Yet wondrous quick and persant was his spright,*
> *As Eagles eye, that can behold the Sunne.*
>
> *(I, x, 47)*

The contrast between man's eyes, which can perceive God only in his works, the faint reflection of the divine emanations, and the eagle's eye which has the power of direct vision, is thus directly related to the distinction between the eyes of the body and the eyes of the spirit significant for the discussion of the blindness of Cupid.

It comes as no surprise to find that words like 'eye-eyes-see-sight-behold-look' occur twice as frequently in the hymns of beauty as in the hymns of love.[51] We should be aware, however, that two essentially different types of vision are suggested in the two hymns of beauty. Just as the Red Cross Knight approached heavenly Contemplation guided by Mercy, so the Christian of the fourth hymn can ascend 'through heauenly contemplation' by virtue of grace granted by Christ, leaving behind 'this darke world, whose damps the soule do blynd'. So the lover of heavenly beauty is eventually endued with some of the characteristics of the angelic mind (see *HHB* 34, 232). Rereading the hymns we note that in the *Hymne of Love* Cupid is compared to a young eagle:

> *he gan to mount vp hyre,*
> *And like fresh Eagle, make his hardie flight*
> *Through all that great wide wast, yet wanting light.*
>
> *(HL lines 68–70)*

It is ironical that eagle-like Cupid, imitating the Spirit of God in Genesis, flies through *darkness* where the keen eyesight of the eagle can be of no use.

But we should not forget when we read the *Hymne of Heavenly Beautie* that the eagle has wings. In the Bible the eagle was interpreted as a symbol of regeneration and as a type of Christ who lifts the souls of men to heaven on his strong wings.[52] It is sufficient to remind ourselves of the Psalms, 103.5: 'thy youth is renewed like the eagle' and Isaiah, 40.31: 'but they that wait upon the Lord shall renew their strength; they shall mount up with wings as eagles;' we realise something of the fascination that a symbol like the eagle must have had for Spenser. Carrying the ambiguity of Cupid as both type and parody one step further, eagle-like Cupid may even be seen as a kind of travesty of Christian regeneration 'renewing still [his] yeares' (*HL* 8, 55).

The wings and awkward flight of Cupid have already been contrasted to the 'nimble wings' and easy flight of the Angels. In the *Hymne of Heavenly Beautie* the poet-speaker, regenerated through Christ and lifted up on his eagle's wings, compares himself to a young falcon that begins on earth and promises

> *From thence to mount aloft by order dew,*
> *To contemplation of th' immortall sky,*
> *Of the soare faulcon so I learne to fly,*
> *That flags awhile her fluttering wings beneath,*
> *Till she her selfe for stronger flight can breath.*
>
> (*HHB* 4, 24–8)

When he has completed his ascent he can throw himself down in fear and reverence before 'the footestoole of his Maiestie' (*HHB* 21).

The *Hymne of Heavenly Beautie* seems to be the most beautifully structured of all the hymns. While the central stanza of the *Hymne of Beautie* describes the 'deformed tabernacle' of man, the central stanza of the last hymn, stanza 22, gives us a glimpse of the perfect Tabernacle of God as we are urged to fall down before his 'mercie seate'. It is, of course, extremely appropriate and in keeping with the tradition of 'placement in the middest' that in the middle line of this mid-stanza we see God sitting 'vpon the righteous throne on hy' (*HHB* 22, 151).

While the poet of the heavenly hymn ascends to the vision of the perfection of beauty, the poet of the earthly hymn deplores the grievous corruption of beauty through lust (*HB* 22–5, 148–75). The virtue of those 'faire Dames' is a very pale reflection indeed of that 'heauenly vertue' which breeds the 'immortall light' encircling the throne of God

> *hid in his owne brightnesse from the sight*
> *Of all that looke thereon with eyes vnsound:*
>
> (*HHB* 26)

Compared to that light, 'Loue' which can 'illumine' the 'resplendent ray' of the ladies and 'adde more brightnesse' to their 'goodly hew' is a poor substitute (*HB* 26).

The 'faire Dames' are praised as the 'liuely images of heauens light' (*HB* 24, 163). When this phrase is linked with the 'mirrours' mentioned in stanza 26 and related to the parallel group of stanzas in the heavenly hymn, the contrast is made quite clear: weak reflections and indirect vision on the one hand, and true light and direct vision on the other.

In stanza 27 of the *Hymne of Beautie* the ladies are urged to show forth their 'heauenly riches' so that 'men the more admyre their fountaine may'. In stanza 27 of the *Hymne of Heavenly Beautie* we turn from the weak reflections of beauty in the earthly hymn to the divine beauty of heavenly Sapience, the true 'fountaine' of beauty. She rules both in 'the house of God on hy' and on the earth. Her fairness, in contrast to that of her mortal counterparts, exceeds 'all humane thought'.

The description of Sapience sitting in the bosom of the Father ('There in his bosome Sapience doth sit', *HHB* line 183), can be regarded as an echo of Christ's descent

> *Out of the bosome of eternall blisse,*
> *In which he reigned with his glorious syre.*
> (*HHL* lines 134–5)

These closely parallel descriptions of Christ and Sapience can be added to those already suggested by Robert Ellrodt, and to a certain extent they strengthen his theory that Sapience should be interpreted as the second person of the Trinity. There is, however, every probability that 'the ideas of many authors, representative of three traditions, Christian, Platonic, and Kabbalistic' can be 'brought to bear upon Spenser's image of Sapience'.[53] In order to assess the relative importance of these sources, however, we should also know something about how Spenser looked upon the relationship between them. Surely, in the syncretistic philosophy of Spenser it would be wrong to posit any opposition between Christianity and the Neoplatonic philosophy of Ficino and Pico. These authors merely advanced and clarified the dark sayings of Plato which, if unveiled, would be seen to be in accord with the basic truths of the Bible.[54]

Since Sapience is above all the divine person to whom the *Hymne of Heavenly Beautie* is dedicated, we would expect Spenser to make her appearance significant in the manner he has made the appearance of Christ significant. We may note first of all that there are 169 stanzas in the *Fowre Hymnes*, and if 'we subtract the introductory stanzas, the sum total is 153'.[55] This number may refer to the number of fish caught by Simon Peter on Christ's order (John XXI. 11). It was explained by Augustine as the sum of the first seventeen numbers, and 'this was designed to reveal to the initiated the means by which man is to be saved. Man is saved, not by works alone (through obedience to the ten commandments), but by grace (the seven gifts of the Holy Ghost). We must add Grace to the Law, 7 to 10'.[56] It is probable that Spenser made conscious use of the number 153. If we include the introductory stanzas in our count, the description of heavenly Sapience in stanza 27 of the *Hymne of Heavenly Beautie* is stanza 153. Thus in the last hymn Spenser managed to place 'high heauens king' in his appropriate place of majesty, seated on the high throne of his mercy seat in the middle of the heavenly tabernacle, in the middle of the hymn. And yet he was able, by his subtle use of the number 153, which is the triangular number based on 17, to place Sapience at the very pinnacle of his poetical edifice. (It is relevant to note that even the two first hymns contribute in the count and thus form a meaningful base on which the exalted picture of heavenly Sapience may be placed.)

Stanzas 28 to 30 stress the importance of harmony and the incomparable beauty of heavenly Sapience. The contrast between the supreme rule of Sapience, imposing order among all 'lower creatures', and those who 'loosely loue' and reduce love to a 'discordant warre', is pointed out in stanza 28; and in stanza 29 the harmony and heavenly extraction of the 'likely harts' (*HB* 29), are related to the statement about the heavenly origin of all creatures who 'do in state remaine, / As their great Maker did at first ordaine' (*HHB* 29). The idea of adherence to God's original plan is echoed in the next stanza of the earthly hymn, which argues that only those should combine in love 'whom heauen did at first ordaine'; (*HB* 30). The statement (in *HHB* 30) that mortals are unable to describe heavenly beauty, and that it cannot 'on earth compared be to ought,' is an apt comment on the attempt in the earthly hymn to reach heavenly beauty indirectly through earthly beauty. The approach is only made possible through Christ's descent to earth, and through his offer to lift up man on his eagle's wings.

It is highly appropriate that the following two stanzas in the *Hymne of Heavenly Beautie* (lines 211–24), should show Venus dethroned.

She is no more the high goddess and queen of beauty. 'Had she remained still' the poets who had spent their 'plenteous vaine in setting forth her prayse' would certainly regret their former activity. Spenser's disparaging remarks on the 'fabling wits' of the poets who had praised Venus reflects badly on his second hymn. The deposal of Venus in the last hymn can also be taken as a reference to the second hymn (lines 260–6): where the poet expresses his hopes that she will place her throne in men's hearts and spread her 'louely kingdome ouer all'.

The task of picturing heavenly Sapience makes the poet come closer to despair as his muse is much 'too weake and faint' (line 230). The lover in the *Hymne of Beautie*, however, has no such qualms. The sharp eyesight of the lover enables him to discover the hidden pleasures of the exquisite beauty of the beloved (lines 232–8). The description that follows is a true banquet of sense, very properly with an allusion to the gods that feed on 'Nectar in their bankets free' (lines 239–52). A few stanzas earlier the lover insisted on his ability to extract from the sight of the beloved a form which he presented to his mind 'free from fleshes frayle infection' (line 217), of which he would shape a 'heauenly beautie to his fancies will' (line 222). But in stanzas 35 to 38 he seems content to delight in those aspects of her beauty which present themselves to his senses. He has indeed been too bold and has allowed his fancy to run wild; in this deluded state the lover sees 'many wonders' 'that others neuer see' (stanza 36). He adopts an attitude that finds no room in the heavenly hymns for God 'hath scattered the proud in the imagination of their hearts' (Luke I.51). The lovers who *'behold'* and *'vnfold'* the beauty of the beloved in the *Hymne of Beautie* are contrasted to the Angels who *'behold'* the beautiful face of heavenly Sapience

> *And those most sacred mysteries* vnfold,
> *Of that faire loue of mightie heauens king.*
> (*HHB* lines 234–5, my roman)

The contrast between the happiness enjoyed by the earthly lover and that of the lover of heavenly beauty is highlighted in the description of the extreme joy and superlative happiness of those whom Sapience allows into her presence. The close relationship between the two sections is underlined by the appearance of the rhymes 'free-bee' in stanza 36 in both hymns.

The *contemptum mundi* attitude of the last stanzas of the *Hymne of Heavenly Beautie* is perhaps no surprise. The effect on those who are allowed to take part in the heavenly pleasures is, of course, to root out all 'fleshy sense, / Or idle thought of earthly things' (lines 267–8). When they have seen her divine beauty and experienced heavenly bliss 'All other sights but fayned shadowes bee' (line 273). Earthly love and honour 'seem to them basenesse, and all riches drosse' (line 279). From their high vantage point

> *that faire lampe, which vseth to enflame*
> *The hearts of men with self consuming fyre,*
> *Thenceforth seemes fowle, and full of sinfull blame;*
> (*HHB* 40, 274–6)

In contrast to the earthly lover who delights in the beauty he can perceive with his eyes, the heavenly lovers can delight in nothing

> *But in th' aspect of that felicitie,*
> *Which they haue written in their inward ey;*
> (*HHB* 41, 284–5)

Leaving the deceitful shadows of earthly beauty behind and forgetting the time when they were 'with false beauties flattering bait misled' (line 290), they look up to the light of perfect beauty which inspires love of God and

> *which loathing brings*
> *Of this vile world, and these gay seeming things;*
> (*HHB* 43, 299)

Having reached this point their journey is at an end, and the rising movement which started in rapturous, ravished thought has found its supreme end in eternal rest. This circular quality of the last hymn is also underlined by the recurrence of rhymewords. Thus the rhymes 'sight-delight', and 'light-spright' in stanzas 41 and 43 echo the rhymes 'sights-delights-sprights', 'Spright-light', and 'sight-delight' in stanzas 1 to 3. Above all, however, we should note that the *rest* achieved in the last stanza of the *Hymnes* also marks the end of the problems of the lover who started the first hymn by complaining that Cupid had subdued his heart and was 'raging' 'therein with *restlesse* stowre' (*HL* 1). Thus the structural unity of the *Fowre Hymnes* seems to bear out that the problems of the lover-sinner find their solution not through hymns in praise of Cupid and Venus but in the mind's journey to God as described in the last pair of hymns.

Apart from the opening stanzas the tyranny of Cupid and Venus

over man which dominated substantial parts of the first hymn, has
been largely absent from the second. But in the last three stanzas of
the *Hymne of Beautie* the lord-vassal relationship and the lover's
prostrate adoration of Cupid and Venus is back in full force. The
poet is Venus's vassal and her 'poore liegeman', and he has composed
this hymn in praise of Venus in order that she may grant him success
in love.

The praise offered to the poet's beloved in the penultimate stanza
and particularly in the last stanza is excessive in almost every respect.
Her beauty is said to have such power that she 'can restore a damned
wight from death'. This could, of course, simply mean that the pains
of frustrated love have worked such changes and such sorrows in
him that he now seems more dead than alive. If the beloved can be
moved to give him grace at last he will once more be able to enjoy
life. But if we see this statement as part of the general pattern of
conscious contrasts between earthly and heavenly love and beauty,
the mock-religious description of the power of the lady is clearly
reminiscent of Christ of whom the poet says: 'He gaue vs life, he it
restored lost' (*HHL* line 181) and 'vs wretches from the second death
did saue' (*HHL* line 193). Similarly, when the poet asks the lady
in a beautiful line to 'deigne to let fall one drop of dew reliefe', so
that there may be an end to his grief and sorrow, this reminds the
reader not only of similar statements in the first two hymns but also
of the poet's prayer to the Holy Spirit in the *Hymne of Heavenly
Love* to

> *Vouchsafe to shed into my barren spright,*
> *Some little drop of thy celestiall dew.*
>   (*HHL* lines 45–6)

The lady is also called '*Venus* dearling'. The word *dearling* is used
only twice in the hymns, the second time in the crucial stanza 27 of
the *Hymne of Heavenly Beautie* where Sapience is introduced and
described as the 'soueraine dearling of the *Deity*'. If this is not enough
to bring out the ambiguity and blasphemy of the poet's praise of the
beloved in the last stanza of the second hymn, consider the poet's
praise of his beloved as the 'flowre of grace'. This phrase recurs in
the *Hymne of Heavenly Love* where Christ is called 'floure of grace'.
He alone deserves the epithet. None of the epithets used about the
lady are exceptional in themselves. Spenser had described ladies in
like fashion earlier, but the significant way in which these phrases

are echoed in later descriptions of Christ and Sapience makes the reader aware of the excessiveness of the poet's praise.

The last stanza of the *Hymne of Beautie* is particularly significant, not simply because of its excessive, mock-Christian praise of the lady, nor merely because it is the last stanza of the first pair, but mainly because it is the central stanza of the whole work. That is to say, that of the 169 stanzas in the *Fowre Hymnes* this is stanza 85. This assertion may seem a little puzzling since I have argued above that stanzas four to six of the *Hymne of Heavenly Love* in praise of the triune Deity are the central stanzas of the *Fowre Hymnes*. It is obvious that in a poem with some stanzas that are more or less clearly marked as introductory the poet may have chosen to include or exclude the introductory stanzas from the total number. It is also clear that if we exclude the introductory stanzas the central stanza of the *Fowre Hymnes* is the second stanza proper of the *Hymne of Heavenly Love*. This seems highly appropriate since that stanza is devoted to the second person of the Trinity. In my discussion of the significance of the number 153 in relation to the *Fowre Hymnes* I have shown that this number is relevant to our understanding of the structure of the *Fowre Hymnes* even when we include the introductory stanzas. It is possible that Spenser has invested his *Hymnes* with a double centre.[57] The triune Deity occupies as it were the affirmative centre and Venus and the beloved the negative centre. It is important that the reader realises that the crucial final stanza of the second hymn is preceded by 84 stanzas in praise of earthly love and beauty, and is succeeded by an equal number of stanzas in praise of heavenly love and beauty. And the central stanza around which they are grouped is seen to refer not only to Venus and the beloved, but also to Christ and Sapience. The two pairs are thus not only opposed but also closely related. The poet-speaker of the *Hymne of Beautie* is perhaps not led on to the search for heavenly beauty, but the author of the *Fowre Hymnes* has seen to it that the reader is.

IV

Spenser could have turned his back on his first two hymns when they met with criticism and asked forgiveness of God and man. But he chose a more complex, though not necessarily more pharisaical, solution. He was, first of all, a poet, and it was as such that he was criticised. He felt the need to defend his art, and he possessed the genius to be able to do so, not in an elaborate, philosophical treatise, but by proving in practice that poetry is so powerful that it may guide man to virtue even when it apparently takes the form of a paean to the 'snowy bosome' of Pleasure.

On their own the first pair give a distorted picture, but when they are combined with the second pair a true picture is seen to emerge although the first, distorted picture is still a part of it. This is what Spenser has tried to say in the dedicatory epistle, and this is the effect he has achieved. If we read the hymns as two distinct pairs they may seem mutually exclusive, but when we read the four hymns as a whole, as the *Fowre Hymnes*, we discover that Spenser has managed to create harmony in discord—*discordia concors*.

By means of such devices as foreshadowing, contrast, parallelism, verbal echoes, and elaborate structural patterns Spenser has succeeded in making the first two hymns point to the heavenly love and beauty of the last two hymns. In this way even the first pair may be said to glorify the generous love and divine wisdom of Christ and Sapience, not so much through direct statements, as through the subtle interplay with the last pair. In so doing he has utilised the chief asset of poetry: it can move the reader's imagination so that he makes the right choice in spite of his infected will.

APPENDIX

A List of Verbal Echoes in Spenser's Fowre Hymnes

The list presents verbal echoes of the first pair of hymns found in the second pair. All the instances listed may not constitute verbal echoes in the strictest sense, but the cumulative effect justifies their inclusion. My selection has, of course, been guided by my interpretation of the poem as a whole.

Abusd, abused	HB 150, 172	HHL 242
Admyre	HB 224	HHB 16
Adornd, adorne	HB 151	HHB 188
Affection	HB 76	HHL 11, 157
Against	HL 81	HHL 84
Aloft	HL 68	HHB 24, 136
Amiable	HB 131	HHL 273
Approch	HL 248	HHB 100
Aray, arayd	HL 285	HHL 228
Aspect	HL 217	HHB 284
Aspyre	HL 109	HHL 88
Assayes	HB 88	HHL 235
Assure	HL 297	HHL 97
Attend	HB 261	HHL 68, HHB 97
Auengefull	HL 30	HHB 150
Author	HL 128	HHL 256
Bait	HB 152	HHB 290
Basenesse	HL 191	HHB 279
Beauty	HB 15	HHB 21
Bee	HL 119, HB 250	HHL 119, HHB 252
Begot	HL 53	HHL 30

Beheast	HL 93	HHB 202
Behold	HB 253	HHB 232
Behoue, behoues	HB 184	HHL 178
Being	HL 96	HHL 191
Bitter	HL 5	HHL 245
Blame	HL 288, HB 155	HHL 18, 149, HHB 276
Bleed, bleede	HL 12	HHL 248
Bleeding	HL 142	HHL 164
Blemish, blemishment	HB 215	HHL 149
Blesse, blessed, blest	HL 210, 284	HHL 184
Blind, blynd, blinding	HL 226, HB 77	HHL 262, 280, HHB 137
Blisse, blisses	HL 23, 207	HHL 134, HHB 243
Bosome	HL 289 (see 'lap' HL 24, 62)	HHL 134, HHB 183
Bountie	HL 284	HHL 223
Bowre, bowres	HL 23, HB 202	HHB 249
Breast, brest	HL 27, 224, HB 3	HHL 259, 269
Bright, brighter	HB 56	HHB 188
Brightnes, brightnesse	HB 11, 178	HHB 178, 189
Cleare	HB 11	HHB 189
Commend	HB 263	HHB 222
Contented, contentment	HL 246	HHB 287
Cradle, cratch	HL 51	HHL 226
Crowne, crownd	HL 292	HHL 243, HHB 190
Cruell	HL 14, 32	HHL 151
Damned	HB 287	HHL 89
Darknesse	HL 60	HHL 73, 90
Dearling	HB 281	HHB 184
Death	HB 287	HHL 193
Delight	HL 281, HB 16, 123, 151	HHL 272, HHB 17, 258
Deserued, deseruer	HL 159	HHL 160
Desire, desyre	HB 5	HHL 268
Dew, deaw	HB 27	HHL 46
Dewty	HB 17	HHB 20

Dislike, dislikes	HL 86	HHL 34
Downe	HB 109	HHL 136
Drop	HB 277, 284	HHL 46
Eagle, eagles	HL 69	HHB 138
Earth	HL 111, 214	HHB 210, 283
Earthly	HL 185	HHL 5
Eldest	HL 56	HHL 31
Embrace	HL 111	HHL 261
Endewd, endewed	HB 135	HHL 112
Enlarge	HL 105	HHL 52
Entire, entyre	HB 223	HHL 271
Exceed, exceede	HB 231	HHB 209
Excell	HB 41	HHB 206
Ey, eye	HL 132, 216, HB 226	HHL 276, HHB 23, 144, 285
Eyes, eyne	HL 118, HB 20, 72, 232–4	HHL 222, 280, 283, HHB 123, 179
Face	HB 41, 168	HHL 171, HHB 204, 207
Faire	HL 72, HB 139, 281	HHB 133, 216
Fairenesse	HB 231	HHB 204
Fairer, fairest	HL 216, HB 230	HHB 102
False	HL 261	HHL 240
Fancies, fansie	HL 254, HB 222	HHB 289
Fashiond	HB 33	HHL 109
Fayne, fayning	HL 216, 254	HHB 216, 223
Feare, feares	HL 223, 226	HHB 141, 146
Feeble	HL 185, HB 3, 24	HHL 5, 269, HHB 123
Feed, feede	HL 38, HB 248	HHL 196, HHB 29
Felicitie, felicitye	HL 217	HHB 284
Fierie	HB 241	HHB 95
Fixe, fixed, fixeth	HB 228	HHB 139, 272
Flight	HL 69	HHB 28
Floure, flowre	HB 282	HHL 169
Flowing	HB 55	HHL 100
Foes	HL 263	HHL 161, 234, HHB 156
Force, forse	HL 8, 229	HHL 250

Fount, fountaine	HB 186	HHL 99, HHB 21
Free	HL 154, HB 249	HHL 183–4, HHB 251
Gazefull	HB 12	HHB 29
Golden	HL 178	HHL 1
Grace	HB 27, 277, 282	HHL 44, 99, 169
Great	HB 5	HHL 268
Grieue, grieued	HL 129	HHL 252
Grone	HL 129	HHL 252
Guilt, guilty	HL 290, HB 157	HHL 141, 167
Happie	HL 209	HHB 239
Hart, harts	HL 123, 142	HHL 156
Heast, heasts	HL 160	HHL 161
Heauenly	HL 169, 302, HB 119, 185, 222	HHL 6, 112, 229, HHB 21, 248, 262
Heauens	HL 189, 215, HB 109	HHL 2, 7, 57, 88, HHB 235
Hell, hellish	HL 253, 265	HHL 89, 130
Hew	HB 150	HHB 231
Hid, hidden	HL 59	HHB 178, 248
Higher, see Hyer, hyre		
Hight	HL 189, HB 109	HHL 2, 57, 88, HHB 67
Hope	HL 206	HHL 122
House	HB 117	HHB 193
Hungrie, hungry	HL 198	HHL 196, HHB 288
Hyer, hyre	HL 68	HHB 19
Hymne, hymnes	HL 41, 302, HB 10, 21, 272	HHL 6, 70
Idle, ydle	HL 66, 256	HHB 268, 289
Image	HL 132, 197	HHL 259, HHB 105, 114
Images	HB 163	HHB 3
Immortall	HB 23	HHB 13, 169
Increast	HL 96	HHB 203
Inner	HL 124	HHL 158

Inspire, inspired inspyre	HL 27, 98, HB 2	HHL 281
Ioy	HL 206, 240	HHB 243, 264, 271, 287
Kindle, kindled	HL 28, 65, 124, 203, HB 180	HHL 86, 287, HHB 5
Kindleth	HL 187	HHB 297
King	HL 305	HHL 7
Lampe	HL 131, HB 59, 99	HHL 43, 170, HHB 274
Lie, lye	HL 136	HHL 129
Lieu	HB 274	HHL 176
Life, lyfe	HL 125, 265, HB 63, 279	HHL 181, 183
Light	HL 70	HHL 69
Liue	HL 154, 244, HB 278	HHL 210
Maiestie, maiesty	HB 271	HHB 186
Mangled	HL 143	HHL 250
Might	HL 43, 49, HB 54, 124	HHL 4, 37, 172
Mind, minds, mynd	HL 43, 204, HB 223	HHL 260
Mould	HB 32, 207	HHL 116, 198
Mount	HL 68, 188	HHB 24, 136
Near	HL 248	HHB 100
Obserued, obseruation	HL 93	HHB 202
Ordaine	HB 206	HHB 201
Paine, paines	HL 253, 278, 295	HHL 126, 235, 246
Part	HL 4, 144	HHL 158
Partake, partakes, partakers	HL 275, HB 43	HHL 63, HHB 200
Peares, peerelesse	HL 56	HHB 186
Perfect	HB 40	HHB 296
Pierce, pierst, piercing	HL 30, 123, HB 72	HHL 156

Please, pleased	HB 54	HHB 270
Pleasure	HL 287	HHL 75, HHB 264
Pleasures	HL 275, HB 259	HHL 220, HHB 256, 300
Plumes	HL 178	HHB 134
Powre	HL 1, HB 271	HHB 186, 196
Praise, prayse	HL 301, 307, HB 7–8	HHL 9, HHB 220, 263
Praises, prayses	HL 10	HHL 14, HHB 233
Purest	HL 178, HB 105, 109	HHL 98, HHB 47
Quench, quenched	HL 102, 202, HB 175	HHL 18
Rage, raging	HL 117, HB 4, 73	HHB 1
Rauisht	HB 12	HHL 268, 281, HHB 1
Remaine, remained	HL 92	HHL 125
Resplendent	HB 177	HHB 126
Restore, restored	HL 164, HB 287	HHL 139, 181
Riches	HB 119, 185	HHL 112, HHB 248
Rigour	HL 152	HHB 158
Sake	HL 72	HHL 147
Satietie, satiety	HL 201	HHB 282
Seat, seate	HL 66	HHL 82, HHB 148, 159
See	HL 118, 226, HB 38, 234	HHL 118, 283, HHB 117, 255
Sense	HB 77	HHL 278
Shadow, shadowes	HB 168	HHB 291
Shame	HL 290	HHL 19, 151
Sharp, sharpe	HL 16, 121	HHL 235
Shew	HB 286	HHB 114
Shine, shynes, shyning	HB 168, 175	HHB 169
Sight	HL 119, 195, HB 18, 131, 166, 220	HHL 5, 287, HHB 15, 178, 281
Sing	HL 10, 21, 302	HHL 6, 14
Sit	HL 24	HHB 183
Skie, sky	HL 178	HHB 25
Sore, sores	HL 143	HHL 162, 166
Sorrow, sorrowes	HL 16, HB 28	HHL 251

Soule, soules	HB 14, 60, 137, 159, 248	HHL 196, 251, HHB 137, 288
Spright	HL 106	HHL 110
Stirre	HB 73	HHL 263
Striue, striueth	HL 247	HHB 77
Sunne	HB 220	HHB 139
Sweet, sweete	HL 190, HB 199, 245, 252	HHL 273, HHB 4, 257, 269, 300
Swerue, swerued	HL 165	HHL 161
Taking	HL 64	HHL 146
Thinke, thinks	HL 205	HHB 266
Thought	HB 224	HHB 223
Thraldome, thrall, thrals	HL 136, HB 278	HHL 124, 137, 184
Thrise	HL 209	HHB 239
Throne	HB 265	HHB 151–2
Time	HL 61	HHL 36
Tongue	HL 264	HHB 204
Truth	HL 176	HHB 11, 159
Vnfold	HB 255	HHB 234
Voide	HB 215	HHL 32
Vouchsafe	HL 19, HB 19	HHL 45, HHB 8
Wings	HL 64	HHL 1, 66
Wound, wounds	HL 143, HB 63	HHL 156, 245
Wretches	HL 265	HHL 193
Yre	HL 84, 234	HHL 86, HHB 182

2

Elaborate song

CONCEPTUAL STRUCTURE IN MILTON'S 'ON THE MORNING OF CHRIST'S NATIVITY'

MAREN-SOFIE RØSTVIG

As Milton explains in his *Animadversions* (1641), the imperfections of man extend to the very words of praise that he offers to the Deity: as a rule his 'thanke-offering' must be a 'plain ungarnish't present' only, but when the glorious acts of God have been fully achieved, he 'may then perhaps take up a Harp, and sing thee an elaborate song...'[1]

The poetic perfection envisaged here is of course unattainable within our fallen world, but it must nevertheless be permissible to characterise Milton's *Nativity Ode*—his ceremonial gift to the infant Christ—as 'elaborate song' rather than a 'plain ungarnish't present' snatched up in a hurry. And if his words of praise should be felt to possess some measure of perfection, this is so partly because they have been made to reflect the very structures by means of which God perfected and accomplished his glorious acts. Augustine would have appreciated the art with which this has been done, and so would poets like Edmund Spenser and Giles Fletcher. The task that I have set myself here is to explain this art, and although I hope to make my argument sufficiently persuasive for acceptance, I shall also feel a major obligation to try to convey the conceptual richness of the structures selected by Milton as appropriate, and their intrinsic aesthetic beauty.

I have seldom come across structures that yield greater aesthetic delight, and it is possible that they are there, in the poem, not so much to persuade as to move. Although they relate to matters of faith they seem designed, to borrow the words of William Whitaker, 'to give pleasure, not to coerce assent',[2] or, to quote a modern scholar, 'to deepen and change the meaning of the narrative from the specific to the general and universal.'[3] It does not necessarily follow that Milton must have believed implicitly in the presence of these structures, in the Bible and the created universe, if he saw fit to use them. As long as they were felt as powerfully evocative images they would do to adorn his song.

The major images of the Christian religion are very complex, and structural images are no exception. Such images, by the way, connect so closely with the traditional kind of verbal image that they cannot be kept absolutely apart. The Tree of Life, for example,—in the Garden of Eden, on Golgotha, and in the Heavenly Jerusalem— acquires added symbolic richness by being seen as a structuring element placed at the beginning, middle, and the end. The semantic complexity of the structures attributed to the glorious acts of God posits a very real problem in literary criticism: if the critic, in his attempt to elucidate a particular poetic structure, were to follow the example set by Biblical exegetes, he might easily be encouraged to range so far afield that the connection with the text may be obscured. I hope I have avoided this hazard, but I have nevertheless on occasion included arguments that some readers perhaps may find objectionable as going beyond the limits set by Milton's text. My defence for so doing is a simple one: it seemed to me that since the structures possess this conceptual complexity, then the point of incorporating them in a poem on the Nativity must be to invoke the nexus of ideas that they embody. If my first critical premiss, therefore, is that the structures are there as the result of conscious planning rather than instinctive artistic tact, my second is that the entire conceptual range may be drawn on in an *explication de texte,* even if this should mean going beyond the strict limits of what I am tempted to refer to as the para- phrasable prose content. But the use of such material for the purpose of literary criticism presupposes sufficient familiarity and sympathy with certain ways of thinking typical of much Renaissance theology, Protestant as well as Roman Catholic, and sufficient critical tact in assessing the degree of relevance.

The analysis presented here will be found to stress the concepts of the circle, the centre, and the 'well-balanced world' hung on 'hinges', my argument being that these images have been worked into the structure of the poem to permit Milton's gift to the child to consti- tute an image of his acts as Creator and Redeemer. My structural units are stanza-length (respectively seven and eight lines), the number of stanzas in each part (4 and 27), and the sum total of lines (28 and 216).[4]

My 'warrant' for considering structure in this manner is taken primarily from traditional interpretations of the Psalms, especially Psalm 119 (Vulgate 118) and the fifteen Psalms of Ascent (Psalms 120–34). My inclusion of the Platonic *lambda*-formula has similar Biblical authority, the appropriate points of reference in this case being comments on the Mosaic account of creation and the creation-passage in *Job* 38:4–8 (echoed by Milton in stanza 12). However, my most important frame of reference for interpreting the structural numbers was provided by theological glosses on the Apocalyptic passages invoked by Milton's vision of Christ as universal King and of the complete perfection that will be ours at the end of Time.

The basic structure in the hymn proper is created by a thematic movement focussed around a triple centre-piece so that the overall pattern may be presented as a sequence of 12—3—12 stanzas. For H. Neville Davies, writing without knowledge of my analysis, the thematic movement seemed to indicate a division into 15—11—1. His thematic analysis of the first fifteen stanzas, however, not only is compatible with my own but supplements it, and the same is true of his analysis of the last twelve stanzas as a sequence of 11 plus 1. Biblical exegesis similarly offers examples of the attribution, to the same work, of different structures. Thus the Psalms could be divided in various ways—into three times fifty, for example, or a sequence of 70 plus 80—and each arrangement carried its own symbolic significance. When Cassiodorus discusses various ways of dividing the books of the Bible into groups (*Institutiones*, I, 14), he recommends them all because a 'careful consideration and inspection' will show that so far from conflicting they tend 'to make one another mutually intelligible'. Statements by the Fathers on this matter 'are not contradictory but varying'; through the divisions they recommend, all of them have created structural expressions of the contents of divine revelation. The actual phrase used by Cassiodorus is that they 'through their divisions have adapted the sacred books to appropriate mysteries'.

When poets like Vaughan and Cowley appropriated structures as well as themes from the works of their predecessors, they reveal that different poets could 'read' a structure in slightly different ways, or put a given structure to a somewhat different use. But similarity need not necessarily indicate borrowing. The presence of fairly similar structures in poems possessed of thematic similarities may quite simply constitute evidence of the extent to which certain themes were associated with certain structures. If Cowley for example wrote his 'Hymn to the Light' without awareness of Milton's use of related themes and structures, one must perforce conclude that Cowley drew on a general tradition which enabled him to achieve the degree of similarity to Milton's ode that I discuss below.

In assessing structural analyses, then, one must take into account the fact that a poem may accommodate more than one structural effect. A structural image, in other words, may possess the same kind of willed ambiguity that we have been accustomed to recognise in verbal imagery. I suppose it is because structures seem so unambiguous —a seven-line stanza is a seven-line stanza—that certainty has been more or less expected. When a poet takes the trouble to explain the meaning invested in a structure, certainty is of course achieved, but such authorial glosses are the exception rather than the rule, and for good reasons: they reduce the 'mystery' of the poem, to use the word so popular among Biblical expositors. As Augustine puts it in his *De doctrina Christiana* (II, vi, 7), things that are easily discovered 'seem frequently to become worthless', while 'what is sought with difficulty is discovered with more pleasure.'[5] But our understanding of the message of salvation does not depend on these more difficult passages; that which is stated obscurely and with great art can always be found elsewhere in phrases easily grasped by all. This argument seems to me to apply to Milton's poem as well; one can enjoy it without perceiving the elaborateness of its art. It conveys its basic message both simply and memorably.

As far as Milton's structural rhetoric is concerned, I wish I could assert with Augustine's supreme confidence that the more obscure the prophetic eloquence, the sweeter it becomes when explained *(De doctrina Christiana,* IV, vii, 15).

I. *Structural Exegesis*

To begin with the beginning is, I believe, to begin with Psalm 119 (Vulgate 118) and with a summary of the symbolism attributed to its form, since it was this symbolic import which made the form appropriate for Nativity hymns.

Psalm 119 is an acrostic poem, the sequence of initial letters spelling out the 22 letters of the Hebrew alphabet. It consists of 22 groups of 8 verses, each of which begins with the appropriate letter in the alphabet, a technique used in *Lamentations* 1–4, where it may be better known today. As I have explained elsewhere,[6] a prophetic message was attributed to the textual arrangement of this Psalm, partly in terms of its use of the alphabet and partly in terms of its structural numbers (8 and 22). The idea of fullness or completeness was conveyed (so it was argued) by using all the letters in the alphabet, a concept seen as appropriate since the Psalm presents all the precepts required for the achievement of eternal life. A summary of patristic interpretations may be found in the *Commentarium In Librum Psalmorum* (Lugduni, 1611–1613) by the Jesuit Lorinus. Thus Lorinus observes that Cassiodorus followed Augustine in admiring the perfection of this Psalm, a perfection revealed by the Tree in the middle of the Garden of Eden: *sub similitudine arboris, quae in medio paradisi erat, Augustino hunc psalmum reuelatum fuisse.*[7] Why the structure should seem like the Tree which is Christ is explained more fully by Bonaventura in his *Collationes in Hexaemeron* (XVII, 12). Augustine apparently had a vision of a tree with 22 branches each of which had 8 twigs from which issued *guttae dulcissimae*, and he suddenly understood that this tree was the Psalm which begins *Beati immaculati in via* ('Blessed are the undefiled in the way, who walk in the law of the Lord . . .'). To realise this one must follow Augustine in connecting the form of Psalm 119 with the contents of Psalm 1 as Bonaventura explains, conveniently quoting the first few lines to display the similarity in theme and phrasing ('Blessed is the man that walketh not in the counsel of the ungodly . . . But his delight is in the law of the Lord . . . And he shall be like a tree planted by the rivers of water . . .').[8] The tree in Psalm 1 was universally accepted as an allusion to the Tree of Life in the Garden of Eden, both being images (or types) of Christ, and Augustine reveals a visual, almost architectural or spatial approach to textual structure when he has this vision of Psalm 119 as a tree full of the sweetest sap. In Psalm 1 as in *Genesis* this image of Christ is verbal, while it is the literary structure that conveys it in Psalm 119, and the ease with which it was possible to turn from verbal to structural images or the other way round is typical of the tradition extending from Hilarius and Augustine to Lorinus.

Representative comments on the conceptual content of the structural numbers may be fetched from a Renaissance edition of the medieval Bishop Haymo's *Pia, Brevis Ac Dilucida In Omnes Psalmos Explanatio* (Freiburg, 1533). The structure shows that the Law (10) and apostolic doctrine (12) combined (so as to make 22) lead to beatitude (the Octonarius represented by the groups of eight verses). In this manner God rescues man from the confusion which is the consequence of the Fall, to a state of order. Similar remarks are found in the commentary written by a Protestant theologian, Johannes Bugenhagius *(In Librum Psalmorum Interpretatio,* 1524). Bugenhagius felt that the form had been selected to show that this Psalm contains everything stated in the sacred Scriptures concerning the attainment of perfection—a comment bearing on the alphabetical technique of composition. He goes on to explain that the number 8 must refer to the resurrection because Christ rose on the eighth day which signifies the time of grace. This time of grace cannot pertain to the seven days of this world, all of which terminate with a night so that they cease being days. All those will be resurrected who walk with God and *not* according to the elements of this world *(secundum mundi elementa).*

All this, and more, could be adduced as legitimate commentary by exegetes convinced that structure conveyed part of the prophetic message. After reading a fairly wide range of commentaries on selected parts of the Bible, I have formed the conclusion that the truly basic reason for associating the structure of Psalm 119 (or of *Lamentations)* with Nativity hymns must be its highly ordered form, and the connection made between this form and Christ as the creative Logos. The creative Word imposes order on chaos, and hence the words of praise offered to Christ in celebration of his Nativity must themselves be highly ordered. The standard example cited by exegetes is Sedulius' Nativity hymn beginning *A solis ortus cardine*,[9] but I am unable to say how common the practice actually was.[10] Venantius Fortunatus employed an alphabetical structure on one occasion, but not in a Nativity hymn,[11] and when he wrote a poem that might qualify as such thematically, he devised structural patterns of such ingenuity that one can only marvel at the skill with which he manipulated his 33 lines, each consisting of 33 letters, at the centre of which is the letter which itself holds the centre of the alphabet.[12]

Augustine reinforced the association between Christ and a meaningful arrangement of letters and numbers in his comment on the supposed prophecy, by the Sibyls, of the birth of Christ in an acrostic poem consisting of 27 lines. Augustine found the number appropriate because it is a cube (3^3), since cubes symbolise the permanence and stability of the divine *(De civitate Dei* XVIII, 23). This use of classical number lore in a purely Christian context illustrates a syncretistic tendency extending through the Middle Ages and into the Renaissance, when it received renewed impetus.[13] The way in which classical myth was interpreted so as to convey the same truths that we find in divine revelation has been explored by Edgar Wind and Don Cameron Allen,[14] and it was of course much easier for classical number lore to be subsumed under a Mosaic revelation than for pagan myth; numbers figure so importantly in so many Biblical passages that it must have seemed eminently logical to assume a Hebrew source for the Pythagorean and Platonic numerical accounts of creation. I have discussed this assumption elsewhere,[15] so suffice it here to quote one or two arguments advanced by Francesco Giorgio in his *Problemata* (1536, 1574, and 1622),[16] a collection of Biblical cruxes. Problem III, i, 26 discusses the reason for the alphabetical composition employed in Psalm 119 and *Lamentations* (and, in so doing, refers to and quotes from Sedulius' Nativity hymn), while V, ii, 176 associates the music of the spheres inferred from *Job* 38 with the inaudible music of the divine numbers used in the work of creation, adding that it is of this divine order that the prophet sings in Psalm 119. This inaudible music was given mathematical expression by Plato and Pythagoras, as theologians with a syncretistic bias took care to remind their readers, adding that the ultimate source for this classical number lore was in Moses and the prophets. Strictly speaking, therefore, one should not refer to this lore as 'pagan' if one wishes to represent the point of view of theologians like Augustine, Aquinas or Cornelius à Lapide.[17] If readers of this essay, therefore, should hesitate to attribute to conscious intent the fact that Milton's ode has three cubes as the chief structural numbers (8, 27, and 216 are the cubes of 2, 3, and 6), and that 8 and 27 represent the inaudible music of the divine numbers used in the work of creation,[18] they must take care to do so for reasons that can be accepted. It would be an historical anachronism to argue that such number lore would be inadmissible in a poem on the Nativity.

Milton may not have read Mantuan's comments on the form of Psalm 119, but his familiarity with the symbolism attributed to its structure can be taken for granted. He would have studied this *lusum poeticum* (to borrow Mantuan's words)[19] with complete awareness of the belief that the formal arrangement of this particular Psalm as of all the Psalms as a whole had been so designed by the Holy Ghost as to convey a message of its own. Distinctly odd as this belief seems to us today, it must nevertheless be classified as being well within the orthodox fold in the age itself. We must remember that the first half of the seventeenth century in England was virtually obsessed by typological exegesis, and that typology exploits numbers. Typological imagery, therefore, spilled over into the pages of poets as well as preachers, as all readers of George Herbert and John Donne will know. This marked interest in typology was in large measure a direct consequence of that belief in Providence and in England as God's chosen nation that for a time made the Millennium seem at hand. And to think typologically is to think in terms of meaningful, carefully balanced patterns imposed by the hand of Providence on the course of human history, which is one reason why structure assumed such great significance. The concern with structure, therefore, should be seen as a direct manifestation of a way of thinking that must be characterised as widespread, and even a poet who may have refused to commit himself fully to it as an article of faith, would have felt its poetic potentiality—its power to move the minds and hearts of men.

If this belief in the prophetic or conceptual import of structure was at all widely known, poets other than Milton must have felt the attraction of imitating patterns attributable to divine inspiration. And so they did, as we may see from the poetry of Giles and Phineas Fletcher and most clearly, perhaps, from Giles Fletcher's *Christ's Victory and Triumph* (Cambridge, 1610). His defence of poetry in the prefatory epistle to the reader invokes the poetic passages in the Bible and the example set by 'sedulous Prudentius' and 'prudent Sedulius' and the 'choicest witts of Christendome'. What Giles Fletcher himself refers to as 'poetical diuinity' no doubt prompted his choice of an eight-line stanza in imitation of Psalm 119. This may seem a bold assertion, but readers may possibly agree on studying the last stanza of the last part. This concluding stanza deplores man's inability, caught up as he is in the web of Time, to grasp the vision of Eternity that the poet has tried to present in the preceding 50 stanzas:

> *Impotent words, weak lines, that strive* in vain
> In vain, *alas! to tell* so heavenly sight,—
> So heavenly sight, *as none greater* feign,
> Feign *what he can, that seems of greatest* might:
>   Might *any yet compare with* Infinite?
>   Infinite *sure those joys, my words but* light;
> Light *is the palace where she dwells—O blessed wight!*[20]

Giles Fletcher has given structural expression to the links in the chain of Time by means of phrasal repetition as indicated typographically by romans. But not only have the lines been linked in a circular pattern, their number has been reduced from 8 to 7. This is the only stanza that has been tampered with in this unusual manner, and the linking of the lines explains why. If the stanzaic structure is to reflect the nature of Time as it revolves around the ever-repeated cycle of weeks, the number of lines must be seven. I consider these structural phenomena as adequate proof of intent, and on the strength of the formal symbolism displayed in this last stanza I conclude that the eight-line stanza should be taken to reflect the eighth 'day' of Eternity in the manner familiar to students of Psalm 119 and of the 15 Psalms of Ascent. The fact that there are 15 such Psalms was interpreted as showing that the ascent takes us from the 7 of Time to the 8 of Eternity.[21] Giles Fletcher may conceivably have trusted some of his readers to realise why he shortened the Spenserian stanza to eight lines in a poem concerned with Christ's victory and triumph, but he underlined his artistic purpose by creating a final stanza whose departure from the established norm explains the reason for the norm.

II

The Structure of Milton's Ode

I find it inconceivable that Milton, who must have studied Fletcher's poem with considerable care,[22] should have failed to observe how the last stanza underlines the symbolism invested in the stanzaic pattern. I find it more reasonable to suppose that he was inspired by Giles Fletcher and the exegetical tradition Fletcher invokes, to exploit the same polarity between Time and Eternity in the two stanza-patterns he created for his ode. Like Giles Fletcher (and, of course, Spenser before him), Milton encouraged his readers to adopt a structural perspective by providing verbal clues to the conceptual content of the chosen form. 'This is the month,' he proclaims in the first line of the four seven-line stanzas that constitute the introduction, 'and this the happy morn' when the Son 'Forsook the courts of ever-lasting day / And chose with us a darksome house of mortal clay.' A reader accustomed to structural exegesis and to the use of Biblical structures in religious poetry, would have observed the care with which the poet has observed structural decorum and would have enjoyed it as an aspect of his art. The structural numbers of the introduction—4, 7, and 28—enact the weekly and seasonal cycles of Time; in its capacity as the lunar cycle the sum total of lines, 28, aptly represents the mutability of this world of 'mortal clay', but it may also suggest that our earthly existence borrows its light from that Son who is the Sun of our spiritual existence.

The transition to the eight-line stanza of the hymn with its varied rhythmical movement is strongly felt, but a sense of continuity is suggested by the concluding alexandrine. This rhythmical element is shared, thus showing that the worlds of Time and Eternity, although separate, must not be entirely unconnected. The point of the incarnation is to enable man to achieve the ascent.

The introduction provides another important clue when it presents Christ as King, seated 'at heaven's high council-table' 'the midst of trinal unity'. This recalls the greatest Biblical vision of Christ as King as presented in the Book of Revelation. As St John puts it (*Rev.* 4:1–5 and 5:8–14), 'a door was opened in heaven' and he saw 'a throne set in heaven, and one sat on the throne', and 'there was a rainbow round about the throne'. Also there are around the throne 'four and twenty seats: and upon the seats I saw four and twenty elders sitting'. These elders fall down before the Lamb, 'having every one of them harps', and so Christ is worshipped with 'a new song', the voices of 'every creature which is in heaven, and on the earth' being added to praise him 'that sitteth upon the throne'. It is interesting that Milton should begin his introduction by invoking this most familiar and most impressive Apocalyptic vision of Christ as King; he is clearly concerned to fuse the two images—of Christ as eternal King surrounded by the elders and worshipped with 'a new song', and of Christ as the 'heaven-born-child' in the manger hymned by cherubim and seraphim. As the singer of his own hymn, Milton joins his voice to both 'quires'. The importance, to Milton, of the Apocalyptic vision, is brought out again in stanzas 13–15, where we recognise direct verbal echoes. Thus heaven 'as at some festival' is seen to 'open wide the gates of her high palace hall' to provide a glimpse of what the introduction refers to, in a phrase reminiscent of Giles Fletcher, as 'the courts of everlasting day'. These gates are envisaged as opening when the 'ninefold harmony' (13) has been fully achieved so that 'hell itself will pass away' and permit the return to Earth of Truth and Justice, 'Orbed in a rainbow', with Mercy sitting 'between' (15).

When these Apocalyptic echoes are recognised, one perceives that stanzas 13–15 form a triple centre-piece depicting the glory of the Heavenly Jerusalem. The points of transition are easily felt: the passage begins with the joyous command to the spheres to 'ring out' and it is at an end when we reach the emphatic retraction. 'But wisest fate says no.' It must be stressed that the vision invoked in the introduction and in this triple centre-piece is a vision whose meaning was explained almost entirely in terms of its structural symbolism. To think of this vision was to think of its structural import.

But before this import is discussed we must consider the thematic movement through the twelve stanzas that precede the centre, and the twelve that follow. There is a strongly felt contrast between the central section and the rest of the poem, as well as between the two flanking sections of equal length. While the centre-piece presents the perfection of the Heavenly Jerusalem when God's glorious acts will have been fully achieved, the rest of the hymn describes the impact of the incarnation, beginning and concluding with a stanza showing the child in the manger. We observe, however, that in the first stanza it is Nature who pays homage to the incarnate Deity, while it is the angels who do so in the last. And as we read on from the first stanza to the centre-piece, we realise that they form a carefully planned sequence showing the impact of the incarnation on the world of Nature and of man, concluding with a climactic last stanza (12) recalling Christ's work as Creator—his first act within the world of Time. And after we have passed through the three stanzas on the harmony of Eternity (consequent on the completion of his glorious acts), we are made to envisage his last work in the world of Time when the 'trump of doom' announces Judgement Day. The centre-piece, therefore, is surrounded by stanzas devoted to respectively the first and the last day of Time, and to the first and the last work of Christ. Stanza 17, moreover, shows us Christ seated on his throne 'in middle air' sentencing souls, thus indicating that this second major thematic movement (stanzas 16–27) is devoted to a different sphere of life, namely a realm of spiritual powers and principalities to invoke *Ephesians* 6:12. In this sphere, too, the superior power of the Son is manifested. In some ways this overall thematic movement reminds one of the many representations in sacred art of Christ surrounded on the one hand by the orderly ranks of the blessed and, on the other, by a confused array of the damned. Even more appropriate, perhaps, is a comparison with Spenser's use of so-called encyclo-paedic infolded images as explained by Gerald Snare.[23] When pre-sented iconographically the key figure—God, for example, or man—

is placed seated within a circle surrounded by its attributes or acts as circular emanations. But to return to Milton, we observe that the two sequences I have indicated (1–12 and 16–27) are dominated by the concept of reign or rule. In the first earthly kings acknowledge their 'sovran Lord', just as the Sun hides his head to see 'a greater Sun appear', but in the realm of man and Nature Christ is no hostile power. He purifies and fulfils, but does not expel: Nature 'was almost won / To think her part was done, / And that her reign had here its last fulfilling' (10). In the second sequence on the effect of the incarnation within a realm of spiritual powers, the purification is partly by expulsion, partly by replacement: evil powers are overcome and the imperfect foreshadowings replaced by full and final revelation.[24] The idea of kingship is again strongly stressed: Christ evicts from their thrones powers that have usurped his place. Their spurious kingdoms must needs fail the moment they feel the 'dreaded infant's hand'.

Before I consider the two sequences in greater detail, I would like to stress the importance of the chronological structure indicated by stanzas 1/27 and 12/16. The circular effect created by letting the hymn begin and end with the babe in the manger is easily felt, but it is surely an equally striking structural phenomenon that the first sequence concludes with Christ's work of creation (12), while the second begins with Judgment Day (16). Since Christ was born not only *in medio noctis* but also *in medio annorum*, a beautiful temporal scheme is perceived. When we reach the centre of the hymn we are referred back to the beginning of Time (as stated at 14:3) and to its end (16:8)—a chiastic arrangement recalling the fusion of beginning and end in Eternity. Conversely the true mid-point is found at the beginning (1) and at the end (27). Not only is the chronological scheme plainly circular, but the great circle of Time is shown as issuing out of Eternity and returning to it again. Such is the beauty and the theological appropriateness of this structure that it becomes an object of contemplation in its own right. And if one tries to fuse this abstract structural pattern with the poem, one's ability to experience it as a whole is perceptibly increased. It becomes possible to hold the poem in one's mind in an act almost disconnected with the world of Time: sequential reading is supplemented by an almost visual act of instant perception.

But Christ is the beginning, middle, and end in other respects as well. Such is the connotative richness of the structure I have indicated that it may be as well to explain some of the theological concepts involved by referring to Bonaventura, a writer whose epigrammatic style invites quotation. Bonaventura begins his *Collationes in Hexa-emeron*[25] by showing the many ways in which Christ 'holds the middle' at the same time that he circumscribes everything. We are reminded of the well-known rule for epic poetry when Bonaventura writes that we must always begin with the middle, that is Christ (*incipiendum est a medio, quod est Christus*; I, 10), who became our true mid-point through his incarnation (*Hoc medium fuit Christus in incarnatione*; I, 20). The theological appropriateness of letting Christ circumscribe the whole poem (1 and 27) and the centre (12 and 16) is brought out when Bonaventura writes that Christ *habet rationem principii, medii et finis ultimi* (I, 13), or again when he compares Christ as our beginning, middle, and end to the circle and its centre in his most famous work, the *Itinerarium mentis in Deum*:

> Rursus revertentes dicamus: quia igitur esse purissimum et absolutum, quod est simpliciter esse, est primarium et novissi-mum, ideo est omnium origo et finis consummans.—Quia aeternum et praesentissimum, ideo omnes durationes ambit et intrat, quasi simul existens earum centrum et circumferentia.— Quia simplicissimum et maximum, ideo totum intra omnia et totum extra, ac per hoc 'est sphaera intelligibilis, cuius centrum est ubique et circumferentia nusquam' (Alan. ab Insulis, Theolog. Regul. 7).—Quia actualissimum et immutabilissimum, ideo 'stabile manens moveri dat universa' (Boeth., III de Consolat., metr. 9).—Quia perfectissimum et immensum, ideo est intra omnia, non inclusum, extra omnia, non exclusum . . . ideo est omnia in omnibus (I Cor 15, 28) . . .
>
> (*Itinerarium mentis in Deum*, V, 8)

To paraphrase this loosely, as pure being Christ is the first and the last and the end of everything; because he is eternal and most present he circumscribes and enters into everything so that he is as it were both the centre and the circumference of all things. He is at once inside and outside everything because he is highest unity, or most One, and the greatest (both *simplicissimum* and *maximum*). Thus he is 'an intelligible sphere whose centre is everywhere and whose circumference nowhere'. He is in everything without being enclosed by it, and he is outside everything without being excluded. In short, he is all in all despite the fact that 'all' is multiplicity (*omnia sunt multa*) and he is One (*ipsum non sit nisi unum*).[26]

I have quoted so extensively in order to show the wealth of associations connected with a fairly simple structural concept involving beginning, middle and end, or circle and centre. Unless these associations are present as we consider the highly ordered structure of Milton's poem, it will seem but a *lusus poeticus* and a pretty idle one, to quote Mantuan, rather than a device whereby *omnia sunt prophetica.*[27]

The juxtaposition, in stanzas 12 and 16, of Christ as creator and judge, anticipates the similar effect in *Paradise Lost* where the first half concludes with Christ as triumphant victor and judge, while the second half begins by showing Christ as omnipotent creator. In both poems Christ 'holds the middle' as our *sol iustitiae* (*Malachi* 4:2) who expels the powers of darkness.

The fact that stanzas 1 and 27 and again 12 and 16 display strong thematic linking may be an indication of the presence of recessed symmetry around the centre, and this supposition is borne out by an analysis of the thematic movement as indicated in my diagram. I would not insist on a pattern worked out in terms of one to one equivalents; the thematic movement seems based on groups of stanzas. One observes that the most magnificent images have been placed closest to the centre, stanzas 11–12 and 16–17 focussing on Christ. Stanzas 12/16 display the acts of Christ on the first day (as creator) and the last (as judge), while 11/17 describe the homage paid by the angelic hosts to 'heaven's new-born heir' (11) and his appearance as 'dreadful judge in middle air' (17).

Stanzas 2–10 and 18–26 praise the acts of Christ within the world of Time, the first sequence being concerned with the world of man and nature, the second with the world of spiritual powers. The thematic pairing is emphatic in 2/26, where the common denominator is guilt: Nature hides her 'guilty front' (2) just as guilty spirits are seen to vanish into their 'infernal jail' (26). At the other end of the thematic 'chain' the linking is equally clear: in stanza 10 Nature hopes to see her reign fulfilled, while in stanza 18 Satan's 'usurped sway' ceases. In both spheres of life the true ruler has appeared. The stanzas that fall in between are linked through related themes; 'universal peace' is the theme of stanzas 3–5, while the absence of peace is stressed in the stanzas placed equidistant from the centre on the other side (23–5). The next group of stanzas (6–7 and 21–2) magnify the *true ruler* by revealing the inadequacy of the acts performed by man and Nature or by spiritual powers. The next thematic key word is *true revelation* of the divine to men (8–9) and to powers, whether these be false or merely inadequate (19–20). The symmetrical structure also manifests itself in the rising movement of stanzas 2–10 and the corresponding falling movement of stanzas 18–26. Initially one ascends in contemplation from Earth with its elements and societies of men to the stars and the sun (6–7), and from there one moves to the heavenly voices heard by the shepherds (8) and to the theme of the harmonious union between Heaven and Earth (9–10). This rising movement continues in the stanzas that take us into the realm of Christ as related to the world of man and Nature (11–12), the peak being reached in the three stanzas on the heavenly Jerusalem (13–15). After this centre has been passed we begin at the same high level with two stanzas (16–17) presenting Christ in his relationship to a world of spiritual powers. The spatial connotations of the stanzas that follow are realised on remembering that the dragon whose reign ceases (18) falls from Heaven (*Rev.* 20:2), and that the 'straiter limits' imposed on him are on a cosmic scale. The false idols and deities are connected with the stars (22) or the elements (23) and when these are ousted from their 'wonted' seats (21) Satan's sway is indeed reduced. The descent is also a spiritual descent from lesser goods to absolute evil: stanzas 19–21 describe pagan myth and ritual in terms that reveal an awareness of intrinsic beauty, and this beauty must be recognised for the simple reason that pagan myth foreshadows the incarnation. The Pan who is ousted in stanza 20 is a type of the true, or 'mighty Pan' whose coming is announced in stanza 8. Similarly the Sun who hides his head for shame is a natural type of Him who is the source of all light. Without Christ the Sun is as inadequate a ruler as the rites of stanza 21 are inadequate, and for the same reason. The impact of pure evil is strongly felt in the stanzas that follow (22–5), and the thematic movement concludes when we are taken underground with the fettered ghosts that 'Troop to the infernal jail' (26).

As my diagram shows, the overall 12—3—12 pattern modifies into one of three groups of nine, one for each part of the triple world. It is a particularly felicitous arrangement that the sphere of Christ and Eternity should be at the centre (11–17) at the same time that it circumscribes them all in stanzas 1 and 27. To do justice to the structure my diagram ought to have been three-dimensional so as to allow for the spatial effect of ascent and descent. The appropriateness of having three groups of nine is obvious, since this is the traditional pattern of the threefold world. However, Milton has varied this pattern in a manner which recalls Cusanus' Circulus Universorum (*De coniecturis* I, xvi).[28] He has fused the macrocosmic and the microcosmic, inserting a world of spirits and powers between a hierarchically structured heaven and the world of Nature and man. As a consequence one receives a strong impression that man is placed in a world where spiritual powers manifest themselves everywhere and at all times, and the thematic alignment between these two spheres underlines their interconnection. Thus in stanzas 6 and 5 (reading from the centre outwards to each side) Christ commands the stars and the elements, in 22 and 23 idols and powers associated with the stars and the elements. And in 4 and 3 the hand of Peace pacifies the world of men and 'sea and land', while conversely the 'dreaded infant's hand' deprives the powers of evil of all rest in 24 and 25. The thematic alignment between stanzas or groups of stanzas is clearly the result of tracing the impact of the incarnation through spheres of life that are subtly interconnected. One may derive a purely aesthetic pleasure from a contemplation of the beauty of order as manifested in this poem, but there is even greater pleasure in discovering that the order of the poem is the order imposed by him whom the poem celebrates. As a consequence of this discovery a problem has been resolved which has puzzled many readers—why Milton paid such sustained attention to the theme of the cessation of oracles and the expulsion of false gods.

To summarise: the overall structure combines two patterns, a sequence of 12—3—12 and another of 1—9—7—9—1 stanzas. The first resembles that of the created universe (as described in stanza 12), the 27 stanzas being 'hung' on 'well-balanced' stanzaic 'hinges'. The balance of each sequence is equally perfect, as it must be to mirror the perfect unity of the Creator. Symmetry is a matter of *aequalitas*, so that *aequalitas*-structures should be considered as a poetic *mimesis* of the unity which is the supreme attribute of the Deity. No one has brought out the emotional impact of this intellectual argument more strongly than Augustine in his *De vera religione*, the treatise which, together with the *De libero arbitrio*, provides the theoretical basis for the use of conceptual structures in religious poetry. Since our minds suffer the mutability of error, Augustine writes, the standard called truth must be above our own minds in the mind of God, and by this standard we perceive that beauty is harmony. 'In all the arts that which pleases is harmony [*convenientia*], which alone invests the whole with unity and beauty. This harmony requires equality and unity either through the resemblance of symmetrically placed parts, or through the graded arrangement of unequal parts.'[29] We delight in harmony because we delight in absolute equality, which is the similitude of Him who created it; by perceiving this *aequalitas* in the universe or in a work of art, our minds are led back to God. So far Augustine. Milton's ode achieves *aequalitas* in many ways—most strikingly perhaps in the structures indicated here, but also by means of what Augustine calls 'graded arrangement'. This is where the *lambda*-formula becomes relevant, since the key numbers of this formula, 8 and 27, are the key numbers of the hymn.[30] It can be added that each of these numbers illustrates *aequalitas* by being a cubed number, since cubes consist of sides that must needs be of equal size.

So far I have commented on the 12—3—12 sequence largely in terms of its poised symmetry or in terms of its *mimesis* of the great circle of Time which issues out of, and returns to, that Eternity of which it is an image. The two chief metaphors of Christ as *light* and *harmony* are fully realised in the three central stanzas (13–15) on the 'ninefold harmony' of 'heaven's deep organ' and the glorious appearance of Truth, Justice, and Mercy 'Throned in celestial sheen' as an image of the Trinity. Each is also embodied in the structure: the concept of harmony in the *lambda*-numbers and the ninefold arrangement of the three spheres,[31] and that of light in the solar symbolism traditionally invested in the Apocalyptic vision of the Lamb seated amidst the 24 elders. The 12—3—12 sequence may be seen either as a straight sequence of 12 plus a three-in-one centre plus 12, or as a three-in-one centre surrounded by thematically paired stanzas that constitute 12 pairs or circles. The sequence, therefore, enacts both the 24-hour cycle of the sun and the annual cycle of 12 months as the sun passes through the 12 signs of the zodiac. And the image of Christ as our *sol iustitiae* commanding the celestial constellations or again as *lux vera* illuminating the whole earth in its daily and annual cycles, was virtually fused with the image of Christ as the head of the 12 tribes in the Old Testament and of the 12 Apostles in the New. This may be illustrated by a passage in Rabanus Maurus (*Enarrationes in librum numerorum* III, 9) as quoted by Pietro Bongo towards the end of the sixteenth century:

Horis ergo 24 Sol mundanus totem Orbem vndiq. illustrat,

atque noctis tenebras suo ambitu fugat. Qui. n. fidei lumine, quod per Apostolos atque Prophetas prædicatum est, mentis suæ oculos illuminat, peccatorum tenebras euitare decertat.[32]

To paraphrase: just as the Sun illuminates the whole Earth in the course of 24 hours, chasing away the darkness of night, the light of our true faith revealed by the Prophets and the Apostles illuminates the eyes of the mind, overcoming the darkness of sin. And as readers of the Apocalypse will recall, the number 12 prevails also in the structure of the Heavenly Jerusalem with its carefully measured walls and its numbered doors or gates, and all these occurrences of the number 12 in the universe, in the history of man, and in Heaven itself would be summarised in Renaissance expositions of the meaning of the vision of Christ as King seated amidst the 24 elders.

No wonder, therefore, that the number was applied to the Nativity, as we see from Cassiodorus' comments on Psalm 13 and again on the thirteenth Psalm of Ascent (Ps. 131).[33] As he puts it, the ordinal numbers of these Psalms indicate that Christ was to be born on the thirteenth day after the winter solstice, thus showing that he was to be the head of the 12 Apostles (symbolised by the 12 days). Rabanus Maurus attributed the same symbolism to the literary structure of the New Testament when he wrote that the account of the acts of the 12 Apostles is followed by the Apocalypse as a thirteenth section the purpose of which is to reveal Christ in his full glory as their head.[34] On studying glosses of this kind one sees how easily the transition is achieved from the *liber creaturarum* to the Scriptures and back again, the two being all but fused through the analogies traced between them.

This exposition may seem ingenious, but I hope that I have made it perfectly clear that the ingenuity is not mine. Neither the selection of symbolic significances nor even their collocation can be credited to my account. Once the connection had been made with the structure of Psalm 119 and with the Apocalyptic vision of Christ in glory, all that remained was to consult representative theological accounts of the import attributed to these structures. Bongo's chapter on the number 24 has the vision of the elders as its point of departure, thus stressing its importance in Biblical exegesis, and among the sources drawn on by Bongo are the *Glossa ordinaria*, Augustine, Bede, Jerome, and Rabanus Maurus—orthodox sources as one would expect from a handbook authorised by the Roman Catholic church.

As is the practice in numerical exegesis, Bongo resolves the number into various groupings, for example into two twelves or three eights, letting the meaning of the whole number emerge from a consideration of its parts. As the centre-piece in Milton's ode consists of three eight-line stanzas (24 lines), this section, therefore, neatly balances the two twelves provided by the flanking 12-stanza sequences, but I would not stress this particular example of balance or *aequalitas*, nor the point that the three eights of the centre traditionally represent the name of Christ (888). These are, perhaps, unnecessary flourishes more apt to vex the modern reader than to please. What is truly important, however, is the fact that Bongo's summary of received opinion shows quite clearly that the vision of the elders was considered as a clue to a proper understanding of the entire Providential scheme for our redemption, and that this was done on the basis of a numerical argument of the kind that I have used here. What my analysis has shown, therefore, is quite simply that Milton's structure invokes this Providential scheme and on the basis of the same vision. This structure should be seen as a non-verbal, abstract image of this design and of him who realised it through his incarnation and crucifixion. The abstract character of this image is its chief virtue—a strength, not a weakness—since its appeal is to our understanding and not to the world of sense. It moves our minds rather than our passions, but the passions are stirred by the beauty of the intellectual vision.

III

Structural Analogues in Sidney and Cowley

Helen Gardner has observed that in Protestant thought Christ was primarily the Redeemer and the King of Heaven, not the babe in the manger or the crucified Christ. Even when contemplating the crucifixion, in 'The Sacrifice', George Herbert aims at completeness of theological statement: 'As Christ speaks, he reveals not simply the love for man that made him endure a shameful and agonizing death, but the whole economy of salvation . . . He implies the whole scheme that began with Adam's eating of the apple . . . '[35] This is an important observation, and I wonder to what extent this insistence on the whole scheme is indebted to a habit of thinking structurally. This habit was certainly encouraged by typological exegesis with its careful balancing of event against event, so that to think of Christ was to think of certain patterns woven by God through space and time to secure salvation for fallen man. These patterns can be perceived by 'the eye of the mind, only cleared by faith' to quote Sir Philip Sidney, that is, by the man whose mental vision has been purified through regeneration. Just as Augustine put his conversion to the test by submitting his analysis of the Mosaic account of creation in the last three books of his *Confessions*, Milton may be said to indicate the quality of his inner vision by building into his poem on the Nativity those patterns—spatial, chronological or historical—by means of which the creative Word manifests its power. The highly abstract character of these patterns is somewhat softened by their connection with the world of sense. Although these abstract principles may be recognised 'inside ourselves without reference to any material object' as Augustine explains, initially one depends on an act of sense perception (*Confessions* X, 12). Augustine applies this argument to the aesthetic appreciation of works of art in a memorable part of his treatise on Free Will. Through the beauty of his creation God beckons man to consider the beauty of the Creator:

> Wherever you turn, wisdom speaks to you through the imprint it has stamped upon its works.[36] When you begin to slip toward outward things, wisdom calls you back, by means of their very forms, so that when something delights you through the bodily senses, you may see that it has number and may ask whence it comes . . .
>
> (*De libero arbitrio,* II, xvi)

Similarly all artists 'have numbers by which they organize their works' so that when the patterns they see have been transferred to the world of sense in the work of art, 'it delights the inner judge who gazes upward upon numbers'. The artist, like God,'somehow beckons the spectator' to proceed from the 'beauty of the work he has made' to the superior beauty of the 'eternal and immutable Form'. This eternal Form 'is neither contained by nor, as it were, spread out in space, neither prolonged nor changed by time', but through this Form every temporal object receives its form so that it 'can manifest and embody number in space and time'.[37]

The ascent from the visible to the invisible was sufficiently familiar to the Renaissance and sufficiently orthodox by being read into *Romans* 1:20, but the point which requires emphasis today is its connection with the contemplation of numerical form or ordered arrangement as explained by Augustine. As the beauty of the world is a matter of its organisation in terms of number, weight, and measure (*Wisdom* 11:20), the ascent from this beauty to that of God could be achieved through a contemplation of number as the basic aspect of Form. This is why numbers could be used to structure poetic compositions and prose treatises, too: they represent the basic elements of existence. All acts of creation presuppose number, so that if you 'remove measure, number, and order, nothing at all remains' (*De libero arbitrio*, II, xx, 203).

This view of creation (whether artistic or divine) has moved away from the Platonic concept of abstract Form or Idea to structure or pattern,[38] and its popularity in the Renaissance may possibly be connected with the firm belief in the Providential view of history as shaped into a meaningful design by the hand of God. If so, then Plato and Neoplatonic thought may have been less influential, as far as Renaissance poetics is concerned, than the argument advanced by Augustine in his discussion of Free Will and Providence.

It is an unfortunate circumstance that our ignorance of the conceptual use of numbers by thinkers like Augustine and Nicolas Cusanus, and our awareness of the fairly widespread Renaissance fondness for a 'hidden sense' have collaborated to create the impression that all speculations concerned with numbers must be classified as esoteric if not positively occult, and certainly well beyond the limits set by orthodox theology. This is not the place for a refutation of this particular superstition, but I would like to conclude this essay by comparing Milton's use of conceptual structure with that of Sir Philip Sidney and Abraham Cowley. This will widen the perspective somewhat, not merely because it may be wise to indicate the prevalence of the structural approach, but also because the comparison will provide a better perspective on Milton's poem.

Among the eclogues that Sir Philip Sidney inserted between Books III and IV of the *Old Arcadia* is an epithalamion which is one of the first English poems of this kind.[39] Its structure is of unusual interest because of its similarity to Milton's hymn. Its eleven nine-line stanzas fall into a sequence of 6—4—1; the first six stanzas request various good qualities for the two that are to be married, while the four that follow denounce various ills. The eleventh stanza summarises the contents of the ten preceding ones. Although each substructure concludes with a climax, a sense of unity is achieved by letting the last stanza constitute an affirmation: all the good qualities have been fully achieved and the ills expelled, and hence the refrain, too, is changed from the optative to the affirmative mode.

The last stanza in the first, positive movement represents a very real climax. Each of these six stanzas invokes personified powers and deities, the sixth—Virtue—being the most important one:

> *Virtue, if not a god, yet God's chief part,*
> *Be thou the knot of this their open vow:*
> *That still he be her head, she be his heart,*
> *He lean to her, she unto him do bow;*
>   *Each other still allow,*
>   *Like oak and mistletoe,*
>   *Her strength from him, his praise from her do grow.*
>   *In which most lovely train,*
>   *O Hymen long their coupled joys maintain.*

That which the whole poem celebrates is brought into sharp focus here in this apostrophe to Virtue as the 'knot of this their open vow'. It is numerically appropriate that this should be said in the sixth stanza, since 6 is the marriage number fusing 2 (the female principle) and 3 (the masculine one) in the formula 2×3. The tying of the knot of concord between opposite principles—male and female—is given syntactical expression in the varied arrangements between the personal pronouns (lines three and four present an a-b-b-a pattern and line seven the reversed form b-a-a-b).

But the stanza on Virtue is not only the climax of the positive sequence; it is also the textual centre of the whole poem, five stanzas preceding and five following. That Virtue has been placed where she should be, *in medio*, is true not merely in a numerical sense but rather because the stanza constitutes the centre for a sequence of paired stanzas. The pairing is achieved by pitting positive against negative versions of the same aspect of marriage—honest trust against jealousy, for example, or healthy procreation against disease-ridden sexual license ('foul Cupid'). A table will indicate the thematic links:

Honest open love image: elm & vine	2	10	*Distrust* ('vile jealousy, / The ill of ills') image: snake
Purity ('That they all vice may kill') image: 'lilies pure'	3	9	*Vice:* pride and sluttishness images: 'peacock pride' and 'sink of filth'

Union in life and death	4	8	*Strife*
image: union of 'two			image: strife in the house and
rivers sweet'			with neighbours
Healthy sex, procreation	5	7	*Diseased sex* ('foul Cupid')
image: younglings of the			image: Cupid's golden dart
herd			'shall here take rust'

At the centre of this sequence, then, Virtue holds the middle, thus permitting the structure to express the theme of unity. But symmetry is displayed in other ways as well, as we see on studying the movement within each stanza. Thus a simile is presented in the last four lines of each of the first six stanzas, at the same time that the syntactical movement in the first five lines is so organised as to permit the fifth to constitute the climax. This means that the line which is at the centre, numerically, has been given the key phrase of the whole stanza. The absence of a concluding simile in the negative sequence (stanzas seven to ten) somewhat blurs this image of stanzaic symmetry, but here, too, the fifth line has been awarded the climactic statement ('Avoids thy hurtful art', 'Be hence ay put to flight', 'For ever hence away', and 'Go snake, hide thee in dust'). And in stanza eleven all lines are used to present the summary, except the fifth, which apostrophises bride and groom as 'Happy man, happy wife', thus providing a perfect example of a symmetrically structured stanza. Placed as it is at the stanzaic centre and outside the pattern of affirmative summary, the exclamation helps to create that sense of a final grand climax which is needed to round off the poem as a whole. This need is the greater as the sense of linear movement is so much stronger than the sense of balance around a central stanza. True, we know that Virtue is in the middle in every sense, but the movement through stanzas seven to ten is primarily felt as a linear progression through a catalogue of ills climaxed by the denunciation of jealousy as the 'ill of ills' embodied in the image of the snake. This strongly felt linear movement through ten stanzas may be said to constitute an image of unity through the significance invested in the number 10 as the return to unity. The epithalamion therefore provides an arithmetical image of unity by progressing through a sequence of 10 stanzas concluded with a coda whose function it is to serve as a summary and an affirmative full stop.

Milton's hymn, too, establishes linear progression through two movements combined with balanced symmetry, the symmetry being achieved by letting a positive thematic movement (concluded with a climax) be followed by a negative one concerned with the theme of expulsion. And in both poems the climax of the first movement becomes the centre around which the whole poem is focussed. The central accent is more strongly felt in Milton's poem, partly because he has fused the thematic movement with a chronological pattern showing how Time issues out of, and returns to, Eternity. One's impression that Sidney's structure is more linear while Milton's is decidedly spatial is the result also of that steady rise towards the vision of Eternity (in the triple centre) and the subsequent descent to the level where the hymn began.

On observing this general structural similarity one wonders whether the fairly simple structural formula employed by Sidney[39a] could have been sufficiently well known to have helped Milton to his choice of form. If Milton thought in terms of a progressive sequence of stanzas leading up to a climax, followed by a somewhat shorter regressive sequence so organised that stanzas equidistant from the centre are paired off against each other, then this would help to explain why he saw fit to devote so many stanza units to the theme of expulsion: these constitute the counter-movement required to create the subtle interplay between linear progression and recessed symmetry around a centre.

Abraham Cowley's version of the same basic formula, in his 'Hymn to the Light', indicates that it was not restricted to the epithalamic tradition, but it would have been perfectly appropriate for Milton to invoke this tradition in a poem on the incarnation. The Biblical epithalamion, the *Song of Solomon*, was considered as an Old Testament prophecy, written allegorically, of that final union with Christ in the Heavenly Jerusalem which St John describes in the Apocalypse. At its beginning, middle, and end the Bible was supposed to have not only an image of Christ (as the Tree of Life) but also an image of marriage or union. The marriage between Adam and Eve foreshadowed the union between God and man through the incarnation (and the crucifixion), both pointing forward to the final union in Eternity. Francesco Giorgio is one Renaissance theologian who makes these points, and with unwonted brevity, in his *De harmonia mundi* III, viii, 9. The first three stanzas of Milton's hymn seem to me to invoke epithalamic overtones of the kind associated with Biblical exegesis. Since the incarnation joins Heaven and Earth, this may be why Milton begins by showing an Earth suddenly confronted by that 'greater sun' on whose coming the physical sun must be instantly rejected as inferior. Her feeling of guilt and her desire to hide her 'foul deformities' should perhaps be related to the bride's feeling of unworthiness ('Look not upon me, because I am black . . . ' *Song of Solomon* 1:6), while her 'naked shame' reflects the feeling of our first parents after their fall. As Giorgio puts it in the passage referred to, Christ covers our nudity by regenerating us. His action, in so doing, is like that of the sun: he gives of his riches to all.[40]

Similar epithalamic overtones are felt in Cowley's 'Hymn to the Light' (*Verses Written on Several Occasions*, 1663)[41] which presents the action of Light on the Earth as a marriage union. The thematic and structural similarities to Milton's poem are sufficiently striking to make one suspect that Cowley may have written his lines with an eye on the *Nativity Ode*. What caught Cowley's fancy was the confrontation between light and the powers of darkness, and the stately progress of light from the first day of creation to the last, when it merges with the light of Eternity. An allusion to the incarnate Christ may be felt in the first stanza which presents the creation of Light on the first day as a 'lovely Child' on whose appearance Chaos itself 'put on kind looks and smil'd.' The chronological structure is simple: we move from the first day in stanza 1 to the last day in the last stanza. Although the four-line stanza pattern is equally simple the concluding alexandrine suggests a link with the pattern designed by Milton for his ode. A firmer link is found in Cowley's elaboration of the theme touched on initially by Milton in the hymn—the marriage union between Nature and the Sun, 'her lusty paramour'. Cowley relates 'active Nature' to the Sun as bride to groom: 'Thou the Worlds beauteous Bride, the lusty Bridegroom He!' (stanza 3). Milton's lovely description of the descent of Peace 'softly sliding / Down through the turning sphere', 'With turtle wing the amorous clouds dividing' may have inspired Cowley's passage on the cosmic marriage union:

24
Through the soft ways of Heav'n and Air, and Sea,
    Which open all their Pores to Thee;
    Like a clear River thou do'st glide,
And with thy living Stream through the close Channels slide.

Another theme shared by the two poems is the ousting of ghosts and all kinds of evil spirits and powers. In Milton 'speckled vanity' and 'lep'rpus sin' disappear, leaving their mansions 'to the peering day' (14), while in Cowley 'Night, and her ugly subjects' are 'Asham'd and fearful to appear', just as clusters of 'painted Dreams' vanish 'At the first opening of thine eye' (10 and 11):

15

Ev'n Lust, the Master of a hardned Face,
Blushes, if thou be'st in the place,
To darkness Curtains he retires,
In sympathizing Night he rowls his smoaky fires.

16

When, Goddess, thou lift'st up thy wak'ned head,
Out of the Morning's Purple Bed,
Thy Quire of Birds about thee play,
And all the joyful World salutes the rising day.

17

The Ghosts, and Monster-Spirits, that did presume
A Bodies Priv'ledge to assume,
Vanish again invisibly,
And Bodies gain agen their visibility.

This reads like a revised version of two of Milton's most striking images in his penultimate stanza—first of the Sun 'in bed, / Curtained with cloudy red' but about to rise so that he 'Pillows his chin upon an orient wave' and next of each 'fettered ghost' slipping to 'his several grave'.

Cowley's symmetrical structure is both simpler and more emphatic than Milton's. The fact that the Earth is provided with two sources of light induced him to fashion his hymn around a double centre flanked by twelve four-line stanzas. The central stanzas (13–14) are identified as such formally as well as thematically—formally through carefully balanced parallel phrases ('At thy appearance . . .') and thematically by the apostrophe to the achievement of harmony in the microcosmos of man as grief is balanced by joy, fear by hope. Finally the allusion to reflected light in stanza 13 and to sunshine in stanza 14 serves to link the pivotal centre with the two sources of light in the Sun and the Moon. And as in Milton's hymn the flanking stanzas display recessed symmetry created by tracing similar phenomena in two clearly differentiated spheres of life. My diagram shows that the pairing of individual stanzas around the double centre is sufficiently clear to be easily spotted, but that the pairing nevertheless is seen to function in groups of three stanzas. As we move out from the centre in both directions we encounter first a group of three stanzas concerned with the theme of expulsion, then a similar group where the focus is on the way in which Light adorns everything in the two spheres. The next group of three stanzas stresses the creative action of Light, while images of birth and of marriage union dominate the first three stanzas and the three last ones. The division into two spheres so that stanzas 2–12 are concerned with the air and the sky and the upper spheres while the focus is on the Earth and man in stanzas 15–25, is perhaps the most striking structural similarity between the two hymns. Another similarity is the circular effect created by letting the first stanza present the birth of Light on the first day while the last presents its fusion with the light of Eternity on the last day.

The concepts embedded in Cowley's structural numbers are as simple as they are basic to our human existence. The sequence of 12—2—12 stanzas can be seen to incorporate the chief numbers of Time as created by our two luminaries. Around the double centre are stanzaic 'emanations' in imitation of the 12 unequal hours of the day and night and the 12 solar months, and if we divide the hymn into equal halves of 13 4-line stanzas the structure reflects the annual lunar cycle and the number of weeks in the year through the sum total of lines, 52. As S. K. Heninger has remarked à propos of the absurd notion that structures of this kind should imply esoteric lore, what is reproduced is 'the fairly simple pattern of cosmos. A line count is unlikely to disclose anything more arcane than a calendar, a diapason, a tetrad, or a trinity.'[42]

Since Cowley favoured symmetrical arrangements around a centre he need not have borrowed this particular effect from Milton, but the phrasal and thematic similarities suggest that he actually had Milton's poem in mind. If these similarities should be felt as too imprecise to warrant any firm conclusion, we must needs posit a general tradition of sufficient strength to produce this degree of similarity.

The symmetrical structures I have indicated pose an interesting critical problem. I have observed that my perception of this kind of thematic movement away from a centre towards the beginning and the end induces a habit of reading the poem from the centre outwards. One does this, at first, to test the validity of the feeling that a given poem may be organised symmetrically, and if the theory is confirmed, one finds that the structural analysis enables one to bear the whole poem in mind as one reads it progressively from the beginning in the normal way. As one reads the first stanza of Milton's hymn, for example, one knows, at the back of one's mind, that one will meet the babe in the manger again in the last stanza, that the theme of the second stanza will be repeated, with a variation, in the penultimate stanza, and so on until the centre is reached; after the centre the balance is changed, and that which was remembered becomes the experience of the moment, while that which was experienced regresses and becomes memory.

This interaction between progressive and retrospective form affects our reading in many ways. It invests the structural centre with a uniqueness which turns it into a more powerful climax than could have been achieved by mere terminal heightening. But other aspects are involved as well. If the form that one perceives retrospectively is held in mind with sufficient clarity as one re-reads the poem, a kind of unity is perceived which is difficult to put into words. The best I can do is to repeat what I have already said (p. 65): sequential experience is supplemented by an almost instantaneous vision of the whole poem. It is interesting to discover that Paula Johnson, in grappling with the same problem of the interaction between these two modes of perception, picked on much the same phrase. The retrospective mode, so she puts it, achieves 'increased approximation to simultaneity'. Its function is to provide an aid to the normal way of reading a poem, and this assistance is always provided whether or not we happen to be aware of it.[43]

Since his structures are more obvious, the awareness comes more easily to us as we read Cowley, but once we have grasped the main outlines of Milton's ode it is not at all difficult to keep them in mind as one reads. The patterns indicate a tradition of reading poetry in a way that has been largely lost to us since the Romantic period at least. The fact that symbolic numbers may have been used to create the symmetrical effects need worry no one: the Biblical authority for so doing is too explicit and the habit of reading the Bible with attention to structure too ingrained for the technique to be at all tainted by the unorthodox or the esoteric. I would say, instead, that if one reads Milton's poem with an awareness of its formal structure, one reads it in the manner that Milton's generation would have read the Bible or its supposed summary in the Psalms. That the structures are largely identical makes the comparison even more appropriate.

Diagram 1: Milton,
'On the Morning of Christ's Nativity'

				in medio annorum
CHRIST (1)	1 (27)	NATURE pays homage to CHRIST		
MAN & NATURE (9)	2 (26)	NATURE hides her 'guilty front'		
	3 (25)	'universal peace'	in NATURE	
	4 (24)		in the world of MEN	
	5 (23)		in the ELEMENTS	
	6 (22)	the true ruler	by the STARS	12
	7 (21)	recognised	by the SUN	
	8 (20)	true revelation of the divine	'mighty Pan' appears TO MEN	
	9 (19)		heavenly voices ravish MEN	
	10 (18)	NATURE believes her reign fulfilled		

CHRIST (7)	11 (17)	CHRIST hymned as King on Earth		
	12 (16)	CHRIST as Creator		the first day
	13	Heaven's 'high palace		
	14	hall' and its 'ninefold		ETERNITY
	15	harmony'		
	16 (12)	CHRIST as Redeemer and Creator of a new world		the last day
	17 (11)	CHRIST as Judge in 'middle air'		

SPIRITS & POWERS (9)	18 (10)	The reign of SATAN ceases		
	19 (9)	true revelation of the divine	ousts the false ('words deceiving')	
	20 (8)		replaces shadowy types (Pan)	
	21 (7)	the true ruler recognised	various powers leave their seats and false rites cease; idols representing stars are ousted;	12
	22 (6)			
	23 (5)	no peace	for powers connected with the elements	
	24 (4)		for false deities	
	25 (3)		for Typhon, son of Earth	
	26 (2)	Guilty SPIRITS hide in the 'infernal jail'		
CHRIST (1)	27 (1)	ANGELS pay homage to CHRIST		
				in medio annorum

Diagram 2
Abraham Cowley, 'Hymn to the Light'

Generation

Creation of Light the first day	1	26	Light merges with Eternity the last day
Images of union on a cosmic scale (continued)	2	25	Images of union focussed on the Earth (continued)
	3	24	

Action

Creative action in the air; arrows are shot from 'Golden Quivers'; the rainbow is created; the movement compared to swiftest 'Post-Angel'	4	23	Creative action in the Earth; gold is produced (continued) colours are produced; comparison with the goddess Flora
	5	22	
	6	21	

Adornment

The 'flowry Lights' of the stars form a 'Nocturnal Spring' in a 'bright wood of Stars'; and above the Sun Light moves in regal state attended by 'shining Pageants'; and living stars adorn the Earth	7	20	On Earth Light creates the flowers of spring and dresses every thing in royal splendour (continued)
	8	19	
	9	18	

Expulsion

Light ousts the 'ugly Subjects' of the Night	10	17	Light ousts ghosts and spirits, making real bodies appear;
and 'painted Dreams'	11	16	and a joyful, real world awakes
and 'guilty Serpents', 'Ill Omens' and 'ill Sights'	12	15	and 'Ev'n Lust' is expelled

Centre

Harmonious balance between Grief and Joy	13	14	Harmonious balance between Fear and Hope

Stanzas 1–12 trace the power of Light within the whole cosmic sphere including powers of evil

Stanzas 15–26 trace the power of Light within the sphere of the Earth and of man

My comparison between Milton, Sidney and Cowley will have shown that a structure, like all images, may be more or less effective, more or less beautiful, subtle, complex, or appropriate. Like images and themes, structures, too, may be borrowed and, in the process, become elaborated or simplified. Certain structures may be so familiar as to constitute a tradition drawn on by different poets so that a theory of direct indebtedness must be ruled out or at least modified. On the basis of a formal pattern associated with Nativity hymns Milton created a complex structure the perception of which has a profound effect on our response to his poem. Cowley, however, was content with the simplest of structural outlines and with a system of paired stanzas that contributes little or nothing to his main theme. To compare the two hymns is to see a major aesthetic principle in a splendid work of art transferred and transposed to suit the abilities of the lesser poet. The juxtaposition shows up the superior quality of Milton's performance, at the same time that Cowley's proves his familiarity with the tradition drawn on by Milton. Cowley, by the way, documents his familiarity in the footnotes added to his *Pindarique Odes* and his *Davideis*, thus providing the explicit authorial statement so often required by critics as yet unfamiliar with this aspect of Renaissance aesthetics. A footnote appended to the ode on 'The Resurrection' declares quite openly that the Pythagorean doctrine of harmony 'does much better befit *Poetry*, than it did *Philosophy*', while the poem itself announces that it sets the standard for the numbers of Time, which dance to the song 'with smooth and equal measures'. The world, it would seem, is not only God's poem; it is also Cowley's.[44] In this respect, at least, Milton was the more humble poet.

3

Laid artfully together

STANZAIC DESIGN IN MILTON'S
'ON THE MORNING OF CHRIST'S NATIVITY'

H. NEVILLE DAVIES

FOR thirty years now the apparently lax construction and variety of imagery in Milton's *Nativity Ode* have been strongly defended. Although Warton's remark about 'a string of affected conceits' seems a far cry, it is, after all, not utterly at odds with modern criticism.[1] 'String' and 'affected' are loaded words, but it is precisely the choice of imagery and plan of construction that much recent criticism of the poem has attended to. Generally, the modern defence involves dividing the poem into sections, like the movements of a symphony, and then arguing that these movements contrast with and complement each other to cohere in a symphonic whole. Appreciation of the unity of the poem thus depends in part upon perception of the autonomy of the constituent sections. This is a critical strategy of some flexibility, capable of supporting a wide variety of interpretations, and we find it—not surprisingly—linked with many different analyses of the Ode's structure. But on one matter commentators agree: there is a natural break between the four introductory seven-line stanzas (hereafter numbered i–iv) and the twenty-seven eight-line stanzas of the Hymn (hereafter numbered 1–27).

In the Hymn itself different symphonic 'movements' are distinguished by different critics. Comparison of a dozen studies shows it divided into two, three, or four, but usually three sections, the divisions being made in certain general areas, but by no means in exactly the same places.[2] A list of stanzas simply marked with the various divisions suggested in these twelve studies show what degree of unanimity there is:

1 2 3 4 5 6 7 / 8 / 9 / 10 11 12 13 14 15 / 16 / 17 / 18 / 19 20 21 22 23 24 25 26 / 27.

Most of the critics encompassed by this survey seem to regard their own distinctions between sections as not only right but as natural too. When the conflicting or apparently conflicting suggestions are assembled, however, it becomes evident that what is natural to one reader may not be so to another. The disparity is immediately grasped if the number of stanzas included in each section of the Hymn by the critics that I have referred to is set out in tabular form:

Spaeth	8 7 12
Shuster	8 7 12
Barker	8 9 9 1
Brooks & Hardy	15 12 (12 = 11+1)
Allen	7 11 9
Røstvig (1963)	9 9 9 (now refined as 1 9 7 9 1 coexisting with 12 3 12)
Lawry	8 7 11 1
Rajan	8 8 11
Carey	8 10 9
Butler	Endorses Røstvig (1963)
Swaim	8 7 12
Woodhouse & Bush	8 10 8 1

Such statistical information can easily deceive or mislead, and the chronologically arranged list given here needs to be qualified by two observations: firstly that Barker's fine study enjoys something approaching classic status and probably represents the most orthodox view of the structure, and secondly, that notations that look as divergent as 8 8 11 and 8 7 12, or 7 11 9 and 8 10 9 in fact differ over only a single stanza. But even bearing such qualifications in mind, the list records considerable diversity among a distinguished body of critics.

That the *Nativity Ode* is amenable to a multiplicity of analyses is an aspect of its baroque richness. It is clear that the critics disjointing the poem are, at least in some cases, dividing it according to different principles, and so the variety of their views as evident in the table does not necessarily indicate conflict. The fissures in the texture of the poem that they light upon are not open breaches but rather fractures in different layers, each critic studying a different layer, and the poem's essential continuity arising from the joins being staggered. Rigidly to disallow any critical diversity and insist upon crude conformity would be to commit the folly of those 'irrationall men' ridiculed in *Areopagitica* 'who could not consider there must be many schisms and many dissections made in the quarry and in the timber, ere the house of God can be built'.[3] As an example of a structure unified and diverse, Milton described the Temple, whose divine architecture represents a pattern of perfection:

> And when every stone is laid artfully together, it cannot be united into a continuity, it can but be contiguous in this world; neither can every peece of the building be of one form; nay rather the perfection consists in this, that out of many moderate varieties and brotherly dissimilitudes that are not vastly disproportionall arises the goodly and gracefull symmetry that commends the whole pile and structure.[4]

So it is with Milton's *Nativity Ode*. In its fugal texture (to replace a spatial architectural analogy by a temporal musical one), individual voices or strands of interest are variously drawn out, and the complexity of the counterpoint both enhances the assertion of Milton's recent coming of age and enriches a gift to the infant Christ that vies ambitiously with those of the Magi. But this recognition of complexity does not mean that all ways of dissecting the poem are equally helpful. There is a difference between licence and liberty in literary criticism as there is in other areas of activity.

Underpinning the manifest form of the poem, with its evident division into Proem and Hymn, and its other more subtly overlapping strands, are firm structural foundations. It is with these that the present essay is concerned. My purpose—a deliberately limited one—is merely to suggest, without promoting pedantic demarcation disputes, that the impulse of commentators to split the poem into sections is a right impulse, and to propose that the Ode is structured according to an exact and determinable plan, while an overall pattern of 'linked sweetness' unites the separate parts. The approach adopted here is then, in general, similar to that pursued by Maren-Sofie Røstvig in her 1963 account of Milton's poem and now extended in her contribution to the present volume. But although I have learnt much from both her papers, the scheme that I offer differs somewhat from what she had proposed. I leave it to readers, if they so wish, to judge when 'modest varieties' and 'brotherly dissimilitudes' are or 'are not vastly disproportionall'. It needs only to be remarked by me that the decision is not a simple one.

While my approach is through the symbolism of the stanza numbers,

the consequent analysis of the Ode's structure is in accord with what
has been observed by a fair range of critics who have examined the
poem from quite other points of view. I suggest, therefore, that
the Hymn falls into three clearly defined movements of fifteen,
eleven, and one stanzas respectively, and that the recognition of the
symbolic use of numbers in this scheme reinforces the meaning of the
poem, makes sense of the sudden transitions, and gives significance to
what can be naively mistaken for aesthetic disproportion. There is
reassurance to be found in observing that Spaeth and Shuster long
ago recognised the same broad structural divisions, and that Brooks
and Hardy, Lawry, and Swaim have more recently described such a
structure.

I

Stanzas 1–15 of the Hymn describe the coming of Christ to reunite
fallen man and God; and for this purpose, as I shall try to show, a
sequence of fifteen stanzas is appropriate. Since the twelfth century
a ladder of fifteen rungs had been commonly associated with ascent
to God, and Christ as mediator expressed by the figure of this ladder.[5]
It was as a type of Christ that Milton's contemporaries frequently
explained Jacob's ladder. Gervase Babbington, for instance, whose
works were sufficiently in demand to be published in folio in 1615,
1622, and 1637, asserts,

> The ladder is Christ. The foot of it in earth noteth his humanitie,
> man of the substance of his mother borne in the world. The top
> reaching vp to heauen, noteth his divinitie, *God of the substance
> of the Father begotten before all worlds, perfit God, and perfit man,*
> by which vnion of natures, he hath ioyned earth and heauen
> together, that is, God and man.[6]

The Master of St Catharine's Hall during Milton's Cambridge career,
Richard Sibbes, relating Jacob's ladder to Christ, writes of Christ as
'a Mediator' who 'brought God and man together'.[7] Such remarks
are commonplace, but they serve well enough to provide a context
for Milton, and they help to illustrate why it was that Milton in his
De doctrina Christiana, in which he disposed his material into chapters
according to the significance of the chapter numbers, chose Chapter *15*
of Book I to treat of Christ as mediator.[8] In *Paradise Lost* Milton

uses the same number symbolism. The retractable stairs 'Ascending by degrees magnificent / Up to the wall of heaven' which Satan sees on his cosmic flight are described in a series of fifteen lines (III. 501–15) and compared with Jacob's ladder. Another passage of fifteen lines follows shortly afterwards (III. 540–54) in which Satan sits on the bottom step looking enviously and maliciously down onto the newly created world. The stairs rising behind his back, with their suggestion of ascent to God, are now ignored by Satan, but the structure of fifteen lines speaks to the fit reader, or so I have argued elsewhere, of their significance.[9]

The first of these two fifteen-line passages from Book III of *Paradise Lost* alludes to the gate of heaven in its climactic fifteenth line, quoting Jacob's words as he woke from his vision of a ladder: 'This is the gate of heav'n'. A similar climax comes in the fifteenth line of Satan's second speech to Beelzebub:

> *Fallen cherub, to be weak is miserable*
> *Doing or suffering: but of this be sure,*
> *To do ought good never will be our task,*
> *But ever to do ill our sole delight,*
> *As being the contrary to his high will*
> *Whom we resist. If then his providence*
> *Out of our evil seek to bring forth good,*
> *Our labour must be to pervert that end,*
> *And out of good still to find means of evil;*
> *Which oft-times may succeed, so as perhaps*
> *Shall grieve him, if I fail not, and disturb*
> *His inmost counsels from their destined aim.*
> *But see the angry victor hath recalled*
> *His ministers of vengeance and pursuit*
> *Back to the gates of heaven.*
>
> *(I. 157–71)*

The scrupulous reader will notice the discrepancy, ridiculous or blasphemous, between Satan's incitement to rebellion and the pattern of virtuous ascent implied by the form of the speech, a form principally defined by the reference to the gates of heaven in the fifteenth line. Special point is given by the ladder structure to the title 'Fallen cherub' by which Beelzebub is addressed, and the perversion of Creation advocated in lines 162–5 contrasts with the Christian use of Creation:

> *In contemplation of created things*
> *By steps we may ascend to God.*
> *(V. 511–12)*

Such contemplation is the object of Bellarmine's devotional manual *De ascensione mentis in Deum per scalam rerum creaturarum* (1615; English translations 1616 and 1638) with its arrangement in fifteen chapters or rungs.[10] Even while Satan advocates evil, the ordered structure of his speech hints at the alternative, ascent to God.[11] But hints are wasted on the pig-headed. Writing about 'the secret magick of numbers', Sir Thomas Browne noted that

> in this masse of nature there is a set of things that carry in their front, though not in capitall letters, yet in stenography, and short Characters, something of Divinitie, which to wiser reasons serve as Luminaries in the abysse of knowledge, and to judicious beliefes, as scales and roundles to mount the pinnacles and highest pieces of Divinity.[12]

Satan's hell is indeed an 'abysse of knowledge', its new inhabitants intellectually enslaved by a wilfully stupid refusal to recognise the omnipotence of God no matter how strong the evidence to the contrary. Where even capital letters would be ignored, 'the secret magick of numbers' can communicate nothing.

Once the reader has become aware of numerological significance in these fifteen lines, less obviously signalled symbolism becomes apparent. The eleventh line of Satan's speech changes strikingly from the inclusive 'we' form to the assertive first person singular. Both this and the line's reference to grieving and disturbing God are appropriate to its number symbolism, as will become clear later in this paper. (Briefly, eleven is associated with sin and with egotistical transgression.) The futility of Satan's plan is appropriately emphasised in the twelfth line where the ultimate success of God's purpose, his 'destined aim', is admitted. Twelve signifies completion (a piece of number lore which will also be taken up later in this essay). The final three lines of the fifteen-line sequence show God's mercy opposed to Satan's implacable hatred. Another expression of the same divine mercy is the role of Christ as mediator, a role here and elsewhere symbolised by a fifteen-line sequence culminating in a reference to the gates of heaven.[13]

All this material has been adduced only to illuminate Milton's procedure in the *Nativity Ode*. Time is a tedious rehearsal should here have ending and a return be made to the Ode itself where the last line of stanza 15 also refers to the gates of heaven:

> *And heaven as at some festival,*
> *Will open wide the gates of her high palace hall.*

These lines, too, mark the climax of a sequence patterned in a similar way to the fifteen-line passages in *Paradise Lost*. But the association of heaven's gates and the number fifteen is not a private association made only by Milton, like an idiosyncratic Shakespearian image cluster of dogs and sweets. Once again, and unfortunately so since contact with Milton's Ode has only just been renewed, it becomes necessary to digress if the former currency of a now forgotten notion is to be demonstrated.

Giles Fletcher, in the fourth book of *Christ's Victory*, makes the same association in his significantly numbered *fifteenth* stanza with its exuberant reference to Psalm 24:

> *Tosse up your heads ye everlasting gates,*
> *And let the Prince of glorie enter in:*
> *At whose brave voly of sideriall States,*
> *The Sunne to blush, and starres growe pale wear seene,*
> *When, leaping first from earth, he did begin*
> > *To climbe his Angells wings; then open hang*
> > *Your christall doores, so all the chorus sang*
> *Of heav'nly birds, as to the starres they nimbly sprang.*[14]

Writing of Milton's debt to the Fletcher brothers, Joan Grundy characterises the *Nativity Ode* as 'a Christ's victory and triumph in itself'.[15] There can be no doubt that Milton's poem owes more to Giles Fletcher than the single parallel cited in Carey's edition (line 110) might indicate, but it would be quite false to suggest that there is any specific or exclusive indebtedness to Fletcher in Milton's reference to the gates of heaven. Rather, the association seems to be widespread. Bishop Hall, whom Milton also read, has a poem on the death of Dr Whitaker which may equally well have been in Milton's mind as he wrote his *Nativity Ode*.[16] Hall's elegy shows how destruction through death is transcended by eternal life, and Milton would have noticed how the change from the early mournful stanzas to the later triumphant ones is prepared in stanza 14 so that stanza 15 may be the climactic

Open ye golden gates of Paradise,
Open ye wide vnto a welcome Ghost:
Enter, O Soule, into thy Boure *of* Blisse,
Through all the throng of Heauens hoast:
  Which shall with Triumph *gard thee as thou go'st*
  With Psalmes *of* Conquest *and with crownes of cost.*[17]

Hall's witty use of the word 'ghost' instead of the expected word
'guest' is something Milton would surely have enjoyed, just as Hall
would have relished Milton's amusing yet serious interchange of girl
friends and sheep in stanza 8 of the Ode.

Milton's sequence of fifteen stanzas is not merely a simple block
unit. It is itself internally organised. Stanzas 1–8 set the scene of the
Incarnation, stanzas 8–15 recount and elaborate the biblical story. The
sequence is, therefore, divided into equal halves, with stanza 8,
poised 'e'er the point of dawn', acting as a transitional stanza and
having a place in each half. It is a stanza that concludes the expectant
scene setting and introduces the biblical shepherds. The obvious
structural analogy here is with the double-octave musical scale, a
scale of fifteen notes often seen as linking earth and heaven. Such
a cosmic *scala* is set out in an eleventh-century manuscript of Boethius's *De institutione musicae,* and the concept was still valid in Milton's
day.[18] The lower octave is associated with the created world of time,
and the upper, spiritual octave with the supernatural world of eternity.
It is a notion that helps to structure the 'steps of gold to heaven gate'
in Book III of *Paradise Lost* (501–15) where, in the eighth line, there
is a shift from a register of sensual earthly description to a register
of increasingly rarefied suggestion.[19] Similarly, stanza 8 of the
Nativity Ode acts like the central note of a two-octave musical scale,
concluding the octave of preparation in the world of nature while
simultaneously introducing the upper octave of supernatural involvement. The progression shows an unmistakable rising movement.
The Boethius manuscript allocates its lower octave to the sun, moon,
and planetary bodies, the upper octave it allocates to the angels and
their music. The same division is made by Milton.

Within Milton's upper octave (stanzas 8–15) there is further internal
arrangement. The central six of its eight stanzas describe 'the angelic
symphony', an arrangement in accord with the significance of six as
the number of harmony. It was natural for Milton to arrange it thus,
just as it was natural for Marvell to write his *Musicks Empire* in six

stanzas. It is appropriate, too, that Milton's stanza 9 should introduce the angels, just as in Chapter 9 of *De doctrina Christiana*, Book I, Milton writes about angels; and that stanza 10 should emphasise the fulfilment of nature and the perfect union of heaven and earth. It is in Chapter 10 of the first book of *De doctrina* that Milton writes of prelapsarian man.[20]

In short, the first fifteen stanzas of the Hymn defined and profiled with the shapes of traditional or, as Rosemond Tuve would have called them, ancient images display by structural reenactment the mediation of Christ that the Nativity initiates. Earthly imperfection and heavenly perfection are here reconciled because Christ comprehends the whole range. But for Milton to have expressed only that would have been unrealistic. The poem is not yet concluded, the work of redemption only begun. Although Christ brings peace, the angels are armed, and there is no reason to suppose that their arms are merely ceremonial: the evil against which they guard is a potent force.

II

The Incarnation is not the Atonement. We must remember with Traherne that 'the Cross of Christ is the Jacobs ladder by which we Ascend into the Highest Heavens'.[21] The second section of the Hymn comprises eleven stanzas (16–26), the beginning of a new movement being clearly marked by the abrupt termination of the previous line of development:

> *But wisest fate says no,*
> *It must not yet be so.*

These lines form a *volta*, introduced by the typical word 'but' and effectively dividing the hymn, as though it were an enlarged sonnet, into a double octave of stanzas and a double sestet of stanzas. The new section contrasts strongly with the preceding one. The crucifixion in its opening stanza stands out against the nativity scene, and the listing and description of the pagan gods is very different from what has gone before. It is appropriate that eleven, the number of sin, should be chosen for the number of stanzas in this section. In *De doctrina Christiana* Milton devoted the *eleventh* chapter of the first book to the fall of our first parents and to sin. It is, according to the standard handbook of Milton's time, a number 'significans illos qui transgrediuntur Decalogum mandatorum',[22] and is associated also with death. Because of the association with death Milton wrote *Lycidas* in eleven verse paragraphs, and *On the Death of a Fair Infant* in eleven stanzas.[23] Eleven is a number of falling rather than rising and contrasts strongly with fifteen, the number of the ladder:

> Undenarius numerus nullam habet cum divinis, neque cum coelestibus communionem, nec attactum, nec scalam ad supera tendentem.[24]

The opposition between fifteen and eleven which Milton is drawing upon is effectively used by Milton's master, Spenser. Colin's lament for Dido in *The Shepheardes Calender* is appropriately placed in the November eclogue, November being the eleventh month and eleven being associated with death. The lament itself has eleven stanzas with a doleful refrain mourning the death of Dido, followed by four stanzas with joyful refrains celebrating Dido's new life in Elysian fields:

> *There liues she with the blessed Gods in blisse,*
> *There drinks she Nectar with Ambrosia mixt,*
> *And ioyes enioyes, that mortall men doe misse.*[25]
>
>   (194–6)

The four joyful stanzas introduced by a 'but' formula ('But maugre death') make the total up to fifteen, and although there can be no reference to the gates of heaven in a poem adopting non-Christian conventions, there is a ladder-like suggestion that Dido has set up a route between earth and 'heauens hight' that others may follow:

> Dido *is gone afore (whose turne shall be the next?)*
>
>   (193)

The change of refrain in the lament is numerologically appropriate in the same way that Kent Hieatt has shown that the change from positive to negative refrain in Spenser's *Epithalamion* significantly marks the change from day to night.[26] Colin's emblem, '*La mort ny mord*', expresses the process of eleven being transformed by fifteen:

> For although by course of nature we be borne to dye . . . yet death is not to be counted for euil, nor . . . as doom of ill desert. For though the trespasse of the first man brought death into

the world, as the guerdon of sinne, yet being ouercome by the death of one, that dyed for al, it is now made (as Chaucer sayth) the grene path way to lyfe.

(Glosse)

'Death slue not him', says Spenser of Sir Philip Sidney, 'but he made death his ladder to the skies'.[27]

Spenser's organisation of eleven stanzas within the fifteen stanzas of the Lay of Dido could have provided Milton with a model for his juxtaposition of fifteen and eleven stanzas in the Nativity Hymn, but again there is no need to cite the November eclogue as Milton's *specific* source. It is sufficient to recognise that Milton was working within a standard frame of reference. One obvious difference distinguishes Spenser's procedure from Milton's. Spenser's design is compact, subordinating eleven to fifteen. Milton's looser tandem structure requires a final resolving section.

III

Objection is sometimes made to Milton's devoting so many stanzas to the pagan gods. They account for a surprisingly large proportion of the poem. Another common objection is to the elaborate imagery of the penultimate stanza of the Ode, the last stanza of the eleven-stanza section. But excess is appropriate when it is realised that the significance of the number eleven lies in its transgressing ten: 'significans illos qui transgrediuntur Decalogum mandatorum'.[28] Sin is disproportioned, and it is right that stanza 26, the last of the eleven stanzas, should seem to be running away with the poet. However delightful this stanza is, it is in danger of deflecting Milton from his 'destined aim'. One of the characteristically baroque features of the poem is the appearance of exuberant lack of control contained in the discipline of a securely organised structure. The reassertion of poetic control comes suddenly in the final stanza which also forms the final section. The suddenness is itself expressive of God's ultimate omnipotence, as it is in the last two lines of Herbert's 'The Collar' or in the last verse paragraph of Dryden's *Absalom and Achitophel.* Like Spenser's 'But maugre death' and the *Nativity Ode*'s earlier 'But wisest fate' the switch is here also signalled by the word 'but', and the reader is returned to the nativity scene and the angels of the upper octave of the fifteen-stanza section, and to 'the virgin blest' not mentioned since the very first stanza of the Ode.

Colin's lament turned eleven into fifteen. Milton began with fifteen and followed it by eleven. He now turns eleven into twelve to resolve the poem, and as he does so announces that 'Time is our tedious song should here have ending' not merely because the baby is asleep, but because the stanza after the eleventh is an appropriate one with which to conclude the poem. The evil number eleven is resolved by the number twelve, the number of completion: 'Plenae, consummatæq; virtutis est Duodenarius'.[29] The disorder and frantic bustle of the previous stanzas suddenly give way to a quiet, ordered and disciplined tableau presented with all the impressive, stylised dignity of an icon. It is here that the 'perpetual peace' of the first stanza is to be found:

> *But see the virgin blest,*
> *Hath laid her babe to rest.*
>   *Time is our tedious song should here have ending:*
> *Heaven's youngest teemed star,*
> *Hath fixed her polished car,*
>   *Her sleeping Lord with handmaid lamp attending:*
> *And all about the courtly stable,*
> *Bright-harnessed angels sit in order serviceable.*

Perhaps we might even observe that the poem ends in a twelfth stanza just as the Christmas festivities end on Twelfth Night. The twelfth day of Christmas is the Feast of the Epiphany, and it is in the final stanza of the poem that 'Heaven's youngest teemed star' guiding the 'star-led wizards' fixes 'her polished car' over the stable.

The twenty-seventh stanza of the Hymn completes the poem in other ways, as Professor Røstvig has shown.[30] The Proem stresses the numbers four and three. Its four stanzas each have $4+3$ lines, as is appropriate in a poem about the Incarnation, man being compounded of corporeal four and spiritual three. The final stanza of the whole poem, turning eleven into twelve, expresses the same numbers (4×3), and by being the twenty-seventh stanza of the Hymn represents threeness (3^3) in opposition to the beginning of the poem where the four-stanza proem represents fourness. It is appropriate, too, that the angels associated with the six musical stanzas (9–14) should reappear in the final line (line $216=6^3$) in a stanza that harmonises the caco-phonous 'horrid clang', 'hideous hum', and 'loud lament' of the eleven-stanza sequence. The music of the angels cannot now be heard, but its harmonious essence pervades the peaceful scene in the courtly stable. Even Douglas Bush, who so vigorously rejected Professor Røstvig's whole approach, quotes with approval Maynard Mack's remark about 'the number of allusions in this stanza which carry the mind back to earlier symbols' in the poem.[31] It is surely proper to see the number symbolism participating in this resolution.

IV

The *Nativity Ode* was not the first poem in which Milton used in combination the symbolism of fifteen, eleven, and twelve. These numbers are also significant in the Latin elegy he wrote as an undergraduate on the death of the Bishop of Ely. It may be helpful to pause for a while to consider its structure since the elegy draws, in part, on the same repertoire of ideas as the Ode. At first sight this early poem seems to fall into two sections: the poet's lament, followed by a consolation spoken by the spirit of the dead bishop. Underpinning this simple bipartite structure, however, is a neat symbolic scheme the elements of which were to be incorporated into the design of many later works. If the poem is again divided, this time into *equal* halves each of seventeen distichs, it is evident that the first half is composed of the poet's angry reviling of death and the bishop's surprising refutation of this attack, while in the second half the bishop defends death and declares his delight in heavenly bliss. The division of the poem according to speaker is fundamentally less important than division into a section of abjuration and refutation, and a section of praise. A similar structural strategy supports Milton's companion elegy written on the death of the Bishop of Winchester *(Elegia III)* which also falls into two sets of seventeen distichs. The first set describes the poet's grief, and the second describes a dream in which the poet sees Lancelot Andrewes in heaven. The use, in both poems, of two sets of seventeen distichs probably celebrates the inclusion of the two bishops they honour among the blessed.

Similar significance can be found in *Lycidas*, though there the structure is more complex. Setting aside the eight-line coda, the poem may be divided into two parts, a long first part (lines 1–164) mourning because Lycidas is dead, and a short second part (lines 165–85) roundly asserting that Lycidas is after all not dead, but lives in heaven.

The division is thus similar to the formally well marked distinction, from which it ultimately derives, in Virgil's *Eclogue V* where first Mopsus laments the death of Daphnis and then Menalcus celebrates a triumphant apotheosis. But in *Lycidas,* where a single shepherd, as in Spenser's Lament of Dido, delivers both lament and consolation, the structure cannot be marked by a simple change of speaker.[32] Instead, the new beginning is revealed by the way in which the first line of the second section recalls the first line of the whole poem, as Christopher Ricks has noted.[33] The sudden change of direction at the juncture of the two parts has, of course, been frequently commented upon, but it is possibly Rajan who catches the shift most neatly:

> the poem is manoeuvred with startling authority from the desparation into which it has been deliberately plunged into an almost exultant recovery. 'Weep no more, woful Shepherds, weep no more' is a line alive with both serenity and joyousness; the conviction that sings in it is not merely declared but achieved.[34]

The first seventeen lines of the second part record that Lycidas is now with the saints in heaven. They also form a sequence in which the number of lines expresses symbolically the same idea. Their power to comfort lies partly in the ordered structure of the sequence which modulates so reassuringly from injunction to the shepherds to stop their weeping to the full beatitude of the apocalyptic vision ('And God shall wipe away all tears from their eyes') as the reader is pulled firmly onwards by the conjunctive *so*'s and *and*'s. The hoped for pattern is completed in the seventeenth line as the tear image reappears, though with the word 'weep' metamorphosed into 'wipe', and the limited, backward looking 'no more' replaced by the forward looking, unlimited 'for ever', while securely at the centre of the sequence (the ninth of seventeen lines) is Christ, saviour of those who have faith and himself powerfully immune from forces such as those of the 'perilous flood' that have wrecked Lycidas's 'perfidious bark'. The apocalyptic reference that closes the sequence also puts Christ at the centre, though in a way that accords with pastoral elements of the poem. Through Christ all is resolved:

> For the Lamb which is in the midst of the throne shall feed them, and shall lead them unto living fountains of waters and God shall wipe away all tears from their eyes.
>
> (Rev. VII. 17)

We scarcely notice that in the poem it is not God but 'the saints' who wipe the tears away, for Christ at the centre controls the action and the design by determining the placing of the final line so that beginning and end are equally spaced from the centre:

> *Weep no more, woeful shepherds weep no more,*
> *For Lycidas your sorrow is not dead,*
> *Sunk though he be beneath the watry floor,*
> *So sinks the day-star in the ocean bed,*
> *And yet anon repairs his drooping head,*
> *And tricks his beams, and with new spangled ore,*
> *Flames in the forehead of the morning sky:*
> *So Lycidas sunk low, but mounted high,*
> *Through the dear might of him that walked the waves;*
> *Where other groves, and other streams along,*
> *With nectar pure his oozy locks he laves,*
> *And hears the unexpressive nuptial song,*
> *In the blest kingdoms meek of joy and love.*
> *There entertain him all the saints above,*
> *In solemn troops, and sweet societies*
> *That sing, and singing in their glory move,*
> *And wipe the tears for ever from their eyes.*
>
> (lines 165–81)

The shepherds now dry-eyed, the uncouth swain directly addresses Lycidas himself in a brief, four-line statement that returns us, in preparation for the *commiato*, to the fourfold earth.[35]

In all three elegies the number seventeen is important, and it seems likely that Milton was thinking of Saint Augustine's interpretation of seventeen which makes it the union of the ten of the Old Testament Commandments and the seven of the gifts of the Holy Spirit combining to produce a specially famous piece of number lore associated with a saintly life.[36] The triangular form of the number (i.e. 153) was associated with saints in heaven. This association of saintliness and seventeen lies behind the second book of Milton's *De doctrina Christiana* which devotes its seventeen chapters to consideration of the worship or love of God *(de cultu Dei et charitate)*.

In the poem on the Bishop of Ely the first seventeen distichs may be further divided after line 22. The first eleven distichs are appropriately concerned with the poet's grief as he rails against death. In the twelfth a sudden change is introduced, like the final stanza of the *Nativity*

Ode turning eleven into twelve, by the words 'At ecce', and the
sequence is concluded by a twelve-line section (lines 23–34) refuting
the poet's mournful attitude to death. The Bishop's alternative
account is the subject of the second seventeen distichs. Having
rejected the idea of death as destroyer, the second half of the poem
begins with a sequence of fifteen distichs (lines 35–64) that present
death as the means of rising from this world to the next. The sequence
culminates, as we might expect, in images describing the entrance to
heaven:

> *Donec nitentes ad fores*
> *Ventum est Olympi, et regiam crystallinam, et*
> *Stratum smaragdis atrium,*
>
> (lines 62–4)

(until I reached the gleaming gates of Olympus, the palace of
crystal and the forecourt paved with emerald.—*Carey's translation*)

Four concluding lines complete the poem bringing the number of
distichs in the second half from fifteen to seventeen.

The poem on the Bishop of Ely is, then, similar in structure to
Hall's poem on Dr Whitaker. In Hall's elegy there is a single sequence
of seventeen stanzas with the entrance to heaven described in stanza
15. Milton's Latin elegy is shorter because the units are distichs not
six-line stanzas, but the structure is more elaborate because there
are two sequences of seventeen, one of which exploits the eleven to
twelve change, and the other the notion of fifteen. It is appropriate
that Milton's seventeenth distich (second series) presents Bishop
Felton rewarded with eternal felicity just as the seventeenth and final
stanza of Hall's elegy asserts that Whitaker now lives in two ways,
eternally in heaven and in deathless reputation on earth:

> *Is this to die, to liue for euermore*
> *A double life: that neither liu'd afore?*
>
> (lines 101–2)

Analysis of 'In obitum praesulis Eliensis' cannot, of course, in
itself prove that Milton made structural use of certain number symbolism in his *Nativity Ode*, and the obvious pressing question must
be faced. Quite simply, what external evidence is there that the structural scheme for the *Nativity Ode* proposed in this paper would have
been accepted by Milton or could have been recognised by Milton's

early readers? Not surprisingly, there is no relevant direct statement, but there is some reason to suppose that half a century later Dryden would not have found the analysis unacceptable in general outline at least. It is well known that Dryden echoes Milton's Ode in his own Ode on Anne Killigrew. Like Milton's poem, Dryden's can be seen as a nativity poem, an ode celebrating the new life in heaven of Anne, the 'Youngest Virgin-Daughter of the Skies'.[37] Can it be by chance that the first fifteen lines of Dryden's poem share with the last stanza of Milton's the words 'youngest', 'virgin', 'heaven's', 'fixed', 'time', 'star', 'blest', and 'song', and that Dryden's 'Seraphims' recall Milton's 'Bright-harnessed angels'? Like Spenser's Dido, Anne has gone 'As Harbinger of Heav'n, the Way to show', and it is not surprising that the first sentence of Dryden's poem is of fifteen lines and is about Anne's 'Promotion' from earth to heaven:

> *Thou Youngest Virgin-Daughter of the Skies,*
> *Made in the last Promotion of the Blest;*
> *Whose Palmes, new pluckt from Paradise,*
> *In spreading Branches more sublimely rise,*
> *Rich with Immortal Green above the rest:*
> *Whether, adopted to some Neighbouring Star,*
> *Thou rol'st above us, in thy wand'ring Race,*
>   *Or, in Procession fixt and regular,*
>   *Mov'd with the Heavens Majestick Pace;*
>   *Or, call'd to more Superior Bliss,*
> *Thou tread'st, with Seraphims, the vast Abyss:*
> *What ever happy Region is thy place,*
> *Cease thy Celestial Song a little space;*
> *(Thou wilt have Time enough for Hymns Divine,*
>   *Since Heav'ns Eternal Year is thine.)*

The witty afterthought completing the sentence refers to the sufficiency of eternity for Anne's celestial song. Dryden in the world of time does not have this leisure, and we are reminded of Milton's reference to the constraints of time and of his numerological form: 'Time is our tedious song should here have ending' (211). Milton in his Hymn, and Dryden too, is bounded by time; Anne in her 'Hymns Divine' is not. The second sentence, completing Dryden's opening stanza, stresses that Dryden's poetry is mortal, its seven lines indicating, as do the seven-line stanzas of Milton's Proem, that the condition of man is 'a darksome house of mortal clay' (14):

> Hear then a Mortal Muse thy Praise rehearse,
>   In no ignoble Verse;
> But such as thy own voice did practise here,
> When thy first Fruits of Poesie were giv'n;
> To make thy self a welcome Inmate there:
>   While yet a young Probationer,
>   And Candidate of Heav'n.
>
> (16–22)

The first stanza of Dryden's poem, then, juxtaposes a sequence of fifteen lines about Anne's ascent to heaven with a sequence of seven lines about the imperfection of mortal art.

It is the third stanza of Dryden's poem describing Anne's nativity that has previously been particularly associated with Milton's Ode, especially its reference to audibility of the music of the spheres at the time of birth.[38] In Dryden, Milton's six musical stanzas become six musical lines:

> Thy Brother-Angels at thy Birth
> Strung each his Lyre, and tun'd it high,
> That all the People of the Skie
> Might know a Poetess was born on Earth.
> And then, if ever, Mortal Ears
> Had heard the Musick of the Spheres!
>
> (44–9)

The process of adaptation is revealing. Dryden's parenthetical 'if ever' allows him to pay an extravagant compliment while simultaneously denying it and implying that there was nothing special about Anne's birth. There is nothing double-edged about Milton's use of the conditional:

> Ring out, ye crystal spheres,
> Once bless our human ears,
>   (If ye have power to touch our senses so).
>
> (125–7)

Dryden's last stanza, with its reference to the Last Judgement, has also been associated with the *Nativity Ode* (lines 155–6, 163–4).[39]

It is, however, the structure of Dryden's fourth stanza that I wish to compare most closely with the *Nativity Ode*. The stanza presents Anne as a redeeming Christ figure, at once human and superhuman:

Her Wit was more than Man, her Innocence a Child!
(70)

As Christ atones for the sin of man, so Anne atones for the sin of the fallen world of letters. Through her, poets may rise from this 'Second Fall'. The fifteen lines of the stanza deliberately imply, by numerological means, a connexion between Anne and Christ as ladders of redemption, but the structure only reinforces what the words already pointedly imply.

I have argued that the *Nativity Ode* is composed of four sections: a four-stanza Proem, and a Hymn made up of sections of fifteen, eleven, and one stanzas respectively. The same structure is more compactly èvident[40] in Dryden's single stanza which may, like Milton's Hymn, be divided into three sections:

> *O Gracious God! How far have we*
> *Prophan'd thy Heavn'ly Gift of Poesy?*
> *Made prostitute and profligate the Muse,*
> *Debas'd to each obscene and impious use,*
> *Whose Harmony was first ordain'd Above*
> *For Tongues of Angels, and for Hymns of Love?*
> *O wretched We! why were we hurry'd down*
>   *This lubrique and adul'rate age,*
>   *(Nay added fat Pollutions of our own)*
> *T''increase the steaming Ordures of the Stage?*
> *What can we say t'excuse our Second Fall?*
> *Let this thy* Vestal, *Heav'n, attone for all!*
> *Her* Arethusian *Stream remains unsoil'd,*
>   *Unmixt with Forreign Filth, and undefil'd,*
> *Her Wit was more than Man, her Innocence a Child!*

First comes a series of questions expressing the evil into which literature has fallen, suitably composed of eleven lines—the 'steaming Ordures of the Stage' appear like a smoking sacrifice in some obscene rite associated with one of Milton's pagan gods. Dryden's eleven lines are answered by one line, resolving the evil of eleven by the virtue of twelve. The twelfth line serves the same function as the final stanza of Milton's Ode, and in it Anne is seen as both vestal virgin and atoning redeemer. We may appropriately recall the opening of Milton's final stanza which refers to both Mary and Christ:

> But see the virgin blest,
> Hath laid her babe to rest.

Dryden's three concluding lines bring the total for the stanza to fifteen. The structure bears further analysis. A double-octave arrangement is superimposed by distinguishing the first, central, and final lines by metrical irregularity. They are the three lines that correspond to the three soundings of the musical tonic. The use of a quatrain in the middle of the stanza instead of the couplets used elsewhere dovetails the rhyme scheme of the first octave into the rhyme scheme of the second octave just as the median tonic common to both octaves unites the musical scale of two octaves. It is a technique later used by Shadwell.[41] Besides all this, Dryden's choice of his fourth stanza to exploit these structural ideas probably refers to the four stanzas of Milton's Proem as well as being appropriate to the grossness which it is hoped Anne's goodness may purge.

Dryden's use of the numbers four, eleven, and one all contained in fifteen (compact in the manner of Spenser's Lay of Dido) make his stanza a witty and moving epitome of the *Nativity Ode*,[42] but there is more to the parallel than similarity in construction. Milton's Ode is a gift of poetry to Christ, Milton's offering to his maker of the talent with which he was endowed. The gift of poetry concerns Dryden also, but *he* writes of the profanation of the 'Heav'nly Gift of Poesy' in a fallen world. Magi that 'haste with odours sweet' (23) have given way to debauched dramatists who hurry down 'T'increase the steaming Ordures' of the London playhouses.

Other poems, none perhaps more than Cowley's elegy 'On the Death of Mr Crashaw', have contributed to Dryden's achievement in the Anne Killigrew Ode, described by Johnson as the noblest ode in the language,[43] but the shaping force of Milton's 'order serviceable' on that achievement has been unjustly neglected. Comparison of the two odes furthers our understanding of Dryden's poem and provides insight into the way that Dryden read Milton.

V

The *Nativity Ode* is not just a simple accumulation of proem+15 stanzas+11 stanzas+1 stanza. The poem is bound together by an articulating pattern of matching threads appearing and reappearing symmetrically around its centre. This sets up a web of tensions that prevents the accreted units from disintegrating.

The three central stanzas of the poem are clearly marked. The central stanza of the Hymn supposes that

> *if such holy song*
> *Enwrap our fancy long,*
> > *Time will run back, and fetch the age of gold.*
> > > (stanza 14)

The lines suggest a mid-point at which there is a choice between equidistant possibilities: movement forward through history or return to the golden age. 'There are' says Cowley, writing of what he means by 'the *Orb* of *Round Eternity*', 'two sorts of Eternity; from the *Present backwards* to Eternity, and from the *Present forwards*. . . . These two make up the whole *Circle* of *Eternity*.'[44] In the central stanza of Milton's Hymn the poem is poised between movement forward and movement backwards.

The central stanza of the Ode as a whole (i.e. Proem+Hymn; iv+27) is stanza 12 of the Hymn, and it is also marked by a pivotal image: 'the well-balanced world on hinges hung'.[45] These two differently calculated centres frame the magnificent stanza which most readers rightly and instinctively identify as the effective centre of the poem. It is an impressive, splendid, and detachable set piece, grammatically distinguished and heightened by being the only stanza in the Hymn declaimed in the imperative mood. Appropriation of it for downright practical purposes by a nineteenth-century adapter of *Comus* and by a twentieth-century book designer, both relying on the arresting power of the lines to compel attention, is as solid evidence as any of the wide recognition of the stanza's commanding presence and powerful impact. In this way it formed the opening solo and chorus—albeit sadly mutilated—of Macready's 1843 production of *Comus* at Drury Lane,[46] and the opening chorus of the Easter production at the same theatre in 1865.[47] Similarly, it has been exploited graphically on the cover of the Grey Arrow paperback edition of David Daiches's *Milton* (London, 1963). Though such instances may be unimportant in themselves, they are revealing indicators of the way that the lines have been regarded. But to remove the stanza from the poem is to strip it of at least some of its dignity. In its proper context in the Ode Milton gave the stanza pride of place by a setting flanked by two stanzas each a centre in its own right. Like an emperor with kings as attendants, it occupies a position of sovereign honour. In short, placement in the midst enhances the magnificence of the verse while the rhetorical power of the lines distinguishes the place in the poem that they fill. Rhetorical structure and verbal rhetoric combine to reinforce one another.

> *Ring out, ye crystal spheres,*
> *Once bless our human ears,*
> *(If ye have power to touch our senses so)*
> *And let your silver chime*
> *Move in melodious time;*
> *And let the base of heaven's deep organ blow,*
> *And with your ninefold harmony*
> *Make up full concert to the angelic symphony.*

If numerically allusive expression of the 'ninefold harmony' is to be found in the poem, it is probably in the nine words at the heart of this stanza.

Around this centre, stanzas are disposed in linked pairs. Stanzas 12 and 14, which I have already discussed, form a pair of pivotal stanzas flanking the angelic symphony. Together the three stanzas 12–14 make up the nub of the poem. Prompted by the account of the angelic music that precedes them, they describe or invoke the music of the spheres. As Lawrence Stapleton perceptively argued some twenty years ago in a neglected article that draws attention to the importance of both number and central accent in Milton's poem, it is entirely appropriate that this sublime music comes at the centre.[48] The point now needs to to taken up once more, and thus it may be helpful to revive Stapleton's line of investigation.

Stapleton observed a telling similarity between 'the pattern of ideas' in Clement of Alexandria's *Exhortation to the Greeks* and the thematic structure of Milton's Ode. Whether or not Milton himself knew Clement's writings by 1629 (and Stapleton is careful not to claim that Milton *necessarily* had the *Exhortation* in mind), it is clear that familiarity with 'worthy' Clement's vigorous and memorable treatise usefully equips a modern reader of Milton with a ready under-standing of much that is important in the Ode. I have already argued that the structural import of the first fifteen stanzas of Milton's Hymn presents Christ as a saviour who descended to earth so that men may rise to heaven. Turning to the first chapter of Clement's *Exhorta-tion* we find the same concept, but simply stated rather than expressed through structure, and although the actual image of a ladder is not to be found in Clement's treatise, just as it is verbally absent from Milton's poem, the notion of ascent to God through a saviour whose nativity makes that ascent possible is pervasive. Indeed, ascent through Christ is Clement's controlling idea, the very point at which the twin energising forces of the *Exhortation*—Christianity and Platonism —fuse

The first fifteen stanzas of the Hymn and Clement's first chapter also culminate in a similar way. Clement works up to a climactic reference to the gates of heaven opening to disclose a vision of God, an image that can be compared with stanza 15 of Milton's Hymn:

> 'For I am the door,' He says somewhere; which we who wish to perceive God must search out, in order that He may throw open wide for us the gates of heaven. . . . And I know well that He who opens this door, hitherto shut, afterwards unveils what is within, and shows what could not have been discovered before, except we entered through Christ, through whom alone comes the vision of God.[49]

End of chapter. With such a progression in mind, the dramatically truncated version of it found in the Ode, where Milton at the end of his initial fifteen-stanza section cuts straight from the wide open gates of heaven's high palace hall not, like Clement, to a divine vision but instead to the harshly juxtaposed reality of smiling babe and bitter cross, can be seen counterpointed against a pattern that determines the expectations of a properly oriented reader. Only the reader who expects something like Clement's vision can respond fully to the effect gained by Milton's change of direction at stanza 16.

Clement's subsequent chapters describe the pagan gods, and the religious practices and philosophical beliefs of the pre-Christian world. All are either inadequate or evil, and Clement describes them in order to dismiss them just as Milton, in the second section of his Hymn, dismisses types and perversions of Christ. The nativity involves both Milton and Clement in the same sort of rejection of the past.

The general shape of the *Exhortation* as I have here described it is, then, broadly similar to that of Milton's Hymn with its contrasting sections of fifteen and eleven stanzas. Within these similar structures there are many similarities of idea, the most significant being the importance of music in both works. Music accompanies the birth of Christ in the poem and fills its central stanzas; Clement makes Christ himself the musician, a musician far superior even to such wonder-working performers of antiquity as Arion and Orpheus: 'far different is my minstrel', boasts Clement. 'He calls once again to heaven those who have been cast down to earth.'[50] But for Clement, Christ is also the music as well as the musician. He is the new music ousting the old music of pagan shadowy types, though this apparently new music proves after all to be not really new for it is the lost harmony of Creation restored. Clement recalls how 'this pure song, the stay of the universe and the harmony of all things, stretching from the centre to the circumference and from the extremities to the centre, reduced this whole to harmony.'[51] Similarly, Milton gives 'harmonious order' to his poem by arranging it around a musical centre, and while the music is not, for Milton, explicitly identified with Christ, it honours Christ's nativity, as does the whole poem that is centred upon it. Like Clement's music, Milton's too is associated with the music of Creation (stanza 12), and if Clement's syncretistic delight in compiling assertions that God is at the centre of all things is allowed to provide a conceptual basis, it is possible to regard Milton's centralised structure as implicitly identifying the music with Christ.[52] Milton can be seen as suggesting through structure what Clement openly expresses in words.

Milton's distinction between the angelic music attested by the gospels and the unheard music of the spheres is important in the Ode because Milton is careful to distinguish the fabulous or conjectural: 'as 'tis said' (stanza 12), 'If ye have power' (stanza 13), 'For if such holy song' (stanza 14). The distinction also separates the central stanzas from those that precede them. Shape in the triple centre itself is emphasised by surrounding the great call for music to celebrate the Nativity (stanza 13) with framing allusions to the primeval state, unspoiled at the Creation in stanza 12 and regained at the Millenium in stanza 14. It is stanza 13 that celebrates the present time, 'the happy morn' (*Hodie Christus natus est*) while stanza 12 recalls the past and stanza 14 looks to the future. The stanzas that follow this central group are differentiated from it by their non-musical subject matter.

Flanking the triple centre at one remove are stanzas 11 and 15, 'a globe of circular light' (stanza 11) linked with 'orbed in a rainbow' (stanza 15), a link less effectively made, but already present, when, in the first edition, the word 'orbed' was not used. Moving outwards again, we find that the next pair of linked stanzas shows a negative rather than a positive correlation. This is because one of the pair belongs to the fifteen-stanza section of the Hymn (stanza 10) while the other is the first of the eleven contrasting wicked stanzas (stanza 16). The pattern now established continues. The fulfilment of stanza 10 contrasts with the delay of stanza 16, 'This must not yet be so'. Either side of this pair, the 'music sweet' of stanza 9 is set against the 'horrid clang' of stanza 17, and the pastoral eighth stanza contrasts with the 'scaly horror' of the predatory dragon in stanza 18. The sun's respectful response to the 'greater sun' is described in stanza 7, while in stanza 19 the sun god flees. Stanza 6 shows the stars standing still in recognition of the new authority; stanza 20 expresses pagan nature's regret at the passing of the old order. 'Peaceful was the night' in stanza 5 is sharply contrasted with the 'midnight plaint' of stanza 21. Stanza 4 contrasts absence of physical violence, chariots 'Unstained with hostile blood', with the bloody and violent deities of stanza 22, 'wounded Thammuz', Dagon 'the twice battered god', and Baal-Peor for whose sake Cozbi was slain (*Numbers* XXV. 18). Rather similarly, the peace and amity of stanza 3 contrasts with the human sacrifices demanded by Moloch who appears in stanza 23. Stanza 2 describes snow, while in stanza 24 the grass is 'unshowered', and the earlier stanza's reference to a 'saintly veil of maiden white' is contrasted with the later stanza's mention of a shroud (though the primary meaning of 'shroud' may be 'place of shelter or retreat') and of the sable stoles of sorcerers. This pair of stanzas also displays a contrast between 'speeches fair' and 'lowings loud'. 'The heaven-born-child / All meanly wrapped' of stanza 1 becomes in stanza 25 the 'dreaded infant'. The last stanza of the Proem (iv) in which the Magi and the Ode haste *to* Christ is paired by the last stanza of the eleven-stanza section (26) in which shadows, ghosts, and fays flee *from* Christ. The outermost pair of all is composed of stanza iii of the Proem and the final stanza of the whole Ode. In this pair (now that the eleven stanzas have been worked through) Milton reverts to a positive relationship. The 'Bright-harnessed angels sit[ting] in order serviceable' link straightforwardly with 'the spangled host keep[ing] watch in squadrons bright' of the invocation. The two remaining introductory stanzas that precede the invocation lie outside the pattern. They provide a formal statement of the fact and purpose of the Incarnation. It is in response to this statement that the Ode grows, the notion of a gift poem being proposed only in stanza iii.

Bearing in mind how easy it is to make connexions between almost any stanzas in this poem, it is only reasonable to have doubts about whether Milton really did dispose his poem symmetrically around stanza 13.[53] Furthermore, a scheme which seems to ignore two stanzas may seem unsatisfactory, so unsatisfactory perhaps as to be unconvincing. In the face of such doubts, confidence might be strengthened by reflecting that a pattern of positive and negative links between paired stanzas that accords exactly and predictably with the distinction between the eleven stanzas and the stanzas contrasted with them (i.e. the fifteen stanzas that precede them and the single stanza that follows them) indicates that the connexions are unlikely to be fortuitous or casual. The intelligent complexity of the scheme tends to affirm its authenticity. Acceptance of a pattern which excludes two stanzas at the beginning of the poem may be made easier by thinking of a mannerist *trompe l'oeil* painting in which a painted frame forms part of the picture. It is a suggestion that Alastair Fowler has made in relation to the *commiato* of *Lycidas*, but it could be just as helpful in relation to the opening of the *Nativity Ode*.[54] Here the three possible beginnings (the actual beginning of the poem, the invocation of the muse in stanza iii, and the ostensible beginning of the gift-poem inspired by the muse) correspond to three formally denoted points of departure: line 1; the outermost limit of the symmetrical pattern at line 15; the beginning of the Hymn at line 29. The choice of alternatives blurs the distinction between introduction and poem, frame and picture.

The point of the *trompe l'oeil* cleverness lies in Milton's eagerness to race the Magi. 'O run, prevent them' he cries, and we should remember the witty ploy by which Milton later responds to this word 'prevent' in line 8 of the sonnet on his blindness, where he contrives to begin the sestet half a line too early in order to express the haste of patience (the paradoxically active patience of *Hebrews* 12, 1–2, at that). What looks like a blind poet's blunder proves to be a vindication of his undiminished skill:

> *When I consider how my light is spent,*
> *Ere half my days, in this dark world and wide,*
> *And that one talent which is death to hide,*
> *Lodged with me useless, though my soul more bent*
> *To serve therewith my maker, and present*
> *My true account, lest he returning chide,*

> *Doth God exact day-labour, light denied,*
> *I fondly ask; but Patience to prevent*
> *That murmur, soon replies, God doth not need*
> *Either man's work or his own gifts, who best*
> *Bear his mild yoke, they serve him best, his state*
> *Is kingly. Thousands at his bidding speed*
> *And post o'er land and ocean without rest:*
> *They also serve who only stand and wait.*
>
> (Sonnet XVI)

In the *Nativity Ode*, too, Milton anticipates the expected starting point.[55] 'The star-led wizards' are already on the road in the stanza that precedes the Hymn, but Milton 'prevents' (i.e. *comes before*) them by beginning his symmetrical structure one stanza before that. It is revealing that even as Milton asks for inspiration, a pattern is already being formed, and it is significant, if we are to read precisely what is said, that Milton seeks to race the Magi not with a hymn but with a 'humble ode', thus confirming that the gift-poem is not the Hymn, but a larger entity that includes the Hymn. It is almost as if Milton were responding wittily to Lancelot Andrewes's complaint in a Christmas Day sermon for 1622. 'Our Epiphanie', lamented Andrewes, wryly comparing the prompt response of the Wise Men with the dilatoriness of most Christians, 'would (sure) have fallen in Easter-weeke at the soonest.'[56] But Milton is no such laggard. He has given himself a head start, and he has got away unobserved as well, for it is only when the pattern is complete that his plan is revealed. The synoptic view of the poem's symmetrical, concentric form that is required to reveal Milton's strategy is available only in retrospect when the race has been won.[57]

Failing absolutely direct and explicit authorial statement in support of a symmetrical pattern centred round stanza 13, the most encouraging evidence would be confirmation by one of the poem's early readers. It was reassuring to see the relationship between the structure of Dryden's Anne Killigrew stanza and the structure of the *Nativity Ode*. It would be equally reassuring to be able to refer to an imitation of Milton's symmetrical arrangement. But while we can be reasonably sure that in the Anne Killigrew Ode Dryden really was adapting Milton, the relationship between Henry Vaughan's 'The Morning Watch' and Milton's Ode is problematical. Milton's 1645 volume appeared at what was for Vaughan an impressionable time, and it is easy to see why the *Nativity Ode* would have attracted him strongly. It is tempting to conjecture. There is, moreover, *some* evidence that encourages one to recognise the form of Vaughan's poem as an epitome of the symmetry of Milton's Ode. But consideration of this evidence must be accompanied by the text of the poem.

The Morning-watch.
O Joyes! Infinite sweetnes! with what flowres,
And shoots of glory, my soul breakes, and buds!
All the long houres
Of night, and Rest
Through the still shrouds   5
Of sleep, and Clouds,
This Dew fell on my Breast;
O how it Blouds,
And Spirits all my Earth! heark! In what Rings,
And Hymning Circulations the quick world   10
Awakes, and sings;
The rising winds,
And falling springs,
Birds, beasts, all things
Adore him in their kinds.   15
Thus all is hurl'd
In sacred Hymnes, and Order, The great Chime   17
And Symphony of nature. Prayer is
The world in tune,
A spirit-voyce,   20
And vocall joyes
Whose Eccho is heav'ns blisse.
O let me climbe
When I lye down! The Pious soul by night
Is like a clouded starre, whose beames though sed   25
To shed their light
Under some Cloud
Yet are above
And shine, and move
Beyond that mistie showrd.   30
So in my Bed
That Curtain'd grave, though sleep, like ashes' hide
My lamp, and life, both shall in thee abide.⁵⁸   33

E. C. Pettet has already demonstrated the symmetry of 'The Morning-Watch', but the poem's thirty-three lines (the import of *that* number I pass over) are not paired line by line as the stanzas of Milton's Ode are. Such an exacting correspondence would hardly be workable: a line allows too little scope. Instead, a looser plan was adopted by Vaughan:

> With this compulsive, most lyrical opening goes a memorable and satisfying close, which, besides returning us to the beginning, admirably balances with it—in the two long, five-stress lines (appropriately varied by a conclusive rhyme), in the similar density of metaphor, and, above all, in the fact that it epitomises Vaughan's night sensations, the terror and the assurance, as the opening epitomises his spiritual exhilaration at day break.
>
> For further pleasing structural correspondence we may observe how the opening is followed, and the close preceded, by a description, in short lines, of night. Without being unduly repetitive, the second passage recalls the first by its reference to 'cloud' and 'shroud', though at the cost of a repeated rhyme; while the two sections also match in that each is dominated by a single spiritual metaphor, 'dew' in one instance and 'star' in the other.[59]

I have quoted Pettet at such length because his observations are, in the context of the present argument, unbiassed. Having established, then, that it is possible to regard both the *Nativity Ode* and 'The Morning-Watch' as designed symmetrically, it is appropriate to observe particular similarities that may result from conscious borrowing.

We may notice that the central line of Vaughan's poem (line 17) and its two flanking lines,

>   *Thus all is hurl'd*
> *In sacred* Hymnes, *and* Order, *The great* Chime
>   *And* Symphony *of nature. Prayer is* . . .

recall the 'silver chime' and 'angelic symphony' of the notionally central stanza of the *Nativity Ode*. As in Milton's poem the centre is triple. In association with these echoes attention is drawn to structural concerns by possible allusion to Milton's 'order serviceable' and to the numerically symbolic stanza sequence of the Hymn by Vaughan's 'sacred *Hymnes*, and *Order*'. Vaughan's lines

heark! In what Rings,
And Hymning Circulations the quick world
Awakes, and sings;
The rising winds,
And falling springs,
Birds, beasts, all things
Adore him in their kinds.

(lines 9–15)

with their paired images of rising and falling, birds and beasts, and of circles ('Rings' suggests both a circle and the sound invoked in 'Ring out, ye crystal spheres') all implying symmetrical arrangement around a central point, may recall Milton's early morning (Illa sub auroram lux mihi prima tulit) song of adoration ad praesepe symmetrically arranged around a mid-point. Possibly the nine words at the heart of Milton's central stanza (lines 128–9) are remembered in the 9+9 words of Vaughan's three central lines, but more striking is the coincidence that Vaughan's central line is the seventeenth line while the 'central' stanza of Milton's Ode is the seventeenth stanza (i.e. 4 proem+13 Hymn stanzas).[60] This correspondence does not mean, however, that 'The Morning-Watch' has the same number of lines as the Nativity Ode has stanzas. There is good reason for the difference. Because the centre of Milton's poem is a centre between a pair of lesser centres, there are two stanzas at the beginning of the Ode, as has been shown, without corresponding stanzas at the end. Vaughan, untroubled with the complexity of multiple centres, simply added two lines to the end of his poem to balance the two lines at the beginning, thus achieving a symmetrical pattern that comprehends the whole of his poem. In this way, line 17, the notional centre, becomes the arithmetical centre of the poem as well. Vaughan emphasises that his two extra lines are a coda by making them an addendum to the repeating pattern of eight (or in one case seven) lines, and by making them pentameters he matches them with the two opening lines of the poem to give symmetry.

Vaughan's neat adjustment and adaptation of Milton's pattern has been achieved only at the expense of some distortion. There is one piece in the puzzle that will not quite fit without forcing. Vaughan has, appropriately enough, copied the eight-line stanza of Milton's Hymn by adopting a repeating eight-line metrical pattern and rhyme scheme, the units linked syntactically to provide continuity. But strict adherence to this scheme, with a couplet added at the end, would have given thirty-four lines instead of the thirty-three that are required if line 17 is to be central. One of the eight-line units has, therefore, been replaced by a seven-line sequence, or so it seems. It would be typical of Vaughan's art to follow the example of an earlier poem while producing an effect that is all his own, and typical of him to be satisfied with an ambitious scheme that seems not quite to work out; but it may well be better to reserve judgement on the success of Vaughan's manipulations until more is known about numerically determined structures in poetry of the sixteenth and seventeenth centuries, particularly about whether irregularities in form are sometimes actually intended to alert the reader to significant structure.[61]

Milton's poem and Vaughan's have little in common thematically. Both are devotional early morning poems, and there are parallels in imagery and vocabulary. The ladder of mediation set up by Christ's action of becoming man has been turned into its contemplative counterpart, a neoplatonic ascent of meditation:

> *O let me climbe*
> *When I lye down!*

(lines 23–4)

The babe laid to rest in the manger at the end of Milton's poem has been replaced by the poet in his bed at the end of Vaughan's: the bed, like the sun's in Milton's stanza 26, is curtained. All things considered, Vaughan seems to be using Milton's pattern merely because he wants to rather than for any reason significant to the reader. Were it not for the need to account for the curiously irregular seven-line unit beginning at line 17 where an eight-line unit is expected, there would be little reason to take note of a relationship between the two poems. As far as the present essay is concerned the interest lies in what Vaughan's poem may reveal about his awareness of structural pattern in Milton. It seems probable that Vaughan was imitating Milton's concentric symmetry, a probability surely worth entertaining, but like all probabilities it remains no more than just that.

My analysis of the *Nativity Ode* shows three major structural patterns. A manifest structure divides the Ode into proem and Hymn. It is an aspect of the poem's form which this essay largely ignores, not because it is of no importance, but because it has received attention from other commentators and, besides, has been perceived by every reader. Instead the focus here has been on two deeper structures, one aesthetic and one semiotic. The aesthetic structure binds together all but the first two stanzas of the poem in a cohesive and pleasing symmetry of echo and prolepsis. It is a type of arrangement found elsewhere, notably, as Max Wickert has shown, in Spenser's *Epithaamion*, [62] and also in shorter poems like Vaughan's 'The Morning-Watch'. Interlocked with this aesthetic pattern is an agglomerative, semiotic structure composed of numerically significant units, and epitomised in the fourth stanza of Dryden's ode on Anne Killigrew. In his sixth elegy, Milton described for Charles Diodati the composition of the *Nativity Ode* begun early on Christmas morning, 1629:

> I am writing a poem about the king who was born of heavenly seed, and who brought peace to men. I am writing about the blessed ages promised in Holy Scripture, about the infant cries of God, about the stabling under a poor roof of Him who dwells with His Father in the highest heavens, about the sky's giving birth to a new star, about the hosts who sang in the air, and about the pagan gods suddenly shattered in their shrines. These are the gifts I have given for Christ's birthday: the first light of dawn brought them to me. [63]

Such a programme modestly conveys no hint that the poem would be anything other than 'a string of affected conceits'. It alludes to *dona*, 'gifts' for Christ's birthday, not to a single gift. In fact, the 'humble ode' is a magnificent presentation piece constructed with all the art and learning that Milton, newly arrived at his majority, could command. It is the offering of a magus. Milton is determined not only to race the Wise Men, but also to produce a gift to rival theirs. The magnificence of the gift honours the recipient, of course, but it also indicates the status of the donor, his allegiance, his taste, his judgement, and the resources at his disposal.

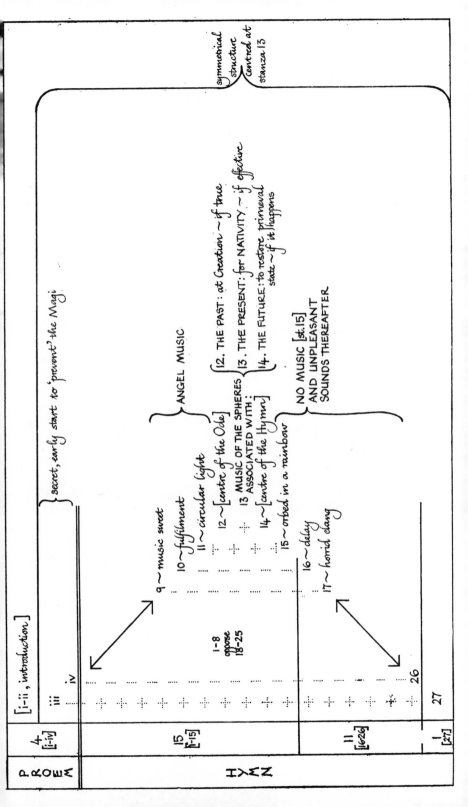

symmetrical structure centred at stanza 13

secret, early start to 'prevent' the Magi

ANGEL MUSIC

9 ~ music sweet
10 ~ fulfilment
11 ~ circular light
12 ~ [centre of the Ode]
13 MUSIC OF THE SPHERES ASSOCIATED WITH:
14 ~ [centre of the Hymn]
15 ~ orbed in a rainbow

12. THE PAST : at Creation ~ if true
13. THE PRESENT : for NATIVITY ~ if effective
14. THE FUTURE : to restore primeval state ~ if it happens

NO MUSIC [st.15] AND UNPLEASANT SOUNDS THEREAFTER

16 ~ delay
17 ~ horrid clang

1-8 oppose 18-25

26

27

PROEM

HYMN

4 [i-iv]	[i-ii, introduction] iii iv
15 [1-15]	
11 [16-26]	
1 [27]	27

4

Dryden's Rahmenerzählung:

THE FORM OF 'AN ESSAY OF DRAMATICK POESIE'

H. Neville Davies

RYDEN'S critical essays, relaxed in style and often engagingly frank in their observations, give every appearance of openness; yet although the style persuades us otherwise, their evasive author was not a directly communicative writer. He was certainly never the man to disclose professional secrets, and his *Essay of Dramatick Poesie,* apparently so rich in circumstantial detail, is a case in point. Such teasing mysteries as the real life identities of the four disputants disguised under the 'borrowed names' Neander, Lisideius, Eugenius, and Crites, and, indeed, the whole question of what in the *Essay* is fiction and what is reportage pose perennial problems for investigation. But some mysteries are more easily penetrated, and it is high time that one of them, the literary form of Dryden's major prose work, was better understood; high time, not only because a better understanding is not hard to come by, but also because such an understanding aids a full response to the *Essay* and helps us to appreciate what Dryden was trying to do in what was, after all, a novel venture. 'To a considerable extent Dryden's dialogue form is an adaptation of the Ciceronian dialogue along both pre-Ciceronian and original lines' assert the latest and most thorough of Dryden's editors.[1] And so it is. Of course the *Essay* has something of the form of a Ciceronian dialogue, and thereby deliberately aligns itself with a great tradition of sceptical inquiry, but to see it simply as a Ciceronian dialogue adapted along 'pre-Ciceronian and original lines' (i.e. like Cicero, only different) is unhelpful. Considering how markedly unlike any classical dialogue, Latin or Greek, the *Essay* is, the notion of adaptation along 'original lines' is patently inadequate, while the glib explanation that 'Dryden returns to Plato in developing the *mise en scène,* especially for the initial dramatic scene, to lengths further than those favored by Cicero'[2] is unlikely to satisfy any reader who stops to compare the *Essay* with the *Phaedo*, the *Symposium*, or the *Republic*.

Where the California editors have gone astray is in insisting that 'Dryden's debts are classical' (p. 351). The following pages attempt to challenge their assumption, and accordingly my first task is to re-examine the form of the *Essay* and to argue that its structural basis is to be found in the framework of an English, late sixteenth-century collection of tales resourcefully transformed, the inset stories replaced by long speeches. The book in question can best be introduced by a short preamble which must begin by recording the death in 1588 of Dick Tarleton. The demise of this great Elizabethan entertainer did not bring to an end the publication of stories and jests associated with him, and in 1590 'Robin Goodfellow' published two editions of *Tarltons Newes Out of Purgatorie. Onelye Such a Jest as his Jigge, Fit for Gentlemen to Laugh at an Houre* . . . which offers yet another set of Tarleton anecdotes, this time posthumous ones. The narrator claims to have been visited, while asleep, by the spirit of the late comedian, and to have reproduced in his book the stories he was then told about the people Tarleton had met in purgatory, 'Eight scurrilous tales, anti-papal and distinctly bawdy', as Muriel Bradbrook describes them.[3] This astutely promoted publication, recently attributed to Robert Armin, was answered by *The Cobler of Caunterburie. Or an Inuectiue against Tarltons Newes Out of Purgatorie. A Merrier Iest than a Clownes Iigge, and Fitter for Gentlemens Humors* . . . (1590), an entertaining collection of six tales set in a carefully engineered and inventive framework. It is a book that amounts to very much more than a mere answer to *Tarltons Newes*, and, to judge from subsequent reprintings, one that seems to have been more popular than fake Tarleton. *Tarltons Newes* was reprinted in 1630, but the *Inuectiue* against it was reissued in 1608, 1614, 1681 (and probably in 1600), as well as being ineptly adapted in 1630 as *The Tinker of Turvey* and imitated in 1620 by *Westward for Smelts*. But despite this seventeenth-century popularity, its use by Dryden, possibly *The Cobler of Caunterburie's* greatest claim to fame, has passed unrecognised.[4]

Described by Margaret Schlauch, and justly so, as 'a minor anonymous masterpiece',[5] *The Cobler of Caunterburie* is regrettably little known today, perhaps because it has not been fully reprinted since Ouvry's edition of 1862. A summary must therefore be offered, and a summary that concentrates on structure will be pertinent to the argument that follows. The volume opens with a vigorous epistle by the titular Cobbler, in which he introduces himself somewhat in the style of Nashe's future Jack Wilton, and offers his book as a desirable alternative to *Tarltons Newes*. A second, shorter epistle follows, signed 'Yours in choller, *Robin Goodfellow*', in which Tarleton's pretended amanuensis in the *Newes Out of Purgatorie* angrily complains about a cobbler turning author. Thus a context of rival literary factions is established by two preliminary documents before we pass on to the main body of the text. The work itself begins like this with the Cobbler as narrator:

> Sitting in the Barge at Billinsgate expecting when the tide would serue for Graues-end diuerse passengers of all sorts resorted thither to go downe: at last it began to ebbe, and then they cryed away when I came to ye staires though I was resolued to go downe in a Tilt-boat, yet seeing what a crew of mad companions went in the Barge and perceiuing by the winde, there was no feare of raine, I stept into the Barge and tooke vp my seate amongst the thickest: with that the Barge-men put from the staires, and hauing a strong ebbe, because there had much raine water fallen before, they went the more merrily downe and scarce had we gotten beyond Saint Katherines, but that a perrye of winde blewe something loude, that the watermen hoyst vp sailes, and laide by their Oares from labour. Being thus vnder Saile going so smugly downe, it made vs all so merry, that we fell to chat, some of one thing and some of another, all of mirth, many of knauery . . . (p. 5).

These opening sentences deftly set the scene in a barge going down the Thames, a host of details lending authenticity to the occasion. As conversation continues, a Gentleman, whom we may suppose preferred to remain aloof, pulls out a book and starts to read. His sociable fellow passengers are not to be so easily ignored, and the Cobbler engages him in conversation by asking what book it is that he is reading. The reply to this tiresome question is predictable: 'mary quoth he a foolish toy, called *Tarltons newes out of Purgatorie*'. The information, unenthusiastically given though it is, immediately prompts a critical discussion about the merits of the book: 'some commended it highly, and sayd it was good inuention, and fine tales: tush quoth another, most of them are stolne out of *Boccace Decameron*: for all that, quoth the third, it is pretie and wittie'. The Cobbler (now presented in the third person instead of writing as a first person narrator) magisterially gives *his* considered opinion: 'Maisters, quoth he, I haue read the booke, and tis indifferent, like a cup of bottle ale, halfe one and halfe the other: but tis not merrie enough for *Tarltons* vaine, nor stuffed with his fine conceits: therefore it shall passe for a booke and no more' (p. 6). As his touchstone of excellence this confidently dismissive critic shows commendable taste in naming 'old father *Chaucer*'; and since, as he says, 'wee are going to Graues-end, and so (I thinke) most of vs to *Canterburie*', the Cobbler's own home town, he proposes that they tell tales 'to passe away the time till we come off the water, and we will call them *Caunterburie* tales' (p. 6). The company agrees, and the Cobbler himself puts his plan into operation by telling the first of these stories. His contribution is followed by five others, and then, on arrival at Gravesend, the enterprising initiator of the scheme makes a further proposal: 'I can (quoth the Cobler) remember—all the tales told on the way, 'and very neere verbatim collect and gather them together: which by the Grace of God gentlemen, I meane to do, and then set them out in a pamphlet vnder mine owne name, as an inuective against *Tarltons newes out of Purgatorie:* and then if you please to send to the *Printer*, I will leaue a token, that euery one of you that told a tale, shall haue a booke for his labor' (p. 83).

The debt to Chaucer extends further than this summary so far indicates. In the first place, each of the six tales is prefaced by a character sketch of the teller written in pastiche Chaucerian verse and modelled on the descriptions of the pilgrims in Chaucer's General Prologue. In the second place, the contention between Chaucer's Reeve and Miller is imitated so as to become a major structural feature in the later work. The Cobbler's opening tale tells how a prior of Canterbury cuckolded a smith, but the passengers on the barge happen to include a Smith, and angered by the Cobbler's tale he responds by relating how a jealous cobbler was cuckolded by none other than a smith. The first two tales, therefore, form a pair, both involving cuckoldry. The next two stories also form a pair. First the Gentleman tells a story of treacherous love in which a naïve Cambridge scholar falls in love with a beautiful but wicked girl from the nearby village of Cherry Hinton. The girl makes a fool of her lover by callously leading him on, and by a particularly cruel trick almost brings about his death from pneumonia, but some years later, after her marriage to another man, the scholar, now more experienced in the ways of the world, gains his revenge by cuckolding her husband and exposing her infidelity. The reply to this harsh, indelicate story comes from a Scholar who tells a touching tale of true love, and in an attempt to raise the tone of the narratives relates the only tale in the collection in which adultery does not occur. His story is of two idealised young lovers separated by various cruel misfortunes. Eventually reunited, they find themselves condemned to death, but as they are about to be burnt at the stake a friend of their parents recognises them, they are reprieved, and a happy ending ensues. The high romance and Mediterranean setting of this elevated tale distinguishes it from the other five, and makes it an admirable contrast to the Gentleman's tale about the Cambridge scholar and the heartless girl from Cherry Hinton.

The final two stories also form a pair, with the tellers both recalling Chaucerian figures, and with both of them telling stories that hinge on the use of clever excuses in an adulterous situation. First of all an Old Wife, clearly related to Chaucer's Wife of Bath, tells a triangular story about a husband, a wife, and the wife's lover: the clever wife tricks her wary husband by persuading him that he was drunk at the time when he thought he had discovered her infidelity. A Summoner, the last of the passengers to tell a tale, thinks it appropriate that he should conclude the series since he practises the same profession as one of Chaucer's pilgrims and since *The Canterbury Tales* has, from the outset, furnished a model for their entertainment on the barge. He also tells about a husband, a wife, and the wife's lover, but this time, as befits a male narrator, it is the lover who cleverly dupes the husband. (In accordance with *fabliaux* conventions, husbands are the butts of male and female narrators alike.) And because the series of tales began with one about a prior, the Summoner thinks it suitable to come full circle by telling a story about an abbot, the abbot taking the role of the resourceful lover. But while the clever wife in the previous story persuaded her husband that he was drunk, the abbot in this story goes one stage further and persuades the husband that he was actually dead and has been revived.

The structure within which the six stories are framed is a lively and attractive one articulated with intelligence and skill. Reduced to its simplest outline it can be conveniently represented by a summary diagram

Billingsgate

Cobbler — | — *Smith*
Gentleman — | — *Scholar*
Old Wife — ↓ — *Summoner*

Gravesend

Unity is given by the focus on cuckoldry, with the exceptional Scholar's tale only sharpening the impression by so deliberately diverging from the pattern. And while the river journey suggests progress, a satisfying sense of completion is also conveyed by terminal recapitulation when a story about an abbot at the end of the sequence matches a story about a prior at the beginning, and when the Chaucerian allusions of the last two story-tellers remind us of the model initially proposed by the Cobbler.

With this summary in mind, the structure of Dryden's *Essay of Dramatick Poesie* can be profitably looked at afresh. First of all there is a general similarity in situation linking the Elizabethan story collection and the Restoration dialogue. In both works a small group of people from London is travelling by barge on the Thames, and although both works are largely taken up with recording the words supposed to have been spoken during that journey, each author takes care, in his own way, to establish the occasion in a lively manner.[6] The opening of Dryden's *Essay*, set against the menacing boom of distant gunfire, is too well known for there to be any need to quote from it here; and the opening of *The Cobler of Caunterburie* has only just been quoted. In both books informal conversation at the beginning leads to more formalised discourse in which the speakers speak at length, uninterrupted, and according to a set plan, and in both books it is discussion about bad literature that gives rise to this more formal discourse. In *The Cobler of Caunterburie* bad literature is represented by *Tarltons Newes Out of Purgatorie*, and in Dryden's *Essay* by the 'ill verses' that are sure to be written to celebrate the English naval victory off Lowestoft. The same number of long speeches is found in both works, and, like the author of *The Cobler of Caunterburie*, Dryden organises his in three answering pairs that provide the vehicle for three debates:

Ancients v. *Moderns*
French v. *English*
blank verse v. *rhyme*

Like the Cobbler, Dryden is both participant (Neander) and presenter, but by presenting himself as Neander he avoids the awkward change from first person to third person narration that jolts the reader of *The Cobler of Caunterburie*. The difficulty of combining reportage and participation is a problem never really solved by the author of the earlier book. Dryden not only copes without difficulty in this respect, but even exploits the situation when as author he allows his spokesman Neander to appear slightly ridiculous in the final paragraph. Lastly, both works begin with a conflict, and although there is an enormous difference in scale between the naval battle of the *Essay* and the merely verbal altercation between the Cobbler and 'Robin Goodfellow', I hope to show later that the basic issue is much the same.

For all that the connexion between the two books is a substantial one, Dryden can certainly not be accused of following his source blindly. For instance, he took the setting for his debates from *The Cobler of Caunterburie*, but the chattily inconsequential, dateless information of the Cobbler he excitingly replaced by a superb evocation of a memorable historical occasion. The transformation is as remarkably inventive in its inception as it is in its execution. But the outstanding alteration is, of course, the substitution of debate speeches for stories. The conceptual shift involved in this change, however, was less violent than the modern reader might at first suppose, for the vocabulary of Dryden's time tends to blur the distinction. Dryden refers to his *Essay* as 'discourse' on more than one occasion: 'I confess I find many things in this Discourse which I do not now approve' he warns Lord Buckhurst; the short preface 'To the Reader' begins by referring in a wittily nautical image to 'The *drift of the ensuing Discourse*'; and in the *Essay* itself the conversation of the four men is regularly termed 'discourse'. It is a word that recalls Corneille's 'Discours des trois unités' and 'Discours du poëme dramatique', to which the *Essay* is much indebted. But 'discourse' is also the word used in the 1620 translation of the *Decameron* to refer to the inset *novelle* when the Induction is headed 'The Induction of the Author, to the Following Discourses'. Similarly, in the 1654 translation of the *Heptaméron* we read that Marguerite de Navarre '*hath surpassed* Boccace *in the elegant Discourses which she hath made on every one of her Accounts*'.[7] For Dryden, the word *discourse* applied equally well to either a narration (OED *sb.* 4) or an argument (OED *sb.* 3), or even to a whole treatise (e.g. the *Essay* itself: OED *sb.* 5), and since the one term covered all these forms the switch from paired narrative to debate would have been more easily made then than now.[8]

The noisy, confident, 'merie cobler', 'the quaintest Squire in all Kent', 'iudiciall Censor of other mens writings', is very much the central, cohesive figure in *The Cobler of Caunterburie*, a robust, red-faced, bald-headed man never at a loss for words. It is he who discovers that one of the passengers is reading *Newes Out of Purgatorie*,

and it is he who offers the most authoritative judgement on that unfortunate book. It is the Cobbler who proposes the telling of tales, and
who tells the first of them ('I myselfe will be ring-leader'). It is the
Cobbler again who undertakes to write down the tales and have them
printed. As an interloper in the literary world, brash, energetic,
and aggressive, he is a new man, a neander, but it is a very different
figure from Dryden's Neander that this upstart presents. Adopting
a totally different tone, Dryden's dedicatory epistle refers modestly
to the *Essay* (a modest title in itself) as 'an amusement', admits its
'rude and indigested manner', apologises for 'many errours', and
discloses that the principal object in publishing it is merely to stimu-
late Lord Buckhurst's literary activities: 'I confess I have no greater
reason, in addressing this Essay to your Lordship, then that it might
awaken in you the desire of writing something, in whatever kind it
be, which might be an honour to our Age and Country' (p. 5). It
is the aristocratic Eugenius, probably a portrait of Buckhurst himself, who proposes the debate, and who earlier breaks the 'strict
silence' on the barge to congratulate the rest on 'that happy Omen of
our Nations Victory' as the sound of gunfire recedes. It is at the invitation of Eugenius that Neander first addresses his three companions. The barge, and the definition of a play, are provided by the
francophile Lisideius who thus supplies the indispensable bases for
both the journey and the debates. Crites, 'a person of a sharp judgment,
and somewhat too delicate a taste in wit', censorious critic of 'ill
verses' and objector to Lisideius's definition, is perhaps the most
vividly drawn of the four men, and the one most like the Cobbler.
He is the first to speak in the formal debate. Neander does not dominate socially in the way that the Cobbler does. We could, for example,
never make even a fleeting comparison between Neander and Shakespeare's Bottom, though such a comparison would not be entirely
wide of the mark in the case of the Cobbler.

Apart from concurring in general decisions, Neander makes no
contribution until the others have all spoken at length and until invited to speak by Eugenius. When he eventually makes his *début*, in
answer to Lisideius, he speaks only 'after a little pause', and when he
later answers Crites he is careful (unlike Crites himself on other
occasions) not to interrupt. We can imagine Neander rather ill at
ease in the company of persons whose 'witt and Quality have made
known to all the Town', his social awkwardness being amusingly
caught at the end of the *Essay* when he pursues his 'Discourse so

eagerly, that *Eugenius* had call'd to him twice or thrice ere he took notice that the Barge stood still' (p. 80). But Neander's clumsy failure to fit his discourse elegantly and unaffectedly into the time allotted him, and, worse still, his insensitive lack of awareness that the barge had become stationary, enable Dryden to draw attention unostentatiously to the larger authorial skill in the contrivance of the framework.[9] As Dryden mentions Eugenius's unavailing attempts to attract Neander's attention, attempts which Dryden would not have known about were he at this point entirely identified with Neander, there is a useful separation between reporter and participant. The readily apparent social failure is deliberately achieved by Dryden's less immediately obvious yet all-embracing artistic control, and serves to make palatable the overriding point that it is Neander who had won the last two debates. Furthermore, the absurdity of Neander's speech overrunning while he is actually recommending rhyme as a means of circumscribing the over-luxuriant fancy, renders pleasantly acceptable his smart observation, which might otherwise have seemed too self congratulatory, that second thoughts are usually best 'as receiving the maturest digestion from judgment' (p. 80), a general proposition of some significance since Neander has spoken second in both of the last two debates. The Cobbler dominated by thrusting himself forward, but Dryden, in his own person and through his spokesman, Neander, establishes himself by more subtle means. Neander's victory in the war of opinions reflects something of the Cobbler's vindication of himself from the disparaging onslaught of 'Robin Goodfellow', and mirrors the English victory in the naval engagement that 'had allarm'd the Town' on that July afternoon; but the Cobbler's unsophisticated assertiveness is dispensed with. 'Their wit', wrote Dryden of the Elizabethans, 'was not that of gentlemen; there was ever somewhat that was ill-bred and clownish in it.'[10] His own age he sees as an age of 'gallantry and civility', though he well knew how often it fell short of its ideals. 'Dryden intends to show that literary debates can be conducted with candour and civility' explains Donald Davie, echoing Dryden's own words. I do not agree with Davie that 'It cannot be said that he succeeds.'[11] As early as 1661, Robert Boyle had, in his dialogue *The Sceptical Chymist, or, Chymico-Physical Doubts and Paradoxes*, employed 'a style more fashionable than that of mere scholars is wont to be', and deliberately provided 'an example how to manage even disputes with civility; whence perhaps some readers will be assisted to discern a difference betwixt bluntness of speech and strength of reason, and to find that a man may be a champion for truth without being an enemy to civility; and may confute an opinion without railing at them that hold it'.[12] Dryden attempts to set before literary critics an example like that which Boyle provided for natural scientists. And, like *The Sceptical Chymist*, Dryden's *Essay* is 'a book written by a gentleman, and wherein only gentlemen are introduced as speakers', neither ill-bred nor clownish.

It will have been noticed that Crites and Neander speak twice in the debates, Lisideius and Eugenius only once, and this disparity shows up another modification that Dryden made to the structure that he found in *The Cobler of Caunterburie*. Because the six narrators are replaced by only four debaters, two of Dryden's cast have to speak twice. The arrangement that he arrives at is plausible enough, with the two more urbane characters speaking only once, and the two others showing less restraint. In each of the debates the second speaker has the advantage, and thus it is Neander-Dryden and Eugenius-Buckhurst who occupy the three winning positions:

> Crites v. *Eugenius*
> Lisideius v. *Neander*
> Crites v. *Neander*

Dryden's use of a smaller body of speakers than is to be found in his source has the effect of pulling the *Essay* more tightly together than it would be were the simple and obviously schematised debate structure not cross grained with an apparently more natural interplay between characters.

One last difference that calls for comment is the distinction between a single and a return journey. The Cobbler and his 'mad companions' go down river from Billingsgate to Gravesend; the four men of Dryden's *Essay* make a journey down river and then return to Somerset Stairs. Both books are shaped by having endings that hark back to the beginning, and both have a progressive element. In *The Cobler of Caunterburie* it is the final inset stories that recall the opening, while the movement of the barge indicates progress, an arrangement that gives importance to the journey and pattern to the story-telling. But while the journey is important to the travellers, it is of no consequence to the reader, and the patterning of the stories though pleasing is ultimately pointless. In the *Essay* the functions are rightly reversed, so that the river journey neatly rounds off the book by concluding where it began, while the truly important inset debates supply the progressive element as one subject leads to another and the debates shift from broader to narrower discriminations: the *Ancients* v. *Moderns* debate followed by a debate discriminating among the *Moderns*, and the *French* v. *English* debate followed by a debate about just one aspect of dramatic composition. Dryden happily put the logical momentum into the discourses and relegated the formal patterning to the underlying river journey, a journey that gets nowhere but serves a literary function by providing a context for the discussion on board the barge.

A return journey (as opposed to a single journey) has three significant moments: the beginning, the end, and the turning point. The importance of London, the city threatened by the Dutch fleet, is emphasised in the *Essay* by its being the beginning and end of the journey. The turning point divides both the journey and the *Essay* into two parts. The down river trip is largely silent, the atmosphere on the barge tense. But eventually, after it is realised that the Dutch fleet is retreating, conversation flows, at first unrestrained, in the now relaxed atmosphere. Gradually the talk becomes less miscellaneous, and an issue arises when Crites and Eugenius disagree about the respective merits of ancient and modern literature. For the purposes of argument they agree to 'limit their Dispute to *Dramatique Poesie*', and Lisideius provides further discipline by supplying a definition of a play. It is at this signal moment that the order is given 'to the Water-men to turn their Barge', and the sequence of six long speeches that occupy the return journey begins (p. 15). Thus three stages are represented on the excursion: 1. silence while the men are apprehensive and the fate of England is uncertain; 2. lively but initially undisciplined conversation prompted by the removal of fear and expressing relief and elation ('the Muses . . . ever follow peace'), this gradually leading to . . . 3. an artful, settled, structured series of debates dependent upon agreed limitations and the acceptance of the authority of a workable even if 'not altogether perfect' definition, and dependent also upon the confidence that stems from the naval victory and a consequent sense of national security.[13] Cultural activity depends upon peace, but it is only when the first adolescent excitement is organised in artful discipline that full cultural maturity is achieved. The turning point on the journey draws attention to the change between the third stage of development and the earlier immature phases, and on the return trip the frightening noise of cannon fire is replaced by its civilised counterpart, verbal contest between friends. Like the naval battle, the war of opinions also leads to an English victory, so that Neander brings back to London another victory to complement the one that is already being celebrated there, while Dryden as author of the whole *Essay*, supplies an example of cultural behaviour to set before his fellow writers.[14] The claim that Dryden had 'no greater reason, in addressing this Essay to your Lordship, then that it might awaken in you the desire of writing something, in whatever kind it be, which might be an honour to our Age and Country' (p. 5) is not false. It flatters Lord Buckhurst in its suggestion of exclusiveness, but Dryden's wish to promote writing that 'might be an honour to our Age and Country' is genuine.

Almost thirty years ago, George Williamson showed that Dryden's *Essay* undertook, among other things, to defend England against the slighting strictures of Samuel Sorbière.[15] The honour of his 'Age and Country' is one of Dryden's main preoccupations in the *Essay*. In 1663 Sorbière, Louis XIV's historiographer, had been courteously received by the newly incorporated Royal Society, and generally entertained by English intellectuals. On his return to France he published an arrogant and ill-informed account of what he had observed of English life, and this *Relation d'un voyage en Angleterre où sont touchées plusieurs choses qui regardent l'état des sciences, et de la religion, et autres matières curieuses* (Paris 1664) angered his late hosts so much that Thomas Sprat interrupted his writing of a history of the Royal Society, a project that was in itself a celebration and commendation of the new life of Restoration London as expressed in the aims and methods of the Society, to reply to Sorbière's ungracious publication with some *Observations on Monsieur de Sorbier's Voyage into England. Written to Dr Wren, Professor of Astronomy in Oxford* (1665). Wren, who happened to be visiting Paris in 1665, is addressed not only because he was the most impressive representative of contemporary English intellectual life, a Restoration complete man prodigiously successful in many spheres, frequently praised for his modesty, but also, presumably, because he was the unofficial title-holder in what amounted to an Anglo-French mathematical contest. In 1658 Pascal had challenged English geometers to solve a problem, and it was Wren who had met the challenge by proposing constructions from which the solution could be derived. He then counterchallenged with a problem originally formulated by Kepler, and to which the French savants had no reply, so it was indeed suitable that 'Thomas Sprat, Fellow of the Royal Society', as he proudly styles himself on the title-page, should address his *Observations* to his colleague Christopher Wren.[16] Among the wide range of issues that Sprat took up, Sorbière's disparaging remarks about English drama are vigorously refuted. Dryden, too, responds to Sorbière's disparagement of English drama in the second of the *Essay*'s three debates, but it is not only when Neander replies to Lisideius that Dryden answers Sorbière. As a riposte to the complaint that the English are 'very much united amongst themselves against Strangers'[17] the final paragraph of the *Essay* shows the French community in London enthusiastically celebrating the victory of their adopted country by dancing in the streets. There can be no doubt about the French *émigrés'* wholehearted identification with English aspirations. In *Annus Mirabilis* Dryden had already contrasted Louis and Charles,

> Lewis *had chas'd the* English *from his shore;*
> *But* Charles *the* French *as Subjects does invite*
> (stanza 43)

and boasted that

> *Were Subjects so but onely by their choice,*
> *And not from Birth did forc'd Dominion take,*
> *Our Prince alone would have the publique voice;*
> *And all his Neighbours Realms would desarts make.*
> (stanza 44)

In the *Essay* Dryden neatly shows this to be so by his inclusion of the description of a 'crowd of *French* people' dancing outside the Savoy where Charles had granted them regular use of the chapel.[18]

In other ways, too, the *Essay* replies to Sorbière's *Relation*. In response to his observation of an aggressive attitude in England towards the Dutch, we see a telling example of Dutch aggression, the naval battle itself; and as a comment on Sorbière's claim that English naval power had declined, Dryden gives us an English naval victory.[19] Sorbière's criticism that the English are lacking in eloquence is magnificently refuted by the eloquence of the speeches that Dryden professes to be recording in the *Essay*, while the serious nature of the subject matter of that eloquence makes nonsense of the contention that the learned men of England are not communicative.[20] Perhaps Dryden claims more for England than Sprat had. Sprat confessed that 'we yield to the *French* in the Beauty of their *Cities*, and *Palaces*'[21] and while Dryden attempts no defence of London's architecture—a city devastated by fire when the *Essay* was published, but with ambitious plans for rebuilding ('New deifi'd she from her fires does rise', *Annus Mirabilis*, line 1178)—his references to Somerset Stairs and to 'the *Piazze*' at Covent Garden, which even Sorbière compared favourably with the *Place-Royale* (*la place des Vosges*), modestly indicate that London is not without architectural interest.[22] It is as a whole, then, that the *Essay* parries the verbal onslaught from France, and it does this as determinedly as the navy is shown to have repulsed the Dutch attack by sea, and as adroitly as an executioner 'who separates the head from the body, and leaves it standing in its place' or as a satirist who makes 'a man appear a fool, a blockhead, or a knave, without using any of those opprobrious terms'.[23] Dryden, well able to follow Boyle's advice and 'confute an opinion without railing at them that hold it', exposes Sorbière's conceited book as the maladroit impertinence of a slow witted ignoramus, without demeaning himself by so much as a single allusion to its author. We cannot help observing that Sprat's straightforward, angry rejoinder to Sorbière is, in comparison, 'a plain piece of work, a bare hanging'.[24] Dryden's response is oblique, just as Wren's response was to Pascal's problem.

Writing of the structure of English plays, Sorbière offensively explained that the English 'do not matter tho' it be a Hodch Potch, for they say, they mind only the Parts as they come on one after another, and have no regard to the whole composition'.[25] Sorbière's English readers must have found the arrogance of this remark even more offensive in view of the rambling, formless nature of the book in which it appeared. With nonchalant suavity Louis's historiographer had presumed that his reader would 'take some pleasure in the Irregularity of my Stile, and be glad to hear my Notions and Adventures: I desire therefore that you would not expect any Method or Ornament in my Writing, but be pleased with the Freedom of my Thoughts upon some very Important Subjects which fall in among the Trifles I shall recount unto you'.[26] Despite an apology for the 'rude and indigested manner' of his *Essay*, for Dryden, too, can display modest *politesse*, Dryden's work is the very opposite of formless.

There is wit in Dryden's choice of the dialogue, a quasi dramatic form, for an enquiry into dramatic poesy, and there is even greater wit in the use of that form to respond to Sorbière's specific criticism of English plays. Sorbière had complained about the neglect of the unities;[27] Neander points out that English dramatists prefer liveliness to the statuesque perfection that servile observation of the unities can give. But that English writers are quite capable of observing the unities when they think it appropriate to do so is brilliantly demonstrated by the achievement of the *Essay* itself which triumphantly mocks the rules by simultaneously observing and flouting them, leaving legalistic pedants bewildered whether to scold or applaud. Thus unity of place is provided by the barge, but because the barge is a moving vehicle there is continuous *variety* of place, though by beginning and ending in London the moving barge can be described, in one sense, as having made no progress. Furthermore, Dryden's choice of place, and the decision to adapt the river journey of *The Cobler of Caunterburie,* wittily cocks a snook at Sorbière's complaint that English authors 'frequently never cite the Books from whence they Borrow, and so their Copies are taken for Originals'.[28] Sorbière had sailed from Calais to Dover, and then, instead of proceeding by coach directly to London, as he could have done, went to Canterbury. From there he travelled overland to Gravesend, 'where for the greater Expedition, I took the Boat, and the Opportunity of the Tide', to London.[29] Dryden has, therefore, found in *The Cobler of Caunterburie,* where the travellers go by boat to Gravesend and then on by road to Canterbury, a 'voyage' complementary to Sorbière's to supply the formal basis for his reply, and then by citing Plato and Cicero has teasingly planted promising looking clues that source hunters three centuries later are still pursuing down the false trail of the classical dialogue.

Unity of time is strictly observed in the *Essay* in so far as the action is continuous and confined to a few hours; but although the excursion is composed of two parts of equal distance (the journey there and the journey back), the turning point is very obviously not placed so as to come half way through the *Essay*. The first tenth, approximately, of the *Essay* describes a largely silent journey down the river, while the remaining nine tenths reproduce the words spoken on the way back. The two halves are grossly disproportionate, but as Lisideius, who admires French observance of the unities, explains, 'some parts of the action [of a play may be] more fit to be represented, some to be related' (p. 40). Dryden's transition from a foreshortened time scale to something like real time in no way disconcerts the reader, especially since a down-river journey, with the current, may plausibly be rapid ('made haste to shoot the Bridge', page 8), while a leisurely progress up stream, against the current,

will be slower. In a finely paced sentence that by its syntactical movement gently establishes a leisurely stroke, the watermen are asked to
'row softly' so that their passengers 'might take the cool of the Evening in their return' (p. 15). Once again, the pedant who seeks to
determine whether unity is or is not observed according to the rules
finds himself confounded by a nicely balanced instance of Dryden
having it both ways. Dryden's treatment of unity of action similarly
mocks the rules. The naval battle and victory celebrations can be
thought of as a sub-plot, or 'under-plot' to use Lisideius's term,
related thematically to a main plot in which the participants are
Lisideius himself and the three men with whom he shares a barge;
thematically linked because in both plots England successfully strives
to vindicate her honour. Furthermore, sub-plot decorously mirrors
main plot in its nautical setting. Like the vigorous, upstart cobbler
seeking to set up as author in spite of the professional disapproval
of the literary establishment as represented by 'Robin Goodfellow',
the English fleet in Dryden's *Essay* defies European naval power,
Neander defies French rules, and Dryden himself debunks Sorbière.
But is it, after all, appropriate to distinguish between a sub-plot and a
main plot when one grows out of the other, and when it is difficult
to say which grows out of which? Is the naval engagement not
perhaps better thought of as the main plot? Or perhaps, after all,
the action is single? Certainly Lisideius would have found Dryden's
presentation of the battle 'both convenient and beautiful':

> But there is another sort of Relations, that is, of things hapning
> in the Action of the Play, and suppos'd to be done behind the
> Scenes: and this is many times both convenient and beautiful:
> for, by it, the *French* avoid the tumult, to which we are subject
> in *England*, by representing Duells, Battells, and the like; which
> renders our Stage too like the Theaters where they fight Prizes.
>
> (p.39)

That Dryden knows how to 'avoid the tumult' the *Essay* itself
demonstrates, though the word 'avoid', with its suggestion of mani-
festly deliberate strategy, fails to do justice to the grace of Dryden's
art. The delight of the *Essay* lies not in arresting contrivance, but in
sprezzatura.

II

So far I have described a structure in which a sequence of three debates is contained within a private river excursion, and in which the river excursion is itself framed, in turn, in the context of the public events of 'that memorable day'. I have tried to show too that the *Essay* is not, in essence, a series of debates, attractively packaged in wrappings that must eventually be discarded before we engage with what is really important—some supposed core of meaning stated in the debates themselves; but that, like an onion, the *Essay* is composed of layers that are themselves the necessary substance of the whole. Even this comparison is a dangerous one, however. To strip away the layers of an onion is to be left with a smaller and smaller onion; to reduce Dryden's *Essay* by a similar process is to destroy it instantly, for the *Essay* depends upon the exhilaratingly patterned interplay between constituent parts which coalesce in an organic whole. Peeling an onion reduces its bulk, not its complexity or flavour.

These are suitable remarks to make before reminding the reader that the outermost frame of the *Essay* is not provided by the account of the events of 3 June, 1665. Dryden's dedicatory letter, which precedes the relation of those events in the physical make up of the book, presents his work as the product of an enforced retreat into the country in time of plague, and as a communication to Lord Buckhurst prompted by a serious patriotic purpose. Both the account of the circumstances of composition, and the decision to address Lord Buckhurst personally are important features, and it is to them that we should now turn. Once again the relationship between frame and inset is significant, a significance that is by no means limited to the obvious connexion between the framing figures of author and dedicatee and the two successful debaters of the inset who represent them, Eugenius and Neander.

The years 1665 and 1666 revealed the new and exciting life of Restoration London to be a precarious affair, subject, despite all its energy and brilliance, to the onslaught of plague, fire, and foreign foe. A frightening alternative from the recent past heightened the sense of alarm, while feelings of guilt, whether for present ungodliness or previous regicide, fostered a sense of insecurity whenever confidence faltered. When Dryden wrote his *Essay*, London society had been forced to disperse, and the theatres, which symbolised the new spirit more strikingly than any other aspect of Restoration life, were closed. The time was not a reassuring one. Dryden took advantage of his retirement to take stock, and the *Essay* is, in part, a nostalgic evocation of all that was best in those years immediately following the re-establishment of the monarchy. But the nostalgia is not just wistful languishing among purling brooks. The *Essay* is both an energetic recreation that provides a lively memorial to the achievement of half a decade, and, at the same time, an original creation that resourcefully provided an imaginative substitute for the way of life frustrated by 'the violence of the last Plague'. The 'violence'of the plague had 'driven' Dryden from London, but Dryden in rural exile, as determined as the English fleet when attacked by the Dutch, builds with the triumphant permanence of art a lovingly realised London of the mind. Even more challengingly, the *Essay* seems to have been a deliberate attempt to raise morale by depicting England at a moment of cultural and military victory; and in its incitement of Buckhurst to write, and its pretense that the ideal discourse on the barge is faithful to the actuality of London life, looks to an even more glorious future when men will proudly serve their country through the practice of writing, and when the art of civilised discourse will be such that what was once a courtly ideal will have become an accepted norm.

It was in the summer of 1667, the summer when Dryden published the *Essay*, that the Treaty of Breda brought the Second Dutch War to an inglorious end after a series of naval disasters. The battle off Lowestoft, it is true, had been a handsome English victory, but by noting only the first 'happy Omen of our Nations Victory', the sound of retreating gun fire, Dryden avoids any reference to the failure to consolidate the defeat of the Dutch by destroying their entire fleet in a vigorous pursuit. A month after Lowestoft an attack on Dutch ships sheltering in Bergen failed wretchedly, while the two following summers each produced further naval disasters for England: in 1666 the resounding defeat of the Four Days' Battle in the Channel, and in 1667 the final humiliation of a successful Dutch raid on Chatham harbour when ships of the line were burnt at their moorings, the flagship captured and towed away, and the Thames shown to be patently open so that London itself could have been bombarded. During the autumn of 1667 and the spring of 1668 the mismanagement of the war was to be debated in the Commons, and it was in this context that Dryden published his account of the events of 'that memorable day' when England triumphed at sea and in debate. It seems likely that the publication of the *Essay* so that it would be read in the late summer and autumn of 1667 was calculated to boost national morale.

Dryden's reference to the disastrous epidemic of bubonic plague which raged in London in 1665 is usually taken to be a purely topical allusion opening up no wider significance. But the habitual mode of Dryden's poetry and prose is one of suggestive allusiveness, and, as Achsah Guibbory has observed in a study of Dryden's views of history, Dryden likes to locate 'his subjects within a historical framework through allusions which are, in fact, historical parallels'.[30] Just such a historical parallel is provided by the plague reference, and the allusion is one, I suggest, that expands the *Essay*'s meaning in the mode characteristic of Dryden's writings. The 'last Plague' finds its parallel in the notorious outbreak that occurred in Florence in 1348, and which Boccaccio described so horrifyingly in the Induction to his *Decameron*. Like Boccaccio's 'seven honourable ladies, and three noble gentlemen' who left plague-stricken Florence for the wholesome countryside, Dryden left London; and like *The Cobler of Caunterburie*, from which Dryden derived the form of his Thames debates, the *Decameron* is a framework collection of tales or 'discourses'. The link between the *Essay* and the *Decameron* is both direct and indirect for *The Cobler of Caunterburie,* which constitutes an indirect link, is itself considerably indebted to Boccaccio's collection, notwithstanding the objection raised to *Tarltons Newes* by one of the Cobbler's fellow passengers that most of its stories 'are stolne out of *Boccace Decameron*'.[31] In fact, *The Cobler of Caunterburie* is open to just that charge.[32] There are, however, two closely connected motives not found in the Elizabethan collection which Dryden has taken over directly from Boccaccio, and disconnected from each other. Flight from a plague-stricken city to a country retreat is one, and associated by Dryden with the story of how he came to write the *Essay*, while a series of framed 'discourses' spoken by supposedly real people, their identities deliberately hidden by pseudonyms,[33] is the other, and a model, in combination with *The Cobler of Caunterburie,* for the ordering of the primary events which the *Essay* apparently recalls. The conflicting claims of two framework collections, the *Decameron* and *The Cobler of Caunterburie,* are cleverly resolved in the *Essay* by the use of a double frame, but because *The Cobler of Caunterburie* is itself derived from the *Decameron*, the conflict is a temporary difficulty and affects only Dryden's opening. The combination of war and plague, and, indeed, of reported speeches as well, may suggest yet another literary parallel, but if Dryden remembered Thucydides's vivid description of plague-stricken Athens in the second year of the Peloponnesian War he does not encourage readers of the *Essay* to pursue the parallel.

At the end of his *Essay* where an allusion to the end of the *Decameron* provides a suitable conclusion, Dryden contrives a neat fusion by transferring the Boccaccio allusion to the inset account of the events of 3 June. In this way, the *Decameron* frame is completed without any harking back to the circumstances attending the writing of the *Essay*. One implication following from this is that any notion that Dryden wrote the *Essay* with its present ending and then, at a later stage, added a dedicatory letter not previously envisaged must be rejected out of hand, no matter how well supported by Dryden's hoary old bluff about finding the *Essay* while looking through his 'loose Papers'. The 'loose Papers' topos is a stock formula included for reasons of decorous modesty. Clearly, the final paragraph and the dedicatory letter were written with each other in mind.

Dryden's terminal allusion to the *Decameron* might easily pass unnoticed were it not that expectations arising from a symmetrical structure alert the reader to its presence. Boccaccio, it will be remembered, records that his story-tellers returned 'to Florence, where the three Gentlemen left the seven Ladies at the Church of Santa Maria Novella, from whence they went with them at the first. And having parted with kinde salutations, the Gentlemen went whether themselves best pleased, and the Ladies repaired home to their houses' (vol. iv, p. 312). Dryden's final sentence is a witty variation of this. His company returns to the city from which it set out, and lands at Somerset Stairs. 'Walking thence together to the *Piazze* they parted there; *Eugenius* and *Lisideius* to some pleasant appointment they had made, and *Crites* and *Neander* to their several Lodgings' (p. 81). Rather as Boccaccio's ladies go dutifully home, while the men went freely 'whether themselves best pleased', Dryden's two less courtly characters (the two who had spoken twice in the debates) return to their lodgings while the more aristocratic pair proceed 'to some pleasant appointment', Boccaccio's innuendo becoming slightly broader in Dryden's version. Dryden's choice of the fashionable *Piazza* at Covent Garden as the point of dispersal combines a reference to Italy with a convincing piece of social realism. In conjunction with this allusion it may also be that the *al fresco* dancing of the French people which Dryden's four men witness on their moonlit walk from the barge is intended to recall the songs and dances with which Boccaccio's Florentines concluded each day as described, for instance, in the passage immediately preceding the account of the return to Florence.

The framing allusions to the *Decameron* provide a delicate means for Dryden to make certain large claims. In the first place, they help to project the exemplary character of the *Essay*, as becomes apparent if we recall the title of the 1620 English translation of the *Decameron*, a title that styles it *The Modell of Wit, Mirth, Eloquence and Conversation*. Just such a model is afforded by the *Essay*. But more important even than the presentation of the *Essay* as a new *Decameron*, is the alignment of Renaissance Florence and Restoration London.

Before Dryden's time, Englishmen looking towards the cities of Italy were dazzled above all by the lustre of Venice, while after Dryden's time it was increasingly the civilisation of Florence that they admired. According to J. R. Hale, the shift in emphasis can be seen for the first time in James Howell's *A German Diet* (1653), an ingeniously structured collection of debates written by Dryden's predecessor in the office of Historiographer Royal.[34] But whatever the truth of Hale's precise assertion, the esteem of Florence as the city where preeminently the new learning had flourished had always been recognised.[35] Its cultural achievements were to endure with a permanence denied the transitory political success of any other Italian city. Florence was also distinguished as the seminal city from which Renaissance thinking spread through Italy, to France, and to England. It is the names of three Florentines, Dante, Petrarch, and Boccaccio, that we, like Dryden, associate most immediately with the new impetus, and in many respects it is Boccaccio, biographer of Dante and scholar of his works, close friend of Petrarch, who is the most representative early Renaissance figure. The *Decameron* is, of course, Boccaccio's most considerable work.

The preeminence of Florence is intimately connected with its role in the establishment of the Italian language. It was the writers of Florence who refined the Tuscan dialect to produce a literary language; and the reputation of the *Decameron* rests, as much as upon anything, on its linguistic elegance. Boccaccio's concern for this aspect of his work is a concern he shares with Dryden, for, like Boccaccio, Dryden saw the refinement of the language as being the particular responsibility of his own time. Both men had the advantage of being able to build on the work of an earlier generation, so that just as 'Dante had begun to file their language, at least in verse', and I use Dryden's own words, so had the poets Waller and Denham initiated a process of linguistic refinement in England. 'The reformation of their prose was wholly owing to Boccace himself, which is yet the standard of purity in the Italian language', recorded Dryden at the end of his life, and the *Essay* may surely be seen as an attempt to set up a similar 'standard of purity' for English prose.[36] Such an approach explains why Dryden went to the uncharacteristic trouble of correcting points of language when he revised the text for the edition of 1684. But to present the *Essay* as a model comparable in mid-seventeenth-century England with that provided by the *Decameron* in *trecento* Italy is to make a very considerable claim, one better made, as Dryden seems to have realised, by suggestive implication than by crudely categorical assertion. In the Preface to the *Fables* Dryden chooses to compare Boccaccio and Chaucer, but this should not blind us to a possible comparison between Boccaccio and Dryden himself.

The state of the English language was inextricably bound up, for Dryden, with the defence of England from French sneers, Dutch naval power, natural calamity, and bad writing. His sense of patriotism is very much in the spirit of Renaissance humanism, and he would certainly have agreed, for instance, with what Milton had to say in a letter (10 September 1638) to the Florentine philologist, Benedetto Bonmatthei:

> Nor is it to be considered of small consequence what language, pure or corrupt, a people has, or what is their customary degree of propriety in speaking it. . . . For, let the words of a country be in part debased by wear and wrongly uttered, and what do they declare, but, by no light indication, that the inhabitants of that country are an indolent, idly-yawning race, with minds already long prepared for any amount of servility? On the other hand, we have never heard that any empire, any state did not flourish moderately at least as long as liking and care for its language lasted.

Milton even suggests that the fall of Athens 'and its low and obscure condition followed on the general vitiation of its usage in the matter of speech'.[37]

Boccaccio's celebration of Florentine life and Dryden's celebration of London life afford another point of comparison. Just as the *Decameron* is suffused with the new spirit of Boccaccio's Florence, even while the Black Death brings about its near collapse, so Dryden's *Essay* celebrates the new and threatened life of 'The Metropolis of Great Britain, the Most Renowned And Late Flourishing City of London', to quote the dedication of *Annus Mirabilis*, a poem prompted by thoughts similar to those which lie behind the *Essay*. Dryden's use of local colour evokes not only London, however, but reaches out towards Italy also. The references to Somerset Stairs and Covent Garden at the end of the *Essay* seem particularly well calculated to display the London of the mid 1660s as the possible inheritor of the Italian Renaissance tradition. The splendid, monumental portico of Corinthian columns which Inigo Jones had built onto the west end of St Paul's Cathedral, begun in 1635, was the most imposing example of building in the Italian manner in London, but the destruction of the body of the cathedral by fire in 1666 made any reference to it unsuitable, given that Dryden's object was to raise morale. The unhappy regicide associations of the Banqueting House at Whitehall rendered yet another important building unsuitable for mention; but both Somerset Stairs and Covent Garden were without taint, and lay west of the area destroyed by the Fire. Both are remarkable examples of Inigo Jones's use of classical forms, and fit without strain in the slight narrative thread of the *Essay*.

Covent Garden, built during the 1630s, was the first geometrically laid out urban space to be designed in England. Thirty years later, in the 1660s, it was still unique. St Paul's Church, on the west side of the square, was a particularly important building, the first post-Reformation church to be erected in London on a new site. Inigo Jones had responded vigorously to the Earl of Bedford's commission to provide a parish church as cheaply as possible ('I would not have it better than a barn') for the new residents of Covent Garden by undertaking to build 'the handsomest barn in England'. Sir John Summerson has explained the rationale of the building:

> A church which was to be of the simplest, cheapest kind could not inappropriately be a temple structure incorporating the Tuscan order. As such it would have classical dignity at the vernacular level: it would be the 'handsomest barn' of the anecdote.[38]

Hence it became the first building in England to have a classical
portico with detached columns, and in a London not yet equipped
with Wren's fifty-two churches, St Paul's Covent Garden must have
presented a forcefully Italianate impression. At a time when the
rebuilding of the City churches destroyed in the Fire was a matter of
major public interest, the style that Jones chose for the Earl of Bedford's church at Covent Garden must have attracted a great deal of
careful attention. According to Sir John Summerson, it was not merely
the church that exploited the Tuscan order. He sees the whole development as having a unified design. The houses on the north and east
sides of the square, raised over arcades known by Londoners as
'piazzas', were, he argues, part of 'a continuous exercise in the
Tuscan':

> Covent Garden therefore was Tuscan from beginning to end,
> a comprehensive essay in the Tuscan mood—Tuscan all the way
> from the high sophistication of the portico to the vernacular
> of the houses—a new vernacular, the first statement of what we
> naturally think of today as the Georgian house.[39]

Evelyn's diary and a biographical note on Inigo Jones published in
1725 seem to indicate that Covent Garden was thought, by some, to
be based on the piazza in the *Tuscan* city of Leghorn, and Dryden
too may have imagined the British Vitruvius to have been remembering an Italian original.[40] The 'Tuscan' architecture and the
particular association with Leghorn all tend to link Covent Garden
with Tuscany, and so with Florence, its chief city. But even if Dryden
saw no specifically Tuscan connexion, or did not associate the Tuscan
architectural style with the geographical area of Tuscany, the more
general Italian association remains.[41] It is, I suppose, even possible that
in some way Dryden may have actually associated Jones's portico
at Covent Garden directly with the famous façade which the Florentine Vitruvius, Alberti, had built onto the medieval structure of the
Decameron's S. Maria Novella in the second half of the fifteenth
century. If so, Dryden would have been thinking of the Florentine
church as it was a century or more after Boccaccio's time, but
such anachronistic associations are easily made, and, in an age less
well supplied with handy reference books than our own, easily
accepted.

It is difficult to be quite sure what the water stairs at Somerset
House, built by Inigo Jones between 1628 and 1631, looked like in

the 1660s, but both John Webb's drawing of the gateway (possibly an unexecuted design) and early eighteenth-century views of Somerset House and the river show neo-classical structures of considerable distinction.[42] Like Covent Garden, they recall the architecture of Renaissance Italy. The stairs also bring to mind Somerset House itself where Jones carried out a great deal of work for Queen Henrietta Maria during the 1630s.

If, then, by literary and architectural allusion Dryden is drawing a parallel, or even merely hinting at a parallel between Renaissance Italy and Restoration England, in the way that I have suggested, he is not doing so for the first time. In a commendatory poem addressed 'To My Honored Friend, Dr Charleton' and prefacing Charleton's *Chorea Gigantum* (1662) Dryden had already associated the restoration of the monarchy and the restoration of learning. Earl Wasserman has shown, in a fine elucidation of the poem, how Dryden made use of the notion that 'Scholasticism was to the history of European thought as the Interregnum was to English political history' and assumed a close relationship between recent political changes and cultural developments.[43] The Restoration was, for Dryden, not just the restoration of Charles to his throne, but a full restoration of the liberal spirit in all possible manifestations, indeed a renaissance comparable with the Italian Renaissance. The advancement of scientific learning in England and the coronation of Charles II came to represent for Dryden the overthrow of tyranny, intellectual and political, and in the new age that was dawning literature could be expected to flourish.

> And though the fury of a Civil War, and Power, for twenty years together, abandon'd to a barbarous race of men, Enemies of all good Learning, had buried the Muses under the ruines of Monarchy; yet with the restoration of our happiness, we see reviv'd Poesie lifting up its head, & already shaking off the rubbish which lay so heavy on it.
>
> *(Essay*, p. 63)

While the verses to Dr Charleton announce this new Renaissance, the *Essay* elaborately attempts to substantiate the claim. Even the choice of the dialogue form, with its generic allusion to the classical past, recalls at the same time the academies of Renaissance Italy. But the form adopted by Dryden also allows him to make the *Essay* massively comprehensive. Crites and Eugenius debate the merits of

Ancients and Moderns, while the *Essay* itself draws richly on both; Ancients Greek and Latin, Plato and Cicero, and Moderns from Boccaccio to Buckhurst. French and English literature are compared in debate, but Dryden as essayist draws with equal assurance on Corneille's *discours* and on the Elizabethan *The Cobler of Caunterburie.* Above all, a strenuous debate between the conflicting claims of rhyme and blank verse is conducted through the medium of an ambitious and impressively well achieved new model for prose composition.

In his reply to Sorbière, Sprat had complained that England was unjustly slighted by arrogant Europeans:

> The *Italians* did at first indeavour to have it thought, that all matters of Elegance, had never yet pass'd the *Alps:* but being soon overwhelm'd by Number, they were content to admit the *French*, and the *Spaniards*, into some share of the honour. But they all three still maintain this united opinion, that all wit is to be sought for no where but amongst themselves: It is their established Rule, that good sense has alwayes kept neer the warm Sun, and scarce ever yet dar'd to come farther then the forty ninth degree Northward.[44]

Dryden does not complain, he acts, and the *Essay* shows that at fifty-one degrees north lies a city that the world would do well to take seriously.

Restoration prose has been well described by J. R. Sutherland. It is, in the main, he tells us,

> a slightly formalised variation of the conversation of gentlemen. The gentleman converses with ease, and with an absence of emphasis which may at times become a conscious and studied underemphasis, but which is more often a natural expression of his poise and detachment. He is imperturbable; nothing puts him out, or leads him to quicken his pace; indeed, a certain nonchalance and a casual way of making the most devastating observations are characteristic of him, for if he is always polite he is never mealy-mouthed, and has no middle-class inhibitions. He will never betray too great eagerness, or ride his ideas too hard, or insist too absolutely, for that is to be a bore; he will not consciously exploit his personality, or indulge in eccentricity or whimsies, for that is to be selfish, to think too much about

himself. On all occasions, like a good host, he will consult the convenience and the pleasure of those he is entertaining; and he will therefore try to express himself clearly and politely and unpedantically, and, if he can manage it, with a witty turn of thought and phrase. He will not dogmatize, or proselytize, or appeal exclusively to the emotions; to do that is the mark of the ignorant zealot and the godly fanatic, of whom no Restoration gentleman wished to be reminded.[45]

As a neat description of what I have been trying to show about Dryden's *Essay* Professor Sutherland's words could hardly be bettered. The way in which Dryden adapted *The Cobler of Caunter-burie*, the unassertive delicacy of the framing references to the *Decameron*, the nonchalance of the devastating response to Sorbière, the lack of dogmatism inherent in the debate form, the entertaining nature of the setting for the debates, and the nimble wit all reveal Dryden as a gentleman. So does the prose style, and Dryden's achievement in this respect is partly the result, as Sutherland has also pointed out, of casting a large part of the *Essay* as a formalised conversation between gentlemen.[46] But the debates are not straightforwardly presented in a simple dialogue form, for the whole piece is a communication to Lord Buckhurst which the general reader just happens to be able to share. The familiar style of the letter provides Dryden with an intermediate mode of discourse lying between conversation and impersonal prose:

> we should write [letters] as we speak; and that's a true familiar Letter which expresseth one's Mind, as if he were discoursing with the Party to whom he writes,

says James Howell, in the first of his familiar letters.[47]

Dryden encloses the dialogue in a report or letter to Lord Buckhurst because in this way he ensures that he writes in the appropriate style: 'This, my Lord, was the substance of what was then spoke on that occasion; and *Lisideius*, I think was going to reply, when he was prevented thus by *Crites*' (p. 64 with Q1 reading). But however effective the device of personal address might have been to Dryden as a compositional aid, especially in his earliest prose pieces, it need have no relevance to the reader, and when Dryden revised the *Essay* for a second edition he removed the explicit reference to 'my Lord' in the passage just quoted. The framework provided by direct address to Buckingham is mere scaffolding. The framework provided by *The Cobler of Caunterburie* and the *Decameron*, on the other hand, is the essential and elegant structure of the whole edifice. Our delight in the texture of the *Essay* should be combined with delight in its significant and splendidly vigorous design.

5

Tom Jones
and the Choice of Hercules

MAREN-SOFIE RØSTVIG

PICO DELLA MIRANDOLA'S *Oration on the Dignity of Man* is perhaps the best known expression of the humanist belief in man as a being whose freedom is such that he may turn himself into what he pleases, angel or beast,[1] and if one looks for a similar theme in Renaissance art, nothing can be more appropriate than the Choice of Hercules.[2] The many Renaissance versions of this theme present the situation of the young man who has to choose between two contrasting modes of existence and the values they embody. At its simplest the choice is between Virtue and Vice; a more philosophical variant posits a choice between an active and a contemplative life, while the subtlest version contrasts mere sensual pleasure with the supreme beauty which reconciles Pleasure to Virtue. Milton's companion poems may be said to confront the reader with a choice between an active and a contemplative life, while *Comus* shows a protagonist already irrevocably committed to the path of virtue and deaf to all the seductive speeches of her opponent. *Paradise Lost*, however, invites us to analyse the various steps involved in the process of choosing. But Adam's choice, although fatal is not final; when the epic reaches the concluding lines infinite vistas of choice are opened up: 'The world was all before them, where to choose / Their place of rest, and providence their guide'.

This is the passage Henry Fielding invokes as Tom Jones, after his expulsion from Paradise Hall, ponders the nature of *his* choice; as Fielding puts it, his problem is 'what course of life to pursue'.[3] And if we turn to another eighteenth-century writer fascinated by the theme of choice, Samuel Johnson, we find him invoking the same Miltonic passage when he lets Rasselas exclaim, after his escape from the Happy Valley, 'I have here the world before me; . . . surely happiness is somewhere to be found.'⁴

As I hope to show, the story of *Tom Jones* is an eighteenth-century dramatisation of the Choice of Hercules, but before I can present my argument a context has to be established. By way of introduction, therefore, I want to show, first, that Fielding may have fetched from the Earl of Shaftesbury not only his moral philosophy but also his application of the principle of harmony to literary composition. Once this has been discussed, a study of narrative structure in *Tom Jones* will reveal the thematic importance of the concept of choice, and at this point it will finally be possible to compare Fielding's story with some literary and iconographical versions of the myth of Hercules, and particularly that of the choice as transmitted by the Earl of Shaftesbury and by an artist like William Hogarth.

I

Moral and religious pessimists are content to associate the choice of Virtue with eternal bliss in a Heavenly Jerusalem; as far as this life is concerned the fate of the virtuous will be thorns and brambles rather than roses and raptures. It is a measure of their optimism that Renaissance humanists could envisage a choice of Virtue reconciled to Pleasure,⁵ but although Dr Johnson shared the typically humanist belief in Free Will, he would have nothing to do with any facile belief in virtue rewarded. To his disillusioned eye Virtue and Pleasure were irreconcilable powers joined in a desperate struggle 'which will always be continued while the present system of nature shall subsist'. The records of poetry and history can exhibit nothing more than 'pleasure triumphing over virtue, and virtue subjugating pleasure'.⁶

Since his best known moral thesis concerns the keenness of the pleasure derived from virtuous action, the Earl of Shaftesbury may perhaps be said to present an early eighteenth-century version of the humanist theme of Pleasure reconciled to Virtue. This pleasure is largely a matter of observing the supreme beauty of moral action. The pleasure and the delight which we take in contemplating order, proportion, and symmetry in the external world, superior though it is to the pleasures of mere sense experience, nevertheless is itself 'far surpassed' by observing 'a *beautiful, proportion'd,* and *becoming* Action.'⁷ The primacy of this experience of moral beauty is clearly indicated when Shaftesbury derives the artist's ability to imitate the order of nature from his experience of the beauty of moral order in the microcosmos of man. His *Advice to an Author* puts this quite succinctly: an artist is capable of imposing order on his work only to the extent that he perceives 'the inward Form and Structure of his Fellow-Creature' and of himself; it is this which enables him to 'imitate the Creator' and become 'a just PROMETHEUS, under Jove'.[8]

Shaftesbury is equally explicit when it comes to explaining exactly what he understands by the imposition of order on a work of art—a part of his argument that has tended to be overshadowed by his discussion of moral harmony. We must take care not to read into his comments on literary structure merely an Aristotelian insistence on a beginning, middle, and end; his views concerning artistic unity should be related to the fusion between Platonic and Christian theories of creation associated with Augustine and with Renaissance syncretists.[9] Like these Shaftesbury posits two steps in the creative procedure: (1) a pre-conceived pattern, and (2) the disposition of the subject-matter according to this pattern so that unity may be achieved. The artist's purpose is to form 'a *Whole*, coherent and proportion'd in it-self, with due Subjection and Subordinacy of constituent Parts'. Before a piece of writing may be considered as 'legitimate', therefore, it must possess '*exterior Proportion* and *Symmetry* of Composition' and this means devising 'a Pattern or Plan of Workmanship.'[10]

Shaftesbury presents the same ideas in a playful manner in his *Miscellaneous Reflections*, his point of departure being the deplorable absence, among modern writers, of a sense of form. They are content to scatter their ideas abroad without any plan or pattern, while a competent writer must behave like 'an able Traveller' who knows how important it is to plan the stages of his journey ahead of time. He measures the distance 'exactly' and 'premeditates his Stages, and Intervals of Relaxation and Intention, to the very Conclusion of his Undertaking'. He knows, too, how to vary his pace: 'He is not presently *upon the Spur*, or in his full *Career*; but walks his Steed *leisurely* out of his Stable, settles himself in his Stirrups, and when fair Road and Station offer, puts on perhaps to *a round Trot*; thence into *a Gallop*, and after a while *takes up*'. He suits his pace to the condition of the road to save his horse so as not to 'bring him puffing, and in a heat, into his last Inn.'[11]

Fielding repeatedly exploits the same metaphor, first in *Joseph*

Andrews II, 1 and then in *Tom Jones* II, 1 and XVIII, 1. True, Fielding varies the metaphor—in *Joseph Andrews* II, 1 it is the reader who travels through the book, looking for entertainment and suitable resting-places—but the context is the same. Like Shaftesbury, Fielding's concern is with the disposition of his material into books and chapters, or as stated in the chapter heading, with 'divisions in authors'. *Tom Jones* II, 1 takes up the issue of varied pace; his own writing, so Fielding argues, is totally unlike that of newspapers which always have the same number of words 'whether there be any news in it or not'. Newspapers are in this respect to be 'compared to a stage-coach, which performs constantly the same course, empty as well as full'. A journalist keeps 'even pace with time, whose amanuensis he is', but not so Fielding whose readers will find 'some chapters very short, and others altogether as long'. They must not be surprised, therefore, 'if my history sometimes seems to stand still, and sometimes to fly'.

Shaftesbury's metaphor is directly echoed in a passage towards the end of *Tom Jones* XI, 9 when Fielding, after having conducted Sophia Western safely to London, pauses to compare his 'history' to 'the travellers who are its subject'. 'Good writers will indeed do well to imitate the ingenious traveller' who knows to 'retard his pace' when confronted by scenes worthy of his attention, 'which delay he afterwards compensates by swiftly scouring over the gloomy heath of Bagshot' or over uneventful, open plains where one spots little more than a single tree in the course of sixteen miles. 'Not so travels the money-meditating tradesman' or the 'offspring of wealth and dulness. On they jogg, with equal pace, through the verdant meadows, or over the barren heath . . . ' Fielding leaves it to his sagacious reader to apply his metaphor to 'the Boeotian writers' renowned for their dullness and 'to those authors who are their opposites'. If we take this advice at all to heart, we are compelled to observe that Fielding has just retarded his own pace from weeks and days to two twelve-hour spans in the two books prior to Book XI, so that these must presumably contain matter well worth perusing with particular care. And sagacity is apparently required to unravel the author's meaning; the lazy reader will miss as much as the lazy traveller:

> Bestir thyself therefore on this occasion; for tho' we will always lend thee proper assistance in difficult places, as we do not, like some others, expect thee to use the arts of divination to discover our meaning, yet we shall not indulge thy laziness where nothing

but thy own attention is required; for thou art highly mistaken
if thou dost imagine that we intended, when we begun this
great work, to leave thy sagacity nothing to do, or that, without
sometimes exercising this talent, thou wilt be able to travel through
our pages with any pleasure or profit to thyself.

Fielding was not content to adapt a popular Renaissance theme;
to alert his reader he also adopts the Renaissance stance of the author
who challenges his public to discover the meaning of the 'dark conceits' scattered through his work. And I agree with Fielding that the
'arts of divination' are superfluous; the clues are there in the text.

The last of Fielding's prefatory chapters (XVIII, 1) reverts to the
stage-coach metaphor as the author bids farewell to his fellow-
travellers, all of whom must certainly agree that the tour has been
extremely well planned from beginning to end. But this is what we
would expect from an author who commands his readers to trust
his ability as a planner in the following frequently-quoted passage
from chapter X, 1:

... we warn thee not too hastily to condemn any of the incidents
in this our history, as impertinent and foreign to our main design,
because thou dost not immediately conceive in what manner
such incidents may conduce to that design. This work may,
indeed, be considered as a great creation of our own; and for a
little reptile of a critic to find fault with any of its parts, without
knowing the manner in which the whole is connected . . . is a
most presumptuous absurdity.

Fielding, then, is completely at one with Shaftesbury in his insistence
on unity of design; his work is an ordered cosmos, a creation of his
own.

When Shaftesbury later on in his *Miscellaneous Reflections* returns
to the issue of the necessity of using 'a *Model* or a *Plan*', he adds a
three-page footnote by way of comment[12] and in the course of this
footnote the reader is referred back to the passage on the 'able Traveller' who premeditates the stages of his journey. The footnote is
interesting in itself as a discussion of purely literary topics, but its
interest is increased on noticing how closely Fielding follows Shaftesbury's lead in some of his own observations on the art of writing.
Thus when Shaftesbury states that if a poet's fiction is to convince, he
must take as his guide 'not *the Possible,* but *the Probable* and *Likely*',
this is of course what Fielding says when he discusses the marvellous

in *Tom Jones* VIII, 1. The two are in complete agreement also with regard to character portrayal: patterns of angelic perfection or diabolical depravity fail to interest readers, let alone to influence their moral behaviour. But when a good character suffers the evil effects of his vices, 'we are not only taught to shun them for their own sake, but to hate them for the mischiefs they have already brought on those we love' (*Tom Jones* X, 1). Shaftesbury had already advanced the same argument, but somewhat more philosophically. After having analysed the vices and virtues of various Homeric heroes, he concludes that this is how the poet imparts his moral lesson. His fable shows how 'the *Excesses* of every Character' are redressed:

> And the Misfortunes naturally attending such Excesses, being justly apply'd; our Passions, whilst in the strongest manner engag'd and mov'd, are in the wholesomest and most effectual manner corrected and *purg'd.*

In short, 'in *a Poem* (whether *Epick* or *Dramatick*) a compleat and *perfect Character* is the greatest *Monster*, and of all Poetick Fictions not only the least *engaging*, but the least *moral* and *improving*.'

Shaftesbury's footnote is at its most interesting when it touches on unity of design. Shaftesbury is not content with a general sense of unity; the principle of unity entails placing episodes with such exactness that they cannot be fitted in anywhere else without disastrous consequences:

> 'Tis an infallible proof of the want of just *Integrity* in every Writing, from the *Epopee* or *Heroick* Poem, down to the familiar Epistle . . . if every several Part or Portion fits not its proper place so exactly, that the least Transposition wou'd be impracticable. Whatever is *Episodick*, tho perhaps it be *a Whole*, and in it-self *intire*, yet being inserted, as a *Part*, in a Work of greater length, it must appear only in its *due Place*. And that Place alone can be call'd its *due*-one, which alone befits it. If there be any Passage in the Middle or End, which might have stood in the Beginning; or any in the Beginning which might have stood as well in the Middle or End; there is properly in such a Piece neither Beginning, Middle, or End. 'Tis a mere *Rhapsody*; not a Work . . .

If *Tom Jones* is a 'great creation' in the sense defined here by Shaftesbury, this would entail a careful placing of the digressions and not only of the various episodes that constitute the plot that Ronald S. Crane has taught us to appreciate.[13] While we recognise and honour the kind of unity which emerges from a successful fusion of incidents that at first seem very loosely related, an easily perceived symmetrical disposition of parts is apt to strike us as a mechanical device of doubtful aesthetic value. No particular admiration has been stirred by observing Fielding's neat division of his story into three equal parts: six books on Allworthy's estate, six on the road, and six in London. The division has been recognised but not explored. It is important, however, to realise that this tripartite arrangement is combined with a central accent on Books IX and X as indicated by the chronological scheme; as we approach the textual centre the narrative pace slows down from years and months to weeks and days and, finally, to the two twelve-hour spans of Books IX and X. After we have passed through this centre with its setting in the inn at Upton, the speed is again increased, but only in terms of days. Since the plot indicates the central role of the events that take place in the inn at Upton, the chronological pin-pointing of Books IX and X as the textual centre merely confirms what we already know, but since it is these books that present Fielding's version of the Choice of Hercules, the structural clue is far from superfluous. It compels the reader to 'bestir himself on this occasion' to discover the author's meaning.

If Fielding took Shaftesbury's advice concerning unity of design at all seriously, it must be possible to show that the notorious digression on the Man of the Hill not only belongs in the pattern, but that it could have been placed nowhere else. It occurs just prior to Books IX–X, in the last six chapters of Book VIII. And on the other side of the textual centre we find that chapters 2–7 of Book XI present the story of Mrs Fitzpatrick as told to Sophia Western. This symmetrical disposition around the centre suggests that the digressions have a bearing on important thematic issues, and that they have been placed where these issues had to be underlined. If this were not so, then the symmetrical structure would be nothing but a mere stylistic flourish. It is hard to believe this, the more so since Douglas Brooks has shown how closely the interpolated tales in *Joseph Andrews* are related to their immediate context in the story.[14]

Since the Man of the Hill, unlike Mrs Fitzpatrick, has no function in the plot, his story can possess thematic relevance only. Critics, however, have found little to interest them in this story of a misspent life apart from the warning which it contains to beware of bad company in London. But if this were its chief thematic relevance, its proper placing would have been just prior to Tom's arrival in London in Book XIII, and not before the events in the inn at Upton. Since the story of the Man of the Hill leads up to these events, its purpose must be to point the reader's attention in the right direction.

It will be remembered that the story falls into two parts. The first phase in the life of the Man of the Hill shows him in eager pursuit of the pleasures of sense and the gifts of fickle Fortune: drinking, gambling, and loving constitute the sum of his achievement—his love being for a woman of easy virtue and a friend so enslaved by the spirit of gambling that everything is sacrificed to it. These characters are exactly what they seem; they never pose as other than what they are— slaves of sensual delights and of Fortune—and so their behaviour is entirely predictable. The disastrous issue of events, therefore, is the consequence of poor judgement and self-deception. The pleasures so eagerly pursued are mere phantoms of the imagination. When the Man of the Hill finally turns his back on the world in disgust, the basic bias of his character remains unchanged. Although he has forsworn drink and all human company, he persists in his pursuit of pleasure—so much so that an initial capital letter is distinctly in order. The only difference is that his quest is now for the pleasures of the mind alone. Both phases in his career, therefore, illustrate the conscious choice of Pleasure. His life is so designed as to illustrate, not vice abandoned in favour of virtue, but the pursuit of two contrary kinds of pleasure, each taken to an excess. That the second phase should be condemned as thoroughly as the first appears from two considerations: despite the fact that he has a gun he remains a mere spectator as Mrs Waters is attacked, and his solitary existence is depicted in such a manner as to constitute a conscious caricature of the Epicurean ideal of the happiness of complete solitude. In its wealth of clearly visualised, significant details Fielding's caricature of this ideal comes fairly close in spirit to Hogarth's paintings, and I would suggest that this is how we ought to view a number of the episodes in Fielding's novel—as a series of satirical pictures conveying a specific moral lesson.[15] The last 'painting' in this particular series shows the hermit on the brow of his hill, watching Mrs Waters in the hands of her cruel assailant 'with great patience and unconcern'. To recognise the caricature one must of course know the original, in this case the Epicurean ideal of happiness current during the last few decades of the seventeenth century, partly in a plainly hedonistic version and partly in a more elevated philosophical alternative capable of appealing to the more serious-minded. As I have shown elsewhere,[16] many Restoration poets favoured Lucretius' picture of the Happy Man as a detached and unconcerned spectator of the follies of men, placed on top of a hill from which he may contemplate the spectacle of the mad pursuit of Fortune. Because this man has taught himself to limit his desires to the pleasures of the mind as enjoyed in solitude, his invulnerability was supposed to be absolute. The basic concept in poems concerned with this type of *beatus vir* is that of conscious choice, a word sometimes found in the title itself, and 'The Choice' would be an entirely appropriate heading for Fielding's interpolated tale. As Tom Jones himself points out, the man's misfortunes were due to his 'want of proper caution in the choice of friends and acquaintance'. But it is a choice of life which is entailed and not merely a choice of friends, and the narrative itself comments ironically on the second choice of complete solitude by underlining its hazards. No retreat from the world can remove a man from the reach of Fortune; the only power capable of providing some measure of protection is divine Providence. But Providence can do no more than place Tom Jones in a position where he may serve as the rescuer; it is Tom's prompt response that saves the life first of the Man of the Hill and next of Mrs Waters.

The life-story of the Man of the Hill invites analysis in terms of an Aristotelian contrast between defect and excess; the pleasures of the body illustrated in the first phase exclude those of the mind, and the other way round. One could also say that the Man of the Hill begins by bestowing his love too freely and on unworthy objects, while he concludes by entirely withdrawing his love from men and bestowing it on the Deity instead. The relevant argument has in fact already been presented by Mr Allworthy in his discussion of charity in Book II, ch. 3. The whole drift of the New Testament proves that charity must entail moral action to relieve the distressed, such actions being their own reward as they engender such exquisite sensations of delight in those who perform them that they become 'in some degree epicures'. This, then, is one way in which pleasure and virtue may be reconciled. Allworthy goes on to add that a man can harden his heart to the distresses of others only if he should become convinced that all men are depraved: '. . . this persuasion must lead him, I think, either into atheism or enthusiasm; but surely it is unfair to argue such universal depravity from a few vicious individuals . . . ' This persuasion is dramatised in the career of the Man of the Hill, the first part of which is marked by an atheistic hedonism of the grossest kind, while he ends his life as a religious enthusiast. As he passes from the one extreme to the other, the Man of the Hill enjoys a brief period of harmony which comes to an end with the death of his father. Fielding had already pursued a similar Aristotelian pattern of defect, a Golden Mean, and excess in *Joseph Andrews,* where the structure is just as obvious if not more so. A sequence of three chapters is so arranged as to take the reader through three scenes illustrating, first the complete lack of charity in Parson Trulliber (II, 14), then the unexpected generosity of the pedlar (II, 15), and finally the fine gentleman's profuse, but false, verbal professions (II, 16). Once one has spotted the Aristotelian structure one can virtually predict the nature of the third episode on the strength of the first two.

To revert to *Tom Jones,* the two extremes dramatised in the life of the Man of the Hill have been refuted in advance by Mr Allworthy, the gist of whose argument (II, 5) is repeated by Tom Jones in his rejection of the view that human nature is 'necessarily and universally evil' (VIII, 15). The enthusiastic phase may also be refuted in terms fetched from Shaftesbury: an appreciation of the beauty of the universe is perfectly useless unless related to the higher beauty of just harmony and proportion in the world of moral action, and it is this superior beauty that Tom Jones displays as he rescues Mrs Waters. The contrast between the two men, therefore, is a contrast between false and true virtue (or moral beauty) and false and true pleasure.

A similar contrast is established between Mrs Fitzpatrick and Sophia Western, each of whom has made her choice, and it is a reflection of their status as women that it turns on a choice of husband. The story of Mrs Fitzpatrick's marriage shows that she, too, has erred grossly in her choice, but in contrast to the Man of the Hill she has been deceived by a pleasing appearance in the man she married. Yet she has erred just as grossly in her second choice: elopement with the Irish peer. The contrast between the two women is strongly underlined: Mrs Fitzpatrick's air of virtue is mere hypocrisy, while Sophia has 'a heart as good and innocent, as her face was beautiful' (X, 5).

Both digressions, then, turn on the theme of *choice*—the choice of pleasures subsequently revealed as false or deceptive, and as opposed to virtue. We can now examine the intervening books in order to assess the possible relevance of this theme.

II

No sooner has Tom Jones proved the superior beauty of moral action as he rescues Mrs Waters with 'his trusty oaken stick', than his attention is riveted on her exposed breasts so that 'for a few moments they stood silent, and gazing at each other' (IX, 2). No reader is likely to forget how, during their progress to Upton, Mrs Waters succeeds in keeping her female attributes in view, and in the inn Mr Jones must again use his 'cudgel' to defend the honour of the lady. Once this honour has been vindicated the hero proceeds to satisfy his hunger, and no sooner has this been done than he falls a victim to the amorous warfare conducted by Mrs Waters. But before this is permitted to happen Fielding pauses, strangely enough, to describe the man with whom we ought to be perfectly familiar: he is a veritable Adonis with regard to beauty and a Hercules with regard to strength. The author also pauses to characterise the kind of love involved in this episode as mere appetite. The ensuing description of the amorous warfare is a particularly delightful example of Fielding's mock epic style: it is conducted throughout in complete silence by means of looks and sighs, the hero's best protection being his tremendous appetite:

> First, from two lovely blue eyes, whose bright orbs flashed lightning at their discharge, flew forth two pointed ogles. But happily for our heroe, hit only a vast piece of beef which he was then conveying into his plate, and harmless spent their force. The fair warrior perceived their miscarriage, and immediately from her fair bosom drew forth a deadly sigh ... so soft, so sweet, so tender, that the insinuating air must have found its subtle way to the heart of our heroe, had it not luckily been driven from his ears by the coarse bubbling of some bottled ale, which at that time he was pouring forth.

But when the cloth is removed, so are his defences, and 'without duly weighing his allegiance to the fair Sophia', he surrenders.

This episode alone might have sufficed to inform contemporary readers that this is a mock epic version of the Choice of Hercules, one of the most popular of themes among painters since the Renaissance. It was Ronald Paulson's study of *Hogarth, His Life, Art, and Times* (1971) that drew my attention to the frequency with which the theme of a choice between Virtue and Vice (or Pleasure) informs Hogarth's work, and a particularly good example is presented by the popular print called *The Lottery* (1724).[17] In his comments on Hogarth's various versions of this basic theme Paulson draws on Shaftesbury's brief treatise entitled *A Notion of the Historical Draught or Tablature of the Judgment of Hercules* (1713) included in the third volume of the *Characteristics*.[18] To read Shaftesbury's account is to realise the use that Fielding has made of this tradition; this use is so obvious that it is virtually unnecessary to re-read *Tom Jones*, IX–X, to spot the parallels. This is particularly true of the temptation scene in IX, 5. When Fielding prefaces his mock epic passage on the amorous warfare with the remark that this is 'a description hitherto unessayed either in prose or verse', he is, in fact, quite right; the theme of the Choice of Hercules had been the peculiar province of painters. As Erwin Panofsky has shown, the iconographical tradition of the choice does not extend back in time beyond the middle of the fifteenth century,[19] but literary versions of various aspects of the Heracles myth are of course another matter. Although Fielding draws on literary traditions, too, and not only on iconographical versions of the Choice, for the moment I want to focus on Fielding's adaptation of the latter as summarised by Shaftesbury.

This can best be done by listing the main points that serve to identify the mid-section in Fielding's narrative as a mock epic version of the Choice of Hercules. As we have seen, Fielding pauses to describe Tom Jones as a Hercules at the very moment when Mrs Waters (as Pleasure/Vice) reaches the climax of her persuasive efforts, and the hero has been given the prime Herculean attribute of a stick or cudgel which he wields to good effect. But even more significant is Mrs Waters' free display of her bosom together with her rhetoric of silent persuasion, while the last, decisive link in the chain is the fact that Fielding places his hero at a cross-road to make his choice. As for Sophia, Fielding uses descriptive terms indicating beyond doubt that he presents her as the kind of superior Beauty where Virtue and Pleasure are reconciled.

If my argument holds, then Tom Jones should be seen not as merely having yet another illicit amour in the inn at Upton, but as Hercules at the crossroads confronted by the contrary persuasions of Pleasure and Virtue. And if this is indeed so, then the story told by the Man of the Hill concerning his choice of life leads directly on to this decisive event in Tom's life, and no 'reptile of a critic' must 'presume to find fault' either with the contents of this digression or its placing. And as far as Fielding's art is concerned, this interpretation, if accepted, would show that the use of mock epic mythology extends from the descriptive terms into the action itself. While *Joseph Andrews* provides the male protagonists with an added dimension by invoking the Biblical Joseph and Abraham, classical myth performs much the same service in *Tom Jones*. Fielding's narratives, like Hogarth's modern history painting, score important points by placing the contemporary world, as Ronald Paulson has put it, 'in relation to conventions of biblical or mythological resonance . . .'[20]

My theory that Fielding drew on Shaftesbury's discussion of the Choice of Hercules is supported by the many instances that *Tom Jones* affords of Shaftesbury's pervasive influence. It is possible, of course, that Fielding may have turned to William Shenstone's early poem on *The Judgment of Hercules* (1740),[21] a work clearly inspired by Shaftesbury's treatise, or that he knew the iconographical tradition even better than the noble Earl, but a comparison between Shaftesbury's *Judgment of Hercules* and *Tom Jones* IX–X nevertheless shows several distinct points of similarity that are more easily accounted for by positing a conscious use, by Fielding, of Shaftesbury's argument.

Thus Shaftesbury stipulates that the setting should be 'in the Country, and in a place of Retirement, near some Wood or Forest' to suggest 'Solitude, Thoughtfulness, and premeditated Retreat'. This is certainly true of Fielding's narrative, where the encounter with the Man of the Hill is the preface to his meeting with Mrs Waters in X, 2. The hero has indeed had his moment of philosophical reflection in a place whose sole function is to serve as a setting for complete retirement from the world. To revert to Shaftesbury, he observes that during the first phase when Hercules is accosted by Pleasure and persuaded by her, the 'Reign of Silence must be absolute'. Hercules must be silent to preserve his dignity, Pleasure because her appeal is to the senses. Her language, Shaftesbury remarks, must be that of the eyes, the persuasive power of rational speech being the attribute of Virtue. Pleasure should be associated with objects suggesting 'the Debauches of the Table-kind', while other 'indulgences' may be suggested by 'certain Draperys thrown carelessly on the ground, and hung upon a neighbouring Tree, forming a kind of Bower and Couch for this luxurious Dame . . .' Shaftesbury does not say that Pleasure should expose her bosom to view, but this is true of most pictorial representations of this 'luxurious Dame', including the picture which adorns the title-page of Shaftesbury's treatise—a plate by S. Gribelin of a painting by Paolo de Matteis.[22] Hogarth's version of the Choice of Hercules in *The Lottery* in the same manner shows a half naked figure surrounded by objects of a similar kind, as Ronald Paulson has remarked.[23]

My enjoyment of Fielding's narrative is distinctly enhanced by observing the use that he makes of a theme made familiar by a host of painters and sometimes in a satirical vein as in the case of Dürer[24] and Hogarth. The character of the amorous Mrs Waters epitomises the seductiveness of sensual pleasure: as such she seems to me curiously at variance with the homely and grammatically inclined Jenny Jones whom we met in the first part, so that it is difficult to avoid the conclusion that at this point Fielding sacrificed consistency of character to the needs of this important occasion. Perhaps consistency of character is not to be expected in such a minor character, or can it be that we are to suppose that the intervening years have achieved this striking metamorphosis? However this may be, Mrs Waters is certainly as delightful as the occasion requires; Shaftesbury's rule that every action in a history-painting must display '*Probability*, or *seeming Truth*'[25] has been fully realised.

It is interesting that Fielding should present as the alternative choice to Vice/Pleasure the kind of Virtue that represents the highest kind of Beauty, the enjoyment of which creates the highest pleasure that mortal man is capable of. The iconographical tradition usually stresses the contrast between Vice and Virtue rather than more subtle philosophical concepts, and in some emblems Vice is an old hag hiding behind a beautiful mask, while Virtue has been so totally deprived of sex as to appear in the shape of an old man with a book.[26] The painters, however, usually present Virtue as a beautiful woman, her beauty being combined with a lofty serenity that is positively awe-inspiring. Beauty is of course Sophia Western's primary characteristic, and when she is introduced in X, 3 as the foil to Mrs Waters this is the aspect which is given reiterated emphasis. As Fielding remarks, there is 'in perfect beauty a power which none almost can withstand' (X, 3), and certainly not Tom Jones. Her second attribute would have seemed strange in any other context than the Choice of Hercules, and this is the sweetness of her voice, a quality associated with penetration in musical thought.[26a] As Shaftesbury explains, it is the privilege of Virtue to persuade through rational speech, and

To dirtie drosse, no higher dare aspyre,
Ne can his feeble earthly eyes endure
The flaming light of that celestiall fyre,
Which kindleth loue in generous desyre,
And makes him mount aboue the natiue might
Of heauie earth, vpto the heauens hight.

Such is the powre of that sweet passion,
That it all sordid basenesse doth expell,
And the refyned mynd doth newly fashion
Vnto a fairer forme, which now doth dwell
In his high thought, that would it selfe excell;
Which he beholding still with constant sight,
Admires the mirrour of so heauenly light.

Whose image printing in his deepest wit,
He thereon feeds his hungrie fantasy,
Still full, yet neuer satisfyde with it,
Like *Tantale*, that in store doth steruedly:
So doth he pine in most satiety,
For nought may quench his infinite desyre,
Once kindled through that first conceiued fyre.

Thereon his mynd affixed wholly is,
Ne thinks on ought, but how it to attaine;
His care, his ioy, his hope is all on this,
That seemes in it all blisses to containe,
In sight whereof, all other blisse seemes vaine.
Thrise happie man, might he the same possesse;
He faines himselfe, and doth his fortune blesse.
                                                            And

Yet thus farre happie he him selfe doth weene,
That heauens such happie grace did to him lend,
As thing on earth to heauenly, to haue seene,
His harts enshrined faint, his heauens quene,
Fairer then fairest, in his fayning eye,
Whose sole aspect he counts felicitye.

Then forth he casts in his vnquiet thought,
What he may do, her fauour to obtaine;
What braue exploit, what perill hardly wrought,
What puissant conquest, what aduenturous paine,
May please her best, and grace vnto him gaine:
He dreads no danger, nor misfortune feares,
His faith, his fortune, in his breast he beares:

Thou art his god, thou art his mightie guyde,
Thou being blind, letst him not see his feares,
But cariest him to that which he hath eyde,
Through seas, through flames, through thousand
        swords and speares:
Ne ought so strong that may his force withstand,
With which thou armest his resistlesse hand.

Witnesse *Leander*, in the Euxine waues,
And stout *Æneas* in the Troiane fyre,
Achilles preasing through the Phrygian glaiues,
And *Orpheus* daring to prouoke the yre
Of damned fiends, to get his loue retyre:
For both through heauen & hell thou makest way,
To win them worship which to thee obay.
                                                            B iij

2. Hercules between Pleasure and Virtue. Engraving by Sim. Gribelin of a painting by Paulo Matthaeis reproduced from the fourth edition of Shaftesbury's *Characteristicks* (172 III, 345.

3. Hercules at the crossroads between Virtue and Vice. From Geoffrey Whitney, *A Choice of Emblemes* (Leyden, 1586). *(Bodleian Library.)*

this is surely why Fielding goes out of his way, again and again, to stress this attribute. Sophia is said to possess 'a voice much fuller of honey than was ever that of Plato, though his voice is supposed to have been a bee-hive' (X, 9). Not only does her beauty eclipse that of Mrs Fitzpatrick as the sun and moon do the stars, but her voice ravishes landladies and beasts as well as men (XI, 3 and X, 9). The climactic assertion occurs just after the comparison to the voice of Plato:

> Reader, I am not superstitious, nor any great believer in modern miracles. I do not, therefore, deliver the following as a certain truth; for, indeed, I can scarce credit it myself: but the fidelity of an historian obliges me to relate what hath been confidently asserted. The horse, then, on which the guide rode, is reported to have been so charmed by Sophia's voice, that he made a full stop, and exprest an unwillingness to proceed any farther. (X, 9)

The real reason is that the guide has stopped using his 'armed right heel', but the point has been made and in a manner appropriate to mock epic. The sweet voice of reason charms that archetypal image of the unruly passions, the horse. Shaftesbury makes the same point when he states that Virtue may be shown as having a bit or bridle to indicate her ability to restrain. However, in the very next chapter— XI, 2—Sophia neglects 'the management of her horse' and so sustains a fall which is an affront to her modesty, and a second fall of the same kind which is witnessed by a number of bystanders. Fortune 'seems to have resolved to put Sophia to the blush that day', and one wonders why; one possible reason is a desire, on the part of Fielding, to stress the modesty of Virtue as contrasted with the patent immodesty of Vice. Just after Mrs Waters has displayed her tempting female attributes, then, Sophia Western is shown as experiencing 'a violent shock' to her modesty. This experience occurs when Sophia is in the company of false Virtue (Mrs Fitzpatrick), when they have found 'a wide and well-beaten road' leading to 'a very fair promising inn' (compare *Matthew* 7:13–14). Fielding's descriptive terms—a 'wide and well-beaten road' and 'very fair promising inn'—places the fall from the horse in a context that is easily identified. This is the kind of prospect which in emblematic representations of the Choice is associated with Vice. In this 'fair promising inn' Sophia Western is in bad company indeed; Mrs Fitzpatrick's true character is perceived readily enough, her appearance of virtue being a mere mask put on to deceive the world. Conversely Sophia herself is taken for Jenny Cameron, a common whore albeit a royal one, and her reputation suffers even more from the intemperate behaviour of Mrs Honour. Book XI concludes with 'a Hint or two concerning Virtue' and with the parting of the two cousins.

The portrayal of Mrs Waters and of Sophia Western, then, is entirely in keeping with the tradition of the Choice of Hercules as explained by Shaftesbury, but so far I have discussed only the first phase in the process of the Choice: the momentary leaning, by Tom Jones/Hercules, in the direction of Pleasure/Vice in Book IX. The second phase begins when Tom Jones discovers Sophia's muff—an event which causes what the chapter-heading (X, 6) refers to as 'the Madness of Jones'—and when he resolves 'never more to abandon the pursuit' of Sophia (X, 7); it concludes with the last Book in this division, XII. Once Sophia has been brought safely to London at the end of Book XI, the narrative returns to Tom Jones and to the theme of his Choice. After leaving the inn at Upton, Tom Jones and Partridge reach the cross-roads where Tom has a second fit of madness at the end of which he chooses to follow the paths of Glory in a truly Herculean spirit (XII, 3). By 'mere chance' he happens to pursue the very road taken by Sophia, and the next chapter confronts him with yet another cross-roads where he meets a lame fellow in rags who has found Sophia's pocket-book. This makes up Tom's mind for him: he grabs occasion by the forelock and with passionate intensity he proceeds to pursue Sophia and Sophia alone.

But at this point the narrative insists on slowness: Tom wants to push on as quickly as possible to the place where the book was found, but the lameness of his guide compels him to moderate his pace to one mile an hour, the distance being more than three miles. Afterwards, however, his speed is such that Partridge must beg him 'a little to slacken his pace' (XII, 5). 'Our heroe' forgoes food and sleep and carries on through darkness and rainy weather 'with the utmost eagerness' (XII, 8), and in the end he rides post. During all this time Fortune favours him with as much grace as before she had vented her malice on his unfortunate person; indeed, the very chapter-heading proclaims that Fortune seems in a better mood with Jones. This benignant aspect carries over into the last third when Tom, as soon as he has arrived in London, sets out 'in pursuit of Sophia'. He succeeds in finding the place he is looking for, 'whether it was that Fortune relented, or whether it was no longer in her power to disappoint him'. After he has begun his eager pursuit of Sophia the absolute power of Fortune, so it would seem, has become abrogated. The introduction of reflections on state lotteries at this point (XIII, 2) shows how much the issue of Fortune occupies the author's mind, and one understands why on recalling one or two points in connection with emblematic representations of Fortune in relation to Virtue. As Rudolf Wittkower explains in an essay on 'Chance, Time, and Virtue'[27] man grasping Occasio-Fortuna by the forelock may be interpreted as Virtue overcoming Chance, Virtue often being represented as Hercules. This theme may be found in literature as well; a play performed before Lucrezia Borgia in 1502 shows Hercules as the champion of Virtue in her battle with Vice. And if we are to judge from what happens to Sophia in Book XI, she certainly needs a champion. But the curious episode of Tom's limping progress still remains to be explained. It fits very neatly into the context I have suggested so far, when seen as an emblematic representation, in a manner appropriate to mock epic, of the proverb quoted by Partridge on first meeting Tom Jones: *festina lente* (VIII,4). The posture that Shaftesbury recommends for Virtue (in a representation of the Choice of Hercules) is one foot planted on the ground and the other lifted on a piece of rock to suggest respectively firmness of purpose and aspiration. This is a posture also associated with emblematic representations of *festina lente*,[28] the lifted foot often being shown as winged to indicate speed. Geoffrey Whitney uses a juxtaposition of crab and butterfly to convey the same point in an emblem of this kind,[29] and I take it, therefore, that the picture of Tom 'hurrying slowly' in the company of a lame man is Fielding's narrative version of this emblem, which exhorts us to combine speed with patience, daring with prudence. It is the role of Fortune to admonish to speed, while Wisdom imposes firmness, and whoever reconciles the two is bound to succeed. Fortune must favour men guided by Virtue, as we learn from one of George Wither's emblems[30] or from one of Erasmus' *adagia* incorporating a quotation from Cicero: *Duce virtute comite Fortuna*.[31] To be led by Virtue and accompanied by Fortune is indeed an enviable position, and it is pleasant to see Tom Jones enjoying it as he hurries towards the 'Elysian fields' of London with its ample quota of Cerberus-like porters guarding the entrance to his Sophia. The attempted rape of Sophia in this underworld is yet another narrative link with the myth of Hercules.

Fielding's allusion to the emblematic representation of *festina lente* serves very neatly to link Tom Jones with the other mythical character whom he resembles, Adonis. As Edgar Wind informs us,[32] the extremely popular Renaissance story of the chastising of Adonis (unchaste love), the *Hypnerotomachia Poliphili*,[33] contained more than eighty woodcuts on the theme of *festina lente*. Tom is described as an Adonis by Fielding himself (IX, 5) and by Lady Bellaston (XV, 7), and it is just after Partridge has quoted the proverb to Tom (VIII, 4) that the very first comparison occurs. The myth of Adonis, then, combines with that of Hercules to provide the penumbra of associations that Fielding desired. It may be my ignorance of the former that makes me load the scales in favour of Hercules, but the myth of Hercules seems to me to provide the basic groundwork for Fielding's story. Before I consider some further uses of this myth, however, I would like to compare Fielding's version of the Choice with Hogarth's as presented in his print of *The Lottery*.[34]

Hogarth's drawing is dominated by two gigantic wheels, one governed by Fortune and the other by Wantonness. Two wheels are required since the one draws a number and the other a paper indicating whether it is a blank or a prize. On the bottom left is an unfortunate wretch who has drawn a blank, while Good Luck forms the central figure in a tableau on the right. Good Luck is shown as a Hercules importuned by a half naked personification of Pleasure on the one hand and, on the other, by Fame who persuades him to raise fallen Virtue. This overall composition recalls the central section of *Tom Jones*, where the beginning of Tom's peregrinations is heralded by his singular misfortune in losing his banknotes, just as his retrieval of Sophia's note marks their end in Book XII. Hogarth's Herculean Good Luck is placed between Pleasure and Virtue—the latter in a fallen position on the ground—and the figure of Glory is encouraging him to raise sinking Virtue. Fielding's narrative equivalents are located in Books XI–XII, where Sophia Western sustains her fall from her horse in XI, 2 and where the hero, in the opening chapters of Book XII, briskly opts for an active life devoted to the pursuit of Glory. Partridge does very nicely as Fielding's version of Folly (drawn by Hogarth in a cap and bells).

I do not want to press this parallel between Fielding and Hogarth too far; for one thing, Hogarth's print is far from unique in combining the concept of Fortune with the Choice of Hercules. Thus the title-page of George Wither's *Emblemes* (1635) shows Fortune with her sail at the centre where the choice is being made, together with a cauldron from which lots are being drawn. That this drawing is based on the Pythagorean Y may not be immediately apparent, but the composition is nevertheless sufficiently clear once it is realised that the bottom part represents childhood. The letter Y was taken to represent the Herculean choice by virtue of its shape, the first, undivided part symbolising the period of childhood prior to the moment of choice. The arms of the letter may be seen in the two towering hills, one embodying the open road to Pleasure and perdition, the other the arduous path to Virtue and eternal life.[35] One sees how the children (dressed like adults) emerge from the subterranean fountain to wander up the path of life to the place where the choice has to be made.

Wither's emblematic title-page underlines the Christian import of the choice, an import usually documented by referring to *Matthew* 7:13–14 on the choice between the two gates and the two roads. However, *Proverbs* 16 will be found to provide an interesting nexus of apt quotations. Thus verses 17 and 25 tell us that 'the highway of the upright is to depart from evil: he that keepeth his way preserveth his soul', while conversely 'there is a way that seemeth right unto a man, but the end thereof are the ways of death'. And as for Dame Fortune, the lot may be cast into the lap, 'but the whole disposing thereof is of the Lord' (verse 33), just as a man's heart may devise his way, 'but the Lord directeth his steps' (verse 9). The sweet voice of Wisdom is equally proverbial: 'The wise in heart shall be called prudent: and the sweetness of the lips increaseth learning.' 'Pleasant words are as an honey-comb, sweet to the soul, and health to the bones' (verses 21 and 24).

III

As we have seen, the entire mid-section (Books VII–XII) is influenced by the theme of the Choice of Hercules to a greater or lesser extent, beginning with the expulsion from Paradise Hall. But the material adduced so far cannot explain all the details, nor can it account for the overall thematic movement of the whole novel. A better perspective will be achieved by enlarging the scope to include other aspects of the Hercules myth. The literary tradition includes both comic and serious versions as we may learn from G. Karl Galinsky's recent book on *The Herakles Theme. The Adaptations of the Hero in*

Literature from Homer to the Twentieth Century (Oxford, 1972).
Fielding himself glances in the direction of Theocritus (*Idyll* 13)
when he says of Squire Western that he called for the missing Sophia
'in as hoarse a voice, as whileom did Hercules that of Hylas' (X, 8).
This is a poem which presents Hercules as the lover struck with
madness when he loses the handsome boy. The madness of Hercules
is given serious treatment in Greek tragedy, but in Aristophanes'
Frogs this well-known theme is parodied in a manner which distinctly resembles Tom Jones's two fits of madness (X, 6 and
XII, 3).

There is, then, ample literary precedent for Fielding's comic
version of the Heracles theme, and particularly for the scenes showing
the hero's deplorable drunkenness (towards the end of Book V)
and his obvious gluttony (IX, 5), a gluttony which prevents him from
even noticing the seductive behaviour of his female companion. The
situation is exactly parallel to the scene in Alexis' *Hesione* when the
girl whom Hercules rescues from a sea monster is similarly ignored
the moment that food is served:

> *When he saw two serving-men bring in the tray*
> *With motley side-dishes abounding gay,*
> *He had no eyes for me.*[36]

The comic Hercules was immoderately addicted to wine, food, and
women in that order,[37] and if one re-reads the chapters describing
Jones's drunkenness and his amorous encounter with Molly Seagrim,
one observes how strongly Fielding brings out the passionate nature
of his hero—his 'naturally violent animal spirits' (V, 9). His wrath
is as powerful as his mirth, but both are outdone by his amorous
propensities. Just as the drunken Hercules, in Propertius' version
(*Elegy* IV, 9), hears the giggle of girls from a shady shrine which
fires his sexual passion, Tom Jones is suddenly confronted by a
giggling Molly in a shady grove characterised as the 'temple of *Venus
Ferina*'. Galinsky calls Propertius' burlesque version 'the most
comical and witty treatment of Herakles in Latin literature',[38] but
there is little reason to suspect an immediate source, the figure of the
comic Hercules being far too popular with poets and playwrights
alike for any one source to be at all likely. Rubens, for example,
painted a picture of the drunken Hercules reproduced by Galinsky,
who also includes Dürer's satirical version of the Choice among his
plates. Then, too, various French operas from the second half of the

seventeenth century present Hercules as a Don Juan, and the same is true of Handel's *Admeto* (1727) and his oratorio *Hercules* (1744).[39]

Many readers will have felt that the comic episodes are more frequent and more uproarious in the first twelve books than in the last six. Tom Jones discovering Mr Square squatting behind the arras in Molly Seagrim's attic, or Tom Jones defending the honour of Molly Seagrim, or 'fondly overcome with female charm' in the inn at Upton—this is what springs to mind the moment we consider the novel in terms of its greatest comic scenes. The reason for the uneven distribution is not difficult to fathom: towards the end the hero must be shown to have acquired enough wisdom to be worthy of the lovely Sophia. And for this purpose, too, Fielding could draw on the myth of Hercules for his most telling effects, the myth in this case being that of the Gallic Hercules—a dignified humanist version closely connected with the theme of the Choice. This means that it was actually possible for Fielding to suggest the ambiguous moral character of his hero by drawing on various traditions associated with Hercules. He could use Xenophon's account of the Choice in the *Memorabilia* (2.1.21–34) as his point of departure, since it presents the young Hercules as a simple lad possessed of a high degree of good nature. This must be improved by a knowledge of virtue which will enable him to deliberate before acting. By adducing just enough of the legend of the drunken Hercules Fielding suggests how vulnerable his hero is to the persuasive powers of Pleasure, while later on he may invoke the dignified image of the Gallic Hercules to show the mental powers of his hero—powers enabling him to become that benefactor of his friends whom Xenophon praises in his fable of the Choice. It is entirely in keeping with this progress that the hero's exploits initially are largely on the level of physical action, while towards the end he must depend on the powers of his mind. No oaken stick, however trusty, can perform the labour of uniting Nancy Miller to the man whose child she carries; for this particular purpose Tom Jones calls upon, and commands, all the powers of rhetoric associated with the Gallic Hercules.

The Gallic Hercules is the male embodiment of wisdom and especially of the irresistible powers of eloquence. Renaissance emblems show this power by letting the words issuing out of the mouth of Hercules, form a golden chain which keeps the audience captive in the most literal manner.[40] It was widely held that the French kings were descended from this prototype of the good orator and the good ruler, and this belief was still sacrosanct in the early eighteenth century so that Nicolas Fréret was imprisoned in the Bastille for four months in 1715 for having cast doubts on it in a memorandum addressed to the Academy.[41]

It is in Book XIV, chs. 6–8 that Tom Jones makes his decisive appearance as the Gallic Hercules. His pursuit of Sophia, in complete disregard of physical discomforts, has proved his total commitment to his choice; the episode of Nancy Miller will prove his ability to assist fallen Virtue. On learning the facts of Nancy Miller's case, he at once promises to persuade young Nightingale to marry the girl he has betrayed, adding that 'I think the picture which I shall lay before him, will affect him.' And the 'picture' is a classical example of persuasive rhetoric at the end of which Nightingale exclaims: 'I wanted not your eloquence to rouse me.' The tempering of anger, greed, and the taste for pleasure is the role usually assigned to the Gallic Hercules, as explained for example by Ripa in his *Iconologia*, and the subduing of Avarice is the motif on a medal reproduced by Rudolf Wittkower in his essay on 'Chance, Time and Virtue.'[42] Avarice is, of course, the besetting sin of old Mr Nightingale, and in tackling him Tom Jones is undertaking 'an impossibility' as his friend points out (XIV, 7). In describing this episode Fielding uses the word 'labour' in a fairly obtrusive manner; thus he writes that 'Mr Jones was acting the most virtuous part imaginable in labouring to preserve his fellow-creatures from destruction' (XV, 1), and as Tom Jones presents himself to old Mr Nightingale, the latter twice exclaims that 'he would lose his labour' (XIV, 8). And so he does, since 'neither history nor fable have ever yet ventured to record an instance of anyone, who by force of argument and reason hath triumphed over habitual avarice' (XIV, 8). But the labour of securing Nancy Miller's marriage is fully achieved, and Tom's reward is to feel the highest form of pleasure on seeing a whole family raised from a state of misery—'more perhaps than worldly men often purchase to themselves by undergoing the most severe labour, and often by wading through the deepest iniquity' (XV, 8).

It was only to be expected that once our hero has entered into the 'Elysian fields' of London he should again be assaulted by the votaries of mere sensual Pleasure. And Pleasure (personified by Lady Bellaston) pursues him appropriately enough in the 'temple' presided over by 'the great high-priest of pleasure' during a fashionable masquerade (XIII, 7). Ronald Paulson has drawn attention to the many occasions on which Hogarth includes the various appurtenances of a masquerade as emblems of licentious pleasure, but similar iconographical details are typical of Renaissance versions of the Choice of Hercules. One sees this on leafing through the plates included by Erwin Panofsky in his *Hercules am Scheidewege* (1930). Masks are displayed next to the figure of Pleasure/Vice in Annibale Caracci's famous painting of the Choice (Plate 44), and in versions painted by Sebastiano Ricci, Jan Lyss, and Michel Corneille le Jeune (Plates 50–2). The masks suggest the falseness of the pleasures offered by Vice, and Lady Bellaston is drawn so as to resemble the figure of vicious Pleasure as seen for example in George Wither's emblem on the Choice (number I, 22). The emblem shows her as possessed of devilish attributes hidden from view partly because they are placed at the back, partly by the interposition of a mask held in front of the leering face. As Wither's poem puts it, 'her Face / Was but a painted *Vizard*, which did hide / The foul'st Deformity that ever was.' The identification is reinforced by so shaping the scene when Lady Bellaston enters Tom's bedroom (XV,7) as to repeat some of the features of the scene with Mrs Waters in the inn at Upton. Tom is again compared to Adonis ('you might at this instant sit for the picture of Adonis'), and the attack is again mounted in silence by means of looks ('a look, in which the lady conveyed more soft ideas than it was possible to express with her tongue'). But as far as Tom Jones is concerned the illicit relationship entails no pleasure, and it is surely this point that Fielding is concerned to make. He wanted to show how firmly the hero resists the combined allure of wealth, high social rank, and pleasure, and he could not have foreseen that later generations would take such a serious view of the sexual relationship that this would overshadow the stout refusal to be caught in the snares of Pleasure. Circumstances conspire against Tom Jones to compel him against his will to engage in an affair for which he has no relish. (This richly comic situation prevents Tom Jones from sharing the fate of Joseph Andrews vis-à-vis Lady Booby.) The fact that Tom Jones, despite the intensity with which he pursues his Sophia, goes out of his way to be a true benefactor of his friends and acquaintances, proves his moral mettle. The role played by rhetoric in this part of the novel is underscored when Lady Bellaston persuades Lord Fellamar to undertake the rape of Sophia. As the chapter-heading explains, 'she applies her Eloquence to an ill Purpose' (XV,4). She acts, to use Fielding's words, 'like a true orator' and is only too successful. Her

words 'sunk deeper into his lordship than anything which Demos-
thenes or Cicero could have said on the occasion'. Her power to
corrupt is proved in the case of Lord Fellamar, just as Tom Jones's
persuasion of young Nightingale proves his ability to advance the
cause of Virtue.

It is sufficiently plain that Tom Jones is no paragon of sexual
virtue even in the third part, but we must not permit the immorality
of his affair with Lady Bellaston to obscure the features that identify
him as the Hercules who has made his choice. And with Sophia
herself as the pledge of his constancy (as the hero craftily argues in
the penultimate chapter) the reader is willing to believe that he will
persist. One may perhaps feel that Fielding has loaded the scales too
heavily in favour of the lovely Sophia so that the choice was only too
easy, if not downright tempting. Who would not be pleased to make a
similar choice if lucky enough to be presented with it? The answer
must be that Tom Jones obtains his Sophia only after he has proved
his ability to act like the Gallic Hercules. He has learnt to add the
powers of his mind to his instinctive good nature, progressing from a
comic Hercules addicted to the life of the senses to the dignified
Hercules who may rightly be the consort of the female personification
of wisdom.

But if Sophia Western serves as a virtually irresistible image of
perfection, must not Fielding be said to have violated the principle
that characters of angelic goodness or diabolical depravity must be
avoided? Sophia's perfection, however, is sufficiently modified by the
comic mode to be fully acceptable; she has as it were two faces in
the manner attributed by Shaftesbury to the 'philosophical HERO' of
the dramatic dialogues of Antiquity. As he explains in his *Advice to
an Author*, this hero

> was in himself *a perfect Character*: yet, in some respects, so
> veil'd, and in a Cloud, that to the unattentive Surveyor he seem'd
> often to be very different from what he really was: and this
> chiefly by reason of a certain exquisite and refin'd Raillery
> which belong'd to his Manner, and by virtue of which he cou'd
> treat the highest Subjects, and those of the commonest Capacity
> both together, and render 'em explanatory of each other.

In this manner the '*heroick* and *the simple, the tragick,* and *the comick
Vein*' were fused, yet in such a fashion that despite the 'Mysteriousness
of the principal Character, the *Under-parts* or *second Characters*

shew'd human Nature more distinctly, and to the Life.' This sort of writing, therefore, constitutes a pocket-mirror in which we may see two faces: the 'commanding Genius' and 'that rude, undisciplin'd and head-strong Creature, whom we our-selves in our natural Capacity most exactly resembled'.[43]

Fielding fully exploits the ambiguity inherent in this joco-serious approach, and Sophia, too, is exposed to that 'exquisite and refin'd Raillery' which permitted him to treat the highest subjects together with the most common ones so that they illuminate each other. But in the case of Fielding's use of various aspects of the Hercules myth the comic mode has so obscured the pattern which it modifies that it has been virtually ignored. Yet it is by playing the two against each other that we perceive what Shaftesbury calls the two faces: the myth embodying the abstract concepts of Beauty, Wisdom, and Virtue in all their dignity, and the actual events that are their manifestation in the world we all know. If we are blind to the former, the latter will lose much of their resonance.

The vision of ideal beauty afforded by the lovely Sophia has its formal counterpart in the highly ordered structure of the work. Fielding may have been inspired by the Earl of Shaftesbury to achieve this juxtaposition of the beauty of ordered structure with the beauty of moral harmony in the world within, but the presence in his library of several editions of Plato indicates an interest in the Platonic tradition and so does his copy of Ralph Cudworth's *True intellectual System of the Universe* (1678).[44] It is nevertheless convenient to draw on Shaftesbury for comments explaining this interesting collaboration between form and content, or external and internal harmony. The platonic vision of ideal beauty may be glimpsed in a character such as Sophia or in the formal organisation of the work itself, the two being interdependent. Shaftesbury links the two in the following passage taken from his *Advice to an Author*:

> HOWEVER difficult or desperate it may appear in any Artist to endeavour to bring *Perfection* into his Work; if he has not at least the *Idea* of PERFECTION to give him Aim, he will be found very defective and mean in his Performance. Tho his Intention be to please the World, he must nevertheless be, in a manner, *above it*; and fix his Eye upon that consummate *Grace*, that Beauty of *Nature*, and that *Perfection* of Numbers, which the rest of Mankind, feeling only by the Effect . . . suppose to be

a kind of *Charm,* or *Inchantment,* of which the Artist himself can give no account.[45]

It is impossible to tell whether Shaftesbury here uses his key phrases ('consummate *Grace*', 'Beauty of *Nature*' and *Perfection* of Numbers') to refer to external or internal harmony, to structural organisation or to character portrayal, but this is exactly the point: the two cannot be kept separate. It seems both possible and probable that Fielding similarly related his theme of moral harmony to the structural harmony imposed upon the text by various kinds of symmetrical arrangements. The undoubted presence of these structural features lends strong support to an interpretation along the lines suggested here: behind all the comedy we should perceive the 'highest Subjects' and the most 'consummate *Grace*' to use Shaftesbury's phrases, and it is particularly important to do this as we consider Tom Jones himself in his role as a richly comic eighteenth-century Hercules. We should do him an injustice if we fail to perceive how he first enacts the famous Choice and then achieves the higher level represented by the Gallic Hercules. Fielding must have invented the Nancy Miller/Nightingale subplot primarily to enable his hero to engage in actions that may underline his new role; we already know that he possesses an instinctive good nature, but we need to discover that he is perfectly capable of other than merely physical exploits. Since the sweetness of rational discourse is the attribute given to Sophia in her role as Virtue, Tom Jones becomes a proper mate for her when he, too, is seen to possess it.

IV

Readers who find it difficult to accept this favourable reading of Tom Jones's character will find a strong ally in Dr Johnson, whose reaction to the story was entirely predictable. He condemned it because it shows a morally ambiguous hero (as explained in *Rambler* 4), and because it links the idea of lasting happiness with the idea of conscious choice. That Samuel Johnson read *Tom Jones* as a story based on the theme of choice may, I think, be inferred from the pages of *Rasselas*. Johnson rejects out of hand the notion that choices can be made so as to ensure a lasting state of happiness; only a God can survey the whole of existence so that a valid choice can be made, and only a God can ensure the duration of the state ultimately chosen. Johnson's annoyance with Fielding's analysis of human existence must have been just as great as Fielding's with Richardson's. *Rasselas* is an analysis and a refutation of all pleasing visions of lasting happiness, and it is distinctly interesting that the narrative should pursue a tripartite, symmetrical structure consisting of three groups of sixteen chapters and a conclusion.[46] Could Johnson have arranged his material in this manner to permit the structural similarity to *Tom Jones* to underline the thematic antithesis? This seems a possibility on observing how the later writer almost parodies the thematic movement through the three parts of *Tom Jones*. While Tom Jones is expelled from a Paradise Hall whose owner is an eighteenth-century *imago Dei*, in Johnson's story the hero laboriously makes his escape from a valley which at first seems a perfect paradise of pleasure. At the point of exodus (as the first third moves into the second) each hero is intent on choosing his future way of life, but *Rasselas* contains no major confrontation scene issuing in a final choice—only a sequence of choices paraded in front of readers and travellers alike, each of which is eventually rejected as false. Johnson is intent on letting his travellers experience what has been called a pattern of comic disillusion,[47] and the choices examined in the mid-section (chapters 17–32) constitute closed systems of unhappiness of the kind associated with Pope's couplet rhetoric.[48] The same evils prevail whether a man's state be private or public, high or low, and grief and joy are equally transient whatever the circumstances under which one lives. In the last third the rescue of the mad astronomer may serve as Johnson's counterpoint to Tom Jones's rescue of Nancy Miller, the power of rhetoric, or persuasion, being replaced by normal human fellowship. The astronomer is saved quite simply by being introduced to human society at its best; good conversation plus the diversions of every-day life restore his sanity. The undramatic character of this episode is remarkable; in comparison Tom Jones's persuasion of his friend seems virtually melodramatic.

The comment that Johnson's *Rasselas* offers on Fielding's vision of life is conveyed as much structurally as through the turn of the narrative, and nowhere more so than in the last chapter, the 'conclusion, in which nothing is concluded'. This is a chapter which presents a sequence of four choices, all of them different. These choices are so arranged and described that readers familiar with Renaissance thought (or with classical philosophy) will observe that they constitute a complete circle or quaternion in the manner of the four elements and the four qualities.[49] This is one reason why the conclusion is inconclusive: through these four choices it presents a complete 'wheel of life'.

Pekuah's choice comes first. She is 'weary of expectation and disgust' and 'would gladly be fixed in some unvariable state'. And the state she prefers is one of complete seclusion from the world. The last choice—that of Imlac and the astronomer—represents the exact opposite: a willing acceptance of a state of flux. The two are 'contented to be driven along the stream of life without directing their course to any particular place'. Two choices are entailed in each case: one of a state of mind, another of environment. Despite the complete contrast with regard to environment (Pekuah seeing herself as totally apart from the world or out of it, Imlac and the astronomer being completely immersed), the two states have one element in common: the absence of desire. Both display *stasis* of mind.

In between these extremes (the first choice and the last) fall the choices of the brother and sister, both of whom are said to *desire*: 'She desired first . . . ' and 'The prince desired . . . ' Both are prompted by desire to act, rejecting the state of mental passivity, the difference between them being one of chosen environment. She chooses a private sphere ('a college of learned women'), he one which is completely public. His kingdom, however, is to be a small one so that he himself as head of state may 'administer justice in his own person'. What they have in common is commitment to an active life.

The pattern traditionally attributed to the four elements and the four qualities is exactly analogous. Although the elements of earth and fire are completely contrary in that the one is hot and the other cold, they share the quality of dryness, and if one presents the sequence in tabular form, one perceives that a link is always provided between each element and the next, the last connecting with the first so that the circle is closed:

earth	water	air	fire
dry & cold	cold & moist	moist & hot	hot & dry

This is why Augustine and Milton can say that the 'quaternions' of the elements and of the seasons 'run / Perpetual circle'.[50]

The four choices listed in the last chapter of *Rasselas* are similarly connected by links into an all-encompassing circle or cycle. Two of the qualities attributed to the elements were supposed to be active (hot and cold), the other two passive, and Johnson, too, posits two active and two passive qualities or aspects. The mental attitude to life may be active or passive, just as one's physical environment may be private or public. One may be out of the stream of life (apart) or immersed in it, as indicated in the following table:

Pekuah:	Nekayah:	Rasselas:	Imlac/ astronomer:
passive & apart	apart & active	active & immersed	immersed & passive

The sequence of choices begins with double *stasis* or complete withdrawal from life, mentally as well as physically; the second choice carries on the theme of retirement from the public sphere, but posits intense mental activity ('to learn all sciences' and to 'divide her time between the acquisition and communication of wisdom'). The prince, however, boldly commits himself to an active life in a public sphere, and this progression reaches its climax with total immersion in the flux of life by Imlac and the astronomer. But since they have no desire to direct 'their course to any particular port', they achieve the mental *stasis* characteristic of Pekuah's choice, so that in this respect the last choice connects with the first, and the circle is closed.

These four choices are aligned with the textual division into three parts, Pekuah's choice connecting with the Happy Valley, Nekayah's and Rasselas's with the mid-section, and that of Imlac and the astronomer with the events of the last third.

The first choice recalls the Happy Valley because of its complete seclusion, and because life in the valley imposes complete quiescence (on the basis of the false assumption that all desires are satisfied). But the *stasis* envisaged by Pekuah is voluntary, not imposed, and it stipulates a *rejection* of the quest for pleasure, and not a total commitment to it. Just as Pekuah's choice constitutes a comment on, and rejection of, the first third of Johnson's story, the last choice mirrors the experience of the last third when the travellers are at the mercy of all the hazards of life. The flux, which they experience very much against their will, is willingly embraced by Imlac and the astronomer, while they reject the state of mental flux (the eternal transition from expectation to disgust and back again to expectation). They are content to be carried along by the stream of life. The prince and the princess, too, similarly modify their choices so as to incorporate their experiences of life in the mid-section, where the prince investigates the public sphere and the princess the private.

All this shows how carefully Samuel Johnson plotted the structure of his tale, and how logically thought out his conclusion is. Although the conclusion has always been felt as open-ended, it is now possible to see somewhat more clearly how its inconclusiveness functions. Each traveller has learnt an important lesson enabling him or her so to modify his choice as to avoid the more obvious hazards and perversions. Pekuah's choice avoids the hedonism of the Happy Valley and the see-saw pattern of the hermit, whose life is a never-ending cycle of ascetic solitude and convivial pleasures. The princess on her part tempers her fondness for learning by company, thus avoiding the fate of the astronomer and also the evils that accompany the restriction to mere family life. The prince modifies the size of his kingdom and the scope of his public activities, while Imlac and the astronomer have learnt that we cannot hope to direct our course to a chosen port; life plays with us and we must be content to accept life on these terms.

The four choices, then, represent ideal states modified by experience, but they also represent all possible choices. Between them they cover all the combinations of mentally and physically active or passive states. However, the most important lesson taught by experience is that none of these wishes can be obtained.

Never has a refutation been more complete. Not only does this story about a 'choice of life' conclude by presenting a complete cycle of choices, but no sooner has the cycle been presented than it is withdrawn. 'Of these wishes that they had formed they well knew that none could be obtained. They deliberated a while what was to be done, and resolved, when the inundation should cease, to return to Abissinia.'

Although one may relish Johnson's psychological realism, it is difficult not to prefer Fielding's vision of life. If the choice between Fielding and Johnson is a test of the reader's sense of moral values, I suspect that he who chooses Fielding does so because he believes in the higher beauty represented by Sophia. It is his sincere love of this higher beauty which guarantees the hero's faithful adherence to the path of virtue, and whoever separates virtue from pleasure in this life does so because the humanist version of the Choice of Hercules has ceased to carry conviction. Fielding seems to me to have grasped the true inwardness of this choice and to have succeeded

4. Hercules between Vice and Virtue. From George Wither, *A Collection of Emblemes* (London, 1635). The plates are taken from Gabriel Rollenhagen's *Nucleus Emblematum*, 1611–13. *(Bodleian Library.)*

Eloquentia fortitudine præstantior.

EMBLEMA CLXXX.

5. The Gallic Hercules. From Andreas Alciatus, *Emblematum libellus* (1535), p. 490. *(Bodleian Library.)*

6. The Gallic Hercules.
From Vincenzo Cartari, *Le imagini degli dei degli antichi* (Padua, 1608),
p. 314 (actual size.)
(The Shakespeare Institute, University of Birmingham.)

7. Emblematic title-page showing a Christianised version of the Choice.
From George Wither, *A Collection of Emblemes* (London, 1635).
(Bodleian Library.)

in conveying it to his readers through a mode of writing indebted to the joco-serious tradition so popular in the Renaissance. His 'exquisite and refin'd Raillery', to use Shaftesbury's phrase, permitted a presentation of absolute beauty which strikes one the more strongly because it must perforce be oblique.

6

Mistaken conduct and proper 'feeling': A study of Jane Austen's Pride and Prejudice

GRETE EK

Seldom, very seldom, does complete truth belong to any human disclosure; seldom can it happen that something is not a little disguised, or a little mistaken; but where, as in this case, though the conduct is mistaken, the feelings are not, it may not be very material.

Jane Austen, *Emma* (Ch. XIII)

In a recent study of Jane Austen's novels, *Pride and Prejudice* is described as 'the greatest example of the novel of antitheses'.[1] With few exceptions, critics seem to favour the general concept that the protagonists represent largely opposing attitudes that need to be modified and then finally reconciled within the framework of the comic resolution. Thus Elizabeth is at first proudly independent and contemptuous of convention, whereas Darcy is an equally proud exponent of social stratification. Before being united in mutual affection and mutual allegiance to social and ethical norms, the initial, basic assumptions of both must be transcended and 'improved'.[2]

The reading submitted here presents a different interpretation of the relationship between conflict and resolution. It is possible to argue that the initial conflict is in itself ironic: the very situations and the very response which create antagonism also reveal a basic affinity between hero and heroine. The resolution, then, eventually terminates a process of clarification rather than one of substantial change, and serves to affirm attitudes that are at all times the common property of Darcy and Elizabeth. The 'contrived' conflict necessarily conceals attraction between them, which the reader is nonetheless allowed to suspect while enjoying the inevitable movement towards a climax of misunderstanding. Beneath the antithetical framework we may recognise a substructure based on a gradual and consistent disclosure of facts that invariably contradict the dramatic illusion in the novel's first half.[3]

This is not to say that Jane Austen has found a new way of proclaiming 'whatever IS, is right', or that the conflict is more or less literally a storm in a teacup. Clearly her conception of 'reality' informs the artistic medium—as Lionel Trilling observes when contending that her irony 'is only secondarily a matter of tone. Primarily it is a method of comprehension. It perceives the world through an awareness of its contradictions, paradoxes, and anomalies.'[4] A conflict based on contrasts that are not what they seem is quite proper in a world that makes it possible—nay, highly probable—that people should be led to misunderstand one another. In *Pride and Prejudice* not only immature conduct on the part of the protagonists but also fictional 'alliances' encouraged by the social structure reinforce that lack of knowledge about the self and about others which creates disorder. The discovery of true partnership—which to my mind remains the novel's central issue—accompanies the removal of misconceptions. Darcy and Elizabeth dramatise the issue, seconded by a number of minor characters whose own interrelationships and whose interaction with hero and heroine serve to clarify events on centre stage.

The novel may conveniently be called a mystery story, where the reader accompanies an engaging heroine in her search for the truth about a man she at first comes to despise, and then finally learns to love. It so happens that she discovers herself in the process. The first half is designed so as to baffle and mislead Elizabeth—and to some extent the reader—while at the same time providing adequate preparation for a dénouement gradually effected after the proposal scene. Darcy's conduct must be such as to make Elizabeth's increasing antagonism possible and acceptable and yet anticipate the eventual revelation of his true character. The presentation of Elizabeth caters to even more diverse requirements: she must invite allegiance so that we may share in the suspense, display limitations that will help us to partake of the author's superior understanding, *and* reveal characteristics that make her final union with Darcy highly plausible. What we need to recognise, then, is the extent to which Jane Austen balances the construction of a credible conflict with a concomitant affirmation of certain underlying 'truths' that can only be fully developed and clarified in the second half of the novel. Our awareness of these 'truths' will not only prepare us for the resolution, but increase our sense of dramatic irony, in so far as our knowledge is constantly superior to that of the protagonists. As I have suggested, 'knowledge' in *Pride and Prejudice* is practically synonymous with knowledge of *character*, as character defines itself both in a social and in a more purely personal context.

At the Meryton Assembly, Darcy's refusal to play 'eligible' produces a delightfully absurd response. The norm by which his conduct is judged is set by that paragon of folly, Mrs Bennet, and presumably by a great number of match-making parents and marriageable daughters with an equal claim to 'understanding' and 'judgment'. Dorothy van Ghent observes that Jane Austen turns the novel's opening paragraph inside-out by showing that it is an unmarried woman who is in want of a wealthy husband. Thus the Mrs Bennets are acting in accordance with the realities of an acquisitive society, 'febrile with social and economic rivalry'.[5] Their behaviour is nonetheless silly enough to provide Mr Bennet with constant entertainment, and is activated by a notion of 'prudence' that bears faint relation to the cardinal virtue. Direct authorial comment, informing us that Mrs Bennet 'was a woman of mean understanding, little information, and uncertain temper' (p. 5)[6] combines with ironic exposure in the initial domestic scenes at Longbourn to define both a certain type of woman and her 'code', which invariably conditions our reactions to events in the Assembly room:

> . . . Mr. Darcy soon drew the attention of the room by his fine, tall person, handsome features, noble mien; and the report which was in general circulation within five minutes after his entrance, of his having ten thousand a year. The gentlemen pronounced him to be a fine figure of a man, the ladies declared he was much handsomer than Mr. Bingley, and he was looked at with great admiration for about half the evening, till his manners gave a disgust which turned the tide of his popularity; for he was discovered to be proud, to be above his company, and above being pleased; and not all his large estate in Derbyshire could then save him from having a most forbidding, disagreeable countenance, and being unworthy to be compared with his friend (p. 10).

Darcy commits the sin of not dancing with young ladies he does not know. Public opinion is fickle indeed. 'His character was decided.

He was the proudest, most disagreeable man in the world, and every body hoped that he would never come there again' (p. 11). Mrs Bennet's later vacillation between abuse and approval of Mr Collins —according to his 'usefulness'—effectively parallels that of Meryton in general upon their first meeting with Darcy. At this point, readers might be inclined to make a favourite of Darcy, if only because he manages to mortify his public.

The author, however, balances this impression by including Elizabeth among the characters affronted by Darcy's pride. Whereas his behaviour seems perfectly justified when seen in relation to the expectations of female Meryton, it becomes offensive the minute it narrows down to a concrete act of rudeness directed against the heroine. The insult is repeatedly referred to in subsequent sequences: ' "She is tolerable; but not handsome enough to tempt *me*; and I am in no humour at present to give consequence to young ladies who are slighted by other men . . . " ' (p. 12). As it provides sufficient motivation for Elizabeth's hostility, the episode has considerable dramatic value. Furthermore, it pinpoints her weaknesses as well as his: if Darcy is haughty, Elizabeth certainly has her share of vanity and pride. Even so, any feeble attempt to pronounce moral judgement comes to nought. Elizabeth joyfully concedes to her own short-comings (' " . . . I could easily forgive *his* pride, if he had not morti-fied *mine*" '; p. 20), and Mary Bennet's homiletic speech on vanity and pride does not encourage further edifying reflections in the reader. It is obvious, also, that Elizabeth is too quick in condemning Darcy: in jumping to conclusions on the basis of appearances, she is acting in the best of Meryton traditions. Nor does this take us very far, as everyone, including Darcy, seems to partake of a general inclination to pronounce hasty judgement: 'Darcy . . . had seen a collection of people in whom there was little beauty and no fashion, for none of whom he had felt the smallest interest, and from none received either attention or pleasure' (p. 16). On the surface, then, moral dis-tinctions are blurred, but the conduct of hero and heroine respectively establishes an effective—if morally neutral—contrast between rigidity on the one hand, and resentment of that quality on the other.

As the response of both is largely determined by environmental incompatibility, this contrast is clearly deceptive. Elizabeth is part of a setting unacceptable to Darcy, and for one moment she has become the object of his scorn, unjustly, but understandably so. By the same token, Darcy's haughtiness is reinforced by his association with Mrs

Hurst and Miss Bingley, of whom Elizabeth—very wisely and perceptively—cannot 'approve'. The reader, on the other hand, is invited to join with the author in her assessment of the reality behind the façade: 'In understanding Darcy was the superior', says the reliable commentator in one of her rare direct appearances. 'Bingley was by no means deficient, but Darcy was clever. He was at the same time haughty, reserved, and fastidious, and his manners, though well bred, were not inviting' (p. 16). At the earliest possible stage Jane Austen states outright that her hero's conduct leaves something to be desired, yet he is superior in *understanding*—a compliment of the highest order, given to those whose basic principles are above reproach. Mrs Hurst and Miss Bingley are 'proud and conceited', for no even faintly acceptable reason, and their pride, though related to the quality associated with Darcy, is unaccompanied by any positive virtue. The factual information conveyed is naturally far less significant than the author's reasoning, implying above all that we need to distinguish between characters who display a superficial similarity of manner, and that conduct in a narrow sense is not necessarily an adequate expression of the mind.[7]

The splendid irony of the initial 'conflict' is brought out only when seen in a larger context: the hero and the heroine have in fact— quite plausibly—fallen out over a social code which they both despise. Elizabeth is no more looking for a matrimonial 'prize' than Darcy is willing to be one. Various minor episodes serve to illustrate this affinity. While Elizabeth cannot imitate her father's abuse of Mrs Bennet, she obviously shares his keen sense of the ridiculous and futile in matrimonial machinations. She can only witness the addresses of Mr Collins with numb incredulity—and then emphatically reject both his 'reasoning' and that of her mother. Similarly, Darcy sees fit to rebuff the amorous Miss Bingley: ' "Undoubtedly . . . there is meanness in *all* the arts which ladies sometimes condescend to employ for captivation. Whatever bears affinity to cunning is despicable" ' (p. 40). If there is 'individualism' in *Pride and Prejudice,* Darcy and Elizabeth have an equal share in it, in that they are both defending themselves against unions that are based on an absurdly narrow definition of 'prudence', and that disregard 'essentials'.[8] The juxtaposition of Elizabeth and Charlotte, both single women of no fortune and little consequence, both wooed by a comic monster who offers security, establishes a strong contrast between idealism and its antithesis—which is not to say that Charlotte is condemned. Her position is pitiful in that she surrenders to a one-dimensional existence. It is easy to see this as the darkest aspect of the novel, and perhaps the most troubling, because Charlotte's options are so severely limited. The celebration of integrity clashes somewhat uncomfortably with the obvious need for security, and Elizabeth is conveniently saved from ever having to bear the consequences of her idealism. We must concede that the admirable principles of Elizabeth and Darcy both may not be uniformly applicable within a world 'haunted' by the 'specter of the shabby-genteel spinster'.[9]

It is the most wonderful paradox that the ultimate proclamation of independence comes through Elizabeth's refusal of Darcy himself —a Darcy who clearly resents having been 'captivated'. At that moment, *her* open disregard of social and pecuniary advantage confronts *his* unpleasant but understandable assumption that any woman will accept a man of his consequence. It seems to me indisputable that her idealism and his arrogant defensiveness spring from the same contempt for that universally acknowledged truth.

The question of 'prudent' marriages relates closely to that of social pride, which more than any other element serves to maintain a sense of contrast between the main characters. No one would deny that Darcy betrays a strong feeling of social superiority, or that Elizabeth resents his attitude. The problem is complex, and the presentation deliberately confusing. Thus the one episode which supposedly testifies to a wholly inexcusable awareness of social distinctions on his part, namely his interference to prevent Bingley from marrying Jane, is shown to have far more diverse origins than Elizabeth is at first capable of comprehending. Similarly, Wickham's denunciation of Darcy—which involves accusations of excessive pride—proves to be founded on pure fiction. In both instances, the reader may be inclined to withhold judgement from the beginning, as we receive information second-hand, and our ability to perceive Elizabeth's limitations may prevent us from putting infinite trust in her subsequent interpretations. Such neutrality, however, is counteracted by certain exchanges with the Bingleys that Elizabeth does not witness as well as by momentary glimpses of Darcy's mind: in spirit these revelations seem to correspond with Elizabeth's evaluation of him. He maintains that Jane's and Elizabeth's uncles in Cheapside 'must very materially lessen their chance of marrying men of any consideration in the world' (p. 37), and is even afraid that his conduct may have raised false hopes in Elizabeth:

He wisely resolved to be particularly careful that no sign of admiration should *now* escape him, nothing that could elevate her with the hope of influencing his felicity; sensible that if such an idea had been suggested, his behaviour during the last day must have material weight in confirming or crushing it. Steady to his purpose, he scarcely spoke ten words to her through the whole of Saturday, and though they were at one time left by themselves for half an hour, he adhered most conscientiously to his book, and would not even look at her (p. 60).

His 'wisdom' is at best a partial virtue: as has been shown by Kenneth Moler in particular, Darcy is certainly related to the class-conscious heroes of Richardson and Fanny Burney.[10]

Whereas the conflict is perfectly plausible, it is not necessarily founded on factual disagreement. Elizabeth and Darcy both provide correctives to a superficial assessment of their attitudes. Thus it would be wrong to conceive of a Darcy solidly entrenched behind aristocratic principles: his association with the Bingleys, who have acquired their money 'in trade', in itself defeats such a supposition. This relationship is indeed proper in a society which always allowed a certain amount of interchange between classes. Nor do we have adequate reason to see Elizabeth as an advocate of 'instinct' and 'feeling', as opposed to Darcy's consideration for his social place. It will be remembered that Elizabeth recognises Darcy's right to be proud —a significant remark, in itself untouched by irony, which is 'lost' in the facetious context in which it occurs. Her reactions to his first proposal also testify to her own acceptance of his social superiority: '. . . she could not be insensible to the compliment of such a man's affection, and though her intentions did not vary for an instant, she was at first sorry for the pain he was to receive . . .' (p. 189). While Darcy's pride is somewhat excessive, it is fairly clear that class consciousness as such carries no negative connotation, and we may assume, with Dr Chapman, that a seemingly impassable gulf 'yawned between [Fitzwilliam Darcy] and Mrs Bennet's daughter.'[11] Darcy's own acknowledgement of Elizabeth's and Jane's moral superiority suggests a possible bridging of the gulf: the question of good breeding, predominantly moral in its conception, helps to define alliances that cut across traditional class barriers.

The display of ill breeding by characters whom the social structure aligns with hero and heroine respectively furthers the movement

towards a climax of antagonism; yet the response of Darcy and
Elizabeth offers supreme proof of their affinity. The vulgarity of
Elizabeth's connections at first cements Darcy's feeling of superiority,
and Elizabeth is affronted and humiliated because she must remain
loyal to a family whose follies never cease to amaze her. Paradoxically,
her awareness of his attitude towards indecorous behaviour—an
attitude which she obviously shares—cannot but increase her hostility. When Mrs Bennet visits Netherfield during Jane's illness,
her conduct shocks everyone, including the tolerant Bingley. As is
the case at the Netherfield ball later on, Darcy does no more than
faintly echo Elizabeth's own reactions: 'Darcy only smiled; and the
general pause which ensued made Elizabeth tremble lest her mother
should be exposing herself again' (p. 45). The author emphasises the
similarity of situation and psychological response by rendering
Elizabeth's mortification at the ball in the very same terms: 'It vexed
her to see [Mr Collins] expose himself to such a man' (p. 98). 'To
Elizabeth it appeared, that had her family made an agreement to
expose themselves as much as they could during the evening, it
would have been impossible for them to play their parts with more
spirit, or finer success' (pp. 101–2). What Elizabeth fears is *exposure*,
an unmasking of a reality that involves a violation of propriety,
sense, decorum. Her acute discomfort reveals her own concern for
such essential ethical norms. The absurdity of Mr Collins has always
been obvious to Elizabeth. Darcy is 'eyeing him with unrestrained
wonder' (p. 98). In *Emma*, a similar effect is obtained when Emma
and Mr Knightley display an all but identical attitude to the conduct
of Emma's relatives, preparing us for their ultimate union.[12]

By the same token, Elizabeth resents the offensive snobbery and
ill breeding displayed by Darcy's own acquaintances and relations,
and as her perceptions are far from unbiased, she identifies Darcy
with his environment. There is no reason for the reader to be unaware
of her mistake. Darcy is obviously amused by Miss Bingley's stupidity
and embarrassed by her incivility to Elizabeth: ' . . . Elizabeth had
been at Netherfield long enough. She attracted him more than he
liked—and Miss Bingley was uncivil to *her*, and more teazing than
usual to himself' (pp. 59–60). At Rosings we are explicitly informed
that he disapproves of Lady Catherine's behaviour: 'Mr. Darcy
looked a little ashamed of his aunt's ill breeding, and made no answer'
(p. 173). The author is in fact subjecting Darcy to a process of humiliation that parallels Elizabeth's own, the only difference being that

Elizabeth's mind is always at the centre of our attention, whereas Darcy's reactions are merely hinted at. In both instances, their mortification denotes the soundness of their principles.

We have seen that Darcy and Elizabeth both reject a certain type of social 'code', and that this naturally does not imply a questioning of contemporary values in general. They resent the *parody* of an established virtue, not the virtue itself. Furthermore, their common allegiance to propriety, along with an acceptance of a stratified—if partly flexible—social structure, makes neither protagonist particularly 'individualistic' vis-à-vis inherited norms. On the other hand, moral allegiance obviously crosses the barriers that initially seem to estrange them. A discovery of such allegiance enables the reader—and eventually the maturing protagonists—to see that just as they belong together, people like Lady Catherine, Mrs Bennet, Lydia, and Miss Bingley—to name a few—are of a piece: Lady Catherine and Mrs Bennet both try to pawn off their daughters, and Miss Bingley and Lydia pawn *themselves* off to the best of their ability. All four ladies betray a total lack of true breeding in their relationship with others. The 'exaggerated figures of fun' are not, then, outside the moral scheme because they are caricatures and frequently productive of pure comedy. The unhappy critic might perhaps be made to sound like Mary Bennet if he were to subject each individual to grave moral evaluation, but we may agree that they represent *attitudes* that are potentially subversive, and that Darcy and Elizabeth both detest.[13] It is possible to say, I believe, that the underlying conflict is not between Darcy and Elizabeth at all, but between sound—if faulty—characters on the one hand, and foolishness and indecency on the other. The moral education of the main characters involves no modification of their basic principles, but an awakening to awareness of their own place in the moral scheme. As the *conduct* of both is in some respects immature during the first phase of their relationship, their humiliation is a prerequisite to full awareness of how conduct should be guided by principles. Thus a discovery of moral allegiance involves a recognition of failings and virtues alike.

A total identification with Elizabeth would clearly blur these essential issues. If the author's main problem in *Emma* is one of maintaining sympathy for the heroine despite her 'almost crippling faults', we may surely say that Jane Austen faces the inverse problem in *Pride and Prejudice* when she needs to expose the heroine's weaknesses despite her almost totally disarming charm and delightful good sense.[14] A recognition of Elizabeth's limitations, however, takes us only part of the way. We might easily assume that some of her shortcomings testify to her being different from Darcy in 'essentials', which would not deduct from her attractiveness. We have to take still another look behind appearances. Elizabeth, it is generally agreed, is admirable enough to give reliable commentary at times, and we may frequently recognise the author's ironic voice in that of her heroine. If we go one step further, however, we see that Elizabeth is unwittingly judging herself. She is allowed the privilege of having very sound principles indeed, her conduct being sometimes at splendid variance with her own assumptions. A minor episode will bear this out. Jane has met Bingley, and is expressing her admiration for his sense, good humour, and happy manners: ' "He is also handsome," replied Elizabeth, "which a young man ought likewise to be, if he possibly can. His character is thereby complete" ' (p. 14). Elizabeth's irony is obviously directed against superficial assessments. In a later exchange with Charlotte she states her belief that partnership must be based on a thorough knowledge of the other person's *character*. There is little doubt that in this respect Elizabeth expresses the ideal norm of the novel, as contrasted with the maxims of Charlotte, and with the unhappy reality of the Bennet household, where 'the experience of three and twenty years had been insufficient to make his wife understand [Mr Bennet's] character' (p. 5). Significantly, Darcy subscribes to Elizabeth's own theory when he warns her not to judge him on the basis of report: ' " . . . I could wish, Miss Bennet, that you were not to sketch my character at the present moment, as there is reason to fear that the performance would reflect no credit on either" ' (p. 94). Anyone who is not blind to Elizabeth's faults will appreciate the complex irony of her remark to Jane, as it comments on her own reactions to Darcy at the Meryton Assembly, and later on backfires with a vengeance, mocking her stubborn persistence in a dislike for Darcy based on 'first impressions', as well as her infatuation with a man who recommends himself chiefly through a handsome exterior and agreeable manners.[15] May we not say that the conduct is mistaken, though the feelings are not?

To be sure, a battalion of admirable precepts will by no means fully account for Elizabeth's excellence, or make her future lover one whit more palatable than Edmund Bertram. Robert Louis Stevenson once remarked that when Elizabeth opened her mouth he wanted to go down on his knees; male infatuation aside, his statement pretty

nearly defines the general response to the heroine.[16] Darcy's performance is at all times less immediately appealing. It is therefore
important to appreciate those significant correctives to Elizabeth's
prejudice—and ours—that the author does provide. If Darcy were
in fact rigid and stationary—however morally sound the basis of his
posture—he would hardly inspire affection either in the reader or in
Elizabeth. But he does inspire affection, and our awareness of attraction between hero and heroine should be complemented by our
recognition of a shared system of values. Darcy's growing attachment to Elizabeth possibly 'redeems' him more completely than any
other element that may modify our initial conceptions and produce
true sympathy for him. Everyone will notice how Jane Austen
occasionally dips into his mind to tell us in no uncertain terms that
he is falling in love:

> . . . no sooner had he made it clear to himself and his friends
> that she had hardly a good feature in her face, than he began
> to find it was rendered uncommonly intelligent by the beautiful
> expression in her dark eyes. To this discovery succeeded some
> others equally mortifying. Though he had detected with a critical
> eye more than one failure of perfect symmetry in her form, he
> was forced to acknowledge her figure to be light and pleasing;
> and in spite of his asserting that her manners were not those of
> the fashionable world, he was caught by their easy playfulness
> (p. 23).

The examples might be multiplied: ' . . . Darcy had never been so
bewitched by any woman as he was by her' (p. 52). 'He began to
feel the danger of paying Elizabeth too much attention' (p. 58).
The disclosure of such delightful sentiment frequently occurs in a
troublesome context: as often as not it coincides with his fear of
attracting a socially inferior woman. Thus response to his reflections
on social inequality will necessarily condition the effect of his more
'tender' emotions. In the light of such privileged information, however—further provided by exchanges between Darcy and Miss
Bingley—incidents that naturally seem insignificant to Elizabeth
become evidence of Darcy's infatuation. When 'Mr. Darcy drew his
chair a little towards her' (p. 179), when he puts off his departure
from Rosings, when he is so often silent, we suspect reasons that
Elizabeth cannot divine. I cannot agree, then, that the effect of his
first proposal is one of 'overwhelming surprise'.[17] If we accept also

that the social gap between them is a real obstacle to their union, Darcy's struggle with himself becomes understandable and meaningful.

Naturally Elizabeth is stunned when Darcy asks her to marry him. She has misinterpreted every one of his actions, and she despises him to the best of her ability. Yet she is clearly fascinated by him. His presence never fails to provoke an emotional response in her, and because the author suggests—however subtly—that her resentment is not factually justified, we are made to feel that 'fascinated but clear dislike' may become an equally strong positive emotion once the reasons for dislike have been removed.[18] Surely the intensity of her resentment is an indication of emotional involvement from a very early stage: she may despise him, but she is never indifferent to him. Significantly, Elizabeth's interest in Wickham springs from her preoccupation with Darcy himself: '. . . she was very willing to hear him, though what she chiefly wished to hear she could not hope to be told, the history of his acquaintance with Darcy' (p. 77). We shall miss an essential ingredient in Elizabeth's response to Darcy unless we grasp the splendour of the man as our bewitching heroine must have done—or she would never have cared for his reactions. G. B. Stern's observations may well be a bit facetious, but I believe they are true to the spirit of the novel:

> I seem to have caught this insistence that he is tall. Obviously glamour heroes have to be tall. He has authority and a certain lordliness . . . His bearing is symbolical; he steps down from the heights as from Mount Olympus—or from the hills of Hollywood. The remote legends of his wealth and great estates in Derbyshire are also in the true hero and Prince Charming tradition. . . . Yes, he is remote, lordly, exclusive. And so *very* tall.[19]

We smile at the effusion, perhaps, and yet we should be thankful that the fascination Darcy held for Elizabeth should not have been lost completely in twentieth-century dissertations on social inequality.

Although Darcy frequently does not appear to his advantage in his verbal encounters with the glorious, slightly impertinent Elizabeth, his exchanges with Miss Bingley reveal his ability to be both witty and resourceful—qualities that Elizabeth possesses to a far higher degree. Furthermore, analyses by Reuben Brower and Howard Babb go to prove that the dialogues between Elizabeth and Darcy carry more than surface meaning. 'It is important', says Brower, ' . . . that in these ironic dialogues no comment is included that makes us take

Darcy's behaviour in only an unpleasant sense.'[20] He points to the dramatic function of these dialogues: they serve to maintain a contrast between the characters so that their estrangement seems logical, while suggesting a different interpretation which may account for the opposite line of development in the second part of the novel. Quite naturally, the illusion of incompatibility will carry over from the social situation to the simple confrontation between two personalities; by the same token, our awareness of their basic attitudes to a total social and moral context will enable us to see to what extent the apparent contrast is real or imaginary. An appreciation of the largely fictitious basis of their disagreement is nowhere more vital than during the first proposal scene, when the mistaken conduct of both reaches an absolute climax and more strongly than ever reinforces whatever sense of contrast our enjoyment of the dramatic illusion may have brought about. Darcy's addresses are couched in language that is uncomfortably wooden, the Richardsonian echoes being no happy addition to his idiom.[21] His reflections on social inequality seem almost preposterously rude: ' " . . . Could you expect me to rejoice in the inferiority of your connections? To congratulate myself on the hope of relations, whose condition in life is so decidedly beneath my own?" ' (p. 192). His arrogance is matched only by her supreme disregard for anything beyond her biased perceptions, which effectively blurs their affinity. At that moment the opposing positions are seemingly so rigidly defined that all subsequent development would appear totally implausible if we did not already possess adequate information to invalidate a substantial part of their disagreement.

After the proposal scene, a predominantly scenic presentation gives way to 'internalised' drama: the mystery has been presented, complete with genuine and misleading clues, and the resulting conflict—aided by the immaturity of both protagonists—has moved to its inevitable climax. It remains for Elizabeth to come to terms with a reality which has been implicit only, and which the reader has been allowed to suspect. The change in narrative technique reflects the author's concern with Elizabeth's development to maturity; the parallel with *Emma* leaps to the eye, though in that novel the 'reported thought process' is even more pronounced.[22] Darcy's explanatory letter is little short of a dramatic device designed to turn the course of the action. It seems a convenient enough means of removing certain factual misconceptions, Elizabeth's reaction being far more important than the information conveyed. Apart from the specific circumstances surrounding Wickham, the letter tells us little that we should not have suspected already. The conclusions Elizabeth reaches between the receipt of the letter and her visit to Pemberley may be regarded as a stepping-stone between the first and the second phase of progression, equally vital to the consistency of both: while providing 'correct' interpretations to the ambiguous statements and actions of the first cycle, they logically introduce the evolution that brings Darcy and Elizabeth together.

Much praise has been bestowed upon the internal dialogue that presents Elizabeth's reassessment of the other characters and of her own past conduct. Reuben Brower calls her thought-pattern 'legalistic': the evidence is submitted to a thorough examination, and judgement is passed on the basis of this evidence alone.[23] The sympathetic reader will delight in the heroine's ability to free herself of that prejudice which has thwarted her judgement, which decreases distance between character and observer:

> . . . every line [of the letter] proved more clearly that the affair, which she had believed it impossible that any contrivance could so represent, as to render Mr. Darcy's conduct in it less than infamous, *was capable of a turn which must make him entirely blameless throughout the whole* (p. 205).[24]

Elizabeth has never been greater than in the recognition of her own folly: she proves to be a truly *rational* person, fully capable of acting upon the extent of her knowledge:

> She grew absolutely ashamed of herself.—Of neither Darcy nor Wickham could she think, without feeling that she had been blind, partial, prejudiced, absurd.
> 'How despicably have I acted!' she cried.—'I, who have prided myself on my discernment! . . . Had I been in love, I could not have been more wretchedly blind. But vanity, not love, has been my folly.—Pleased with the preference of one, and offended by the neglect of the other, on the very beginning of our acquaintance, I have courted prepossession and ignorance, and driven reason away, where either were concerned. *Till this moment, I never knew myself*' (p. 208).[25]

If we accept Elizabeth at this point, we must necessarily accept the woman who falls in love with Fitzwilliam Darcy. If we accept her reading of his past behaviour—and we do only to the extent that the 'truth' is in part known to us already—we will not be surprised to find that he is a man worthy of her love:

> . . . proud and repulsive as were his manners, she had never, in the whole course of their acquaintance, an acquaintance which had latterly brought them much together, and given her a sort of intimacy with his ways, seen any thing that betrayed him to be unprincipled or unjust—any thing that spoke him of irreligious or immoral habits (p. 207).

Like Emma, Elizabeth has to 'understand, thoroughly understand her own heart' before committing herself to another person.[26] Emma and Elizabeth both gain wisdom from their association with the men they eventually marry. And here the parallel ends. Reuben Brower contends that a drama of irony should end once the ambiguities have been removed; consequently, the latter part of *Emma* is more success-ful than that of *Pride and Prejudice*.[27] I am not convinced that the comparison is a happy one. The moment Emma understands her own heart, her knowledge is complete, for conflict has arisen solely as a result of her own shortcomings. Mr Knightley is an invariable quality, an ever-present, ever-known residuary of wisdom and virtue, who is waiting to receive her the moment she perceives her own folly. In *Pride and Prejudice* knowledge pertains to others as well as to the self, and Darcy is an *unknown* quality, whose own conduct has contributed to the misunderstandings that are the basis of the plot. Darcy must be unmasked, not only to the extent that reasons for dis-like no longer apply, but to the extent that he unambiguously displays those qualities that have been implicit only. Mid-way through the novel, Elizabeth merely realises that her reasons for disliking him have been illusory, and that he is a fundamentally upright person: 'His attachment excited gratitude, his general character respect; but she could not approve him; nor could she for a moment repent her refusal, or feel the slightest inclination ever to see him again' (p. 212). In very simple terms: Emma has always known and always needed Mr Knightley. Elizabeth must learn to know Darcy and then to need him before she can become his wife.

The episodes following Elizabeth's return from Rosings serve to consolidate the conclusions so painfully arrived at during the scene of re-evaluation, each episode being a dramatisation of the points Darcy advanced in his defence: 'She felt anew the justice of Mr. Darcy's objections; and never had she before been so much disposed to pardon his interference in the views of his friend' (p. 229). Clearly her response to the general conduct of her family—and to Lydia's indecorous behaviour in particular—recalls her previous disapproval; there is a difference in degree, not in kind, her gravity betraying a stronger awareness of the consequences of immoral habits: ' ". . . Our importance, our respectability in the world, must be affected by the wild volatility, the assurance and disdain of all restraint which mark Lydia's character . . ." ' (p. 231). Her turning away from Wickham is a near-symbolic act. A rejection of him is a rejection of the novel's 'essential' negatives: a serious character, he combines impropriety and false prudence. As we have seen, Elizabeth's basic principles are constant, but the ability to distinguish between mask and reality, and the wisdom to act according to one's basic assumptions, belong to the mature individual. As Elizabeth prepares to go on that journey which will take her to Pemberley, we are shown what she leaves behind and indirectly what she will some day seek. By virtue of a humiliation that has in fact elevated her, Elizabeth's fate will never be that of her father:

> . . . captivated by youth and beauty, and that appearance of good humour, which youth and beauty generally give, [he] had married a woman whose weak understanding and illiberal mind, had very early in their marriage put an end to all real affection for her. Respect, esteem, and confidence, had vanished for ever; and all his views of domestic happiness were overthrown (p. 236).

Having once herself set the ideal norm for compatibility, the mature Elizabeth cannot but base her affection on respect, esteem, and confidence.

Elizabeth's visit to Pemberley falls into two distinct parts, the first providing basic information about Darcy, the second portraying the actual meeting. The Pemberley episode relates closely to all the episodes in the first cycle that reveal both characters' concern for decorum, the half-hidden truths having anticipated a subsequent unambiguous presentation of a residuary of common values. Just as Sir Thomas Bertram's estate may be called the moral centre of *Mansfield Park*, Pemberley is at once the thematic and dramatic centre of gravity in *Pride and Prejudice*: the union of Darcy and Elizabeth—the end-all of the novel's movement—is effected at and through Pemberley, which incorporates the 'essentials' of both.

Mansfield Park receives Fanny, and Pemberley receives Elizabeth; for all their differences, both heroines find a moral home to which they have always aspired by virtue of their sense and sanity.

A seemingly minor episode anticipates both Darcy's position in regard to the estate he has inherited and Elizabeth's reaction to it:

> 'I am astonished,' said Miss Bingley, 'that my father should have left so small a collection of books.—What a delightful library you have at Pemberley, Mr. Darcy!'
>
> 'It ought to be good,' he replied, 'it has been the work of many generations.'
>
> 'And then you have added so much to it yourself, you are always buying books.'
>
> 'I cannot comprehend the neglect of a family library in such days as these.'
>
> 'Neglect! I am sure you neglect nothing that can add to the beauties of that noble place. Charles, when you build *your* house, I wish it may be half as delightful as Pemberley.'
>
> . . .
>
> Elizabeth was so much caught by what passed, as to leave her very little attention for her book . . . (p. 38).

Pemberley, then, represents a living tradition guarded and improved by Darcy, and Elizabeth's interest in the conversation betrays her awareness of the connection between the man and his estate.[28]

The amount of detail in the description of Pemberley is surprising and hence highly significant. By contrast, Rosings is never clearly visualised, beyond very general statements. Our introduction to the estate reads more or less like an inventory of neo-classical aesthetic concepts: there is not only grandeur, but order and harmony tempered by variety; the morally edifying open prospect is not neglected (it will be remembered that Sotherton, that breeding-ground of indecorous conduct, has high walls that impede the view), and the proprietor further betrays his commendable principles by following nature, not distorting it. Elizabeth is rapturous: 'She had never seen a place for which nature had done more, or where natural beauty had been so little counteracted by an awkward taste' (p. 245). Clearly Pemberley commands such close attention on account of its emblematic significance.[29] It is a complex emblem: we note how the word 'taste' relates not only to the proprietor, but indirectly also to the beholder, Elizabeth. We need divine no direct Shaftesburian influence to perceive its ethical connotations. A true child of an age which insisted on the interaction between ethics and aesthetics, Jane Austen not surprisingly sees taste as one of the essential elements of human character. Thus Anne Elliot is said to have been 'an extremely pretty girl, with gentleness, modesty, taste, and feeling',[30] while Edmund Bertram 'encouraged [Fanny's] taste, and corrected her judgment'.[31] Through her later reactions to the union of Jane and Bingley, Elizabeth stresses the importance of having a similarity of taste; in this context, it seems to me equally obvious that the word carries all its ethical implications: '. . . Elizabeth really believed all [Bingley's] expectations of felicity, to be rationally founded, because they had for basis . . . a general similarity of feeling and taste between her and himself' (pp. 347–8).

By the same token, Elizabeth realizes that the master of Pemberley must command not only respect, but also admiration. The Age of Pope is not far removed: Pemberley might well have belonged to Burlington, Darcy might well have been praised in an epistle included among the poet's *Moral Essays*. In her description of Pemberley, Jane Austen includes a direct reference to Lady Catherine's estate, which establishes a contrast between good taste and what Pope termed 'a false Taste of Magnificence':

> The rooms were lofty and handsome, and their furniture suitable to the fortune of their proprietor; but Elizabeth saw, with admiration of his taste, that it was neither gaudy nor uselessly fine; with less of splendour, and more real elegance, than the furniture of Rosings. (p. 246).

The 'grandeur' of Rosings represents a distortion of true magnificence, just as Lady Catherine's ridiculous pride is a distortion of a proper feeling. As in Pope, the gaudy and preposterous (very properly extolled by none other than Mr Collins) sets off what is 'suitable', harmonious, and consequently proof of true virtue.

The subsequent insistence on Darcy's benevolence, as revealed by his housekeeper, naturally accompanies his responsible and tasteful care of the estate. The personal morality of the landowner invariably takes on social implications: his is the responsibility to 'ease, or emulate the care of Heav'n'. Nor is the disclosure of his benevolence acceptable and logical merely within the framework of the Pemberley episode as such. Ironically, it is Wickham's portrayal that provides the most complete preparation for a total vision of Darcy: he places the master of Pemberley in his total context, as someone whose duty and privilege it is to judge and dispose. Even in Wickham's terminology, Darcy is often 'liberal and generous', and he is known to 'give his money freely, to display hospitality, to assist his tenants, and relieve the poor' (p. 81). Wickham's presentation of facts is such as to impute Darcy's benevolence to pride, and all positive virtue is negated by his supposedly uncharitable treatment of Wickham himself. Once fact has been extracted from Wickham's fiction it is easy to see that Darcy has not 'saved up a formidable change to deliver as one lump in the scene at Pemberley',[32] but that the total presentation of him has been carefully prepared for. Similarly, Elizabeth's one-time abhorrence of his alleged unkindness to Wickham clearly demonstrates her own appreciation of the virtue of benevolence.

Towards the end of the novel, Jane asks her sister how long she has loved Darcy. Elizabeth's answer is obviously ironic, and yet there is a grain of truth behind the playful façade: ' "It has been coming on so gradually, that I hardly know when it began. But I believe I must date it from my first seeing his beautiful grounds at Pemberley" ' (p. 373). Following Sir Walter Scott's remark that the heroine 'does not perceive that she has done a foolish thing until she accidentally visits a very handsome seat and grounds belonging to her admirer',[33] a number of critics have chosen to interpret Elizabeth's response to Pemberley as an indication of acquisitiveness. Far from making Elizabeth less attractive, this 'worldliness' supposedly renders her even more 'warmly human'.[34] It is obvious that such a reading of the text would be inconsistent with her previous idealism, and I also find it totally incompatible with the actual events at Pemberley. It is Darcy's *character* that fascinates Elizabeth, as was indeed the case in the days when she despised him, and nothing short of the gradual discovery of his true nature can warm her heart towards him:

> The commendation bestowed on him by Mrs. Reynolds was of no trifling nature. What praise is more valuable than the praise of an intelligent servant? As a brother, a landlord, a master, she considered how may people's happiness were in his guardianship!—How much of pleasure or pain it was in his power to bestow!—How much of good or evil must be done by him! *Every idea that had been brought forward by the housekeeper was favourable to his character* . . . (pp. 250–1).[35]

Mrs Reynolds explains that her master is affable to the poor. 'Elizabeth listened, wondered, doubted, and was impatient for more. Mrs. Reynolds could interest her on no other point. She related the subject of the pictures, the dimensions of the rooms, and the price of the furniture, in vain' (p. 249). It amazes me how anyone should manage to extract a 'sense of property' from such a response.

At one time Elizabeth disliked Darcy so intensely that she went out of her way to have her ill opinion of him confirmed. During that first extensive interview with Wickham, she was also impatient for more information about Darcy: she was 'unwilling to let the subject drop' (p. 77), she 'found the interest of the subject increase, and listened with all her heart' (p. 78). At Pemberley the pattern repeats itself. Again Elizabeth searches for Darcy through another person. The similarity of psychological situation and subject-matter along with the structural parallelism of the two scenes—with their widely different outcomes—serve to emphasise the nature of the progression Elizabeth has gone through; also, our recollection of the earlier scene reminds us of the constant interest she displays for him.

The Pemberley episode is far more than a plot device vital to the disclosure of Darcy's true character and to Elizabeth's parallel change of sentiment towards him. A social and moral code invested in Pemberley suffuses the novel: its traditions 'demand' commitment to propriety and decency, and a responsible interaction with the social and human environment. The various characters in *Pride and Prejudice* invariably define themselves in relation to the ideal, which is not static in its conception: a new generation will always have to be 'buying books' for the 'family library'. The eventual meeting of Darcy and Elizabeth is a meeting between characters whose moral allegiance has been made clear through their response to the claims of Pemberley, implicitly in the novel's first half, explicitly when juxtaposed in face of the estate itself.

Beginning with that unexpected meeting between the two in the woods of Pemberley, the final scenes of *Pride and Prejudice* turn what might have been little more than plausible theory into an immediate experience for the heroine: Elizabeth is not to love the image of a good and decent man, but rather the full personification of that image, as presented to her through actions that apply to her own situation. It is the pattern of the letter episode repeated: what has been suggested already—only this time unambiguously—is emphatically confirmed, the facts themselves being secondary in importance to

Elizabeth's response to them. Artistic unity is achieved as the author brings the 'correct' reading of each initial episode to its logical conclusion. The scenes that finally bring Darcy and Elizabeth together quite naturally echo those that estranged them, showing how greater maturity on the part of both leads to unification rather than estrangement. The prelude to Darcy's easy acceptance of the Gardiners is, of course, his previous acceptance of Elizabeth and Jane: like the Bennet sisters, their uncle recommends himself by intelligence, taste, and good manners. Thus Darcy's 'reformation' is in fact far less fundamental than the dramatic illusion might lead us—and Elizabeth—to believe. That his conduct should finally reflect his finer principles is entirely appropriate and indeed satisfying, in that it recalls Elizabeth's own evolution to maturity. In both instances, a very proper process of humiliation helps to modify a pride that prevented the full realisation of a largely admirable social and moral code: ' ". . . As a child I was taught what was *right*, but I was not taught to correct my temper. I was given good principles, but left to follow them in pride and conceit. . . . By you, I was properly humbled . . ." ' (p. 369). Darcy's words might apply to both. It is perhaps easier to accept Elizabeth's development because we are allowed to witness every progressive step of that process, whereas we merely observe the *effects* of Darcy's parallel struggle with himself. This does not make his conduct inconsistent, merely less immediately predictable—and herein lies the suspense of the action.

The world at large has not changed, and because their essential principles are unaltered, their response to it remains very much the same. Darcy continues to rebuff Miss Bingley—as he always did—and just as he was once ashamed of his aunt's ill breeding he now appreciates Elizabeth's firmness and dignity in face of Lady Catherine's foolish snobbery. Similarly, he will never learn to condone Mrs Bennet's vulgarity, nor is he expected to. Elizabeth will never cease to be vexed at the conduct of her family. The concluding scenes at Longbourn re-emphasise that common concern for decorum which we observed in Darcy and Elizabeth both from the beginning.

When Lydia and Wickham run away together, they carry impropriety to its logical extreme, and Wickham dramatises the marriageability issue by becoming Lydia's husband upon the receipt of money. The obvious thematic relevance being thus established, it is impossible to dismiss the episode as merely conventional and productive of 'irrelevantly directed moral judgment'.[36] The fact that contemporary sentimental fiction abounds with elopements does not make Jane Austen's use of the convention any less effective. Lydia is naturally no fully realised individual, but neither are a number of other 'simple' characters, who remain safely within the novel's moral scheme. Nor do I find it correct to say that neither the conduct of the imprudent couple nor the reactions of Darcy and Elizabeth have been adequately prepared for. Wickham certainly presents a full dress rehearsal in his attempt to elope with Georgiana Darcy, and Lydia has always been second to none in her brainless vulgarity. It is precisely Lydia's behaviour that appals Elizabeth when she returns from Rosings. Darcy's own conduct betrays the intimate connection between concern for propriety and the virtue of benevolence. It is the promise of Pemberley fulfilled: through his treatment of Lydia and Wickham, Darcy reasserts his sense of decorum and his goodness—to Elizabeth most of all. Darrell Mansell—who certainly would not agree with the above attempt to explain the episode in 'realistic' terms—makes the fine point that the elopement epitomises Elizabeth's final, necessary 'humiliation', forcing her to admit that she cannot escape from being a Bennet. Darcy undergoes a parallel process in that Lydia's actions recall those of his own sister: 'Thus Lydia's elopement has the effect of uniting these two in a common shame for a common "family" frailty in their blood.'[37] Even so, I find that the episode primarily serves to set the protagonists apart from foolishness and impropriety, in whatever social class these attitudes might appear. Its dramatic effectiveness cannot be denied: it brings about Elizabeth's ultimate realisation of her love for Darcy.

For *Pride and Prejudice* is above all a story of love—a love that blurs the identity of neither, however similar those principles without which their union would be impossible. From the beginning to the end, Darcy is sometimes silent, sometimes grave, often awesome— as when he asks Elizabeth's hand in marriage—and he has yet to learn to be laughed at by a woman who never loses her sprightliness. Yet every event subsequent to the Meryton assembly goes to prove that difference in temperament is no barrier to intensity of feeling, be it hatred or love: what began as a confrontation between two strong personalities terminates in a union where both retain their individuality. For that we should be grateful. Darcy and Elizabeth are not 'comply-ing' or 'easy', like Jane and Bingley, nor would we wish them ever to become so. For all his good qualities, Darcy is not perfect, merely 'exactly the man, who, in disposition and talents, would most suit

[Elizabeth]' (p. 312)—the man for whom she has nourished every possible feeling—except indifference.

It is all too easy for the post-Romantic reader to underrate the intensity of Elizabeth's affection for Darcy and conclude that his love for her is somehow stronger because more intuitive. As a young girl, I was informed that Elizabeth's mind is 'firmly in control of her emotions; and notwithstanding that she is "in love" with Darcy we cannot imagine that she will be a passionate or adoring wife to him.'[38] This is the kind of response that Jane Austen must have anticipated as she mockingly addressed her public:

> If gratitude and esteem are good foundations of affection, Elizabeth's change of sentiment will be neither improbable nor faulty. But if otherwise, if the regard springing from such sources is unreasonable or unnatural, in comparison of what is so often described as arising on a first interview with its object, and even before two words have been exchanged, nothing can be said in her defence, except that she had given somewhat of a trial to the latter method, in her partiality for Wickham, and that its ill-success might perhaps authorize her to seek the other less interesting mode of attachment (p. 279).

The 'less interesting mode of attachment' is not, of course, incompatible with depth of feeling, which does but gain in plausibility from being 'reasonable and just' (p. 334). Elizabeth's gradual awakening to a full realisation of her attachment is described with shrewd psychological insight, through those subtle touches that are far more revelatory than any number of emotional outbursts. The elopement episode serves to clarify her feelings: the events at Pemberley told her that he cared for her still and that she had every reason to value such a man's affection; at the moment when she believes he is gone forever, she sees that she cannot afford the loss:

> She became jealous of his esteem, when she could no longer hope to be benefited by it. She wanted to hear of him when there seemed the least chance of gaining intelligence. She was convinced that she could have been happy with him; when it was no longer likely they should meet (p. 311).

There is nothing very sensible about staying awake at night because you suspect that a man may never come back.

When Darcy does come, we recognise in the description of Elizabeth the hand that was to create Anne Elliot. A small gesture may betray emotion, silence may speak more eloquently than words: '... Elizabeth, to satisfy her mother, went to the window—she looked,—*she saw Mr. Darcy with [Bingley], and sat down again by her sister*' (p. 333).[39] The visit is entirely unexpected, and all Elizabeth does is sit down. All we hear is a silly conversation between Kitty and her mother. Elizabeth's lively mind has been an open book to us—suddenly there is nothing but silence and inactivity. Her numbness is as real as Anne's, when she 'descried, most decidedly and distinctly, Captain Wentworth walking down the street. . . . For a few minutes she saw nothing before her. It was all confusion.'[40] Again as in *Persuasion* a story can be told by the expression on a person's face: 'The colour which had been driven from [Elizabeth's] face, returned for half a minute with an additional glow, and a smile of delight added lustre to her eyes . . . ' (p. 334).[41] And as in the later novel, the closed rooms with a crowd of people, where only glances and polite phrases can be exchanged, create almost a feeling of claustrophobia which intensifies the uncertainty of the woman, whose reactions fluctuate between hope and resignation. Only Elizabeth is younger, more impetuous, less chastened than Anne: 'She followed him with her eyes, envied every one to whom he spoke, had scarcely patience enough to help anybody to coffee; and then was enraged against herself for being so silly!' (p. 341). She has all the energy of a Mary Crawford, and so she can form a 'desperate resolution' (p. 365) and approach Darcy on the delicate subject of his generosity to Lydia and Wickham. The author does, in fact, dispense with an unusual amount of reticence when allowing Elizabeth to have tears in her eyes and tell her father how much she loves Darcy. 'I am happier even than Jane;' she writes to Mrs Gardiner, 'she only smiles, I laugh' (p. 383). And this is as far as Jane Austen will ever take her reader. Like all her lovers, Darcy and Elizabeth ' "walk off the stage into a cloud"— where it would be indecent to attempt to follow them.'[42] To be sure, *Persuasion* presents a fuller and far more moving picture of human emotion, because it is all about a mature woman's love. Elizabeth had to learn what Anne already knew.

There is nothing unfinished, however, about the image of love that *Pride and Prejudice* ultimately projects. The search for a partner becomes a moral act, which is reflected in the novel's structure. It is a movement from conflict based in part on ignorance to order grounded in awareness. In recognising both their mistaken conduct and their essential affinity the protagonists are made to overcome elements that created chaos and to realise those possibilities for harmony that were implicit even in that initial state of disorder—implicit in their common value system and in their capacity for emotional commitment.

Notes

1. Spenser's defence of poetry:
some structural aspects of the *Fowre Hymnes*

EINAR BJORVAND

¹'Fides enim non res est salutantis corporis, sed credentis animi.' St Augustine, *De Catechizandis Rvdibvs: Liber Vnvs*, translated by J. P. Christopher (Washington, D.C., 1926), pp. 30 and 31.

²All references to Spenser's *Hymnes* are to *The Works of Edmund Spenser: A Variorum Edition*, Volume VII, *The Minor Poems*, Volume 1, edited by C. G. Osgood and H. G. Lotspeich (Baltimore, 1943).

³See Josephine Waters Bennett, 'The Theme of Spenser's *Fowre Hymnes*', *Studies in Philology*, 28 (1931), 49–57; and Robert Ellrodt, *Neoplatonism in the Poetry of Spenser* (Geneva, 1960), pp. 13–24.

⁴See F. M. Padelford, 'Spenser's *Fowre Hymnes*: A Resurvey', *Studies in Philology*, 29 (1932), 216.

⁵See J. W. Bennett, *Studies in Philology*, 28, 49–52; and Ellrodt, p. 14.

⁶J. B. Fletcher, 'A Study in Renaissance Mysticism: Spenser's "Fowre Hymnes"', *PMLA*, 26 (1911), 452–75. Fletcher is refuted by Padelford, 'Spenser's *Fowre Hymnes*', *JEGP*, 13 (1914), 418–33.

⁷J. B. Fletcher, 'Benivieni's Ode of Love and Spenser's *Fowre Hymnes*', *Modern Philology*, 8 (1911), 545–60; R. W. Lee, 'Castiglione's Influence on Spenser's Early Hymns', *Philological Quarterly*, 7 (1928), 65–77; W. L. Renwick, *Daphnaida and Other Poems* (London, 1929), pp. 210–11; the best arguments in favour of this view still seem to be those presented by Joan Waters Bennett in *Studies in Philology*, 28, 18–27, and in 'Spenser's *Fowre Hymnes*: Addenda', *Studies in Philology*, 32 (1935), 131–57. Ellrodt undertakes a refutation of their interpretations, pp. 130–40.

⁸Ellrodt, p. 117.

⁹Sir Philip Sidney, *Defence of Poesie*. The quotation is taken from a stimulating article by Andrew D. Weiner, 'Moving and Teaching: Sidney's *Defence of Poesie* as a Protestant Poetic', *The Journal of Medieval and Renaissance Studies*, 2 (1972), 259–78 (p. 270).

¹⁰William Nelson, *The Poetry of Edmund Spenser: A Study* (New York and London, 1963), p. 99.

¹¹See Paula Johnson, *Form and Transformation in Music and Poetry of*

the English Renaissance (New Haven and London, 1972), pp. 125–31 and 152–3, and William Nelson, pp. 97–115.

[12]The first attempt at a full structural analysis of the *Epithalamion* was by A. Kent Hieatt in *Short Time's Endless Monument: the Symbolism of the Numbers in Edmund Spenser's 'Epithalamion'* (New York, 1960), later discussed and refined by among others Max A. Wickert in 'Structure and Ceremony in Spenser's *Epithalamion*', *ELH*, 35 (1968), 135–57, and by Alastair Fowler in *Triumphal Forms: Structural Patterns in Elizabethan Poetry* (Cambridge, 1970), pp. 103–07 and 161–73. Much of Hieatt's analysis still holds good, but Wicker's more recent analysis of the strictly symmetrical structure seems more convincing than the pairing suggested by Hieatt.

[13]See J. W. Bennett, *Studies in Philology*, 28, 54–6, and volume 32, 152; and Sears Jayne, 'Attending to Genre: Spenser's *Hymnes*', abstract in the *Spenser Newsletter*, 3 (1972), 6.

[14]See Ellrodt, pp. 20–21; 123–24.

[15]Hereafter the hymns will be referred to as *HL, HB, HHL,* and *HHB,* and stanza and line references are given in numerals, e.g. (*HL* 14, 114–16). When reference is made to lines only, this is indicated, e.g. (*HL* lines 114–16).

[16]Alastair Fowler, *Triumphal Forms*, p. 62.

[17]The contrast between 'Love the tyrant and Love the redeemer' has also been pointed out by Paula Johnson, *Form and Transformation*, p. 130.

[18]Paula Johnson, p. 129.

[19]John Mulryan, 'Spenser as Mythologist: A Study of the Nativities of Cupid and Christ in the *Fowre Hymnes*', *Modern Language Studies*, 1 (1971), 13–16 (p. 15).

[20]See Maren-Sofie Røstvig, 'Milton and the Science of Numbers', *English Studies Today*, Fourth Series (Rome, 1966), 283–84.

[21]Michael Wilding, 'Allusion and Innuendo in *MacFlecknoe*', *Essays in Criticism*, 19 (1969), 359–60.

[22]William Nelson, p. 100.

[23]The word 'aspyre' occurs only once more in the heavenly hymns, in stanza 40 of the *Hymne of Heavenly Beautie*, which describes the essential 'basenesse' of 'that pompe, to which proud minds aspyre'. The same set of rhymewords, 'aspyre-fyre-desyre', recurs in stanza 27 of the first hymn, where it is used to underline the lack of these qualities in the lover who succumbs to lust. For this and similar information, see my *A Concordance to Spenser's 'Fowre Hymnes'* (Oslo, 1973).

[24]William Nelson, p. 101. See also Paula Johnson, p. 129.

[25]Paula Johnson, p. 128.

[26]Enid Welsford, *Spenser, 'Fowre Hymnes', 'Epithalamion': A Study of Edmund Spenser's Doctrine of Love* (Oxford, 1967), p. 152.

[27]Paula Johnson, p. 128.

[28]William Nelson, p. 102.

[29]See illustration, facing p. 160.

[30]See *The English Works of Sir Thomas More*, edited by W. E. Campbell, 2 vols (London and New York, 1931), I, 332–35.

[31]Erwin Panofsky, *Studies in Iconology: Humanistic Themes in the Art of the Renaissance* (New York, 1939), pp. 125–26.

[32]Ibid., p. 125.

[33]*Pagan Mysteries in the Renaissance*, revised and enlarged edition (Harmondsworth, 1967), p. 52.

[34]Quoted by Wind, p. 58.

[35]From the *Conclusiones*, quoted by Wind, p. 51. Wind's views have been reaffirmed by C. D. Gilbert in 'Blind Cupid', *JWCI*, 33 (1970), 304–05: 'For Ficino and Pico, Love was not blind because it was irrational but because it was above reason' (p. 305).

[36]Translated by J. B. Fletcher in *Modern Philology*, 8 (1911), 545–60 (p. 549).

[37]See Philip B. Rollinson, 'A Generic View of Spenser's *Four Hymns*', *Studies in Philology*, 68 (1971), 298.

[38]John Block Friedman, *Orpheus in the Middle Ages* (Cambridge, Mass., 1970), p. 57.

[39]Ibid.

[40]Friedman, p. 125.

[41]See Enid Welsford, p. 145.

[42]I take the use of a capital 'G' in God in this line to be significant.

[43]See J. W. Bennett, *Studies in Philology*, 28, 36.

[44]See M.-S. Røstvig's comments on the *Fowre Hymnes* in 'The Hidden Sense: Milton and the Neoplatonic Method of Numerical Composition', in *The Hidden Sense and Other Essays*, edited by M.-S. Røstvig et al. (Oslo, 1963), p. 90.

[45]'in veteri testamento est occultatio novi, in novo testamento est manifestatio veteris.' Augustine, *De Catechizandis Rvdibvs*, pp. 28 and 29.

[46]Edgar Wind, p. 38.

[47]St Bonaventura, *The Mind's Road to God*, translated by George Boas (Indianapolis, 1953), p. 28.

[48]See Paula Johnson, pp. 130–31.

[49]William Nelson, p. 102.

[50]This parallel is not noted in the *Variorum Edition*. Robert Ellrodt cites a parallel in Leone Ebreo's *Dialoghi d'Amore*, but it seems unlikely that any particular source can be pinned down since the simile was, in all probability, a commonplace. See Ellrodt p. 186.

[51]See my *Concordance*, 'Appendix I: A Word-frequency Index'.

[52]See John Block Friedman, pp. 50–2.

[53]See Jon A. Quitslund, 'Spenser's Image of Sapience', *Studies in the Renaissance*, 16 (New York, 1969), 181–213 (p. 212).

[54]See also William Nelson, pp. 114–15.

[55]M.-S. Røstvig, *The Hidden Sense*, p. 90.

[56]Ibid.

[57]See Alastair Fowler, *Triumphal Forms*, pp. 62–124. See also Davies's discussion of the double centre in Milton's 'On the Morning of Christ's Nativity' below, pp. 105–106.

2. Elaborate song: conceptual structure in Milton's 'On the Morning of Christ's Nativity'

M.–S. RØSTVIG

[1]'O perfect, and accomplish thy glorious acts; for men may leave their works unfinish't, but thou art a God, thy nature is perfection . . . When thou hast settl'd peace in the Church, and righteous judgement in the Kingdome, then shall all thy Saints address their voyces of joy, and triumph to thee . . . And he that now for haste snatches up a plain ungarnish't present as a thanke-offering to thee, . . . may then perhaps take up a Harp, and sing thee an elaborate song to Generations.' Quoted from *Complete Prose Works of John Milton*, ed. Don. M. Wolfe (New Haven and London, 1953), I, 706 by Jason P. Rosenblatt, 'The War in Heaven in *Paradise Lost*,' *PMLA*, 87 (1972), 38.

[2]William Whitaker, *A Disputation on Holy Scripture, Against the Papists* (1588) as quoted by Andrew D. Weiner, 'Moving and Teaching: Sidney's *Defence of Poesie* as a Protestant Poetic,' *The Journal of Medieval and Renaissance Studies*, 2 (1972), 273.

[3]Weiner, p. 276. Mr Weiner rightly insists on the importance of contemporary habits of reading the Bible: 'Through their reading of the scriptures and their attendance at sermons, the Elizabethans . . . must have developed the habit of reading slowly and painstakingly, and Sidney clearly expects his readers to bring the same reading habits to poetry . . . We must, in short, read very carefully, paying attention not only to the surface of the narrative but also to the signs which may be embedded in it.' (276 f.) Weiner does not include numbers among such 'signs', although these are specifically discussed as such by Augustine in his *De doctrina Christiana*. The numbers used to create conceptual structures were classified by a Renaissance poet like Guy le Fevre de La Boderie as allegorical; see

his preface to his translation of Francesco Giorgio's *L'Harmonie du Monde* (Paris, 1578 and 1579).

⁴ have excluded the microstructure of each stanza (the number of feet or syllables, for example) as too conjectural. It may be noted here, though, that the abstract metrical pattern in the hymn posits 36 syllables, the square of 6, which is a circular number. (A circular number is a number which returns to itself in the last digit when multiplied with itself.) The sum total of lines, 216, is the cube of 6 which means that it represents a perfect sphere or globe, since 6 is circular. Many theologians observed that the Hebrew letters in the name of God are circular numbers (5, 6 and 10) so that the name describes the nature of the Deity—his all-encompassing aspect and his eternal existence.

⁴ᵃCassiodorus, *Divine and Human Readings,* tr. Leslie Webber Jones (New York, 1966), p. 102.

⁵My quotations are from Saint Augustine, *On Christian Doctrine,* tr. D. W. Robertson Jr (The Library of Liberal Arts: New York, 1958).

⁶See my monograph on 'Structure as Prophecy' in *Silent Poetry: Essays in Numerological Analysis,* ed. Alastair Fowler (London, 1970), 32–72, and especially pp. 50–53.

⁷*Commentarium in librum Psalmorum* (1611–16), III, 479.

⁸Bonaventura, *Collationes in Hexaemeron. Das Sechstagewerk. Lateinisch und Deutsch* (Darmstadt, 1964), pp. 536 f. It must be borne in mind that the structure of the 150 Psalms was believed to constitute a summary and abridgement of the whole Bible, beginning with the Garden of Eden and the tree in Psalm 1 and concluding with the hymns in honour of Christ in the Heavenly Jerusalem as described in the Book of Revelation.

⁹Migne, *Patrologia latina,* 19 (Paris, 1846), columns 765–70.

¹⁰See Francesco Giorgio, *Problemata* (Venice, 1536 and Paris, 1574 and 1622), III, i, 26 and Gasparius Sanctius, *In Ieremiam Prophetam Commentarii* (1618). Both make the point that the alphabetical technique of composition was adopted in Nativity hymns, and both quote the opening lines of Sedulius' hymn. Cornelius à Lapide, *Commentaria In Ieremiam* (1621), like Sanctius, associates the technique with the classical art of memory, the letters serving instead of images. This is a technique which permits one to keep the whole poem in mind at once—an argument which applies to all kinds of conceptual structure, whether alphabetical, numerical, or symmetrical.

Giles Fletcher refers to Sedulius and Prudentius in his preface to *Christ's Victory and Triumph* (1610).

¹¹'Hymnus de Leontio episcopo,' Migne PL 19; see also M. Nisard, ed., *Collection des Auteurs Latins, avec la traduction en français. Ausone, Sidoine Apollinaire, Venance Fortunat* (Paris, 1887), pp. 55–57. The poem is numbered I, 16 in all collected editions.

[12]'Ad Syagrium episcopum Augustidunensem,' pp. 138–41 and 146–48 in Nisard's edition.

Fortunatus himself explains the significance of the chosen structure in an accompanying letter. Since he wrote the poem to serve as a gift or ransom to secure the liberty of a prisoner of war, its subject had to be the ransom offered by Christ to redeem fallen man. And in order to celebrate Christ the poem had to consist of 33 lines of 33 letters each, thus creating a perfect square. At its centre meet five acrostic lines traced through the square formed by the letters, the unifying centre being the letter which is *permedia* of the 23 letters in the Latin alphabet. (This letter, because of its position, clearly symbolises Christ.)

The structure, therefore, presents an image of Christ as our unifying centre, and the firmness of the form reflects the firmness of the providential scheme for our redemption. Thematically the poem falls into two equal parts: lines 1–16 describing the creation of man, his fall and expulsion, a centre-line affirming our eternal damnation under the Law (modified by the presence of the centrally placed letter representing Christ), and a counter-movement (lines 18–33) of redemption through the incarnation and the crucifixion.

[13]For the Middle Ages, see Robert M. Jordan, *Chaucer and the Shape of Creation* (Cambridge, Mass., 1967) and Wolfgang Haubrichs, *Ordo als Form. Strukturstudien zur Zahlenkomposition bei Otfrid von Weissenburg und in karolingischer Literatur* (Tübingen, 1969). D. P. Walker's useful studies in the *prisca theologia* are now available in book form: *The Ancient Theology. Studies in Christian Platonism from the Fifteenth to the Eighteenth Century* (London, 1972).

[14]Edgar Wind's *Pagan Mysteries in the Renaissance* needs no recommendation: to it may be added D. C. Allen's *Mysteriously Meant. The Rediscovery of Pagan Symbolism and Allegorical Interpretation in the Renaissance* (Baltimore and London, 1970).

[15]See note 6 and my essay entitled 'Ars Aeterna: Renaissance Poetics and Theories of Divine Creation,' *Mosaic*, 3 (1970), 40–61. This essay can also be found in *Chaos and Form*, ed. Kenneth McRobbie (Winnipeg, 1972), 101–19.

[16]Giorgio's importance in his own age and his usefulness as a source is being increasingly recognised today. The large extent to which he draws on orthodox theology requires emphasis, as he is too often associated with esoteric traditions. Frances Yates does this persistently, but references to and quotations from Augustine are frequent throughout the pages of his *De harmonia mundi* (Venice, 1525 and Paris, 1545, 1546, and 1564 and, in French translation, 1578 and 1579). For a brief account of his life and works see J.-F. Maillard, 'Le "De harmonia mundi" de Georges de Venise,' *Revue de l'Histoire des Religions*, 179 (1971), 181–203.

[17]Cornelius à Lapide published a number of commentaries on parts of

the Bible during the first few decades of the seventeenth century, and these draw extensively on patristic interpretations. Cornelius à Lapide must be the last major exegete to pursue a fourfold method of interpretation.

For Aquinas' comments on *Job* 38 see his *Opera*, vol. 13 (Antverpiae, 1612). Aquinas, too, refers the harmony of creation to the Pythagorean theory of the music of the spheres and to the 'musical' arrangement of the angelic hierarchies. The 'music' of both is a matter of an order embodying the crucial mathematical ratios.

¹⁸The fact that harmony is a matter of mathematical ratios (as explained in commentaries on Plato's *Timæus*) scarcely requires documentation today. In the study referred to in note 6, 'Structure as Prophecy,' I have shown that Platonic and Pythagorean number lore can be found in Biblical exegesis so that it cannot be considered as at all remarkable that Christian poets could exploit this tradition. The analysis submitted here, in terms of Biblical concepts, should be taken to supplement and modify, but not replace, the analysis offered primarily in terms of classical concepts in my study of 'The Hidden Sense: Milton and the Neoplatonic Method of Numerical Composition' published in *The Hidden Sense and Other Essays* by M.-S. Røstvig et al. (Oslo, 1963), pp. 1–112. The absorption of classical number lore into Christian theology is a topic I shall discuss more fully in a forthcoming publication.

¹⁹I have picked these words from Mantuan's comments on Psalm 119; see Baptista Spagnuolus Mantuanus, *In omnes Davidicos Psalmos . . . commentaria* (Rome, 1585).

²⁰The romans are my own. I have used the edition published in the Ancient and Modern Library of Theological Literature, London, no date.

²¹The same argument applies to the sum total of Psalms, 150, their division into a sequence of 70 plus 80 being taken to convey the same message. The progression from 7 to 8 is one of Augustine's favourite numerical arguments; see for example his sermon on Psalm 150. The number 7 was associated with the Old Testament, 8 with the New.

²²To read *Christ's Victory and Triumph* is to be reminded again and again of themes and phrases in Milton's poem. See for example IV, 13 and IV, 19–21. Fletcher's twice-repeated line, 'So Him they lead along into the courts of day' (IV, 19 and 20), may have prompted Milton's 'the courts of everlasting day' in the introduction. Milton's 'globe of circular light' (stanza 11) is usually compared to Fletcher's 'A globe of wingèd angels' (IV, 13), where *globe* means *troop*.

²³'Spenser's Fourth Grace,' *JWCI*, 34 (1971), 354: 'The picture of a great figure seated within a circle while its attributes are in a circle about it certainly is not original with Spenser. The traditional iconography of the microcosm often pictures man or God within a circle while their attributes

or acts were personified around them. Ficino had pictured the emanations of God in such a way.'

²⁴In an essay on 'Christ's Nativity and the Pagan Deities', *Milton Studies*, 2 (1970), 103–12, Lawrence W. Hyman argues that Milton's attitude to the pagan past was one of regret; a conflict must necessarily inhere 'in any action which banishes a world which we also find beautiful.' But this is to ignore the typological approach to human history as a gradual revelation of the truth, first through 'veils and shadows' (*per vela et umbra*) and at last fully and quite clearly through the incarnation. The world of Nature and the world of pagan myth contained their types as well as the Biblical narrative, and these types must necessarily be beautiful since otherwise they would not point to Him who is the source of beauty and truth. His incarnation is that which they prophesy, however obscurely, and like the mere shadows they are, they must flee the moment that the true Sun of Justice appears. When, in the penultimate stanza, the 'yellow-skirted fays' and the 'moon-loved maze' are seen as beautiful, this is so, not because Milton was the victim of an unresolved inner conflict, but because the 'flocking shadows pale' belong in a typological context.

²⁵See note 8 for the edition used.

²⁶*Itinerarium mentis in Deum* (München, 1961), p. 134. See also VI, 7 pp. 144–47.

²⁷See note 19.

²⁸Nikolaus von Kues, *Philosophisch-Theologische Schriften*, Vol. II (Wien, 1966), p. 74. Cusanus' diagram figures prominently, but without acknowledgement or reference, in the preface written by Nicholas le Fevre de La Boderie to the one-volume edition of Pico's *Heptaplus* and Giorgio's *De harmonia mundi* published in French translation by himself and his brother Guy at Paris in 1578 and 1579. I reproduce this diagram in 'The Hidden Sense' (see note 18). In their prefaces the brothers Guy and Nicholas le Fevre de La Boderie refer quite frequently to 'le docte Cusanus' and so do Pico and Giorgio.

²⁹*De vera religione*, xxx, 55. For the Latin text and a reliable translation into French, see *Oeuvres*, vol. 8 (Paris, 1951), p. 103. The translation into English is my own. See my discussion of this passage in 'Ars Aeterna,' *Mosaic*, 3 (1970), 49 f.

³⁰For comments on the symbolism invested in this formula readers are referred to 'The Hidden Sense' or to Christopher Butler's *Number Symbolism* (London, 1970).

In his *De Trinitate* IV Augustine stressed the importance of the ratio 2:1 (the octave or diapason) in the work of creation and the scheme of redemption. This ratio conveys the idea of return or the closing of the circle, and so does the *lambda*-formula as a whole. The last number in this formula, 27, may represent them all as constituting the sum of the other numbers. These are the numbers that organise the perpetual descent from and ascent to the Deity, and this is true also of the shorter *tetractys*-formula associated with Pythagoras. In Christian thought both formulas were associated with Jacob's Ladder, and with the idea of Christ as the Ladder joining Heaven and Earth.

[31]See my diagram.

[32]Pietro Bongo, *De Numerorum Mysteria* (Bergomi, 1591), p. 448. Bongo's chapter on the number 24 begins by connecting it with the vision of the 24 elders in *Rev.* 4.

[33]For a modern edition of the *Expositio Psalmorum* see the *Corpus Christianorum* vols. 97–98 (Turnholti, 1958).

[34]Wolfgang Haubrichs, *Ordo als Form* (Tübingen, 1969), pp. 64–70, summarises patristic and early medieval expositions of the number 13.

[35]Helen Gardner, *Religion and Literature* (London, 1971), p. 179.

[36]Compare *Wisdom* 8:1; the imprint is the 'sweet order' imposed by Wisdom on 'all things' *(disponit omnia suaviter)*.

[37]Saint Augustine, *On Free Choice of the Will*, tr. Anna S. Benjamin and L. H. Hackstaff (Library of Liberal Arts: New York, 1964), pp. 73–75.

[38]The two are fused in Tasso's *Discorsi del Poema Eroico;* see Annabel M. Patterson, 'Tasso's Epic Neoplatonism,' *Studies in the Renaissance*, 18 (1971), 108 f.: Tasso accepted the fusion, 'achieved by Augustine and Aquinas . . . of two radically different meanings of the term "Idea". The original transcendental absolutes . . . have become confused with any preconception or design in the mind of an artist or craftsman of what he is about to make.'

[39]*The Countess of Pembroke's Arcadia*, ed. Jean Robertson (Oxford, 1973), pp. 245–48.

[39a]It is well known that Sidney's poem is indebted to an epithalamion in Gil Polo's continuation of Montemayor's *Diana*: see Jean Robertson's comment in her introduction to the edition of *The Countess of Pembroke's Arcadia*, p. xx. For the text of Bartholomew Yong's translation of Gil Polo, see Judith M. Kennedy's *A Critical Edition of Yong's Translation of George of Montemayor's Diana and Gil Polo's Enamoured Diana* (Oxford, 1968), pp. 378 f. Yong's translation of Gil Polo's epithalamion was included in *England's Helicon* (1600, 1614); see Hyder Rollins' ed. (Cambridge, Mass., 1935), I, 133 f.

On comparing Sidney's poem with Yong's translation the indebtedness is obvious, but so are the differences. The earlier poem is much shorter; its seven nine-line stanzas move towards a clear terminal climax in the sixth stanza, the seventh forming a coda. Central accent is established, however, by placing a direct apostrophe to the bride and groom in the fourth stanza, and there is some evidence indicating a symmetrical grouping around the centre. The structure of Sidney's epithalamion is much firmer and bolder. Sidney's revision therefore indicates that he desired a more complex structural effect and one which could be sustained through eleven stanzas, thus affording more opportunities for thematic pairing.

For a later example of structural reorganisation of a borrowed theme, see Abraham Cowley's version of Casimire Sarbiewski's ode 'E Rebus Humanis Excessus' in the Pindaric ode entitled 'The Ecstasy'. What Cowley did was to use the last stanza as a pivotal centre, adding an appropriate number of stanzas on an original theme in such a manner that the second thematic movement balances the first through thematic pairing. See my essay on 'Structural Images in Cowley and Herbert: A Comparison', *English Studies*, 54 (1973), pp. 4 f.

I am grateful to H. Neville Davies for drawing my attention to B. Yong's version of Gil Polo's poem.

[40] *L'Harmonie du Monde* (Paris, 1579), pp. 777–79.

[41] I have used the folio edition of Cowley's works published in 1700.

[42] S. K. Heninger Jr in *Renaissance Quarterly*, 25:3 (1972), 335 (in a review of Christopher Butler's book on *Number Symbolism*).

[43] Paula Johnson, *Form and Transformation in Music and Poetry of the English Renaissance* (New Haven and London, 1972), pp. 14 f. See also p. 72, where the point is made that we usually fail to recognise how important a perception of retrospective form is for our understanding of a work. Finally see p. 94 for comments on our attitude to the concept of artistic unity.

[44] Augustine's characterisation of the world as God's poem was well known to the Renaissance, and Cowley refers to it at length in a footnote on the *Davideis*, Book I: 'I have seen an excellent saying of St. *Augustines*, cited to this purpose, *Ordinem sæculorum tanquam pulcherrimum Carmen ex quibusdam quasi antithetis honestavit Deus—sicut contraria contrariis opposita sermonis pulchritudinem reddunt, ita quadam non verborum sed rerum eloquentia contrariorum oppositione sæculi pulchritudo componitur.* And the *Scripture* witnesses, that the World was made in *Number, Weight,* and *Measure;* which are all qualities of a good *Poem.* This order and proportion of things is the true *Musick* of the World . . .' Cowley's Scriptural reference is to *Wisdom* 11:20 *(omnia in mensura, et numero, et pondere disposuisti).*

3. Laid artfully together: stanzaic design in Milton's 'On the Morning of Christ's Nativity'

H. Neville Davies

[1] *Poems upon Several Occasions . . . by John Milton,* edited by Thomas Warton (London, 1785), p. 267.

[2] Sigmund Spaeth, *Milton's Knowledge of Music* (Princeton, 1913), reprinted (Ann Arbor, Mich., 1963), pp. 90–92; George N. Shuster, *The English Ode from Milton to Keats* (New York, 1940), pp. 67–70; A. E. Barker, 'The Pattern of Milton's "Nativity Ode"', *UTQ*, 10 (1941), 167–81, reprinted in *Milton: Modern Judgements,* edited by A. Rudrum (London, 1968), pp. 44–57; *Poems of John Milton. The 1645 Edition,* edited by Cleanth Brooks and J. E. Hardy (New York, 1951), pp. 95–104; D. C. Allen, *The Harmonious Vision* (Baltimore, Md, 1954), chapter II; Maren-Sofie Røstvig, 'The Hidden Sense' in *The Hidden Sense and Other Essays,* by Røstvig et al. (Oslo and London, 1963), pp. 44–58; Jon S. Lawry, *The Shadow of Heaven: Matter and Stance in Milton's Poetry* (Ithaca, N.Y., 1968), pp. 27–41; Balachandra Rajan, 'In Order Serviceable', *MLR*, 63 (1968), 13–22, reprinted as chapter II in Rajan's *The Lofty Rhyme* (London, 1970); John Carey, *Milton* (London, 1969), chapter II; Christopher Butler, *Number Symbolism* (London, 1970), pp. 140–43 (although Butler takes issue with Røstvig, he accepts a basis of $9+9+9$); K. M. Swaim, ' "Mighty Pan": Tradition and Image in Milton's *Nativity Hymn*', *Stud. in Philol.*, 68 (1971), 484–95; *A Variorum Commentary on the Poems of John Milton,* Volume II, edited by A. S. P. Woodhouse and Douglas Bush (London, 1972), part 1, pp. 69, 81, 94–95, 109. Bush specifically rejects (p. 48) any division between stanzas 15 and 16 for reasons strangely at odds with the text of the poem.

[3] Edited by William Haller in *The Works of John Milton,* edited by F. A. Patterson, 20 vols (New York, 1931–40), IV (1931), p. 342

[4] *Areopagitica,* p. 342. See also James R. McAdams, 'The Pattern of Temptation in *Paradise Regained*', *Milton Studies,* 4 (1972), 177–93 (p. 177).

[5] See H. N. Davies, 'The Structure of Shadwell's *A Song for St Cecilia's Day, 1690*', in *Silent Poetry. Essays in Numerological Analysis,* edited by Alastair Fowler (London, 1970), pp. 205–20. Reference should have been made in that essay to Hugh Hare, Lord Colarane's translation of Loredano, *The Ascents of the Soul* (Wing L3065) and his own *La scala sancta* (Wing L3069) both edited by his wife, Lucy, and published in 1681. Even in the twelfth century the concept was widely disseminated as chapters IV and V

of the Old Norse Maríu saga demonstrate: see O. Widding and H. Bekker-Nielsen, 'The Fifteen Steps of the Temple. A Problem in the Maríu Saga', *Bibliotheca Arnamagnæana*, 25 (1961), 80–91.

For William Hazlitt, Poussin 'was among painters (more than anyone else) what Milton was among poets' (*Complete Works*, edited by P. P. Howe, 21 vols (London, 1930–34), VIII (1931), p. 169), and this affinity has been recognised by others, too, especially by Mario Praz ('Milton and Poussin' in his *On Neoclassicism*, translated by A. Davidson, 2nd edn (London, 1969), 11–39). Poussin's 'The Holy Family on the Steps,' completed in 1648, depicts the Holy Family positioned on a flight of steps, possibly steps to the Temple, and it has been suggested that these steps allude to Mary as the *scala coelestis* by which the Son of God descended into the world and through which we can ascend to heaven. But the allusion is not numerological since the steps continue outside the picture. See Howard Hibbard's monograph, *Poussin: The Holy Family on the Steps* (London, 1974), chapter IV.

[6]This and other passages are quoted in C. A. Patrides, 'Renaissance Interpretations of Jacob's Ladder', *Theologische Zeitschrift*, 18 (1962), 411–18 (p. 413).

[7]Quoted by Patrides, p. 413.

[8]The numerological plan of *De doctrina* is discussed by M.-S. Røstvig in *The Hidden Sense*, pp. 39–41.

[9]For a fuller discussion of *Paradise Lost*, III, 501–15 and 540–54 see H. N. Davies, 'The Structure of Shadwell's *A Song for St Cecilia's Day, 1690*', pp. 209–215. Milton's poems are quoted from John Carey and Alastair Fowler's Longmans Annotated English Poets edition (London, 1968).

[10]See H. N. Davies, 'The First English Translations of Bellarmine's *De ascensione mentis*', *The Library*, 25 (1970), 49–52.

[11]If God is a joker taunting Satan with the dangling stairs at III. 523–25, as Michael Wilding has it (*Milton's 'Paradise Lost'* (Sydney, 1969), p. 29), then the fifteen-line structure of I. 157–71 may afford a similar cruel joke whereby Satan is made to taunt himself ('my self am hell)'. Alternatively, the structure of Satan's speech may, by dramatic irony, distance the alert reader from the speaker who can be supposed to blunder inadvertently into a symbolic pattern antithetically opposed to what he is saying. In either case, we observe that the newly fallen angel, like a fallen autumn leaf discoloured but not yet decayed, still retains in his mind and instinctively uses patterns associated with his former life, if, that is, the concept of ascent would have had any meaning in a sinless state. But the main point is, of course, that the pattern jars horribly with the sentiment.

[12]*Religio medici* (I.12), edited by L. C. Martin (Oxford, 1964), p. 12.

[13]For Christ as the number fifteen see François Secret, *L'ésoterisme de*

Guy Le Fèvre de La Boderie, études de philologie et d'histoire 10 (Geneva, 1969), p. 94. Secret quotes La Boderie's *La Galliade (*1578), fol. 91: 'Mais l'homme. Dieu Jesus, le Christ, l'Oint, le David/Qui de David l'esprit par son esprit ravit, / Du systeme formel est la quinziesme chorde / Et le dixieme neuf du divin Decachorde . . . ' I am grateful to Professor Røstvig for this reference.

[14]Giles and Phineas Fletcher, *Poetical Works*, edited by F. S. Boas (Cambridge, 1908), I, 78.

[15]*The Spenserian Poets* (London, 1969), p. 207. See also M. M. Mahood, *Poetry and Humanism* (London, 1950), pp. 171–75.

[16]Cf., for instance, Hall's stanza 4 and Milton's line 125. The similarity between the two poems was brought to my notice by Mrs E. E. Duncan-Jones but it is interesting that her perception of the relationship was without any reference to number symbolism. My numerological connexion is, therefore, an additional link between poems already recognised as related.

[17]*Poems of Joseph Hall*, edited by A. Davenport (Liverpool, 1949), p. 4.

[18]See Kathi Meyer-Baer, *Music of the Spheres and the Dance of Death* (Princeton, N.J., 1970), pp. 80–82, and P. J. Ammann, 'The Musical Theory and Philosophy of Robert Fludd', *JWI*, 30 (1967), 202. In a much less exact form, the scale of music and a ladder linking earth and heaven are still sometimes associated. See, for example, Karen Blixen's story 'The Deluge at Norderney' in Isak Dinesen, *Seven Gothic Tales* (London, 1934), p. 211.

[19]H. N. Davies, 'The Structure of Shadwell's *A Song for St Cecilia's Day, 1690*', p. 210.

[20]The symbolism of the numbers alluded to in this paragraph is too common to need careful documentation. Such documentation can be readily found in Vincent F. Hopper, *Medieval Number Symbolism* (New York, 1938; reprinted New York, 1969); Alastair Fowler's two books, *Spenser and the Numbers of Time* (London, 1964) and *Triumphal Forms* (Cambridge, 1970), and a volume of essays collected by Fowler, *Silent Poetry* (London, 1970); and Christopher Butler, *Number Symbolism* (London, 1970).

[21]Cent. I, med. 60. *Centuries, Poems, and Thanksgivings*, edited by H. M. Margoliouth (Oxford, 1958), I, 31. Cf. Tilley, *Proverbs*, C840.

[22](Signifying those who transgress—*literally* 'step beyond'—the decalogue of the Commandments.) Pietro Bongo, *De numerorum mysteria* (Basel, 1618), p. 377. This book is an expansion of Bongo's *Mysticae numerorum significationis* (Bergamo, 1585).

[23]D. Brooks, 'Symbolic Numbers in Fielding's *Joseph Andrews*' in *Silent Poetry*, p. 259, n. 61, and A. Fowler, ' "To Shepherd's Ear": The Form of Milton's *Lycidas*', *Silent Poetry*, p. 171.

[24](The number eleven has no connexion with the divine, or with the

heavenly, nor has it any contact, nor is it a ladder pointing to those things that are above.) Bongo (1618), p. 377.

²⁵Spenser is quoted from *The Works . . . A Variorum Edition,* edited by E. Greenlaw et al., 9 vols (Baltimore, Md, 1932–57).

²⁶See M.-S. Røstvig, '*The Shepheardes Calender*—A Structural Analysis', *Renaissance and Modern Studies,* 13 (1969), 69–71. Cf. Spenser's *Doleful Lay of Clorinda* which also has an 11 +4 structure, though there then follow three more stanzas which return to the mourners. A line from stanza 15, 'There liveth he in euerlasting blis' makes the same point as stanza 15 of Dido's lament (line 194). Hieatt's book about Spenser's *Epithalamion* is *Short Time's Endless Monument* (New York, 1960).

²⁷Spenser's 'An Epitaph vpon the right Honourable sir Phillip Sidney knight' has fifteen stanzas. The words quoted are from 'Another of the same' (line 20), a poem of ten stanzas.

²⁸Bongo (1618), p. 377.

²⁹Bongo (1618), p. 386. Different numbers may, of course, have similar significance, and here the significance of twelve rather resembles that of ten. Douglas Brooks in his *Number and Pattern in the Eighteenth-Century Novel* (London and Boston, Mass., 1973) discusses the change from *eleven* to *twelve.*

³⁰*The Hidden Sense,* p. 58.

³¹*A Variorum Commentary on the Poems of John Milton,* Vol. II, edited by A. S. P. Woodhouse and Douglas Bush (London, 1972), part 1, p. 109.

³²It could be so marked, as has just been observed, in *In obitum praesulis Eliensis;* but in that poem two structural principles are at work: a narrative surface structure indicated by a change of speaker, and a deeper structure recording basic thematic layout. The former is presumably generated from the latter, while the delight given by the poem lies partly in the delicate balance in the narrative between wayward neglect of and boring subservience to the controlling thematic structure.

³³*English Poetry and Prose, 1540–1674,* edited by Christopher Ricks, Sphere History of Literature in the English Language, vol. II (London, 1970), p. 262.

³⁴Balachandra Rajan, *The Lofty Rhyme. A Study of Milton's Major Poetry* (London, 1970), p. 52.

³⁵The significance of lines 165–85 forming the *tenth* paragraph of the poem is discussed in J. A. Wittreich, Jr, 'Milton's "Destin'd Urn": The Art of *Lycidas*', *PMLA*, 84 (1969), 60–70 (p. 67). See also Fowler's "To Shepherd's Ear": The Form of Milton's *Lycidas*' in *Silent Poetry,* pp. 171–72.

³⁶The symbolism of seventeen as explained by Saint Augustine has been frequently outlined. See, for example, Butler, *Number Symbolism,* p. 27.

[37]Dryden's poem is quoted from *The Works of John Dryden*, III, edited by Earl Miner and V. A. Dearing (Berkeley and Los Angeles, Calif., 1969), pp. 109–15.

[38]John Heath-Stubbs, 'Baroque Ceremony. A Study of Dryden's "Ode to the Memory of Mistress Anne Killigrew" (1686)', *Cairo Studies in English* (1959), p. 80; Arthur W. Hoffman, *John Dryden's Imagery* (Gainesville, Florida, 1962), pp. 105–06.

[39]Hoffman, p. 116.

[40]Cf. the relationship between Spenser's *Epithalamion* and Cowley's 'The Long Life' as described in Alastair Fowler's *Triumphal Forms*, pp. 13–15.

[41]Davies, 'The Structure of Shadwell's *A Song for St Cecilia's Day, 1690*', p. 222. Lines 39–53 of Shadwell's poem employ a rhyme scheme similar to Milton's, and for a similar reason. They differ slightly in that Shadwell ends with a couplet preceded by a triplet while Milton has the couplet before the triplet.

[42]Other aspects of the numerological form of the poem are treated in Fowler's *Triumphal Forms*, pp. 113–15. Fowler rightly rejects the analysis attempted by John T. Shawcross in *Hartford Studies in Literature*, I (1969).

[43]*Lives of the English Poets*, edited by L. A. Hind, Everyman Library, 2 vols (London, 1925), I, 244.

[44]D. B. Morris, 'Drama and Stasis in Milton's "Ode on the Morning of Christ's Nativity"', *Stud. in Philol.*, 68 (1971), 210–11.

[45]The central stanza of the Ode as a whole is miscalculated as stanza 16 in Fowler's *Triumphal Forms*, pp. 115–16, n. 3.

[46]Quoted from the prompt-book in C. H. Shattuck, 'Milton's *Comus*: A Prompt-Book Study', *JEGP*, 60 (1961), 736.

[47]The printed text (D. H. Stevens, *Reference Guide to Milton*, Chicago, Ill., 1930, item 420), apparently adapted from Macready by Edmund Falconer, is ignored by Shattuck and by the article that Shattuck is supplementing, A. Thaler, 'Milton in the Theatre', *Studies in Philol.*, 17 (1920), 269–308.

[48]'Milton and the New Music', *UTQ*, 23 (1954), 217–26.

[49]*Exhortation to the Greeks*, with an English translation by G. W. Butterworth, Loeb Classics (London, 1919), p. 27.

[50]*Exhortation*, p. 9.

[51]*Exhortation*, p. 13.

[52]See especially pp. 157–63.

[53]The ease of making connexions is particularly evident in Lawrence W. Kingsley, 'Mythic Dialectic in *The Nativity Ode*', *Milton Studies*, 4 (1972) 163–76.

[54]' "To Shepherd's Ear": the Form of Milton's *Lycidas*', in Fowler's *Silent Poetry*, p. 174.

⁵⁵In both poems a poetic gift is important, and the angels in the Ode provide a ready example of those who serve being in attendance. Perhaps, as he looked back over his poetic career when writing this sonnet, Milton remembered his first major poem. The way in which Milton as gift bearer shows his eagerness by beginning the symmetrical pattern of his *Nativity Ode* two stanzas before the expected starting point, is similar to the way in which Jonson demonstrates the officious eagerness of the pikes to present themselves as tribute in *To Penshurst*. Alastair Fowler divides Jonson's poem into three 'draughts', each of seventeen couplets. Violating this formal division, the pikes scrape into the last line of the first draught 'As loth, the second draught, or cast to stay' ('The "Better Marks" of Jonson's *To Penshurst*', *RES*, n.s. 24 (1973), 276). Fowler might also have noted the speed of the 'Fat, aged carps' that enmesh themselves in just one line, and before the end of the first 'draught'.

⁵⁶Lancelot Andrewes, *Seventeen Sermons on the Nativity. A New Edition,* "The Ancient and Modern Library of Theological Literature' (London, n.d.), pp. 253–54.

⁵⁷For a discussion of retrospective form, see Barbara Herrnstein Smith, *Poetic Closure. A Study of How Poems End* (Chicago, Ill., and London, 1968), pp. 11–13, 36–37, and Paula Johnson, *Forms and Transformations in Music and Poetry of the English Renaissance* (New Haven, Mass., and London, 1972), pp. 14–15, 71–74, *et passim.* A retrospective summary of Milton's Ode in the form of a diagram follows this essay.

⁵⁸*The Works of Henry Vaughan*, edited by L. C. Martin (Oxford, 1914), II, 424–25.

⁵⁹*Of Paradise and Light* (Cambridge, 1960), p. 126.

⁶⁰Henry Vaughan may well have been interested in numbers through association with his brother. See *The Works Of Thomas Vaughan*, edited by Arthur E. Waite (London, 1919), pp. 302–06.

⁶¹See Bjorvand's discussion of the shortened six-line stanza in Spenser's *Hymne of Love*, pp. 26–28, and Røstvig's comments on Giles Fletcher's similar use of a shortened stanza in *Christ's Victory and Triumph*, p. 62.

⁶²M. A. Wickert, 'Structure and Ceremony in Spenser's *Epithalamion*', *ELH*, 35 (1968), 135–37. See also Røstvig's analysis of Sidney's epithalamium, pp. 74–77. Three recent books studying this type of structure are A. Fowler, *Triumphal Forms: Structural Patterns in Elizabethan Poetry* (Cambridge, 1970), M. Rose, *Shakespearean Design* (Cambridge, Mass., 1972), and D. Brooks, *Number and Pattern in the Eighteenth-Century Novel* (London and Boston, Mass., 1973). Rose's Chapter 4 should be read in conjunction with K. Brown, ' "Form and Cause Conjoin'd", *Hamlet* and Shakespeare's Workshop', *Shakespeare Survey* 26 (1973), 11–20. It is becoming common to notice structural patterns of this sort, and to refer to them as patterns of 'recessed symmetry'. It is not only in Renaissance

literature that they are to be discovered. What seems like free-flowing association in Molly's monologue at the end of Joyce's *Ulysses* has recently been shown to be organised in eight paragraphs forming an *a b c d d c b a* sequence. See D. Tolomeo, 'The Final Octagon of *Ulysses*', *James Joyce Quarterly* 10 (1973), 439–454.

[63]Carey's translation, p. 119.

4. Dryden's Rahmenerzählung: the form of *An Essay of Dramatick Poesie*

H. NEVILLE DAVIES

[1]*The Works of John Dryden*, XVII, edited by S. H. Monk et al. (Berkeley and Los Angeles, Calif., 1971), p. 351. All quotations from the *Essay* are from this edition.

[2]California edition, p. 351.

[3]M. C. Bradbrook, *The Rise of the Common Player. A Study of Actor and Society in Shakespeare's England* (London, 1962), p. 169.

[4]The books mentioned in the foregoing paragraph are most conveniently available as follows: *Tarlton's Newes* in *Tarlton's Jests*, The Shakespeare Society, (London, 1844), a volume that reprints extensive extracts from *The Cobler* in an appendix, *The Tinker of Turvey* (London, 1859), and *Westward for Smelts*, The Percy Society, volume 22 (London, 1848); all three edited by J. O. Halliwell[-Phillipps]. *The Tinker of Turvey* is also to be found in Charles C. Mish's *Short Fiction of the Seventeenth Century* (New York, 1963), and *Tarltons Newes* in facsimile in *The Collected Works of Robert Armin*, edited by J. P. Feather, 2 vols (New York and London, 1972), vol. I. The complete text of *The Cobler*, collating the editions of 1590 and 1608, was edited by Frederic Ouvry (London, 1862): references here are to this edition. Walter R. Davis thinks *The Tinker* 'an interesting revision' subtly structured *(Idea and Act in Elizabethan Fiction*, Princeton, N.J., 1969, p. 240), but I incline to Mish's view that 'Whoever made the alteration was not very well advised' ('English Short Fiction in the Seventeenth Century', *Studies in Short Fiction*, 6, 1969, 265). It is a pity that the title of his anthology led Mish to reprint the inferior adaptation. The possibility that Dryden's *Essay* was based on a derivative of *The Cobler* can be reasonably discounted since the structure of *The Cobler* is more like that of the *Essay* than are those of either *The Tinker* or *Westward for Smelts*. Possibly the adaptations encouraged Dryden to attempt a more radical adaptation. Malone, who possessed a slightly imperfect copy of the first

edition of *The Cobler*, does not seem to have connected the book with Dryden's *Essay*.

[5]*Antecedents of the English Novel 1400–1600 (from Chaucer to Deloney)* (Warsaw and London, 1963), p. 157.

[6]The California editors note that Cicero's *De legibus* 'boasts a river scene' (p. 356, n. 74), but Cicero's location is a rural one on the *banks* of a river, and on an island, and seems to me to be quite unlike Dryden's river setting. There are rivers in Macedon and Monmouth, too.

[7]*Heptameron, or the History of the Fortunate Lovers . . . Now made English by Robert Codrington* (London, 1654), A4 ᵛ.

[8]See also H. James Jensen, *A Glossary of John Dryden's Critical Terms* (Minneapolis, Minn., 1969), p. 41.

[9]'Any comparison with the dialogues of Plato . . . is wildly out of place' asserts George Watson (*Of Dramatic Poesy and Other Critical Essays*, 2 vols, Everyman's Library, edited by G. Watson (London, 1962), I, 12). But perhaps Dryden intends us to draw a parallel between Neander and Socrates as he is presented in the *Symposium*, late for the feast because lost in a fit of abstraction, and, at the end, still talking (about drama) when nearly everyone has gone, two of his last three listeners, the comic dramatist Aristophanes and his host, the tragic dramatist Agathon falling asleep before he has finished, the third listener only half awake. Incidentally, the speakers in the *Symposium* and in Dryden's *Essay* are celebrating victories.

[10]'Defence of the Epilogue' (1672). *Dryden: Of Dramatic Poesy and Other Critical Essays*, edited by G. Watson, Everyman's Library, 2 vols (London, 1962), I, 180.

[11]'Dramatic Poetry: Dryden's Conversation Piece', *Cambridge Journal*, 5 (1952), 553–61 (554).

[12]*The Sceptical Chymist*, edited by M. M. Pattison Muir, Everyman's Library (London, 1937), p. 7.

[13]Cf. Paul Ramsey, *Explicator*, 13 (1955), 46.

[14]The relationship between English naval victory in the battle and English literary victory in the debates was pointed out by Charles Kaplan in *Explicator*, 8 (1950), 36.

[15]George Williamson, 'The Occasion of *An Essay of Dramatic Poesy*', *Mod. Philol.*, 44 (1946), 1–9, rptd in Williamson's *Seventeenth Century Contexts* (London, 1960), pp. 272–88, and *Essential Articles for the Study of John Dryden*, edited by H. T. Swedenberg (London, 1966), pp. 65–82.

[16]John Summerson, *Sir Christopher Wren* (London, 1953), p. 59, gives a short account of the 'contest'.

[17]*A Voyage to England . . . Done into English from the French Original* (London, 1709), p. 5. See also p. 46, and cf. *Observations* (1665), p. 77.

[18]Norman G. Brett-James, *The Growth of Stuart London* (London, 1935), ·d 489.

[19]*Observations*, pp. 167–69. Sorbière's observation of an aggressive attitude was probably not mistaken, though it is a fact that Obdam, the Dutch admiral, had orders to seek his enemy even into the Thames.

[20]*A Voyage*, p. 70. *Observations*, pp. 174, 256–57.

[21]*Observations*, p. 45.

[22]*A Voyage*, pp. 13–14. For current developments in Paris see Michael Greenhalgh, 'Bernini in France, 1665', *History Today*, 23 (1973),398–406.

[23]'A Discourse Concerning the Original and Progress of Satire' (1693). *Dryden: Of Dramatic Poesy and Other Critical Essays*, II, 136–37.

[24]'A Discourse', p. 137.

[25]*A Voyage*, p. 70.

[26]*A Voyage*, p. 5.

[27]*A Voyage*, p. 69.

[28]*A Voyage*, p. 70.

[29]*A Voyage*, p. 3.

[30]A. Guibbory, 'Dryden's View of History', *Philol. Quart.*, 52 (1973), 187–204 (190).

[31]Ouvry's edition, p. 6.

[32]*Decameron* viii, 7; v, 6 and v, 2; vii, 1 and vii, 8; and iii, 8 underlie the last four of *The Cobler of Caunterburie's* six tales.

[33]Cf. *The Decameron . . . Translated into English Anno 1620*, edited by E. Hutton, The Tudor Translations, 4 vols (London, 1909), I, 26–27. All references are to this edition.

[34]J. R. Hale, *England and the Italian Renaissance* (London, 1954), pp. 35–36. The structure of *A German Diet* is somewhat more complex than Hale allows.

[35]See Herbert Weisinger, 'Who Began the Revival of Learning? The Renaissance Point of View', *Papers of the Michigan Academy of Science, Arts, and Letters*, 30 (1944), 625–38 (630).

[36]Preface to *Fables Ancient and Modern* (1700). *Dryden: Of Dramatic Poesy and Other Critical Essays*, II, 271–72. The title-page of the 1620 translation of the *Decameron* calls Boccaccio 'The First Refiner of Italian Prose'.

[37]Masson's translation of letter 8, reprinted in *The Works of John Milton*, edited by F. A. Patterson, 20 vols (New York, 1931–40), vol. XII (1936), p. 33.

[38]John Summerson, *Inigo Jones* (Harmondsworth, 1966), p. 88.

[39]*Inigo Jones*, p. 93.

[40]*The Diary of John Evelyn*, edited by E. S. de Beer, 6 vols (Oxford, 1955), II, 184 (21 October 1644). Inigo Jones, *Stone-Heng*, 2nd. edition [*with related works by Charlton and Webb*] (London, 1725), 'Memoirs', sig. al[v].

[41]For further description of Covent Garden see James Lees-Milne, *The Age of Inigo Jones* (London, 1953), pp. 84–86. A painting of Covent Garden,

c. 1649, is reproduced in the catalogue by John Harris, Stephen Orgel, and Roy Strong of the Jones quatercentenary exhibition held at the Banqueting House, Whitehall, *The King's Arcadia: Inigo Jones and the Stuart Court* (London, 1973), p. 185. Wenceslaus Hollar's etching of St Paul's Covent Garden, *c.* 1640, is reproduced in Margaret Whinney, *Wren* (London, 1971), p. 15, and M. Whinney and Oliver Millar, *English Art 1625–1714,* Oxford History of English Art (Oxford, 1957), pl. 4b.

⁴²Summerson, *Inigo Jones,* p. 75. Webb's drawing is reproduced in *The King's Arcadia,* p. 152. An eighteenth-century engraving of Somerset House, including the water stairs, is reproduced from *Nouveau Théâtre de la Grande Bretagne* (1724) in the California edition of Dryden's *Essay,* facing p. 8. The likely route taken by the four men from the river to Covent Garden, passing Somerset House with its well planned grounds and the Savoy, can be followed in Philippa Glanville's *London in Maps* (London, 1972). Plate X shows a large scale map by Wenceslaus Hollar, *c.* 1658, which gives a vivid three-dimensional effect by representing buildings in isometric projection. The contrast between the layout of Covent Garden and the older, unplanned areas is particularly striking.

⁴³Earl Wasserman, *The Subtler Language* (Baltimore, Md., 1959), pp. 15–33, rptd in *Dryden. A Collection of Critical Essays,* edited by B. N. Schilling (Englewood Cliffs, N.J., 1963), pp. 71–85.

⁴⁴*Observations,* pp. 226–63.

⁴⁵*Restoration and Augustan Prose,* papers delivered by James R. Sutherland and Ian Watt at the Clark Library Seminar, 14 July, 1956, (Los Angeles, Calif., 1956), pp. 5–6. Cf. Sutherland, *On English Prose,* The Alexander Lectures, 1956–57 (Toronto, 1957), pp. 67–68.

⁴⁶*Restoration and Augustan Prose,* p. 16; *On English Prose,* pp. 69–70.

⁴⁷*Epistolæ Ho-Elianæ. The Familiar Letters of James Howell Historiographer Royal to Charles II,* edited by Joseph Jacobs, 2 vols (London, 1892), I, 17.

5. *Tom Jones* and the Choice of Hercules

M.-S. RØSTVIG

¹'O great liberality of God the Father! O great and wonderful happiness of man! It is given him to have that which he chooses and to be that which he wills . . . At man's birth the Father placed in him every sort of seed and sprouts of every kind of life. The seeds that each man cultivates will grow and bear their fruit in him. If he cultivates vegetable seeds, he will become a

plant. If the seeds of sensation, he will grow into brute. If rational, he will come out a heavenly animal. If intellectual, he will be an angel, and a son of God . . . it is not the rind which makes the plant, but a dull and non-sentient nature; not the hide which makes a beast of burden, but a brutal and sensual soul; not the spherical body which makes the heavens, but right reason; and not a separateness from the body, but a spiritual intelligence which makes an angel.' Pico della Mirandola, *On the Dignity of Man, On Being and the One, Heptaplus* (New York, 1965), pp. 5 f.

[2]The classical study of this theme in Renaissance art is Erwin Panofsky's *Hercules am Scheidewege* (Leipzig, 1930) published as vol. 18 in the Studien der Bibliothek Warburg. See also note 40.

[3]*Tom Jones* VII, 2. All quotations are from the Penguin ed. published in 1966.

[4]*Rasselas* ed. J. P. Hardy (Oxford, 1968), ch. 16.

[5]See, for example, Ben Jonson's masque, *Pleasure Reconciled to Virtue* in *Works*, ed. C. H. Herford and Percy and Evelyn Simpson (Oxford, 1925–52), VII, 473–91. For a discussion of the theme, see Edgar Wind, *Pagan Mysteries in the Renaissance* (Harmondsworth, 1967), pp. 81–96.

[6]James Boswell, *The Life of Samuel Johnson, LL.D.* (London: Everyman's Library, 1946), I, 254 f.

[7]Anthony Ashley Cooper, Earl of Shaftesbury, *Characteristicks Of Men, Manners, Opinions, Times* (London, 1727), II, 104 f. All quotations are from this edition.

[8]Shaftesbury, I, 207.

[9]See my study 'Ars Aeterna: Renaissance Poetics and Theories of Divine Creation,' *Mosaic* 3 (1970), 40–61; reprinted in *Chaos and Form*, ed. Kenneth McRobbie (Winnipeg, 1972) pp. 101–19.

[10]Shaftesbury, I, 336.

[11]Shaftesbury, III, 25 f.

[12]Shaftesbury, III, 259–63.

[13]R. S. Crane, 'The Plot of *Tom Jones*,' *Twentieth-Century Interpretations of Tom Jones*, ed. Martin C. Battestin (Englewood Cliffs, New Jersey, 1968), pp. 68–93.

[14]Douglas Brooks, 'The Interpolated Tales in *Joseph Andrews* again,' *MP*, 65 (1967–68), 208–13. The tales of 'The Unfortunate Jilt' and 'The History of Two Friends' are seen by Mr Brooks to 'answer each other across the novel. They are linked not only by being based on a common model but also by the similarity of events in each . . . the vain Leonora abandons the worthy Horatio . . . the vain Leonard abandons the innocent and perplexed Paul.' Each tale is interrupted by a scene of frantic activity as when Adams defends Joseph (II, 5) or Joseph Fanny (IV, 11). (This is true of *Tom Jones* as well, where the tales told by the Man of the Hill and by Mrs Fitzpatrick are followed by acts of violence.)

[15]This has been suggested by Douglas Brooks in relation to *Joseph Andrews;* see his essay on 'Abraham Adams and Parson Trulliber: the Meaning of "Joseph Andrews", Book II, Chapter 14,' *MLR*, 63 (1968), 794–801. Brooks sees Parson Trulliber as an incarnation of Gluttony as depicted for example by Cesare Ripa or Spenser (*FQ* I, iv, 21–23).

[16]*The Happy Man, Studies in the Metamorphoses of a Classical Ideal*, Vol. I: 1600–1700 (2nd ed., Oslo, 1962), pp. 227–310. See also Vol. II: 1700–1760 (2nd ed., Oslo and New York, 1971), pp. 184 f.

[17]Reproduced by Ronald Paulson, *Hogarth. His Life, Art, and Times* (New York, 1971), I, 122 (plate 30).

[18]Not included in the modern edition of Shaftesbury's *Characteristics*, ed. J. M. Robertson (London, 1900). As always, my references are to the fourth edition of 1727.

[19]Panofsky, *Hercules am Scheidewege*, p. 155.

[20]Paulson, I, 276.

[21]William Shenstone, *Poetical Works*, ed. George Gilfillan (Edinburgh, 1854), pp. 186–201. Shenstone makes the point usually observed by painters that the breasts of Pleasure are exposed ('Exposed her breast . . . ' line 111).

[22]Reproduced by Panofsky, plate 77.

[23]Paulson, I, 274.

[24]Edgar Wind, ' "Hercules" and "Orpheus": Two Mock-Heroic Designs by Dürer,' *JWI*, 2 (1938–39), 206–18.

[25]Shaftesbury, III, 349.

[26]See George Wither, *A Collection of Emblemes 1635* (Menston, 1968), p. 22 (Emblem I, 22), or the collection to which he is indebted, Gabriel Rollenhagen's *Nucleus Emblematum*.

[26a]See H. Neville Davies, 'Sweet Music in Herbert's "Easter", '*Notes & Queries*, 213 (1968), 95 f. and G. L. Finney, *Musical Backgrounds for English Literature: 1580–1650* (New Brunswick, n.d.), pp. 76–101. Sweet music could pierce the mind and make it receptive to love.

[27]Rudolf Wittkower, 'Chance, Time, and Virtue,' *JWI*, I (1937–38), 313–21.

[28]Wind, *Pagan Mysteries*, p. 103 and plate 54.

[29]Geoffrey Whitney, *A Choice of Emblemes* (1585), p. 121. This device adorns the coins of the Emperor Augustus, as Wind informs us *(Pagan Mysteries*, p. 107).

[30]Wither, *Emblemes*, p. 139 (Emblem III, 5): '*Good* Fortune *will with him abide,* | *That hath true* Vertue, *for his guide.'*

[31]Wittkower, pp. 316 f. The device is found in Alciati's emblems.

[32]Wind, *Pagan Mysteries*, p. 103.

[33]For an account of this work see Anthony Blunt, 'The Hypnerotomachia Poliphili in 17th Century France,' *JWI*, I (1937–38), 117–37. Passages

from the *Hypnerotomachia* are incorporated verbatim in the fifth book of Rabelais' *Gargantua*. A new translation of the *Hypnerotomachia* into French appeared as late as 1703.

[34]See note 17.

[35]Christian versions of the Choice of Hercules would invoke Matthew 7:13–14. An iconographical half-way stage between the mere letter Y and the two hills is represented by emblems showing various objects hanging from each arm of the letter. See Zacharias Heyn, *Emblemata. Emblemes Chrestienes et Morales* (1625), discussed by Purvis E. Boyette, 'Milton's Abstracted Sublimities: The Structure of Meaning in *A Mask,' Tulane Studies in English*, 18 (1970), 45.

[36]G. Karl Galinski, *The Herakles Theme* (Oxford, 1972), p. 93.

[37]P. 96.

[38]P. 156.

[39]P. 234. Handel 'took pains to dissociate his hero from any trace of crudely selfish love' and saw to it that the story was given a happy end. Themes connected with Hercules were popular during the 1740s; to Shenstone's *Judgment of Hercules* (1740) and Handel's oratorio from 1744 must be added Joseph Spence's *Polymetis* (1747) which includes a poem in twenty-seven stanzas on the Choice.

Fielding's own library contained many classical texts concerned with the Hercules myth; see the library catalogue reproduced by Ethel Margaret Thornbury, *Henry Fielding's Theory of the Comic Prose Epic* (Madison, 1931), pp. 168–89. Item 621 is *Xenophontis Opera* (Paris, 1625) where we find the fable of the Choice in Xenophon's *Memorabilia*. Fielding's shelves were stocked with all the important Greek and Latin playwrights including Aristophanes.

[40]See Edgar Wind, ' "Hercules" and "Orpheus",' and Robert E. Hallowell, 'Ronsard and the Gallic Hercules Myth,' *Studies in the Renaissance,* 9 (1962), 242–55.

[41]Hallowell, p. 255.

[42]See note 27.

[43]Shaftesbury, I, 194–96.

[44]See note 39 for the reference to the catalogue of Fielding's library.

[45]Shaftesbury, I, 332.

[46]Emrys L. Jones, 'The Artistic Form of *Rasselas,' RES*, 18 (1967), 387–401.

[47]Paul Fussell, *The Rhetorical World of Augustan Humanism* (Oxford, 1969), pp. 276 f.

[48]C. Rawson, 'Order and Cruelty,' *Essays in Criticism*, 20 (1970), 36.

[49]E. M. W. Tillyard, *The Elizabethan World Picture* (London, 1950), p. 65 aligns the elements and the qualities with the four humours. For a

popular Renaissance survey, see Pierre de La Primaudaye, *The French Academie* (London, 1618), pp. 726–28.

⁵⁰Milton, *Paradise Lost*, V, 181 f. and Augustine, *De doctrina Christiana*, II, xvi, 25. See my discussion of Milton's use of quaternions in 'Images of Perfection,' *Seventeenth-Century Imagery* ed. Earl Miner (Los Angeles, 1971), p. 11.

6. Mistaken conduct and proper 'feeling': a study of Jane Austen's *Pride and Prejudice*

GRETE EK

¹Alistair M. Duckworth, *The Improvement of the Estate: A Study of Jane Austen's Novels* (Baltimore and London, 1971), p. x.

²Besides Duckworth's valuable study, other recent works offering interpretations along such lines are for example A. Walton Litz, *Jane Austen: A Study of Her Artistic Development* (London, 1965), and Kenneth L. Moler, *Jane Austen's Art of Allusion* (Lincoln, Nebraska, 1968). These works reflect the welcome tendency of later years to consider how a social, ethical, and intellectual context finds expression in Jane Austen's novels. The first overt application of the 'art-nature dichotomy' to *Pride and Prejudice* is found in Samuel Kliger, 'Jane Austen's *Pride and Prejudice* in the Eighteenth-Century Mode', *University of Toronto Quarterly*, XVI (1947), 357–70. For a predominantly socio-economic approach, see especially Dorothy van Ghent, *The English Novel: Form and Function* (New York, 1961), David Daiches, 'Jane Austen, Karl Marx, and the Aristocratic Dance', *The American Scholar*, XVII (1948), 289–96, and Mark Schorer, 'Pride Unprejudiced', *Kenyon Review*, XVIII (1956), 72–91. The argument of largely opposing attitudes moving towards synthesis permits a view of Darcy as a character in his own right, not merely as a 'function' subordinated to Elizabeth's development. The approach of Marvin Mudrick, for example, reduces Darcy to a 'choice' for Elizabeth (*Jane Austen: Irony as Defense and Discovery* (Princeton, 1952)). The most recent study that focuses squarely on the heroine's psychology is Darrel Mansell, *The Novels of Jane Austen: An Interpretation* (London, 1973).

³Howard S. Babb, who offers an exhaustive analysis of the dramatic function of dialogue in *Pride and Prejudice*, contends that Darcy renounces none of his essential values in the course of the novel, and that Elizabeth comes to endorse his assumptions. See *Jane Austen: The Fabric of Dialogue* (Columbus, Ohio, 1962).

[4]'Mansfield Park', *The Opposing Self* (New York, 1955), pp. 206–7.

[5]*The English Novel*, p. 101. See Ronald Paulson, *Satire and the Novel in Eighteenth-Century England* (New Haven and London, 1967), p. 296, for an excellent analysis of the matchmakers' society.

[6]All citations of Jane Austen's fiction are based on the edition of R. W. Chapman (5 vols., 3rd ed., Oxford, 1933). Page references to *Pride and Prejudice* are inserted directly into the text.

[7]In the first part of his article 'Jane Austen and the Moralists', *The Oxford Review*, 1 (1966), 5–18, Gilbert Ryle discusses Jane Austen's 'wine-taster's technique of comparative character-delineation', involving a differentiation between degrees of the same quality. He pays particular attention to the concept of pride in *Pride and Prejudice*.

[8]Paulson makes this point (see especially pp. 298–301). The tenor of his argument, however, differs from mine in that he sees the basic conflict as one between 'a conventional and limiting system of values and the freedom and integrity of the individual' (p. 301), the ending being partly pessimistic because 'one can never get rid of the Collinses and Wickhams, let alone the Mrs Bennets and Lydias' (p. 304). For a similar interpretation, see D. W. Harding, 'Regulated Hatred: An Aspect of the Work of Jane Austen', *Scrutiny*, VIII (1940), 346–62. I believe that we need to distinguish between a parody of convention—which fools and knaves invariably embrace—and positive norms grounded in sense. See p. 186.

[9]The quotation is from Daiches, 289.

[10]Moler sees the portrait of Darcy as basically inconsistent, ascribing the 'flaw' to remnants of a parody figure in the first version of the novel. Darcy's possible 'ancestors' are also discussed in Q. D. Leavis, 'A Critical Theory of Jane Austen's Writings', *Scrutiny*, X (1941), 61–87, in Henrietta Ten Harmsel, *Jane Austen: A Study in Fictional Conventions* (London, The Hague, and Paris, 1964), and in Frank W. Bradbrook, *Jane Austen and Her Predecessors* (Cambridge, 1966). The charges of inconsistency levelled at Darcy recur with considerable frequency, Mudrick being one of his most prominent detractors. See *Irony as Defense and Discovery*, especially pp. 116–17. For a different view, see Babb.

[11]*Jane Austen: Facts and Problems* (the Clark lectures, 1948; rpt. Oxford, 1967), p. 192.

[12]*Emma*, pp. 98–107.

[13]Mudrick insists that the 'simple' characters are beneath moral judgement. His conception of 'morality' in *Pride and Prejudice* is one that excludes the application of 'conventional' norms: ' . . . the power of choice is all that distinguishes [the individual] as a being who acts and who may be judged' (p. 124). The caricatures cannot choose and thus cannot be judged.

[14]See Wayne C. Booth, *The Rhetoric of Fiction* (Chicago and London, 1961), pp. 243–66.

¹⁵See Babb for a full treatment of Elizabeth's limitations.

¹⁶Robert Louis Stevenson's remark is referred to in Elizabeth Jenkins, *Jane Austen: A Biography* (1938; rpt. London, 1948), p. 160.

¹⁷Babb, p. 114.

¹⁸The quotation is from Everett Zimmermann, 'Pride and Prejudice in *Pride and Prejudice*', *Nineteenth-Century Fiction*, XXIII (1968), 68. Zimmermann argues against an 'antithetical' interpretation of the novel.

¹⁹Sheila Kaye-Smith and G. B. Stern, *Talking of Jane Austen* (London, 1943), pp. 56–57.

²⁰'Light and Bright and Sparkling: Irony and Fiction in 'Pride and Prejudice', *The Fields of Light: An Experiment in Critical Reading* (1951; rpt. London, Oxford, and New York, 1968), p. 175.

²¹E. E. Duncan-Jones notes that Darcy's opening 'address' (" "In vain have I struggled . . . " " ') may be a direct echo of Mr B—'s letter to Pamela announcing his honourable intentions. ' "In vain my Pamela, do I struggle against my affection for you . . . " ' ('Proposals of Marriage in *Pride and Prejudice* and *Pamela*', *Notes and Queries*, CCII (1957), 76). See my note 10.

²²See W. A. Craik, *Jane Austen: The Six Novels* (London, 1965), p. 79.

²³Brower, p. 176.

²⁴Italics added.

²⁵Italics added.

²⁶*Emma*, p. 412.

²⁷Brower, pp. 180–81.

²⁸The most detailed treatment of the Pemberley episode is given by Duckworth. His excellent analysis is too comprehensive to be fully summarised here; let me note briefly that he sees Pemberley as the meeting-point of two attitudes that are partly admirable, partly in need of modification. Darcy's commitment to tradition needs the addition of 'individual energy'; it is Elizabeth who eventually supplies this vitality, after having herself realised that 'individual energy must be generated within social contexts, for, lacking social direction and control, it turns too easily to withdrawal from society, or to irresponsibility and anarchy' (p. 132). I see this antithesis as apparent only.

²⁹The tradition of the country house poem is naturally pertinent in this context. G. R. Hibbard in his survey of the genre points out that the country house is expressive of an attitude to life. See 'The Country House Poem of the Seventeenth Century', *Journal of the Warburg and Courtauld Institutes*, XIX (1956), 159–74. C. Molesworth sees this 'attitude' as the poet's ideal conception of the cause-and-effect relationship between virtue and property, pitted against a rising tendency to regard money as the basis of property. See his 'Property and Virtue: The Genre of the Country-House Poem in the Seventeenth Century', *Genre*, I (1968), 141–57. For a discussion of Jonson's *To Penshurst* which focuses on the timeless moral and

even religious significance of the description, see Alastair Fowler, 'The "Better Marks" of Jonson's *To Penshurst*', *The Review of English Studies*, n. ser., XXIV (1973), 266–82. However 'virtue' be defined, the general view remains that 'in every country house poem the structure and the people who inhabit it are the same. Their virtue creates their environment; their environment, their property, is a perfect expression of their virtue.' (Molesworth, 153–54.)—A useful, if necessarily sketchy, review of the emblematic use of the country house in poetry and fiction has been recently provided in Richard Gill, *Happy Rural Seat: The English Country House and the Literary Imagination* (New Haven and London, 1972), pp. 227–52. See especially pp. 243–46, where Gill discusses Jane Austen's place within this tradition: he pays particular attention to *Mansfield Park*, where 'individual characters are portrayed in terms of their contrasting and changing relationships with Mansfield Park and its mode of life' (p. 244). Similarly, 'the good taste manifest at Pemberley deepens Elizabeth Bennet's appreciation of Darcy's qualities' (p. 243). See also Litz, pp. 103–04, for the idea that the Pemberley episode should be interpreted in the light of eighteenth-century conceptions of taste.

[30]*Persuasion*, p. 26.

[31]*Mansfield Park*, p. 22. See also Ann Banfield, 'The Moral Landscape of *Mansfield Park*', *Nineteenth-Century Fiction*, XXVI (1971), 1–24.

[32]Mansell, p. 100.

[33]Review of *Emma*, in B. C. Southam, *Jane Austen: The Critical Heritage* (London and New York, 1968), p. 65.

[34]The quotation is from Van Ghent, p. 108. In *Jane Austen's Literary Manuscripts* (London, 1964), B. C. Southam contends that it is the 'sense of property which warms her heart towards Darcy' (p. 60).

[35]Italics added.

[36]Mudrick, p. 119. Generally speaking, the elopement episode invites scant enthusiasm on the part of critics. Brower, for example, feels that it belongs 'to a simpler world where outright judgments of good and bad or of happy and unhappy are in place' (p. 180).

[37]*Jane Austen: An Interpretation*, p. 101.

[38]A. C. Ward, 'Introduction' to *Pride and Prejudice*, Longmans edition (London, 1958), p. xviii.

[39]Italics added.

[40]*Persuasion*, p. 175.

[41]Cp. *Persuasion*, p. 245. Anne is described as 'Glowing and lovely in sensibility and happiness', which is all the more striking because we have been told that 'her bloom had vanished early' (p. 6).

[42]Chapman, *Facts and Problems*, p. 193. The idea is that of Mary Lascelles (*Jane Austen and Her Art* (London, 1939)); I have been unable to trace the exact passage.

Textual appendix

JOHN MILTON

'On the Morning of Christ's Nativity'

I

This is the month, and this the happy morn
Wherein the Son of heaven's eternal King,
Of wedded maid, and virgin mother born,
Our great redemption from above did bring;
5   For so the holy sages once did sing,
    That he our deadly forefeit should release,
   And with his Father work us a perpetual peace.

II

That glorious form, that light unsufferable,
And that far-beaming blaze of majesty,
10 Wherewith he wont at heaven's high council-table,
To sit the midst of trinal unity,
He laid aside; and here with us to be,
    Forsook the courts of everlasting day,
   And chose with us a darksome house of mortal clay.

III

15 Say heavenly Muse, shall not thy sacred vein
Afford a present to the infant God?
Hast thou no verse, no hymn, or solemn strain,
To welcome him to this his new abode,
Now while the heaven by the sun's team untrod,
20   Hath took no print of the approaching light,
   And all the spangled host keep watch in squadrons
      bright?

IV

See how from far upon the eastern road
The star-led wizards haste with odours sweet,
O run, prevent them with thy humble ode,
25   And lay it lowly at his blessed feet;
Have thou the honour first, thy Lord to greet,
    And join thy voice unto the angel quire,
From out his sècret altar touched with hallowed fire.

The Hymn

1

It was the winter wild,
30   While the heaven-born-child
    All meanly wrapped in the rude manger lies;
Nature in awe to him
Had doffed her gaudy trim,
    With her great master so to sympathize:
35   It was no season then for her
To wanton with the sun her lusty paramour.

2

Only with speeches fair
She woos the gentle air
    To hide her guilty front with innocent snow,
40   And on her naked shame,
Pollute with sinful blame,
    The saintly veil of maiden white to throw,
Confounded, that her maker's eyes
Should look so near upon her foul deformities.

3

45   But he her fears to cease,
Sent down the meek-eyed Peace,
    She crowned with olive green, came softly sliding
Down through the turning sphere
His ready harbinger,
50   With turtle wing the amorous clouds dividing,

And waving wide her myrtle wand,
She strikes a universal peace through sea and land.

4

No war, or battle's sound
Was heard the world around
55   The idle spear and shield were high up hung,
The hooked chariot stood
Unstained with hostile blood,
    The trumpet spake not to the armed throng,
And kings sat still with awful eye,
60 As if they surely knew their sovran Lord was by.

5

But peaceful was the night
Wherein the Prince of Light
    His reign of peace upon the earth began:
The winds with wonder whist,
65 Smoothly the waters kissed,
    Whispering new joys to the mild ocean,
Who now hath quite forgot to rave,
While birds of calm sit brooding on the charmed wave.

6

The stars with deep amaze
70 Stand fixed in steadfast gaze,
    Bending one way their precious influence,
And will not take their flight,
For all the morning light,
    Or Lucifer that often warned them thence;
75 But in their glimmering orbs did glow,
Until their Lord himself bespake, and bid them go.

7

And though the shady gloom
Had given day her room,

The sun himself withheld his wonted speed,
80 And hid his head for shame,
As his inferior flame,
    The new enlightened world no more should need;
He saw a greater sun appear
Than his bright throne, or burning axle-tree could bear.

8

85 The shepherds on the lawn,
Or ere the point of dawn,
    Sat simply chatting in a rustic row;
Full little thought they then,
That the mighty Pan
90   Was kindly come to live with them below;
Perhaps their loves, or else their sheep,
Was all that did their silly thoughts so busy keep.

9

When such music sweet
Their hearts and ears did greet,
95   As never was by mortal finger strook,
Divinely-warbled voice
Answering the stringed noise,
    As all their souls in blissful rapture took:
The air such pleasure loth to lose,
100 With thousand echoes still prolongs each heavenly close.

10

Nature that heard such sound
Beneath the hollow round
    Of Cynthia's seat, the airy region thrilling,
Now was almost won
105 To think her part was done,
    And that her reign had here its last fulfilling;
She knew such harmony alone
Could hold all heaven and earth in happier union.

11

At last surrounds their sight
110 A globe of circular light,
    That with long beams the shame-faced night arrayed,
The helmed cherubim
And sworded seraphim,
    Are seen in glittering ranks with wings displayed,
115 Harping in loud and solemn quire,
With unexpressive notes to heaven's new-born heir.

12

Such music (as 'tis said)
Before was never made,
    But when of old the sons of morning sung,
120 While the creator great
His constellations set,
    And the well-balanced world on hinges hung,
And cast the dark foundations deep,
And bid the welt'ring waves their oozy channel keep.

13

125 Ring out, ye crystal spheres,
Once bless our human ears,
    (If ye have power to touch our senses so)
And let your silver chime
Move in melodious time;
130   And let the base of heaven's deep organ blow,
And with your ninefold harmony
Make up full consort to the angelic symphony.

14

For if such holy song
Enwrap our fancy long,
135   Time will run back, and fetch the age of gold,
And speckled vanity
Will sicken soon and die,
    And lep'rous sin will melt from earthly mould,

And hell itself will pass away,
140 And leave her dolorous mansions to the peering day.

15

Yea Truth, and Justice then
Will down return to men,
    Orbed in a rainbow; and like glories wearing
Mercy will sit between,
145 Throned in celestial sheen,
    With radiant feet the tissued clouds down steering,
And heaven as at some festival,
Will open wide the gates of her high palace hall.

16

But wisest fate says no,
150 This must not yet be so,
    The babe lies yet in smiling infancy,
That on the bitter cross
Must redeem our loss;
    So both himself and us to glorify:
155 Yet first to those ychained in sleep,
The wakeful trump of doom must thunder through
        the deep.

17

With such a horrid clang
As on Mount Sinai rang
    While the red fire, and smould'ring clouds out brake:
160 The aged earth aghast
With terror of that blast,
    Shall from the surface to the centre shake;
When at the world's last session,
The dreadful judge in middle air shall spread his
        throne.

18

165 And then at last our bliss
      Full and perfect is,
        But now begins; for from this happy day
      The old dragon under ground
      In straiter limits bound,
170   Not half so far casts his usurped sway,
      And wroth to see his kingdom fail,
      Swinges the scaly horror of his folded tail.

19

      The oracles are dumb,
      No voice or hideous hum
175   Runs through the arched roof in words deceiving.
      Apollo from his shrine
      Can no more divine,
        With hollow shriek the steep of Delphos leaving.
      No nightly trance, or breathed spell,
180 Inspires the pale-eyed priest from the prophetic cell.

20

      The lonely mountains o'er,
      And the resounding shore,
        A voice of weeping heard, and loud lament;
      From haunted spring, and dale
185 Edged with poplar pale,
        The parting genius is with sighing sent,
      With flower-inwoven tresses torn
      The nymphs in twilight shade of tangled thickets mourn.

21

      In consecrated earth,
190 And on the holy hearth,
        The lars, and lemures moan with midnight plaint,
      In urns, and altars round,
      A drear and dying sound
        Affrights the flamens at their service quaint;

195 And the chill marble seems to sweat,
While each peculiar power forgoes his wonted seat.

22

Peor, and Baalim,
Forsake their temples dim,
   With that twice battered god of Palestine,
200 And mooned Ashtaroth,
Heaven's queen and mother both,
   Now sits not girt with tapers' holy shine,
The Libyc Hammon shrinks his horn,
In vain the Tyrian maids their wounded Thammuz
    mourn.

23

205 And sullen Moloch fled,
Hath left in shadows dread,
   His burning idol all of blackest hue;
In vain with cymbals' ring,
They call the grisly king,
210   In dismal dance about the furnace blue;
The brutish gods of Nile as fast,
Isis and Orus, and the dog Anubis haste.

24

Nor is Osiris seen
In Memphian grove, or green,
215   Trampling the unshowered grass with lowings loud:
Nor can he be at rest
Within his sacred chest,
   Nought but profoundest hell can be his shroud,
In vain with timbrelled anthems dark
220 The sable-stoled sorcerers bear his worshipped ark.

25

He feels from Juda's land
The dreaded infant's hand,

The rays of Bethlehem blind his dusky eyn;
Nor all the gods beside,
225 Longer dare abide,
Not Typhon huge ending in snaky twine:
Our babe to show his Godhead true,
Can in his swaddling bands control the damned crew.

26

So when the sun in bed,
230 Curtained with cloudy red,
Pillows his chin upon an orient wave,
The flocking shadows pale,
Troop to the infernal jail,
Each fettered ghost slips to his several grave,
235 And the yellow-skirted fays,
Fly after the night-steeds, leaving their moon-loved maze.

27

But see the virgin blest,
Hath laid her babe to rest.
Time is our tedious song should here have ending:
240 Heaven's youngest teemed star,
Hath fixed her polished car,
Her sleeping Lord with handmaid lamp attending:
And all about the courtly stable,
Bright-harnessed angels sit in order serviceable.

Index

INDEX OF FICTIONAL CHARACTERS

INDEX OF CRITICS CITED IN TEXT